# AGING AND COGNITIVE PROCESSES

# ADVANCES IN THE STUDY OF COMMUNICATION AND AFFECT

Volume 1 • NONVERBAL COMMUNICATION
Edited by Lester Krames, Patricia Pliner, and Thomas Alloway

Volume 2 • NONVERBAL COMMUNICATION OF AGGRESSION
Edited by Patricia Pliner, Lester Krames, and Thomas Alloway

Volume 3 • ATTACHMENT BEHAVIOR
Edited by Thomas Alloway, Patricia Pliner, and Lester Krames

Volume 4 • AGGRESSION, DOMINANCE, AND INDIVIDUAL SPACING
Edited by Lester Krames, Patricia Pliner, and Thomas Alloway

Volume 5 • PERCEPTION OF EMOTION IN SELF AND OTHERS
Edited by Patricia Pliner, Kirk R. Blankstein, and Irwin M. Spigel

Volume 6 • ASSESSMENT AND MODIFICATION OF EMOTIONAL BEHAVIOR
Edited by Kirk R. Blankstein, Patricia Pliner, and Janet Polivy

Volume 7 • SELF-CONTROL AND SELF-MODIFICATION OF EMOTIONAL BEHAVIOR
Edited by Kirk R. Blankstein and Janet Polivy

Volume 8 • AGING AND COGNITIVE PROCESSES
Edited by F. I. M. Craik and Sandra Trehub

A Continuation Order Plan is available for this series. A continuation order will bring delivery of each new volume immediately upon publication. Volumes are billed only upon actual shipment. For further information please contact the publisher.

ADVANCES IN THE STUDY OF COMMUNICATION AND AFFECT

Volume 8

# AGING AND COGNITIVE PROCESSES

Edited by

F. I. M. Craik and Sandra Trehub

*University of Toronto*
*Mississauga, Ontario, Canada*

PLENUM PRESS • NEW YORK AND LONDON

Library of Congress Cataloging in Publication Data

Main entry under title:

Aging and cognitive processes.

(Advances in the study of communication and affect; v. 8)

Papers presented at the 10th annual psychology symposium held at the Erindale Campus of the University of Toronto in the summer of 1980.

Includes bibliographical references and index.

1. Aged—Psychology—Congresses. 2. Aging—Psychological aspects—Congresses. 3. Cognition—Congresses. I. Craik, Fergus I. M. II. Trehub, Sandra, 1938- . III. Series. [DNLM: 1. Aging—Congresses. 2. Cognition—In old age—Congresses. W1 AD8801 v.8/WT 150 A2656 1980]

BF724.85.C64A37 1982 155.67′182-18129

ISBN 0-306-40946-1


A Division of Plenum Publishing Corporation
233 Spring Street, New York, N.Y. 10013



Printed in the United States of America

# Contributors

BRIAN P. ACKERMAN

*Department of Psychology, University of Delaware, Newark, Delaware*

DAVID ARENBERG

*Gerontology Research Center, National Institute on Aging, Baltimore, Maryland*

A. JOHN ARROWOOD

*Department of Psychology, University of Toronto, Toronto, Ontario, Canada*

JERRY AVORN

*Division on Aging, Harvard Medical School, Boston, Massachusetts*

PAUL BALTES

*College of Human Development, The Pennsylvania State University, University Park, Pennsylvania*

ROBIN A. BARR

*Department of Experimental Psychology, University of Oxford, Oxford, England*

MARK BYRD

*Department of Psychology, Erindale College, University of Toronto, Mississauga, Ontario, Canada*

FERGUS I. M. CRAIK

*Department of Psychology, Erindale College, University of Toronto, Mississauga, Ontario, Canada*

JOHN L. HORN

*Department of Psychology, University of Denver, Denver, Colorado*

IRENE M. HULICKA

*Faculty of Natural and Social Sciences, State University College at Buffalo, Buffalo, New York*

JANET L. LACHMAN

*Department of Psychology, University of Houston, Houston, Texas*

ROY LACHMAN

*Department of Psychology, University of Houston, Houston, Texas*

MARY W. LAURENCE

*Department of Psychology, University of Toronto, Toronto, Ontario, Canada*

D. R. CRAPPER MCLACHLAN

*Department of Physiology and Medicine, University of Toronto, Toronto, Ontario, Canada*

DAVID B. MITCHELL

*Institute of Child Development, University of Minnesota, Minneapolis, Minnesota*

MORRIS MOSCOVITCH

*Department of Psychology, Erindale College, Mississauga, Ontario, Canada*

MARION PERLMUTTER

*Institute of Child Development, University of Minnesota, Minneapolis, Minnesota*

TED L. PETIT

*Scarborough College, University of Toronto, Toronto, Ontario, Canada*

PATRICK M. A. RABBITT

*Department of Experimental Psychology, University of Durham, Durham, England*

Jan Rabinowitz

*Department of Psychology, Erindale College, University of Toronto, Mississauga, Ontario, Canada*

David Schonfield

*Department of Psychology, University of Calgary, Calgary, Alberta, Canada*

Don W. Taylor

*Department of Psychology, University of Houston, Houston, Texas*

David A. Walsh

*Department of Psychology and Andrus Gerontology Center, University of Southern California, Los Angeles, California*

Nancy C. Waugh

*Department of Experimental Psychology, University of Oxford, Oxford, England*

Sherry L. Willis

*College of Human Development, The Pennsylvania State University, University Park, Pennsylvania*

Gordon Winocur

*Department of Psychology, Trent University, Peterborough, Ontario, Canada*

Diana S. Woodruff

*Department of Psychology, Temple University, Philadelphia, Pennsylvania*

# Preface

For a variety of reasons, there has been an explosion of interest in research on aging over the past few years. The reasons include an awareness that a large and growing proportion of our population is over 65 and that research findings can contribute to their health, satisfaction, and efficiency as members of society; the fact that funding agencies have endorsed the need for more research effort in the area by setting up special programs; and also the fact that researchers themselves are turning more to practical problems as many theoretical issues (in experimental psychology at least) seem to remain as intractable as ever. Thus, at present there is widespread interest in aging, but there is also a lack of knowledge as to what has already been accomplished in the area, what the theoretical issues are, and what factors contribute to the methodological and practical difficulties. The time is propitious for meetings of experts in various aspects of the aging process, both to discuss among themselves latest advances in the field and also to integrate known information for researchers and practitioners.

In the summer of 1980 we organized such a meeting as the 10th annual psychology symposium to be held at the Erindale Campus of the University of Toronto. The topic chosen was *Aging and Cognitive Processes,* and the edited contributions to the symposium form the chapters of the present book. It is possible to argue that intellectual functioning, broadly speaking, is *the* central topic for a full understanding of the aging process and its ramifications. The processes of attending, remembering, comprehending, thinking, talking, and acting are crucial for the satisfaction and enjoyment an older person gets from living, for his or her mental health, and for his or her continuing ability to function well as a member of the work force and of society generally. How are we to understand the changes in cognitive functioning that take place as the person grows older? Do the changes depend on underlying physiological changes in the nervous system or in other body systems—if so, are these changes inevitable? Can cognitive changes be understood in terms of failures or differences in psychological components of specific cognitive processes? And are such differences due to disuse, to environmental changes, to inevitable maturational changes; are they changes in structures or changes in processes; alternatively, are the widely reported declines in cognitive functioning with age greatly exaggerated—is there evidence that under appropriate circumstances older people do as well as or better than their younger counterparts? The contributors to the present volume address these and related issues.

The book is organized in four sections, broadly following the organization of the symposium itself. The first section deals with underlying neuroanatomical and neurophysiological changes with age and their possible relations to changes in cognitive abilities; the second reports empirical and theoretical developments in perception and memory; the third deals with age differences in higher mental processes; and the fourth section reports work with more directly practical consequences for further research and practice.

We would like to thank various people and organizations for their support at various stages of the project. First, the symposium was funded jointly by grants from Erindale College, from the Programme in Gerontology at the University of Toronto, and from the Natural Sciences and Engineering Research Council of Canada. We are extremely grateful to these bodies; the meeting and the consequent volume would not have been possible without their support.

The meeting itself was opened by Dr. Blossom Wigdor, Director of the Programme in Gerontology at the University of Toronto, and we would like to thank her both for these opening remarks and for her support of the project. The symposium included papers by three people who were unable to contribute to the present volume—David Drachman, Jonathan Freedman, and Marcel Kinsbourne—we are very grateful for their excellent contributions to the meeting.

Finally, we wish to record our gratitude to various members of the Department of Psychology and the Centre for Research in Human Development at the Erindale Campus, University of Toronto, for their help at every stage during the organization of the meeting and editing of this volume. They include Maureen Patchett, Gayle Dyckman, Shannon Thompson, and Susan Curry. We are most appreciative of all their help.

Fergus I. M. Craik
Sandra Trehub

# Contents

Chapter 17



Chapter 18

CHAPTER 1

# Neuroanatomical and Clinical Neuropsychological Changes in Aging and Senile Dementia

Ted L. Petit

*Scarborough College*
*University of Toronto*
*Toronto, Ontario, Canada*

> Throughout recorded history, the tragedy of aging has been, not that it comes, but that so often it brings with it a host of changes in the psychosocial patterns of the individual, changes that may degrade and enfeeble the most gallant and competent. We cannot fail to share, as psychiatrists and as human beings, the pain of subject, family, and friends walking this bitter path together. But we must not lose sight of the fact that where substrate mechanisms can be identified, there is hope, if not of a way back, then at least of a gentler path which may give to more of the aged, some measure of those much-celebrated compensations of age. (Scheibel & Scheibel, 1977, p. 39)

What is to follow must be considered merely a temporary review of the present state of the art. Research on aging, the brain, and behavior is in an explosive state; out of what appeared a very long history of ignorance and neglect there is emerging a rapidly growing field of research. Changes are occurring so rapidly in the field that this review will probably be outdated before it reaches the press, and considering the crucial importance of the research, I hope that it will be.

## Aging: Normal versus Pathological

It is important for those interested in aging and cognitive processes to understand those concomitant changes occurring in the human brain with aging, for these neural changes may underlie the observed cognitive changes. But perhaps more importantly, psychologists frequently discuss behavioral findings in the "normal old" or cognitive differences between the "normal old" and the demented with the incorrect assumption that the two are organically qualitatively different. This chapter should be of as much importance to those who are interested in "normal aging" as it is to those interested in senile dementia, because in the human, "normal" individuals and individuals displaying symptoms of senile dementia are organically quantitatively, not qualitatively, different. It should also be of personal interest, as some of these changes are already well underway in all of us.

At this point, there are about 23 million people over the age of 65 in the United States and Canada, or a number approximately equal to the entire population of Canada. Of these, 10–15% are said to show some signs of senile dementia, and the prevalence is much higher in the eighth and ninth decades (Wisniewski & Terry, 1976; Wang, 1977). Approximately 4–5% of the over 65 age group are classified as seriously demented, giving us approximately 1,000,000 seriously demented people in North America.

Until recently, it was commonly assumed that senile dementia was caused by arteriosclerosis. Fisher (1968), however, reported that the amount of cerebral vessel arteriosclerosis bears little, if any, relation to the degree of clinical dementia. There is an observable decrease in cerebral blood flow in the demented, but it is presently believed that this is more likely a *result* of lost cerebral cortical tissue, not the *cause* of it. In contrast, Alzheimer's disease, which was originally classified as a presenile disorder, was known to cause basically identical symptoms of senile dementia in individuals under the age of 65. We now realize that this age distinction is no longer valid; the majority of cases of senile dementia beyond the age of 65 are caused by Alzheimer's disease (Terry & Davies, 1980) and, what is more, these pathological changes of Alzheimer's disease occur usually to a lesser degree in almost all intellectually preserved old people.

Autopsy studies have indicated that the majority (50–70%) of demented individuals show morphological changes identical to Alzheimer's disease and thus suffer from senile dementia of the Alzheimer's type (SDAT) (Tomlinson & Henderson, 1976; Wisniewski & Terry, 1976; Wells, 1978). Another 15–20% of the cases have a mixture of vascular and Alzheimer's changes, but the impression of most investigators is that the Alzheimer's changes are the contributing factor to the behavioral dementia. Approximately 10–20% of the cases involve vascular disorders or gross infarcts, with the remaining small percentage of the cases caused by a number of other degenerative diseases. Thus, SDAT is the most common known cause of senile dementia, with a prevalence of 3 per 1,000 of the general population.

SDAT appears to be an age-related disease with increased frequency of onset beyond the age of 65, just as measles occurs most frequently in youth and cancer beyond the age of 50. Interestingly, SDAT occurs in all patients with

Down's syndrome beyond the age of 40 (De Boni & Crapper McLachlan, 1980) and there is a 3- to-5-fold increase in SDAT in first-degree relatives of SDAT patients (Wisniewski & Terry, 1976). The life expectancy of individuals with SDAT is very short. From the onset of symptoms, 50% are dead in 3 years, 95% are dead in 5 years. This makes SDAT the fourth largest killer, causing over 130,000 deaths in North America each year. Yet SDAT is not on the list of top killers because the direct cause of death is usually secondary infection. Because of the above findings, it now seems apparent that SDAT is, as its name implies, the result of a specific disease process, not an inevitable consequence of advancing years. As yet, however, there is no known cause or cure for SDAT.

Although SDAT may be a disease, it appears to be manifest to some degree in all old people, even those who are intellectually intact. Senile changes as well as areas of ischemic destruction occur frequently in the elderly without noticeable effect on mental function (Tomlinson & Henderson, 1976). Tomlinson and Henderson reported that 79% of their normal aged "controls" had senile plaques, 73% had granulovacuolar degeneration, and 59% had neurofibrillary degeneration (see below for description of these changes). Indeed, 100% of individuals over 80 have some degree of neurofibrillary degeneration. Just as there are clinically normal persons with marked histological changes, there are also severely demented patients with minimal histological changes (Katzman, Terry, & Bick, 1978; Blessed, Tomlinson, & Roth, 1968). Thus, the correlation between the amount of neuropathological change and the presence, absence, or severity of dementia is less than perfect (Sherwin & Selzer, 1977).

Nonetheless, a strong correlation between the amount of neuropathological change and the degree of the dementia does exist. There is a significantly greater severity of the above-noted changes in the demented than in the nondemented population. In about 75% of the demented, the severity of the changes is greater than that found in almost any cases in the nondemented (Tomlinson & Henderson, 1976). Therefore, quantitative rather then qualitative differences exist between normal aging and SDAT. This has led Wisniewski and Terry (1976) to suggest that "normal aging is simply that stage of pathology without clinical expression. The presence or absence of the clinical manifestation does not mean that the cellular process is different except in degree" (p. 266).

## Neuroanatomical Changes

There are a number of changes seen in the aging brain. They can be divided into those seen inside the cell, at the electron microscopic level, those seen outside the cell, within the tissue, at the light microscopic level, and those observable by gross visualization of the brain. In this review, I will start at the finest level, looking at changes within the cell. I will then step back and look at changes in the tissue, then, stepping back further, look at changes in the brain as a whole. Finally, I will step outside the individual and look at changes in behavior. In discussing each of the anatomical changes, I will attempt insofar as possible to define each of the changes and then discuss what causes them, where the changes are found, what neural or behavioral effects we think the changes may have, and what relationships may exist between the observation of these changes and the presence or degree of behavioral changes of dementia.

## *Electron Microscopic Observations*

*Lipofuscin.* Lipofuscin is the accumulation in the cell of a yellow to brown pigment, as fine granules 1–3 μm in diameter or as clumped masses (Figure 1; Brizzee, Harkin, Ordy, & Kaak, 1975). Lipofuscin, the "age pigment," shows a slow, steady accumulation in the cell body with increasing age. Lipofuscin is also known to accumulate in certain other neuropathological conditions, as well

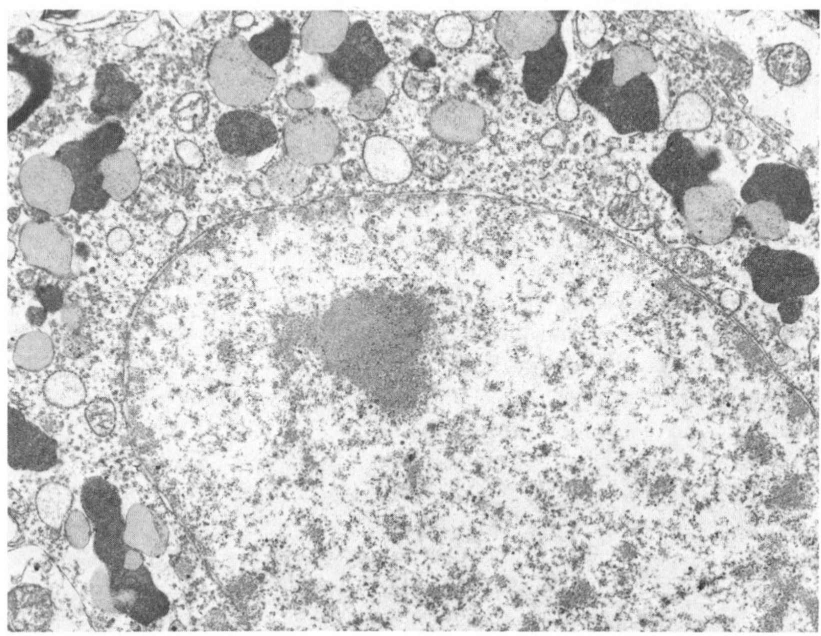

Fig. 1. Lipofuscin bodies forming polar cap in perikaryon at base of apical dendrite in pyramidal cell neuron of human frontal cerebral cortex. Lipofuscin bodies show electron-lucent and electron-dense components. × 12,000. (From Brizzee *et al.*, 1975, with the permission of the author and publisher.)

as in epilepsy, anoxia, and alcoholism (Siakotos, Armstrong, Koppang, & Muller, 1977).

Lipofuscin is accumulated in different regions of the central nervous system (CNS) at different rates. The accumulation has been observed quite early in certain neural centers; for instance, lipofuscin has been observed in the spinal cord of fetuses and in the inferior olive of 3-month-old children (Brizzee, Harkin, Ordy, & Kaak, 1975).

While the inferior olive and dentate nucleus usually both show appreciable degrees of pigment storage by the sixth to tenth *year* of life (Hopker, 1951), the palladium accumulates significant amounts of lipofuscin only after the seventh or eighth *decade* (Wahren, 1957). Lipofuscin accumulation has been observed in a number of animal species. For example, in the rhesus monkey, as in the human, the earliest accumulation of lipofuscin is seen in the inferior olive at 3 months, with all CNS structures, except the medial nucleus of the superior olive, showing lipofuscin accumulation by 10 years of age (Brizzee, Ordy, & Kaak, 1974).

It appears, therefore, that lipofuscin accumulation begins early in life and shows a gradual but dramatic age-dependent accumulation in the brain. Different parts of the brain also appear to accumulate lipofuscin at different rates. The rank order found by Brizzee *et al.* (1974) for lipofuscin accumulation from the lowest to the highest regional means was: (1) cerebellum, (2) neocortex, (3) pons, (4) midbrain, (5) hippocampus, and (6) medulla. Some neurons, such as the medial nucleus of the superior olive, accumulate almost no lipofuscin.

Within the cell, lipofuscin tends to accumulate deep to the base of the apical dendrites in pyramidal neurons in the rat motor cortex and rat and monkey hippocampus (Brizzee, Cancilla, Sherwood, & Timiras, 1969). In most other types of neurons, the distribution is variable and appears to be randomly distributed in the cell body.

The origin and exact structure of lipofuscin is presently unknown. Electron microscopic examination indicates that lipofuscin is composed of two major components: a granular, electron-dense component and a vessicular, probably lipid-containing, electron-lucent component. The entire lipofuscin granule is contained within a single limiting membrane (Brizzee *et al.*, 1975).

Lipofuscin is composed predominantly of lipid (50%) and protein (30%). Different researchers have argued that lipofuscin originates from lysosomes, golgi apparati, or mitochondria (see Brizzee *et al.*, 1975). Recent histochemical and electron microscopic evidence leads most researchers presently to agree on a lysosomal origin (Hasan & Glees, 1972, 1973). It has been suggested that lipofuscin develops by the continuous fusion of lysosomes with lipid globules or lipid-filled lysosomes (Siakotos *et al.*, 1977).

A number of researchers have attempted to understand the function and potential effects of lipofuscin accumulation, but here is little present understanding. On the negative side, researchers have suggested that lipofuscin may interfere with transport and movement of elements within the cytoplasm, thus clogging the cell. Others have suggested that it might accumulate, interfering with cell metabolism to the point at which cell death occurs (Brody, 1976). Brizzee *et al.* (1976) found that the accumulation of lipofuscin in layer IV cells of rhesus monkey somatosensory cortex was correlated with a loss of cells in that area.

However, cells of the inferior olive, which have the largest accumulation of lipofuscin in the CNS, show no evidence of decreasing cell number with age, while in the cerebral cortex, where lipofuscin deposits never reach a high level, cell number does decrease with age (Brody, 1976). Thus, each cell may have a different capacity for surviving with lipofuscin, or lipofuscin may not have any effect on cell survival. To date, there is no *direct* evidence that it is harmful to cells or that there is an increased amount of lipofuscin in dementia (Mann & Sinclair, 1978; Terry & Davies, 1980). Some researchers have suggested that it is a harmless product of normal cell metabolism, while others have even suggested that lipofuscin may be helpful as an intracellular oxygen stock, storing oxygen for critical times (Karnaukhov, 1973).

One must not dismiss the possibility of harmful effects of lipofuscin too quickly, however, for, as we will see, no single agent or neuropathological change is capable of explaining the dramatic withering and loss of cells observed in the aging human brain.

It is possible to dissolve lipofuscin from the cell with the drug meclofenoxate (Lucidril, Centrophenoxine) (Nandy & Bourne, 1966; Nandy, 1968; Riga & Riga, 1974). Such a treatment prolongs the median life span and improves the learning capacities of old mice (Hochschild, 1973a,b; Nandy & Lal, 1978). This information suggests that lipofuscin may be exerting a detrimental effect on neurobehavioral functions, although its exact nature is unknown.

*Neurofillamentous Tangles.* There are two major types of neurofibrous cell organelles in adult neurons: neurotubules, 24 nm in diameter, and neurofilaments, 10 nm in diameter. In normal neurons, neurotubules and filaments are long, straight, thread-like fibers running through and parallel to the long axis of axons and dendrites.

It now appears that the major function of the neurotubule is to transport substances within the cytoplasm to distant regions of the dendrite or axon (Schubert & Kreutzberg, 1975). This active transport system is crucial in neurons, where, unlike most other cells of the body which are generally quite compact, neuronal processes can extend great distances from the cell body (up to 3 feet in man). Thus, a transport mechanism is essential for the growth and survival of distal cell processes; while small molecules may be picked up from the immediate environment, the distal processes depend on the transport of macromolecules, essential for cell life, from the soma. Disruption of neurotubules leading to a disruption of cytoplasmic transport disrupts dendritic growth (Petit & Isaacson, 1977) and causes atrophy of dendrites in the adult (Petit, 1977; Petit, Biederman, & McMullen, 1980). Although the role of neurofilaments is less well understood, they are presently thought to assist in this transport mechanism.

Neurofilamentous tangles commonly seen in the aging brain are abnormal intraneuronal accumulations of masses of paired helical filaments, that is, paired 10 nm filaments twisted in a double helix with an average periodicity of 80 nm (see Figure 2; Kidd, 1964; Wisniewski, Narang, & Terry, 1976). As tangles progressively fill the cytoplasm, they eventually push the nucleus to one side and often extend out into the axons and dendrites (Terry & Davies, 1980). In SDAT, they are found in 1–10% of neurons at death (De Boni & Crapper McLachlan, 1980).

The exact cause or composition of neurofilamentous tangles is not presently known. Most researchers agree that they are probably a result of a disturbance of normal neurotubules or neurofilaments. The chemical analysis has indicated that the tangles are composed of a new protein, which some researchers suggest most closely resembles neurofilaments and others suggest most closely resembles neurotubules; there is still some debate on the issue (Iqbal, Grundke-Iqbal, Wisniewski, Korthals, & Terry, 1976; Terry & Davies, 1980).

The first accumulations of such tangles are observed in the hippocampus (Morel & Wildi, 1952); where they can be seen in middle age (Tomlinson & Henderson, 1976). Tomlinson (1972) has stressed that when tangles are observed in intellectually intact old people, they are found predominantly in the hippocampus. In fact, considerable numbers of tangles are observed in the hippocampus and subiculum of the intellectually intact aged, and by the tenth decade few individuals have no such lesions (Tomlinson & Henderson, 1976).

Neurofilamentous tangles appear later in the layer III pyramids of the prefrontal and superior temporal neocortex. The frequency of tangles increases markedly in both the neocortex and HI region of the hippocampus in SDAT (Terry & Davies, 1980). Tangles are found predominantly in the cerebral cortex, mesencephalon, and lower rhombencephalon; the cerebellum, basal ganglia, lower rhombencephalon, and spinal cord are rarely affected (Iqbal, Wisniewski, Grundke-Iqbal, & Terry, 1977). In particular, cerebellar Purkinje cells, dorsal root ganglion cells, and primary sensory nuclei of the brainstem never appear to be involved (see De Boni & Crapper McLachlan, 1980).

Neurofibrillary tangles are not unique to SDAT; they are observed in other neuropathological conditions such as Parkinsonism, amniotropic lateral sclerosis, and Down's syndrome. They are, however, unique to the neurons of man, and are not seen in aging or other neurological diseases of other animals.

While neurofibrillary tangles are found in the normal aged, heavy tangle formation throughout the cortex is invariably associated with dementia. Further, the concentration of tangles is quantitatively strongly correlated with the degree of psychometric deficiency of the patients (Tomlinson & Henderson, 1976).

Although the exact effects of tangle accumulation are unknown, the high correlation with dementia scores suggests a detrimental effect. A number of

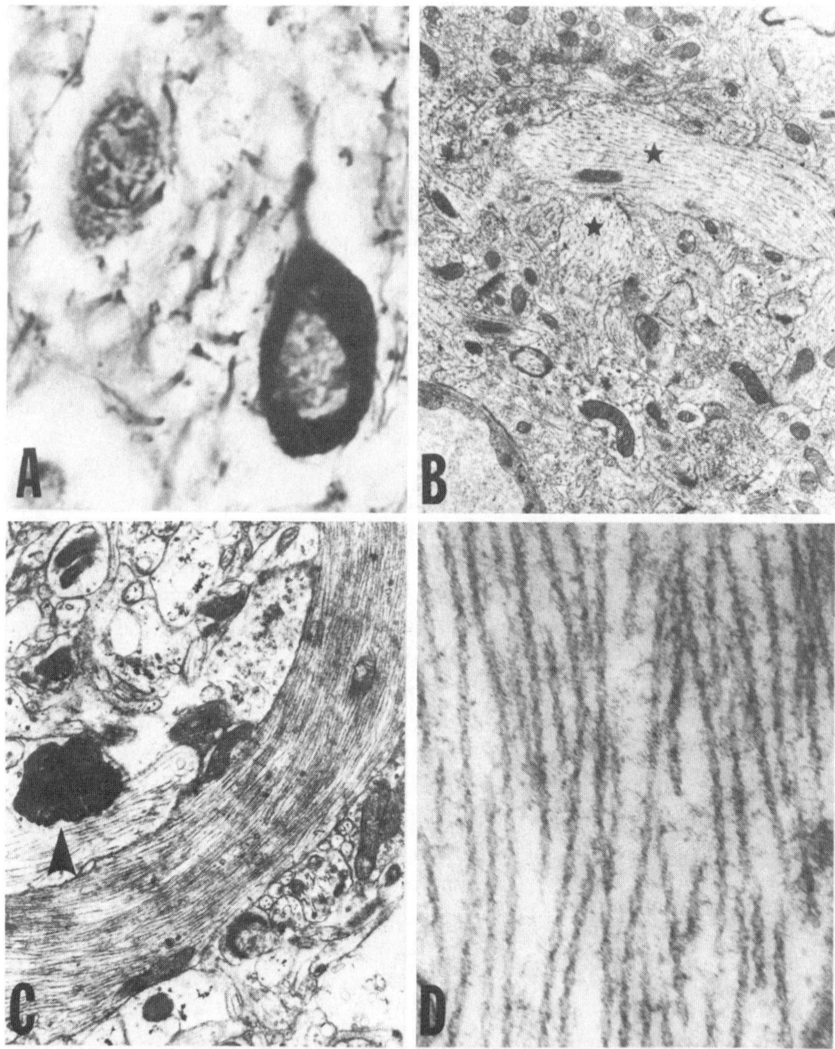


Fig. 2. (A) Neuron (right) with perinuclear aggregate of argentophilic neurofibrillary degeneration. Normal neuron at left (Bielchowsky stain, × 700). (B) Ultrastructure of normal human neuropil, with abundant microtubules in neuronal cytoplasma (⋆) (glutaraldehyde/osmium preparation, × 8000). (C) Ulstrastructural appearance of aggregate of paired helical filaments in cerebral cortical neuron of patient with Alzheimer's disease. Electron-dense particle (arrow head) is lipofuscin or ''age pigment'' (glutaraldehyde/osmium preparation, × 19000). (D) Higher power micrography of paired helical filaments characteristic of Alzheimer's disease. Note regular period of approximately 800 Å (glutaraldehyde/osmium preparation, × 94000). Reduced 31% for reproduction. (From DeBoni & Crapper McLachlan, 1980, with the permission of the author and publisher.)

researchers have suggested the possibility that tangles may interfere with normal cytoplasmic transport, thus blocking normal cellular functioning and potentially leading to atrophy of distal cell processes and ultimately to cell death (Mehraein, Yamada, & Tarnowska-Dziduszko, 1975; Petit, Biederman, & McMullen 1980; Scheibel & Scheibel, 1975, 1977). It is of interest to note that cytoplasmic transport is reduced in aged animals that do not show neurofibrillary tangles (Geinisman & Bondareff, 1976; Komiya, 1980; McMartin & O'Connor 1979).

*Granulovacuolar Changes.* Granulovacuolar changes are characterized by the presence of small vacuoles in the neuronal cytoplasm, or at the base of the dendrite (see Figure 3; Scheibel & Scheibel, 1975). Electron microscopic examination indicates that these vacuoles are surrounded by a limiting membrane and consist of an electron-lucent particle with a small central electron-dense granule (Hirano, Demlitzer, Kurland, & Zimmerman, 1968). Their origin and function or effect are unknown, but the presence of these small intracellular granules is limited to hippocampal pyramidal neurons.

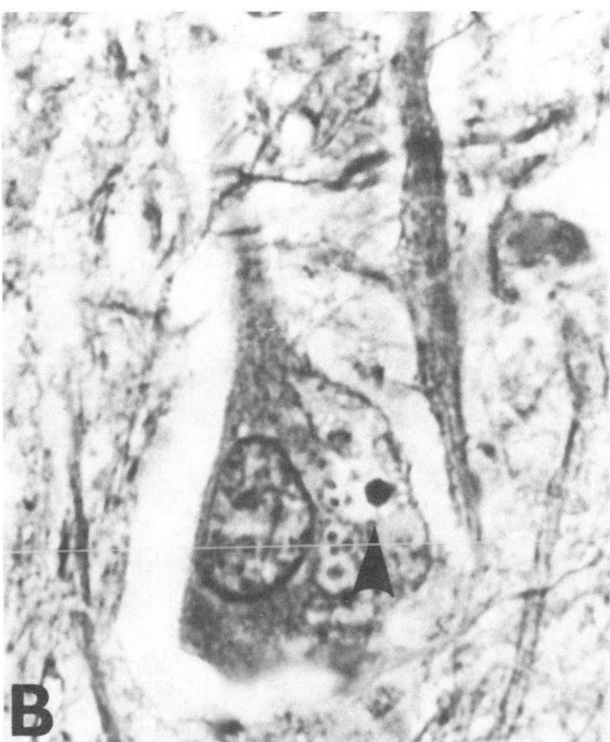


Fig. 3. Granulovacuolar degeneration in pyramidal neuron of hippocampus in patient with Alzheimer's disease (Bielschowsky stain, × 700). (From DeBoni & Crapper McLachlan, 1980, with the permission of the author and publisher.)

Granulovacuolar changes are seen in 75–80% of the intellectually intact aged, but in the majority the number of affected cells is small (Sherwin & Seltzer, 1977; Tomlinson & Kitchener, 1972). However, both the incidence and degree of granulovacuolar change are significantly higher in the brains of the demented (Ball, 1978; Tomlinson, Blessed, & Roth, 1968, 1970). Tomlinson and Kitchener (1972) found that 90% of the subjects with more than 9% of their hippocampal neurons involved were demented. There is a strong correlation between the severity of granulovacuolar changes and the degree of dementia, neurofibrillary tangles, and senile plaques (Ball & Lo, 1977; Tomlinson & Kitchener, 1972; Woodard, 1972). In cases of SDAT, granulovacuolar changes can be so extensive as to involve virtually all hippocampal pyramids (Scheibel & Scheibel, 1975).

## *Light Microscopic Changes*

*Dendritic Atrophy.* One of the most striking effects of aging and SDAT on the brain is the marked atrophy of dendritic processes (see Figure 4). The dendrites are the major receptive area of the cells and are responsible for receiving

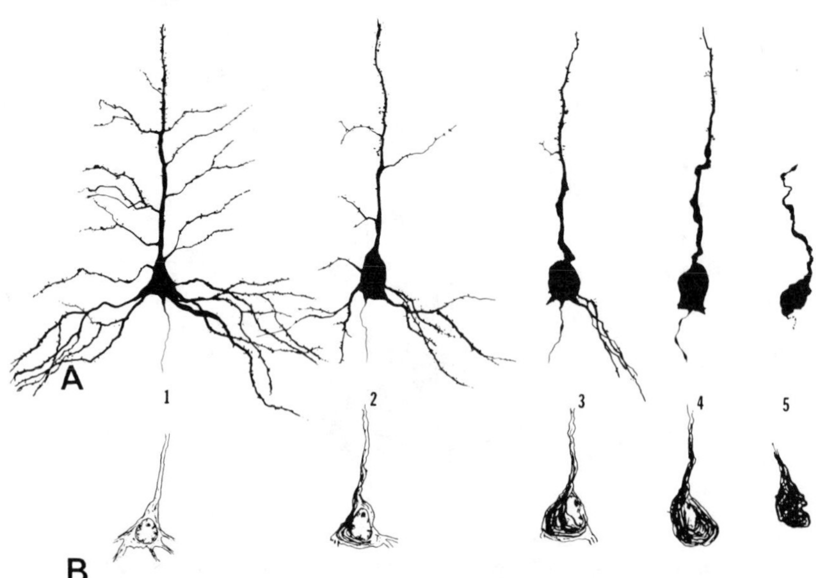


Fig. 4. Progression of senile changes in cortical pyramids as seen in Golgi impregnations (A) and in Bielchowsky stains (B). (From Scheibel & Scheibel, 1975, with the permission of the author and publisher.)

and integrating neuronal information. Scheibel and Scheibel (1975, 1977) have demonstrated a dramatic loss of the dendritic processes with advancing age. The earliest change they noted in neocortical cells involved a bulging and irregular swelling of the cell body. Shortly thereafter, local areas of swelling develop along the dendritic shafts, and the basilar dendrites begin to decrease in length and number. The basilar dendrites continue to diminish by either shrivelling up or completely disappearing as if they had been cut off. There is a progressive loss of dendritic spines as well as horizontal and oblique dendritic branches, with a progressive dying back toward the original vertical apical shaft. "The final stages of senile deterioration show that the apical shaft becomes shorter and more tortuous and and may begin to break up as the soma enters the final stages of distortion, pyknosis, and neuronopathy" (Scheibel & Scheibel, 1975). A similar stripping of dendritic spines and distortion and dismembering of dendritic branches culminating in a swollen, dying cell body has been described in hippocampal pyramidal and granule cells and pyramidal cells of the entorhinal cortex (Machado-Salas & Scheibel, 1979; Scheibel & Scheibel, 1977). The loss of dendritic spines in the demented has been quantified by Mehraein *et al.* (1975), who also noted a shortening of vermal Purkinje cell dendrites in SDAT patients. However, Cragg (1975) did not find the number of synapses per unit area of electron micrographs to be reduced in the demented.

These signs of dendritic atrophy were observed in the intellectually intact aged as well as the demented. However, the dendritic atrophy is greater in SDAT than in age-matched controls, and the Scheibels suggest that these changes are correlated more closely with the patient's antecedent level of psychomotor capacities than his calendar age. Nonetheless, "it is clear that similar changes, in milder form and to varying degrees invariably characterize the aging process" (Scheibel & Scheibel, 1977).

While this knowledge of dendritic atrophy may present a particularly gloomy picture of advancing age, recently Buell and Coleman (1979) indicated that there may be two populations of cells, those undergoing atrophy and those not. They found an increase in dendritic branching in elderly nondemented individuals compared to middle-aged adults, indicating that healthy old dendrites continue to grow and branch with age.

Similar changes in dendritic structure have been reported in nonhuman animals, although the degree of change does not appear to be as severe. Mervis (1978) has shown similar changes in aged primates and dogs. The most extensive research has centered on the rat (Feldman, 1974, 1977; Geinisman & Bondareff, 1976; Geinisman, Bondareff, & Dodge, 1977; Vaughan, 1977). The complexity of branching is reduced in layer V basal and oblique dendrites in the visual and auditory cortex. The neocortical neuronal cell body decreases in size, and there is a decrease in the number of synapses in the neocortex and hippocampal dentate gyrus. The thinning of dendritic spines and processes observed in the rodent neocortex, although somewhat similar to that observed in the human, is not nearly so severe. The extreme dendritic atrophy culminating in cell death appears to be confined to the human brain.

*Senile Plaques.* Senile plaques are spherical masses or areas found in cortical tissues (see Figure 5). They are composed of a central core of amyloid surrounded by what appears to be an area of intracellular and extracellular debris. Amyloid is a substance which appears to be of immunoglobulin origin and may result from phagocytic catabolism of antigen–antibody complexes (Wisniewski & Terry, 1976; Brizzee, 1975). The plaque is frequently surrounded by astrocytic processes and microglia (typically a sign of neuronal degeneration) and is often found adjacent to a capillary. Closer examination of these plaques with the electron microscope indicates that surrounding the amyloid core are masses of neural processes which contain large numbers of lamellar dense bodies and many mitochondria in various stages of degeneration (Terry & Davies, 1980). Despite the enlargement of the neuronal processes with pathological organelles, the plasma membrane is well preserved, and synaptic contacts appear normal

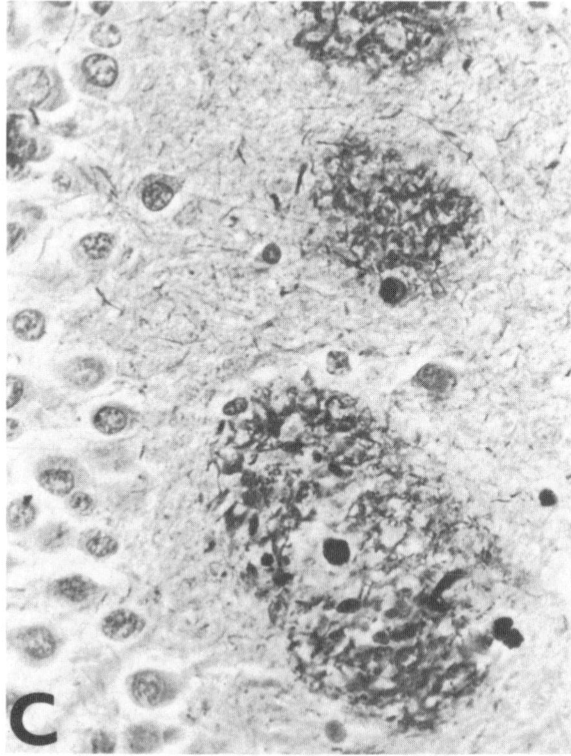


Fig. 5. Three senile plaques adjacent to granule cell layer (left) in hippocampus of patient with Alzheimer's disease. Note core in largest plaque × 300. (From DeBoni & Crapper McLachlan, 1980, with the permission of the author and publisher.)

(Gonatas, Anderson, & Evangelista, 1967; Wisniewski & Terry, 1976). This has led some researchers to suggest that the majority of the neuronal processes found in the plaque area are alive and connected to the cell body, thus raising the hope of functional recovery (Wisniewski & Terry, 1976).

The formation of plaques begins with a small group of enlarged axonal and dendritic processes containing clusters of mitochondria and dense lamellar bodies of presumed lysosomal origin (Brizzee, 1975; Terry & Wisniewski, 1970; Wisniewski & Terry, 1973). Amyloid is generally first seen after the plaque contains at least five distended processes. The plaque appears to grow with the accumulation of more glial cells and degenerating axons and dendrites and an enlargement of the amyloid core. In the final stages, the amyloid core continues to grow but with a reduction in neural processes, until the formation of the "burned out" plaque, which consists primarily of amyloid with a few peripheral processes rich in unusual intracellular inclusions.

Senile plaques are found primarily in the frontal, temporal, and occipital lobes of the cerebral cortex and in the hippocampus. Senile plaques are also found in the neocortex of aged dogs (Wisniewski *et al.*, 1970) and monkeys (Wisniewski, Ghetti, & Terry, 1973). They are also seen in other brain diseases of man and animals, sometimes associated with viral etiologies, implicating an infectious agent in SDAT (Bruce & Fraser, 1975; Bruce, Dickinson, & Fraser, 1976; Wisniewski, Bruce, & Fraser, 1975).

Senile plaques are also numerous in the brains of the intellectually and emotionally intact aged and are absent in some cases of obvious SDAT (Scheibel & Scheibel, 1975). Tomlinson and Henderson (1976) found that 15% of the general population in their 50s, 50% of individuals in their 70s, and 75% of individuals in their 90s have senile plaques. However, the number of plaques remains small in the undemented, and the plaque number tends to increase with the degree of dementia, showing an inverse correlation between plaque concentration and the subject's ability to perform on psychological tests (Roth, Tomlinson, & Blessed, 1966).

*Cell Loss.* From earlier discussions of dendritic atrophy culminating in cell death, it is not surprising to find a decrease in neuron number in SDAT. Of the brain areas studied, the hippocampus and neocortex appear to be the most affected, with the cerebellum suffering substantial loss as well. Within the neocortex, cell loss appears to be most prominent in the prefrontal and superior temporal areas (Brody & Vijayoshankar, 1977; Tomlinson & Henderson, 1976). In the most affected cortical areas, 50% of the cells are lost (Brody, 1955, 1973; Tomlinson & Henderson, 1976).

Cell loss in the cerebellum does not become appreciable until the 60th year, after which there is an average loss of 25% of the cerebellar Purkinje cells in the very old (Hall, Miller, & Corsellis, 1975; Harms, 1944).

Not all brain areas show cell loss. Certain areas of the cerebral cortex (e.g., inferior temporal gyrus), as well as many brainstem nuclei, particularly the inferior olivary nucleus, show little or no cell loss (Brody, 1973; Brody & Vijayashankar, 1977).

A larger cell loss was expected in cases of dementia than in the normal aged, but this was not borne out. Tomlinson and Henderson (1976) found that both groups had equally wide scatters of cell number, and no cases of dementia had cell numbers below those of the nondemented population for the age. This would indicate that dementia is not due to a massive loss of cell number but may represent aberrations in the remaining cells' structure or function.

A decreased cortical neuron number has also been reported in aged monkeys (Brizzee, Ordy, Hanschee, & Kaak, 1976). In aged rodents however, there appears to be less of a consensus on cell loss, with some researchers reporting cell loss and others not (Buetow, 1971; Brizzee, Sherwood, & Timiras, 1968; Dayan, 1971; Johnson & Erner, 1972; see Freund, 1980). Even if such a cell loss occurs, it would seem to occur only in the very oldest rodents, and it is apparently not of the same magnitude as that observed in the human.

## *Gross Changes*

As the brain ages, there is a progressive loss of neural tissue (Figure 6). This is most obviously seen as a marked atrophy of neocortical gyri and a widening of sulci (Andrew, 1971; Ordy, Kaak, & Brizzee, 1975). The ventricular system frequently becomes dilated, secondary to the often perceptibly shrunken cortical gray and white matter (Arendt, 1972; Scheibel & Scheibel, 1975). Total brain mass shrinks 10–15% in the normal aged (Wisniewski & Terry, 1976) or 5% by age 70, 10% by age 80, and 20% by age 90 (Minckler & Boyd, 1968).

The majority of the tissue loss in normal aging is in the cerebral cortex, where Corsellis (1976) found a 2% (female) to 3.5% (male) drop per decade from age 20. The atrophy is most marked over the frontal lobes, although parietal and temporal lobes suffer heavy losses.

Like most other changes discussed so far, there is no perfect correlation between brain loss and dementia. Some reports indicated increased brain loss in SDAT (Wisniewski & Terry, 1976; Corsellis, 1976). However, Tomlinson, Blessed, and Roth (1970) found that many senile dements do not have brains of smaller weight than "normal" controls. More recently, Terry and Davies (1980) reported that the mean brain weight in SDAT is not significantly below that of age-matched normals. Their measurements of cortical thickness in the frontal and superior temporal regions were also similar in the two groups.

Thus, while there is serious loss of brain (especially cortical) tissue with aging, like cell loss, this alone does not seem capable of explaining the behavioral changes in SDAT. However, as Terry and Davies point out, dementia is only diagnosed when there is considerable deterioration on a wide range of cerebral functions. It would appear that all aged people are suffering from cell

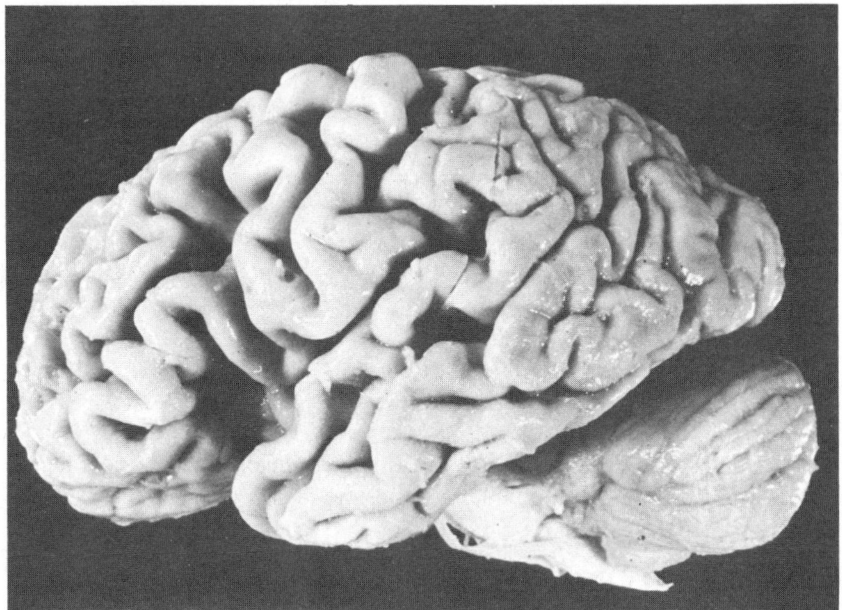

Fig. 6. Photograph of the brain of a patient with Alzheimer's disease. Note the diffuse atrophy that is slightly more severe in the frontal and temporal lobes. (From Schochet & McCormick, 1976, with the permission of the author and publisher.)

and tissue loss and are perhaps functioning organically at just below clinical levels. The behavioral manifestations probably become apparent when those neurons remaining reach a level of significant dysfunction.

## Clinical Neuropsychological Changes

The earliest symptoms of SDAT are usually subtle, with the patients showing lessened spontaneity and initiative and becoming quiet, apathetic, and withdrawn (De Boni & Crapper McLachlan, 1980; Joynt & Shoulson, 1979; Sherwin & Seltzer, 1977, Terry & Davies, 1980). They may also show some forgetfulness, an accentuation of prior behavioral traits to the point of eccentricity, and an inability to handle multiple mental operations (Joynt & Shoulson, 1979). As the condition progresses, along with disorientation and general decreases in judgement and memory, behavioral symptoms of the frontal, temporal, and parietal neuropathology become prominent. One typically finds (1) frontal lobe signs such as indifference to social decorum along with a loss of care about personal hygiene, interest in the environment, and insight; (2) parietal lobe signs such as tactile agnosia and apraxia; and (3) temporal lobe signs of speech and language problems, appearing first in word-finding difficulties and later in increasing simplification of language.

In the final stages, the patients may become boisterous, hyperactive, and assaultive, with a profound loss of higher mental functions, losing urinary and fecal control, necessitating total nursing care. Death usually results from secondary infections.

## Conclusions

Certain things seem apparent after examining research in the area of human aging. The first is that senile dementia is most frequently caused by Alzheimer's disease (not arteriosclerosis) and thus this review centered on that disease. SDAT itself appears to be a disease, not just a consequence of passing years. However, it is a disease of which virtually everyone shows neuropathological signs beyond the age of 65. The signs of the disease progressively accumulate, the rate varying in different individuals. There appears to be some critical point at which these neuropathological changes become manifest behaviorally. Therefore, most "normal" old people are suffering from subclinical cases of SDAT.

Perhaps the most important question left is "What causes SDAT?" The question may be examined at several levels. In terms of what causes the behavioral changes, dendritic atrophy and cell death appear to be major underlying factors. What, then, causes the dendritic atrophy culminating in cell death? Neurofibrillary tangles do not appear to be the cause because such tangles are not observed in cerebellar Purkinje cells which undergo 25% cell death. Granulovacuolar changes cannot account for the cell atrophy as these changes are only found in the hippocampus. Lipofuscin does not seem adequate as an explanation either, since large lipofuscin deposits are found in areas of no cell death and only small deposits are seen in areas of marked cell loss. It remains a possibility that cells are undergoing secondary degeneration following deafferentation from lack of cholinergic input. However, such marked atrophy seems hardly reasonable, and neural atrophy does not seem to be confined to areas of ACh input.

Therefore, there is not one known neuropathological change that can explain the neuronal atrophy observed in SDAT. It remains a possibility that several of the above noted changes, alone or in combination, are capable of producing neural atrophy. Conversely, some element not yet realized may be responsible.

The ultimate cause for SDAT is yet to be understood. Crapper McLachlan has suggested the possibility of aluminum involvement secondary to a viral infection. Certainly the hypothesis of a slow virus seems reasonable considering our knowledge of slow viral involvement in other CNS degenerative diseases. However, I will leave further discussion of this hypothesis to Crapper McLachlan in the following chapter.

The final question concerns cures or potential cures for SDAT. We have made some headway. We are now capable of dissolving lipofuscin, which results in increased cognitive abilities. With the recent knowledge of acetylcholine involvement, there is the possibility of pharmacological enhancement of the cholinergic system. Preliminary research with the acetylcholine precursor, choline, has been dissapointing, but this would be expected since the cells utilizing choline may be dead or dying. Cholinergic receptor enhancers, such as the anticholinesterase physostigmine, may be of more benefit. Much research is presently underway to understand the neurochemistry of neurofibrillary tangles and their genesis, and more research will undoubtedly be devoted to understanding the viral agent possibly responsible for SDAT. Thus, at this point there are some pharmacological agents of assistance, but for the foreseeable future we must rely on more psychological and medical symptomatic help.

Even if the cause of SDAT were known and a cure available, the problem of human aging would remain paramount. Many of the psychological problems of aging are independent of SDAT and reflect the difficulties of coping with aging and its other effects. These will wane only when man is able to free himself from the shackles of the aging process as a whole. Aging was an unfortunate concomitant of the evolution of sexual reproduction found in all but primitive organisms. It now seems likely that the whole process called development and aging may be intimately locked in our DNA structure and controlled by our histones. With our most recent advances in DNA research, perhaps we may some day be able to stop the biological clock ticking in all of us. Then man may finally be free of the medical and psychosocial difficulties inherent in growing older today.

## References

Andrew, S. *The anatomy of aging in man and animals.* New York: Grune & Stratton, 1971.

Arendt, A. Altern des Zentralnervensystems. In H. Gottfried (Ed.), *Handbuch der allegemeiner Pathologie.* New York: Springer, 1972.

Ball, M. J. Topographic distribution of neurofibrillary tangles and granulovacuolar degeneration in hippocampal cortex of aging and demented patients. A quantitative study. *Acta Neuropathologica,* 1978, *42,* 73–80.

Ball, M. J., & Lo, P. Granulovacuolar degeneration in the aging brain and in dementia. *Journal of Neuropathology and Experimental Neurology,* 1977, *36,* 474–487.

Blessed, G., Tomlinson, B. E., & Roth, M. The association between quantitative measures of dementia and senile changes of the cerebral gray matter of elderly subjects. *British Journal of Psychiatry,* 1968, *14,* 797–811.

Brizzee, K. R. Gross morphometric analyses and quantitative histology of the aging brain. In J. M. Ordy & K. R. Brizzee (Eds.), *Neurobiology of aging*. New York: Plenum Press, 1975.

Brizzee, K. R., Cancilla, P. A., Sherwood, N., & Timiras, P. S. The amount of distribution of pigments in neurons and glia of the cerebral cortex. *Journal of Gerontology*, 1969, *24*, 127–135.

Brizzee, K. R., Harkin, J. C., Ordy, J. M., & Kaak, B. Accumulation and distribution of lipofuscin, amyloid and senile plaques in the aging neurons system. In H. Brody, D. Harman, & J. M. Ordy (Eds.), *Aging* (Vol. 1). New York: Raven, 1975.

Brizzee, K. R., Ordy, J. M., Hansche, J., & Kaak, B. Quantitative assessment of changes in neuron and glial cell packing density and lipofuscin accumulation with age in the cerebral cortex of nonhuman primate (macaca and mulatta). In R. D. Terry & S. Gershon (Eds.), *Neurobiology of aging*. New York: Raven Press, 1976.

Brizzee, K. R., Ordy, J. M., & Kaak, B. Early appearance and regional differences in intraneuronal and extraneuronal lipofuscin accumulation with age in the brain of a non-human primate (macaca & mulatta). *Journal of Gerontology*, 1974, *29*, 366–381.

Brizzee, K. R., Sherwood, N., & Timiras, P. S. A comparison of cell populations at various depth levels in cerebral cortex of young adult and aged Long-Evans rats. *Journal of Gerontology*, 1968, *23*, 289–297.

Brody, H. Organization of the cerebral cortex. III. A study of aging in the human cerebral cortex. *Journal of Comparative Neurology*, 1955, *102*, 511–556.

Brody, H. Aging in the vertebrate brain. In M. Rockstein (Ed.), *Development and aging of the nervous system*. New York: Academic Press, 1973.

Brody, H. An examination of cerebral cortex and brainstem aging. In R. D. Terry & S. Gershon (Eds.), *Neurobiology of aging*. New York: Raven Press, 1976.

Brody, H., & Vijayashankar, N. Cell loss with aging. In K. Nandy & I. Sherwin (Eds.), *The aging brain and senile dementia. Advances in behavioral biology* (Vol. 23). New York: Plenum Press, 1977.

Bruce, M. E., Dickinson, A. G., & Fraser, H. Cerebral amyloidosis in scrapie in the mouse: Effect of agent strain and mouse genotype. *Neuropathology and Applied Neurobiology*, 1976, *2*, 241–278.

Bruce, M. E., & Fraser, H. Amyloid plaques in the brains of mice infected with scrapie: Morphological variation and staining properties. *Neuropathology and Applied Neurobiology*, 1975, *1*, 189–202.

Buell, S. J., & Coleman, P. D. Dendritic growth in the aged human brain and failure of growth in senile dementia. *Science*, 1979, *206*, 854–856.

Buetow, D. E. Cellular content and cellular proliferation changes in the tissues and organs of the aging mammal. In I. L. Cameron & J. D. Thresher (Eds.), *Cellular and molecular renewal in the mammalian body*. New York: Academic Press, 1971.

Corsellis, J. A. W. Some observations on the Purkinje cell population and on brain volume in human aging. In R. D. Terry & S. Gershon (Eds.), *Neurobiology of aging*. New York: Raven Press, 1976.

Cragg, B. G. The density of synapses and neurons in normal, mentally defective, and aging human brains. *Brain*, 1975, *98*, 81–90.

Dayan, A. D. Comparative neuropathology of aging studies on the brains of 47 species of vertebrates. *Brain*, 1971, *94*, 31–32.

DeBoni, U., & Crapper McLachlan, D. R. Senile dementia and Alzheimer's disease. A current view. *Life Sciences*, *27*, 1–14, 1980.

Feldman, M. L. Degenerative changes in aging dendritis. *Gerontologist* 1974, *14* (Supp.), 36.

Feldman, M. L. Dendritic changes in aging rat brain. Pyramidal cell dendrite length and ultrastructure. In K. Nandy & I. Sherwin (Eds.), *The aging brain and senile dementia. Advances in behavioral biology* (Vol. 23). New York: Plenum Press, 1977.

Fisher, C. M. Dementia in cerebrovascular disease. In R. G. Siekert & J. P. Whisnant (Eds.), *Cerebral vascular disease, Sixth Conference*. New York: Grune & Stratton, 1968.

Freund, G. Cholinergic receptor loss in brains of aging mice. *Life Sciences*, 1980, *26*, 371–375.

Geinisman, Y., & Bondareff, W. Decrease in the number of synapses in the senescent brain: A quantitative electron microscopic analysis of the dentate gyrus of molecular layer in the rat. *Mechanisms of Aging and Development*, 1976, *5*, 11–23.

Geinisman, Y., Bondareff, W., & Dodge, J. T. Dendritic atrophy in the dentate gyrus of the senescent rat. *American Journal of Anatomy*, 1977, *152*, 321–330.

Gonatas, N. K., Anderson, W., & Evangelista, I. The contribution of altered synapses in the senile plaque: An electron microscopic study in Alzheimer's dementia. *Journal of Neuropathology and Experimental Neurology* 1967, *26*, 25–39.

Hall, T. C., Miller, A. K. H., & Corsellis, J. A. N. Variations in the human Purkinje cell population according to age and sex. *Neuropathology and Applied Neurobiology*, 1975, *1*, 267–292.

Harms, J. W. Altern und Somatod der Zellverbandstiere. *Zeitschrift für Alternforschung*, 1944, *5*, 73–126.

Hasan, M., & Glees, P. Genesis and possible dissolution of neuronal lipofuscin. *Gerontologia*, 1972, *18*, 217–236.

Hasan, M., & Glees, P. Lipofuscin in monkey "lateral geniculate body." An electron microscope study. *Acta Anatomica*, 1973, *84*, 85–95.

Hirano, A., Demlitzer, H. M., Kurland, L. T., & Zimmerman, H. M. The fine structure of some intraganglionic alterations. Neurofibrillary tangles, granulovacuolar bodies, and rod-like structures as seen in Guam amyotrophic lateral sclerosis and Parkinson-dementia complex. *Journal of Neuropathology and Experimental Neurology*, 1968, *27*, 167–182.

Hochschild, R. Effect of dimethylaminoethyl-p-chlorphenoxy-acetate on the life span of male Swiss Webster albino mice. *Experimental Gerontology*, 1973, *8*, 177–183. (a)

Hochschild, R. Effect of dimethylaminoethanol on the life span of senile male A/J mice. *Experimental Gerontology*, 1973, *8*, 185–192. (b)

Hopker, W. Das Altern des Nucleus dentatus. *Zeitschrift für Alternsforschung*, 1951, *5*, 256–277.

Iqbal, K., Grundke-Iqbal, I., Wisniewski, H. M., Korthals, J. K., & Terry, R. D. Chemistry of neurofibrous proteins in aging. In R. D. Terry & S. Gershon (Eds.), *Neurobiology of aging*. New York: Raven Press, 1976.

Iqbal, K., Wisniewski, H. M., Grundke-Iqbal, I., & Terry, R. D. Neurofibrillary pathology: An update. In K. Nandy & I. Sherwin (Eds.), *The aging brain and senile dementia Advances in behavioral biology* (Vol. 23). New York: Plenum Press, 1977.

Johnson, H. A., & Erner, S. Neuron survival in the aging mouse. *Experimental Gerontology*, 1972, *7*, 111–117.

Joynt, R. J., & Shoulson, I. Dementia. In K. E. Heilman & E. Valenstein (Eds.), *Clinical neuropsychology*. New York: Oxford, 1979.

Karnaukov, V. N. On the nature and function of yellow aging pigment lipofuscin. *Experimental Cell Research*, 1973, *80*, 479–483.

Katzman, R., Terry, R. D., & Bick, K. L. (Eds.). *Alzheimer's disease: Senile dementia and related disorders*. New York: Raven Press, 1978.

Kidd, M. Alzheimer's disease—An electron microscopical study. *Brain*, 1964, *87*, 307–319.

Komiya, Y. Slowing with age of the rate of slow axonal flow in bifurcating axons of rat dorsal root ganglion cells *Brain Research*, 1980, *183*, 477–480.

Machado-Salas, J. P., & Scheibel, A. B. Lymbic system of the aged mouse. *Experimental Neurology*, 1979, *63*, 347–355.

Mann, D. M. A., & Sinclair, K. G. A. The quantitative assessment of lipofuscin pigment, cytoplasmic RNA, and nuclear volume in senile dementia. *Neuropathology and Applied Neurobiology*, 1978, *4*, 129–135.

McMartin, D. N., & O'Connor, J. A., Jr. Effect of age on axoplasmic transport of cholinesterase in rat sciatic nerves. *Mechanisms of Aging and Development, 1979, 10,* 241–248.

Mehraein, P., Yamada, M., & Tarnowska-Dziduszko, E. Quantitative study on dendrites and dendritic spines in Alzheimer's disease and senile dementia. In G. W. Kreutzborg (Ed.), *Physiology and pathology of dendrites. Advances in neurobiology (Vol. 12).* New York: Raven Press, 1975.

Mervis, R. Structural alterations in neurons of aged canine neocortex: A golgi study. *Experimental Neurology,* 1978, *62,* 417–432.

Minckler, T. M., & Boyd, E. Physical growth. In J. Minckler (Ed.), *Pathology of the nervous system* (Vol. 1). New York: McGraw-Hill, 1968.

Morel, F., & Wildi, E. Clinique pathologique générale et cellulaire des altérations seniles et préséniles du cerveau. *Proceedings of the First International Congress on Neuropathology,* Rome, 1952, *2,* 237.

Nandy, K.,Further studies on the effects of centrophenoxine on the lipofuscin pigment in the neurons of senile guinea pigs. *Journal of Gerontology,* 1968, *23,* 82–92.

Nandy, K., & Bourne, G. H. Effect of centrophenoxine on the lipofuscin pigments in the neurons of senile guinea pigs. *Nature* (London), 1966, *210,* 313–314.

Nandy, K. & Lal, H. Neuronal lipofuscin and learning deficits in aging mammals. In P. Deniker, C. Radouco-Thomas, & A. Villenuve (Eds.), *Neuropsychopharmacology.* New York: Pergamon Press, 1980.

Ordy, J. M., Kaak, B., & Brizzee, K. R. Life-span neurochemical changes in the human and non-human primate brain. In H. Brody, D. Harman, & J. B. Ordy (Eds.), *Aging* (Vol. 1). New York: Raven Press, 1975.

Petit, T. L. Dendritic atrophy following colchicine-induced neuroplasmic transport disruptions: Implications for brain aging. *Society for Neuroscience Abstracts,* 1977, *3,* 351.

Petit, T. L., Biederman, G. B., & McMullen, P. A. Neurofibrillary degeneration, dendritic dying back, and learning–memory deficits after aluminum administration: Implications for brain aging. *Experimental Neurology,* 1980, *67,* 152–162.

Petit, T. L., & Isaacson, R. L. Deficient brain development following colcemid treatment in postnatal rats. *Brain Research,* 1977, *132,* 380–385.

Riga, S., & Riga, D. Effects of centrophenoxine on the lipofuscin pigments in the nervous system of old rats. *Brain Research,* 1974, *72,* 265–275.

Roth, M., Tomlinson, B. E., & Blessed, G. Correlation between score for dementia and counts in senile plaques in cerebral gray matter of elderly subjects. *Nature* (London) 1966, *209,* 106.

Scheibel, M. E., & Scheibel, A. B. Structural changes in the aging brain. In H. Brody, D. Harman, & J. M. Ordy (Eds.), *Aging* (Vol. 1). New York: Raven Press, 1975.

Scheibel, M. E., & Scheibel, A. B. Differential changes with aging in old and new cortices. In K. Nandy & I. Sherwin (Eds.), *The aging brain and senile dementia. Advances in behavioral biology* (Vol. 23). New York: Plenum Press, 1977.

Schubert, P., & Kreutzberg, G. W. Parameters of dendritic transport. *Advances in Neurology,* 1975, *12,* 255–268.

Sherwin, I., & Seltzer, B. Senile and pre-senile dementia: A clinical overview. In K. Nandy & I. Sherwin (Eds.), *The aging brain and senile dementia. Advances in behavioral biology* (Vol. 23). New York: Plenum Press, 1977.

Siakotos, A. N., Armstrong, D., Koppang, N., & Muller, J. Biochemical significance of age pigment in neurons. In K. Nandy & I. Sherwin (Eds.), *The aging brain and senile dementia. Advances in behavioral biology* (Vol. 23). New York: Plenum Press, 1977.

Terry, R. D. & Davies, P. Dementia of the Alzheimer type. *Annual Review of Neuroscience,* 1980, *3,* 77–95.

Terry, R. D., & Wisniewski, H. The ultrastructure of the neurofibrillary tangle and the senile plaque. In G. E. W. Wolstenholm & M. O'Connor (Eds.), *Ciba Foundation symposium on Alzheimer's disease and related conditions.* London: J. and A. Churchill, 1970.

Tomlinson, B. E. Morphological brain changes in non-demented old people. In H. M. Van Praag & A. V. Kalverboer (Eds.), *Aging of the central nervous system*. New York: De Ervon F. Bohn, 1972.

Tomlinson, B. E., Blessed, G., & Roth, M. Observations on the brains of nondemented old people. *Journal of Neurological Science*, 1968, *1*, 331–356.

Tomlinson, B. E., Blessed, G., & Roth, M. Observations on the brains of demented old people, *Journal of Neurological Science*, 1970, *11*, 205–242.

Tomlinson, B. E., & Henderson, G. Some quantitative cerebral findings in normal and demented old people. In R. D. Terry & S. Gershon (Eds.), *Neurobiology of aging*. New York: Raven Press, 1976.

Tomlinson, B. E., & Kitchener, D. Granulovacuolar degeneration of the hippocampal pyramidal cells. *Journal of Pathology*, 1972, *106*, 165–185.

Vaughan, D. H. Age related deterioration of pyramidal cell basal dendrites in rat auditory cortex. *Journal of Comparative Neurology*, 1977, *171*, 501–516.

Wahren, W. Neurohistologischer Beitrag zu Fragen des Alterns. *Zeitschrift für Alternsforschung*, 1957, *10*, 343–357.

Wang, H. S. Dementia of old age. In W. L. Smith & M. Kinsbourne (Eds.), *Aging and senile dementia*. New York: Spectrum, 1977.

Wells, C. E. Role of stroke in dementia. *Stroke*,1978, *9*, 1–3.

Wisniewski, H. M., & Terry, R. D. Reexamination of the pathogenesis of the senile plaque. In H. M. Zimmerman (Ed.), *Progress in neuropathology* (Vol. 2). New York: Grune & Stratton, 1973.

Wisniewski, H. M., & Terry, R. D. Neuropathology of the aging brain. In R. D. Terry & S. Gershon (Eds.), *Neurobiology of aging*. New York: Raven Press, 1976.

Wisniewski, H. M., & Terry, R. D., & Hirano, A. Neurofibrillary pathology. *Journal of Neuropathology and Experimental Neurology*, 1970, *29*, 163–176.

Wisniewski, H. M., Ghetti, B., & Terry, R. D. Neuritic (senile) plaques and filamentous changes in aged rhesus monkeys. *Journal of Neuropathology and Experimental Neurology*, 1973, *32*, 566–584.

Wisniewski, H. M., Bruce, M. E., & Fraser, H. Infectious etiology of neuritic (senile) plaques in mice. *Science*, 1975, *190*, 1108–1110.

Wisniewski, H. M., Narang, H. K., & Terry, R. D. Neurofibrillary tangles of paired helical filaments. *Journal of Neurological Science*, 1976, *27*, 173–181.

Woodard, G. S. Clinicopathologic significance of granulovacuolar degeneration in Alzheimer's disease. *Journal of Neuropathology and Experimental Neurology*, 1962, *21*, 85–91.

CHAPTER 2

# Cellular Mechanisms of Alzheimer's Disease

D. R. Crapper McLachlan

*Department of Physiology and Medicine*
*University of Toronto*
*Toronto, Ontario, Canada*

Among those brain insults which result in dementia, particularly in older people, Alzheimer's disease is the most common. The disease is distinguished by several brain cell changes which include brain cell loss, brain shrinkage, a protein change within neurons known as neurofibrillary degeneration, and a peculiar degenerative change of neuron terminals in which another type of fibrillary material called amyloid may accumulate in the extracellular spaces (Terry, Gonatas, & Weiss, 1964). This latter histopathological change is known as the senile plaque. Although each of these changes may occur in disease other than Alzheimer's disease, it is the unique combination of histopathological changes which distinguishes this relentlesly progressive, invariably fatal, and untreatable condition from other nervous system disease.

In Alzheimer's disease, brain function fails in a characteristic pattern. Initially, there appears to be a period in which the density and distribution of lesions does not attain sufficient magnitude to affect function. However, this asymptomatic stage is followed by changes in memory function, and it appears that the most severely affected regions include brain structures which sustain memory, namely, the hippocampal formation and medial temporal lobes. Following the early stages of the illness, lesions occur in increasing number on the lateral surface of the temporal lobe and appear to spread slowly out from the temporal-parietal-

This work was supported by the Ontario Mental Health Foundation, Medical Research Council of Canada, and the Canadian Geriatrics Research Society.

occipital junction to involve large areas of these lobes. The lesions also occur in the frontal lobe and brain stem. The disease does not invade the spinal cord or cerebellum. The anatomical distribution for several cases of Alzheimer's disease has been carefully documented by Brun and Gustafsen (1976).

The functional deficits resulting from the underlying pathology account well for the sequence of clinical signs which include the loss of impulse control, motor dyspraxia, and sensory and motor agnosia. Because the pathology involves brain stem and extrapyramidal motor regions, there are changes in muscle tone and locomotion. Eventually so much of the cerebral cortex and brain stem is affected that the patient becomes bedridden and usually succumbs to bronchopneumonia or systemic infection. The course of the illness averages about 8 years, but there is considerable variation and the illness may range in duration from as short as 5 years to as long as 19 years.

When Down's syndrome is present, the condition may be more difficult to detect because cognitive functions are already impaired. However, once focal neurological signs are apparent, the clinical course appears to be identical to that found in the normal population.

There are many mysteries concerning this disease. One of the most intriguing is the mechanism underlying the apparent spread of the degenerative changes, a process which occurs over several years. In some individuals the degenerative process involves only a limited area of the brain, resulting in a relatively stable amnestic syndrome, although more commonly the process is relentlessly progressive and involves vast areas of the neocortex. Furthermore, the primary sensory and motor areas of the brain are relatively resistant to degenerative changes, whereas the large association areas of the cortex are particularly affected.

The slow march of the disease from the medial temporal lobes over the neocoretx is compatible with the possible release from cell to cell of a factor which induces degeneration in adjacent cells. One such mechanism might be a slow virus, but although this hypothesis is under active investigation in many laboratories of the world, there is no definitive evidence in support of a viral cause for this illness (Crapper & De Boni, 1978). Repeated attempts to reproduce Alzheimer's disease with all its pathological manifestation in animals has also failed (Crapper & De Boni, 1980).

Recent work from several laboratories suggests that an early event in Alzheimer's disease is a reduction in the flow of genetic information. An uninterrupted flow of genetic information is necessary for normal cell function. A consequence of reduced transcription appears to be reduced RNA content (Bowen, Smith, White, Goodhardt, Spillane, Flack, & Davidson, 1977), a reduced ratio of RNA to DNA (Bowen, Smith, & Davidson, 1973), a reduced ratio of microsomal-associated proteins to total proteins (Dayan & Ball, 1973), reduced nucleolar volume (Mann & Sinclair, 1978; Ringborg, 1966) and reduced ratio of total proteins to total lipids (Suzuki, Katzman, & Korey, 1965). While the factors which alter transcription are incompletely known, it appears that there are changes in the physical state of chromatin which reduce the probability that sites which carry genetic information are accessible to the enzymes which read the genetic messages.

The DNA message is associated with protein and this complex structure is called chromatin. The interaction of DNA with various proteins and $Mg^{++}$, $Ca^{++}$, and $K^{+}$ ions determines which regions of DNA are available for transcription. One mechanism of regulation of transcription involves DNA folding in such a manner as to render the DNA messages inaccessible for transcription. There appear to be several states of DNA folding and degrees of gene repression. Chromatin can be separated into several fractions by a variety of techniques. One procedure is based upon the physical properties of chromatin. When chromatin is exposed to mechanical shearing by ultrasound, a fraction of chromatin is split from chromatin which is heavy and precipitates from solution. This chromatin is called heterochromatin and is not transcribed by RNA polymerase enzymes *in vitro*. A second class of chromatin separated by the mechanical shearing technique is called euchromatin and can be divided into two components: an intermediate weight euchromatin and a soluble light euchromatin fraction. These two chromatin fractions are capable of transcription *in vitro*. We have found in Alzheimer's disease that the amount of heterochromatin is almost twice that found in other forms of dementia and age-matched controls (Crapper, Quittkat, & De Boni, 1979). The amount of intermediate and light euchromatin is proportionately reduced. This would suggest that transcription loci normally available in the human brain may be masked and unavailable for transcription in Alzheimer's disease. Furthermore, both neurons and glia are affected by the process which leads to heterochromatization.

While it is not yet possible to study the transcription process in living human brains, these observations predict that the number of sites on DNA which may be available for attack by enzymes would also be reduced in brains affected by Alzheimer's disease. Recently our laboratory, in collaboration with Dr. P. Lewis, Department of Biochemistry, of the University of Toronto, has applied another technique for examining chromatin structure. This involves treating the extracted brain cell chromatin with the polynucleotide-hydrolyzing enzyme, micrococcal nuclease. This enzyme digests special regions of the chromatin called the linker regions. The linker regions are about 60 nucleotides in length and join special regions of DNA which are tightly wrapped about a special histone core and called the nucleosome. The linker is partly masked by a protein called histone $H_1$. As predicted, material extracted from Alzheimer-affected brain shows a marked reduction in the number of sites available for micrococcal nuclease digestion compared to control chromatin. This is compatible with the proposal that DNA in Alzheimer's disease is more extensively folded than in control brain.

When digested segments composed of two nucleosomes and the linker regions were chemically treated to separate the proteins which are associated with these chromatin fragments, the Alzheimer digest contained considerably more of a certain protein than control dinucleosomes. This protein has many properties resembling a protein known as histone $H_1^o$. This lysine-rich subspecies of histone $H_1$ appears in cell systems when the cells shift from a high state of genetic transcription to a low state of genetic transcription. For instance, during development when the myoblast ceases to divide, the amount of histone $H_1^o$ increases several fold (Limas & Chan-Stier, 1978). Thus, it has been speculated that $H_1$ may be a general repressor-protein involved in the shut-down of certain segments of DNA by holding the chromatin tightly folded and thus preventing transcription. There are several known mechanisms of gene repression associated with other proteins, particularly the acidic proteins, and their role in Alzheimer's disease, if any, is unknown.

Since Down's syndrome predisposes to Alzheimer's disease, it is speculated that close to the genetic loci which regulates the Down's trait is a locus which predisposes the brain to the development of Alzheimer's disease. Although our data on the alteration of chromatin in Alzheimer's disease are preliminary, we offer the speculation that the genetic predisposition to Alzheimer's disease in Down's syndrome may be related to a gene which codes for the overproduction of histone $H_1^o$. Furthermore, we would speculate that this protein may have a genetic domain on chromosome 21, perhaps closely associated with those genetic loci which determine the Down's syndrome trait. If this hypothesis were correct, it would predict that in the brains of Down's syndrome patients which do not yet exhibit the histopathological changes of Alzheimer's disease there would be an increase in the amount of histone $H_1^o$. Indeed, we have data which support this hypothesis. From a single case of Down's syndrome, age 26, chromatin extracts from this brain have been examined. This brain contains more histone $H_1^o$ than is found in age-matched controls and less than that which is found in fully developed Alzheimer's disease. However, until more brains with Down's syndrome are examined and until we know more about the functional significance of these speculations, they must be verified by further work.

There are several implications to brain function which follow from the hypothesis that the primary pathogenic event in Alzheimer's disease alters chromatin structure and thereby reduces protein synthesis. For instance, this hypothesis would predict that the known deficits in the concentrations of hippocampal enzyme choline acetyltransferase (Bowen, Smith, White, Goodhardt, Spillane, Flack, & Davidson, 1976) and beta dopamine hydroxylase (Cross, Crow, Perry, & Kimberlin, 1980) may be related to reduced protein synthesis. The accumulation of the neurotoxic agent aluminum upon neurons with neurofibrillary degeneration may also represent a failure of the brain in Alzheimer's disease to produce proteins necessary for the chelation and removal of this element (Crapper, Quittkat, Krishman, Dalton, & De Boni, 1980). Finally, certain hormones such as adrenal corticosteroid and thyroid hormones which bind to chromatin may have defective binding, and therefore the brain may not be able to respond to systemically produced signals important in regulating brain metabolism. It is of importance to note that chromatin binding sites of thyroid hormone receptor protein (T3) are related to domains which are susceptible to micrococcal nuclease, sites which we believe are fewer in number in Alzheimer's disease. All of these hypotheses are currently under investigation.

## References

Bowen, D. M., Smith, C. B., & Davidson, A. N. Molecular changes in senile dementia. *Brain*, 1973, *96*, 849–856.

Bowen, D. M., Smith, E. B., White, P., Goodhardt, M. J., Spillane, J. A., Flack, R. H. A., & Davidson, A. N. *Brain*, 1976, *99*, 459–496.

Bowen, D. M., Smith, C. B., White, P., Goodhardt, M. S., Spillane, J. A., Flack, R. H. A., & Davidson, A. N. Chemical pathology of the organic dementias I. Validity of biochemical measurements in human post-mortem brain specimens. *Brain*, 1977, *100*, 397–426.

Brun, A., & Gustafsen, L. Distribution of cerebral degeneration in Alzheimer's disease. *Archiv für Psychiatrie und Nervenkrankheiten*, 1976, *223*, 15–33.

Crapper, D. R., & De Boni, U. Brain aging and Alzheimer's disease. *Canadian Psychiatric Association Journal*, 1978, *23*, 229–233.

Crapper, D. R., & De Boni, U. Models for the biochemical study of dementia. In P. J. Roberts (Ed.), *Biochemistry of dementia*. New York: Wiley, 1980.

Crapper, D. R., Quittkat, S., & De Boni, U. Altered chromatin conformation in Alzheimer's disease. *Brain*, 1979, *102*, 483–495.

Crapper, D. R., Quittkat, S., Krishman, S. S., Dalton, A. J., & De Boni, U. Intranuclear aluminum content in Alzheimer's disease; dialysis encephalopathy and experimental aluminum encephalopathy. *Acta Neuropathologica* (Bulletin), 1980, *50*, 19–24.

Cross, A., Crow, T., Perry, E., & Kimberlin, R. Brain dopamine-B-hydroxylase activity in Alzheimer's disease. *Abstract 148*, 12 CINP Congress, 1980.

Dayan, A. D., & Ball, M. J. Histometric observations on the metabolism of tangle bearing neurons. *Journal of the Neorological Sciences*, 1973, *19*, 433–436.

Limas, C. J., & Chan-Stier, C. Nuclear chromatin changes during post-natal myocardial development. *Biochemica et Biophysica Acta*, 1978, 521, 387–396.

Mann, D. M. A., & Sinclair, K. G. A. The quantitative assessment of lipofuscin pigment, cytoplasmic RNA and nucleolar volume in senile dementia. *Neuropathology and Applied Neurobiology*, 1978, *4*, 129–135.

Ringborg, U. Composition of RNA in neurons of rat hippocampus at different ages. *Brain Research*, 1966, *2*, 296–298.

Suzuki, K., Katzman, R., & Korey, S. R. Clinical studies on Alzheimer's disease. *Journal of Neuropathology and Experimental Neurology*, 1965, *24*, 211–224.

Terry, R. D., Gonatas, N. K., & Weiss, M. Ultrastructural studies in Alzheimer's pre-senile dementia. *American Journal of Pathology*, 1964, *44*, 269–297.

# CHAPTER 3

# Advances in the Psychophysiology of Aging

Diana S. Woodruff

*Department of Psychology*
*Temple University*
*Philadelphia, Pennsylvania*

The decade of the seventies has witnessed some major advances in scientific knowledge about physiology and behavior relationships in aging. These advances have been achieved by the invention and application of new measuring tools and by a change in assumptions about the aging individual. The newly invented tools have provided clearer perspectives of the living, responding brain. They have also enhanced the descriptive knowledge of brain and behavior relationships. The change in assumptions about aging has led us to modify the notion that aging in the nervous system is fixed and irreversible, and we have begun to explore the impact of interventions on aging physiology.

## Novel Descriptive Techniques: Windows into the Brain

Description has been the main activity in the psychophysiology of aging since its inception in the early decades of this century. Psychophysiologists have described behavior and aging nervous system relationships with measures of autonomic nervous system function such as the galvanic skin response (GSR),

Portions of this research were supported by National Institute on Aging grant AG01069.

heart rate or electrocardiogram (EKG), and blood pressure, and with measures of the central nervous system such as the electroencephalogram (EEG). Although a great deal of useful information has accumulated with the application of these measures (e.g., Marsh & Thompson, 1977; Thompson & Marsh, 1973; Woodruff, 1973, 1975a), they provided little direct information about the brain's response to stimulation or about physical aspects of the brain. The advent of computers has led to the development of new brain measures which identify the brain's electrical responses in one case and topography in the other case. Event-related potentials (ERPs) are computer-averaged EEG responses to experiment-controlled stimuli. Computerized axial tomography (CAT) involves computer analysis of X-Ray density scans of the brain and provides a picture of internal brain structures. Both of these brain measures are useful at all phases of the life cycle, and they have been used by gerontologists to gain insight into brain changes with aging.

### *Event-Related Potentials*

Brain electrical responses to specific stimuli are usually not apparent in recordings of ongoing EEG, but by taking a number of epochs in which the same stimulus event has occurred and summing or averaging across these epochs, the activity related to the stimulus becomes apparent. The assumption is that random activity not associated with the stimulus cancels to a flat voltage pattern, while activity time-locked to the stimulus cumulates and emerges from the random background "noise" of the ongoing EEG. A number of different bioelectric signals exhibit stable temporal relationships to a definable external event, and these can be elicited in most of the sensory modalities. Most research involves auditory, visual, or somatosensory stimulation. The general term for these signals is *event-related potentials,* and a number of categories of ERPs exist. These include (1) very early potentials generated in peripheral sensory pathways, (2) sensory evoked potentials, (3) long latency potentials related to complex psychological variables, (4) steady potential shifts, (5) motor potentials, and (6) potentials of extracerebral origin. The distinction between these classes can pose problems, as more than one class of potential may be recorded simultaneously, but since the classes are usually treated separately in the ERP literature, we will follow that convention. Most studies of ERPs in aging subjects have involved class 2, sensory evoked potentials, but categories 1, 3, and 4 have received more attention recently and have generated some excitement in the psychophysiology of aging. Motor potentials and extracerebral potentials will be considered as artifacts in the measurement of cortically generated potentials related to psychological constructs. Although class 5 and 6 potentials will not be discussed, they cannot be ignored in ERP recording. Motor potentials can contaminate steady potential shifts, and peripheral factors such as pupil size, eye blinks, and eye-movement potentials can contaminate ERP data when they are not controlled. This issue is of special concern in aging studies since the effects of eye artifacts appear to be more severe in some groups of older adults (Schaie, Syndulko, & Maltzman, 1976).

Event-related potential correlates of sensation, perception, and cognition can be recorded. Figure 1 depicts an auditory potential combining categories 1 and 2, very early potentials and sensory potentials. This response was recorded from a young adult who was sitting and listening to clicks, but he was not processing the clicks in any meaningful way. He was not counting or particularly attending to the clicks. The ERP reflects sensation to the click. Characteristic waveforms at various latencies appear in most individuals, and amplitude and latency of various waves provide information on the auditory pathway from the auditory nerve to the cortex. Louder clicks elicit greater amplitude in some of the

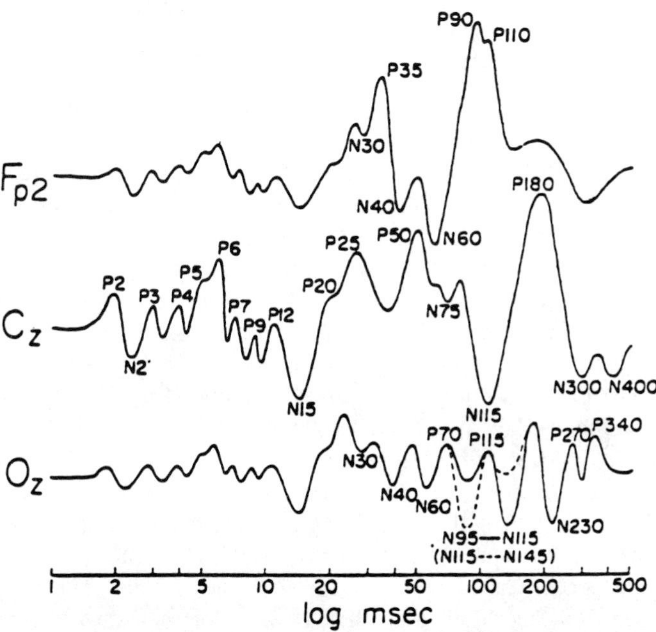


Fig. 1. Schematic summary of the human auditory evoked potential (AEP) is shown as it would typically be recorded in a normal awake adult subject not performing a specific task in relation to a click stimulus. Recording is referential to ears. A similar AEP would be recorded to click stimulation of both ears or to brief tone bursts. No amplitude calibration is shown since the P2–P9 complex is much smaller (typically .1–.5 μv) than later components (typically 1–20 μv) and for purposes of illustration is not drawn to the same amplitude scale. Components are not necessarily largest in the locations shown. Components N15, P20, N30, P35, a portion of N40, a portion of N60, N75, P90, and P110 are thought to be myogenic; all others are thought to be neurogenic. (From Goff, Allison, & Vaughan, 1978. Reprinted by permission.)

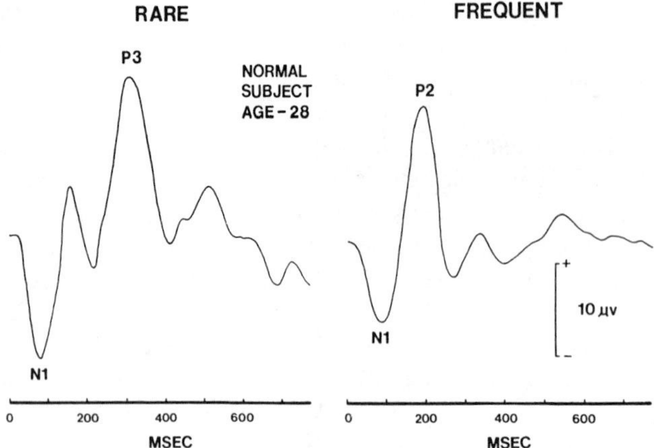


Fig. 2. Evoked-potential waveforms recorded from the vertex (Cz) for one normal subject, age 28. Separate averaged waveforms are presented for the rare (left) and frequent (right) tones. (From Squires, Goodin, & Starr, 1979. Reprinted by permission.)

waves and shorter latency in some waves. Most of the activity is completed by 200 msec after stimulation.

When subjects are asked to process auditory information, different waveforms emerge. Figure 2 shows the ERP of a young adult subject who has listened to a sequence of 400 tones, 85% of which had a frequency of 1000 Hz and 15% of which had a frequency of 2000 Hz. He was asked to count the occurrence of rare tones, and the attachment of significance to these tones leads to the emergence of a large wave identified as P3 in this figure. Figure 2 combines categories 2 and 3 potentials, sensory potentials and long latency potentials related to complex psychological variables. Category 1 potentials do not appear in this recording as they are of smaller amplitude and require additional amplification to be detected. Whereas most of the activity in Figure 1 was completed after 200 msec, the greatest amplitude waveform in the rare stimuli condition is at around 300 msec when the subject is processing the meaning of the stimulus. Thus, the P3 wave appears to be a brain correlate of information processing which is independent of the sensory response to the stimulus. This potential was first identified by Sutton and his colleagues in 1965, and since that time it has received intensive investigation, including application to aging.

*Long Latency Potentials Related to Complex Psychological Variables.* The P3 wave of the ERP is prominent only when the stimulus which has elicited the ERP has some meaning or significance to the subject. A number of studies have indicated that the amplitude of the P3 component, regardless of the stimulus modality, is inversely related to the degree to which the subject expects the stimulus to occur (e.g., Duncan-Johnson & Donchin, 1977; Squires, Wickens,

Squires, & Donchin, 1976; Sutton, Tueting, Zubin, & John, 1967; Tueting, Sutton, & Zubin, 1971). The factor which appears to determine the latency of the P3 component is decision time, more specifically, the time required for the subject to perceive and categorize the stimulus according to a set of rules (e.g., Kutas, McCarthy, & Donchin, 1977; Ritter, Simson, & Vaughan, 1972; Ritter, Simson, Vaughan, & Friedman, 1979; Roth, Ford, & Kopell, 1978; Squires, Donchin, Squires, & Grossberg, 1977). When task difficulty is increased, young subjects have prolonged processing times and longer P3 latencies.

Comparisons of the P3 in young and old subjects have led gerontologists such as Thompson and Marsh (1973; Marsh & Thompson, 1977) to suggest that the ERPs of the two age groups are more similar during active processing than during passive stimulation. The amplitude and shape of the P3 component have been similar in many of the age-comparative experiments. However, the result which has been consistent since the first report of P3 research in aging (Marsh & Thompson, 1972) is the fact that the latency of P3 is delayed in older subjects. Thus, the P3 research offers direct confirmation of the aging phenomenon to which behavioral studies have been pointing for decades. Processing time is slower in the aged central nervous system.

Using the task described previously in which the subject is asked to count the number of occurrences of an infrequent tone, Goodin, Squires, Henderson, and Starr (1978) tested 40 healthy subjects between the ages of 15 and 76 years. Data from six subjects in this experiment ranging in age from 15 to 71 years are presented in Figure 3. The primary result of this study was that the latency of P3 component systematically increased with age. Regression analysis indicated that P3 component latency increased at a rate of 1.64 msec/year. This results in almost a 100 msec increase in the P3 component in the decades between the 20th and 80th year. Some of the other components increased in latency with age, but the magnitude of these latency increases was not more than half of the magnitude of the P3 latency. Goodin *et al.* (1978) demonstrated that these age changes were not a function of auditory sensitivity by noting that behavioral performance (detection of higher frequency tones) was equal in young and old, all subjects reported that they could hear the tones clearly, and the N1 component which is dramatically affected by tone intensity was only different by 6 msec between the young and old subjects. Thus, ERPs provide differential information about the effects of aging and auditory acuity.

Other more difficult tasks have been used to demonstrate the effects of age upon P3 latency (e.g., Ford, Hink, Hopkins, Roth, Pfefferbaum, & Kopell, 1979; Ford, Roth, Mohs, Hopkins, & Kopell, 1979). In a selective attention task, Ford and her associates (1979) not only demonstrated that P3 latency was greater in old subjects but also demonstrated the elegance with which the ERP can be used to differentiate behavioral effects on information-processes. It has been established that the N1 component of the ERP, a negative component

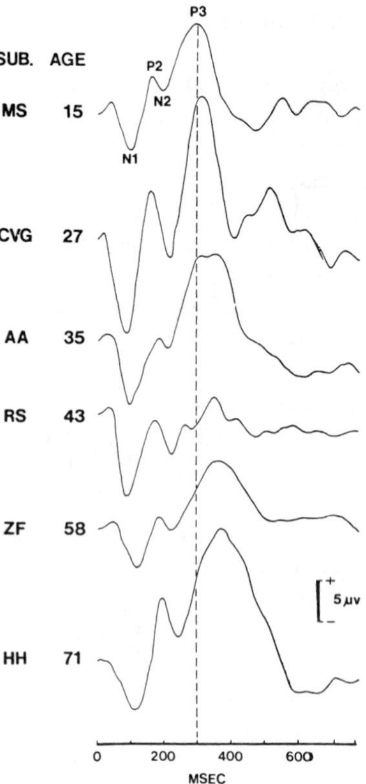


Fig. 3. Rare-tone evoked-potential waveforms for six normal subjects shown in order of increasing age (top to bottom). The dashed line represents 300-msec post-stimulus onset. (From Squires, Goodin, & Starr, 1979. Reprinted by permission.)

occurring about 100 msec after stimulation, varies in amplitude with an attended stimulus (Hillyard, Hink, Schwent, & Picton, 1973). Ford and her associates used a task in which tone bursts of 800 and 840 Hz were presented to the right ear while tone bursts of 1500 and 1560 Hz were presented to the left ear. The lower-pitched bursts in each pair (i.e., 800 and 1500 Hz, respectively) were each presented about 49% of the time and were called frequents. The higher-pitched tones (840 and 1560 Hz, respectively) were presented 1% of the time each and were called infrequents. The sequence of tones was presented to each subject twice, with the task being to count the infrequents in the right ear one time and to count the infrequents in the left ear one time. Data analysis revealed no age differences in the N1 component amplitude, indicating that both age groups were attending at an equal level. Frequent tones in the attended ear had higher N1 amplitude than frequent tones in the unattended ear to an equal degree in the young and old, indicating that both young and old were attending selectively to the relevant channel. P3 amplitude, which is an index of stimulus probability, did not differentiate the age groups. This suggests that young and old were using stimulus probability information equally well. The only ERP difference between young and old was P3 latency, which was 80 msec longer for old subjects. The old appeared to take longer to decide whether a stimulus was a target and that they should count it, and behavioral data indicated that the old performed more poorly on the task. They were less accurate in their count of the infrequent tones. Thus, the behavioral data indicated that there were selective attention deficits in the old subjects, but the electrophysiological data demonstrated that attention was equal in young and old. What seemed to be different in the old was the latency of their decision. In this manner, what appeared to be a deficit in selective attention was actually caused by slower decision making.

Squires, Chippendale, Wrege, Goodin, and Starr (1980) also concluded that cognitive deficit in the elderly may be accounted for by slower decision time. Furthermore, they demonstrated that increases in task difficulty interacted with age to prolong P3 latency disproportionately in older subjects. In 44 healthy subjects between the ages of 8 and 82 years, P3 latency increased by an estimate of .79 msec/year on an easy auditory discrimination and by 1.49 msec/year on a difficult auditory discrimination. Just as increasing task difficulty disproportionately delays reaction time in the aged, so it delays the CNS response.

In addition to elucidating the nature of the effect of aging on behavior, Squires and his associates (1980) have concluded that the P3 is the most effective electrophysiological measure for evaluating variations in mental status associated with neurological disease. P3 data have been collected on a total of 151 patients using the paradigm of counting higher-pitched tones which occur 15% of the time (described previously). There were three groups of patients: 58 neurological patients diagnosed as demented due to organic causes, 33 psychiatric patients with no known deficits in mental function, and 60 neurological patients with no known deficits in mental function. The latency of P3 clearly differentiated the patients on the basis of mental status. The average P3 latency of the demented patients exceeded the mean value of normal subjects by 3.61 SD, and using the criterion of P3 latency in excess of 2 SD, 80% of the demented patients were successfully identified. Thus, P3 latency is a useful measure in the diagnosis of individual patients. Figure 4 illustrates the dramatically slower P3s in demented patients and demonstrates the normal aging function of P3 latency in psychiatric patients who have normal mental capacity.

Squires and his colleagues (1980) also demonstrated that in individual patients showing changes in mental status, P3 latency accompanies the change. Declines in mental status were accompanied by increases in P3 latency, while improvements in mental status were accompanied by decreases in P3 latency. P3 latency thus provides a sensitive measure for differentiating organic dementia from functional disorders such as depression or disorders of movement or lin-

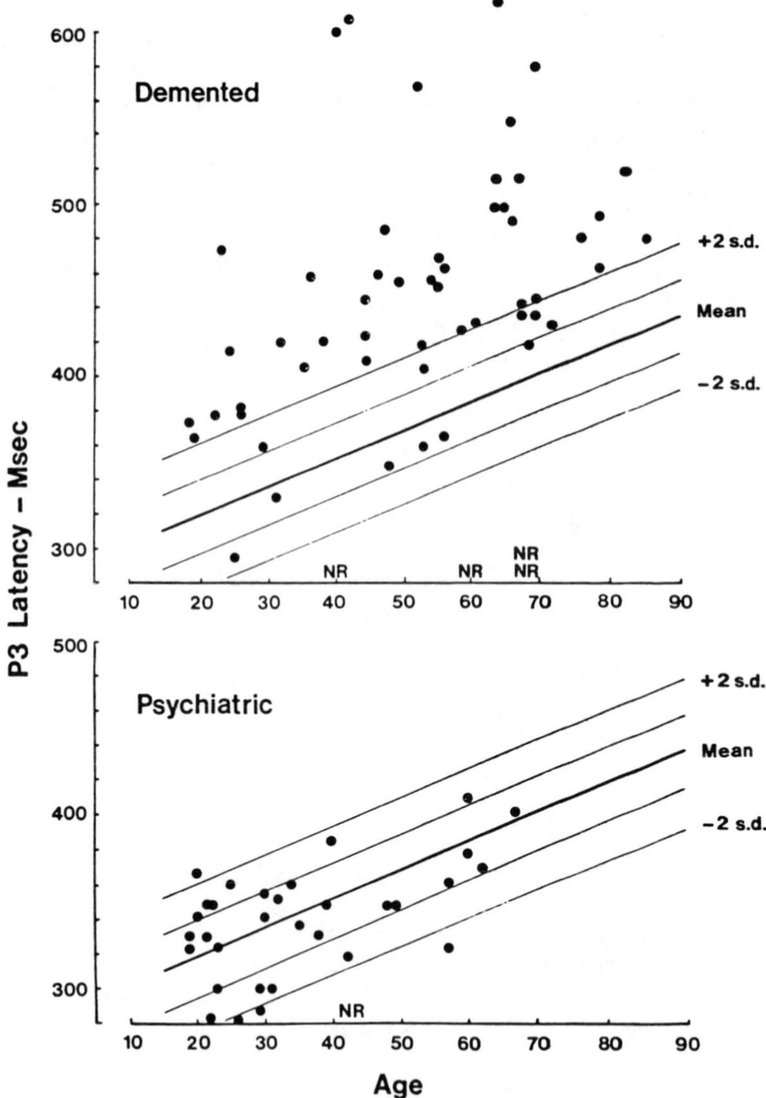


Fig. 4. Latencies of the P3 components from the rare-tone evoked-potential waveforms for individual demented and nondemented psychiatric patients as a function of age. Also shown are the regression line and 1 and 2 standard deviation (*SD*) bands derived from the data for normal subjects. (From Squires, Chippendale, Wrege, Goodin, & Starr, 1980. Reprinted by permission.)

guistic skills. Because such disorders are difficult to distinguish, the P3 can be an extremely useful measure in clinical neurological practice.

*Steady Potential Shifts.* Most investigations of steady potential shifts have focused on the *contingent negative variation* (CNV), a term that denotes a class of negative slow potential shifts lasting in the order of seconds (as compared to milliseconds of duration of most other ERPs) that occur in conjunction with certain sensory, motor, and cognitive activities. Donchin, Ritter, and McCallum (1978) described the CNV as a cortical change that occurs when an individual's behavior is directed toward a planned action in response to a sequence of two or more events. The action referred to can be an overt motor response, the inhibition of a motor response, or a decision. The optimal situation first demonstrated by Walter and his colleagues (1964) for the production of the CNV is a simple reaction time task in which the first stimulus (S1) serves as a ready signal for a second stimulus (S2) to which an operant motor response is made. Walter (1968) suggested that a massive depolarization of the dendrites in the frontal cortex was likely to be involved in the generation of the CNV. This waveform has been of interest to gerontologists because it has been conceived as a measure of attention and arousal (Tecce, 1972).

Initial studies of the CNV in aging yielded no age differences in CNV amplitude in scalp locations over central motor areas (Marsh & Thompson, 1973; Thompson & Nowlin, 1973). However, Loveless and Sanford (1974) found age differences in the shape of the CNV in long S1–S2 intervals, and they suggested that the aged failed to modulate arousal as efficiently as the young. Recent CNV studies involving a wider array of electrode recording sites and more complex tasks have found significant age differences.

Tecce (1979a) identified a CNV rebound effect occurring when a short-term memory task, demanded of subjects on half of the CNV trials, was absent. A normal CNV developed in a control condition when the typical S1–S2 reaction time paradigm was used, but when three letters were presented between the S1 and S2 which the subject later had to remember, CNV amplitude was diminished. On half of the trials in the short-term memory condition, the letters were not present. This is when the CNV rebound effect occurred. CNV amplitude was greater than in the control condition or when letters were present. Reaction time to S2 was also faster when the letters were not present. Young subjects verbalized a strategy of recognizing after a certain time interval past S1 that the letters would not appear. Then they concentrated solely on responding to S2. The supranormal increase in CNV amplitude was interpreted as reflecting a switching of attention from the divided attention set intrinsic to letters trials to an undivided attention set in no-letters trials. Tecce (1979b) tried this task in older subjects and found that the CNV rebound effect was diminished in fronto-central brain areas. None of the older subjects verbalized the strategy of realizing that no letters were coming and hence preparing only for S2, and their CNV indicated that they did not use this strategy. The older subjects also made significantly more perseverative responses than young subjects on the Wisconsin Card Sorting Test, a finding associated with frontal lobe patients (Milner, 1963). Tecce concluded that the diminution of CNV rebound in the older group appeared to indicate a perseverative attention set which was mediated significantly by fronto-central brain areas and which interfered with the switching of attention. Figure 5 depicits the lower amplitude CNV in fronto-central areas in the old subjects which was found in Tecce's laboratory.

Using a task similar to the task employed by Tecce (1979a), Michaelewski, Thompson, Smith, Patterson, Bowman, Litzelman, and Brent (1980) independently produced the same result. In this study the subjects heard letters in every trial, but on one block of trials they had to remember the letters, whereas they were not required to remember the letters on another block of trials. There was also a block of trials using the classical S1–S2 CNV paradigm with no letters. Frontal CNVs for the older individuals were reduced in every condition com-

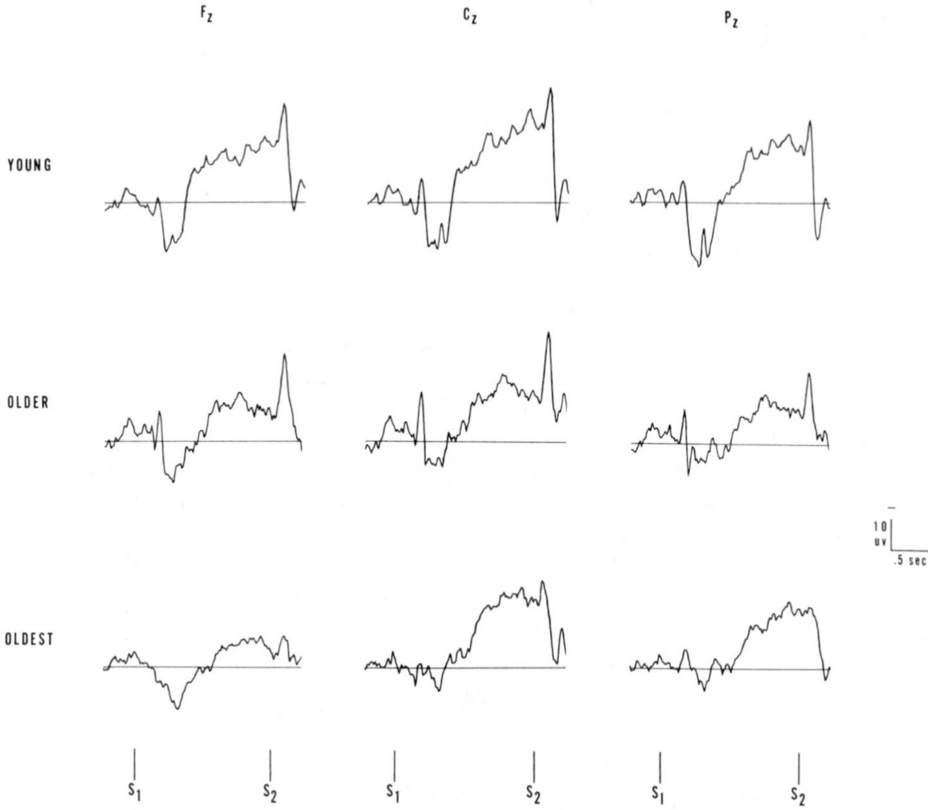


Fig. 5. Examples of CNV traces for frontal (Fz), central (Cz), and parietal (Pz) recording sites of young and older subjects. Averaged CNVs are based on 22 trials for the young subject and 14 and 18 trials for the older and oldest subjects, respectively. Relative negativity at Fz, Cz, and Pz (referred to linked earlobes) is depicted upward.

pared to the young group. Changes in midline activity were the same for both age groups. Michaelewski *et al.* (1980) pointed out that this overall reduction in frontal CNV activity in the aged suggests a process of selective aging in the frontal lobes. Albert and Kaplan (1980) reviewed the neuropsychological evidence which suggested that many behavioral deficiencies which are apparent in the elderly resemble behavioral deficits in patients with frontal lobe lesions. Scheibel and Scheibel (1975) identified losses of dendritic masses in prefrontal and temporal areas of aging brains in histological studies. Thus, the reduced CNV in frontal areas may reflect a cellular change.

Pfefferbaum, Ford, Roth, Hopkins, and Kopell (1979) appear to have anticipated the results of Teccee (1979b) and Michaelewski *et al.* (1980). In a group of extraordinarily healthy and active old women they noted a marked reduction in frontal recording sites in a wave they called the late sustained potential (SP). This wave occurs as a negative wave 300–450 msec after a stimulus. The SP is maximal at frontal recording sites and is similar in form to the CNV. Thus, the brain generators of the two waveforms may be the same. Pfefferbaum *et al.* (1979) suggested that the diminished SP might result from a loss in dendritic mass in frontal areas in the elderly.

Three independent laboratories have reported diminished electrophysiological activity at frontal recording sites in brains of normal elderly subjects. The generators of these CNV and SP waveforms are thought to be dendritic layers in the frontal lobes. In two of the laboratories the diminished frontal activity occurred as a correlate of diminished capacity to switch attention. These data, coupled with behavioral and histological evidence, begin to point rather compellingly to a selective aging of the frontal lobes which impairs the capacity of the elderly to modulate attention.

*Sensory Evoked Potentials.* In a recent review of the literature on aging and ERPs, Smith, Thompson, and Michaelewski (1980) found 33 primary research papers. Most of these studies were descriptive and dealt with category 2 potentials, sensory evoked potentials. The first paper appeared in 1963 and involved research on the visual evoked response and aging by Kooi and Bagchi. They reported that there was an increase in visual evoked potential amplitude with age and an increase in latency with age. The most comprehensive study of sensory evoked responses was carried out in the Salt Lake City laboratory of Dustman and Beck who, with Schenkenberg, measured auditory, visual, and somatosensory potentials in males and females over the life span. This research began to appear in 1966 (Dustman & Beck, 1966), and was followed by a series of reports (Dustman & Beck ,1969; Schenkenberg, 1970; Schenkenberg, Dustman, & Beck, 1971). Figure 6 shows a sample of these data. The major age change which they identified was a greater latency in the waveforms, particularly in the later waves appearing after 100 msec. Amplitude in later waves also decreased in later life. A change limited to the visual evoked response was an increase in amplitude in an early component. General hypotheses were advanced to explain these age changes. The general slowing in the nervous system was associated

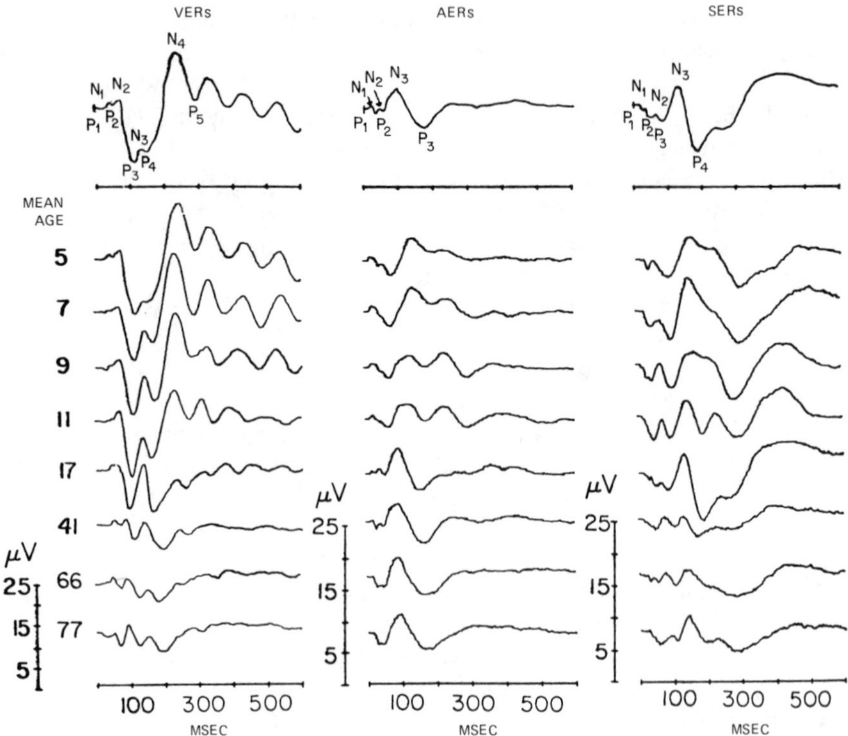


Fig. 6. Composite VERs, AERs, and SERs of subjects in eight age groups. Each plot is a composite of 20 subjects: 10 males and 10 females in each age group. VERs are from left scalp; AERs and SERs are from left central scalp. P = positive peak; N = negative peak. (From Dustman, Beck, & Schenkenberg, 1977. Reprinted by permission.)

with latency increases, and decreases in the amplitude and latency of the later components were associated with age changes in the secondary system—the ascending reticular arousal system (ARAS)—perhaps involving age changes at the synapse. To explain the increase in visual evoked response amplitude in early components, it was suggested that a decrease in inhibition was occurring. In the late 1960s and early 1970s these kinds of general hypotheses were the only ones which could be offered because sensory evoked potentials had not been related to specific hypotheses about age changes.

*Brain Stem Auditory Evoked Responses.* Although we still do not have concrete information about the generators of the sensory potentials of class 2, a new type of potential has been identified in the decade of the seventies which can be linked to specific generators and thus provides direct information about the intactness of the brain pathways. This is a category 1 potential—very early potentials generated in peripheral pathways. The visual and somatosensory pathways have been studied with this method, but the greatest amount of research and excitement has been generated in the auditory modality by potentials which have been named brain stem auditory evoked responses. (BAERs). These very small (measured in tenths of microvolts) potentials provide information about hearing acuity, about the functional capacity of the auditory pathway through the brain stem, and about the speed of conduction of neural impulses through this pathway.

The immediate history of the BAER began in 1967 when Somer and Feinmesser observed that auditory nerve activity could be recorded from the human scalp. The BAER itself was discovered in 1971 by Jewett and Williston, who reported that in addition to the auditory nerve response, four more waves time-locked to the stimulus (a click) could be recorded. They compared these waves to similar events recorded from animals and concluded that the human BAER is a signal resulting from click stimuli, which travels up the brain stem en route to the cortex. Laboratories in many parts of the world have confirmed and extended these discoveries, and this work is summarized in Figure 7. This remarkable figure represents a very recent development in the study of human electrophysiological responses—the ability to link individual waves to their generators in the brain and spinal cord. This measure is one of the rare instances in which functional activity from known brain sites can be recorded.

Anatomical mapping of the waves in animal and human autopsy data indicates that wave I originates in the auditory nerve, wave II is from the cochlear nucleus, waves III and IV are in the pons, wave V is in the inferior colliculus, and waves VI and VII are in the thalamus and thalamic radiations, respectively. Wave V is particularly well correlated with the intensity of the auditory signal in normal and pathological ears, and therefore it is useful diagnostically. At higher intensities the latency of wave V is shorter, and when the signal is not detected by the nervous system, the wave does not appear (e.g., Amadeo & Shagass, 1973).

The BAER has been shown to change with development (Hecox & Galambos, 1974). Figure 8 demonstrates the developmental curve from infancy to age 42. The most rapid development of the auditory system occurs in the first 16 months, as reflected in the rapid decrease in wave V latency. Adult values are reached around age 16 months and are maintained at least until middle age. Studies of the BAER in old age have been underway only in the past several years, and the early data suggest that wave V latency does not change dramatically in old age. (Gott, Mephan, & Van Der Maulen, 1979; Harkins & Henhardt, 1981; Patterson, Michalewski, Thompson, & Bowman, 1980; Rowe, 1978). Rowe (1978) showed about .3 msec slowing in all BAER waves when he compared 25 young (mean age 25.1 years) and 25 old (mean age 61.7 years) subjects with normal hearing. Patterson *et al.* suggested that there may be a delay in wave III which occurs at the level of the pons. Again, the slowing was slight, only about .2 msec. The emerging picture from the BAER is that at peripheral

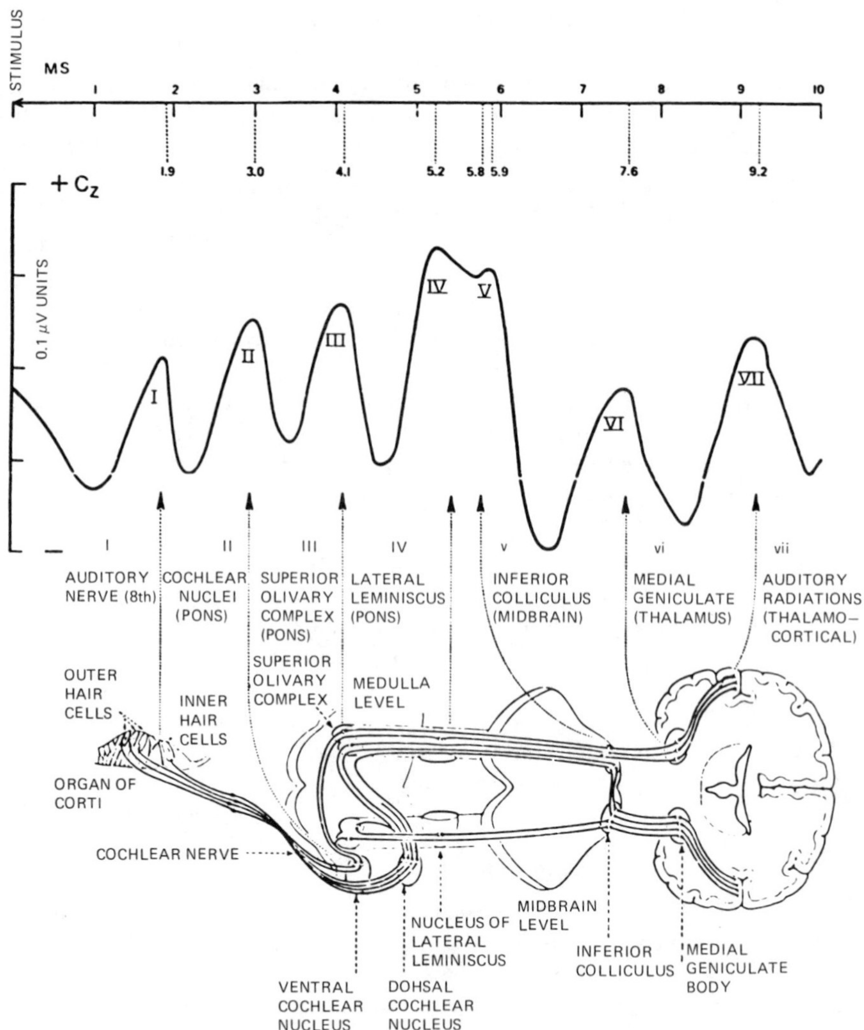


Fig. 7. Diagram of normal latencies for vertex-positive brainstem auditory potentials (waves I through VII) evoked by clicks of 60 dBHL (60 dB above normal hearing threshold) at a rate of 10/sec. Lesions at different levels of auditory pathway tend to produce response abnormalities beginning with indicated components, although this does not specify the precise generators of the response; the relative contributions of synaptic and axonal activity to the response are as yet unknown. Intermediate latency (5.8 msec) between those of waves IV and V is mean peak latency of fused wave IV/V when present. Cz+, Cz− = vertex positivity, represented by an upward pen deflection, and vertex negativity, represented by a downward pen deflection. (From Stockard, Stockard, & Sharbrough, 1977. Reprinted by permission.)

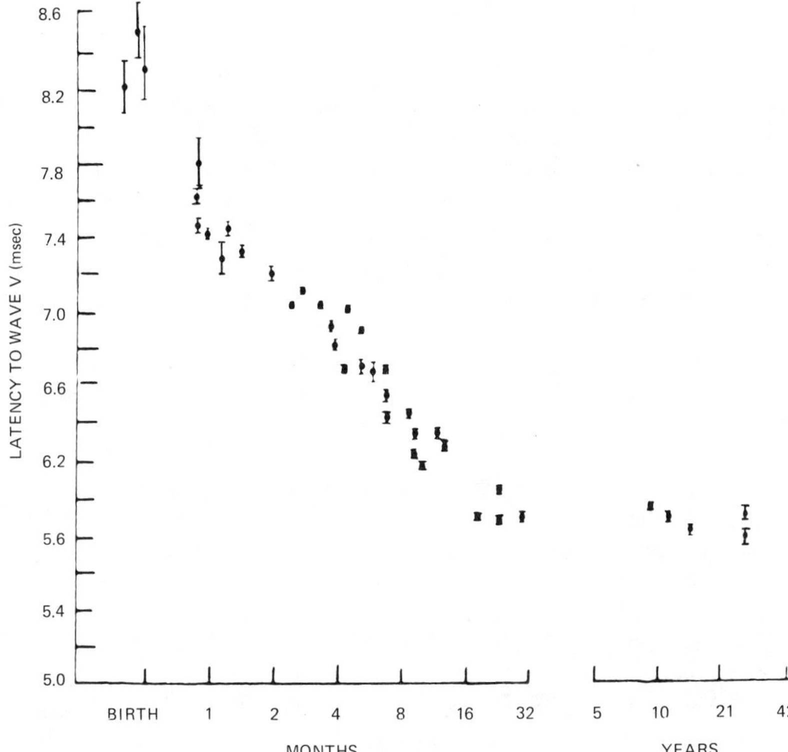


Fig. 8. Latency of wave V to 60 db clicks is represented as a function of age. Latencies decrease as subjects get older particularly between the first postnatal month and 12–18 months after birth. At this time, the latency stabilizes and is similar to latency in childhood, adolescence, and young adulthood. Norms for older subjects are just beginning to become available (cf. Harkins & Lenhardt, 1980.) (From Hecox, K., & Galambos, T. 1974. Copyright 1974, American Medical Association. Reprinted by permission.)

levels, the older nervous system performs about the same as the younger nervous system. It is when brain potentials are recorded from structures at higher levels of the brain that the slowing is significant.

The gerontological applications of the BAER may be primarily clinical. The BAER is clearly of significance in the evaluation of hearing ability, which declines in a significant proportion of the elderly population. The BAER is particularly useful as a diagnostic tool for hearing in patients who are unable to respond (e.g. Woodruff, 1980a). In addition to its clinical usefulness in hearing assessment, the BAER is a neurological assessment tool in that it provides a measure of the intact nature of the auditory pathway. Brain stem lesions can be detected with this painless measure, and the BAER is an improvement over the EEG in the assessment of brain death.

## *Computerized Axial Tomography*

Another brain measure which as primarily clinical applications is the CAT scan. Until quite recently the assessment of patients with behavioral disorders has involved indirect measures of nervous system function or dangerous invasive techniques that involved risks and potential complications to patients (e.g., angiography, pneumoencephalography). Computerized axial tomography is a safe and painless procedure which provides a picture of the living brain. It is a method of visualizing cerebral structures including a ventricular system and cortical sulci. The value of this technique in neurological assessment of patients of all ages is so great and has been recognized so rapidly that many hospitals throughout the country have installed the relatively expensive apparatus required for this procedure, even though it has become commercially available only since the mid-1970s. Thus, the CAT scan can be used in most large cities in the United States to assess geriatric patients showing symptoms of cerebral impairment, and it can be undertaken upon referral by the attending physician.

The CAT scan involves a rotating X-ray source which takes over 28,000 readings in approximately 5 minutes. This usually consists of a scan that has viewed two contiguous slices of brain tissue in a transaxial plane at a selected level of the brain. The entire procedure takes less than half an hour. Readings are processed by a computer which calculates 6400 absorption values for each brain slice. The computer calculates the density of tissue scanned by the X-ray beam, and different densities of tissue are translated into lighter or darker areas on a cathode ray tube display. A Polaroid photograph is then taken of the display so that a permanent record can be assessed by a neuroradiologist or neurologist. The data are also stored on magnetic tape.

The resultant photograph is essentially a picture of a transaxial slice of the brain. Bone and calcified areas that are dense look white in the computerized tomograms, grey matter of the brain looks grey, and the least dense areas, the ventricles, look almost black.

Huckman, Fox, and Topel (1975) have devised and validated specific quantitative criteria for evaluation of cerebral atrophy and senile dementia. They have indicated that both enlarged ventricles and enlarged sulci are necessary for a reliable diagnosis of senile dementia, and they have provided numerical standards for the width of the ventricles at two points and for the width of the four largest sulci that can be considered atrophied (Huckman *et al.*, 1975). It has also been demonstrated by these investigators that these criteria applied to tomograms yielded results as reliable as assessments based on pneumoencephalographic examination and pathological examination at autopsy.

CAT scans have been used to diagnose senile dementia and to identify geriatric patients with treatable brain pathology (Huckman *et al.*, 1975; Nathan, Gonzales, & Laffey, 1975). This technique has also been used in conjunction with behavioral assessment to determine the relationship between behavioral capacity and brain structure. Kaszniak (1977) assessed the memory of 50 patients for whom a CAT scan was available, and he demonstrated that CAT scans predict behavioral changes. However, his correlations were moderate, and more recent evidence indicates that the severity of dementia cannot be predicted by CAT scan data (Fox, Kaszniak, & Huckman, 1979; Kaszniak, Garron, Fox, Bergen, & Huckman, 1979). In 78 hospital patients aged 50 years or older with suspected changes in mentation in the absence of focal or other organic brain disease, EEG slowing was the strongest and most general pathological influence on cognition (Kaszniak *et al.*, 1979). Physiological functioning of the brain rather than neuroanatomical structure was the best correlate of cognitive function. Thus, although the CAT scan is a powerful tool in evaluating patients with dementia and can be used to rule out potentially treatable disorders, it is not terribly useful in demonstrating the severity of dementia or the ultimate prognosis.

Ford and Pfefferbaum (1980) reported preliminary results of their attempt to correlate ERP changes with structural changes in the brain as assessed by the CAT scan. They derived measures of the proportion of fluid to tissue in the frontal and parietal cortex and a measure of ventricular volume from CAT scans of 14 patients who had participated in their ERP experiments. Among their findings was a high correlation ($r = .77$) between the increase in the ratio of fluid compared to brain tissue (meaning less brain tissue) and longer latency P3 waves. This result linking decreases in brain tissue with longer latency P3 waves is in accordance with the data of Squires *et al.* (1980) that P3 latency increases dramatically in dementia patients. Ford and Pfefferbaum also found a high correlation ($r = .81$) between more negative slow waves recorded over the frontal area and less brain tissue. This result is in line with Smith, Thompson, and Michalewski's (1980) suggestion that behavioral, neuroanatomical, and ERP data are converging to suggest a deficit with age in the frontal lobes.

The main application of CAT scan data may be clinical, and this tool has great significance in the diagnosis of senile dementia. However, CAT scans are beginning to be used in conjunction with ERP and behavioral measures to provide greater precision of information about brain and behavior relationships in aging.

## Intervention: Plasticity in the Aging

Research in the psychology of aging has been characterized by intervention studies in the decade of the seventies. Once it was established that cohort differences might account for more of the behavioral variance in age-comparative studies than could age changes, numerous attempts were made to ameliorate the deficits in performance shown by older cohorts. A recent volume on intervention studies over the life span edited by Turner and Reese (1980) collects much of the research which has been carried out from this perspective.

Intervention research has been based on the notion that the older individual has the capacity to learn and adapt to change his or her behavior. No longer is it assumed that biological decrement accounts for all aging changes or that aging involves inevitable, irreversible decrement. If one assumes that behavior and physiology interact and affect one another, then it is logical to assume further that if intervention can affect behavior in old age, it can also affect physiology (Woodruff, 1980b).

One of the first to demonstrate physiological effects of intervention was deVries (1970), who devised an exercise regimen for older men (and later for older women, Adams & deVries, 1973) and demonstrated physiological improvements in efficiency of the cardiovascular and pulmonary systems as a result of this behavioral intervention. More recently, Treadway (1978) has demonstrated that physical exercise has a positive effect upon mood in the elderly. This work, coupled with other studies (e.g., of Dru, Walker, & Walker, 1975; Miller, Groves, Bopp, & Kastin, 1980), has led us to modify our assumptions about plasticity in the aging organism at a physiological as well as a behavioral level.

Intervention has been demonstrated to be effective in the domain of the aging EEG as well. The intervention research in which I have been involved has used the biofeedback training techniques to alter EEG frequency in young and old individuals (Woodruff, 1975b,c). The EEG alpha rhythm was chosen as the physiological age function on which to intervene as the greatest age changes in the EEG are manifested in the slowing of the alpha rhythm (see Obrist & Busse, 1965, for a review). Groups of young and old subjects were trained to increase the amount of modal alpha frequency, and then they were trained to increase output at frequencies two Hz faster and two Hz slower than the modal frequency. The results of this training are presented in Figure 9, which shows the actual learning trials for young and old. All subjects were able to carry out the task, and a high performance criterion at the modal condition was reached in many fewer trials than at the slow or fast condition. Increasing EEG activity faster than the modal activity proved to be the most difficult task, and it required the most trials to criterion. Young subjects showed consistently better performance when required to produce fast brain activity, but old subjects were better at producing slow brain activity.

We had demonstrated some plasticity in the older nervous system by showing that old as well as young subjects could increase the amount of fast as well as slow brain wave activity in the alpha frequency bandwidth, but we were also interested in the effects on behavior. Simple reaction time was tested when subjects were producing fast, modal, and slow frequency alpha waves. It was found that alpha frequency was related to reaction time, as when subjects were producing fast alpha activity their reaction time was significantly faster than

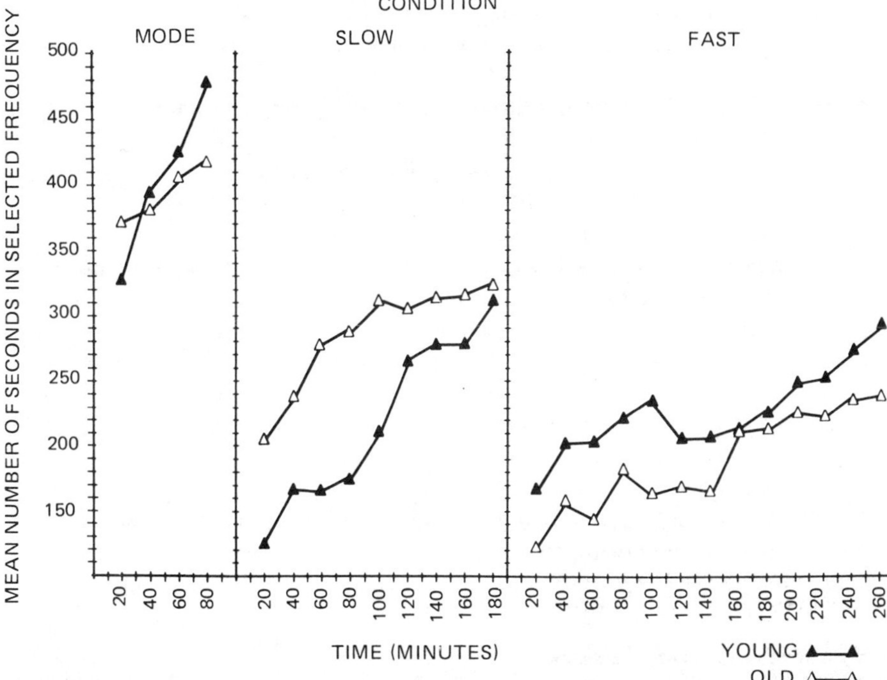


Fig. 9. Change in abundance of modal alpha frequency is shown for 10 young and 10 old experimental subjects who received biofeedback at three different brain wave frequencies (modal frequency, 2 Hz slower than modal frequency, 2 Hz faster than modal frequency). It is apparent that the task of producing alpha frequency 2 Hz slower than mode was carried out much more quickly than the task of producing alpha frequency 2 Hz faster than mode. This difference was statistically significant at the .001 level of confidence. (From D. S. Woodruff, 1975. Copyright 1975, The Society for Psychophysiological Research. Reprinted with permission.)

when they were producing slow brain waves. Mean reaction time was 20 msec faster in old subjects in the fast brain wave condition and 7 msec faster in the young subjects. One hundred percent of the old subjects demonstrated this effect and 70% of the young subjects had faster reaction times in the fast brain wave condition.

Research underway at the present time involves examination of concurrent and long-term effects of biofeedback on brain wave frequency and behavior. In the present research, we are examining a number of cognitive and mood behaviors as well as reaction time as a function of long-term training at the biofeedback task. Biofeedback training consists of a sequence of 10 1-hour training sessions after baseline performance on EEG and behavioral measures has been determined. In this research we are using very stringent criteria for success at the biofeedback task, and we are finding that not all subjects can control their brain activity to the degree that we have specified. Of the subjects who have been able to demonstrate remarkable control of alpha activity, more have been old than young. This result is interesting inasmuch as old subjects perform more poorly on most learning tasks.

Since there were such large between-subject performance differences in our data, we decided to attempt to identify characteristics which differentiated the good from the poor biofeedback learners. Although all of the analyses are not complete, we have identified one characteristic on which the two groups are different. This is habituation. Those who are successful in learning the biofeedback task are slower to habituate or do not habituate at all to an auditory signal which is presented 20 times over a 7-minute period. The measure of habituation is alpha blocking, and the subjects with successful biofeedback control present the alpha blocking response to most trials, while most nonsuccessful learners do not. Thus, learners maintain attention and alertness while the nonlearners may relax more and be less attentive to stimuli.

Comparing EEG alpha reactivity to repetitive tone stimulation in our young and old subjects, we found patterns of response characteristic of young subjects to be different from the response patterns of the old. Young subjects were responsive at the beginning of the 7-minute period, but they became drowsy in the middle by the tenth stimulus. Then they became more reactive again, and showed their initial level of reactivity by the end of the period. The old subjects showed a consistent lessening of reactivity. They gradually became more drowsy throughout the 7-minute reactivity session, and they did not show the return to initial level of alpha blocking that the young subjects showed. Baseline alpha activity also dropped off in the old subjects, whereas it dropped and then returned to initial session levels in the young subjects. The exception to the old pattern of reactivity was shown in the two older women who showed great control of alpha activity. One of these women showed the young pattern of lowered reactivity in the middle of the session with a return to initial level, while the other showed no decline in reactivity over the 20 stimulus trials. Thus, we may have a means to predict which subjects will do well on the biofeedback task. (Echenhofer & Woodruff, 1980).

Biofeedback control of alpha activity turns out to be quite a difficult task that requires the maintenance of effort for long periods. Although young subjects have shown evidence of learning control after 10 or more hour-long biofeedback training sessions, none have shown the magnitude of control exhibited by several old subjects. More women have demonstrated control of their EEG than have men. Control subjects who hear tape-recorded feedback signals show no changes or decline in their alpha activity. Thus, we have identified a task which may be optimal for older women, and we are learning more about the unique skills older women possess which provide them with this capacity to control their brain electrical activity (Woodruff, 1981).

# Conclusions

The psychophysiology of aging is an area of psychology which has made considerable advances in the last decade. New tools have been used to provide insights which were not possible in preceding years. A new outlook on the potential for the older brain to change has also resulted in research demonstrating brain plasticity in aging. From the research reviewed in this paper the following conclusions can be made.

1. Studies using paradigms eliciting the P3 waveform have confirmed what behavioral studies have been indicating for decades: Central processing time is slower in older brains. Dementia exacerbates the effects of normal aging so that demented patients have much greater latency P3 waves. Indeed, the P3 can be used to identify dementia. Central slowing is disruptive to cognitive processing and may desynchronize processing so that the individual fails at a task completely rather than simply performing it more slowly.

2. CNV studies, coupled with neuropsychological and neuroanatomical data, provide strong evidence of a selective decline in frontal areas of the brain which results in a difficulty in older people to modulate attention.

3. BAER studies suggest that there is little change with age in the peripheral pathways leading to the cortex. Latencies at least to the level of the pons remain almost unchanged in late life in individuals with normal hearing.

4. CAT scan measures of neuroanatomy suggest that brain mass or brain atrophy is not a strong correlate of behavioral capacity. While there are moderate correlations between brain atrophy and behavior, measures of the functioning brain, such as EEG slowing, correlate better with behavior in patients with impaired mental function.

5. A few intervention studies have been carried out and have shown modifiability of physiology in aging, but a great deal more research is necessary before we have fully tested the limits of plasticity in aging.

6. Biofeedback control of the EEG alpha rhythm is a difficult task, and it may be best learned by older women. The women who learned to control their alpha activity have shown uncharacteristic alertness in a repetitive task. The ability and willingness to maintain alertness in such a situation may be related to the skills necessary in learning to control EEG alpha activity.

# References

Adams, G. M., & deVries, H. A. Physiological effects of an exercise training regimen upon women aged 52–79. *Journal of Gerontology*, 1973, *28*, 50–55.

Albert, M. S., & Kaplan, E. F. Organic implications of neuropsychological deficits in the elderly. In L. W. Poon, J. Fozard, L. Cermak, D. Arenberg, & L. W. Thompson (Eds.), *New directions in memory and aging: Proceedings of the George A. Talland Memorial Conference.* Hillsdale, N.J.: Lawrence Erlbaum, 1980.

Amadeo, M., & Shagass, C. Brief latency click-evoked potentials during waking and sleep in man. *Psychophysiology,* 1973, *10,* 244–250.

deVries, H. A. Physiological effects of an exercise training regimen upon men aged 52–88. *Journal of Gerontology,* 1970, *25,* 325–336.

Donchin, E., Ritter, W., & McCallum, W. C. Cognitive psychophysiology: The endogenous components of the ERP. In E. Callaway, P. Tueting, & S. H. Koslow (Eds.), *Event-related brain potentials in man.* New York: Academic Press, 1978.

Dru, D., Walker, J. P., & Walker, J. B. Self-produced locomotion restores visual capacity after striate lesions. *Science,* 1975, *187,* 265–266.

Duncan-Johnson, C., & Donchin, E. On quantifying surprise: The variation of event-related potentials with subjective probability. *Psychophysiology,* 1977, *14,* 456–467.

Dustman, R. E., & Beck, E. C. Visually evoked potentials: Amplitude changes with age. *Science,* 1966, *151,* 1013–1015.

Dustman, R. E., & Beck, E. C. The effects of maturation and aging on the wave form of visually evoked potentials. *Electroencephalography and Clinical Neurophysiology,* 1969, *26,* 2–11.

Dustman, R. E., Beck, E. C., & Schenkenberg, T. Life span changes in man. In J. E. Desmedt (Ed.), *Cerebral evoked potentials in man: The Brussels International Symposium.* London: Oxford University Press, 1977.

Echenhofer, F. G., & Woodruff, D. S. *The effects of repetitive stimulation upon EEG reactivity and arousal in young and old adults.* Paper presented at the 33rd Annual Scientific Meeting of the Gerontological Society, November 1980.

Ford, J. M., & Pfefferbaum, A. The utility of brain potentials in determining age-related changes in central nervous system and cognitive functions. In L. W. Poon (Ed.), *Aging in the 1980s: Psychological issues.* Washington, D.C.: American Psychological Association, 1980.

Ford, J. M., Hink, R. F., Hopkins, W. F., Roth, W. T., Pfefferbaum, A., & Kopell, B. S. Age effects on event-related potentials in a selective attention task. *Journal of Gerontology,* 1979, *34,* 388–395.

Ford, J. M., Roth, W. T., Mohs, R. C., Hopkins, W. F., & Kopell, B. S. Event-related potentials recorded from young and old adults during a memory retrieval task. *Electroencephalography and Clinical Neurophysiology,* 1979, *47,* 450–459.

Fox, J. H., Kaszniak, A. W., & Huckman, M. Computerized tomographic scanning not very helpful in dementia—nor in craniopharyngioma. (Letter) *New England Journal of Medicine,* 1979, *300,* 437.

Goff, W. R., Allison, T., & Vaughan, H. G., Jr. The functional neuroanatomy of event related potentials. In E. Callaway, P. Tueting, & S. Koslow (Eds.), *Event related potentials in man.* New York: Academic Press, 1978.

Goodin, D., Squires, K., Henderson, B., & Starr, A. Age-related variations in evoked potentials to auditory stimuli in normal human subjects. *Electroencephalography and Clinical Neurophysiology,* 1978, *44,* 447–458.

Gott, P. S., Mephan, M. T., & Van Der Maulen, J. P. *Brain stem auditory evoked response variations with adult age and hearing threshold.* Paper presented at the 33rd Annual Meeting of the American Electroencephalographic Society, Atlanta, September 1979.

Harkins, S. W., & Lenhardt, M. Brainstem auditory evoked potentials in the elderly. In L. W. Poon (Ed.), *Aging in the 1980s: Psychological issues.* Washington, D.C.: American Psychological Association, 1980.

Hecox, K., & Galambos, T. Brain stem auditory evoked responses in human infants and adults. *Archives of Otolaryngology,* 1974, *99,* 30–33.

Hillyard, S. A., Hink, R. F., Schwent, V. L., & Picton, T. W. Electrical signs of selective attention in the human brain. *Science,* 1973, *172,* 1357–1360.

Huckman, M. S., Fox, J., & Topel, J. The validity of criteria for the evaluation of cerebral atrophy by computed tomography. *Radiology,* 1975, *116,* 85–92.

Jewett, D. L., & Williston, J. S. Auditory evoked far fields averaged from the scalp of humans. *Brain,* 1971, *94,* 681–696.

Kaszniak, A. W. Effects of age and cerebral atrophy upon span of immediate recall and paired associate learning in older adults. *Dissertation Abstracts International,* 1977, *37*(7-B), 3613–3614.

Kaszniak, A. W., Garron, D. C., Fox, J. H., Bergen, D., & Huckman, M. Cerebral atrophy, EEG slowing, age, education, and cognitive functioning in suspected dementia. *Neurology,* 1979, *29,* 1273–1279.

Kutas, M., McCarthy, G., & Donchin, E. Augmenting mental chronometry: The P300 as a measure of stimulus evaluation. *Science,* 1977, *197,* 792–795.

Loveless, N. E., & Sanford, A. J. Efforts of age on the contingent negative variations and preparatory set in a reaction-time task. *Journal of Gerontology,* 1973, *28,* 52–63.

Marsh, G., & Thompson, L. W. Age differences in evoked potentials during an auditory discrimination task. *Gerontologist,* 1972, *12,* 44.

Marsh, G., & Thompson, L. W. Effects of age on the contingent negative variation in a pitch discrimination task. *Journal of Gerontology,* 1973, *28,* 56–62.

Marsh, G., & Thompson, L. W. Psychophysiology of aging. In J. E. Birren & K. W. Schaie (Eds.), *Handbook of the psychology of aging.* New York: Van Nostrand–Reinhold, 1977.

Michalewski, H. J., Thompson, L. W., Smith, D. B. D., Patterson, J. V., Bowman, T. E., Litzelman, D., & Brent, G. Age differences in the contingent negative variation (CNV): Reduced frontal activity in the elderly. *Journal of Gerontology,* 1980, *35,* 542–549.

Miller, L. H., Groves, G. A., Bopp, M. J., & Kastin, A. J. A neuroheptapeptide influence on cognitive functioning in the elderly. *Peptides,* 1980, *1,* 55–57.

Milner, B. Effects of different brain lesions on card sorting. *Archives of Neurology,* 1963, *9,* 90–100.

Nathan, R. J., Gonzalez, C. F., & Laffey, P. *Correlations between computerized transaxial tomography and the extent of dementia.* Paper presented at the 28th Annual Meeting of the Gerontological Society, Louisville, Kentucky, October 1975.

Obrist, W. D., & Busse, E. W. The electroencephalogram in old age. In W. P. Wilson (Ed.), *Applications of electroencephalography in psychiatry.* Durham, N.C.: Duke University Press, 1965.

Patterson, J. V., Michalewski, H. J. Thompson, L. W., & Bowman, T. E. *Age differences in the human auditory brainstem response.* Paper presented at the Annual Meeting of the Western Psychological Association, Honolulu, May 1980.

Pfefferbaum, A., Ford, J. M., Roth, W. T., Hopkins, W. F., & Kopell, B. S. Event-related potential changes in healthy aged females. *Electroenceophalography and Clinical Neurophysiology,* 1979, *46,* 81–86.

Ritter, W., Simson, R., & Vaughan, H. G., Jr. Association cortex potentials and reaction time in auditory discrimination. *Electroencephalography and Clinical Neurophysiology,* 1972, *33,* 547–555.

Ritter, W., Simson, R., Vaughan, J. C., Jr., & Friedman, D. A brain event related to the making of a sensory discrimination. *Science,* 1979, *203,* 1358–1361.

Roth, W. T., Ford, J. M., & Kopell, B. S. Long-latency evoked potentials and reaction time. *Psychophysiology,* 1978, *15,* 17–23.

Rowe, M. J. Normal variability of the brain-stem auditory evoked response in young and old adult subjects. *Electroencephalography and Clinical Neurophysiology,* 1978, *44,* 459–470.

Schaie, J. P., Syndulko, K., & Maltzman, I. *Time estimation of the elderly and performance in a forewarned reaction time task.* Paper presented at the Meeting of the Western Psychological Association, Los Angeles, April 1976.

Scheibel, M. E., & Scheibel, A. B. Structural changes in the aging brain. In H. Brody, D. Harmon, & J. M. Ordy (Eds.), *Aging* (Vol. I). New York: Raven Press, 1975.

Schenkenberg, T. *Visual, auditory, and somatosensory evoked responses of normal subjects from childhood to senescence.* Unpublished doctoral dissertation, University of Utah, 1970.

Schenkenberg, T., Dustman, R. E., & Beck, E. C. Changes in evoked responses related to age, hemisphere, and sex. *Electroencephalography and Clinical Neurophysiology,* 1971, *30,* 163–164.

Smith, D. B. D., Thompson, L. W., & Michalewski, H. J. Status and prospects for averaged potential research in aging. In L. W. Poon (Ed.), *Aging in the 1980s: Psychological issues.* Washington, D. C.: American Psychological Association, 1980.

Sohmer, H., & Feinmesser, M. Cochlear action potentials recorded from the external ear in man. *Annals of Otolaryngology,* 1967, *76,* 427–435.

Squires, K. C., Goodin, D. S., & Starr, A. Event related potentials in development aging and dementia. In D. Lehman & E. Callaway (Eds.), *Human evoked potentials.* New York: Plenum Press, 1979.

Squires, K. C., Wickens, C., Squires, N. K., & Donchin, E. The effect of stimulus sequence on the waveform of the cortical event-related potential. *Science,* 1976, *193,* 1142–1145.

Squires, K. C., Chippendale, T., Wrege, K. S., Goodin, D. S., & Starr, A. Electrophysiological assessment of mental function in aging and dementia. In L. W. Poon (Ed.), *Aging in the 1980s: Psychological issues.* Washington, D.C.: American Psychological Association, 1980.

Squires, N. K., Donchin, E., Squires, K. C., & Grossberg, S. Bisensory stimulation: Inferring decision-related processes from the P300 component. *Journal of Experimental Psychology: Human Perception and Performance,* 1977, *3,* 299–315.

Stockard, J. J. Stockard, J. J. & Sharbrough, F. W. *Mayo Clinic Proceedings,* 1977, *52,* 761–769.

Sutton, S., Braren, M., & Zubin, J. Evoked-potential correlates of stimulus uncertainty. *Science,* 1965, *150,* 1187–1188.

Sutton, W., Tueting, P., Zubin, J., & John, E. R. Information delivery and the sensory evoked potential. *Science,* 1967, *155,* 1436–1439.

Tecce, J. J. Contingent negative variation (CNV) and psychological processes in man. *Psychological Bulletin,* 1972, *77,* 73–108.

Tecce, J. J. *Frontal diminution of CNV rebound in older subjects.* Paper presented at the NATO symposium on *Event Related Potentials in Man: Applications and Problems,* Konstanz, Federal Republic of Germany, August 1978.

Tecce, J. J. A CNV rebound effect. *Electroencephalography and Clinical Neurophysiology,* 1979, *46,* 546–551. (a)

Tecce, J. J. Diminished CNV rebound and perseverative attention set in older subjects. In D. Lehmann & E. Callaway (Eds.), *Human evoked potentials: Applications and problems.* New York: Plenum Press, 1979. (b)

Thompson, L. W., & Marsh, G. Psychophysiological studies of aging. In C. Eisdorfer & M. P. Lawton (Eds.), *The psychology of adult development and aging.* Washington, D.C.: American Psychological Association, 1973.

Thompson, L. W., & Nowlin, J. B. Relation of increased attention to central and autonomic nervous system states. In L. F. Jarvik, C. Eisdorfer, & J. E. Blum (Eds.), *Intellectual functioning in adults: Psychological and biological influences.* New York: Springer, 1973.

Treadway, V. A. *Mood effects of exercise programs for older adults.* Paper presented at the 86th Annual Meeting of the American Psychological Association, Toronto, September, 1978.

Tueting, P., Sutton, S., & Zubin, J. Quantitative evoked potential correlates of the probability of events. *Psychophysiology,* 1971, *7,* 385–394.

Turner, R. R., & Reese, H. W. *Life-span developmental psychology: Intervention.* New York: Academic Press, 1980.

Walter, W. G. The contingent negative variation: An electro-cortical sign of sensori-motor reflex assocation in man. In E. A. Asratyan (Ed.), *Progress in brain research.* Vol. 22: Brain Reflexes. Amsterdam: Elsevier, 1968.

Woodruff, D. S. The usefulness of the life-span approach for the psychophysiology of aging. *Gerontologist,* 1973, *13,* 467–472.

Woodruff, D. S. A physiological perspective on the psychology of aging. In D. S. Woodruff & J. E. Birren (Eds.), *Aging: Scientific perspectives and social issues.* New York: Van Nostrand, 1975. (a)

Woodruff, D. S. Biofeedback conditioning of the EEG alpha rhythm in young and old subjects. *Journal of Biofeedback,* 1975, *1,* 16–24. (b)

Woodruff, D. S. Relationships between age, EEG alpha rhythm, and reaction time: A biofeedback study. *Psychophysiology,* 1975, *12,* 673–681. (c)

Woodruff, D. S. Brainstem auditory evoked response in assessment of infancy. *Neonatal neurological assessment and outcome.* Columbus, Ohio: Ross Laboratories, 1980. (a)

Woodruff, D. S. Intervention in the psychophysiology of aging: Pitfalls, progress, and potential. In R. Turner & H. W. Reese (Eds.), *Life-span developmental psychology: Intervention.* New York: Academic Press, 1980. (b)

Woodruff, D. S. *Successful biofeedback conditioning in young and old and its predictors.* Paper presented at the 12th International Congress of Gerontology, Hamburg, Germany, July 1981.

CHAPTER 4

# A Neuropsychological Approach to Perception and Memory in Normal and Pathological Aging

Morris Moscovitch

*Department of Psychology*
*Erindale College*
*University of Toronto*
*Mississauga, Ontario, Canada*

The neurophysiological mechanisms responsible for producing cognitive changes in old age are poorly understood. Chapters 1 and 2 mention a number of striking changes in neuronal physiology and structure that occur with normal aging and that are accelerated and more widespread during pathological states such as Alzheimer's disease. Some of these, such as neurofibrillary tangles and senile plaques, are highly correlated with cognitive impairment; others, such as lipofuscin, are not; whereas still others, such as the production of chromatin, have an uncertain status in this regard. Whatever changes in cellular physiology are finally shown to be related to cognitive changes associated with aging, it must be borne in mind that these cellular changes do not affect psychological function directly but rather indirectly by altering the working of neuronal systems. From a psychologist's point of view, then, the psychological consequences of neurophysiological or biochemical changes with age might be best understood by focusing on the larger systems than on the microstructure of those systems. For example, although neurofibrillary degeneration is associated with cognitive deficits, the particular deficits that are noted in each individual will be determined by the brain structures that are most severely affected. The vulnerability of the hippocampus to this type of pathology and the relative sparing of primary sensory cortex (Tomlinson, Blessed, & Roth, 1970) help explain why most Alzheimer patients have severe memory deficits but relatively intact sensory processes (Schlotterer, 1977; see below for a more precise formulation). Apart from the view that one has to examine the larger systems in order to ascertain a particular neuron's function, there is a more practical purpose for concentrating on them. Most of our knowledge, however imperfect, of the relation between neurological structure and psychological function is derived from this level of analysis. Although operating at this level may not be fruitful for those interested in physical intervention, such as drug therapy, it is, at the moment, the most useful one for providing neuropsychological explanations of cognitive changes with age. It is for these reasons that I have adopted this approach in most of my research.[1]

The research on which I will report has been conducted in collaboration with Gordon Winocur. In Chapter 9, Winocur describes a series of experiments on the effects of interference and contextual cuing on memory in the aged. The studies that I shall describe are not as focused in the sense that they do not address a single domain or activity in which old people are known to be impaired. Instead, the studies were designed to explore the performance of old people on a variety of tasks that ranged from those that were laboratory-based and purely perceptual to those that tested long-term memory in real-life situations. Our purpose in casting such a wide net was not simply to get an idea of the capacities of old people but to see whether our neuropsychological approach was feasible—and we could know this only if we sampled a wide range of functions. Essentially, we wanted to see whether there was a reasonable fit between older people's performance on a variety of tasks and the level of performance predicted on the basis of the neurological deficits known to accompany old age. By and large, our studies are encouraging in this regard.

The subjects whom we tested were usually noninstitutionalized alumni from the University of Toronto between the ages of 65 and 75 who could be compared with our undergraduate control subjects. Occasionally, however, we also tested older institutionalized patients between the ages of 70 and 85 as well as patients believed to be in the early stages of Alzheimer's disease. These patients were diagnosed by Dr. McLachlan, who also collaborated with us on this research.

## Visual Perception: The Effects of Backward Masking on the Identification of Letters and Words

There is a large literature indicating that information processing slows with age (see Chapters 3 and 6). We reasoned, therefore, that perception of a target

[1] Those who are concerned with neurotransmitter characteristics of the system are subscribing to a simple variation of this basic approach. There is, however, another neuropsychological approach that pays little attention to the neuroanatomical locus of the deficit but merely uses the breakdown of psychological function associated with neurological damage to fractionate a particular function into its various components.

would be susceptible to disruption by a succeeding visual stimulus (mask) over a larger temporal interval in old people than in young. We chose to look at the effects of two different types of mask because they are known to involve different perceptual processes and are presumed to act at different neurological loci (Coltheart, 1980; Turvey, 1973). One mask, a homogeneous noise field (a light flash in our case) is assumed to act peripherally because it is effective only if it is presented to the same eye as the target. The other type of mask was a pattern of lines that contained elements present in the target which, in our work, was either a letter or a word. This pattern mask is assumed to act centrally as well as peripherally because it is effective even when it is presented to the eye opposite the target. Neurophysiological and neuroanatomical evidence indicates that in primates information from the two eyes converges first in the striate cortex and then even more so in the prestriate region and in areas anterior to it (Hubel & Wiesel,1968, 1977; Van Essen & Zeki, 1978; Zeki, 1978). The locus of the central effects of pattern masking must, therefore, be at or beyond the striate cortex. By the same reasoning, a peripheral mask probably exerts its effects earlier in the system. Because the degenerative processes associated with Alzheimer's disease generally spare the primary sensory areas, such as striate cortex, but not prestriate and the posterior temporal lobes, the performance of Alzheimer patients under the two masking conditions might help us determine more precisely the locus at which the two types of mask are operating. Specifically, if the homogeneous mask acts at or prior to the striate cortex, the Alzheimer patients' performance on that task should be comparable to that of normal old people. A deficit on the pattern masking task should be noted if that mask acts beyond the region of the striate cortex. If performance on both masking tasks is normal, it would mean that both masks act at or prior to striate cortex.

The hypothesis was tested by Schlotterer (1977). First he determined the thresholds for detecting the target perfectly in the absence of a mask. The target was a single letter chosen from a set of 11 letters that were symmetrical about the vertical. Once that duration was found, he increased the stimulus onset asynchrony (SOA) between the mask and target from 0 by 2 msec steps until the subject identified the target correctly on four successive trials. This critical SOA at which the target escaped the effects of the mask was determined for each subject for both the homogeneous and the pattern mask.

As Figure 1 shows, Schlotterer found that in both masking conditions the young were able to identify the target at a shorter critical SOA than were the normal elderly and the Alzheimer patients. Interestingly, the latter two groups differed from each other only in the pattern masking condition. According to our hypothesis, these results suggest that the pattern mask acts anterior to the striate cortex where the pathological process associated with Alzheimer's disease is pronounced, whereas the homogeneous mask presumably acts at the striate cortex or prior to it, areas that are relatively unaffected by the disease.

The spatial frequency contrast sensitivity function of Alzheimer patients provides additional evidence that their striate cortex is functionally normal. In

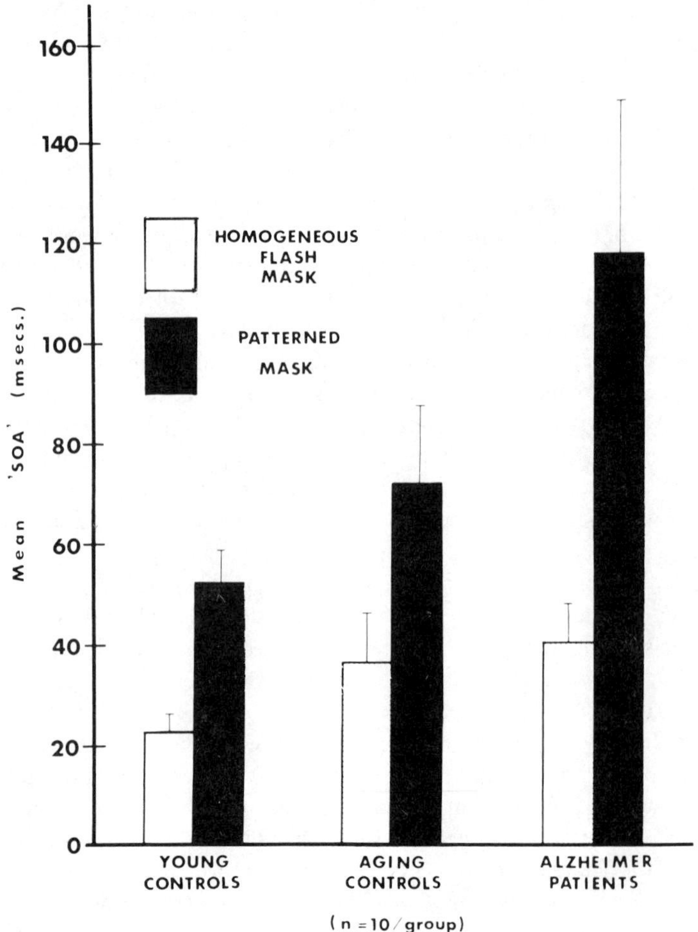


Fig. 1. Critical SOA at which a single letter target escaped the effects of a flash or pattern mask in young people, healthy old people, and Alzheimer patients.

this test, subjects were presented with sinusoidal gratings of different spatial frequencies on an oscilloscope. The spatial frequency of the grating is defined as the number of oscillations through a light and dark region that occur within a degree of visual angle. The higher the spatial frequency the finer the grating. The contrast between the light and dark regions was varied until they were just distinguishable from a uniform field. Previous research (see Campbell, 1974; Campbell & Robson, 1968; Cornsweet, 1970) had shown that normal people are differentially sensitive to gratings of different spatial frequencies. Damage to the striate cortex causes a loss of sensitivity to high spatial frequency (Bodis-Wolner, 1972). Schlotterer found that in comparison to the young, both old people and Alzheimer patients showed a loss of sensitivity across the entire range of spatial frequencies, but especially in the areas of lowest sensitivity, namely, in the high and low spatial frequency range (see Figure 2). This picture is consistent with anatomical evidence showing mild, yet noticeable, diffuse cell loss in the aged throughout the geniculostriate system beginning with the retina (Blessed, Tomlinson, & Roth, 1968; Tomlinson, Blessed, & Roth, 1968, 1970). The reasons for the discrepancy between our results and those of Sekuler, Hutman, and Owsley (1980), who found a loss of sensitivity only for low spatial frequencies in the aged, is not clear. What is important from our point of view is that patients with Alzheimer's disease did not differ markedly from normal age-matched controls, confirming the impression that pathological processes in Alzheimer's disease generally spare the striate cortex.

It would be wrong to conclude from these studies that the changes in visual functions that accompany normal aging originate peripherally, that is, at or prior to the striate cortex, whereas the changes typical of Alzheimer's disease also

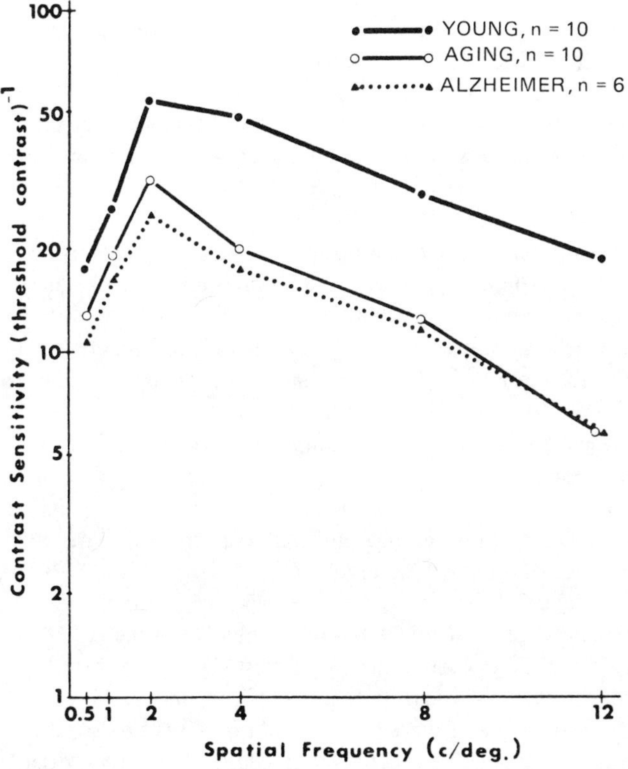


Fig. 2. Spatial frequency contrast sensitivity (threshold) in young people, healthy old people, and Alzheimer patients.

implicate more central structures. Were this true of normal aging, we would expect performance on tasks that presumably involve central processes, such as pattern masking, to be highly correlated with performance on more "peripheral" tasks, such as homogeneous or noise masking. As Walsh (Chapter 6) notes, however, this is not the case. The central changes that are commonly found in old people seem to be independent of the peripheral ones.

Rather than rely on correlational data, Mark Byrd and I compared the performance of old and young people on a homogeneous and pattern masking task that differed from the one used with Alzheimer patients in the following ways: (1) The target was a three-letter word presented vertically rather than a letter. (2) Performance was assessed by monitoring the accuracy of identification at various preselected SOAs, rather than by determining only the critical SOA when identification was nearly perfect. This enabled us to chart the differences between old and young at various points in the identification process. (3) The targets were presented either to the right or left of fixation but the mask was presented bilaterally. By presenting the target laterally, we could project it initially to the left or right hemisphere and thus test the hypothesis that in old people the right hemisphere deteriorates before the left (Borod & Goodglass, 1980; Brown & Jaffe, 1975; Clark & Knowles, 1973). (4) Only those subjects who could detect the targets perfectly at an exposure duration of 2 msec without a mask present were admitted to the experiment. By this procedure we hoped to exclude all those subjects whose peripheral processes were impaired. In fact, about one third of our elderly subjects could not satisfy our criterion.

As Figure 3 shows, for those subjects who met our criterion, there was little difference between the old and young subjects on homogeneous masking conditions at all SOAs. There was, however, a highly significant age difference on the pattern masking condition, and this difference was evident at every SOA sampled at which any identification was possible. These results support the view that central visual deficits in the elderly can be independent of peripheral deficits and can occur even when peripheral processes are intact.

With respect to hemispheric specialization, we found a similar right visual field advantage in old and young people in the pattern masking condition, but no visual field difference in the homogeneous condition. These results are consistent with previous evidence that visual hemispheric asymmetries are central and first appear at or beyond the prestriate cortex (Moscovitch, 1979; Moscovitch, Scullion, & Christie, 1976). The present study does not support the idea that the right hemisphere deteriorates more quickly with age than the left.

If it is generally true, as our data suggest, that in some old people and in most Alzheimer patients visual processes anterior to the striate cortex are the ones that deteriorate most severely, it should be possible to use these patients to elucidate more clearly which functions are mediated by the prestriate cortex and the areas anterior to it and which functions can survive damage to these regions. In a current study, for example, Jill Moscovitch, McLachlan, and I have been

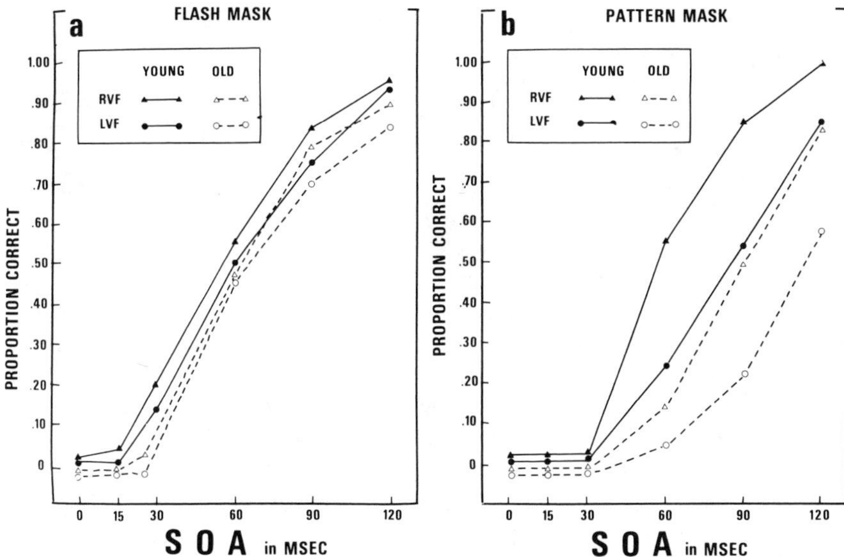


Fig. 3. Proportion of words followed by either a flash (a) or pattern (b) mask that were identified correctly at different SOAs in the right or left visual field by young and old subjects.

investigating color perception in Alzheimer patients because damage to prestriate regions are known to affect color perception selectively (Meadows, 1974; Ratcliff & Cowey, 1979). Preliminary evidence suggests that their color discrimination as measured by their performance on the Farnsworth-Munsell 100 hue test is severely impaired as compared to age-matched controls, whereas their performance is not significantly different from that of even young subjects on a similar and equally difficult brightness discrimination test (see Figure 4). This result is consistent with Zeki's finding that an area (V4) in the prestriate cortex is critical for color vision in macaque monkeys (Zeki, 1973) and suggests that a

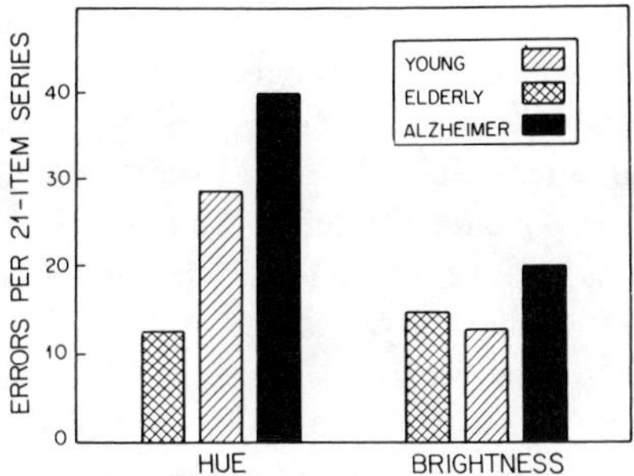


Fig. 4. Average errors per 21 items set on the Farnsworth-Munsell 100 hue test one on a similar brightness discrimination test.

homologous region may serve a similar function in humans (Pearlman, Birch,& Meadows, 1979; Ratcliff & Cowey, 1979).

## Primary and Secondary Memory: Free Recall, Cued Recall, and Recognition of Words and Faces

Previous studies of adult patients with focal cortical lesions have shown that damage to a variety of cortical areas lead to a small but noticeable loss in primary verbal memory, whereas it is only damage to the left anterior mesial temporal lobe and hippocampus that is related to a secondary verbal memory loss (Moscovitch, 1982; Moscovitch & Milner, in preparation). On the basis of these results, we predicted that the diffuse cortical cell loss that accompanies old age would be associated with some negligible primary memory impairment but that the most noticeable deficit would be in secondary memory because it is the anterior temporal lobes and hippocampus that are most severely affected by neural deterioration with age (Malamud, 1972; Tomlinson *et al.*, 1968). Both deficits would be exaggerated in Alzheimer patients. Although there is ample evidence in the literature that this is indeed the case, we nonetheless wanted to confirm it for ourselves, in particular since there is some disagreement as to whether primary memory deficits exist at all in normal aging (Craik, 1977).

In addition, we wished to test another idea related to the role of frontal lobes in memory and their supposed deterioration in the aged person. In our studies of brain-damaged patients (Moscovitch, 1981; Moscovitch & Milner, in preparation) we found that failure to show a release from proactive interference (PI) was associated with damage to the left frontal region and was not strongly related to overall memory performance.

To test these ideas we used Craik and Birtwistle's (1971) modification of Wicken's (1970) release from PI test. Subjects were presented with four successive different lists of items chosen from the same taxonomic category, followed by a fifth list of items from a different category. PI is built up during the first four lists and is typically released on the fifth list. The procedure was repeated twice so that there was again a buildup of PI from list 5 to 8 with a second release on list 9. Because each list contained 9 items, we could look at recall accuracy at different serial positions to determine whether the item was recalled from primary or secondary memory (Glanzer & Cunitz, 1966). According to Tulving and Colotla (1970), an item is considered to be recalled from primary memory if it is recalled within seven items of its presentation. Otherwise, it is considered to be recalled from secondary memory. We chose this measure because of the many ones available it carries the least theoretical baggage and gives a very consistent estimate of primary memory (Watkins, 1974).

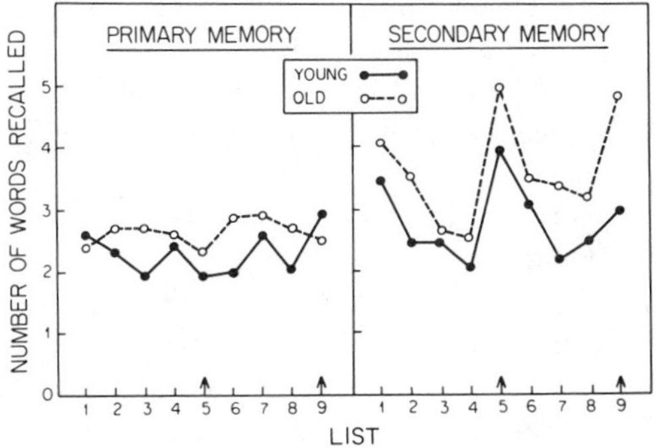


Fig. 5. Number of words recalled in each list from primary and secondary memory by young and old people. PI was built up during lists 1–4 and 5–8 and released in list 5–9.

As Figure 5 shows, the elderly have a slight deficit in primary memory and in secondary memory. The old people, like young controls, however, showed a normal release from PI. Performance of these old people on the Wisconsin Card Sorting Test (WCST), which is indicative of frontal damage, was in the normal range for the group. Performance on this test did not correlate very well with performance on release from PI as it did in brain-damaged people, but then the deficit that some of the elderly showed on the card sorting test seemed distinctly different from that observed in frontal patients. Unlike the frontal patients, the elderly did not perseverate on the old categories; they were simply unable to arrive at a correct new one. This was not the case when we tested institutionalized but mentally alert elderly subjects. As a group, they failed to show a consistent release from PI (see Figure 6) and to do well on the WCST. Here, too, however, performance on the WCST test was not always predictive of performance on the release from PI task.

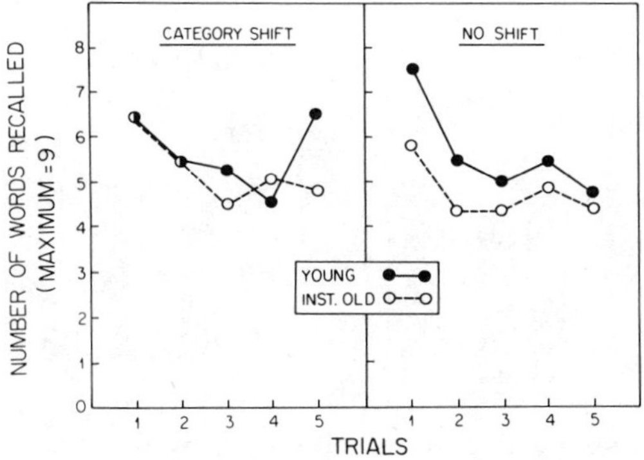


Fig. 6. Number of words recalled by institutionalized elderly and young controls. PI was built up in list 1–4 and released in list 5 in the category shift condition, but not in the no-shift condition.

The primary and secondary memory deficits seen in normal elderly people are exaggerated in Alzheimer patients. Because preliminary investigation revealed a severe memory loss in these patients, we did not administer a release from PI test but simply asked them to recall a list of nine unrelated or categorized words presented auditorally. Their performance relative to age-matched controls on a similar test is illustrated in Figure 7.

Our studies support our neuropsychological approach only partially. The slight deficit in primary memory and the more noticeable deficit in secondary memory are consistent with suggestions that neural deterioration is present throughout the secondary zones of the cortex but most prominently in the hippocampus. This pattern is exaggerated in Alzheimer patients, and their extremely severe secondary memory deficit is consistent with this picture. The normal noninstitutionalized elderly person's performance on the WCST and the release from PI task, however, suggests either that frontal loss in the elderly is not sufficiently severe to affect performance on these tasks or that the presumed loss of frontal tissue may have been compensated for in other ways. What does emerge from these data is that absolute performance on the WCST is not always a good predictor of performance on the release from PI test, suggesting that it is not always the same mechanism that subserves performance on both tests. For patients with focal cortical lesions, performance on the WCST may have been a good predictor of performance on the release from PI test because the lesion may have affected, by chance, an area large enough to affect both functions. Alternatively, it may be that performance on each of these tests is mediated by the same or closely adjacent areas and in the elderly other factors affect performance on these tests.

From a neuropsychological perspective, our results are consistent with the hypothesis that the secondary memory deficit observed in the elderly and in Alzheimer patients results, in part, from diffuse cell loss or damage in the hippocampus. This hypothesis, however, is not concerned with specifying the

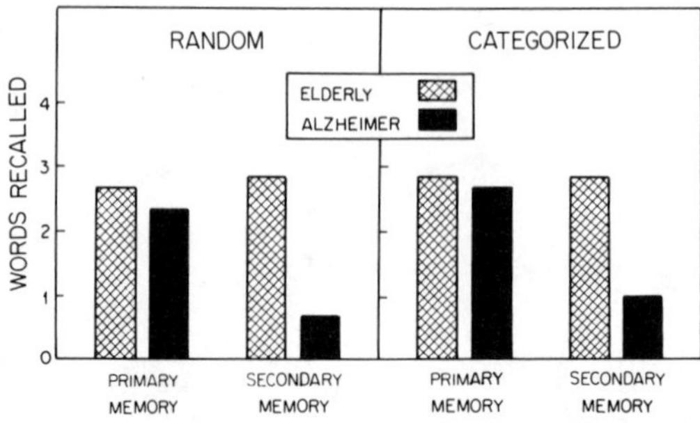


Fig. 7. Number of words recalled from primary and secondary memory by healthy old people and Alzheimer patients.

psychological processes whose impairment leads to a loss of secondary memory. An exploration at a functional, psychological level, rather than at a structural, neurological one, would contribute to our understanding of memory processes in the elderly as well as to our knowledge of hippocampal function.

One such psychological explanation that is very popular at Erindale College was proposed by Craik (1977) and is based on his levels of processing framework for memory research. According to Craik, the more deeply an event is encoded initially, the better it will be remembered, provided that similar deep cues are used at retrieval. Old people have a poor memory because they do not spontaneously encode information to a deep semantic level, nor do they use deep, semantic cues at retrieval to recreate the initial encoding situation. If they are forced to encode events deeply and are given appropriate retrieval cues, the performance of the elderly is markedly improved. Conversely, if young people are forced to encode information at a shallow level, their memory will be no better than that of elderly persons under similar circumstances.

These predictions were confirmed in experiments conducted by Sharon White (cited by Craik, 1977) and by Eysenck (1974). Edith Hughes and I were interested in replicating their studies for two reasons. Pilot experiments on patients with anterior temporal and hippocampal damage suggested that even when these patients were forced to encode deeply their memory for verbal material did not reach a normal level even if they were tested after a brief delay. Moreover, when these patients were induced to encode at a shallow level, the difference between their memory and that of normal subjects was not eliminated but, if anything, was exaggerated. More recent formal studies by Reed (1981) and Raines (1981) have confirmed this impression. If elderly people indeed suffer from deterioration of the hippocampus, their performance should resemble that of these patients and also be at variance with some of the predictions of levels of processing theory. Lastly, we wished to test old people's memory for nonverbal material, such as faces, since almost all the previous research had been concerned with verbal memory.

The subjects in our study were university undergraduates and alumni who had graduated about 50 years ago. They were divided into three groups, each of which received different encoding instructions. The *intentional* group was asked simply to study a series of 40 words and 40 faces for a later memory test; the *deep encoding* group was asked to judge the pleasantness of the words or faces; and the *shallow* encoding group was asked to judge the size of the material. After a 5-minute distraction, all subjects were asked to recall the words and later, after a further distraction, to identify the presented words and faces by choosing the correct word from a set of three and the correct face from a set of two.

The results, shown in Table 1, indicate that regardless of encoding condition the alumni recalled fewer words than the undergraduates. Although the performance of both groups improved markedly when memory was tested by

*Table 1. Percentages of Correct Performance by University Educated Young and Old People*

| | Mean percentage recall of words | | |
|---|---|---|---|
| | | Encoding condition | |
| Group | Size | Pleasantness | Intentional |
| Young | 7.5 | 25.0 | 20.6 |
| Old | 1.9 | 13.8 | 11.7 |
| | Mean percentage recognition | | |
| | Words | | |
| Young | 68.7 | 100.0 | 86.9 |
| Old | 61.6 | 96.9 | 86.3 |
| | Faces | | |
| Young | 82.5 | 81.9 | 86.1 |
| Old | 71.9 | 80.0 | 80.9 |

recognition and the difference between the two groups was reduced, alumni still performed more poorly than the undergraduates. Contrary to predictions based on the levels of processing framework, however, the differences between the old and young were greatest in the shallow, size judgment condition and least in the intentional condition. For faces, as for words, the elderly performed worse than the young in all conditions, the largest differences again being in the size condition. Size judgment, however, may not have induced as shallow a level of processing for faces as it did for words since recognition accuracy was only slightly worse in this condition.[2]

Our results are consistent with the levels of processing framework insofar as purportedly deeper encoding leads to better memory and appropriate retrieval cues reduce the difference between old and young for deeply encoded information. Contrary to the levels of processing framework, however, the gap between the old and young was never fully bridged and it remained widest for material encoded at a shallow level. These findings suggest that unless the encoding and retrieval environment is made extremely supportive, elderly subjects will always remember more poorly than the young. The impaired hippocampal function of the elderly may not be completely overcome by psychological means. No matter how hard one tries, information that is accessible to conscious recollection may never be fully consolidated (i.e., fixed) or retained once the hippocampus is damaged.

[2] Subsequent experiments by Hughes revealed that judging the sex of faces leads to very poor memory whereas a similar judgment on words (is this word ''feminine'' or ''masculine'') leads to excellent memory. Clearly it is not always possible to determine the level of processing induced by a particular orienting task. The same task may induce a different level for different materials.

## Procedural or Skill Memory

Even patients with extensive, bilateral damage to the hippocampus or other medial limbic structures who are profoundly amnesic can nonetheless learn some things quite well. This may seem paradoxical, but their behavior strongly suggests that it is important to distinguish between two modes of remembering. I refer to one of them as *conscious recollection* (Moscovitch, 1982); it is the kind of memory that is typically assessed by traditional tests of recall and recognition. In these tasks, there is usually a conscious effort by the subject to recall the information requested or to decide which of the alternatives are familiar to him. The other form of memory is referred to as *procedural or skill memory* (other investigators have characterized it differently). By *skill* or *procedure* I follow Kolers's (1976) usage to mean a set of procedures or operations that are brought to bear on a particular task. As such, the term applies equally to motor acts and cognitive processes. Procedural or skill memory is assessed by having the subject perform an operation or execute an action or relearn a task to see if there is improvement with practice or any saving from the initial presentation. In these tasks, the subject is never asked to remember, but merely to perform. Indeed, amnesic patients who demonstrate considerable savings on a large range of tasks often have no conscious recollection of ever having performed them. These tasks include mirror and pursuit rotor drawing (Corkin; 1968; Milner, Corkin, & Teuber, 1969; Starr & Phillips, 1970) identifying pictorial and verbal Gollin figures (Warrington & Weiskrantz, 1970), classical eyelid conditioning (Weiskrantz & Warrington, 1979), solving anagrams and jigsaw puzzles (Baddeley, 1982; Brooks & Baddeley, 1976), learning to read geometrically transformed script (Cohen & Squire, 1980), applying a new mathematical rule (Kinsbourne, & Wood, 1975), and solving a complex block arrangement problem such as the Tower of Hanoi (Cohen & Squire, 1981).

If it is true that the memory deficits in the aged and Alzheimer patients are related to impaired hippocampal function, then procedural or skill memory should be less severely affected than conscious recollection. To date, we have tested this hypothesis using two different paradigms which involve verbal material.

In the first experiment, we used young undergraduates, older alumni living at home, institutionalized elderly people, and four patients with memory disorders, three who were believed to be in the early stages of Alzheimer's disease and one whose condition was due to anoxia. The subjects were required to read, as quickly as possible without making mistakes, sentences in normal or geometrically transformed script, in which each letter was rotated about its vertical axis (see Kolers, 1976). Their reading speed was timed. The sentences were derived from a brief essay on the recent history of popular music. On the first day they read 14 sentences in each of the two scripts; two hours later they read 7 new and 7 old sentences of each type and were required to indicate whether they had read each sentence before. Two weeks later, they read 28 sentences of each type, 7 of which they had seen only on the first presentation, 7 of which they had seen only on the second presentation, 7 of which they had seen both times, and 7 of which were new. Again, they had to identify the sentences as old or new.

As Table 2 shows, recognition accuracy for old sentences gets worse as we proceed from young adults to memory-disordered patients. Institutionalized old people performed almost as poorly as the memory-disordered patients on this task despite their having a clearly superior memory in everyday situations. For example, only one of the patients had a subjective sense of familiarity with the task, whereas all the elderly subjects remembered it well. The high accuracy scores for the institutionalized elderly and memory-disordered patients on the new sentences merely reflected their judgment that almost all the sentences, even the old ones, were unfamiliar or new and in this case they were correct.

Contrary to our expectations, however, the evidence is not very strong that procedural memory as reflected by the speed and accuracy of reading transformed script is relatively spared in the normal and institutionalized elderly (see Table 3). As a group, their improvement, both proportionately and absolutely, parallels their performance on the recognition task. The simplest interpretation of these group data is that for normal elderly patients, either institutionalized or not, their deficits are such as to affect both types of memory. If we look at the performance of some individual subjects, however, there is a suggestion that the two types of memory are differentially affected. Some subjects who performed especially poorly on recognition, nonetheless, indicated by their reading skills that they were especially sensitive to the effects of prior presentation.

What is merely suggestive in the old people's performance is seen clearly in that of the memory-disordered patients. Although recognition accuracy is almost at chance, their reading showed at least as much improvement as that of the noninstitutionalized elderly, whose recognition performance was far superior. Moreover, we see that it is not just a generalized skill that they acquired, but rather a specific one as well, in the sense that they found sentences that they had seen twice easier to read than those they had seen once, which in turn were easier to read than new sentences, despite the fact that they cannot consciously distinguish one type of sentence from another.

Because the results of this experiment were encouraging, we decided to test our hypothesis using a different paradigm—a lexical decision task in which some words and nonwords were repeated at various lags after the initial presentation. Recent studies by Scarborough and his colleagues (Scarborough, Gerard, & Cortese, 1979; Scarborough, Cortese, & Scarborough, 1977) showed that the latency to make a lexical decision, that is to judge whether a string of letters forms a word, decreases on the second presentation of that word. This reaction time advantage, known as the repetition priming effect, does not decrease signif-

*Table 2. Recognition Accuracy for Geometrically Transformed Sentences*[a]

| | Young | | | | Community old | | | | Institutionalized old | | | | | Memory disordered | | | |
|---|---|---|---|---|---|---|---|---|---|---|---|---|---|---|---|---|---|
| | A | B | C | D | A | B | C | D | A | B | C | D | | A | B | C | D |
| Initial | √ | √ | | | √ | √ | | | √ | √ | | | | √ | √ | | |
| 1–2-hour delay | 98.0 | — | 99.0 | — | 93.9 | — | 93.9 | — | 67.1 | — | 81.3 | — | | 42.9 | — | 67.6 | — |
| 2-week delay | 96.9 | 78.6 | 78.6 | 82.6 | 81.6 | 54.1 | 60.2 | 80.6 | 35.7 | 24.1 | 30.0 | 82.9 | 4–14 day delay | 71.4 | 60.7 | 46.4 | 53.5 |

[a]Sets A, B, C, and D each consist of seven sentences. The numbers indicate the percentage of correct recognition of the previously seen sentences and the rejection of new sentences.

*Table 3. Reading Speed (in Seconds) of Geometrically Transformed Sentences*[a]

| | Young | | | | Community old | | | | Institutionalized old | | | | | Memory disordered | | | |
|---|---|---|---|---|---|---|---|---|---|---|---|---|---|---|---|---|---|
| | A | B | C | D | A | B | C | D | A | B | C | D | | A | B | C | D |
| Initial | 18.5 | 19.6 | — | — | 34.8 | 36.9 | — | — | 42.2 | 44.7 | — | — | | 41.8 | 44.3 | — | — |
| 2-hour delay | 9.1 | — | 15.7 | — | 23.0 | — | 33.0 | — | 35.5 | — | 44.3 | — | | 26.1 | — | 36.8 | — |
| 2-week delay | 7.7 | 9.7 | 11.3 | 12.5 | 19.2 | 22.9 | 26.2 | 26.5 | 32.1 | 36.1 | 38.2 | 37.4 | 4–14 day delay | 19.5 | 26.3 | 29.5 | 34.5 |

[a]Sets A, B, C, and D each consist of seven sentences.

icantly with lag even for lags as long as 31 items. On a recognition task, in which subjects must decide whether a word was presented earlier, decision latencies increase significantly with lag. One can consider the repetition priming effect as dependent on procedural memory and recognition performance as dependent on conscious recollection. We would predict, therefore, that performance on a recognition task will be more sensitive to the effects of aging and Alzheimer's disease, at least in the early stages, than performance on a repetition priming task.

In our test, 144 items, divided equally between words and pronounceable nonwords, were presented on the display screen of a PET microprocessor. One third of the items were repeated at lags of 0, 7, and 29; there were 216 trials in each condition. Because each subject was tested on both repetition priming and recognition, two different sets of stimuli were assembled. We tested 10 young and 10 old subjects in each condition.

As Figure 8 shows, the repetition priming effect is virtually identical in young and old subjects. There is very little influence of lag on performance. Recognition, however, is affected by lag, but contrary to our expectations, there was no interaction with age. Age seemed only to affect overall speed but not the slope of the RT function with lag.

To see if we could exaggerate the lag effects on the two types of task and produce an interaction with age, we had subjects add two numbers that were displayed on the screen between each trial. Figure 8 shows that our attempt was not successful. Again, the functions remained similar to that in the no-match condition except that all RTs were increased. Our results do support the hypothesis that repetition priming and recognition are mediated by different mnemonic processes insofar as lag affects the latter much more than the former.

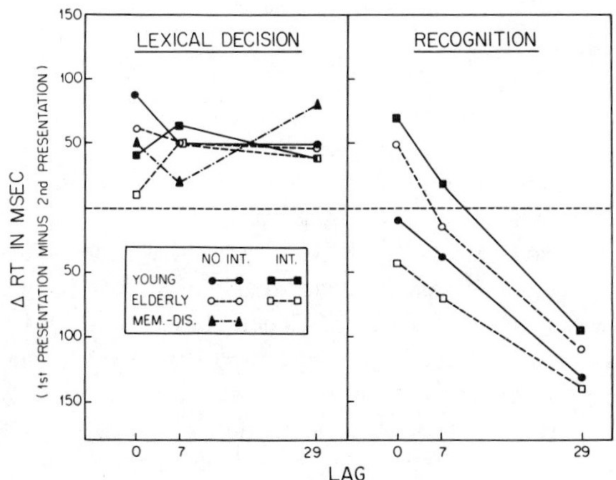


Fig. 8. Differences in RT between the first and second presentation of a word in lexical decision and recognition tasks. The second word was presented at lags of 0, 7, and 29 items. INT refers to interference produced by an interpolated math task between each trial.

Moreover, we had to discard about one-third of our elderly patients because they produced too many errors on the recognition test for their RT data to be interpretable. There were no such "failures" on the lexical decision task.

This pattern appeared in an exaggerated form in patients suspected to be in the early stages of Alzheimer's disease. All patients showed a normal repetition priming effect (Figure 8). On the recognition test, however, none of the patients performed consistently above chance even at a lag of 0, so their RT results were not useable.

The performance of patients in the early stages of Alzheimer's disease on both the reading task and the word recognition and lexical decision tasks seems to be similar to that of amnesic patients with confirmed or suspected bilateral damage to the hippocampus or midline limbic structures. This similarity reinforces our impression that the memory deficits of Alzheimer patients who are not yet severely demented are strongly related to hippocampal and temporal lobe pathology that occurs early in these patients. Our results also support the hypothesis that the presumed hippocampal damage affects performance primarily on tasks that require conscious recollection rather than procedural or skill memory.

A similar but somewhat hazier picture emerges from our experiments on old people. Performance on the word recognition and lexical decision tasks indicates that conscious recollection is much more severely affected than skill memory by age, but results from the reading task suggest that both forms of memory are impaired. At this stage, the safest conclusion is that although conscious recollection is likely to be more severely affected, the neural deficits accompanying old age are sufficiently widespread that performance on some skill memory tasks may also be impaired.

## Remote Memory

There is some controversy as to whether remote memories are impaired in organic amnesics. Warrington and her colleagues (Sanders & Warrington, 1975; Warrington & Sanders, 1971) and Kinsbourne and Wood (1975) claim that all memories are equally impaired whereas others, such as Milner (1966), Albert, Butters, and Levin (1979), Squire and Cohen (1982), and Marslen-Wilson and Teuber (1975) claim that there is a strong temporal gradient in amnesia such that the amnesia is most severe for events occurring after the onset of the syndrome and, perhaps, just prior to it. Memory for remote events is relatively spared. My impression of the current status of this debate (Squire & Cohen, 1982; Moscovitch, 1982) is that all amnesics show a temporal gradient in amnesia. Korsakoff patients, however, have an impaired memory for events extending through their entire lifespan, although it is most severe for more recent material. Non-Korsakoff amnesics have a normal memory for remote events.

In light of this controversy and the often stated impression that recent but not remote memory is impaired in old age (Ribot, 1882), we thought it might be interesting to look at the performance of old people and Alzheimer patients on the famous faces test of Albert *et al.*, 1979.

In the famous faces test, subjects must identify photographs of personalities who became known in different decades beginning with the 1920s and running through the mid-1970s. Some personalities are well known and easy to identify and others are more obscure and harder to identify as determined by the performance of a group of 50-year-old control subjects living in the Boston area. If the subjects had difficulty identifying the personality, they were given a semantic and then a phonemic hint. Figure 9 shows that old people tend to remember personalities from the remote past better than those from the more recent past, a pattern, not surprisingly, that is the opposite of that of our undergraduates. In fact there is a steady decline in old people's memory for faces from the 1920s to the 1960s with a slight upswing for the 1970s. This latter fact is important because it implies that the old people's poorer memory for personalities in the 1960s and 1950s does not arise because they did not acquire that information but rather because it is not now readily available, either because it decayed or because it is difficult to retrieve.

The memory disordered patients, all but one of whom were in the early stages of Alzheimer's disease, performed at a level equal to that of old people, except for identification of personalities from the 1970s. The Alzheimer patients' performance resembles that of the organic amnesic and the patients who have

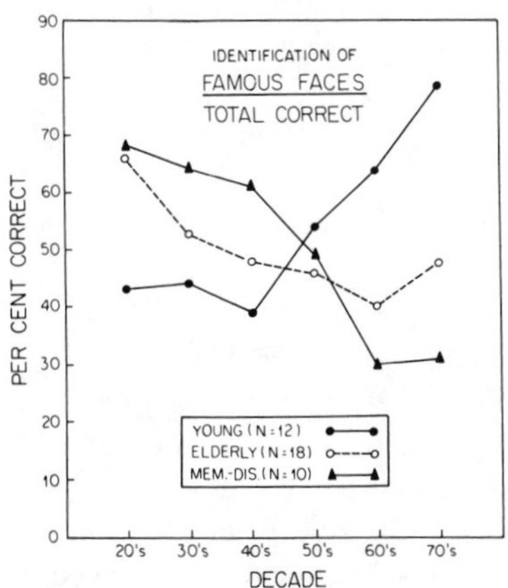


Fig. 9. Proportion of personalities who first became famous in different decades that were identified correctly with the help of semantic and phonemic cues by young people, healthy old people, and memory disordered patients.

received multiple ECT treatments (Squire & Cohen, 1982). We are not sure what neurological effects ECT treatment produces but, even if we were, it would still be imprudent to infer that the elderly and Alzheimer patients suffer from similar deficits. For these reasons, we think it best to reserve judgment on the neurological determinants of remote memory performance in old people and Alzheimer patients.

## Memory in Everyday Life

The impression one gets from reading the experimental literature is that in the absence of appropriate cues normal old people have a mild to moderate memory impairment. It is unlikely that this impairment is restricted to laboratory situations. Old people commonly complain that their memory is not as good as it once was and young people often voice similar sentiments in dealing with the elderly. Despite this, there are very few studies that test memory performance in everyday situations. Moreover, responses on questionnaires show surprisingly little effect of age on subjective evaluation of memory performance. Perhaps the cues are so very strong in most everyday situations that for the most part they can prop up memory functions that are beginning to show the effects of age.

With this as background, Nina Minde and I decided to compare memory performance in old and young people in a telephone-appointment study. Subjects were simply given a date and time at which to call a telephone answering service; we wished to see how close to the appointed time the call was placed.

We chose this paradigm for a number of reasons. First, it is an activity that most of us carry out regularly. Second, keeping appointments or remembering to carry out chores at appointed times is one of the things that old people claim to find difficult. Third, it is an activity that one can monitor carefully. Lastly, if we wished, we could intervene in various ways to see if we could modify performance.

In the first experiment, we had a group of 10 young and 10 old people call in every day for two weeks at the same time. The time was chosen by the subject to be one that was convenient. To our surprise, only one old person missed the appointment, whereas eight of the young people missed at least one appointment and, of those, some missed several. We do not think that the differences arose because the old people led relatively empty lives in which a phone call to an answering service was the highlight of their day or because the young people led especially full lives that interfered with placing the call. Many of our old subjects led very active lives, either in business or in community affairs. In questioning the subjects, the single most relevant factor that affected performance seems to have been the use of mnemonic devices. Those young people who trusted their memory ("I have an internal alarm that always goes off at the right time") were the ones who missed their appointments. The ones who gave themselves reminders, such as a note on the telephone or a shoe near the door, were the ones who always called on time. Invariably, the old people made full use of these external mnemonic devices.

In a second study, we decided to make things more difficult by setting up only two appointments, one a week, at a time of our choosing, not the subject's. The results were similar to the first study, although the differences between the old and young subjects were not as large.

In a last, desperate attempt to force the old people to forget an appointment, we had to make them promise that they would not resort to any mnemonic tricks. They were to write down the telephone number and put it in a place where it would not be easily noticed. The time of the two appointments, however, they were to keep in their heads. Finally, we succeeded in getting about half of the old people to miss an appointment by more than five minutes. They were still no worse than our young controls. What was interesting, however, was how unwilling the old people were to part with their mnemonic aids. For example, despite instructions to the contrary, some of our subjects still carried the piece of paper bearing the telephone number in a prominent place in their wallets.

With more effort, we are sure we can bring old people's memory to its knees in everyday situations, but that hardly seems to be the point of this research. The main lesson of this venture into the dangerous, real world is that old people have learned from experience what we have so consistently shown in the laboratory—that their memory is getting somewhat poorer—and they have structured their environment to compensate for this loss in some situations.

## Summary

The neuropsychological framework that we adopted in our research rests on the assumption that cognitive changes with age result primarily from structural changes in the nervous system. Although this assumption is probably accurate when applied to individuals with presumed neural pathology, such as Alzheimer patients, it is probably overstated when applied to normal, healthy old people for whom psychological factors may play an important role as well. Moreover, we have also assumed that the effects of progressive neural deterioration with age on certain structures are similar to the effects of damage resulting from trauma, a rather strong assumption given the literature suggesting that there may be important differences between them. Despite these uncertain assumptions, the neuropsychological approach was generally useful. In some instances, such as the studies on visual masking and on primary and secondary memory, the performance of old people and Alzheimer patients was consistent with the predictions we made on the basis of their presumed neuropathology, if such a strong term could also be used to describe the relatively slight but normal deterioration that occurs with age. In other cases the fit was not so good. Performance on the WCST and the release from PI task was not wholly consistent with predicted effects of presumed frontal damage in the elderly. Similarly, we failed to find the clear dissociation between procedural memory and conscious recollection in the elderly that we predicted on the assumption that the memory deficits in old people resulted primarily from hippocompal or limbic system damage.

One can use these partial failures to discredit our neuropsychological approach. At this moment, it seems premature to do so. The more sensible tactic is to refine our neuropsychological hypotheses. The variability in performance among old people of similar background is much higher than it is among the young. One can assume as well that there is similar variability in the locus and extent of neural degeneration.

New behavioral, electrophysiological, and radiological techniques such as the CAT and PET scan may help us localize the regions of impaired function more precisely and thereby reduce a major source of variance among our elderly subjects. This will not remove some of the other problems that we mentioned earlier, especially the one concerning the compensatory processes that accompany slow neural degeneration. If the techniques are sufficiently sensitive, however, they will enable us not only to test our hypotheses more precisely but also to discover new correlations between neural structure and function.

# References

Albert, M. S., Butters, N., & Levin, J. Temporal gradients in the retrograde amnesia of patients with alcoholic Korsakoff disease. *Archives of Neurology*, 1979, *36*, 211–216.

Baddeley, A. D. Amnesia: Minimal model and an interpretation. In L. S. Cermak (Ed.), *Human memory and amnesia*. Hillsdale, N.J.: Lawrence Erlbaum, 1981.

Blakemore, C. Central visual processing. In M. S. Gazzaniga & C. Blakemore, (Eds.), *Handbook of psychology*. New York: Academic Press, 1975.

Blessed, G., Tomlinson, B. E., & Roth, M. The association between quantitative measures of dementia and of senile changes in the cerebral grey matter of elderly subjects. *British Journal of Psychiatry*, 1968, *114*, 797–811.

Bodis-Wolner, I. Visual acuity and contrast sensitivity in patients with cerebral lesions. *Science*, 1972, *178*, 769–771.

Borod, J. C., & Goodglass, H. Lateralization of linguistic and melodic processing with age. *Neuropsychologia*, 1980, *18*, 79–83.

Brooks, D. N., & Baddeley, A. D. What can amnesic patients learn? *Neuropsychologia*, 1976, *14*, 111–122.

Brown, J. W., & Jaffe, J. Hypotheses on cerebral dominance. *Neuropsychologia*, 1975, *13*, 107–110.

Campbell, F. W. The transmission of spatial information through the visual system. In F. O. Schmitt & F. G. Worden (Eds.), *The neuronsciences: Third study program*. Cambridge: MIT Press, 1974.

Campbell, F. W., & Robson, J. G. Application of Fourier analysis to the visibility of gratings. *Journal of Physiology*, 1968, *197*, 551–566.

Clark, L. E., & Knowles, J. B. Age differences in dichotic listening performance. *Journal of Gerontology*, 1973, *28*, 173–178.

Cohen, N. J., & Squire, L. R. Preserved learning and retention of pattern-analyzing skill in amnesia. Dissociation of knowing how and knowing that. *Science*, 1980, *210*, 207–210.

Cohen, N. J., & Squire, L. R. Paper presented at the meeting of the International Neuropsychological Society, Atlanta, February 1981.

Coltheart, M. Iconic memory and visible persistence. *Perception and psychophysics*, 1980, *27*, 183–228.

Corkin, S. Acquisition of motor skill after bilateral medial temporal-lobe excision. *Neuropsychologia*, 1968, *3*, 255–265.

Cornsweet, R. N. *Visual perception*. New York: Academic Press, 1970.

Craik, F. I. M. Age differences in human memory. In J. E. Birren & K. W. Schaie (Eds.), *Handbook of the psychology of aging*. New York: Van Nostrand Reinhold, 1977.

Craik, F. I. M., & Birtwistle, J. Proactive inhibition in free recall. *Journal of Experimental Psychology*, 1971, *91*, 120–123.

Eysenck, M. W. Age differences in incidental learning. *Developmental Psychology*, 1974, *10*, 936–941.

Glanzer, M., & Cunitz, A. R. Two storage mechanisms in free recall. *Journal of Verbal Learning and Verbal Behavior*, 1966, *5*, 351–360.

Hubel, D. H., & Wiesel, T. N. Receptive fields and functional architecture of monkey striate cortex. *Journal of Physiology*, 1968, *195*, 215–243.

Hubel, D. H., & Wiesel, T. N. Functional architecture of Macaque monkey visual cortex. *Proceedings of the Royal Society of London*, 1977, *198*, 1–59.

Kinsbourne, M. & Wood, F. Short-term memory processes and the amnesic syndrome. In D. Deutsch & A. J. Deutsch (Eds.), *Short-term memory*. New York: Academic Press, 1975.

Kolers, P. Reading a year later. *Journal of Experimental Psychology: Human Learning and Memory*, 1976, *2*, 554–565.

Malamud, N. Neuropathology of organic brain syndromes associated with aging. In C. M. Gaitz (Ed.) *Aging and the brain*. New York: Plenum Press, 1972.

Marslen-Wilson, W. D., & Teuber, H. L. Memory for remote events in anterograde amnesia: Recognition of public figures from news photographs. *Neuropsychologia*, 1975, *13*, 347–352.

Meadows, J. C. Disturbed perception of colours associated with localized cerebral legions. *Brain*, 1974, *97*, 615–632.

Milner, B. Amnesia following operation on the temporal lobes. In C. W. M. Whitty & O. L. Zangwill (Eds.), *Amnesia*. London: Butterworth, 1966.

Milner, B., Corkin, S., & Teuber, H. L. Further analysis of the hippocompal amnesic syndrome. *Neuropsychologia*, 1968, *6*, 215–234.

Moscovitch, M. Information processing in the cerebral hemispheres. In M. S. Gazzaniga (Ed.) *Handbook of behavioral neurobiology, Vol. II: Neuropsychology*. New York: Plenum Press, 1979.

Moscovitch, M. Multiple dissociations of function. In L. S. Cermak (Ed.), *Human memory and amnesia*. Hillsdale, N.J.: Lawrence Erlbaum, 1982.

Moscovitch, M., & Milner, B. Release from proactive interference with an analysis of short- and long-term memory deficits in free recall in patients with unilateral frontal or temporal lobectomy. In preparation.

Moscovitch, M., Scullion, D., & Christie, D. Early vs late stages of processing and their relation to functional hemispheric asymmetries in face recognition. *Journal of Experimental Psychology: Human Perception and Performance,* 1976, *2,* 401–416.

Pearlman, A. L., Birch, J., & Meadows, J. C. Cerebral colourblindness: An acquired deficit in hue discrimination. *Annals of neurology,* 1979, *5,* 253–261.

Raines, D. Personal communication, June, 1981.

Ratcliff, G. & Cowley, A. Disturbances of visual perception following cerebral lesions. In D. J. Oborne, N. M. Greeneberg, & J. R. Eiser (Eds.). *Research in psychology and medicine.* New York: Academic Press, 1981.

Reed, D. Papers presented at the Canadian Psychological Association Meeting. Toronto, June 1981.

Ribot, T. A. *The diseases of memory.* New York: Appleton, 1882.

Sanders, H., & Warrington, E. K. Retrograde amnesia in organic amnesic patients. *Cortex,* 1975, *11,* 397–400.

Scarborough, D. L., Cortese, C., & Scarborough, H. Frequency and repetition effects in lexical memory. *Journal of Experimental Psychology: Human Perception and Performance,* 1977, *3,* 1–17.

Scarborough, D. L., Gerard, D., & Cortese, C. Accessing lexical memory: The transfer of word repetition effects across task and modality. *Memory and Cognition,* 1979, *7,* 3–12.

Schlotterer, G. *Changes in visual information processing with normal aging and progressive dementia of the Alzheimer type.* Unpublished Doctoral thesis, University of Toronto, 1977.

Sekuler, R., Hutman, L. P., & Owsley, C. J. Human aging and spatial vision. *Science,* 1980, *209,* 1255–1256.

Squire, L. R., & Cohen, N. J. Remote memory, retrograde amnesia, and the neuropsychology of memory. In L. S. Cermak (Ed.), *Human memory and amnesia.* Hillsdale, N.J.: Lawrence Erlbaum, 1981.

Starr, A., & Phillips, L. Verbal and motor memory in the amnesic syndrome. *Neuropsychologia,* 1970, *8,* 75–88.

Tomlinson, B. E., Blessed, G., & Roth, M. Observation on the brains of non-demented old people, *Journal of Neurological Sciences,* 1968, *7,* 331–356.

Tomlinson, B. E., Blessed, G., & Roth, M. Observation on the brains of demented old people. *Journal of Neurological Sciences,* 1970, *11,* 205–242.

Tulving, E., & Colotla, V. A. Free recall of trilingual lists. *Cognitive Psychology,* 1970, *1,* 86–98.

Turvey, M. On peripheral and central processes in vision: Inferences from an information-processing analysis of masking with patterned stimuli. *Psychological Review,* 1973, *80,* 1–52.

Van Essen, D. C., & Zeki, S. M. The topographic organization of Rhesus monkey prestriate cortex. *Journal of Physiology,* 1978, *277,* 193–226.

Warrington, E. K., & Sanders, H. I. The date of old memories. *Quarterly Journal of Experimental Psychology,* 1971, *23,* 432–442.

Warrington, E. K., & Weiskrantz, L. Amnesic syndrome: Consolidation or retrieval? *Nature,* 1970, *228,* 628–630.

Watkins, M. J. Concept and measurement of primary memory. *Psychological Bulletin,* 1974, *81,* 695–711.

Weiskrantz, L., & Warrington, E. K. Conditioning in amnesic patients. *Neuropsychologia,* 1979, *17,* 187–194.

Wickens, D. Encoding categories of words: An empirical approach to memory. *Psychological Review,* 1970, *77,* 1–15.

Zeki, S. M. Colour coding in Rhesus monkey prestriate cortex. *Brain Research,* 1973, *53,* 422–427.

Zeki, S. M. Uniformity and diversity of structure and function in Rhesus monkey prestriate visual cortex. *Journal of Physiology,* 1978, *277,* 273–290.

CHAPTER 5

# How Do Old People Know What to Do Next?

Patrick M. A. Rabbitt

*Department of Experimental Psychology*
*University of Durham*
*Durham, England*

## Introduction

A very large, though fragmentary and disconnected, literature shows that as people grow old their cognitive efficiency declines. Gerontologists try to specify the precise details of this decline, to calibrate its relative extent in various components of cognition function, and to understand the nature of the changes which bring it about. To do this they have traditionally depended on empirical techniques and functional models of cognitive performance developed by human experimental psychologists working with normal young adults. There are signs that this dependence has now become so complete that it stifles original work. This has not occurred because of the lethargy or dullness of gerontologists but rather because the models currently used by human experimental psychologists have a particular crucial, and very general, limitation. They are all models for steady-state systems working under optimal conditions in the able young. They do not allow us to describe the nature of *changes* in human performance. Gerontologists are primarily concerned with descriptions and explanations of *change*.

A survey of gerontological literature leaves the impression that most workers are too diffident to do more than replicate on elderly populations experiments originally carried out to answer particular, sometimes very narrow, theoretical questions about young adults. This would be a reasonable way to proceed if models for functional processes such as memory, decision making, perceptual motor control, or selective attention were sufficiently developed to allow us to interpret the nature of the changes which our experiments reveal. Surprisingly, however, we do not even have any plausible model for any single subsystem or process which allows us to discuss how people improve with practice (Rabbitt, 1980a,b). In all cognitive tasks people spontaneously become more efficient when they are practiced, even when they are given no special training or guidance. This is true even of the easiest possible choice–reaction time (CRT) tasks in which people have only to respond as fast as they can to each one of a set of possible events. In such tasks extended practice may increase speed and reduce errors by 100 or 200%. Improvements continue over indefinitely long periods and may be maintained without further training (e.g., Mowbray & Rhoades, 1959; Rabbitt, Cumming, & Vyas, 1979). Changes due to extended practice are much larger than those due to such factors as stimulus discriminability, stimulus and response compatibility, the number of stimulus and response alternatives between which subjects choose, or sequential effects. Further, the effects of all these latter variables may be reduced, altered, or completely abolished by extended practice. Yet most reaction-time experiments and all functional models for CRT have been concerned with the relatively minor and transitory effects of such variables (Rabbitt, 1980b).

This would not matter if we could accept what appears to be the general tacit assumption that the functional models we have developed are adequate to explain the effects of practice because we need only suppose that as people practice they carry out the same functional operations in precisely the same way—only they carry out each operation faster and more accurately. But this assumption is certainly unreliable since we know that practice does not merely improve the efficiency with which people carry out these tasks but also changes the *ways* in which they do so (e.g., Kristofferson, 1977; Mowbray & Rhoades, 1959; Rabbitt, 1980a,b; Rabbitt, Cumming, & Vyas, 1979).

This is a serious situation for gerontology since whenever we find that elderly people do not perform as efficiently as the young we do not know whether this is a permanent difference or whether differences between old and young may not be mitigated by appropriate training. There are two other distinct and severe handicaps. First, if we do not have useful models to describe change within a person, we cannot interpret changes which may occur as he ages. A second limitation is that even in very simple CRT tasks the most impressive feature of age comparisons is not the fact that the *average* level of performance of large groups of people declines as older samples are tested. It is rather that *variability* of performance dramatically increases in older groups. The present author has sampled the reaction times of some 1800 adults aged from 20 to 80 years. Within each successive decade, variance in individual differences in speed and accuracy steadily and sharply increases. In the oldest group, aged from 70 to 80 years, about 10% of the sample still have speed and accuracy scores equal to, or significantly better than, the means for the youngest age groups. Of course, another way to put this is that about 90% of 70- to 80-year-olds are grossly slower and less accurate than the young. However, the point is that even for such a very simple skill the performances of individuals seem to change with age at very different rates. It is precisely this increased diversity of performance within members of an aging population that is one of the most intriguing phenomena of human aging. The study of aging is, inescapably, the study of widening individual differences in performance. The lack of reasonable models for change implies a lack of models for individual differences in *rates* of change, and this is a crucial handicap to further progress.

This generalization about limitations of current models would merely be tetchy and unhelpful if it could not be sharpened by suggestions based on work directly concerned with active adaptations to change.

My colleagues and I have tried to understand how humans actively adapt to changes in their own abilities and in task demands in very easy, serial, self-paced CRT tasks. It now seems clear that even in such elementary tasks people must actively monitor and adjust their response-speed so as gradually to optimize performance with extended practice (e.g. Rabbitt, 1980a,b; Rabbitt & Vyas, 1970). They optimize subtly to cope when signals occur at unpredictable intervals (Rabbitt, 1980c). They also optimize to compensate for changes which occur with advancing age (Rabbitt, 1979a, 1980a,b; Rabbitt & Vyas 1980b).

A generalization which emerges from these experiments is that people very rarely behave as simple systems which are passively controlled by sequences of external events. They much more frequently behave as active, self-adjusting systems which can seek out an appropriate one among many possible optimization procedures in order to adjust to their own limitations and to task constraints. Changes in performance with practice may involve a series of successive choices among optimization procedures to approximate to optimal control. Changes in performance accompanying old age may similarly involve active selection among strategies to mitigate specific decrements. A general feature of aging seems to be a gradual loss of flexibility of active control and consequent reduction in possibilities for self-optimization. The nature of performance change in old age may be usefully approached by asking what specific decrements in CNS function may lead to such loss of control and what residual degrees of freedom for adaptation an aged human information-processing system may retain and use.

This general distinction between adjustments which are externally driven, or imposed by external events, and adjustments which are actively made on the basis of acquired experience parallels earlier theoretical discussions by Norman and Bobrow (1975a,b). The purpose of the present chapter is to go beyond simple CRT tasks to discuss some questions of more general interest: How do people control their performance actively to optimize their attentional selectivity in the face of rapidly changing events? How do they make optimal decisions as to what to do next from moment to moment during rapid, complex tasks? What factors may reduce the efficiency of *control* of performance as people grow older? What implications do such changes in efficiency of control have for the ways in which elderly people cope with everyday life?

## Passive and Active Control of Momentary Changes in Selective Attention

Norman and Bobrow's (1975a,b) useful distinction between data-driven and memory- or response-driven systems may be illustrated by considering how sequences of operations carried out on a simple programmable calculator may offer crude analogies for some psychological functions. First consider a case in which no program is entered. When any digit key is pressed, a corresponding number appears on the display. The display is now passively data-driven by immediate inputs. The calculator may be said to simulate simple reflex responses to external stimuli. Next consider a program which will display the squares or square roots of numbers which are entered. The calculator is still data-driven, but its internal hardware resources act upon input to present complex transformations of numbers entered. An analogy might be with cases in which complex output sequences (e.g., the stepping reflex) are passively initiated in response to simple external stimuli (pressure on a paw). Next consider a program which allows the machine to accept and display a digit only if it is entered twice in immediate succession. Here each new data input resets the machine and momentarily adjusts its selectivity. The machine may, not too fancifully, be said to display the classic "stimulus repetition effect" (Bertelson, 1965; Rabbitt, 1968). Finally, consider a case in which a program is entered which allows the machine to accept and display only some digits (e.g., 4 and 7) but which clears the display when any other digit is entered. This may be taken as a logical analogy to types of selective attention which are memory-driven—that is, which accept only inputs corresponding to information held in memory in accordance with instructions also held in program memory.

These cases also illustrate that the locus of control of selectivity may shift within a system from direct control by momentary input through control by input transformed by internal resources to control of input by previously acquired information held in memory.

Rabbitt (1979b) and Rabbitt and Vyas (1980b) have compared tasks in which subjects' momentary fluctuations of attentional selectivity are directly controlled by external events, are controlled by transformations of input based on previously learned associations, or are controlled entirely by information held in memory. Comparisons between young and elderly people suggested that while input-driven control of selectivity may remain unaffected by age, elderly people may lose the ability to control efficiently momentary changes in selectivity on the basis of previously learned information. Two recent experiments by Rabbitt and Fleming (1980) may serve to illustrate and extend these ideas.

### *Recency Effects Determined by Stimulus Characteristics or by Previously Learned Associations*

Lists of 200 words were made up from sets of 20 Thorndike–Lorge AA nouns. These words were presented in sequence one at a time on a computer-controlled display. Subjects responded to each by pressing one of two keys. In one condition they carried out a letter-detection task pressing one key if a word contained, for example, the letter "E" and another if it contained the letter "A." In the other condition they pressed one key to identify words which were names of members of one semantic category (e.g., fish) and the other to identify members of another (e.g., mammals). Each word list was made up so that it could be orthogonally classified either in a letter-detection or semantic classification task. Since the words occurred in random order, individual words might recur on immediately successive trials (1 back) or after 1 to 40 other intervening trials (2 back to 41 back). Half the subjects classified half the lists in the letter detection task and half in the semantic classification task. The remainder classified the same lists in opposite ways. Each response was identified, timed, and stored. Subjects were asked to respond as fast and accurately as possible.

Subjects' responses were sorted to separate and pool all cases in which identical words immediately recurred (1-back repetitions), recurred after 1, 2, or 3 intervening trials (2-, 3-, or 4-back recency effects), or after 4 or more intervening trials (5+ recency effects). Data obtained from 19 triads of young (18- to 25-year-old), late middle-aged 50- to 65-year-old), and elderly (65- to 75-year-old) people, matched for adjusted Mill–Hill verbal IQ, were sorted in this way, and group means are given in Table 1.

The point of interest was the extent to which immediate, or recent, recurrence of an item facilitated its categorisation in these tasks. For all groups letter detection was facilitated only up to 1-back recurrences. In contrast, in the semantic categorization task, classifications were facilitated when words recurred after as many as 3 intervening trials.

It seems that the more complex a decision made about a word, the longer the human information-processing system retains information about it which may facilitate subsequent reclassification. This is what might be predicted from the levels of processing hypothesis put forward by Craik and Lockhart (1972) and others since.

Although classification speed was slowed by age in both tasks, subjects of all ages benefited equally from repetition and recency effects. We may suggest that this facilitation occurs because each new word, briefly, selectively activates a particular stimulus encoding pathway in the human information-processing

*Table 1. Repetition Effects in Experiment 1*

| | 1-back | | 2-back | | 3-back | 4-back | 5-back |
|---|---|---|---|---|---|---|---|
| **Letter detection task** | | | | | | | |
| Young | 576 | <[a] | 627 | | 643 | 642 | 667 |
| Middle | 656 | <[a] | 721 | | 750 | 744 | 759 |
| Old | 753 | <[a] | 812 | | 843 | 849 | 845 |
| **Taxonomic categorization task** | | | | | | | |
| | 1-back | | 2-back | | 3-back | 4-back | 5-back |
| Young | 630 | <[a] | 694 | <[a] | 749 | 770 | 741 |
| Middle | 734 | <[a] | 855 | <[a] | 910 | 907 | 901 |
| Old | 799 | <[a] | 914 | <[a] | 992 | 1009 | 1013 |

[a] $p < .01$.

system. Because pathways activated when words are semantically encoded are more elaborate, some activation may be retained in parts of more extensive pathways. Any new input using a pathway which is still partly or completely active will be more rapidly processed than new input requiring use of a new inactive pathway (Posner & Snyder, 1975; Rabbitt & Vyas, 1979a,b). This is a model for data-driven modulation of selective attention and in terms of such a model it seems that the efficiency of data-driven selectivity does not change with old age, as other experiments reviewed by Rabbitt (1979b) also suggest.

A second experiment tested whether facilitation might also be observed when different words with common semantic associations were successively classified. Lists of 160 ''AA'' words were made up of 40 nouns, each of which was the name of an animate or an inanimate object. Unknown to subjects, the names of animate objects included equal numbers of names of insects, birds, fishes, and mammals and the names of inanimate objects names of gemstones, metals, articles of furniture, and tools. The experiment was run precisely as before except that subjects only made semantic classifications, responding to all names of living organisms on one key and to all names of inanimate objects on the other. Immediate repetitions of the same word never occurred but responses were sorted as before to identify cases of 2-back to 5+ back recurrences of identical words. Responses were also sorted to identify and pool all instances where a member of one of the covert subcategories (e.g., horse = mammal) was followed after 0 to 5+ intervening trials by another, different, word from the same subclass (e.g., pig = mammal). Means of individual mean RTs for both sorts for matched groups of 20 elderly (65 to 75-year-old) and young (18- to 25-year-old) matched pairs are given in Table 2.

When identical words recurred, we see that, as before, recency effects for semantic classifications extended over two or three intervening trials and were

*Table 2. Repetition and Recurrence Effects in Experiment 2*

| | Repetition of identical words | | | | | | | |
|---|---|---|---|---|---|---|---|---|
| | 1-back | | 2-back | | 3-back | | 4-back | 5-back |
| Young | — | | 699 | $<^{b}$ | 749 | $<^{a}$ | 791 | 783 |
| Old | — | | 805 | $<^{b}$ | 874 | $<^{a}$ | 956 | 982 |
| | Subcategory recurrence | | | | | | | |
| | 1-back | | 2-back | | 3-back | | 4-back | 5-back |
| Young | 661 | $<^{b}$ | 724 | $<^{a}$ | 761 | $<^{a}$ | 795 | 792 |
| Old | 931 | $<^{a}$ | 984 | | 979 | | 991 | 985 |

$^{a}p < .05$.
$^{b}p < .01$.

equal in magnitude and duration for young and old. Again there was no evidence that data-driven modulation of selective attention was less efficient in the old.

It is clear that classification is also facilitated when words from the same semantically related subclass recur. But for old subjects this facilitation is less than for the young and is only apparent when words recur in immediate succession. For the young it is apparent even after three intervening trials.

This facilitation cannot be described as directly data-driven since it must be mediated by the activation of previously learned associations between physically different words stored in long-term memory. To this extent it may be called memory-driven. As in other experiments reviewed by Rabbitt (1979b), it seems that this memory-driven modulation of momentary attentional selectivity becomes less efficient in old age.

Is there a plausible model, based on what we know about changes in neuronal function with age (see Chapter 1), which might explain why memory-driven control of selective attention is lost with age faster than data-driven control?

One simple speculation is that the human information-processing system may be considered as a hierarchically organized structure, similar to the pandemonium system envisaged by Selfridge (1966). Peripheral feature-analytic systems (demons) provide information for higher-order classificatory systems (higher-order demons, or "logogens," Morton 1970). A neglected property of such a system is that the numbers of higher-order classificatory demons or logogens must necessarily increase with levels in the hierarchy. This is because higher-order systems respond to unique patterns, or combinations of activated lower-order systems and the number of possible *combinations* of lower-order constructs must always be greater than the number of possible constructs themselves (i.e., there must always be a larger range of "things" than of particular "features of things" in the perceptual world).

We have suggested that unique pathways through such a hierarchical system may be activated from the bottom up (data-driven activation) or from the top down (memory-driven activation). A final postulate is that as a system ages, components at all levels become disabled or cease to be available. We may assume that at each level there will be sufficient redundancy of components for some processing still to occur. The point of this postulate is, of course, that in the human brain there appears to be substantial, and as far as we know random, death or functional impairment of individual cortical units (Chapter 1). Young and old systems are illustrated in Figure 1.

How would these systems respond to data- and memory-driven activation during experiments such as those we have described?

We have assumed that any external input activates a particular pathway from lower to higher levels of the coding system. In spite of demon mortality, there is sufficient redundancy to allow encoding. Any subsequent input requiring reuse of the same pathway or of part of this pathway can be encoded more rapidly. Thus, if a pathway can still be activated at all there is no reason why subsequent (data-driven) facilitation should be impaired.

There is equally no reason why memory-driven facilitation should be impaired if information stored in surviving higher-order units is used to activate *single, particular* pathways through a surviving hierarchy. But in our second experiment, in order for classification of one word to facilitate the subsequent encoding of any of several other, *different,* words in the same semantic subset, we must assume that simultaneous top-down activation of *several different* pathways is possible. As we see from Figure 1, this would become increasingly difficult as redundancy of demon-power is reduced and the possibility of activation of separate pathways requiring analyzers performing similar functions is thereby limited.

On these assumptions as people grow older they can still successfully anticipate single events but they may become increasingly less able to anticipate any of several different events at the same time. Loss of memory-driven control is therefore not necessarily an absolute condition which implies the loss of any inner-directed attentional selectivity. It may rather imply the gradual loss of power simultaneously to use an entire body of useful information held in memory flexibly to anticipate any and all of a wide range of possible *alternative* contingencies. The distinction is thus not necessarily between the availability and lack of availability of information to direct the expectation of contingencies, but rather the distinction between the possession of useful information and the ability to use it. As we grow older we may cease to be able to prepare ourselves to deal with all of many different things which we *know* may happen next.

If this distinction between data-driven and memory-driven selective processes is expanded and qualified, it may help us towards a model of the *processes of change* in the control of selective attention with advancing age. However, this

Fig. 1. An illustration of the pandemonium hierarchies of young and elderly cortical units. (The reader may be able to identify demons in both hierarchies from among colleagues). By V. Z. Pinkava.

distinction alone is obviously too narrow to serve as a descriptive base for all changes in control processes with age.

## Control of Efficient Interrogation of the Environment

Consider how people manage to find their way about structured environments such as city centers, airports, supermarkets, or banks in everyday life. Although a person may be quite unfamiliar with a particular city center, for example he may nevertheless recognise it as a member of a class of environments which he knows to be subject to particular, familiar functional constraints. This will make it possible for him to search efficiently for probable locations for post offices, public lavatories, and check-in counters. The following experiments are simplified attempts to illustrate some of the most elementary techniques which people learn and use to guide their interrogation of their environment and to discover whether, and in what ways, the efficiency with which they control such interrogations changes in old age.

### *Search of Probable before Improbable Locations in Space*

Rabbitt and Vyas (reported by Rabbitt, 1979b) required people to scan circular displays of capital letters for designated targets. Half the displays contained a single target letter, the others did not. When a target was present it might occur most often at a particular spatial location, and with ordered probabilities at other locations. People aged from 18 to 30 rapidly recognized this fact and apparently used it to guide their scans of displays since they detected targets most rapidly at most frequent locations. People aged from 65 to 75, given the same amount of practice, located targets no faster at frequent than at rare locations.

Apparently this was not because the elderly failed to realize that targets occurred more often at some locations than at others since they were all able to give accurate rank-orderings for target probability across display locations. They seemed to be able to recognize, learn, and describe differences in probability but not to be able to use this information to optimize their scans of displays. Of course we cannot say that our elderly subjects could never have learned to use their knowledge, even if they had practiced for indefinitely long periods or, more to the point, even if they had been given appropriate experimental instructions or had been guided by systematic cues on displays. However they clearly seemed to be less efficient than the young at spontaneously developing and using optimal scanning strategies. They also illustrate a dissociation, earlier shown by Sandford and Maule (1971, 1973a,b), between the knowledge and the use of relative probabilities of events at different locations to control search.

### *Guiding Search on the Basis of Cues from Neighboring Background Items*

When we scan an environment unfamiliar to us we typically guide our search by the knowledge that a thing we are looking for is most likely to be near other things with which we are not currently concerned. For example, even in an unfamiliar office we will look for a wastebin near a desk rather than near a fireplace.

Rabbitt and Vyas (unpublished) attempted a simplistic simulation of this by requiring people to search displays of randomly arranged capital letters for special targets. If targets were present they most frequently occurred next to other, particular, background letters. Thus the target letters N or O might occur very frequently embedded among the particular subset of letters R, S, V, P and L. However, these letters were not themselves targets, nor were they reliable cues that a target was present since they might occur in the absence of targets and since targets might occur when none of them was present, or might be remote from any of them.

People aged from 20 to 30 years located targets most rapidly when they occurred among frequent neighbors. They also took longer to decide that no target was present when the frequent neighbors appeared clustered together without a target. People aged from 60 to 78 years found targets no faster when they were embedded among frequent neighbors than when they were not. Most elderly subjects were able to specify correctly which background letters most often occurred next to targets. Thus, again, efficient control of active interrogation of displays seemed to be weakened by two distinct difficulties. First, old subjects were less able to recognize and learn differences in joint locational probabilities of target and background items. Second, they did not use information they acquired to control flexibly and adaptively their scans of displays. An obvious next point of interest was what factors might make people less efficient at recognizing changes in the probabilistic structure of events as they grow older. In other words, what changes underlie their lessening ability to detect and use possibilities for opitimizing their performance by exercising active control of it?

### *Detection of Possibilities for Developing and Using Optimal Scanning Strategies*

It is well known that patterns of eye movements which people use to scan faces, scenes, or objects are systematic rather than random. Those parts of an object or scene which convey most information relevant to a necessary decision are typically scanned first. Subordinate, less crucial parts of the environment are neglected or scanned only late during sequences of eye movements (Gippenreiter, 1978; Monty & Senders, 1976; Yarbus, 1965). The efficiency with which everyday skills such as driving a car in heavy traffic can be carried on depends on the learning and maintenance of such optimal scanning strategies (McDowell & Rockwell, 1978).

Rabbitt, Bishop, and Vyas (unpublished) investigated the learning of scanning strategies during a visual search task. Subjects scanned displays of 20 letters to determine whether designated target letters were present or absent. On all displays letters appeared at randomly selected points on an imaginary 20- × 30-location grid. For each subject, one such random display recurred on 50% of all trials. That is, on these recurrent displays letters appeared at the same, randomly chosen, 20 different spatial locations, though the locations of target and background letters among these positions were never the same on two displays. On the remaining 50% of displays, different patterns of spatial positions were occupied by target and background letters. Thus, the appearance of a recurrent display gave no assurance that a target was present, where a target might be if it were present, or which particular target or background items might be present. It simply provided a pattern of spatial locations which people might learn to recognize as the experiment proceeded and whose familiar structure they might use to develop an efficient scanning strategy.

People aged from 18 to 35 years evidently did use this information since, after 500 trials, they made target detections faster on recurrent than on nonrecurrent displays. People aged from 65 to 78 years showed no advantage for recurrent over nonrecurrent display patterns after 1500 trials.

This result does not necessarily mean that elderly people cannot ever learn or use optimal scanning strategies. Still less that they are unable to use efficient scanning strategies which they have developed since their youth. It does show that they take much longer to develop and use such strategies in an unfamiliar task. It also raises the question as to the relative complexities of scanning strategies which can be developed or used in old age.

A further point is whether elderly people can adapt their scanning strategies flexibly, from moment to moment, to keep pace with a changing visual world. To investigate this, Rabbitt *et al.* (unpublished) first presented subjects with runs of displays which all had the same pattern, in comparison with other runs in which all the displays had different patterns. Subjects of all ages learned to scan recurrent displays faster, although the elderly took longer to do so. These trained subjects were then tested on runs in which half the displays were of the familiar patterns on which they had been trained and half were new, random patterns. The young showed transfer, maintaining their advantage for familiar display patterns. The old did not.

Even when the old can learn and use a specific, efficient scanning strategy they find it difficult to employ it in a situation in which they must rapidly decide, on each trial, whether to use it or not. Apart from possible difficulties in learning efficient scans they show a loss of flexible exercise of control.

Again we have evidence of loss of flexibility and precision of control coupled with evidence of slower discovery and learning of information about the structure of events on which such control depends. This raises the further question as to whether changes in the ability to learn probability structures represent a simple loss of memory efficiency or whether they must be qualified in terms of more subtle deficits which contribute to this loss.

## *Detection of Constant Probability Bias and of Sudden Changes in the Relative Probabilities of Events*

Rabbitt and Vyas (unpublished) have run series of pilot experiments using 3-choice self-paced serial response tasks in which the probability of occurrence of one signal relative to two others was kept constant within runs of 500 trials but systematically varied between such runs to compare runs with small (40%, 30%, and 30%), medium (50%, 25%, and 25%), and gross (66%, 17%, and 17%) differences in probability. To eliminate the effects of immediate repetitions of frequent signals, events were subjectively unpredictable but repetitions of frequent signals were no more common than repetitions of rare signals in all conditions. After 3 runs of 500 trials on each condition, people aged from 18 to 35 years responded fastest to the most frequent signals in each case. With the same amount of practice, people aged from 65 to 78 years responded faster to the frequent signals with gross or medium but not with small probability bias. It seems that as people grow old they become less sensitive to small changes in probability bias, or at any rate they require much more practice before they can detect and use them to improve their performance.

This result contrasts directly with experiments reported by Griew (1962, 1968), who studied the speed with which people can detect sudden, uncued *changes* in the relative frequencies of two possible signals in a variety of tasks. Griew's elderly subjects seemed to detect and use sudden changes in bias more rapidly than the young.

A relatively trivial explanation for this discrepancy in results might have been that Griew did not control for changes in the numbers of immediate repetitions of frequent signals. In his two choice tasks abrupt changes in event probability simultaneously entailed sudden increases in repetitions of frequent signals. Since elderly subjects have been found to show larger repetition effects than the young in some CRT tasks (Jordan & Rabbitt, 1977), confounding of bias and repetition effects might make the old only apparently more sensitive to changes in relative event probability.

An experiment by Rabbitt and Vyas (1980b) suggests that Griew's effect may have a more interesting implication. In serial CRT tasks such as those he used a young person's RT on any one trial has been shown to vary with the transition structure of the immediately preceding string of 3 (Remington, 1969) to 10 (Kirby, 1972) signals and responses. It seems that in order to make running estimates of the relative probabilities of events young people maintain and use running samples of from 3 to 10 previous events. Since the accuracy of detection of bias in a sequence of signals will vary directly with the square root of the sizes of samples taken of this sequence, the longer a running sample a person takes the more accurately small differences in bias will be detected. But if estimates of bias are made on the basis of long running samples, detections of abrupt *changes* in bias will become more sluggish as sample size increases. Rabbitt and Vyas found that whereas for young people RT on any given trial varied with at least two previous events, elderly people were affected only by the immediately previous event. It seems possible that young people base computations of bias on longer running samples of events than do the elderly. This would mean that the young can more accurately detect small, constant differences in bias but that the old may more rapidly respond to sudden gross changes as Griew (1962, 1968) found. No doubt the old also pay for their increased lability by a tendency to mistake brief random perturbations in event probability for actual sudden changes in bias, and this factor contributes to their notoriously spectacular trial-by-trial variations in reaction times during CRT tasks.

In the present context, these results show that in order to study changes in the ability to control active preparation for predictable events we must consider changes in the kinds of information on which such predictions are based. The nature, as well as simply the amount, of available information may change with alterations in the efficiency of immediate memory. In order to study changes in control processes, we must also study changes in the efficiency with which memory can be used to *direct* control. The experiments which follow explored this idea.

## Remembering What to Do Next

We have seen that people do not simply passively accept information from the visual world but rather actively interrogate their environments to seek out what they need to know. This is particularly clear in visual search where they learn and use optimal scanning strategies which guide them in deciding what to look at next. If we consider how such stragegies may be controlled by the information they have acquired while they are practiced at particular tasks, a simple hypothesis is that they refer to an internal, linear program which directs them to look at A, then B, then C, then D and so forth. Such programs may, of course, be more or less elaborate, some containing branches which guide conditioning decisions (e.g., if X is at B, then look at K; if Y is at B, then look at C, etc.).

Our data suggest that subjects discover and learn such programs less efficiently as they grow old. And even when the old have learned such programs they may be unable to use them to control search. What are the minimal requirements for *using* a learned program which the old, apparently, find difficult to meet?

One simple point is that in order to follow a familiar list of instructions held in memory a person has to know what he last did in order to refer to the program to discover what to do next. For example, I may hold, in my long-term memory, a set of instructions for reciting the alphabet. I may fail because I forget some of these instructions and so garble the sequence. But I may also make errors if I am distracted momentarily, forget which letter I said last, and so continue from some other point than that at which I left off.

In reciting the alphabet this latter type of error is unlikely because since each letter in the sequence occurs only once I merely have to recall the single last letter I uttered to be able correctly to reach my long-term memory program and retrieve the next. But consider sequences of the type A, B, C, D, B, C, E, F, D, J, C. . . etc. Here if I can only remember the last letter I spoke, I am sure to make errors. In order to index the correct D in the sequence, I need to recall at least the previous letter (C, D → B or F, D → J), while to index the correct C, I need to know at least the last three letters (A, B, C → D or D, B, C → E). Thus, to index a learned linear program correctly from moment to moment, I always have to keep a running tally of my past responses in immediate memory. This tally may have to be longer or shorter depending on the particular structure of the program which I use.

Note that the complexities of this structure, and the length of tally which it demands, need not have anything to do with the total amount of information contained in the program as assessed by classical information theory (e.g., Garner 1969, 1970). It is not merely the size of vocabulary of possible program events nor the conditional probability constraints on all possible transitions between events which may make it harder to maintain a running tally. A longer tally will be necessary whenever two subsequences of a program are confusible unless indexed by immediate memory for an additional item. More simply, the information value of a program (in bits) will certainly affect the time necessary to learn it. But the difficulty of *using* it will depend on the information value of the minimum length of tally necessary to index it at any necessary point. The program information load may, but need not, affect the information load of the minimum tally necessary to keep place.

As a simple demonstration, Rabbitt and Heptinstall (unpublished) trained people to a criterion of 100 successive perfect repetitions of sequences of 30 key-tapping responses in which all elements might either be unique (adequately indexed by 1 previous item) or repetitions might occur so that indexing required minimum running tallies of at least 2, 3, 4, or 5 previous responses. As expected, elderly subjects took longer to learn all sequences, and this relative difficulty became more marked as sequences demanded longer tallies. When all subjects had learned all sequences to criterion, they were required to perform them while repeating the alphabet aloud, backwards, in time to a metronome beat of 1/1.5 sec. All subjects made more errors and responded more slowly on sequences which required longer tallies, and this difficulty was more marked for the old. Most errors occurred at repeated rather than at unique items, suggesting that distraction interfered with the ability to maintain and use longer tallies.

We have seen how control processes can depend on memory. These experiments stress that they do not depend either on long-term or on short-term memory alone but rather on dynamic interactions between information in each of these (hypothetical) systems. Loss of short-term memory capacity may reduce the efficiency of control possible for the elderly. There is also evidence that loss of short-term memory *capacity* is not their only disability but that they may also fail to maintain effective control by indexing information within immediate memory itself. The experiment which follows illustrates this.

### *Failures to Index Immediate Memory to Maintain Control in a Serial Task*

Thomas (1977) reports a replication of work with a paced serial addition task (PASAT) originally carried out by Gronwall and Sampson (1974) to investigate cognitive changes in patients recovering from mild closed-head injuries. Strings of 50 single digits are presented at constant rates varying from 1/1.5 sec to ⅓ sec. Subjects have to add each digit in turn to its predecessor and to report the results aloud fast enough to keep up with the sequence, thus:

Digits presented 8, 9, 5, 7, 2, 4, 3, etc.
Correct answers –, 17, 14, 12, 9, 6, 7, etc.

Gronwall and Sampson report that patients with closed head injuries make more errors than normal controls, especially when digits are presented at fast rates. Thomas failed to replicate this finding. She found that most errors made by her subjects were omissions of responses which seemed to occur because people gradually lagged behind presented sequences and then paused, ignoring one or more presented digits. Other errors seemed to represent mistakes in addition. However, a more interesting, though rare, class of errors seemed to occur because people correctly added together the wrong numbers. Thus they might, apparently, add a current digit to the last total they had reported or add a current digit not to its predecessor but to one presented two or more trials previously, thus:

Digits presented 8, 9, 5, 7, 2, 4, 3 . . . etc.
Subject's responses –, 17, 22, 12, 9, 11 7 . . . etc.

Although of course such errors were often ambiguous, they occurred sufficiently often for Thomas to be certain that many of her subjects sometimes made them. To verify this she used sequences in which such errors could not be confounded with simple mistakes in addition of successive digits. Although patients with head injuries did not make more of these errors than normal controls, the fact that such errors occurred at all illustrated that performance on this task could not be described in terms of a model which involved simple, passive employment of immediate memory. For instance, conventional theories of trace decay do not readily explain why a more recently presented digit should, apparently, be neglected in favour of one presented earlier which must presumably be considered to have a weaker and less accessible trace. Nor do such passive theories explain the confusions between single-figure digits presented by the experimenter and two-figure totals arrived at by the subject during a run.

In terms of the simplistic analogies with program hand calculators given at the beginning of this paper it seemed that, at any moment during a task, people may hold at least 4 numbers in immediate memory, that is, the currently presented digit and the first two digits before that, together with the last total they have given. Numbers held in storage have to be updated by the input of each new digit and a selection must then be made afresh from each new updated list. Errors sometimes do not represent a simple loss of information from immediate memory but rather a loss of effective control of the indexing and selection of appropriate items from among others held in short-term storage.

Rabbitt and Vyas (unpublished) gave the PASAT task to normal young and elderly people who were simultaneously distracted by performing serial, self-paced choice response tasks. All subjects made more errors on the PASAT task under distraction and the elderly suffered from distraction more than the young. Most errors caused by distraction were omissions and errors of addition, but errors due to correct additions of the wrong numbers (e.g., current number with 2-back previous number, current number with last total, two previous totals, number two back with current total) showed greater relative and absolute increases even allowing for the fact that increases in other types of errors reduced the available opportunities for these rare errors to be observed. Thus, among its other effects, the distracting task evidently disrupted people's efficient control of updating, indexing, and selection of digit strings held in short-term memory. This disruption seemed relatively more severe in elderly people.

## Conclusions

This article began with the complaint that current models in human experimental psychology are of limited use to gerontologists because they only describe steady-state systems and give no adequate account of how such systems may actively adapt and change. A striking feature of human aging is the fact that differences between individuals dramatically increase in elderly populations so that while a minority may continue to perform as efficiently as most young controls the majority occupy various positions along a broad spectrum of decrement. To understand these increasing individual differences we require models of change within and between individuals. In particular we require descriptions of the ways in which people actively optimize their performance to cope with changing task demands, to improve with practice, and to circumvent or minimize growing failures in their own efficiency.

One approach to this problem is to consider how people manage to exercise active control of their transactions with their environments, to consider the choices which they have to make in attempting to exercise this control, to consider the ways in which this active control may break down in old age, and to consider what particular decrements in specific subsystems (such as long- or short-term memory, speed of information-processing, failures in attentional selectivity) may reduce the efficiency of control by limiting the range and power of control strategies still available to the elderly.

A group of experiments on visual search suggested that the efficiency with which people can actively interrogate their visual worlds declines in old age. One cause of this decline seemed to be that older people are slower to recognize and learn regularities in their environments which might lead them to optimize interrogation. Even when such regularities are learned and optimal strategies are used, elderly people may find it difficult to switch between appropriate strategies fast enough to meet task demands (p. 90). Apparently it is also necessary to make a distinction between the acquisition of such information and its possession in long-term memory and the ability to use it efficiently to guide an active search process (pp. 90–95). One possible reason for this is that even when a man can carry a complex sequence of instructions securely in his long-term memory, in order to index such a sequence appropriately to discover what to do next at any juncture during a task he must be able to remember what he has just done. The more complex the program sequence, the more comprehensive the running tally of his recent responses he must maintain in order to guarantee efficient indexing. The size of the tally which can be maintained (p. 93) and the efficiency of accurate indexing within immediate memory itself (p. 94) are reduced by distraction and by old age in combination.

A promising feature of this approach is that it can be applied to analyze the ways in which people cope with everyday life. It is applicable to situations such as finding one's way about unfamiliar environments like strange airports and supermarkets, going through familiar sequences of operations such as making tea, or detecting and coping with sudden changes in the pattern of current events (pp. 88–95). We may begin to understand the mistakes which elderly people make in such situations and perhaps at long last begin to keep the neglected promise made by all applicants for grant support to do gerontological research.

We may even begin to find ways in which laboratory research can *really* help the elderly to cope with daily life.

## References

Bertelson, P. Serial choice reaction time as a function of response versus signal-and-response repetition. *Nature,* 1965, *206,* 217–218.

Craik, F. I. M., & Lockhart, R. S. Levels of processing: A framework for memory research. *Journal of Verbal Learning and Verbal Behavior,* 1972, *11,* 671–684.

Garner, W. R. *Uncertainty and structure as psychological concepts.* New York: Academic Press, 1962.

Garner, W. R. The stimulus in information processing. *American Psychologist,* 1970, *25,* 350–358.

Gippenreiter, I. B. *Dvizheniya chelovecheskovo glaza.* Moscow: Moscow University Press, 1978.

Griew, S. Learning of statistical structure: A preliminary study in relation to age. In C. Tibbets & W. Donahue (Eds.), *Social and psychological aspects of aging.* New York: Columbia University Press, 1962.

Griew, S. Age and the matching of signal frequency in a two-channel detection task. *Journal of Gerontology,* 1968, *23,* 93–96.

Gronwall, D. M. A., & Sampson, H. *The psychological effects of concussion.* Oxford: Oxford University Press, 1974.

Jordan, T. C., & Rabbitt, P. M. A. Response times to stimuli of increasing complexity as a function of aging. *British Journal of Psychology,* 1977, *68,* 189–201.

Kirby, N. H. Sequential effects in serial reaction time. *Journal of Experimental Psychology,* 1972, *96,* 32–36.

Kristofferson, M. The effects of practice with one positive set in a memory scanning task can be completely transferred to a new set. *Memory and Cognition,* 1977, *5,* 177–186.

McDowell, E. D., & Rockwell, T. H. An exploratory investigation of the drivers' eye movements and their relationship to the roadway geometry. In J. W. Senders, D. F. Fisher, & R. A. Monty, *Eye movements and the higher psychological functions.* Hillsdale, N.J.: Lawrence Erlbaum, 1978.

Morton, J. A functional model for memory. In D. A. Norman (Ed.), *Models of human memory.* New York: Academic Press, 1970.

Monty, R. A., & Senders, J. W. *Eye movements and psychological processes.* Hillsdale, N.J.: Lawrence Erlbaum, 1976.

Mowbray, G. H. & Rhoades, M. V. On the reduction of choice reaction time with practice. *Quarterly Journal of Experimental Psychology,* 1959, *11,* 16–23.

Norman, D. A., & Bobrow, D. G. On the role of active memory processes in perception and cognition. In C. N. Cofer (Ed.), *The structure of human memory.* San Francisco: Freeman, 1975. (a)

Norman, D. A., & Bobrow, D. G. On data limited and resource limited processes. *Cognitive Psychology,* 1975, *7,* 44–64. (b)

Posner, M. I., & Snyder, C. R. R. Facilitation and inhibition in the processing of signals. In P. M. A. Rabbitt & S. Dornic (Eds.), *Attention and Performance V.* New York: Academic Press, 1975.

Rabbitt, P. M. A. Repetition effects and signal classification strategies in serial choice response tasks. *Quarterly Journal of Experimental Psychology,* 1968, *20,* 232–240.

Rabbitt, P. M. A. How old and young subjects monitor and control responses for accuracy and speed. *British Journal of Psychology,* 1979, *70,* 305–311. (a)

Rabbitt, P. M. A. Some experiments and a model for changes in attentional selectivity with old age. In F. Hoffmeister & C. Müller (Eds.), *Bayer-Symposium VII, Evaluation of Change.* Bonn: Springer Verlag, 1979. (b)

Rabbitt, P. M. A. Serial RT tasks. In L. Holden (Ed.), *Motor skill.* New York: Wiley, 1980. (a)

Rabbitt, P. M. A. A fresh look at changes in reaction times in old age. In D. Stein (Ed.), *The psychobiology of aging: Problems and perspectives.* New York: Elsevier, N. Holland, 1980. (b)

Rabbitt, P. M. A. The effects of R–S duration on serial choice reaction time: Preparation time or response monitoring time? *Ergonomics,* 1980, *29,* 234–248. (c)

Rabbitt, P. M. A., & Vyas, S. M. An elementary preliminary taxonomy of errors in choice reaction time tasks. *Acta Psychologica,* 1970, *33,* 56–76.

Rabbitt, P. M. A., & Vyas, S. M. Signal recency effects can be distinguished from signal repetition effects in serial CRT tasks. *Canadian Journal of Psychology,* 1979, *33,* 88–95. (a)

Rabbitt, P. M. A., & Vyas, S. M. Memory and data-driven control of selective attention in continuous tasks. *Canadian Journal of Psychology,* 1979, *33,* 71–87. (b)

Rabbitt, P. M. A., & Vyas, S. M. Actively controlling anticipation of irregular events. *Quarterly Journal of Experimental Psychology,* 1980, *32,* 235–247. (a)

Rabbitt, P. M. A., & Vyas, S. M. Selective anticipation for events in old age. *Journal of Gerontology* 1980, *35,* 913–919. (b)

Rabbitt, P. M. A., Cumming, G., & Vyas, S. M. Improvement, learning and retention of skill at visual search. *Quarterly Journal of Experimental Psychology,* 1979, *31,* 441–459.

Remington, R. J. Analysis of sequential effects in choice reaction times. *Journal of Experimental Psychology,* 1969, *82,* 250–257.

Sandford, A. J., & Maule, A. J. Age and the distribution of observing responses. *Psychonomic Science,* 1971, *23,* 419–420.

Sandford, A. J., & Maule, A. J. The allocation of attention in multisource monitoring behavior: Adult age differences. *Perception,* 1973, *2,* 91–100. (a)

Sandford, A. J., & Maule, A. J. The concept of general experience: Age and strategies in guessing future events. *Journal of Gerontology,* 1973, *28,* 81–88. (b)

Selfridge, D. G. Pandemonium: A paradigm for learning. In L. Uhr (Ed.), *Pattern recognition.* New York: Wiley, 1966.

Thomas, C. M. *Deficits of memory and attention following closed head injury.* Unpublished Master of Science thesis, University of Oxford, 1977.

Yarbus, A. L. Rol'dvizhenia glaz v protsesse zreniya. *Nauka,* 1965, *14,* 363–374.

CHAPTER 6

# The Development of Visual Information Processes in Adulthood and Old Age

David A. Walsh

*Department of Psychology and Andrus Gerontology Center*
*University of Southern California*
*Los Angeles, California*

The human world is a visual world. Our ability to see was important to our evolutionary past and will be important to our evolutionary future. Locating prey and escaping predators may be less important in the industrial societies of the twentieth century than they were in our past, but other visual tasks have become important. Adults in the modern world must deal with visual tasks never imagined by even our recent ancestors. The development of high speed transportation systems allows us to travel rapidly through a diversity of environments. These developments have created heavy visual monitoring demands for drivers, pedestrians, pilots, and air traffic controllers. They have increased the demands for acquiring spatial layout information and using the visual information that supports moving about in an urban environment. The industrial world has broadened the need for education and educational materials. While adults in modern society may spend little time tracking animals across fields, they spend ever increasing amounts of time tracking words across printed pages.

The importance of visual functioning has motivated research interest in examining changes in these processes across the adult years. Researchers have examined questions ranging from structural changes in the eye (Weale, 1965) to differences in the ability to acquire spatial layout information for urban environments (Walsh, Krauss, & Regnier, 1981). One line of investigation has examined age differences in visual functioning from the viewpoint of contemporary models of visual information processing drawn from the field of experimental psychology. These investigations will be the focus of this paper.

In general, investigations of age-related differences in visual information processing have tried to provide an empirical data base that has clear theoretical interpretations. In the pages that follow, a model of visual information processing that has directed our own research in this area will be presented. The research paradigms used to investigate questions of aging will be described and the growing data base we have collected will be reported. Special attention will be given to a recent investigation that allows us to examine relations between what we believe to be separate stages of visual information processing.

## A Visual Information Processing Model

The work of Sperling (1960) motivated some related research programs that produced the model of visual information described here. Sperling's investigations set out to determine how much can be seen in a brief visual exposure. The results of his research established the existence of a brief visual storage system that preserves an image for about 250 msec following tachistoscopic presentation. Other investigations by Averbach and Coriell (1961) confirmed Sperling's findings and extended his work by examining some of the cognitive demands of the "partial-report" task developed by Sperling. This task required subjects to report a randomly determined subset of a large visual display. The portion of the display subjects were to report was indicated by an auditory signal in Sperling's investigations while Averbach and Coriell used a visual indicator. The work of Averbach and Coriell showed that the task of attending to the indicator signal and identifying the to-be-reported section of a display required between 100 and 250 msec. The work of Eriksen and his colleagues (Eriksen & Colegate, 1971; Eriksen & Collins, 1969; Eriksen & Hoffman, 1972) has provided additional support for the idea that selectively attending to elements in visual displays requires measurable processing times close to 200 msec.

An important part of the work of Averbach and Coriell (1961) relied on the use of visual backward masking to measure the time required to read information out of iconic memory. Backward masking refers to the perceptual impairment of a leading stimulus by a following one. The time course and visual mechanisms responsible for masking phenomena received considerable investigation as the result of Averbach and Coriell's report. An important question raised by Eriksen and his colleagues (cf. Schultz & Eriksen, 1977) was whether backward masking provided a legitimate tool for studying the time course of visual information processes. The question posed by Eriksen was whether masking resulted from the following stimulus operating to *stop* the processing of the leading stimulus, or whether the two stimuli simply combined into a single, integrated "montage" in which the signal-to-noise ratio was altered so as to degrade the *continued* perceptual analysis of the target.

Research reported by Turvey (1973) and Hellige, Walsh, Lawrence, and Prasse (1979) provided clear evidence for the idea that some forms of visual backward masking arise as a result of the following stimulus stopping the processing of the leading stimulus. This finding is important for demonstrating the legitimacy of backward masking as a technique for studying visual information processing. However, some of the results of Turvey's experiments are even more important in that they demonstrate two qualitatively different masking phenomena.

Turvey (1973) identified separate peripheral and central processes underlying visual perception by observing the types of stimuli that are successful masks, and the form of the resulting masking functions, in a backward masking paradigm. Backward masking occurs when the perception of a leading stimulus (target stimulus) is impaired by a rapidly following stimulus (masking stimulus). Turvey used letters as targets and both visual noise and patterned stimuli as masks. Figure 1 shows examples of the target and visual noise masks that were used in these investigations. When visual noise was presented monoptically (same eye receiving target and mask), an energy-sensitive peripheral masking phenomenon was found. Three characteristics define peripheral masking: First, peripheral masking is an energy-dependent phenomenon; in order for masking to occur, the energy of the mask must exceed the energy of the target. Second, target energy is related to the interstimulus interval ($ISI_c$) necessary to escape masking by a power function. Specifically, target energy $(TE)^b \times ISI_c$ is equal to a constant for masking arising peripherally. Third, the figural characteristics of the mask are noncritical in peripheral masking. Turvey found that visual noise or a homogeneous flash was an effective mask only with monoptic and binocular presentations, those conditions of presentation that permit peripheral interference in all parts of the visual pathway.

Turvey's model of peripheral processes assumes that the visual pathway includes anatomically the retina, lateral geniculate nucleus, and terminal connections at the striate cortex. Conceptually, he characterizes the peripheral pathway as a set of independent neural nets which are specifically attuned to figural

PATTERN MASK

VISUAL NOISE

TARGET STIMULUS

Fig. 1. Examples of masking and target stimuli.

characteristics of visual stimulation but which share many receptor and intermediate neurons (Thomas, 1970). The processing of the target by the neural nets is assumed to be hierarchically organized, and its speed of processing believed to be directly related to the energy of the target—the greater the target energy, the faster peripheral processing is completed.

Masking that arises centrally is described by a completely different set of characteristics. Whereas the energy relation between target and mask is critical in peripheral masking, it is unimportant in masking arising centrally. The critical variable in central masking is the degree of similarity between target and mask features. Furthermore, escape from central masking is determined by the time separating the onset of the target and mask (the stimulus onset asynchrony, SOA). The following three characteristics define the central masking phenomenon: First, a target may be masked by a stimulus of lower energy. Second, an additive relation, target duration (TD) + $ISI_c$ = a constant = SOA, describes escape from masking that arises centrally. Third, central masking is dependent on similarity of figural characteristics between the target and mask.

The additive relationship showing SOA to be the critical variable in central masking is explained by the operating time requirements of central, sequential, decision processes. Turvey's model proposes that these sequential decision nets operate on both stored outputs from peripheral nets and the output of prior decision processes. Later decision nets must await outputs from earlier nets. Central masking occurs when the stored peripheral output of a target is replaced by mask output before all decision processes have completed their operation.

With this summary of Turvey's (1973) distinction between peripheral and central perceptual processes as a base, we can now outline a general model of visual information processing that has directed the research reported below. Figure 2 presents a diagrammatic representation of the model. Light incident on the eye initiates processing by sets of peripheral nets attuned to specific visual features. These nets are assumed to operate in parallel, with the operating speed of each net determined by the visual features to which it is sensitive and the amount of energy incident on the retinal receptors. Concurrent with the operation of the peripheral nets, central decision nets begin to process the output of the peripheral stage. It is assumed that the operation of the central stage is contingent on output from the peripheral stage. Thus, as long as the energy of a visual stimulus is high, and peripheral processes are completed before contingent stages of central processing are ready for that output, then peripheral and central processes can be assumed to operate concurrently. The function of central processing stages, as conceptualized by Turvey, is the synthesis of context-dependent features of the visual input. It is important to understand that the output of the central stage is *not* an identification of the visual input. Rather, this central stage is assumed to yield higher-level sets of visual features which provide the material on which subsequent pattern recognition processes operate.

Output from the central processing stage, as proposed by the model, is stored in a brief visual sensory memory such as that investigated by Sperling

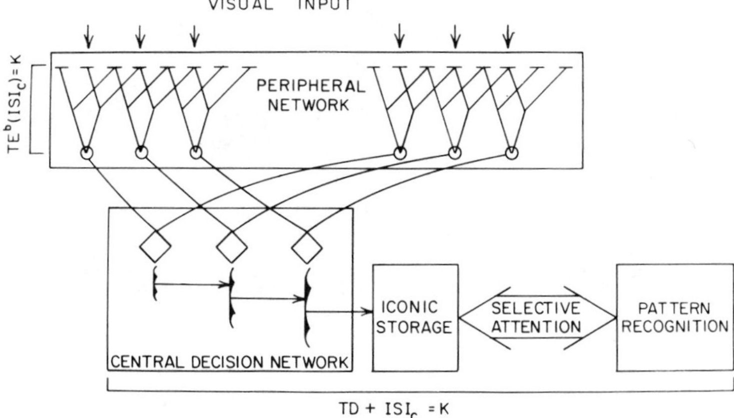


Fig. 2. Diagrammatic representation of a visual information-processing model of human performance. Included are peripheral and central decision networks, iconic storage, selective attention, and pattern recognition stages.

(1960) and Averbach and Coriell (1961) and labeled "iconic memory" by Neisser (1967). Iconic memory provides a temporary storage for to-be-identified context-dependent visual features. This early store in the flow of visual information is assumed to be visual, of large capacity, and susceptible to irreversible decay that is complete in about 250 msec following stimulus onset.

The to-be-identified features in iconic memory are selectively attended to and identified by processes subsequent to the central perceptual processes outlined by Turvey (1973). Our conceptualization of these processes has been heavily influenced by Neisser's (1967) concepts of selective and focal attention. His analysis suggests that subareas of iconic memory can be selectively attended to and that the processing resources available for pattern recognition can be focused on separate areas in order to identify clusters of context-dependent features. An important implication of the work by Averbach and Coriell (1961) is the demonstration that the processes of selective and focal attention which Neisser proposes as support systems for pattern recognition processes take real and measurable amounts of processing time. The latter two stages of Figure 2 represent selective attention and pattern recognition in visual information processing.

## Developmental Questions

Investigations of the adult development of visual functioning using information-processing models have made considerable progress in describing age differences in some of the stages of visual information processing outlined above. Many findings document age differences in the speed of peripheral and central perceptual processes (Hertzog, Williams, & Walsh, 1976; Till, 1978; Walsh, 1976; Walsh, Till, & Williams, 1978; Walsh, Williams, & Hertzog, 1979). The results showing that older adults require longer processing times than young adults to complete both peripheral and central processes can be interpreted as evidence for a general slowing associated with aging (Birren, 1965). However, none of the investigations cited above collected measures of peripheral and central processing speed on the same subject sample. Clearer support for the idea that aging is associated with a general slowing in many stages of information processing could be provided by examining the intercorrelation of subjects' speed of information processing at separate stages. The present paper addresses this question with data from a recent investigation conducted in our laboratory.

The examination of intertask correlations as evidence for or against the hypothesis of a general slowing in the speed of information processing with age is not a simple undertaking. Birren, Riegel, and Morrison (1962) suggest that evidence for a general slowing hypothesis should include increased correlation between individuals' speed of performance on various tasks in addition to increases in mean performance times as they age. The large intersubject variability in speed of processing typically found in old age groups is one factor that could produce higher intertask correlations for old than for young subjects. Furthermore, if the increased variability results from individual differences in the magnitude of age-related slowing, which affects the speed of some individuals' performance on all tasks, then additional increases in intertask correlations could be expected. Although the above factors may produce larger intertask correlations for old than for young subjects, other patterns of intertask correlation could also provide support for the general slowing hypothesis. For example, if aging is associated with a 20 msec increase in task performance for each decade lived, and this 20 msec constant is added to all tasks for all subjects, then no change in intertask correlations would be expected with age. (Adding a constant to each pair of scores for all observations in a sample has no effect on the correlation among the scores.) While the situation described in this example would have no effect on correlations within any age group, it would produce an intertask correlation computed across all age groups that was substantially larger than the intertask correlations within any separate age group.

On the other hand, if aging is not associated with a general increase in processing time, then a different pattern of overall intertask correlations might be observed. For example, if aging is associated with slowing in different stages of information processing for different individuals, then we should not expect to find intertask correlations computed over all subjects that are larger than those found for separate age groups. The possible patterns of correlation outlined above represent clear evidence for or against the idea of general slowing in the rate of visual information processing. Of course, other patterns intermediate to these extremes might be observed. The most likely cases would involve some reliable but modest relation between the speed of processing in separate stages. It is important to recognize that no completely objective criteria are available for assessing the amount of support for the hypothesis of general slowing provided by correlations of different magnitudes. Rather, it will be necessary to consider both the amount of explained and unexplained variance in one task provided by knowledge of performance on another.

## Peripheral Perceptual Processes

Investigations of age differences in peripheral perceptual processes have shown that groups of older adults (60–70 years) require longer processing times than younger adults (18–25 years) to complete peripheral stages of visual information processing. This conclusion is based on three investigations that used visual masking procedures that meet the criteria proposed by Turvey to define masking due to interference in peripheral perceptual processes. These criteria, reviewed at length above, include monoptic or binocular presentation of target and mask to the same visual pathway, the use of low target and high mask energies, and resulting data functions that show the relation of $ISI_c$ to target energy is described by a power function.

Walsh, Till, and Williams (1978) examined two samples of young (average ages of 20 and 24 years) and old adults (average ages of 65 and 68 years) in similar monoptic backward masking tasks. The first investigation measured the accuracy with which subjects could report target stimuli (single letters) presented at 9.6, 19.2, and 38.4 ($cd/m^2 \times$ msec) energy levels. The masking stimulus was always presented at a 1050 ($cd/m^2 \times$ msec) energy level and followed the target at 9 SOAs (0 to 80 msec in 10 msec steps). The second investigation employed the same target and mask energy levels, but an ascending limits procedure was used to determine the interstimulus interval required to report four consecutive target stimuli. The first investigation used forced-choice responding to control for different response criteria that might be used by the separate age groups. Figure 3 presents the results of these investigations which show that the older adults required longer $ISI_c$s to escape the effects of peripheral masking. However, the relation between energy and $ISI_c$ for each age group was found to be described by the same power function: $TE^{.34} \times ISI_c$ = a constant. This outcome demonstrates that changes in target energy result in proportional changes in peripheral processing speed for young and old adults.

An important question associated with the results of Walsh *et al.* (1978) and other investigations of aging and peripheral perceptual processes (cf. Kline & Szafran, 1975; Till, 1978) is the mechanism responsible for the speed differences observed. It is well known that the human eye undergoes many age-related

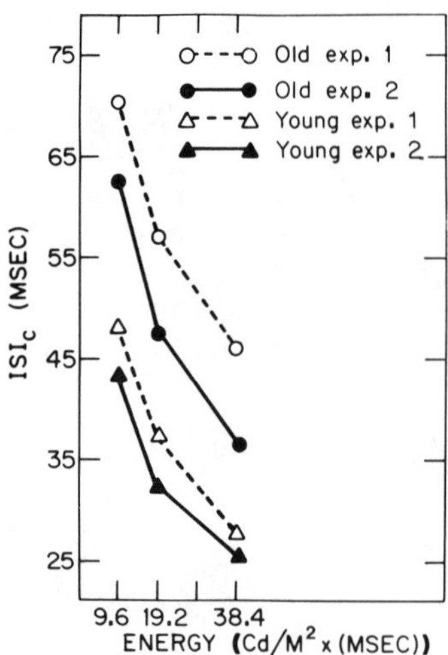


Fig. 3. Effect of target energy on interstimulus interval required to escape peripheral masking (ISI$_c$) for two different groups of young (average ages of 20 and 24 years) and old (average ages of 65 and 68 years) adults. (From Walsh *et al.*, 1978.)

changes that serve to change the amount of energy reaching the retina from a light source. For example, the pupil decreases in size and the crystalline lens yellows, factors which decrease the amount of light reaching the retina. In contrast, the response time of the pupil also increases and could operate to increase the amount of light entering the eye. Although there are large individual differences in the degree to which these changes occur, in general less energy from a light source can be expected to reach the retina of an older eye. These physical changes in the eye could have some important implications for interpreting the differences in the estimates of processing speed shown in Figure 3. The functions relating ISI$_c$ to target energy for each age group show that the former increases as the latter decreases. Thus, it is necessary to consider the possibility that the difference in peripheral processing speed between young and old adults at any given target energy is a result of less energy reaching the retina of the older eye. The Walsh *et al.* (1978) investigation addressed this issue by careful subject selection for their first investigation. A sample of 10 older women were recruited who did not differ from the young sample in the minimum lumination required to report the unmasked target stimuli. The results of that investigation, shown in Figure 3, demonstrate that this exceptional sample of older subjects required longer processing times to escape peripheral masking effects than did a sample of young subjects even when both age groups showed similar target energy thresholds. Furthermore, the results of a second investigation using less select older subjects who had higher target energy thresholds than the young comparison group resulted in similar age differences in peripheral processing speed. These outcomes suggest that the large and reliable differences in processing times between young and old adults required to escape peripheral masking effects cannot be explained completely by the amount of light reaching the retina of a young and old eye. Rather, the results of these investigations suggest that a substantial proportion of the observed slowing probably results from changes in the rate of neural net operation in the peripheral system.

Other investigations provide support for the above conclusions regarding aging and peripheral perceptual processes. Till (1978) extended the results of the Walsh *et al.* (1978) investigation using higher target energies. The results of Till's work replicate the findings of age differences in the speed with which peripheral perceptual processes are completed. Furthermore, they show that similar power functions relating target energy to $ISI_c$ describe the performance of 20- and 55-year-old adults. Another investigation by Kline and Szafran (1975) can be interpreted as further evidence for age differences in peripheral perceptual processes as defined by Turvey's model of these phenomena (cf. Walsh, 1976).

Results from a recent investigation in our laboratory provide some confirmation of the above results and some evidence of other changes in peripheral processes in later life. In this investigation, which will be an important focus for the remainder of this chapter, we collected measures of visual information processing at each of the stages depicted in the model shown in Figure 2, on a sample of 24 young (average age 18.7 years, range 17–21 years), 24 middle-aged (average age 46.5, range 40–53 years), and 24 old adults (average age 70.3 years, range 67–74 years). The processing times required to report target stimuli with 70% accuracy were measured. In general, our procedure involved a measure of the $ISI_c$ that subjects required to report four targets correctly, using the method of ascending limits, followed by a more accurate determination of the processing time required to report 14 of 20 target stimuli correctly (i.e., 70% correct performance). This was accomplished by examining the accuracy of report for 20 stimuli presented at the $ISI_c$ determined with the methods of ascending limits. If performance was above or below 70% correct at $ISI_c$, then ISI was either decreased or increased by one fifth and another set of 20 targets was presented. This procedure continued either until the ISI producing exactly 70% performance was located or until ISIs yielding performance above and below 70% had been determined. In the latter case, we used linear interpolation to estimate the ISI that would produce 70% performance for a subject. These procedures were used in order to assure high reliability of our measures of processing time. The high intercorrelation between repetitive measures of peripheral processing time, shown in Figure 6 (see p. 110), demonstrate that these efforts were quite successful.

Figure 4 presents the results of the peripheral masking conditions. (The target energy levels used in this investigation are the same as those reported by Walsh *et al.*, 1978.) Figure 4 shows that old adults require longer processing times than young adults, as indexed by ISI, to avoid masking resulting from

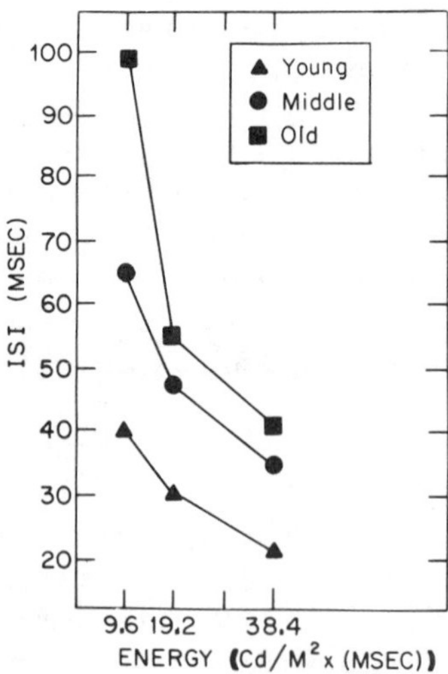


Fig. 4. Effect of target energy on the interstimulus interval required for 70% correct perceptual performance in a peripheral masking paradigm. Twenty-four adults whose average age was 19, 47, and 70 years participated in each age group.

interference in the peripheral processing system. Furthermore, the relation between ISI and target energy is described by similar power functions for the young and middle-aged subjects. The major difference between these results and those of other investigations is the finding that the power function that relates ISI to target energy for the 70-year-old group is different from the power function that describes the data of young and middle-aged adults. The exponents of these functions were determined by transforming the power function $k = TE^b \times ISI_c$ to the logarithmic form of an equation for a straight line. A linear regression analysis was performed on the (log TE, log $ISI_c$) pairs to find the line of best fit. The slope of the regression line provides the best estimate of the exponent in the power function (cf. Walsh *et al.*, 1978). These exponents were $-.46$, $-.46$, and $-.59$ for the young, middle-aged, and old subjects respectively [$F(2,64) = 6.5$, $p < .01$]. Since earlier investigations did not test subjects as old as those studied in this investigation, these results suggest that the rate of change in peripheral processing speed as a function of changes in target energy may be different in adults beyond 65 years.

As in our other investigations, we collected measures of the target energy required to see target stimuli on unmasked trials. Figure 5 shows that the three age groups required different amounts of light energy to achieve equivalent levels of target recognition. This result allowed us to examine the amount of variance in peripheral processing speed that can be predicted from differences in energy thresholds. This relationship is of interest since Turvey's (1973) work demonstrates that the ISI required to escape peripheral masking decreases as target energy increases. Thus, individual differences in the proportion of light entering the eye might play a substantial role in determining the ISI required to escape peripheral masking effects. The less light entering the eye, the longer would be the ISI required to escape masking. While the general form of the relationship between target energy and $ISI_c$ is exponential, a comparison of the fit of exponential and linear models to the relationship between subjects' unmasked energy thresholds and their $ISI_c$ to escape peripheral masking showed that a better fit was obtained with a linear equation. (These comparisons were made by contrasting the correlation between the log of these measures with the correlation between the untransformed values.)

Therefore, the question of the relationship between target energy threshold and peripheral processing speed was examined using linear correlation. Before we discuss these correlations, it is important to note that the reliability of our measures of peripheral processing speed and unmasked threshold was quite high. The average intercorrelation of the ISIs determined for subjects in the 9.6, 19.2, and 38.4 (cd/m$^2$ × msec) energy levels was .83, (range from .77 to .92), while the intercorrelation of unmasked thresholds for the two eyes was .74. Figure 6 presents a scatter plot of the .92 correlation between the ISIs required to escape peripheral masking at the 38.4 and 19.2 (cd/m$^2$ × msec) energy levels. The intercorrelations between the unmasked energy thresholds and the ISIs to escape peripheral masking effects were examined for each of the three target energies and these correlations were computed across all 72 subjects and for each age group. In general, the correlations between unmasked energy threshold and the 9.6 energy level were the lowest, with the strength of the relation for the 19.2 and 38.4 levels being about equal. Table 1 presents these correlations for each

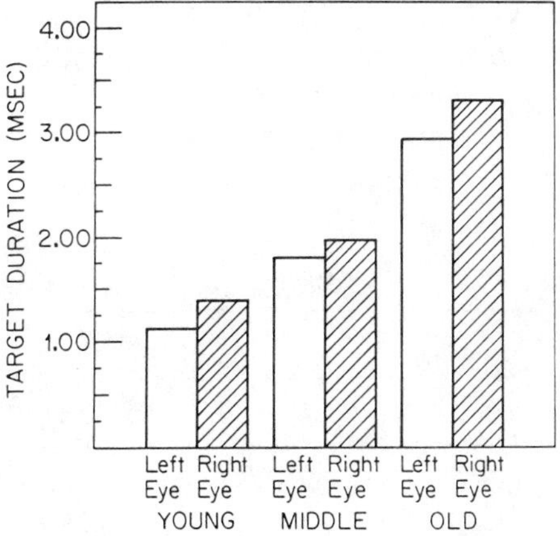


Fig. 5. Target energy thresholds of 19-, 47- and 70-year-old adults. Luminance was held constant at 2.4 cd/m$^2$ and duration was varied (target energy = target duration × luminance).

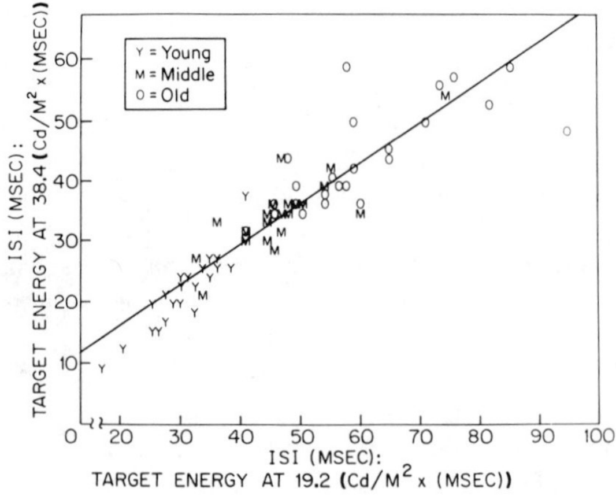


Fig. 6. Scatter plot of subjects' $ISI_c$s in two conditions of peripheral masking. The high intercorrelation reflects the high degree of reliability of the measurement procedures used in this investigation. Subjects in the young (Y), middle-aged (M), and old (O) samples are distinguished in the plot.

age group and all subjects considered together. Overall, 50% of the variance in peripheral processing speed could be accounted for by differences in unmasked target thresholds. However, the strength of this relation was less in each age group considered separately: only 6%, 12%, and 36% of the variance in peripheral processing speed could be accounted for by the unmasked energy thresholds for young, middle-aged, and old subjects, respectively.

Although these results show that a considerable amount of the variance in processing speed is predicted by differences in target energy threshold, there is still 50% of the variance in peripheral processing speed that cannot be predicted from target thresholds. The unexplained variance suggests that some of the differences in $ISI_c$ probably result from age-related differences in the rate of peripheral net operations. Further support for this conclusion is provided by an analysis of covariance on the $ISI_c$s required to escape peripheral masking which

*Table 1. The Correlation of Target Energy Threshold with the $ISI_C$ Required to Escape Peripheral Masking at Three Target Energies*

| | Age group | | | |
|---|---|---|---|---|
| Target energy[a] | Young | Middle-age | Old | All ages |
| 9.6 | .21 | .37 | .40 | .63 |
| 19.2 | .25 | .38 | .67 | .76 |
| 38.4 | .25 | .30 | .69 | .73 |

[a]Target energies are in ($cd/m^2 \times msec$) units.

used subjects' unmasked thresholds as the covariate. This analysis showed the effect of age to be highly reliable even after peripheral masking values were adjusted for differences in unmasked energy thresholds [$F(2,62) = 14.4$, $p < .001$].

## Central Perceptual Processes

Investigations of age differences in central perceptual processes have shown that adults between 60 and 70 years of age require longer processing times than younger adults (18–25 years) to complete central stages of visual information processing. This conclusion is based on the results of three investigations that used visual masking tasks that meet Turvey's criteria of masking that results from interference in central perceptual processes. These criteria, reviewed in detail above, include dichoptic presentation of target and mask, target energies greater than mask energies, similar features composing the target and masking stimuli, and data functions that show an additive relation between target duration and $ISI_c$ ($TD + ISI_c = K$, a constant).

Walsh (1976) investigated the differences between young adults (18–23 years) and old adults (60–68 years) in the $ISI_c$ required to escape masking due to interference in central perceptual processes. Subjects viewed letters as targets and a random arrangement of line segments (pattern mask) as the masking stimulus. Subjects were tested with target durations of 10, 20, and 30 msec using a mask duration of 10 msec in all cases. The target and masking stimuli were presented dichoptically, and in a further condition ISI was held at 0 msec while the target duration required to escape masking was determined. The results of this investigation, shown in Figure 7, revealed that the older subjects required 24% longer processing times than the young subjects to escape the effects of central masking. In addition, the linear functions of Figure 7 fit the additive rule reported by Turvey (1973) to describe central masking phenomena ($TD + ISI_c = K$).

Further support for the finding of age differences in the speed of central perceptual processes is provided by an investigation designed to examine the stability of such differences across five days of practice (Hertzog, Williams, & Walsh, 1976). Twelve young subjects with an average age of 19 years and 12 old subjects with an average age of 66 years participated in a central masking task identical to that used in the Walsh (1976) investigation. During each of five consecutive days, an $ISI_c$ was determined at the beginning and end of a one-hour session. Separating the two $ISI_c$ determinations were 60 practice trials at which target and mask stimuli were presented at ISIs close to the initial measure. One third of the practice trials were presented at the initial $ISI_c$, another third at 5

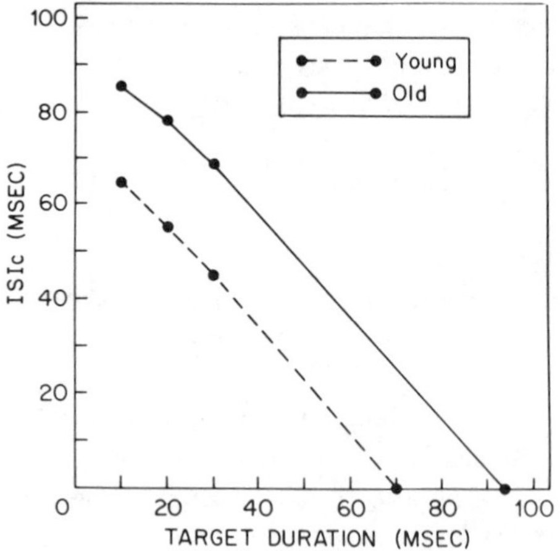


Fig. 7. Critical interstimulus interval ($ISI_c$) and target duration required to escape masking for 20- and 64-year-old adults. The linear functions fit the central rule reported by Turvey: TD + $ISI_c$ = K, a constant. (From Walsh, 1976.)

msec above that value, and the remainder at 5 msec below $ISI_c$. The results of this investigation, shown in Table 2, demonstrate that the age difference in the processing times required to escape the effects of central masking remained stable at about 30 msec across the five days of practice. While both groups showed a substantial reduction in the $ISI_c$ required to escape masking, the rate of decline was best fit by linear functions that did not interact with age. The Hertzog *et al.* investigation is also interesting in that it provides a close replication of the estimates of central processing speed for 20- and 64-year-old adults reported by Walsh (1976). Walsh found average ISIs of 64 and 87 msec for 20- and 64-year-

*Table 2. Means and Standard Deviations of ISI Across and Within Days of Testing (in msec)*

| | | $ISI_1$ | | $ISI_2$ | |
|---|---|---|---|---|---|
| Days | | Young | Old | Young | Old |
| 1 | *M* | 65.00 | 93.25 | 59.67 | 78.00 |
| | *SD* | 10.42 | 33.05 | 7.62 | 21.06 |
| 2 | *M* | 54.67 | 90.25 | 47.42 | 77.75 |
| | *SD* | 8.57 | 23.46 | 9.44 | 26.85 |
| 3 | *M* | 45.58 | 73.92 | 38.25 | 68.33 |
| | *SD* | 8.47 | 21.45 | 14.26 | 18.51 |
| 4 | *M* | 41.50 | 79.75 | 36.25 | 63.25 |
| | *SD* | 10.54 | 39.88 | 14.28 | 16.38 |
| 5 | *M* | 36.50 | 66.33 | 37.83 | 60.08 |
| | *SD* | 10.97 | 21.53 | 7.80 | 20.24 |

old adults respectively, whereas Hertzog *et al.* found prepractice ISIs of 65 msec and 93 msec for 19- and 66-year-old adults. Thus, the Hertzog *et al.* investigation provides strong support for the idea that age differences in the speed of central perceptual processing are stable and highly replicable.

Finally, an investigation by Walsh, Williams, and Hertzog (1979) examined age differences in two components of central perceptual processes suggested by the information processing model depicted in Figure 2. The first stage involves the operation of central decision nets involved in constructing context-dependent features of the to-be-recognized displays. The second stage is pattern recognition (cf. Michaels & Turvey, 1979). Interference in Stage I is believed to occur when output from peripheral nets related to both target and mask is combined into a confused set of context-dependent features on which Stage II pattern recognition processes must operate. Under these conditions, only chance identification of the targets should be expected. However, when Stage I processes separate target and mask features into successive stimuli, then interference in Stage II processes can be observed. Stage II interference is believed to result from the replacement of target features in iconic memory by mask features before pattern recognition of the target is complete. This analysis of the operation of Stage I and II suggests a method for examining age differences in each. The shortest ISI at which target identification increases above chance can be used as a measure of the time required to complete Stage I processes. The slope of the function relating target detection to ISI from chance to asymptote can be used to measure the rate of Stage II processing.

The Walsh *et al.* (1979) investigation examined the accuracy of subjects' target identification as a function of the SOA between target and mask onset. Two important results of that investigation can be seen in Figure 8. First, the performance of the young subjects rises above chance at shorter SOAs than that of the old and, second, the slope of the function relating improvement in accuracy to SOA is greater in the young than in the old sample. These observations have been confirmed by statistical analysis (Walsh *et al.*, 1979). Furthermore, an analysis of relative age differences showed that the older subjects required 38% longer processing times than the young to complete Stage I and 36% longer processing times to complete Stage II. It is interesting to note that the magnitude of this age difference, about 37%, is larger than that reported earlier with samples of comparable age. Walsh (1976) and Hertzog *et al.* (1976) reported age differences of 24% in the times required to complete central perceptual processes. One procedural difference was the use by Walsh *et al.* (1979) of forced-choice responding to control for criterion differences. The larger age differences in that investigation seem to suggest that the young use more conservative criteria than the old, which may lead to increases in measured time of young subjects unless they are forced to respond on each trial.

Recent research in our laboratory has examined further the relation between age and the speed of central perceptual processing. The investigations by Walsh

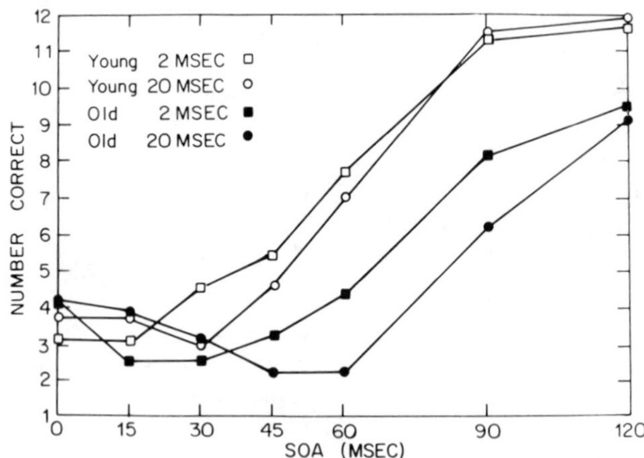


Fig. 8. The perceptual accuracy of 20- and 68-year-old adults as a function of the stimulus onset asynchrony (SOA) between target and mask. Chance responding would result in three letters being reported correctly. (From Walsh *et al.*, 1979.)

(1976), Hertzog *et al.* (1976), and Walsh *et al.* (1979) have focused only on differences between 20- and 65-year-old adults. While the results of those investigations demonstrate that older adults require longer times to complete central processes, they provide little information about the life-span development of this slowing. Our recent work was designed to explore the differences in processing speed between young, middle-aged, and old adults. Dichoptic masking tasks similar to those described above were used, but more reliable measures of processing speed were collected; we used a procedure of ascending limits in combination with measures of perceptual accuracy to determine the ISI required for 70% performance. The result of this investigation, shown in Figure 9, is that 46-year-old adults required processing times intermediate to those of 19- and 70-year-old adults. This suggests that the slower processing speeds of older adults may have a gradual onset beginning in young adulthood.

In addition, we correlated these measures of central processing speed with measures of peripheral processing speed collected on this same sample of subjects. These analyses were carried out in order to examine the possibility that a general slowing with age in the rate of information processing might explain the age differences in average processing time observed for peripheral and central masking masks (cf. Birren *et al.*, 1962).

The model of information processing presented in Figure 2 assumes a concurrent but contingent relation between peripheral and central perceptual processes in the fashion proposed by Turvey (1973). Thus, it would not be surprising to find little relation between the speed of peripheral and central processes in young populations: As long as target energy is relatively high, as was the case in our central masking tasks, we should expect peripheral processes to be completed before contingent central processes are ready to operate on the output from peripheral networks. The intercorrelation of our measures of peripheral and central processes supports this idea. Less than 1% of the variance in the central processing speed of our young sample could be accounted for by the speed of peripheral processes. However, we did find that larger amounts of the variance in central processing speed could be explained by peripheral processing speed in our middle-aged and old samples (17% and 18% of the variance, respectively). This outcome, furthermore, does not provide much support for the hypothesis that a general speed factor underlies the processing time differences between young and old adults. Although it was the case that the correlations between central and peripheral processing speed were positive for the middle-aged sample, the correlations were negative in the old sample. Middle-aged adults with slower central processing speed also tended to have slower peripheral processing speed, but the opposite relation was found in the old population. The slope of the regression equation for the old subjects showed that each 10-msec increase in peripheral processing speed was associated with a 1.3-msec decrease in central processing speed.

The correlation between peripheral and central processing speeds computed across all ages does not provide any support for the idea the general slowing with age underlies the longer processing times required by old adults to complete these stages of information processing. Only 8% of the variance in central processing speed could be predicted from subjects' performance in peripheral processing speed. Of the three correlations that bear on this question, only one was found to be statistically reliable, even though the correlations are based on 72 subjects. Figure 10 shows the scatter plot of subjects' $ISI_c$ required to escape peripheral and central masking effects. As can be seen in Figure 10, a substantial

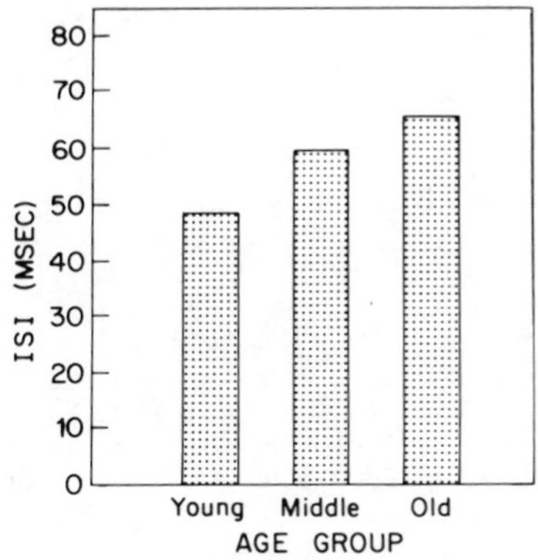


Fig. 9. The ISI required to escape central masking effects for three groups of 24 adults whose average age was 19, 47, and 70 years. The processing times were measured using a dichoptic backward masking paradigm.

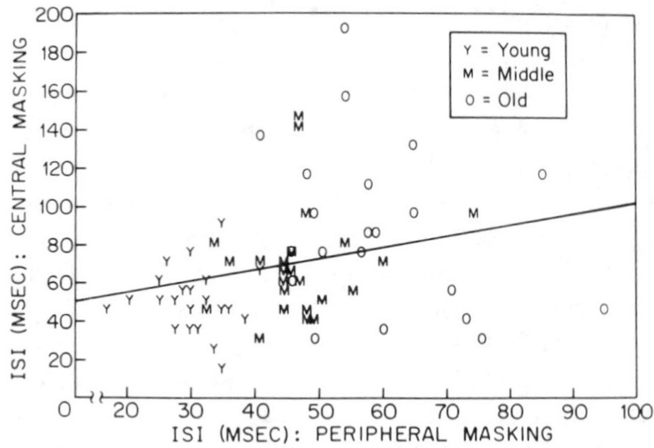


Fig. 10. Scatter plot of subjects' ISIs required to escape peripheral and central masking effects. Subjects in the young (Y), middle-aged (M), and old (O) samples are distinguished in the plot. Estimates of peripheral processing time were collected with target energies of 19.2 (cd/m$^2$ × msec).

portion of the middle-aged and old adults evidence disproportionate slowing in one of the two stages of visual information processing being correlated.

An examination of the intercorrelation of peripheral and central processing speed provides little support for the idea that a general mechanism underlies the often-replicated finding that groups of older adults are slower than groups of young adults in both peripheral and central perceptual processes. However, it is not unreasonable to suggest that a general mechanism might operate to slow the performance of older adults at a number of separate stages of central perceptual processing. The investigation by Walsh *et al.* (1979) examined the processing time required to complete Stages I and II. The results of that investigation, reviewed above, showed that groups of older adults were about 37% slower than groups of young adults in completing both stages of central processes. In the pages that follow, we will focus on age differences in the speed of completing selective attention and pattern recognition stages of central processing as conceptualized by the model (Figure 2). A primary focus of this discussion will be to determine whether older adults show a higher degree of intercorrelation than young adults in the speed with which some separate stages of central processes are completed.

## Selective Attention and Pattern Recognition

The research of Sperling (1960) and Averbach and Coriell (1961) provided much of the impetus for research in visual information processing over the last two decades. Although the results of these investigations focused on characteristics of iconic memory, they also demonstrated the ability of human observers to redirect their attention and identify alphabetic characters with surprising speed. These impressive attentional and pattern recognition abilities can best be understood by considering the diagrammatic representation of the partial-report procedure shown in Figure 11. Subjects in the Averbach and Coriell (1961) experiments were presented with arrays of 16 letters arranged in two parallel rows of 8 items. The letter arrays were displayed for 50 msec and followed at variable intervals by a marker placed over or under the position previously occupied by one of the 16 letters. Subjects in their experiment were able to locate the marker, focus their attention on the designated location, and recognize which consonant of the alphabet was located in that position in about 200 msec.

Our investigations of age differences in selective attention and pattern recognition have been heavily influenced by the conceptual analysis of the partial-report task proposed by Neisser (1967). He suggested that the task involves stages of selective and focal attention followed by pattern recognition. An investigation in our laboratory attempted to use a partial-report task to examine age differences in iconic memory. The results of that investigation suggested that aging might be associated with some major slowing in selective attention and pattern recognition. The surprising finding was that adults over 60 years of age were unable to perform a partial-report task in which the marker appeared at the same time as the letter arrays. The difficulty of the old subjects was in sharp contrast to the performance of the young subjects who showed perfect performance under the identical conditions. Subsequent investigations (cf. Kline & Baffa, 1976; Kline & Orme-Rogers, 1978; Walsh & Thompson, 1978) have

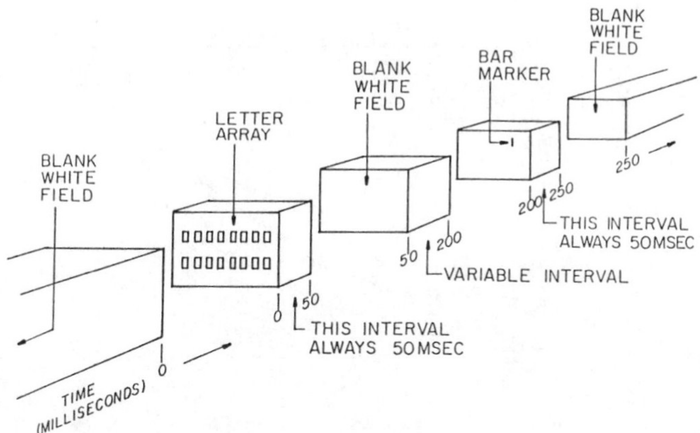


Fig. 11. A diagrammatic representation of the partial report procedure used by Averbach and Coriell (1961). Subjects' task was to report only the one letter indicated by the bar marker. (Copyright 1961 by the American Telephone and Telegraph Company. Reprinted by permission from the *Bell Systems Technical Journal*.)

shown that the difficulty of the older adults was unlikely to result from any substantial age-related decline in the duration of iconic memory.

Two approaches have been taken in our laboratory to examine the role of age differences in selective attention and pattern recognition as explanations for the poor performance of old adults in partial-report tasks. Both approaches have reduced the complexity of visual displays so that acceptable levels of performance for adults of all ages could be obtained. The first approach examined the time required by different age groups to identify displays composed of one, two, or three letters. The logic behind the selection of these conditions is that the readout of letters from these displays is a serial process requiring successive stages of selective attention and pattern recognition. The basic paradigm for this investigation was central masking described above. Displays of one, two, or three letters were presented dichoptically with a pattern mask composed of straight-line segments similar in width to the contours of the target letters. Target and mask energies were relatively high (74 cd/m$^2$), and the stimuli were photographic positives consisting of black figures on a white background. Figure 12 shows that the processing times of young, middle-aged, and old adults increased as a linear function of the number of letters in the display. In general, the relation between the number of items in a display and the $ISI_c$ required to escape masking was linear. For the middle-aged and old subjects the average linear correlation between these two variables was .95. However, the relation between $ISI_c$ and the number of items in a display departed significantly from linearity for six of the young subjects. These six subjects were excluded from the analyses reported below. For the remaining 18 young subjects, the average linear correlation between $ISI_c$ and the number of items in a display was .93—a value which did not differ from the goodness of linear fit found for the other age groups, $F(2,63)$

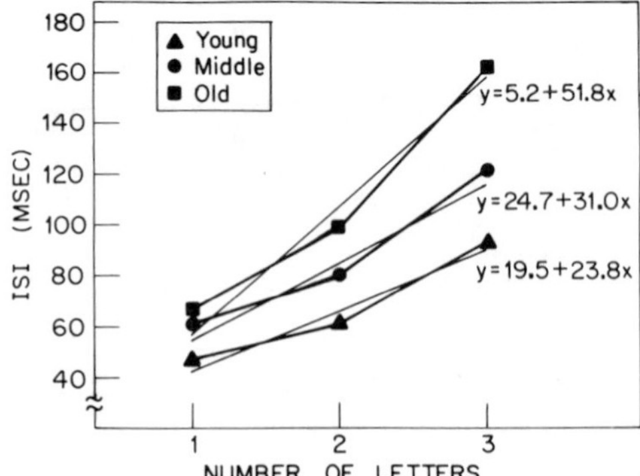


Fig. 12. The interstimulus intervals required by three groups of 24 adults (average ages of 19, 47, and 70 years) to identify 1-, 2-, and 3-letter displays. The slope of the linear functions represents the number of milliseconds required to identify a second and third letter. Processing times were measured using a dichoptic backward masking paradigm.

= .61. The linear functions that have been fit to the masking results of Figure 12 show that the recognition of each additional letter required 23.8, 31.0, and 51.8 msec for the young, middle-aged, and old subjects, respectively. An examination of the 95% level confidence interval on the slope for each age group showed that both the young and middle-aged samples differed from the old sample but not from one another.

The question of a general speed factor underlying age differences in central processes was again examined by inspecting the intercorrelations of our measures. The results of these correlational analyses provide no support for the idea that a common mechanism underlies the age differences between groups of young and old adults in the speed of separate stages of central processes. Specifically, we examined the intercorrelation of subjects' ISI to escape central masking effects when one letter was the target with the slope of the function which describes the increase in ISI required to identify one, two, and three letters. The slope is believed to reflect the amount of time required by subjects to shift their attention and recognize an additional item in the multielement displays. The intercorrelations of the slope values with the ISIs for single letter identifications were −.16, .04, and −.12 for the young, middle-aged, and old adults, respectively. These correlations show that more variance in the slope values could be predicted by variance in central processing times for the young than for the old subjects. Furthermore, the direction of the relations for young and old is opposite to that which would be expected if a single mechanism accounted for the slowing in both tasks. In other words, these results suggest that subjects who completed central processes most quickly were slower in switching their attention and recognizing alphabetic characters. Furthermore, an inspection of the intertask correlations computed across all subjects did not provide support for the hypothesis of a general slowing mechanism. The overall correlation of central processing speed with the readout rate functions was not statistically reliable, and only 1% of the variance in the speed of one process could be predicted by the speed of the other ($r$ = .10, $df$ = 71). Figure 13 shows the scatter plot of the $ISI_c$s subjects required to escape Stage I central processes with the rate of Stage II processes involving selective attention and pattern recognition. As Figure 13 shows, there is little association between the processing rates measured at these two stages of central processing for any age group.

A second approach to investigating age differences in the time required for selective attention and pattern recognition has focused on an analysis of some of the component processes that we believe to be required by the partial-report task. Reference to Figure 11 will help to clarify this analysis. The first requirement of the partial-report task involves the location of a visual marker. A second component involves the "readout" or pattern recognition of the alphabetic character indicated by the marker. Neisser (1967) has suggested that a stage of cognition intermediate to the location of the marker and recognition of the character involves the focusing of attention on the indicated position before pattern recogni-

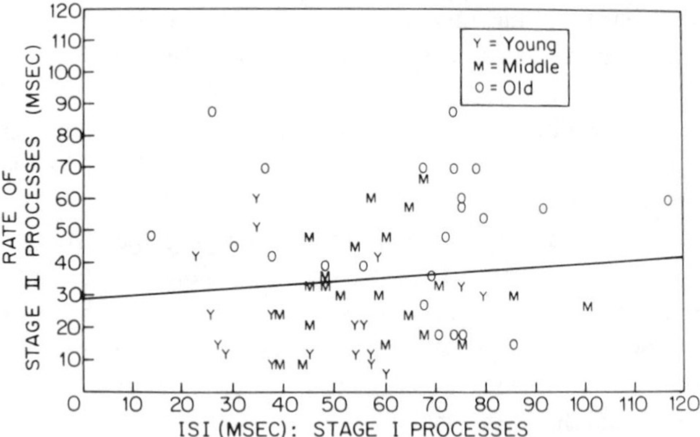


Fig. 13. Scatter plot of the ISI subjects required to escape masking for Stage I central processes and the rate (slope) at which Stage II processes involving selective attention and pattern recognition were completed. Subjects from the young (Y), middle-age (M), and old (O) samples are distinguished in the plot.

tion processes can begin. Three variations of a central masking paradigm that differed in the nature of the target field were used to examine age differences in these processing components. The first target field duplicated the conditions of central masking described above with the modification that target letters with smaller visual angles were used. (These letters could be easily identified by anyone with 20/100 vision or better.) A fixation field appeared 1.5 seconds before each masking trial, clearly indicating the spatial location (center of the viewing field) where the to-be-identified target would appear. Thus, the ISI values required to avoid central masking effects can be thought of as the time required to recognize alphabetic characters unconfounded by visual search and focal attention processing times. The second set of target fields was designed to assess visual-search time alone. Subjects were presented with rectangular viewing fields that contained a *T* in one of four possible positions (corners of the viewing field about 1.5° from fixation in each direction). The target field was preceded by a 1.5-sec fixation field and followed by a field containing four pattern masks that overlapped each of the four areas where a *T* could appear. The third viewing field was designed to assess the processing time required to complete visual search, focal attention, and pattern recognition in combination. Subjects viewed the same fixation and masking fields as in the second condition, but the target field was modified so that one of four letters could appear in any of the four locations previously occupied by a *T*. Thus, the third condition assessed the time required by subjects to locate *and* identify the target character.

The results from these conditions are shown in Figure 14. In general, subjects required longer processing times to complete pattern recognition than visual search. The time required to complete the combined visual-search and pattern-recognition task was greater for each age group than the time required to complete the separate tasks. The pattern of age differences is also clear in Figure 14. The old age group required longer processing times than the middle-aged and young subjects to achieve equivalent levels of performance. While this general finding holds for both males and females, Figure 14 shows that the older males were substantially slower than the older females in each of the three conditions. Although there is some tendency for the older subjects to show a disproportionate increase in the time to complete the combined task relative to the separate tasks, neither the Age × Task nor the Age × Sex × Task interactions were statistically significant.

The intercorrelation of performance on these three processing tasks was examined in search of a common mechanism associated with the longer processing times of older adults in each of the conditions shown in Figure 14. The intercorrelations of performance on the visual search, pattern recognition, and combined task are shown in Table 3. The intercorrelations are reasonably large, but the intercorrelations within the old group were not larger than those within

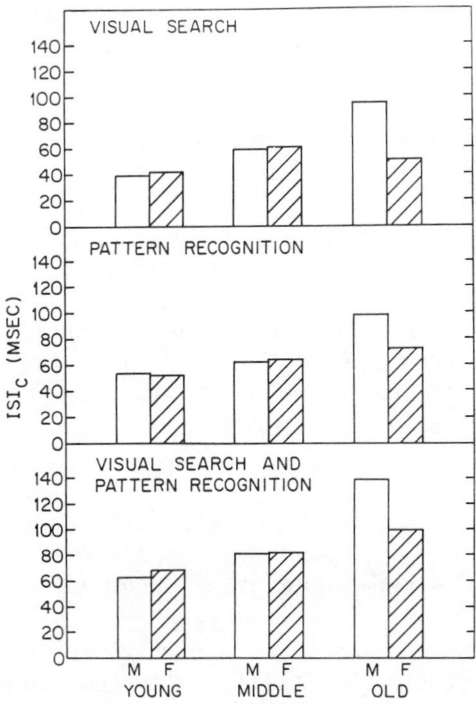


Fig. 14. Processing times ($ISI_c$) required to complete a visual search, pattern recognition, and combined visual search and pattern recognition task. Three groups of 24 adults whose average age was 19, 47, and 70 years served as subjects. Processing times were measured using a dichoptic backward masking paradigm.

*Table 3. The Correlation of Visual Search (VS), Pattern Recognition (PR), and Combined Visual Search and Pattern Recognition (VS & PR) Task for Young, Middle-Aged, and Old Adults*

| | Intercorrelated conditions | | |
|---|---|---|---|
| Age group | VS/PR | VS/VS & PR | PR/VS & PR |
| Young | .44 | .52 | .50 |
| Middle-age | .54 | .63 | .83 |
| Old | .58 | .18 | .55 |
| All ages | .62 | .50 | .72 |

the young and middle-aged groups. As can be seen in Table 3, the correlations between these tasks ranged from about .50 to .60 with two strong exceptions. The low correlation of visual search with the combined task within the old sample suggests that the visual search component of this task changes substantially for the older adults when pattern identification processes are required. The other exception was the high correlation (.83) of the pattern recognition task with the combined task within the middle-aged subjects. The strength of this relationship is consistent with the strong relation found between these two tasks when the correlations were computed on all subjects. This outcome suggests that the pattern recognition component is the most salient aspect of the combined task.

Table 3 also presents the intercorrelations between the three task conditions of Figure 14 computed across all subjects. Although these correlations are large and reliable, they do not differ significantly from those computed within separate age groups. This pattern of correlations shows a considerable relation between the times required by all subjects to complete these three experimental tasks. However, aging does not appear to be associated with the increase in correlations among these tasks that would be expected if a single mechanism, such as general slowing, were responsible for the age differences seen in group averages on each of these three tasks.

## Developmental Implications

The present chapter has reviewed the results of a number of investigations that demonstrate that groups of old adults are slower than groups of young adults in many separate stages of visual information processing. This generalization seems to hold for peripheral processes responsible for the transmission of visual information to the brain and central processes involved in the construction of higher level visual features, visual search, and pattern recognition. The findings provide important descriptions of differences in the speed of visual information processes of adults across the life span, but they do not, by themselves, provide support for a single explanation of these widespread age differences. Although the results of separate investigations might be interpreted as evidence for a general slowing with age, the results of the research reported here provide little support for this hypothesis.

Two sources of evidence have been presented that argue against a general slowing explanation of the age differences seen in many visual information processing tasks. First, the correlations between separate stages of visual information processing computed across subjects of all ages have not been larger than the correlations found within the separate age groups. Furthermore, the regression of processing speed at one stage on the speed of processing at another stage has not accounted for sizable amounts of the variance in processing speed. For example, the results reported above showed that only 8% of the variance in central processing speed could be predicted from peripheral processsing speed and that less than 1% of the variance in central processing speed measured with single letter displays could be predicted by the rate of identifying successive items in multielement displays. Figures 10 and 13 present scatter plots for the intercorrelations of these sets of variables. An inspection of the scatter plots of all subjects' performance in these stages of information processing provides further evidence against a general slowing hypothesis. The plots in Figures 10 and 13 show that only about half of the older adults are proportionately slow in separate stages of processing; the other subjects show disproportionate slowing in one of the two stages being correlated. The performance of this latter group of older adults is incompatible with the general slowing hypothesis. However, the results for the former group are not incompatible with some selective slowing explanations. For example, if the processing speed of different stages is affected by different life experiences, such as disease or dietary factors, then we should expect to see slowing in those stages in which an individual has been exposed to the causal life experiences. Individuals who have experienced more of the causal factors would be expected to show slowing in more stages of processing. Conversely, individuals who have been exposed to a limited set of causal factors would be expected to demonstrate slowing in only a few processing stages.

There are some exceptions to the conclusions stated above. For example, measures of the processing time required to complete a visual search and a pattern recognition task were found to be highly correlated. However, the central masking procedures used in measuring both processing stages were quite similar and the total time required to perform each task probably includes a large and common component of context-dependent feature construction. The correlation of these measures within the three separate age groups was similar in magnitude to the correlation computed across all ages. This result provides some support for the suggestion that the high correlation found between visual search and pattern recognition processing times probably results from the large amount of feature construction time associated with each measure rather than from a general slowing in both visual search and pattern recognition processes.

In conclusion, the research reviewed in this chapter demonstrates that groups of older adults are slower than groups of young adults in all stages of visual information processing. However, research examining the correlation of adults' performance between separate stages of information processing provides little support for the hypothesis that these widespread age differences are the result of a single causal factor. In contrast, the correlational analyses and their associated scatter plots show that a large proportion of the older subjects showed disproportionate slowing in separate stages of visual information processing. These findings have been interpreted as possible support for a hypothesis of selective slowing in which life experiences such as disease or nutritional factors may play a major causal role.

## References

Averbach, E., & Coriell, A. S. Short-term memory in vision. *Bell Systems Technical Journal*, 1961, *40*, 309–328.

Birren, J. E. Age changes in speed of behavior: Its central nature and physiological correlates. In A. T. Welford & J. E. Birren (Eds.), *Behavior, aging, and the nervous system*. Springfield, Ill.: Charles C Thomas, 1965.

Birren, J. E., Riegel, K. F., & Morrison, D. F. Age differences in response speed as a function of controlled variation of stimulus conditions: Evidence of a general speed factor. *Gerontologia*, 1962, *6*, 1–18.

Eriksen, C. W., & Colegate, R. W. Selective attention and serial processing in briefly presented visual displays. *Perception and Psychophysics*, 1971, *10*, 321–326.

Eriksen, C. W., & Collins, J. F. Temporal course of selective attention. *Journal of Experimental Psychology*, 1969, *80*, 489–492.

Eriksen, C. W., & Hoffman, J. E. Temporal and spatial characteristics of selective encoding from visual displays. *Perception and Psychophysics*, 1972, *12*, 201–204.

Hellige, J. B., Walsh, D. A., Lawrence, V. W., & Prasse, M. Figural relationship effects and mechanisms of visual masking. *Journal of Experimental Psychology: Human Perception and Performance*, 1979, *5*, 88–100.

Hertzog, C. K., Williams, M. V., & Walsh, D. A. The effect of practice on age differences in central perceptual processing. *Journal of Gerontology*, 1976, *31*, 428–433.

Kline, D. W., & Baffa, G. Differences in the sequential integration of form as a function of age and interstimulus interval. *Experimental Aging Research*, 1976, *2*, 333–343.

Kline, D. W., & Orme-Rogers, C. Examination of stimulus persistence as the basis for superior visual identification performance among older adults. *Journal of Gerontology*, 1978, *33*, 76–81.

Kline, D. W., & Szafran, J. Age differences in backward monoptic visual noise masking. *Journal of Gerontology*, 1975, *30*, 307–311.

Michaels, C. F., & Turvey, M. T. Central sources of visual masking: Indexing structures supporting seeing at a single, brief glance. *Psychological Research*, 1979, *41*, 1–61.

Neisser, U. *Cognitive psychology*. New York: Appleton–Century–Crofts, 1967.

Schultz, D. W., & Eriksen, C. W. Do noise masks terminate target processing? *Memory & Cognition,* 1977, *84,* 127–190.

Sperling, G. The information available in brief visual presentations. *Psychological Monographs: General & Applied,* 1960, *74,* 1–28.

Thomas, J. P. Model of the function of receptive fields in human vision. *Psychological Review,* 1970, *77,* 121–134.

Till, R. E. Age-related differences in binocular backward masking with visual noise. *Journal of Gerontology,* 1978, *33,* 702–710.

Turvey, M. T. On peripheral and central processes in vision: Inferences from an information-processing analysis of masking with patterned stimuli. *Psychological Review,* 1973, *80,* 1–52.

Walsh, D. A. Age differences in central perceptual processing: A dichoptic backward masking investigation. *Journal of Gerontology,* 1976, *31,* 178–185.

Walsh, D. A., Krauss, I. K., & Regnier, V. A. Spatial ability, environmental knowledge and environmental use: The elderly. In L. Liben, A. Patterson, & N. Newcombe (Eds.), *Spatial representation and behavior across the life span.* New York: Academic Press, 1981.

Walsh, D. A., & Thompson, L. W. Age differences in visual sensory memory. *Journal of Gerontology,* 1978, *33,* 383–387.

Walsh, D. A., Till, R. E., & Williams, M. V. Age differences in peripheral perceptual processing: A monoptic backward masking investigation. *Journal of Experimental Psychology: Human Perception and Performance,* 1978, *4,* 232–243.

Walsh, D. A., Williams, M. V., & Hertzog, C. K. Age-related differences in two stages of central perceptual processes: The effects of short duration targets and criterion differences. *Journal of Gerontology,* 1979, *34,* 234–241.

Weale, R. A. On the eye. In A. Welford & J. Birren (Eds.), *Behavior, aging and the nervous system.* Springfield, Ill.: Charles C Thomas, 1965.

CHAPTER 7

# The Appearance and Disappearance of Age Differences in Adult Memory

Marion Perlmutter and David B. Mitchell

*Institute of Child Development*
*University of Minnesota*
*Minneapolis, Minnesota*

Over the past two decades there has been much support for the commonly held belief that memory deteriorates in later adulthood. However, there has been less progress towards understanding the basis of this decline. Moreover, under some conditions age differences have not been observed. Contrasting the situations in which deficits are and are not observed should be instructive for gaining an understanding of age-related changes in memory. The present chapter includes a presentation of some of our research in which age deficits have been observed and a discussion of how the deficits often have been attenuated and sometimes eliminated. Finally, an attempt is made to integrate these results, as well as other findings in the literature, in a way that may shed light on the mechanisms underlying memory change in adulthood.

A common strategy of recent reviewers of age changes in adult memory (e.g., Salthouse, 1980; Smith, 1980) has been to ascribe older subjects' poorer performance to problems at encoding, storage, and/or retrieval. Although the goal inherent in such a perspective to *localize* the stage of memory deficits is important, further consideration of the *nature* of the deficits is also essential. Several relatively general factors have been hypothesized to underlie age deficits

The authors' research has been supported by grants from the Graduate School of the University of Minnesota and NIH (PHS 1 ROS MH 319801) to Marion Perlmutter, and NICHHD (HD 01136) and NSF (BNS 75 038 16) to the University of Minnesota Center for Research on Human Learning.

in adult memory. For example, interference (e.g., Arenberg, 1973; Botwinick, 1967), quality or depth of processing (e.g., Craik, 1977), capacity or amount of processing resources (e.g., Craik & Simon, 1980), and speed of processing (e.g., Waugh & Barr, 1980) have all been suggested as contributors of age-related declines in memory. The primary goal of this chapter is to elucidate the nature of processing deficits that contribute to age-related declines in memory, although some consideration is also given to the localization of these deficits.

## Summary of Present Research

In all of our own studies, performance of younger males and females in their 20s was compared with that of older males and females in their 60s. The older adults were community dwellers and thus in relatively good health. Level of education was always controlled; thus, it was not confounded with age, as it is in the population at large. A few studies included subjects who had completed only high school, most involved subjects with college-level education, and in one study adults with postgraduate education were included. We have found that higher level of education is related to better performance on all tasks, but each of the educational groups has shown remarkably similar patterns of aging, with virtually parallel age functions obtained in all comparisons. The testing procedures were generally self-paced, although records were kept of the amount of time that subjects spent on each phase of the tasks. In many cases time to prepare for or to complete the task did not vary systematically with age, although in some cases older individuals spent more time on the tasks than did younger individuals, In all experiments analyses in which time was treated as a covariate yielded essentially the same pattern of results as analyses in which time was not considered.

In the first series of studies (Perlmutter, 1978, 1979a) subjects were tested for their memory of lists of words. In one condition, called the *intentional learning* condition, subjects were told to try to memorize the words because they would be tested for retention. In another condition, called the *incidental learning* condition, subjects were given no indication of the impending retention tests. Rather, they were engaged in a task in which they were to generate free associations to words. Subsequently all subjects were tested for recall and recognition.

The results of one of these studies (Perlmutter, 1979a) are presented in Figure 1. The recall data are in the left panel and the recognition data in the right; retention in the intentional condition is shown with solid lines and that in the incidental condition in broken lines. Consider first intentional memory performance. Significant age deficits in both recall and recognition were observed. Of greatest interest, however, was the interaction between age and testing situation. The age difference was greater in recall than in recognition. While all subjects

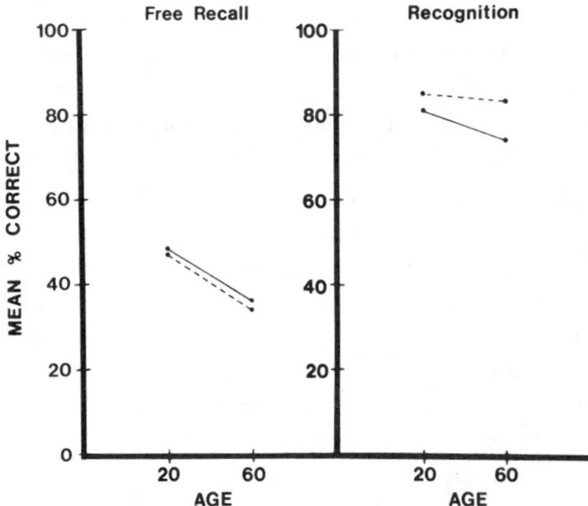


Fig. 1. Mean percentage correct free recall and recognition following incidental and intentional conditions by younger and older adults ( •——• = intentional; •---• = incidental).

benefited from the external retrieval support available in the recognition test, this support benefited the older subjects more than the younger subjects. Apparently not all of the age deficit in recall performance is due to encoding and/or retention differences. Rather, some of older adults' memory deficits appear to be attributable to retrieval difficulties.

On the other hand, the persistent age-related deficit in recognition performance, where retrieval demands were minimized, points to probable age differences in encoding as well. The nature of these encoding differences should be clarified by consideration of the incidental memory performance shown in Figure 1. It was hypothesized that the associative task would lead to a good retention since it required subjects to process the words at a semantic level (cf. Craik & Lockhart, 1972). Indeed, this orienting condition led to recall performance that was virtually identical with that in the intentional condition for both younger and older subjects. Of greater interest, however, was the pattern of results obtained on the recognition test. The incidental learning condition actually led to better recognition than the intentional learning condition; this was especially true for the older adults. Moreover, when encoding processes were directed in this way, and retrieval supports were adequate, age differences were eliminated. Similar results were also obtained by White (cited by Craik, 1977). Apparently, instructions in the intentional learning condition did not induce older adults to carry out processing as effectively as younger adults. Nevertheless, the fact that performance could be equated indicates that older adults were capable of more effective mnemonic processing than they exhibited spontaneously.

The comparable recognition performance of younger and older adults in the incidental condition is suggestive of the two age groups' equal encoding *abili-*

*ties,* but differences in their *spontaneous use* of them. However, this conclusion is qualified by other investigators (e.g., Eysenck, 1974), who have posited that older adults are *less capable* of effective semantic encoding than younger adults. Such evaluations of encoding have been based entirely on inferences from memory performance and thus rely upon circular reasoning. Therefore, additional means of assessing encoding independently of retention were attempted.

One line of research designed to assess encoding independently has been motivated by a desire to analyze more carefully the encoding carried out by subjects in the incidental association condition. In our first study, in which the associative orienting task was used (Perlmutter, 1978), there was some suggestion that older adults generated fewer common associates than did younger adults and that the associations of the older group overlapped with each other less than did those of the younger group. However, the design of that study did not permit adequate assessment of this possibility. Moreover, it was hypothesized that whereas such an age-related increase in between-subject variability might not be relevant to memory performance, it could reflect greater within-subject variability, which could contribute to retrieval difficulties. Thus, a task was designed in which subjects were asked to generate free associations to the same words on each of four trials.

The results of the first such study (Perlmutter, 1979b) are shown in Table 1. The measure of between-subject variability, percentage of associations that were normed as most common, indicated that older subjects produced somewhat fewer common associations. This difference was marginally significant. Two measures of within-subject variability, percentage of same associations generated over four trials and total number of different associations, agreed in suggesting that younger adults were a bit more consistent and older adults a bit more variable in associative productions. Although these differences reached statistical significance, it should be noted that their magnitude was quite small.

*Table 1. Mean Percentage Most Common Associations, Percentage Same Associations, and Number of Different Associations, by Each Age Group*

| | Age group | |
|---|---|---|
| | 20s | 60s |
| Between subject variability | | |
| Percentage most common associations | 31 | 24 |
| Within subject variability | | |
| Percentage same association (over 4 trials) | 45 | 33 |
| Number of different associations (out of 96) | 45 | 51 |

*Table 2. Mean Number of Different Associations in Each Condition by Each Age Group*

| Condition | Age group 20s | 60s |
|---|---|---|
| Free | 49 | 45 |
| Same | 32 | 33 |
| Different | 113 | 113 |

A second study (Mitchell & Perlmutter, in preparation) was carried out in an attempt to replicate these findings. This study included two additional conditions designed to determine whether age differences in the consistency of spontaneous associative productions reflect capacity differences or simply dispositional differences. For four trials, subjects were simply told to generate the first association that came to mind (*free association*), or to try to generate the same association on each trial (*same condition*), or to try to generate a different association on each trial (*different condition*).

Although the data are not yet fully analyzed, the preliminary results are presented in Table 2. As can be seen, younger subjects were actually somewhat less consistent than older subjects, although this difference was not statistically significant. Of further interest was the virtually identical performance of younger and older subjects in both the same and different conditions. Apparently, when so instructed, younger and older adults are equally competent at generating and monitoring their productions of consistent or inconsistent associations. In general, then, the results of these association studies are in agreement with the findings of the memory studies. It appears that when directed to carry out associative encoding younger and older adults engage in similar processing.

We have employed another paradigm to evaluate possible age differences in encoding independently of the retrieval requirements that can contribute to age differences in recall and recognition. In particular, reaction-time patterns have been examined. The use of reaction times as indices of ongoing processing has a long history in cognitive psychology. Across a wide variety of procedures (e.g., Stroop tasks, lexical decision tasks, picture-naming tasks), it has been shown that the nature of the semantic relation between two or more items can produce systematic increases or decreases in reaction time (e.g., Meyer & Schvaneveldt, 1976). Such reaction-time patterns are thought to reflect activation of semantic knowledge structures and thus can provide an index of processing that is independent of episodic memory performance. Furthermore, even unattended stimuli have been shown to increase or decrease response latencies to process target stimuli, depending upon the semantic relatedness between targets and distractors (cf. Shaffer & LaBerge, 1979).

In one study (Mitchell & Perlmutter, 1980) reaction times were recorded as subjects made semantic (animate vs. inanimate) or nonsemantic (upper vs. lower case type) decisions about target words that were paired with distractors. These orienting tasks were followed by expected or unexpected tests of recall and recognition of both targets and distractors. To the extent that distractors influence reaction times, they are assumed to have been processed. Thus, the reaction times provided a relatively direct measure of processing during encoding. If, when engaged in the semantic orienting task, all subjects process information to a deep semantic level, parallel patterns of reaction times, reflecting the semantic relation between target and distractor stimuli, should be obtained for younger and older subjects. On the other hand, if, even when so directed, older adults engage in less deep semantic processing (the processing deficit hypothesis), then their pattern of reaction times under the semantic orienting task should not reflect the semantic relation between targets and distractors but should parallel their reaction times under the nonsemantic orienting task.

The reaction times for correct responses on the orienting tasks are shown in Figure 2. These correct responses represent over 90% of the data. The upper graphs show reaction times on the first trial blocks, when memory tests were not expected, and the lower graphs show reaction times on the second trial block, when memory tests were expected. As can be seen, older subjects were consistently slower than younger subjects. Of greater interest, however, was the similarity in the pattern of reaction times for the two age groups.

Consider, first, reaction times when memory tests were not expected. The predicted patterns were obtained. Semantic processing took longer than nonsemantic processing. Moreover, while distractor type did not affect reaction times in the nonsemantic task, it systematically affected reaction times in the semantic task. In particular, in the semantic task there were no reliable differences in latencies in the presence of same word or related word distractors, but unrelated word and nonword distractors reliably increased latencies. Although there appeared to be a difference between same word and related word distractors for the older group, a separate *t*-test indicated that this difference was not significant.

When memory tests were expected, reaction times were 109 msec longer in the nonsemantic task and 90 msec shorter in the semantic task than when memory tests were not expected. Thus, while semantic processing continued to take longer than nonsemantic processing, this difference was reduced by knowledge of forthcoming memory tests. Moreover, when memory tests were expected, orienting task did not interact with distractor type.

These findings again point to similarities in younger and older adults' processing. The statistically parallel patterns of reaction times suggest that younger and older subjects' encoding was quite comparable, at least when carrying out the orienting tasks that were used. For both age groups distractors had little effect on reaction times in the nonsemantic task, but, as predicted, reaction times varied as a function of the target-distractor relation in the semantic task. The fact

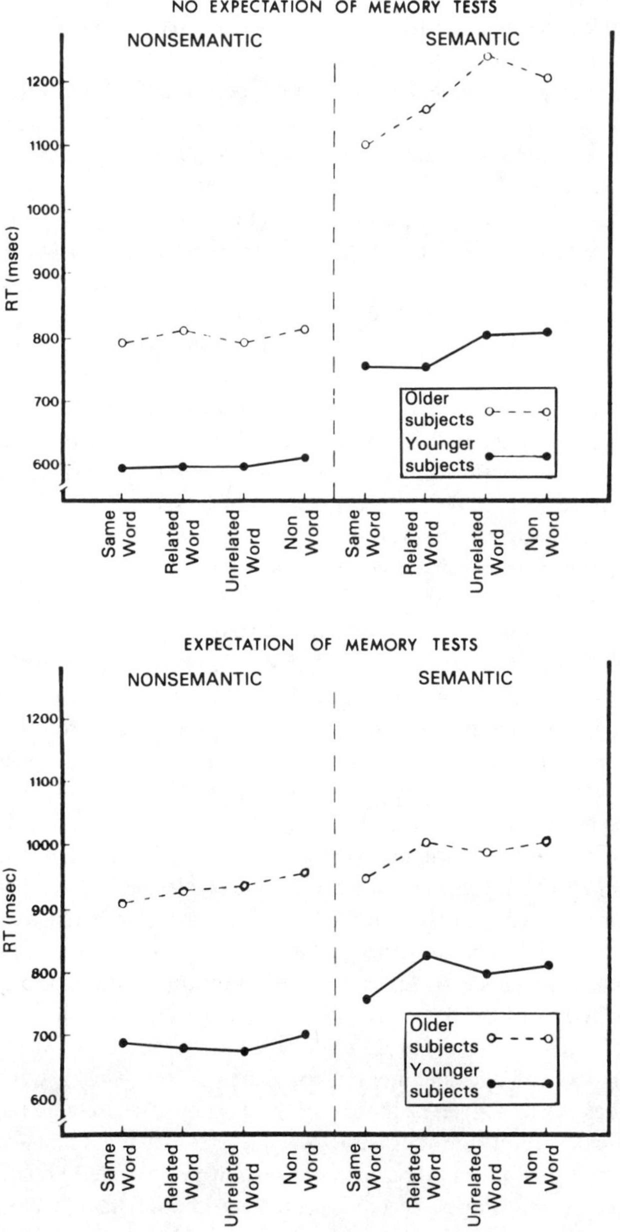


Fig. 2. Mean reaction times for correct responses when memory tests were unexpected or expected, on nonsemantic and semantic orienting tasks, in each distractor condition, for younger and older adults.

that performance of both age groups was sensitive to the type of distractor in the semantic task demonstrates that such reaction-time paradigms may be useful for elucidating encoding processes across adulthood.

The memory data were also of interest, pointing to remarkable similarities in younger and older subjects' processing, as well as important differences. These data are shown in Figure 3. The upper graphs show the mean number of words correctly recalled and the lower graphs show the mean number of words correctly recognized. The left panel of each graph shows performance on the first trial block, when memory tests were not expected, and the right panel shows performance on the second trial block, when memory tests were expected.

Consider, first, performance on the first trial block, when memory tests were unexpected. Since the patterns of recall and recogniton performance were essentially the same, they will be summarized together. The semantic orienting task led to better retention than the nonsemantic orienting task, and target stimuli were remembered better than distractors. Of greater note, however, was the absence of main effects of age or interactions involving age. When encoding was controlled by the rapid-decision orienting tasks, and memory tests were not expected, there were no significant age differences in retention.

The absence of age differences following nonsemantic processing is consistent with most previous studies (e.g., Eysenck, 1974). However, the absence of age differences following semantic processing, particularly in free recall, is at variance with the results of several earlier studies. For example, Eysenck (1974) reported that older adults were unable to benefit as much from semantic processing as were younger adults, and Simon (1979) reported that performance of older adults was actually impaired under a semantic cuing task. The emphasis on rapid decisions in the present procedures may have controlled encoding better and thus contributed to this discrepancy.

Consider, next, performance on the second trial block, when memory tests were expected. Overall performance was better with knowledge of forthcoming memory tests. However, this improvement was evident primarily following nonsemantic processing, and only in younger subjects. Again, targets were remembered better than distractors. In addition, the semantic orienting task led to better retention of targets than the nonsemantic orienting task, but there was no such difference for distractors. Of greater note were the significant main effects of age and interactions of age and item type. When memory tests were expected, younger subjects remembered more than older subjects, although this age trend was statistically significant for distractors only. This finding of an age difference in retention of distractors when memory tests were expected points to strategy and/or capacity advantages in younger adults. Although the older subjects' performance on distractors did not change over trial blocks, the younger subjects' retention of distractors increased dramatically on the second trial block. The knowledge of forthcoming memory tests appears to have encouraged the younger subjects to invoke strategies for encoding and retrieving irrelevant distractors.

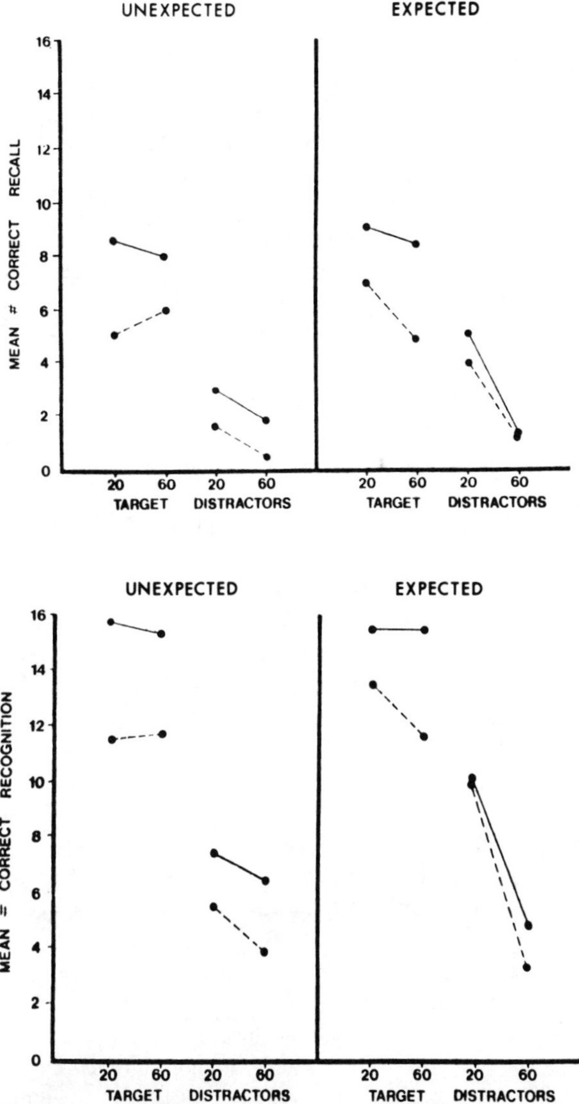


Fig. 3. Mean number correct recall and recognition of targets and distractors, on expected and expected memory tests, following the nonsemantic and semantic orienting tasks, by younger and older adults ( •——• = semantic; •---• = nonsemantic).

This finding indicates that the younger subjects were able to carry out supplemental processing, even while carrying out the orienting tasks. At this point, it remains unclear whether the older subjects did not attempt to modify their processing in this way or whether the processing demands of the orienting tasks left insufficient capacity to do so. Recent evidence suggests that deeper levels of processing require greater proportions of processing capacity (e.g., Eysenck & Eysenck, 1979), but the possibility that these processing demands change differentially across the lifespan has not been investigated. Nevertheless, the finding of age differences only on expected memory tests is consonant with several other studies in which larger age differences have been obtained for intentional relative to incidental memory (e.g., Erber, 1979; Perlmutter, 1978, 1979a).

Thus far, the prevalent type of research on memory and aging has been discussed, that is, research on retention of lists of words. In general, this research has demonstrated age-related deficits when subjects are left to study stimuli in whatever manner they choose. However, when subjects' study is directed in certain ways, age differences are often ameliorated. These findings suggest that an important factor contributing to age differences in memory performance is change in the use of effective strategies. It appears that effective mnemonic processing is within the repertoire of older adults, although it is less likely to be employed by them.

Of course, this perspective has developed mainly from studies involving deliberate retention. In recent theoretical statements about memory it has been suggested that automatic processing should be distinguished from effortful processing (Hasher & Zacks, 1979). In particular, it has been claimed that automatic and effortful operations vary in their attentional requirements. Automatic operations drain minimal energy from the limited-capacity attention mechanism and do not interfere with ongoing cognitive capacity. On the other hand, effortful operations do require considerable capacity and, therefore, interfere with other cognitive activities. Automatic operations are expected to develop earlier in life and to reach a level of maximal efficiency sooner than effortful processes. Thus, development across the life span is expected to have a greater impact on effortful than on automatic processes. The question remains, however, whether there are age-related deficits in retention of information presumed to be encoded automatically.

Processes that encode the fundamental aspects of the flow of information, such as the frequency and recency of events, are generally considered to be automatic (Hasher & Zacks, 1979), and storage of these types of information is assumed to be an obligatory concomitant of normal encoding. That is, such information is acquired without intention and thus is not susceptible to alteration by manipulations such as instructions to remember, practice, or feedback concerning accuracy of performance.

In a recent study (Perlmutter, Metzger, Nezworski, & Miller, 1981) younger and older adults were tested for their retention of the recency of occurrence of stimuli. Age accounted for less than 1% of the variance in performance, with both age groups performing between 60% and 65% correct. Thus, these results are in agreement with the notion that automatic processing does not change over the life span. Similarly, Attig and Hasher (1980) and Kausler and Puckett (1980) found no age-related deficits in adults' retention of the frequency of occurrence of stimuli. Their results apparently add further support to the view that a major factor contributing to memory decline in later adulthood is the decreasing use of effective strategies.

The above analysis is probably incorrect, however. Although age differences were not observed in retention in these studies, it is not clear whether the required encoding interfered with other cognitive activities. For example, Kausler and Puckett (1981) investigated adults' retention of the content and sex of voice of spoken sentences in incidental and intentional conditons. In both conditions only minor age differences in retention of sex of speaker were found. However, intentional encoding of this information significantly diminished older, but not younger, subjects' retention of sentence content. These results seem to point to an age-related decrement in total processing capacity. For older adults, enhanced encoding of nonsemantic information occurred at the expense of encoding of semantic information. For younger adults, the apparently larger capacity of their processing system resulted in virtually no trade-off or adverse effect of additional intentional encoding.

This apparent *processing surplus* in younger adults also seems to be a viable explanation of the one age difference observed in the rapid-decision task discussed earlier (Mitchell & Perlmutter, 1980). The only significant age difference in that study was that older subjects retained fewer distractors than younger subjects on expected memory tests. When expecting memory tests, younger subjects apparently had the capacity to engage in supplemental encoding that could increase their retention of irrelevant stimuli, but such additional processing was not evident in older subjects.

It is interesting, too, that the notion of a processing surplus in younger adults is helpful in interpreting a number of inconsistencies in levels-of-processing studies of memory and aging. Whereas in some laboratories (e.g., Craik & Perlmutter) it has been possible to eliminate age differences with semantic orienting tasks and recognition testing, in other laboratories (e.g., Smith) this amelioration of age differences has not always been obtained. It appears that when orienting instructions are given under incidental learning conditions, age differences can generally be eliminated, but when orienting instructions have been paired with expectation of memory tests age differences persist. Indeed, in a single study Erber (1979) has compared younger and older adults' retention following nonsemantic and semantic orienting tasks that were administered either incidentally or intentionally. For both orienting tasks, younger adults' performance was substantially better with the addition of intentional instructions, whereas older adults' performance was equivalent in the incidental and intentional conditions. A similar result also was reported by Zelinski, Walsh, and Thompson (1978), who found that intentional instructions improved recall of younger but not of older adults.

In summary, much of the age-related deficit observed in our studies of list learning can be accounted for by inefficient use of strategies by older subjects. Although it is possible that further encoding deficits exist, such processing must be evaluated independently of retention. In two attempts to assess encoding independently, similarities in the nature of these processes have been observed across adulthood. On the other hand, there have been recent suggestions of a more severe capacity limitation in older than in younger adults. Such differences in processing capacity are likely to be important in understanding aging of the cognitive system.

## Integration with Previous Research

Age differences in adults' memory have been evident in some studies but absent in others. Examination of our own data, and that of others, points to three factors that may contribute to these apparent inconsistencies. In particular, some understanding of the nature of age deficits in adult memory has been achieved through experiments that have manipulated (1) depth or quality of encoding, (2) goal of encoding activty, and (3) retrieval support at testing.

When depth or quality of encoding is manipulated, subjects are required to carry out different kinds of operations or decisions during presentation of stimuli. For example, subjects might be asked whether words rhyme or not or whether they have pleasant or unpleasant connotations. The latter task requires more meaningful analysis than the former and typically leads to better memory performance. By comparing memory performance of various age groups following such controlled encoding conditions, investigators have made inferences about age differences in *encoding abilities*. Since subjects' processing is directed by the orienting tasks, it has been argued that performance differences can be attributed to subjects' ability to process in the required manner.

When goal of encoding activity is manipulated, knowledge of forthcoming memory tests is varied. If memory tests are expected, adults are assumed to activate mnemonic strategies that will facilitate retention. Thus, by comparing the difference in memory performance of various age groups following incidental versus intentional instructions, investigators have made inferences about age differences in the *spontaneous use of encoding operations*. That is, since subjects' processing is not specifically directed by intentional instructions, performance following such instructions is an index of spontaneous mnemonic processing.

Finally, when retrieval support in the testing environment is manipulated, type of retention test is varied. For example, subjects might be given free recall, cued recall, or recognition tests. When cued recall tests subjects are provided with somewhat more retrieval support than with free recall tests, and with recognition tests maximal retrieval support is provided. In general, increasing retrieval support has been found to increase memory performance. By comparing the relative benefits of added retrieval support to various age groups, investigators have made inferences about age differences in *retrieval skills*. To the degree that retrieval support differentially aids the performance of particular age groups, it has been argued that the subjects themselves are deficient in the required retrieval skills.

Table 3 summarized 12 experiments in which at least some manipulations of depth of processing, goal of encoding activity, and retrieval support, were carried out with younger and older adults. A rather clear picture emerges from these fairly diverse experiments. First, under standard intentional memory instructions, statistically reliable age differences in free recall have been obtained in all relevant experiments, with these differences averaging 13% (range = 8% to 28%). Similarly, when orienting tasks have been paired with expectation of memory tests, age differences in free recall also averaged 13% (range = 2% to 15%) and were statistically significant in all but one instance (Mason, 1979, shallow orienting task). On the other hand, when memory tests have followed orienting tasks in which the forthcoming memory tests have not been expected, age differences in free recall averaged only 5% (range = 0 to 17%), and were statistically significant in only 5 out of 18 instances. This pattern of results suggests that *encoding ability* is probably less central to age differences in adult memory than is the *spontaneous use of optimal encoding operations*. However, all of the results discussed thus far were obtained with free recall procedures. Additional support for this view emerges from the results obtained with recognition procedures, where retrieval demands are minimized.

In recognition, under standard intentional memory instructions, substantial age differences generally have been observed (mean = 19%, range = 5% to 40%); in five out of seven experiments including this condition the age difference was statistically significant. Of the remaining two experiments, Erber's (1979) findings were likely to be limited by ceiling effects, and Mason (1979) reported only d′ scores. While the d′ means were higher for younger than for older subjects, it is still unclear why the difference was not larger.

The suggestion that spontaneous use of efficient strategies contributes significant to the memory advantage of younger adults also emerges from recognition performance following orienting tasks. When orienting tasks have been paired with expectation of memory tests, age differences in recognition averaged 12% (range = 0 to 26%), and were significant in all but the Erber (1979) and Mason (1979) studies. On the other hand, when unexpected memory tests have followed orienting tasks, age differences in recogniton averaged only 5% (range = 0 to 9%), and were never statistically significant. Thus, when retrieval support has been provided and encoding operations directed, age differences seem to vanish. Apparently *encoding abilities* of younger and older adults do not differ, although their *spontaneous use of encoding operations* do.

*Table 3. Mean Percentages of Free Recall and Recognition by Young and Old Adults under Five Processing Conditions, from 12 Experiments*

| | | Orienting tasks | | Subjects | | Free recall (mean percentage) | | | | | Recognition (mean percentage) | | | | |
|---|---|---|---|---|---|---|---|---|---|---|---|---|---|---|---|
| | | | | | | Incidental | | Intentional | | | Incidental | | Intentional | | |
| Study | Stimuli | Shallow | Deep | *n* | Age ranges | Shallow | Deep | Free | Shallow | Deep | Shallow | Deep | Free | Shallow | Deep |
| Craik & Simon, 1980 | 64 unrelated words | 1. type case | 1. category | | (Y) | 5 | 16 | 45 | — | — | 40 | 77 | 83 | — | — |
| | | 2. rhyme | | | (O) | 3[b] | 12[b] | 35[b] | — | — | 31[b] | 69[b] | 54[b] | — | — |
| Erber, 1979 | 28 words | 1. letter search | 1. pleasantness | 60 | 18–31 | 11 | 39 | 37 | 29 | 44 | 73 | 100 | 90 | 85 | 99 |
| | | | | 60 | 65–77 | 9 | 30[a] | 26[a] | 12[a] | 31[a] | 65 | 97 | 85 | 71 | 99 |
| Eysenck, 1974 | 27 words | 1. letter count | 1. adjective | 50 | 18–30 | 26 | 60 | 72 | — | — | | | | | |
| | (9 categories) | 2. rhyme | 2. imagery | 50 | 55–65 | 26 | 45[a] | 44[a] | — | — | | | | | |
| Mason, 1979 | 60 common nouns | 1. type case | 1. category | 86 | 20–39 | — | — | 19 | 7 | 26 | — | — | 1.89 | 1.30 | 2.54 |
| | | 2. rhyme | | 99 | 60–80 | — | — | 9[a] | 5 | 11[a] | — | — | 1.74 | 1.05 | 1.67 |
| Mitchell & Perlmutter, 1980 | 32 nouns | 1. type case | 1. category | 16 | 19–30 | 21 | 36 | — | 34 | 44 | 54 | 73 | — | 73 | 81 |
| | | | | 16 | 59–73 | 20 | 30 | — | 19[a] | 30[a] | 49 | 69 | — | 47[a] | 64[a] |
| Perlmutter, 1978 | 24 words | | 1. free association | 32 | 20–25 | — | 40 | 39 | — | — | — | 68 | 59 | — | — |
| | | | | 32 | 60–65 | — | 23[a] | 28[a] | — | — | — | 61 | 40[a] | — | — |
| Perlmutter, 1979a Experiment 1 | 24 words | | 1. free association | 48 | 18–29 | — | 46 | 48 | — | — | — | 85 | 81 | — | — |
| | | | | 48 | 59–70 | — | 35[a] | 37[a] | — | — | — | 83 | 74[a] | — | — |

| | | | | | | | | | | | | | | | |
|---|---|---|---|---|---|---|---|---|---|---|---|---|---|---|---|
| Smith & Winograd, 1978 | 50 faces | 1. structural feature | 1. face friendliness | 101 | 18–25 | | | | | | | | 62 | 65 | 78 |
| | | | | 115 | 50–80 | | | | | | | | 46[a] | 44[a] | 57[a] |
| Till & Walsh, 1980 | Exp. 1. 16 sentences | 1. word count estimate | 1. pleasantness | 19 | 17–29 | 9 | 39 | — | — | — | | | | | |
| | | | | 17 | 57–81 | 4[b] | 35[b] | — | — | — | | | | | |
| | Exp. 2. 16 sentences | 1. word count estimate | 1. pleasantness | 16 | 18–22 | 4 | 38 | — | — | — | | | | | |
| | | | | 16 | 65–81 | 2 | 33 | — | — | — | | | | | |
| White (in Craik, 1977) | 64 words | 1. type case | 1. category | | (Y) | 6 | 31 | 33 | — | — | 28 | 58 | 73 | — | — |
| | | 2. rhyme | | | (O) | 6 | 17[b] | 18[b] | — | — | 28 | 60 | 33[b] | — | — |
| Zelinski, Walsh, & Thompson, 1978 | 25 high-imagery words (auditory) | 1. letter search | 1. pleasantness | 94 | 18–30 | 18 | 36 | 40 | — | — | | | | | |
| | | | | 49 | 55–70 | 16 | 33 | 32[a] | — | — | | | | | |

| | | Incidental | | Intentional | | | Incidental | | Intentional | | |
|---|---|---|---|---|---|---|---|---|---|---|---|
| | | Shallow | Deep | Free | Shallow | Deep | Shallow | Deep | Free | Shallow | Deep |
| Averaged over studies: $\bar{X}$ (*SD*) | Young | 12.5 (8.2) | 38.1 (11.0) | 41.6 (15.1) | 23.3 (14.4) | 38.0 (10.4) | 48.8 (19.3) | 76.8 (14.5) | 74.7 (12.3) | 74.3 (10.1) | 86.0 (11.4) |
| | Old | 10.8 (8.9) | 29.3 (9.6) | 28.6 (11.1) | 12.0 (7.0) | 24.0 (11.3) | 43.3 (17.2) | 73.2 (14.3) | 55.3 (20.3) | 54.0 (14.8) | 73.3 (22.5) |

[a]Denotes age difference $p < .05$.
[b]Denotes $p$ value for age difference not reported.

It should be noted that this conclusion suggests that intention to remember plays a much greater role in memory performance than the nondevelopmental literature on memory would lead one to expect (e.g., Hyde & Jenkins, 1969; Johnston & Jenkins, 1971; Walsh & Jenkins, 1973). It appears that an understanding of memory based solely on fairly homogeneous samples of college students may lead to some misconceptions.

One additional aspect of the data should be considered, that is, the relative size of age differences in recall and recogniton conditions. This comparison is relevant to the contribution of retrieval factors in the memory difficulties of older adults. As has been indicated, age differences in intentional free recall tests averaged 13%, while in intentional recognition tests they averaged only 9%. This greater age difference in free recall, where retrieval demands were maximal, suggests that retrieval difficulties contribute to age deficits in memory performance. On the other hand, when encoding was directed with orienting tasks, age differences in free recall were only slightly greater than age differences in recognition; the age difference averaged 9% in recall and 8% in recognition. This pattern points to an important interaction between encoding and retrieval conditions and suggests that a more general analysis may be advantageous.

## Conclusions

In summary, older adults' poorer memory of word lists appears to be accounted for by their *inefficient spontaneous use* of encoding and retrieval strategies. While other cognitive limitations may affect their memory performance on other tasks, studies of list learning provide little evidence of deficits in the encoding *abilities* of older adults.

If this *description* of age differences in adult memory is correct, what are the *explanations* for it? Two general domains, environmental demands and biological constraints, are viable factors. Unfortunately, however, there is scant empirical validation of either. Still, it seems extremely relevant that the younger subjects in studies of aging typically are college students who are routinely faced with tasks that are similar to experimental memory tests, while the older subjects typically have been out of school for many years and are rarely faced with comparable tasks. It is likely that recent experience in utilizing mnemonic strategies that are appropriate for memory experiments contributes importantly to the results. Likewise, while there is still little understanding of the relation between biological and cognitive function, there are known age-related changes in the central nervous system, and older adults are often in poorer health than younger adults. These factors are almost surely related to cognitive performance in some way. Since there is great heterogeneity of these conditions in older samples, a more careful analysis of individual differences should be helpful.

# References

Arenberg, D. Cognition and aging: Verbal learning, memory, problem solving, and aging. In C. Eisdorfer & M. P. Lawton (Eds.), *The psychology of development and aging*. Washington D.C.: American Psychological Association, 1973.

Attig, M., & Hasher, L. The processing of frequency of occurrence information by adults. *Journal of Gerontology*, 1980, *35*, 66–69.

Botwinick, J. *Cognitive processes in maturity and old age*. New York: Springer, 1967.

Craik, F. I. M. Age differences in human memory. In J. E. Birren & K. W. Schaie (Eds.), *Handbook of the psychology of aging*. New York: Van Nostrand Reinhold, 1977.

Craik, F. I. M., & Lockhart, R. S. Levels of processing: A framework for memory research. *Journal of Verbal Learning and Verbal Behavior*, 1972, *11*, 671–684.

Craik, F. I. M., & Simon, E. Age differences in memory: The roles of attention and depth of processing. In L. W. Poon, J. L. Fozard, L. S. Cermak, D. Arenberg, & L. W. Thompson (Eds.), *New directions in memory and aging*. Hillsdale, N.J.: Lawrence Erlbaum, 1980.

Erber, J. T. The effect of encoding instructions on recall and recognition memory. *Maximizing the Memory of Older Adults: Encoding in Verbal Memory*. Symposium presented at the meeting of the Gerontological Society, Washington, 1979.

Eysenck, M. W. Age differences in incidental learning. *Developmental Psychology*, 1974, *10*, 936–941.

Eysenck, M. W., & Eysenck, M. C. Processing depth, elaboration of encoding, memory stores, and expended processing capacity. *Journal of Experimental Psychology: Human Learning and Memory*, 1979, *5*, 472–484.

Hasher, L., & Zacks, R. T. Automatic and effortful processes in memory. *Journal of Experimental Psychology: General*, 1979, *108*, 356–388.

Hyde, T. S., & Jenkins, J. J. Differential effects of incidental tasks on the organization of recall of a list of highly associated words. *Journal of Experimental Psychology*, 1969, *82*, 472–481.

Johnston, C. D., & Jenkins, J. J. Two more incidental tasks that differentially affect associative clustering in recall. *Journal of Experimental Psychology*, 1971, *89*, 92–95.

Kausler, D. H., & Puckett, J. M. Frequency judgments and correlated cognitive abilities in young and elderly adults. *Journal of Gerontology*, 1980, *35*, 376–382.

Kausler, D. H., & Puckett, J. M. Adult age differences in memory for sex of voice. *Journal of Gerontology*, 1981, *36*, 40–50.

Mason, S. E. Effects of orienting tasks on the recall and recognition performance of subjects differing in age. *Developmental Psychology*, 1979, *15*, 467–469.

Meyer, D. E., & Schvaneveldt, R. W. Meaning, memory structure, and mental processes. *Science*, 1976, *192*, 27–33.

Mitchell, D. B., & Perlmutter, M. *Encoding processes and memory performance in younger and older adults*. Unpublished manuscript, 1980.

Mitchell, D. B., & Perlmutter, M. *Consistency of associations and recall in young and old adults*. Manuscript in preparation, 1980.

Perlmutter, M. What is memory aging the aging of? *Developmental Psychology*, 1978, *14*, 330–345.

Perlmutter, M. Age differences in adults' free recall, cued recall, and recognition. *Journal of Gerontology*, 1979, *34*, 533–539. (a)

Perlmutter, M. Age differences in the consistency of adults' associative responses. *Experimental Aging Research*, 1979, *5*, 549–553. (b)

Perlmutter, M., Metzger, R., Nezworski, T., & Miller, K. Spatial and temporal memory in 20 and 60 year olds. *Journal of Gerontology*, 1981, *36*, 59–65.

Salthouse, T. A. Age and memory: Strategies for localizing the loss. In L. W. Poon, J. L. Fozard, L. S. Cermak, D. Arenberg, & L. W. Thompson (Eds.), *New directions in memory and aging*. Hillsdale, N.J.: Lawrence Erlbaum, 1980.

Shaffer, W. O., & LaBerge, D. Automatic semantic processing of unattended words. *Journal of Verbal Learning and Verbal Behavior,* 1979, *18,* 413–426.

Simon, E. Depth and elaboration of processing in relation to age. *Journal of Experimental Psychology: Human Learning and Memory,* 1979, *5,* 115–124.

Smith, A. D. Age differences in encoding, storage, and retrieval. In L. W. Poon, J. L. Fozard, L. S. Cermak, D. Arenberg, & L. W. Thompson (Eds.), *New directions in memory and aging.* Hillsdale, N.J.: Lawrence Erlbaum, 1980.

Smith, A. D., & Winograd, E. Adult age differences in remembering faces. *Developmental Psychology,* 1978, *14,* 443–444.

Till, R. E., & Walsh, D. A. Encoding and retrieval factors in adult memory for implicational sentences. *Journal of Verbal Learning and Verbal Behavior,* 1980, *19,* 1–16.

Walsh, D. A., & Jenkins, J. J. Effects of orienting tasks on free-recall in incidental learning: "Difficulty," "effort" and "process" explanations. *Journal of Verbal Learning and Verbal Behavior,* 1973, *12,* 481–488.

Waugh, N. C., & Barr, R. A. Memory and mental tempo. In L. W. Poon, J. L. Fozard, L. S. Cermak, D. Arenberg, & L. W. Thompson (Eds.), *New directions in memory and aging.* Hillsdale, N.J.: Lawrence Erlbaum, 1980.

Zelinski, E. M., Walsh, D. A., & Thompson, L. W. Orienting task effects on EDR and free recall in three age groups. *Journal of Gerontology,* 1978, *33,* 239–245.

CHAPTER 8

# General Encoding of Episodic Events by Elderly Adults

Jan C. Rabinowitz

*Department of Psychology*
*Erindale College*
*University of Toronto*
*Toronto, Ontario, Canada*

and

Brian P. Ackerman

*Department of Psychology*
*University of Delaware*
*Newark, Delaware*

It is almost a truism that memory in older people is much poorer than memory in younger people. These performance differences are most often found in typical laboratory experimental tasks requiring recall (and sometimes recognition) of recently experienced episodic events. The most common tasks require recall of previously studied lists of words, paired associates, or sentences. Age differences in these paradigms are often profound and occur under a wide variety of conditions (see Craik, 1977).

The purpose of the present experiments was to determine the nature of any processing (encoding) differences that might exist between young and old people. In particular, are there qualitative differences in the nature of the encodings or are they simply quantitative? Perlmutter and Mitchell (Chapter 7) argued that

This research was supported by a University of Toronto grant to the Centre for Research in Human Development.

"evaluations of encoding that are based only on inferences from memory performance rely upon circular reasoning, and thus, they are inadequate." The measures of memory performance referred to were comparisons of different encoding conditions across different types of tests (e.g., recall versus recognition). In addition to these memory measures, Perlmutter and Mitchell directly examined performance in various encoding tasks, such as encoding time as a function of distractor type and encoding task, and consistency of associations in a free-association task. Our approach, in contrast, returns to a direct reliance on memory measures, in which recall is measured with different types of retrieval cues. These experiments are based on the logic of the encoding specificity principle (Tulving, 1979). Memory performance is presumed to be determined by the match (informational overlap) between what was originally encoded and the information provided (or generated) at the time of test. The information available for retrieval can be manipulated by varying the type of retrieval cue provided to the subject by the experimenter. To the extent that the relative effectiveness of different types of retrieval cue varies between young and old adults, we can infer differences in the amounts of different types of information initially encoded.

This logic will be demonstrated with a concrete example which will also serve as the starting point for the present investigation. Simon (1979) presented subjects of different ages with sentences, each of which had an underlined to-be-remembered target noun. For different lists, subjects were instructed that their recall of the target nouns would be cued by either phonemic cues (the first two letters of each target noun) or semantic cues (synonyms of the target nouns). Although the younger subjects recalled more than the older subjects, there was an interaction between age and type of recall cue. Younger subjects recalled more words to semantic cues than to phonemic cues, whereas older subjects recalled more words to the phonemic cues than to the semantic cues. Stated another way, the magnitude of the age difference was greater with semantic cues than with phonemic cues.

These results suggest that semantic processing is particularly impaired in old adults relative to young adults. In a second experiment Simon (1979) presented the same stimulus materials to young subjects under speeded presentation conditions. The pattern of cued recall was now the same as that previously obtained with the older subjects. This suggests that the locus of the semantic processing deficit in older adults is primarily at encoding. What, then, is the nature of this semantic processing deficit? Are the semantic encodings of the old similar but quantitatively poorer than those of the young, or do they differ in some qualitative manner?

The hypothesis under investigation is that the semantic encodings of older people differ qualitatively from those of younger people. In particular, it is hypothesized that old people encode material in a rather general, prototypic manner on the basis of similarities with past experiences. Only general, or global, features of the event are encoded at the expense of specific features of the immediate context which are likely to differentiate the event from other similar events. In contrast, the encodings of younger people are likely to be more specific and will include those aspects of the immediate experimental context that are likely to differentiate each event from other similar events.

This hypothesis is supported by data from two recent experiments. Both Rankin and Kausler (1979) and Smith (1975) compared old and young people's performance in recogniton tasks in which the nature of the distractor items was systematically varied. In both of these experiments, older people made significantly more false alarms to distractors that were semantically related to target items (associates or synonyms) than did younger people. They did not differ, however, in their false alarm rates for unrelated distractors. The finding that old people made more false alarms to semantically related distractors than to unrelated distractors suggests that they were, indeed, encoding semantic information about the target items. However, the difference in the false alarm rates to the semantically related distractors as a function of age suggests that the semantic information that the older people encoded was not specific enough to differentiate the target events from other similar events. Rather, they seemed to be encoding global or general semantic information about the target items.

Following the logic of the encoding specificity principle, we directly compared these different types of encodings through the use of different types of retrieval cue. Specific encodings were assessed through retrieval cues that were a part of the initial study context. General encodings were assessed through either category cues which tap general or global properties of specific items, or strong semantic associates, which are presumed to be most similar to previous experiences with a particular item.

## Experiment 1

Two groups of old (mean age = 67) and two groups of young (mean age = 20) subjects participated in an incidental memory task. There were 10 subjects in each of the 4 experimental groups. Each subject was presented with a list of 40 critical words which had been selected so that each word came from a distinct semantic category (e.g., fruit, furniture). The subjects were induced to encode each word semantically by requiring them to generate a semantic associate to each item. Half of the subjects were required to generate a common semantic associate, which was defined as "one which comes quickly to mind, is likely to be generated by you at a later time, and is also likely to be generated by other people." The other half of the subjects were required to generate a unique semantic associate. This was defined as "an association based on some personal life experience with the item, which is also likely to be generated again at a later time, but which is not likely to be generated by other people."

Following the presentation of all of the items, the subjects were given an unexpected cued recall test. Half of the items were cued by the specific associate that the subject had generated for that item earlier. Subjects were required to recall the item to which that associate had been generated. The other half of the items were cued by common category labels. The subjects were told that one item from that category had been presented earlier, and they were to try to recall that item.

Subjects who had generated common associations recalled more words than those who had generated unique associations. This held for both age groups and for both types of retrieval cue. Neither of these latter two factors interacted with the type of association that had been generated; the data were therefore collapsed over this factor.

The proportions of words recalled, as a function of age and type of retrieval cue, are presented in Table 1. The young subjects recalled more words when cued by the association that they had generated earlier in the experiment than when they were cued by category labels. The old subjects recalled just as many words to the category labels as they did to the associations that they had generated. The interaction between these two factors was significant, $F(1,36) = 4.95$, $p < .05$.

A similar result has been reported by Perlmutter (1979). She presented single words to old and young subjects and required them to generate a number of free associations to each word. They were then cued for recall by either the first association that they had generated to each word or the most common associate of each word, based on published word-association norms. Whereas younger subjects recalled significantly more words when cued by their own associations than when cued by normed associations, there was no difference between these two cue types for the older subjects.

These results suggest that older people are just as likely to encode general aspects or properties of the presented material as are young people but are less likely to encode specific features of the presented context, even when this con-

*Table 1. Proportions of Words Recalled in Experiment 1*

| | Retrieval cue | |
|---|---|---|
| | Category | Associate |
| Young | .70 | .87 |
| Old | .66 | .70 |

text is one that they themselves have generated. Our conclusion is that the memory traces of the older people contain relatively more general than specific information as compared with those of the younger people.

## Experiment 2

Many of the standard context effects found in the memory literature are based on the fact that young people integrate the experimental context with the target material at the time of encoding. Access to the target material is then best when the original experimental context is presented again at retrieval. If older people are encoding material generally and integrating the experimental context with the target item to a lesser extent, then many of the standard context effects that have been demonstrated in young subjects should not be so evident with older people.

One of the earliest and most powerful context effects was the one demonstrated by Thomson and Tulving (1970). Contrary to much of the current wisdom of the time, they found that when weakly associated pairs such as *glue–CHAIR* were presented, the word *CHAIR* was better recalled when the original weak cue (*glue*) was re-presented than when a strong associate (e.g., *table*) that had not been originally presented with the to-be-remembered word was presented as a cue for retrieval. That is, weakly related intra-list cues were more effective than strong extra-list cues. We sought to replicate this finding with young people. It was predicted, however, that this finding would not be obtained with older people. If they are encoding items generally and not integrating them with the experimental context, then previously presented weak cues should not be better retrieval cues than strong, extra-list, semantic associates.

Twenty-four young (mean age = 20) and 24 old (mean age = 69) subjects participated in the experiment. The experiment was almost an exact replication of Thomson and Tulving's (1970) Experiment III. Each subject was presented with two lists, under intentional learning instructions. Each list consisted of 24 paired associates. Half of the pairs were weakly related and half were strongly related. The pairs were presented visually, at a rate of 5 sec/pair.

After presentation of the first list, each target word was cued with the word with which it had been originally paired, as the subjects had expected. After a 10-minute filler task, the second list was presented, with identical study instructions. For this list, though, only half of the target items (6 targets from weak pairs and 6 targets from strong pairs) were cued with the words that had originally been presented with them. The remaining items were cued with extra-list cues. Each of the six targets that had been presented as members of weak pairs (e.g., *glue–CHAIR*) was now cued with a strongly associated word (e.g., *table*), and each of the six targets that had been presented as members of strong pairs (e.g., *lake*–WATER) was now tested with a weak associate (e.g., *whisky*). The 24 cue words were randomly arranged in a single column. The subjects were told that they had seen some of the cue words before and that they should try to recall the words that were presented with each of them. They were also informed that other cue words had not been presented before but that they were related to target words from the list. The subjects were asked to try to recall a word that was associated with each of these cues and that was also a target member of one of the pairs that they had seen. They were encouraged to guess when they were uncertain.

The results are shown in Table 2, along with the data from Thomson and Tulving's (1970) Experiment III for comparison. Another group of 16 old subjects were also tested with identical instructions and materials but with a 10 sec/pair presentation rate. These data are also shown in Table 2.

The original "encoding specificity effect," better recall to the same weak cues than to the changed strong cues, was replicated in our sample of young subjects, but the older subjects failed to show this effect. Their recall to the changed strong cues was just as good as their recall to the same weak cues. The locus of this age × cue type interaction, $F(1,46) = 5.07$, $p < .05$, is clear. Recall to the changed strong cues was unaffected by age. Recall to these cues can be taken as an index of the degree to which general aspects of the target nouns have been encoded. Thus, old and young subjects encode general semantic properties equally well. However, young subjects' recall to the same weak cues is better than that of the old subjects. This effect was also observed on list 1. These pairs require subjects to integrate the cue and target in a novel relation, and older subjects were not very successful at this task. Note, however, that the older subjects did quite well at integrating cue–target pairs that tapped common semantic relations, as indicated by the high level of recall to the same strong cues.

*Table 2. Proportions of Words Recalled in Experiment 2*[a]

| | List 1 | | List 2 | | | |
|---|---|---|---|---|---|---|
| | Same cues | | Same cues | | Different cues | |
| | Strong | Weak | Strong | Weak | Strong | Weak |
| Thomson & Tulving (Exp. III, 1970) | .84 | .75 | .83 | .73 | .33 | .04 |
| Young | .94 | .90 | .92 | .85 | .68 | .07 |
| Old | .88 | .68 | .83 | .62 | .63 | .03 |
| Old (10 sec replication) | .94 | .70 | .92 | .62 | .67 | .00 |

[a]Strong and weak cues refer to the type of cue used for retrieval.

## Experiment 3

What determines the degree to which a given encoding is general? This final experiment sought to manipulate the degree to which general, global aspects of a target word are encoded by varying the amount of contextual, semantic elaboration provided by the experimenter. It was predicted that as the amount of contextual elaboration is increased, more specific, unique relations will be encoded, at the expense of general features of the target word. Thus, recall to general (category) cues should actually be worse for items embedded in a rich semantic context as compared to a less rich semantic context. Baker and Santa (1977) demonstrated a similar effect with young subjects who either learned a list of words or elaborated them by linking images of successively presented items. Cued recall to extra-list, strong semantic associates was slightly better for the "learned" words than for the imaged words, while the reverse was true for free recall.

Will the general encodings of older adults be affected in the same manner? If older people make less use of the presentation context to modify their encoding, as the first two experiments suggested, then the general aspects of their encoding should be less affected by the amount of semantic elaboration provided at the time of presentation. Therefore, it was predicted that the effectiveness of general category cues would not vary as a function of elaboration for older subjects, whereas for younger subjects general cues would actually be less effective for material presented in rich, elaborated contexts.

The amount of semantic elaboration was manipulated by presenting target nouns either in adjective–noun pairs or in sentences. An example of a pair is: *diluted–**bourbon**.* The corresponding sentence is: *The frugal businessman served his guests diluted **bourbon**.* The general category cue is *alcoholic beverage*.

Each subject was presented with either 36 critical paired associates or 36 critical sentences. In addition, there were three primacy and three recency items. Thirty-two old (mean age = 69) and 32 young (mean age = 21) subjects participated in the experiment. Half of the subjects in each age group received the sentences, while the remaining half received the adjective–noun pairs.

The subjects were told to study each sentence (or adjective–noun pair) and to pay particular attention to the final noun, which was underlined. They were told that their memory for these nouns would be tested later, although the manner in which the items would be tested was not specified. The subjects were instructed to think of the noun in relation to the adjective (or the rest of the sentence) because this would help them. The materials were presented visually, typed on separate pages of little booklets. The subjects were given 10 seconds to study each sentence or pair.

Following the study phase, the test booklets were given to the subjects. The target nouns had been selected so that each one came from a distinct semantic

*Table 3. Proportion of Words Recalled in Experiment 3*

| | Encoding | |
|---|---|---|
| | P–A | Sentence |
| Young | .65 | .54 |
| Old | .48 | .50 |

category; the test booklet contained the names of these semantic categories. (The 3 primacy and 3 recency items were tested first but were not scored.) The subjects were told that one member of each category had been presented to them as an underlined noun, and they were asked to recall each item in response to its category label. They were required to produce a response to each label even if it meant simply guessing a category instance. All subjects complied with these instructions.

The results are shown in Table 3. Overall, the young subjects recalled more correct words in response to the category labels than did the old subjects. The effect of materials is of particular interest: Young subjects recalled more target nouns from the adjective–noun pairs than from the sentences, whereas the older subjects' recall did not differ as a function of the type of material. While the pattern of these results is exactly as predicted, the age × materials interaction was not significant. These results must therefore be interpreted with some caution.

In general, however, the results support our prediction that the degree to which encoding includes general aspects of the to-be-remembered material will vary as a function of the amount of context provided. The sentences provided rich semantic elaborations in comparison to the adjective–noun pairs, and these specific elaborations were encoded at the expense of general characteristics of the target nouns. Older people, however, were apparently unaffected by the encoding context, at least in terms of the degree to which general aspects of the target nouns were encoded.

## Conclusions

The experiments reported here support the hypothesis that old people encode material more generally, in terms of global semantic characteristics, and are less likely to encode specific, unique features of the experimental context. As a result, they have difficulty integrating novel relations and are less affected by context then are the young. What is the cause of these processing differences? It seems reasonable to suggest that integrating unique features of the experimental context and elaborating the to-be-remembered material can place heavy demands on cognitive resources. Encoding general, or global, semantic characteristics appears to be a well-practiced task, which can be performed relatively automatically (Hasher & Zacks, 1979) or with a minimum of resource. Thus, if older people have fewer processing resources available or are unwilling to expend these resources, their encoding of specific information will suffer, relative to younger people. Instead, they may encode only those general, global aspects of the material that can be encoded with a minimum of cognitive resource.

Craik has recently carried out a series of experiments with young subjects in which the amount of resources available for encoding was reduced by requiring subjects to perform a second concurrent task while studying the to-be-remembered items. Under these divided-attention conditions, subsequent memory performance is impaired, but, more importantly, the qualitiative patterns of performance are similar to those shown by older adults (see Chapter 11). We are currently attempting to produce some of the general encoding effects reported here with older people, in younger subjects under divided-attention conditions.

Two important goals for further research in this area are first, to delineate the reasons why older adults suffer from reduced cognitive resource, as the divided-attention results suggest, and second, to ascertain the degree to which the resulting encoding deficiencies can be remedied through the use of specific orienting tasks or other mnemonic techniques.

ACKNOWLEDGMENTS

The authors are grateful to Fergus I. M. Craik for his continued support throughout this research project and to Marjorie Swanson for coordinating our group of older subjects.

# References

Baker, L., & Santa, J. L. Context, integration, and retrieval. *Memory & Cognition, 1977, 5,* 308–314.

Craik, F. I. M. Age differences in human memory. In J. E. Birren & K. W. Schaie (Eds.), *Handbook of the psychology of aging.* New York: Van Nostrand Reinhold, 1977.

Hasher, L., & Zacks, R. T. Automatic and effortful processes in memory. *Journal of Experimental Psychology: General,* 1979, *108,* 356–388.

Perlmutter, M. Age differences in adults' free recall, cued recall, and recognition. *Journal of Gerontology,* 1979, *34,* 533–539.

Rankin, J. L., & Kausler, D. H. Adult age differences in false recognitions. *Journal of Gerontology,* 1979, *34,* 58–65.

Simon, E. Depth and elaboration of processing in relation to age. *Journal of Experimental Psychology: Human Learning and Memory,* 1979, *5,* 115–124.

Smith, A. D. Partial learning and recognition memory in the aged. *International Journal of Aging and Human Development,* 1975, *6,* 359–365.

Thomson, D. M., & Tulving, E. Associative encoding and retrieval: Weak and strong cues. *Journal of Experimental Psychology,* 1970, *86,* 255–262.

Tulving, E. Relation between encoding specificity and levels of processing. In L. S. Cermak & F. I. M. Craik (Eds.), *Levels of processing in human memory.* Hillsdale, N.J.: Lawrence Erlbaum, 1979.

CHAPTER 9

# Learning and Memory Deficits in Institutionalized and Noninstitutionalized Old People

## An Analysis of Interference Effects

Gordon Winocur

*Department of Psychology*
*Trent University*
*Peterborough, Ontario, Canada*

## Introduction

This chapter addresses several issues related to declining learning and memory performance in the aged. In particular, attention is focused on the role of interference, which for many years was regarded as the single most important factor underlying cognitive decline in old people. Recently, however, it has become apparent that, despite its parsimony and wide appeal, the interference hypothesis lacks a solid empirical base. Design flaws in some of the relevant studies and conflicting results in others have raised considerable doubt as to whether the aged are indeed more susceptible to interference than the young. In view of the theoretical and practical importance of this controversy, a systematic examination of interference effects was undertaken and results of this research are reported here.

Funding was provided by grants from the Medical Research Council of Canada and the Ontario Mental Health Foundation.

A second issue concerns techniques that may be useful in compensating for the cognitive deficits of older people and improving their performance on tests of learning and memory. This is also an area that has attracted increased attention in recent years, and there are now several reports of reduced impairment in aged subjects following specific instruction in the use of various mnemonic or strategic aids. It may be that such techniques exert their benefits by helping the elderly to overcome the negative effects of interference. Several of our experiments that have dealt directly with the potential usefulness of specific cuing procedures have yielded results suggesting that this is, at least partly, the case.

In our experiments, we compare the performance of aged populations living in institutions with those living at home. Intuitively, it is often assumed that institutionalized old people are more handicapped than people at home and that this is reflected in their cognitive functioning. However, there is a surprising lack of data to indicate that differences do, in fact, exist. The present research responds to this lack and in addition is concerned with the nature and extent of any such differences.

Finally, consideration is given to cognitive decline in relation to changes in brain function. There is now a substantial literature that implicates the hippocampus in specific aspects of the learning and memory disorders associated with the aged. Our own research involving brain-damaged animals and humans suggests that the hippocampus may be especially important for tasks involving high interference. Accordingly, the performance of old people on tests involving varying amounts of interference was examined to determine whether a similar pattern emerges.

## Interference

Ruch (1934) was among the first to suggest a relation between impaired cognitive functioning in the aged and a failure to cope with interfering associations. Ruch compared the performance of old and young subjects on a series of verbal and nonverbal tests which included standard measures of pursuit-rotor ability and paired-associate learning involving familiar, logically related words. Other tests required greater reorganization of well-established habits. For example, one test required subjects to learn nonsense equations using alphabet letters (e.g., $L \times P = Q$) while another involved the use of numbers in learning false equations (e.g., $5 \times 3 = 6$). Ruch found that old people were generally inferior to younger subjects but that age differences were greatest for the high-interference tasks.

Gilbert (1941) studied various types of memory loss in the aged as a function of several variables, including interference and meaningfulness. Her test battery included visual and auditory digit span, sentence and paragraph recall, memory for designs, and several paired-associate tasks, including one that involved Turkish stimulus words and their English equivalents as responses. The results indicated a reliable decrease in memory functioning in older subjects, with interference emerging as the single most important factor contributing to their deficit. Differences between young and old people were especially apparent in the high-interference, Turkish–English test. Gilbert commented on the decreased flexibility of old people and attributed their impaired performance to rigid strategies that prevented the types of associations necessary for efficient learning.

In a test of retroactive interference, Cameron (1943) compared the abilities of young and old people to recall a series of three-digit numbers at varying intervals. As in the Ruch and Gilbert studies, old subjects generally performed worse, but differences were greatest when an interpolated task (word spelling) provided a source of interference between original learning and recall.

In recent years experimenters, using more sophisticated experimental designs, have also reported evidence pointing to the importance of interference in age-related learning and memory decline. For example, Lair, Moon, and Kausler (1969) used a cross-associates procedure to demonstrate the importance of explicit response competition in the build-up of interference. Coppinger and Nehrke (1972) used a nonverbal transfer-of-learning test involving intra- and extradimensional stimulus shifts to demonstrate that the aged focus too restrictively on specific stimulus attributes. By neglecting conceptual information that could mediate between related tasks, they learned less efficiently and were more susceptible to interfering influences than younger people. Zaretsky and Halberstam (1968) systematically varied the associative strength of paired-associate items in a comparison of learning ability of young and old people. The results revealed an age-related deficit and a differential effect of associative strength that represented the greater difficulty of elderly subjects on high-interference tasks that involved learning new relations.

Thus, the evidence appeared to support overwhelmingly the notion that increasing age is accompanied by an increased vulnerability to interference (see also reviews by Arenberg, 1973; Welford, 1958). On the other hand, other investigators have questioned the legitimacy of some of this evidence. At least two recent reviews (Arenberg & Robertson-Tchabo, 1977; Craik, 1977) have drawn attention to methodological weaknesses in several early studies. Of particular concern is the frequent failure to equate original learning between young and old subjects. As a result, performance differences may reflect a basic inefficiency, on the part of the aged, in acquiring new information rather than an increased susceptibility to interfering influences. This point is highlighted in an experiment by Hulicka (1967), who tested recall of paired-associate items following varying amounts of interpolated activity. A significant age $\times$ interference interaction was observed when the level of original learning was lower in older subjects. When all subjects were allowed to learn the list to the same criterion, the interaction disappeared. Similar results were reported by Wimer and Wigdor (1958). Unfortunately, in both studies the tasks proved to be more difficult for older subjects, who required more trials to reach criterion than younger adults. Thus, the effect of removing unequal learning levels as a potential confound was to introduce varying amounts of training as another.

Aside from methodological problems, several studies have failed to provide support for an interference interpretation of age-related learning and memory deficits. For example, Gladis and Braun (1958) trained subjects to associate stimulus letter combinations (e.g., TL) with familiar response words (e.g., *insane*) and then presented the same stimuli along with new words of varying similarity to the original response words (e.g., high: *crazy;* medium: *deranged;* low: *balmy;* neutral: *oral*). Finally, subjects were asked to remember as many of the original response associates as possible. The results showed strong main effects of age and similarity between interpolated material and original items, but there was no evidence of an interaction, as would be expected if interference effects were acting differentially upon the aged.

Smith (1975) used a probe technique to study interference effects on short- and long-term memory of paired-associate lists in young and old age groups. The results indicated an age-related decrement in long-term recall, but there was no evidence that interference had a differential effect on either age group.

Unfortunately, procedural flaws can also be identified in some of the studies purporting to show a lack of interaction between age and interference. For example, Canestrari (1966) compared young and old people on a task requiring them to learn new response associates to stimulus words that varied in terms of number of preexisting associations. It was found that all groups experienced comparable amounts of interference or facilitation in learning the new lists. There was no evidence of increased interference in the older groups, but the representativeness of this sample is suspect since only the more highly educated members of the available population were included in the experiment. It is probable, and indeed Gilbert (1941) has evidence to suggest, that bright people are less prone to interference effects with advancing age and consequently suffer less cognitive decline than less intelligent individuals of comparable age.

Sampling procedures may have had a greater biasing effect than previously thought on results obtained with respect to interference. For example, of the studies reported in the last 50 years that deal specifically with intereference effects, the majority of those reporting clearly significant age × interference interaction effects involved subject samples drawn from institutionalized populations. Typical of these are Cameron (1943), Coppinger and Nehrke (1972), and Lair *et al.* (1969). On the other hand, those experimenters reporting no differential effects of interference have tended to draw their subjects from the community at large (e.g., Gladis & Braun, 1958; Nehrke, 1973; Smith, 1975). There are, of course, exceptions to this broad classification (most notably Ruch, who tested only old people living at home). Nevertheless, a review of the literature reveals a clear pattern along these lines.

The effects of institutionalization on the aged has been studied more than any other environmental influence, and substantial information is available concerning, its impact on physical and mental health (see reviews by Kasl & Rosenfield, 1980; Lawton, 1977). Although it is difficult to separate relocation, prior history, and other factors from the effects of institutionalization, the consensus is that the institutionalized elderly, when compared to their community counterparts, suffer higher mortality rates (Goldfarb, 1964), a greater variety and number of psychiatric illnesses (Muller & Lieberman, 1965), and more serious social and morale problems (Kasl, 1972). It is generally assumed that the elderly living in institutions are also worse off with respect to cognitive functioning and, although the little concrete information available on this subject is consistent with this position (e.g., Klonoff & Kennedy, 1966), there is a surprising lack of experimentation dealing with this important subject.

Thus, the present research had two major objectives with respect to interference: (1) to determine whether, indeed, interference differentially affects the learning and memory capabilities of the elderly and (2) to compare the performance of institutionalized and noninstitutionalized old people on our tasks in an attempt to establish a possible link between factors related to institutionalization and susceptibility to interference.

## Control of Learning and Memory Deficits

It is well established that learning and memory impairment associated with the aged can be related, in part, to the adoption of inefficient strategies during information processing. For example, Craik and Byrd (Chapter 11) present evidence indicating that verbal encoding strategies of old people, while normal with respect to structural and phonetic attributes, do not adequately incorporate higher-order semantic meaning. Rabbitt (Chapter 5) discusses the limited processing capabilities of old people and, in particular, focuses on their inability to switch attention on tasks requiring shifts in mental set. During information retrieval, the elderly appear deficient in search operations, as evidenced by their superior performance when required to recognize correctly rather than recall target items.

One area in which strategic aids have proven useful is with respect to the organization of stimulus items. Old people do not spontaneously organize material into manageable groupings that provide for more elaborate encoding, resistance to interference, and generally efficient learning and memory. However, when they are encouraged to do so, their test performance improves significantly. In a study by Smith (reported by Schonfield, 1980), old people were presented with lists of low-associate paired words under whole- or part-learning conditions. In the whole condition the lists were presented without interruption in the usual manner, while in the part-learning condition the items were divided into groups of 2, 3, or 4 stimulus–response pairs. The typically observed age-related impairment was observed when the lists were presented as a whole, but significant improvement occurred when the material was presented in sections. Presumably, old people encoded the stimulus material more efficiently when it was presented in smaller units, although it may be noted that young people benefited comparably from the part-learning procedure.

The memory of old people is also hampered by their failure to organize stimulus material into meaningful units. Laurence (1967) compared old and young people's recall of a 36-word list composed of six different categories. The elderly were significantly impaired under conditions of free recall, but when category cues were provided there were no differences between groups. Cuing only at original learning did not lead to similar results, but in this case procedural factors may have operated against improvement. Hultsch (1969, 1971) found that instructing subjects to organize according to category, in terms of their first letters, or, for that matter, any association that came to mind, was equally effective in improving subsequent recall performance in the elderly.

In a recent study, Hultsch (1974) found that old people spontaneously adopt more efficient organizational strategies with familiar tasks. Two successive multitrial free-recall tests were administered to subjects of various age groups. Analysis of list 2 performance in the aged groups indicated a transition from negative transfer in the early trials to positive transfer during the final stages of learning. The progressive improvement in recall of list 2 was accompanied by improved organization of stimulus items, although young people also benefited from the practice and, as with the Smith study, measures of organization did not interact with age. Taub (1973) used digit strings and obtained similar results by instructing subjects to rehearse between successive tests of recall.

Another way to compensate for age-related decrements in cognitive functioning is to encourage old people to use mediational devices in learning new material. Crovitz (1966) found improved discrimination learning by elderly subjects if they were specifically instructed to verbalize the relevant dimensions of the discriminanda. Crovitz did not test young control groups, but in a related study Hulicka and Grossman (1967) administered a paired-associate task to subjects of varying ages with instructions to employ different strategies in learning the list. Old people's learning was significantly better when they were advised to use verbal or imaginal mediators than when they were given no specific instructions. Young subjects also benefited from mediation instructions but their improvement was relatively less than that of old people.

It has been suggested that in addition to impaired strategies a combination of performance variables, including reduced motivation and heightened anxiety, contribute to learning and memory deficits in the aged. There is evidence that as older individuals become increasingly dependent on others and personal effort becomes less of a factor in attaining goals, a corresponding lowering of aspiration level is likely to occur (see reviews by Elias & Elias, 1977; Wigdor, 1980). Moreover, the frustration of increasing numbers of past failures is likely to raise stress levels and adversely affect performance on demanding new tasks. Since these are acquired and not necessarily irreversible characteristics, it is reasonable to expect that control procedures could effectively counteract their disruptive effects and lead to improved learning and memory performance.

Research dealing with this aspect of age differences has been limited, but two relevant examples may be cited. Ross (1968) administered paired-associate learning tasks to different age groups following pretest instructions that were described as neutral, supportive, or challenging in style. The results indicated that elderly subjects did best following supportive, and worst following challenging instructions. In general, their performance was inferior to controls but the prediction of an interaction whereby age differences would be smallest following supportive instructions did not materialize.

In another study, this time involving institutionalized subjects, Langer, Rodin, Beck, Weinman, and Spitzer (in press) attempted to improve memory for events and pictures by providing specific instructions designed to encourage greater use of cognitive abilities. Motivation was varied in one condition by the type of social interaction between experimenter and subject and, in another, by linking practical rewards to performance. The results showed that either type of incentive was sufficient to bring about significant improvement in performance. Moreover, informal observations indicated that subjects in the high incentive conditions were consistently rated highest in terms of general awareness, activity, and social interaction.

Unfortunately, Langer *et al.* did not include control groups to indicate whether the observed changes also occur in younger people or, for that matter, in old people who are not institutionalized. In fairness, the latter comparisons are rarely made but, as indicated earlier with respect to interference effects, important differences may exist between institutionalized and noninstitutionalized individuals. The general rule seems to be that elderly people residing at home and young people benefit comparably from control procedures (e.g., Hultsch, 1974; Taub, 1973), whereas the institutionalized aged are aided differentially (e.g., Hulicka & Grossman, 1967). The exception may occur when category cues are used to facilitate free recall. Hultsch (1975) found that such cuing helped old people more than young on measures of word and category recall, although the interaction was not significant in terms of the number of words recalled per category. Similar results were reported by Laurence (1967) in the study cited earlier.

The lack of interactions in experiments with noninstitutionalized subjects should not detract from the importance of demonstrating that, with appropriate aids, significant (if not differential) improvement can be achieved in the learning and memory performance of aged people. Such findings, as Schonfield (1980) has already noted, are of considerable practical, if less theoretical, significance. On the other hand, the suggestion that institutionalized people do respond more to cuing and instructional aids may be indicative of fundamental and qualitative changes in their cognitive functioning. This possibility is taken up in the present research, which includes an assessment of potential benefits of specific cueing procedures.

## Brain Mechanisms

Since the pioneering work of Milner in the 1950s, the hippocampus has been widely implicated in the mediation of learning and memory (see Chapter 1). Milner's observations (1959) were based largely on the classic patient, H. M., who in his late 20s sustained a bilateral hippocampectomy in treatment of a severe epileptic condition. The operation successfully relieved the epilepsy but left H. M. with a severe amnesia primarily for postsurgical events. In another study, Milner (1957) examined patients with medial temporal lobe damage and found a significant correlation between degree of memory loss and hippocampal destruction. Although damage in these patients frequently extended beyond the hippocampus, no other structure yielded this pattern. Other investigators (e.g., Lhermitte & Signoret, 1976) have similarly concluded that the intact hippocampus is essential for normal learning and memory, although there is considerable disagreement concerning the precise nature of its involvement (see review by O'Keefe & Nadel, 1978).

The hippocampus seems particularly vulnerable to the aging process, and there have been numerous reports of physical changes in this structure that could underlie the types of learning and memory deficit observed in elderly people (Bondareff, 1980). These changes include an early accumulation of the fatty pigment lipofuscin, which is correlated with a decline in the rate of RNA synthesis in hippocampal cells. The presence of neurofibrillary tangles, which reflect abnormal protein metabolism and ultimately lead to neuronal death, is especially marked in the hippocampus. Senile plaques, which consist of granular debris surrounded by glial cells, occur most frequently in the hippocampus as well as in frontal and temporal cortical areas. Plaques are related to the neurofibrillary neuronal changes and contribute to the degenerative process. Finally, research on the rat brain has indicated an age-related hypertrophic astrocyte reaction that is largely confined to the hippocampal region (Landfield, 1977). This hypertrophy may be a factor in the high incidence of synaptic decay and altered dendrite branching associated with aging hippocampal cells. Electrophysiologically, the effect of such structural changes is to limit severely long-term synaptic potentiation of neural firing, a phenomenon believed to be fundamental to the establishment of a memory trace (Barnes, 1979).

For obvious reasons, there is little opportunity to study the effects of selective hippocampal damage on human cognitive functioning. Instead, research for the most part must be confined to patients with known or suspected hippocampal damage caused by closed head injuries or neurological disease. In recent years, considerable attention has focused on Korsakoff syndrome, a condition involving pathology of limbic-diencephalic mechanisms, typically resulting from excessive alcoholism. Although damage associated with this disease can be extensive, it frequently involves the hippocampal system. Of particular interest are the important parallels that can be drawn between the cognitive performance of Korsakoff patients, H. M., and the normal aged.

Korsakoff patients are, of course, more impaired than old people on most behavioral measures but, allowing for quantitative differences, the patterns of deficit are strikingly similar. There is some controversy regarding short-term retention (see Butters & Cermak, 1975), but both groups exhibit normal primary memory and comparable deficits in learning and recalling new information over extended periods of time. They are, for example, reliably impaired in verbal learning tasks when the associative strength of the words is low. Both groups also tend to perform better on tests of recognition memory than free recall, where no retrieval cues are available. In general, Korsakoff patients and old people benefit in similar ways from cuing techniques and specific instructions that encourage the use of organizational strategies, mediating devices, and more elaborate processing of stimulus material.

Of particular interest is evidence that performance deficits of brain-damaged amnesics are linked to an exaggerated susceptibility to interference effects. For example, Starr and Phillips (1970) found that a postencephalitic amnesic's ability to learn a serial list of familiar words was adversely affected by prior training on similar lists. The patient's tendency was to emit words that had appeared on earlier lists. Interference phenomena in amnesic patients have been systematically studied by Warrington and Weiskrantz (1973), who in one series of experiments attempted to reduce amnesics' learning and memory impairment by providing cues designed to lessen response interference. The procedure was to present fragmented but unrecognizable versions of stimulus materials as cues at retention testing. This treatment led to reduced response competition in amnesic patients and resulted in substantial improvement in recall.

Winocur and Weiskrantz (1976) confirmed amnesics' vulnerability to interference using retroactive- and proactive-interference paradigms. Amnesics' ability to learn and recall lists of high-associate paired words was a direct function of their experience prior to testing. When related tasks were introduced to increase response competition, amnesics' test performance deteriorated and was characterized by large numbers of intrusions from prior learning. However, under conditions of low interference, the performance of amnesics approximated that of controls.

There has been considerable speculation as to the brain regions most directly implicated in the learning and memory deficits associated with the amnesic syndrome. The structure frequently cited as the most likely candidate is the hippocampus and, significantly, animal research involving controlled surgical procedures has strongly supported this position. In a particularly relevant experiment, Correll and Scoville (1965) employed a design that is similar in principle to paradigms frequently used in human research. They found that monkeys with medial temporal lobe lesions (involving extensive hippocampal damage) were impaired in recalling a previously learned visual discrimination when each stimulus had multiple associates but not when associations for each stimulus were minimal. The deficit was attributed to the high level of interference that was built into the task.

Winocur and Mills (1970) studied the effects of more restricted lesions to the hippocampus of rats on a high-interference test involving negative transfer. Subjects preoperatively learned a black-white discrimination and were postoperatively tested on a pattern discrimination which included elements of the original task. All groups took more trials to learn the pattern discrimination with prior training than without, but a significant groups x condition interaction indicated that animals with hippocampal lesions were most affected by the high interference.

For many years, an apparent contradiction in the hippocampal literature was the consistent failure to demonstrate, in hippocampus-damaged animals, the memory loss reliably observed in comparably damaged humans. Indeed, hippocampal animals displayed normal learning and recall on a variety of tasks including classical conditioning, simultaneous discrimination, and continuous reinforcement operant conditioning. These results were taken by some as evidence that the structure mediates different functions in humans and lower animals (see Douglas, 1967). However, closer examination of test procedures across species reveals significant differences that could account for the discrepancy. In contrast to human experimentation, where the potential for interference is considerable, in animal tests of memory special care is usually taken to ensure that original learning and recall conditions are as similar as possible with a minimum of interference. It follows, therefore, that manipulations that increase interference should correspondingly impair memory performance in animals with hippocampal lesions.

This prediction was confirmed in an experiment by Jarrard (1975), using a retroactive-interference design. Groups of hippocampal and control rats were preoperatively trained on a spatial-alternation habit and postoperatively retested with or without interpolated exposure to forced running in a circular activity wheel. All groups displayed good retention in the absence of interpolated activity, but hippocampal animals with such intervening activity were selectively impaired.

In a related experiment (Winocur, 1979), hippocampal and control groups of rats initially learned a pattern discrimination and, before recall testing, were subjected to one of three tasks varying in similarity to the test problem. All groups learned the original discrimination within normal limits and there were no retention differences in the relatively low interference conditions. There was, however, a significant effect in the high-interference conditions where hippocampal animals required more trials to reestablish criterion and showed less savings than the control groups.

As indicated earlier, impairment of organic amnesics and old people can be reduced with the help of cuing techniques that reduce response competition. Analogous experiments conducted with hippocampus-damaged animals have produced similar results. In a test of passive-avoidance conditioning, Winocur and Black (1978) trained groups of hippocampal and control rats to run down an alley for water reward in a distinctive goal box. When approach behavior had stabilized, the goal box was electrified, resulting in a cessation of running by controls on subsequent trials. Animals with hippocampal damage readily learned the approach response but continued to perform that response following punishment. However, when reminded of the aversive experience by being placed in a replica of the goal box prior to testing, passive avoidance behavior of hippocampal animals could not be differentiated from that of controls. Similar results have been obtained by using cuing procedures in other tasks (e.g., maze learning, operant condition, reversal learning) in which animals with hippocampal lesions are typically impaired.

As a cautionary note, it is important to recognize that other structures have also been linked to learning and memory processes. The dorsal medial thalamus has received considerable attention since Victor, Adams, and Collins (1971) identified a high incidence of damage to this region in cases of Korsakoff syndrome. In addition, there is strong evidence linking the frontal lobe, mammillary bodies, and fornix pathway to learning and memory processes.

In an important paper, Horel (1978) has argued that the hippocampus may not necessarily be crucial for operations basic to learning and memory. He cites numerous examples of apparently normal memory in animals and humans with hippocampal damage as well as impaired memory in subjects with intact hippocampi but with damage to other regions. Essentially, Horel argues that in those "hippocampal" cases in which memory defects do occur, careful anatomical analysis consistently reveals damage to the temporal stem, a pathway that connects the temporal lobe and amygdala with a number of subcortical structures including the dorsal medial thalamus and frontal lobe area, but not the hippocampus. When selective lesions were made to the temporal stem or hippocampus in monkeys, far greater anterograde and retrograde amnesia was found in the temporal stem preparations. In support of his position, Horel reports evidence that combined lesions to the amygdala and hippocampus produced profound deficits in acquisition and retention, whereas selective amygdala or hippocampal lesions had little or no effect. The combined lesions, unlike the more restricted lesions, probably caused temporal stem damage which could account for the deficits.

An important feature of Horel's studies is that they involved tasks that are relatively interference-free. For example, some were tests of short-term memory that involved brief intervals of only a few seconds between stimulus presentation and response (e.g., delayed response, delayed matching from sample) with no distractions during that period. Others tested retention of learned simultaneous discriminations, in which the conditions associated with recall were identical to conditions at original learning. In these tests, virtually all the necessary stimulus cues associated with the previously learned responses are readily available so that, in the absence of competing associations, the process of response selection becomes a relatively simple one. When interference is introduced, for example through interpolated experience (Jarrard, 1975; Winocur, 1979), recall of a previously acquired response declines substantially.

Thus, the role of the hippocampus in learning and memory may be an indirect consequence of its more basic function in complex situations requiring the control of interference. It had been widely held that exaggerated perseverative tendencies and failure to suppress inappropriate responses following hippocampal damage are the result of a disinhibitory effect at the behavioral level. However, subsequent research has not supported this view, and recently there has been a shift to more cognitively oriented interpretations (O'Keefe & Nadel, 1978). On the basis of the type of deficit that can be reliably associated with hippocampal damage and the success of cuing procedures in compensating for such deficits, an information-processing dysfunction related to the utilization of available stimulus cues has been proposed (Winocur, 1980, 1982). According to this view, subjects with hippocampal damage are deficient in their ability to extract information from the environment and, as a result, may form less efficient strategies in adapting to situational requirements. Performance is unaffected in relatively straightforward tests of learning and memory, but an intact hippocampus becomes important when tasks are more complex and involve integration of spatially or temporally separated cues, stimuli that change their significance following conflicting experiences or, in the human case, where efficient learning depends on sophisticated semantic analysis. In such cases, hippocampal damage results in incomplete processing, a greater vulnerability to interference, and, ultimately, behavioral deficits.

The notion that the hippocampus is crucial for coping with interference derives support mainly from animal experimentation and to a certain extent from observations of brain-damaged humans. The aging literature has scarcely addressed this issue despite evidence of hippocampal dysfunction in the aging brain and the traditional belief that cognitive processes in the aged are limited by a susceptibility to interference. Thus, an investigation of age-related learning and memory deficits, using tasks believed to bear on hippocampal function, would seem to be appropriate and represents a major objective of the research reported in the following section.

## Empirical Studies

### *Subjects*

Subjects were drawn from populations of young (20–35 years) and old (70–85 years) people living in Peterborough, Ontario, and the surrounding area. All experiments involved three groups: (1) an institutionalized group made up of people living in nursing homes or similar senior citizens' residences, (2) an at-home group consisting of people who lived independently in the community, and (3) a group of young people residing at home. Every possible effort was made, including consulting medical records and physicians, to secure only physically and mentally healthy subjects. Individuals with severe or chronic medical problems thought to affect mental functioning were excluded. Patients receiving medication that could alter psychological processes were also excluded.

All prospective subjects were advised that they were being asked to participate in a university-based study investigating memory processes in different population groups. Special care was taken to emphasize that their participation was voluntary and that any information obtained would be treated in strictest confidence. The experimenters met with subjects prior to testing to answer all questions and provide reassurance concerning the nondemanding nature of the tasks and to reduce anxiety as much as possible.

All groups were made up of roughly equal numbers of males and females. In assigning subjects, care was taken to ensure that such variables as socioeconomic status, educational level, health, and degree of community involvement did not vary substantially between groups. All prospective subjects were administered the Quick Intelligence test and only those who scored within the normal range or better were considered for the experiments. There were no statistically significant differences between any of the groups on this measure.

### *Interference and Learning*

To assess interference effects during new learning, a transfer of training task originally developed for organic amnesics with known or suspected damage to the hippocampus was used (Winocur & Weiskrantz, 1976). Although such patients are clearly more deficient than the normal aged, this task permitted comparisons between the performance of old people, severely brain-damaged individuals for whom data already existed, and young normal people who were to be included in the research.

The task essentially was a variation of the well known AB–AC transfer paradigm in which subjects initially learned to associate specific word combinations and were then tested on a second list in which new response words were to be associated with the original stimulus words. Because amnesics and, to a certain extent, old people have trouble learning unrelated word pairs, the lists were made up of high-associate words so that the test, in effect, became an AA′–AA″ paradigm. Subjects initially received four study trials of list 1, which consisted of 12 pairs of semantically related paired associates (e.g., *battle–soldier*). Sixty seconds after the last presentation, recall was tested by presenting the stimulus words and asking subjects to provide the correct response words. A 20–30 minute interval followed during which subjects were engaged in conversation. The 12 pairs of list 2 words were then presented once only followed by a series of trials in which subjects were to match the new response words to the original stimuli (e.g., *battle–army*). The correct word was always provided after the subject's response and testing was terminated after an errorless trial or when a maximum of 9 trials had been administered.

The results, which for comparison purposes include the performance of an amnesic group from the Winocur and Weiskrantz (1976) experiment, are presented in Figure 1. An examination of list 1 recall scores yielded no significant differences, indicating that original learning was equated between the aged and control groups. For obvious reasons, statistical comparisons did not include the amnesic group but it is apparent that, on this measure, they were comparable to the other groups. Indeed, in the various conditions involving this paradigm no group differences in original learning were observed and subsequent differences in list 2 learning could therefore not be attributed to unequal learning ability.

A clear age effect is apparent in list 2 learning where both institutionalized and at-home groups made significantly more errors than the control group. Response interference was an important factor in this impairment, as is indicated in the error analysis of Table 1. About two thirds of the errors made by old people and amnesics were response intrusions from list 1. That is, given the familiar stimulus, the tendency of these subjects was to emit the previously associated response word.

An interesting aspect of the list 2 results is the poor performance of the institutionalized group relative to the at-home group. Indeed, the institutionalized subjects initially made as many errors as the amnesics and, although they began to improve substantially by trial 3, their performance continued to lag behind the other groups in this experiment. All controls and 8 of 9 at-home subjects reached the criterion of an errorless trial by 9 trials but only 3 of 9 institutionalized subjects were able to achieve this criterion.

This experiment was repeated using phonetically related paired associates

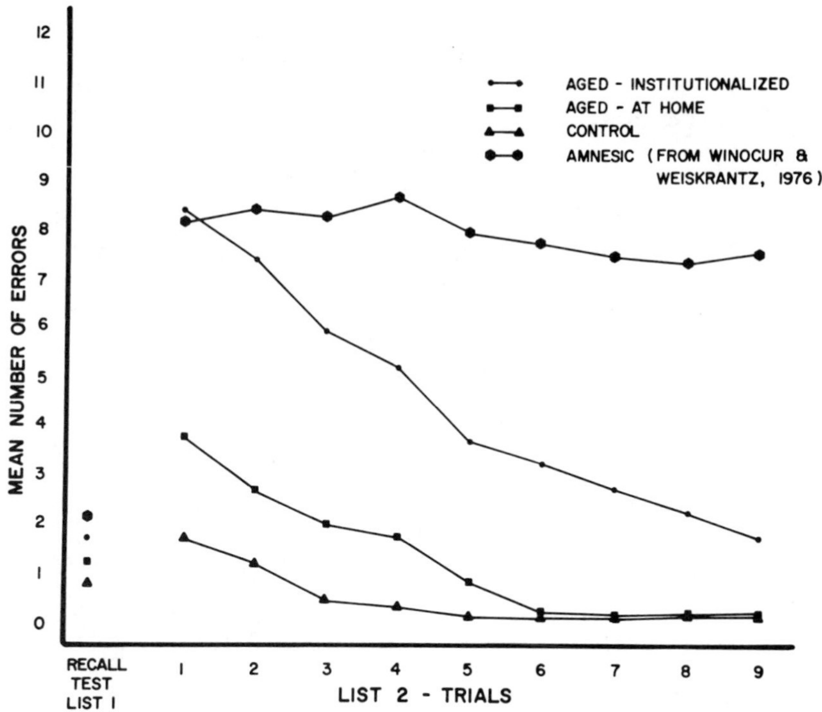


Fig. 1. Performance of aged, amnesic, and control groups in standard transfer test.

(e.g., list 1: *steam–dream;* list 2: *steam–cream*) with essentially the same results (see Figure 2).

In view of disagreement in the literature over interference effects and aging, it was important to ask whether the greater negative transfer displayed by old people in learning list 2 represented an increased susceptibility to interference or was simply part of a proportional decline related to age. Thus, new groups of subjects were presented with the semantically related list 2 items of the previous experiment but without prior training. In accordance with the list 2 testing

*Table 1. Mean Percentage Errors during List 2 Learning in Standard Transfer Paradigm*

| | Semantic | Response intrusion | Omission | Other |
|---|---|---|---|---|
| Amnesic | 20.7 | 73.3 | 6.0 | — |
| Aged (institutionalized) | 11.6 | 63.8 | 19.0 | 4.8 |
| Aged (at home) | 16.8 | 68.8 | 12.3 | 1.1 |
| Control | 59.5 | 37.6 | 2.0 | .9 |

procedure, one study trial was administered followed by a series of trials in which subjects were required to match responses to correct stimuli. A comparison of their performance with that of the groups in the transfer paradigm enabled an assessment of list 2 learning under conditions of high and low interference. The results, shown in Figure 3, revealed a highly significant group × condition interaction that could be attributed to the relatively poor performance of the institutionalized aged group in the high interference condition. No group differences were obtained during list learning without prior training, nor did the at-home aged group differ significantly from controls following training. However, comparisons between the institutionalized aged and the other two groups in the prior training condition yielded significant differences in both cases. These findings indicate that the greater impairment of institutionalized old people can be related to an increased susceptibility to interference created by prior training on the related task. The results for the at-home group, on the other hand, seem to reflect only a nonspecific learning decrement.

In an earlier experiment (Winocur & Kinsbourne, 1978), the same analysis of interference effects was made involving Korsakoff amnesics and alcoholic control groups. Significant main effects were noted but there were no interac-

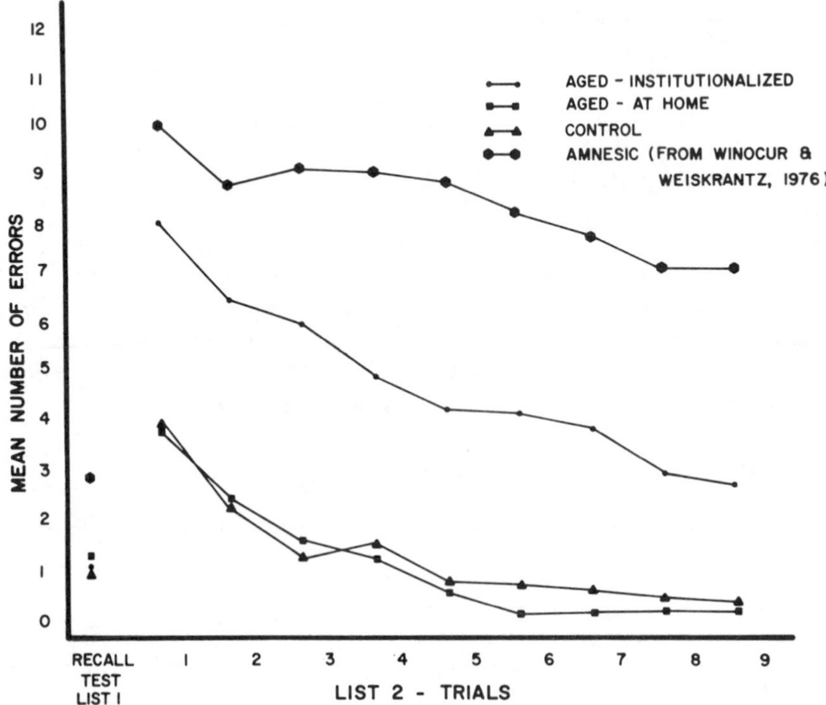


Fig. 2. Performance of aged, amnesic, and control groups in transfer test using rhyming words.

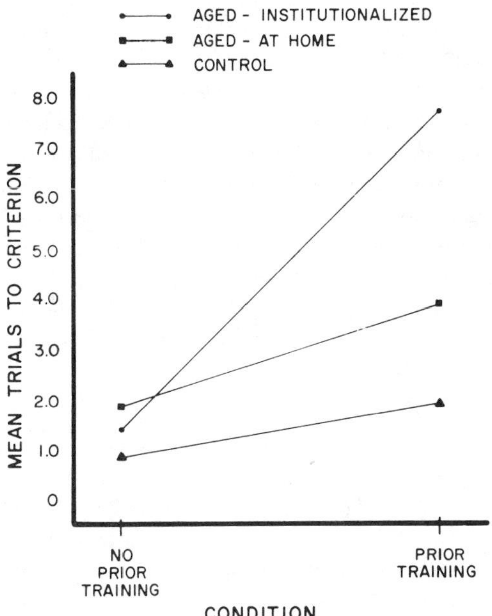


Fig. 3. Performance of aged and control groups in low and high interference conditions.

tions, suggesting that, while amnesics were generally inferior to the control groups, the impairment was not due to an exaggerated reaction to interference. In retrospect, it is necessary to reconsider the assumption that individuals who had been alcoholic for many years could be considered free of memory pathology. In reality, the alcoholic groups performed worse than our present controls and, indeed, perhaps even slightly worse than our at-home aged groups despite being younger by over 20 years. If amnesics were compared to our nonalcoholic controls, interactions similar to those obtained with institutionalized old people could be expected.

In summary, the negative transfer test yielded clear age differences, particularly in comparisons involving the institutionalized subjects. The performance of this group was differentially affected by interfering influences and resembled, in important respects, the behavior of severely brain-damaged amnesic patients.

## *Cuing Effects*

Previous research has shown that the learning and memory deficits of amnesic patients, despite their severity, can be at least partially reversed by appropriate control procedures. Various cuing techniques have also proved effective in reducing response interference and producing better list 2 learning in our negative-transfer test. In one experiment (Winocur & Weiskrantz, 1976) this was accomplished by pairing words in each list according to different rules. Thus, list 1 items were combined with semantically related associates (e.g., *battle–soldier*) while list 2 stimuli and responses were matched phonetically (*e.g., battle–rattle*). In this condition, amnesics improved significantly over their performance in the standard paradigm where only phonetically combined words were used. Identical results were obtained when a phonetic list preceded a semantic list.

The same experiment was conducted with old people and the results for the semantic/phonetic condition are presented in Figure 4. The consistent finding in all groups was a reduction in response intrusions and improvement in list 2 learning, relative to respective performance in the standard test. In proportional terms the degree of improvement was the same, indicating that each group benefited equally from the treatment.

In a sense, these results may not be surprising since they are based on a manipulation that changed the essential character of the test. On the other hand, they do suggest the possibility of reducing negative transfer in the original paradigm if procedures could be developed that help subjects to separate the two tasks and regard them as unrelated problems. This was accomplished with am-

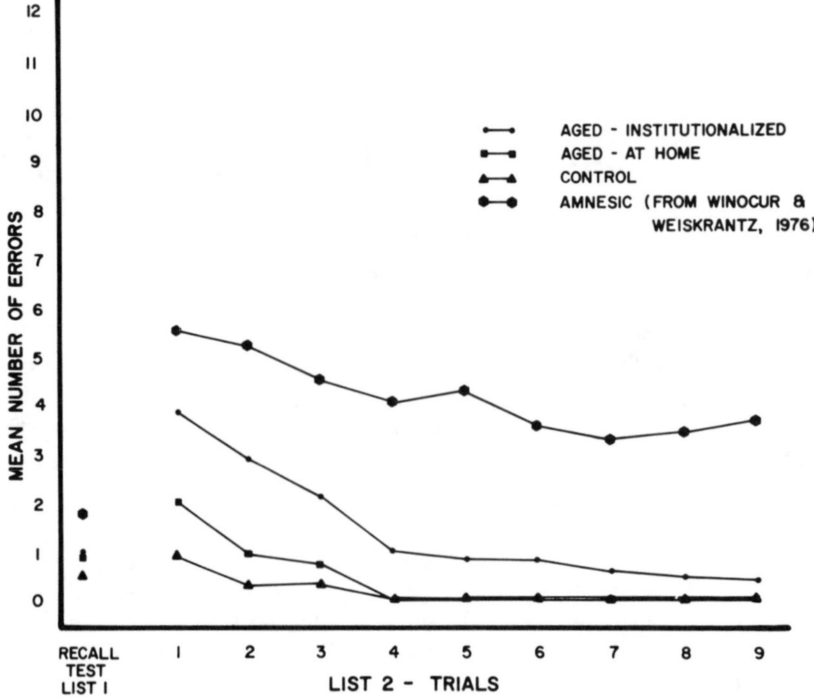


Fig. 4. Performance of aged, amnesic, and control groups in semantic-rhyme transfer condition.

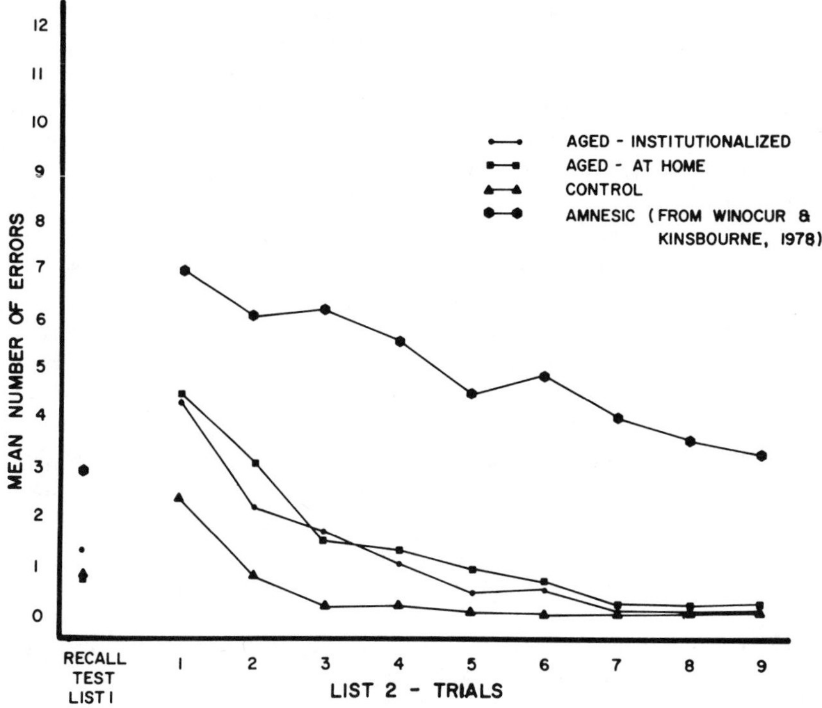


Fig. 5. Performance of aged, amnesic, and control groups in context-shift transfer condition.

nesic patients by drastically varying the context in which each list was presented (Winocur & Kinsbourne, 1978), and so a similar attempt was made with old people.

In this experiment, list 1, which consisted of semantically related paired associates, was presented in a distinctive context provided by a darkened room illuminated only by a bright red lamp and taped music playing in the background. After subjects learned and recalled this list, the room lights were turned on and the music turned off. Twenty minutes later the second list, which consisted of the same stimulus words but new semantically related response words, was presented under standard testing conditions.

The results for this experiment are shown in Figure 5. The most dramatic finding was the improved performance of the institutionalized old people, who learned list 2 as well as did old people living at home. The at-home aged, whose performance was very similar to their counterparts in the standard test, appeared unresponsive to contextual manipulations. Thus, in terms of benefiting from contextual cuing, the institutionalized group showed the same pattern as amnesics, although the latter never attained the performance level of the aged groups.

The control group learned list 2 faster than the aged groups, despite not improving relative to the corresponding control group in the standard test. With respect to controls, it is necessary to consider the possibility of ceiling effects, but it should be noted that the control group in the semantic/phonetic condition made significantly fewer errors in learning list 2 than the control groups in either the standard or context shift conditions. This result suggests that the controls were, in fact, not operating at ceiling.

Figure 6 summarizes the performance of institutionalized and at-home groups in the transfer experiments. It also includes a disruptive condition which involved the standard transfer paradigm but a short inter-list interval during which subjects simply left the testing room and walked about for three minutes. All groups displayed the same learning patterns in this condition as their counterparts in the context shift condition. In general, it can be seen that the institutionalized groups benefited from each treatment designed to improve performance, although they were never able to overcome totally the effects of list 1 interference. In contrast, the at-home groups benefited only when there was a change from one rule to another.

A major difference between the semantic/phonetic condition and the other treatments is that in the latter, interference reduction was accomplished by manipulations that were extraneous to the task itself. In the semantic/phonetic condition, the discriminative cues were intrinsic since they involved changes to the types of associations between word pairs. Thus, the at-home people seemed

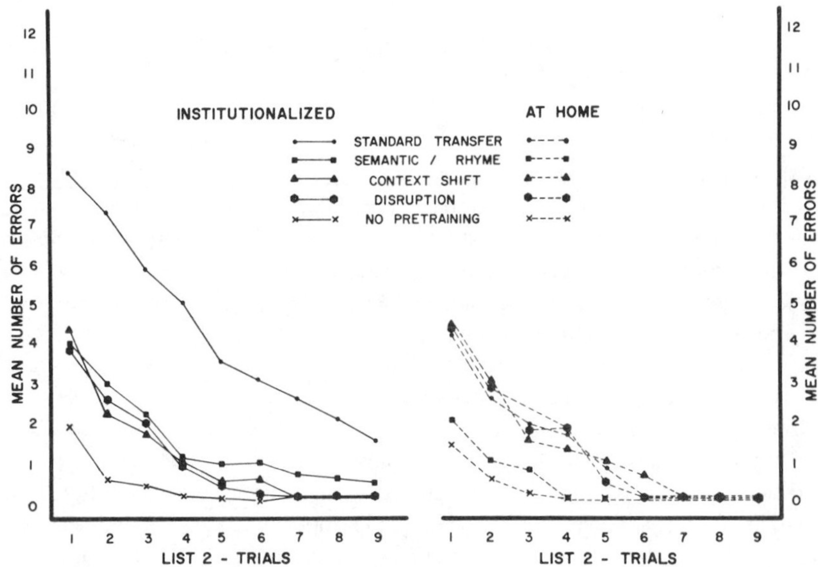


Fig. 6. Comparison of institutionalized and at-home aged subjects on the various transfer tests.

more selective in terms of the cues to which they responded, implying different approaches to the two aged populations.

## *Memory*

In view of our success with cuing procedures in reducing interference, at least in institutionalized old people, it was decided to apply this approach to long-term memory. Considerable potential for interference is built into most tests of long-term memory since they typically involve familiar stimuli presented in settings that already have other experiences associated with them. In addition, intertest intervals frequently last several days and are usually filled with diverse activities which could reduce the distinctiveness of the original learning experience and affect its recall. This problem would, of course, be magnified for institutionalized people for whom more activities occur in the same restricted environment as testing.

If, indeed, memories of old people are adversely affected by interference, procedures that minimize interference should yield improved recall. It was reasoned that information presented in a unique setting that could not easily be identified with other experiences would be resistant to interference effects and therefore more accessible at retrieval. This hypothesis was tested by comparing the learning and recall of paired associates under various conditions of distinctiveness. Groups of aged and young subjects were presented lists of semantically related word pairs under either standard testing conditions or in the highly distinctive setting of the contextual shift transfer experiment. The list was presented four times followed 60 seconds later by a recall test. Forty-eight hours later, subjects returned to the same room to relearn the list.

The results for this experiment are presented in Figure 7. Looking first at the results of the standard recall test, there were no group differences at the time of original learning, but a clear age effect emerged 48 hours later. Although old people generally displayed poorer memory than the controls, the impairment was greater in the institutionalized group. A comparison of the two aged groups revealed a statistically significant difference at recall (trial 1), although this difference disappeared by trial 2. The aged groups were, of course, superior to a group of Korsakoff amnesics tested under comparable conditions (Winocur & Kinsbourne, 1978).

Age differences in recall were still present in the distinctive context condition, but here there were no differences between the aged groups. The institutionalized subjects benefited significantly from the salient cues, as did the Korsakoff patients in the Winocur and Kinsbourne study, but the at-home subjects performed essentially at the same level as their corresponding group in the standard recall test.

Thus, the same pattern detected in the negative transfer experiments

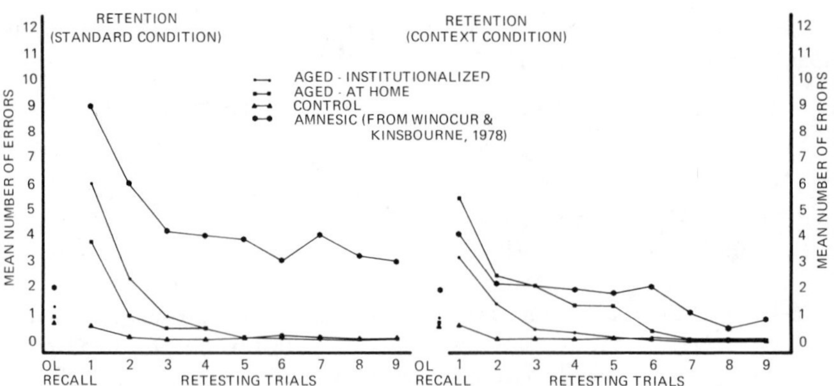


Fig. 7. Performance of aged, amnesic, and control groups on memory test in standard and context conditions.

emerged in the test of memory. Institutionalized old people performed worse than old people living at home when tested under standard, presumably high-interference, conditions. However, in the presence of salient contextual cues, the performance of institutionalized subjects improved in a manner similar to that of brain-damaged amnesics. In contrast, noninstitutionalized subjects, like normal, young adults, were unresponsive to contextual cuing.

## Concluding Comments

A number of tentative conclusions can be drawn from the present research. It is clear that elderly people were generally less efficient than young at learning and recalling new information. Deficiencies were especially marked in the elderly living in institutions, whose pattern of performance was very similar to that of amnesic patients with extensive brain damage thought to involve the hippocampus. In contrast, the behavior of elderly subjects living at home, while also impaired, was more similar to that of young people.

The critical factor underlying the differences between the elderly groups was the institutionalized subjects' exaggerated vulnerability to interference. Taking into account this group's improvement in the cuing experiments, their deficit may be interpreted as a failure to derive enough information from task-inherent cues. More discriminative information was required to dissociate conflicting experiences and suppress competing responses. The tendency of institutionalized old people, it appeared, was to look beyond the task for additional information that could be used to compensate for their deficiency. This strategy proved effective when extraneous cues were sufficiently salient. Young normal adults typically use contextual information during learning only when the problems are very difficult or when the primary cues are highly ambiguous (Keppel, 1972). This was clearly not the case for the present tasks and consequently controls were unaffected by contextual cuing. In this respect, noninstitutionalized old people, who responded only to manipulations that were intrinsic to the tasks, were similar to the control groups.

These results confirm trends in the literature which suggest that old people living at home adopt problem-solving strategies that are fundamentally the same as young adults but that qualitative changes can be associated with institutionalization. The parallels in performance between the institutionalized subjects and organic amnesic patients imply a more advanced state of brain decline in institutionalized than in noninstitutionalized old people of comparable age. One brain region known to be selectively affected by the aging process and likely to be implicated in the behavioral patterns exhibited by institutionalized old people and amnesics is the hippocampus.

The experiments reported in this chapter are essentially analogues of animal studies conducted in our lab and designed to clarify the function of the hippocampus. The studies that bear most directly on the present results involved the use of contextual cues to facilitate learning and memory (Winocur & Olds, 1978). In one experiment, groups of hippocampal and control rats initially learned a pattern discrimination and were subsequently retested with the positive and negative stimuli reversed. When contextual conditions were the same throughout testing, hippocampal animals were severely impaired in reversal learning. However, when the second task was presented in a highly contrasting physical environment in which illumination and sound stimuli were amongst those changed, the effects of hippocampal lesions were dramatically reduced.

Contextual conditions were also varied in a test of memory. All subjects originally learned a discrimination habit in a given context with recall testing occurring in the same or different contexts. Control groups showed excellent savings at retesting under all conditions. In contrast, the hippocampal animals showed good recall only when context was held constant. Their performance, measured in terms of recall and relearning, was markedly impaired in the contextual shift conditions.

The Winocur and Olds (1978) findings clearly implicate the hippocampus in the types of information-processing deficits earlier attributed to organic amnesics and institutionalized old people. Thus, without attributing the broad range of age-related cognitive deficiencies to this structure, it is reasonable to conclude that impairment in high-interference tasks reflects a loss of hippocampal function.

An important question raised, but not answered, by the present research concerns other, nonbiological factors that could have contributed to observed differences between the aged groups. It is undoubtedly too simplistic to differentiate these subjects exclusively according to place of residence. Indeed, it is not clear whether the results represent true institutional effects or differences that already existed prior to institutionalization. Many people are, of course, admitted to institutions precisely because declining faculties prevent adequate self-care. Unfortunately, it was not possible to obtain reliable information concerning the state of each institutionalized subject prior to admission or progressive changes occurring since that time.

Another variable that may not have been adequately considered is the role of stress associated with moving from home to an institution. The effects of relocation on the aged have been extensively studied, and there is considerable evidence pointing to related declines in morale and health, particularly when people are reluctant to enter institutions (see Kasl & Rosenfield, 1980). Only people who had been institutionalized for a minimum period of six months were included in the present research, but this may not have been sufficiently long to allow relocation anxiety to dissipate entirely. Furthermore, there was little information concerning stability in prior living conditions, and some subjects may have relocated several times before finally entering their present institution.

On the other hand, it must be recognized that institutions mean, for many people, reduced freedom and mobility, less contact with family and long-standing friends, and a less enriched life. Such changes have obvious implications for psychological processes generally, but they may also contribute to an accelerated rate of brain decline. Recently, Greenough and Green (1979) have identified a link between environmental factors and structural changes in the aging brain. Although still in its early stages, this research raises the real possibility that the nondemanding and predictable nature of institutional life can contribute to a disuse of brain mechanisms and their more rapid decay. Clearly, this factor must be taken into account by future research designed to assess the impact of institutionalization on cognitive aspects of the aging process.

## Acknowledgments

The aging experiments reported in this chapter were conducted in collaboration with Dr. Morris Moscovitch, University of Toronto.

This research could not have been conducted without the cooperation of the medical and administrative staff of the Peterborough Civic Hospital, Activity Haven, and the following nursing homes: Fairhaven, Extendicare, and Spruce Haven. Their assistance and that of Ann Smith and Sylvia Nesbitt-Papadopolous are gratefully acknowledged. And finally, the subjects, especially the elderly, who willingly, sometimes suspiciously, let us touch their lives: to them, special thanks.

# References

Arenberg, D. Cognition and aging: Verbal learning, memory, and problem-solving. In C. Eisdorfer & M. P. Lawton (Eds.), *The psychology of adult development and aging*. Washington, D.C.: American Psychological Association, 1973.

Arenberg, D., & Robertson-Tchabo, E. A. Learning and aging. In J. E. Birren & K. W. Schaie (Eds.), *Handbook of the psychology of aging*. New York: Van Nostrand, 1977.

Barnes, C. A. Memory deficit associated with senescence: A neurophysiological and behavioral study in the rat. *Journal of Comparative and Physiological Psychology*, 1979, *93*, 74–104.

Bondareff, W. Neurobiology of aging. In J. E. Birren & R. D. Sloane (Eds.), *Handbook of mental health and aging*. Englewood Cliffs, N.J.: Prentice–Hall, 1980.

Butters, N., & Cermak, L. S. Some analyses of amnesic syndrome in brain-damaged patients. In R. L. Isaacson & K. H. Pribram (Eds.), *The hippocampus* (Vol. 2). New York: Plenum Press, 1975.

Cameron, D. E. Impairment of the retention phase of remembering. *Psychiatric Quarterly*, 1943, *17*, 395–404.

Canestrari, R. E., Jr. The effects of commonality on paired-associate learning in two age groups. *Journal of Genetic Psychology*, 1966, *108*, 3–7.

Coppinger, N. W., & Nehrke, M. F. Discrimination learning and transfer of training in the aged. *Journal of Genetic Psychology*, 1972, *120*, 93–102.

Correll, R. E., & Scoville, W. B. Effects of medial temporal lesions on visual discrimination performance. *Journal of Comparative and Physiological Psychology*, 1965, *60*, 360–367.

Craik, F. I. M. Age differences in human memory. In J. E. Birren & K. W. Schaie (Eds), *Handbook of the psychology of aging*. New York: Van Nostrand, 1977.

Crovitz, B. Recovering a learning deficit in the aged. *Journal of Gerontology*, 1966, *21*, 236–238.

Douglas, R. J. The hippocampus and behavior. *Psychological Bulletin*, 1967, *67*, 416–446.

Elias, M. F., & Elias, P. K. Motivation and activity. In J. E. Birren & K. W. Schaie (Eds.), *Handbook of the psychology of aging*. New York: Van Nostrand, 1977.

Gilbert, J. G. Memory loss in senescence. *Journal of Abnormal and Social Psychology*, 1941, *36*, 73–86.

Gladis, M., & Braun, H. W. Age differences in transfer and retroaction as a function of inter-task response similarity. *Journal of Experimental Psychology*, 1958, *55*, 25–30.

Goldfarb, A. The evaluation of geriatric patients following treatment. In P. Hoch & J. Zubin (Eds.), *Evaluation of psychiatric treatment*. New York: Grune & Stratton, 1964.

Greenough, W. T., & Green, E. J. *Experience and the changing brain*. Paper presented at Workshop on Biology and Behavior of the Elderly, Woods Hole, Mass., June 1979.

Horel, J. A. The neuroanatomy of amnesia. *Brain*, 1978, *101*, 403–445.

Hulicka, I. M. Age differences in retention as a function of interference. *Journal of Gerontology*, 1967, *22*, 180–184.

Hulicka, I. M., & Grossman, J. L. Age-group comparisons for the use of mediators in paired-associate learning. *Journal of Gerontology*, 1967, *22*, 46–51.

Hultsch, D. S. Adult age differences in the organization of free recall. *Developmental Psychology*, 1969, *1*, 673–678.

Hultsch, D. S. Organization and memory in adulthood. *Human Development*, 1971, *14*, 16–29.

Hultsch, D. S. Learning to learn in adulthood. *Journal of Gerontology*, 1974, *29*, 302–308.

Hultsch, D. S. Adult age differences in retrieval: Trace-dependent and cue-dependent forgetting. *Developmental Psychology*, 1975, *11*, 197–201.

Jarrard, L. E. Role of interference and retention by rats with hippocampal lesions. *Journal of Comparative and Physiological Psychology*, 1975, *89*, 400–408.

Kasl, S. D. Physical and mental health effects of involuntary relocation and institutionalization—A review. *American Journal of Public Health,* 1972, *62,* 377–384.

Kasl, S. D., & Rosenfield, S. The residential environment and its impact on the mental health of the aged. In J. E. Birren & R. D. Sloane (Eds.), *Handbook of mental health and aging.* Englewood Cliffs, N.J.: Prentice–Hall, 1980.

Keppel, G. Forgetting. In C. P. Duncan, L. Seclrest, & A. W. Melton (Eds), *Human memory: Festschrift for Benton J. Underwood.* New York: Appleton-Century Croft, 1972.

Klonoff, H., & Kennedy, M. A comparative study of cognitive functioning in old age. *Journal of Gerontology,* 1966, *21,* 239–243.

Lair, C., Moon, W., & Kausler, D. H. Associative interference in the paired-associate learning of middle-aged and old subjects. *Developmental Psychology,* 1969, *1,* 548–552.

Landfield, P. W., Rose, G., Sandels, L., Wohlstadler, D. C., & Lynch, G. Patterns of astroglial hypertrophy and neuronal degeneration in the hippocampus of aged, memory-deficient rats. *Journal of Gerontology,* 1977, *32,* 3–12.

Langer, E. J., Rodin, J., Beck, P., Weinman, C., & Spitzer, L. Environmental determinants of memory improvement in late adulthood. *Journal of Personality and Social Psychology,* in press.

Laurence, M. W. Memory loss with age: A test of two strategies for its retardation. *Psychonomic Science,* 1967, *9,* 209–210.

Lawton, M. P. The impact of the environment on behavior. In J. E. Birren & K. W. Schaie (Eds.), *Handbook of the psychology of aging.* New York: Van Nostrand, 1977.

Lhermitte, F., & Signoret, J. L. The amnesic syndrome and the hippocampal-mammillary systems. In M. R. Rosenzweig & E. L. Bennett (Eds.), *Neuromechanisms of learning and memory.* Cambridge, Mass: M.I.T. Press, 1976.

Milner, B. The memory defect in bilateral hippocampal lesions. *Psychiatric Research Reports.* 1959, *11,* 43–52.

Muller, D., & Lieberman, M. A. The relationships of affect state and adaptive capacities to reactions to stress. *Journal of Gerontology,* 1965, *20,* 492–497.

Nehrke, M. S. Age and sex differences in discrimination learning and transfer of training. *Journal of Gerontology.* 1973, *28,* 320–327.

O'Keefe, J., & Nadel, L. *The hippocampus as a cognitive map.* Oxford: Oxford University Press, 1978.

Ross, E. Effect of challenging and supportive instructions on verbal learning in older persons. *Journal of Educational Psychology,* 1968, *59,* 261–266.

Ruch, S. L. The differentiative effect of age upon human learning. *Journal of General Psychology,* 1934, *11,* 261–268.

Schonfield, A. E. D. Learning, memory, and aging. In J. E. Birren & R. D. Sloane (Eds.), *Handbook of mental health and aging.* Englewood Cliffs, N.J.: Prentice–Hall, 1980.

Scoville, W. D., & Milner, B. Loss of recent memory after bilateral hippocampal lesions. *Journal of Neurology, Neurosurgery and Psychiatry,* 1957, *20,* 11–21.

Smith, A. D. Aging and interference with memory. *Journal of Gerontology,* 1975, *30,* 319–325.

Starr, A., & Phillips, L. Verbal and motor memory in the amnesic syndrome. *Neuropsychologia,* 1970, *8,* 75–88.

Taub, H. A. Memory span, practice and aging. *Journal of Gerontology,* 1973, *28,* 335–338.

Victor, M., Adams, R. D., & Collins, G. H. *The Wernicke-Korsakoff syndrome.* Philadelphia, Pa: Davis, 1971.

Warrington, E. K., & Weiskrantz, L. Analysis of short-term and long-term memory defects in man. In J. A. Deutsch (Ed.), *The physiological bases of memory.* New York: Academic Press, 1973.

Welford, A. T. *Aging and human skill.* London: Oxford University Press, 1958.

Wigdor, B. T. Drives and motivation with aging. In J. E. Birren & R. D. Sloane (Eds.), *Handbook of mental health and aging.* Englewood Cliffs, N.J.: Prentice–Hall, 1980.

Wimer, R. E., & Wigdor, B. T. Age differences and retention in learning. *Journal of Gerontology,* 1958, *13,* 291–295.

Winocur, G. The effect of interference on discrimination learning and recall by rats with hippocampal lesions. *Physiology and Behavior,* 1979, *22,* 339–345.

Winocur, G. The hippocampus and cue utilization. *Physiological Psychology,* 1980, *8,* 280–288.

Winocur, G. The amnesic syndrome: A deficit in cue utilization. In L. Cermak (Ed.), *Human memory and amnesia.* Hillsdale, N.J.: Lawrence Erlbaum, 1982.

Winocur, G., & Mills, J. P. Transfer between related and unrelated problems following hippocampal lesions in rats. *Journal of Comparative and Physiological Psychology,* 1970, *73,* 162–169.

Winocur, G., & Weiskrantz, L. An investigation of paired-associate learning in amnesic patients. *Neuropsychologia,* 1976, *14,* 97–110.

Winocur, G., & Black, A. H. Cue-induced recall of a passive avoidance response by rats with hippocampal lesions. *Physiology and Behavior, 1978, 21,* 39–44.

Winocur, G., & Kinsbourne, M. Contextual cueing as an aid to Korsakoff amnesia. *Neuropsychologia,* 1978, *16,* 671–682.

Winocur, G., & Olds, J. Effects of context manipulation on memory and reversal learning in rats with hippocampal lesions. *Journal of Comparative and Physiological Psychology,* 1978, *92,* 312–321.

Zaretsky, H. H., & Halberstam, J. C. Age differences in paired-associate learning. *Journal of Gerontology,* 1968, *23,* 165–168.

CHAPTER 10

# Encoding Deficits in Aging

Nancy C. Waugh and Robin A. Barr

*Department of Experimental Psychology*
*University of Oxford*
*Oxford, England*

The ability to register, retain, and recollect experienced events is basic to every other higher mental process. Remembering is an essential component of problem-solving, concept-formation, and intelligent decision-making. By now there exists a growing mass of evidence that memory undergoes progressive deterioration throughout the late adult years, even in the absence of specific neurological disease. It takes the normal elderly individual longer than it does the young adult to assimilate, search for, and locate information, both verbal and nonverbal—and he is less likely to do so successfully. Different processes may, as Walsh has indicated (Chapter 6), decline at different rates within the same individual, and the pattern is not necessarily the same from subject to subject. This is an important point to consider, all the more so if one wishes to construct and standardize more sophisticated tests of memory function than are currently available. We really ought to measure individual patterns of performance in the study of aging more than we do.

That said, we nevertheless propose to discuss differences in psychological function between the "average" young and elderly adult. These are the differences that are almost invariably reported in the literature, and it is in fact necessary to deal with averages if we are to generalize from samples to populations. It must be borne in mind when doing so that elderly samples are more heterogeneous than young ones, since different people age at different rates. It

The experimental work reported in this chapter was supported by the Social Science Research Council (United Kingdom).

should also be borne in mind that there is overlap between age groups, so that a particular 65-year-old's performance may be indistinguishable from the average 25-year-old's, and a particular 30-year-old's from the average 60-year-old's. Finally, we shall confine most of our remarks to age-related differences in the encoding of information into memory—but not because we believe that retrieval is less important than acquisition. We do so because of limitations of space and because of the nature of the papers we were asked to discuss.

A sturdy common thread runs through what might seem at first glance to be a rather disparate set of papers. That common thread consists of what one might call the elderly subject's encoding inefficiency: the elderly subject is able to register less information than can the young adult over the same interval of time. This "slow-tempo" effect (Waugh & Barr, 1980) is clearly evident at the "building-block" level in studies of both peripheral and central processing of visual signals reported by Walsh and his colleagues (Walsh, 1976; Walsh & Thompson, 1978; Walsh, Till, & Williams, 1978; Walsh, Williams, & Herzog, 1979; Chapter 6). The older subject requires longer SOAs or ISIs for backward masking to be eliminated at a fixed level of target energy. His visual system apparently takes longer to complete the process of registering the information available in a briefly exposed visual target. The information is lost if it has not been registered by the time the masking stimulus appears. This type of very rapid encoding is elementary and essential to higher levels of perception. The elderly subject encodes less of a briefly presented visual signal than does the younger within a fixed period of time. One might almost say that the older subject's encoding of such signals was impoverished. It is of interest that nowhere in Walsh's studies is there an interaction between the subject's chronological age and the parameters of the stimuli.

Turning now to encoding at a different level, we have two similar sets of results reported by Perlmutter (Perlmutter & Mitchell, 1979; Chapter 7) and Rabinowitz and Ackerman (Chapter 8). Both have concluded that the elderly subject is less likely than the young one to encode his own free associate to a target word, since that associate tends to be a relatively ineffective retrieval cue later on. We submit that this is because the older subject is less likely to register and retain what he considers to be irrelevant information. The older subject's reluctance to encode insignificant detail—or his inability to encode such detail within a given temporal interval—is also evident in his diminished ability to remember which distractors he saw in a classification task (Perlmutter & Mitchell, 1979). And the older subject, as Rabinowitz and Ackerman have reported, is *less* likely than the younger one to be put off by too much context at the time of retrieval (Experiment 3). This is probably because he simply failed in the first place to register the verbal context in which a target word was embedded, perhaps because he failed to perceive it as relevant to the task at hand.

The elderly subject also appears less likely than the younger to integrate apparently disparate events, or incoherent pieces of information—in the Rabinowitz and Ackerman experiment, a weak cue and its associated target word. The old subject's reduced likelihood of encoding irrelevant or incoherent information could be said to represent a process of encoding selectivity in the aging subject. The encoding is selective because information perceived to be unimportant or incoherent is not registered.

Finally, Winocur (Chapter 9) has reported that the old are more susceptible than the young to negative transfer in an A–B, A–C paradigm when the B term resembles the C but not when B and C are dissimilar. This finding suggests that the old fail to encode those detailed aspects of an event which will distinguish it from a similar event. Instead, they selectively encode general features of verbal input and so are unable later on to make a temporal discrimination between confusable stimuli.

To summarize what we have said so far, old people quite evidently register and integrate less information per unit time than do young adults. When input is verbal, moreover, they encode the general features of the stimulus and fail to encode seemingly trivial or incoherent detail which could in some instances aid later recall.

These same principles are fully obvious in a very different experimental paradigm which we ourselves have recently used. Our own results also bring out a further point: not only does the older subject encode more selectively than the younger one, he also does so with greater variability.

The subject's task was initially to look at a series of seven items—either pictures or words drawn without replacement from a large pool—projected one at a time onto a screen. The pictures were in color and were, for each list, selected so as to be readily discriminable one from the other yet difficult to describe by distinctive verbal labels. For instance, they might all have been beach scenes, or they might have been pictures of harbors or of wooden houses. The words were balanced for number of syllables and frequency of usage, and they were arranged so as to bear no obvious semantic relation to each other. The picture stimuli were presented at either a fast rate (500 msec on time) or a slow rate (1000 msec on time); the verbal stimuli were presented at the fast rate only. The interstimulus interval was 1.8 sec. Immediately after the last item went off, the subject heard a high-pitched tone. This meant that the next slide would be the first of a set of nine test items. The test slides included the seven original slides plus two that the subject had never seen before. His task was now to decide whether each successive test slide was new or old and, if old, which position on the original list it had occupied. He pressed a key labeled "0" if he thought an item was new, or one labeled "1" to "7" according to where in the original list he thought that item had occurred. Each original serial position was represented with approximately equal frequency in each test position. At least 16 subjects in each of two age groups—18 through 40 and 60 through 75—were tested on 18 lists.

The broad purpose of the experiment was to compare age groups (old versus young), rate of presentation (fast versus slow), and type of material (pictures

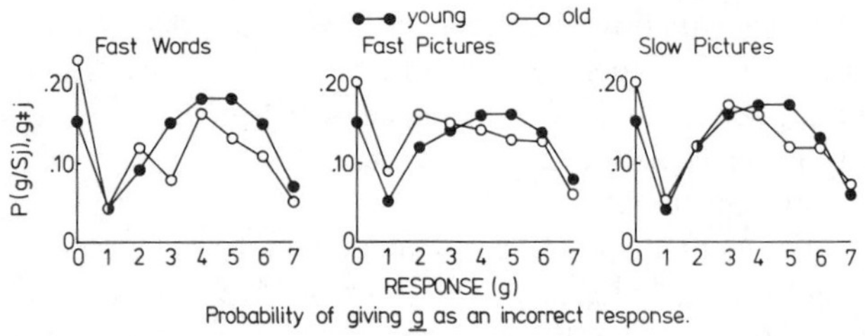


Fig. 1. Frequency with which location *g* was given as an incorrect response expressed as a ratio of the total number of incorrect responses.

versus words). The dependent variable was the frequency with which item *j* in the original list was assigned to category *g*—for instance, the number of times that item 4 was called 1, 2, 3, 4, 5, 6, or 7, or 0.

Any observed differences between the age groups were not caused by different guessing strategies. That much is evident from Figure 1. The two distributions shown in that figure represent the relative frequency with which the old and the young subjects said "0," "1," "2," "3," . . . or "7" *in error*. The patterns of response are exceedingly similar. The overall probability with which "0" was given as an incorrect response represents the overall probability of a miss.

In Figure 2 the relative frequency of a miss is plotted as a function of an item's serial position in the original list, separately for age groups and for conditions. It is clear that the older subjects are likelier than the younger ones to miss both verbal and pictorial items when they are presented at a rapid rate—that is, a rate that exceeds the rate at which incoming information can be handled. There is some tendency for items late in the list to be missed more frequently

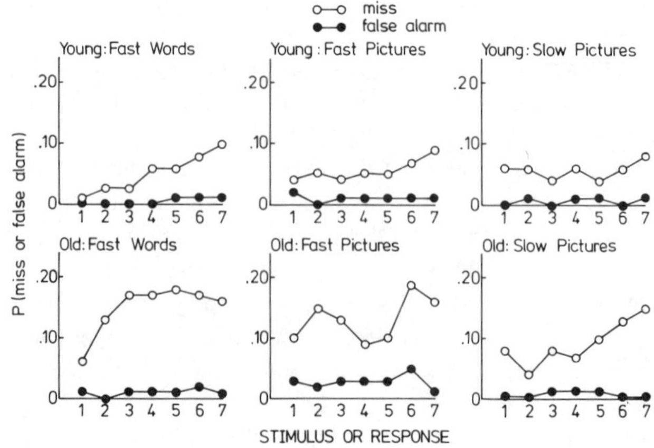


Fig. 2. Relative frequency of a miss or a false alarm as a function of serial position in the exposure list.

than very early ones. Older subjects, then, selectively encode some items at the expense of others; and their encoding is generally inefficient by comparison with that of the younger subjects. Speed of presentation appears to have a disproportionate effect on the rate at which older subjects miss pictorial items.

Also shown in Figure 2 is the proportion of false alarms as a function of response category. There is no obvious trend. Old subjects tended to make more false alarms under the "fast pictures" condition for reasons that escape us. Otherwise, the rates are uniformly low; and there is no marked preference for any one response category. According to a false-alarm criterion, then, both young and old subjects are very good at discriminating old items from new ones—that is, they both show good retention of item (as opposed to order) information.

What about order information? Figure 3 shows the relative frequency with which an item was correctly identified as a function of its position in the original series, pooled across position in the test series. (With only one exception, position in the test series was of no significance whatever. The one exception concerns the last item in the original list, which enjoyed a huge advantage when it was tested first, some two seconds after its offset. Apparently it was available in a very short-term visual store—not iconic storage—but only when it was tested first. This was true both for words and pictures and for young and old subjects.)

The data presented in Figure 3 show that, when words and pictures are presented rapidly, the older subjects are uniformly less correct than the younger ones. The two sets of curves are everywhere separated by some 30 percentage points. When pictures are presented slowly, the gap is considerably narrower—it is approximately 10% for serial positions 3 to 7 and virtually nonexistent for serial positions 1 and 2. We do not at this point, however, wish to draw any firm conclusions about the apparent interaction between age and rate of presentation, since different groups of subjects saw the fast and the slow items.

So far we have discussed measures of amount of information encoded. What about the accuracy with which it is encoded? A technique borrowed from psychophysics allows us to address this issue. In essence, the technique measures variability. Figure 4 shows the median scale values and the interquartile ranges

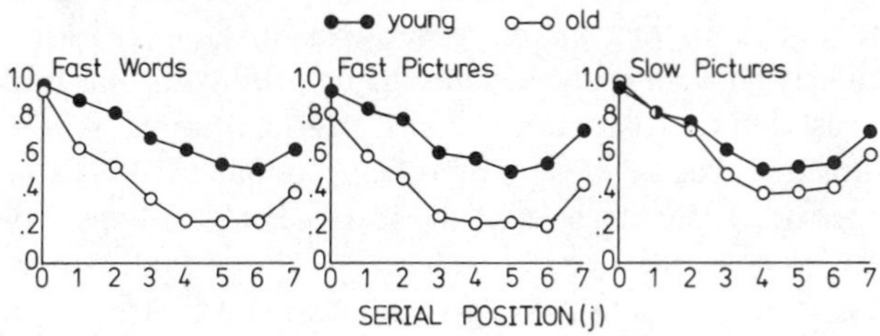


Fig. 3. Relative frequency with which an item was correctly located as a function of its serial position in the exposure list.

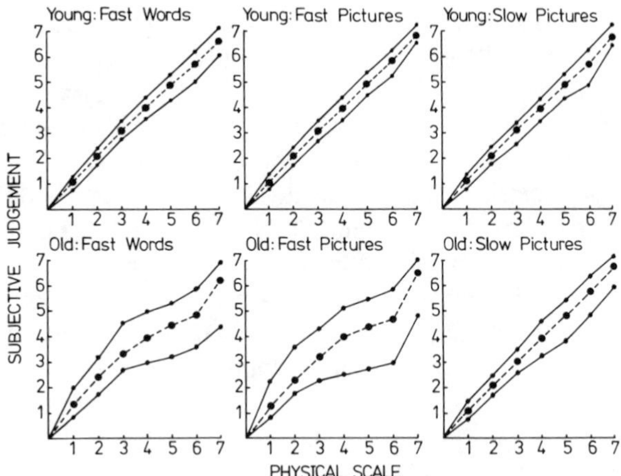


Fig. 4. Median remembered position as a function of original position in the exposure list (large filled circles). The upper and lower sets of points represent the interquartile ranges.

of the subjects' judgments of remembered location. Again it appears to be the case that when information, either verbal or pictorial, is presented rapidly, the old subjects are considerably less accurate than the young—and they are also much more variable. When rate of presentation is slowed down, judgments appear to become more accurate and variability is reduced. Increased variability necessarily produces a decrease in accuracy.

Figure 5 summarizes the entire set of data. We have considered our experiment analogous to a psychophysical absolute identification task in which each of seven stimuli is assigned repeatedly to any of seven categories. The stimulus in this case is an item's position in the original series and is represented on the x-axis. The category to which the stimulus is assigned is its remembered location and is denoted by the parameter. The graphs represent what we have called quasi-psychometric functions. They show, for instance, the probability that the response *1* would be given to item 1, or to items 1 or 2, or to items 1, 2, or 3, and so on. Or, reading now not across a set of points connected by a line, but looking instead at the points arrayed above a given value on the abscissa, we have, for instance, the probability that the response *7* was given to at least item 2. The point immediately above that one denotes the probability that the response *6* was given to at least item 2—that is, to items 1 or 2, and so on.

These functions can be thought of as being cumulated "discriminal dispersions" (Torgerson, 1958) for each of the seven serial positions. For the young subjects, the distributions are exceedingly steep. This is evident in the extremely sharp increase in the functions as we go from item $n$–1 to item $n$, where $n$ is the parameter. The fact that each function crosses the 50% point close to the vertical marks indicates that the median judgments were very accurate. The fact that the functions are more or less parallel to one another means that the psychological distances between the remembered locations of adjacent items are more or less equal. This is everywhere true of the young subjects, and it is almost true of the old subjects under the slow pictures condition.

It is a different story for old subjects under both the fast words and the fast pictures condition. Here the slope of the curves is much shallower. This means that responses were much more variable. There is bunching in the center of the series, and there is even a cross-over between two functions in the middle graph in the lower row. This denotes an utter failure to discriminate between two original list positions.

What this experiment has shown, then, is that when items are presented at a rapid rate older subjects encode some of them at the expense of others. That is, they encode selectively. Second, given that the elderly subject has registered an item in episodic memory, he is much less likely than is his younger counterpart to register its location accurately. This means that he is encoding inefficiently as well as selectively. Older subjects *appear* to perform more accurately when material is presented slowly. We would prefer not to draw this as a firm conclusion, since the fast pictures and slow pictures comparisons are between subjects, and we have reason to believe that the older subjects run under the latter conditions were generally abler than those run under the former.

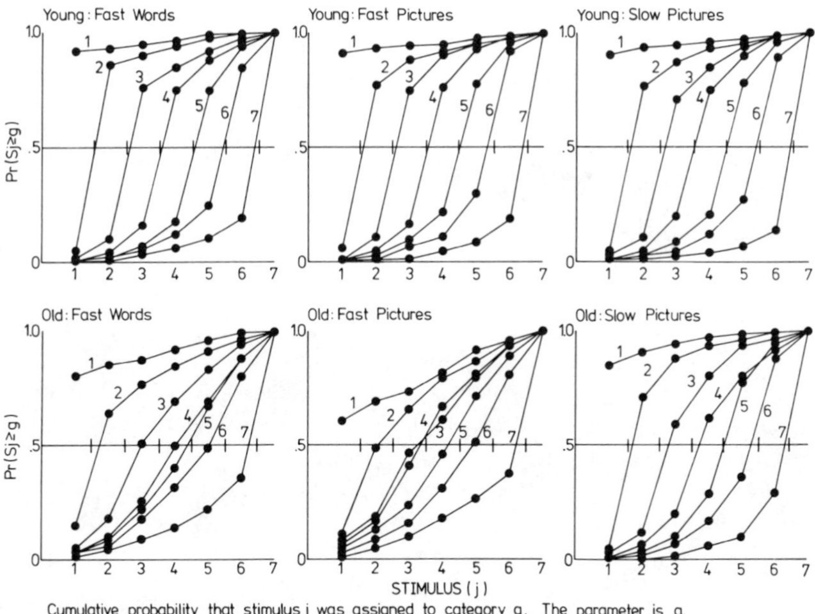


Fig. 5. Cumulated "discriminal dispersions" for each serial position in the exposure list.

In any event, it is an undeniable fact that the older the subject, the less efficiently and the more selectively he encodes—perhaps because when events are externally paced, he simply lacks the time to encode efficiently and comprehensively. This is so regardless of whether he is looking at visual signals presented for only a few msec, or performing a semantic orienting task, or memorizing a set of paired associates, or attempting to register the location of each item in a series of pictures or words. The extent to which inefficient retrieval as well as inefficient encoding is implicated in those memory tasks remains to be determined.

## References

Perlmutter, M. & Mitchell, D. B. *Do levels of processing vary with age level?* Paper presented to the Gerontological Association, Washington, D.C., 1979.

Torgerson, W. R. *Theory and method of scaling.* New York: Wiley, 1958.

Walsh, D. A. Age differences in central perceptual processing: A dichoptic backward masking investigation. *Journal of Gerontology,* 1976, *31,* 178–185.

Walsh, D. A. & Thompson, L. W. Age differences in visual sensory memory. *Journal of Gerontology,* 1978, *33,* 383–387.

Walsh, D. A., Till, R. E., & Williams, M. V. Age differences in peripheral perceptual processing: A monoptic backward masking investigation. *Journal of Experimental Psychology: Human Perception and Performance,* 1978, *4,* 232–243.

Walsh, D. A., Williams, M. V., & Hertzog, C. K. Age-related differences in two stages of central perceptual processes: The effects of short duration targets and criterion differences. *Journal of Gerontology,* 1979, *34,* 234–241.

Waugh, N. C. & Barr, R. A. Memory and mental tempo. In L. W. Poon, J. Fozard, L. Cermak, D. Arenberg, & L. Thompson (Eds.), *New directions in memory and aging.* Hillsdale, N.J.: Lawrence Erlbaum, 1980.

CHAPTER 11

# Aging and Cognitive Deficits

## The Role of Attentional Resources

Fergus I. M. Craik and Mark Byrd

*Department of Psychology*
*Erindale College*
*University of Toronto*
*Mississauga, Ontario, Canada*

The general belief that cognitive abilities decline with age has been somewhat qualified in recent years. Many age-related effects previously demonstrated in studies using cross-sectional designs have been shown to be artifacts of sampling or of the different social and economic conditions experienced by different age cohorts (Schaie, 1973). In addition, older people tested in laboratory studies are usually further removed in time from formal education, and have not had so much recent practice at cognitive skills as their younger counterparts. Older experimental subjects *may* be less motivated to perform well on artificial laboratory tasks, they may have had less formal schooling and may be less healthy. As Avorn (Chapter 17) points out, these factors and others make interpretation of apparent age losses difficult and ought to induce substantial caution before observed deficits are attributed unequivocally to the aging process as such. On the other hand, it does not seem unreasonable to propose that genuine age-related deficits in cognitive functioning do occur. Physical strength, agility, and endurance clearly decline with age, and the various physiological systems of the body (respiratory, circulatory, digestive, excretory) also decline in efficiency as a person grows older (Finch & Hayflick, 1977). It would be rather extraordinary

The work reported in this chapter was supported by grants from the Natural Sciences and Engineering Research Council of Canada and from the University of Toronto.

if the nervous system and its associated psychological functions were found to be immune to these otherwise widespread changes.

In the present chapter we examine the proposition that mental energy declines with age, as physical energy certainly does (Sacher & Duffy, 1978). By *mental energy* we mean the reservoir of psychological energy that enables cognitive operations to be performed. Presumably the psychological notion of mental energy has a physiological correlate, but we will not be concerned with that here. The concept of mental energy has not been much discussed in the literature although theorists have recently distinguished *automatic* from *controlled* (or *effortful*) processes (Shiffrin & Schneider, 1977). Automatic processes are those which run off involuntarily; they require little or no attention (and thus, presumably, consume little mental energy), interfere minimally with concurrent mental operations, and do not necessarily involve conscious awareness. In contrast, controlled operations typically involve a greater degree of conscious awareness, are voluntary and optional, and require the allocation of attentional resources. That is, they *do* consume mental energy. Most complex tasks probably involve a combination of automatic and controlled processes, the overall degree of automaticity being heavily dependent on how practiced the person is at the task. That is, specific operations can change from *controlled* to *automatic* with practice and experience.

By this account, different mental operations and activities will require different amounts of mental energy or attentional resource (Norman & Bobrow, 1975). Also, the observation that human subjects can perform a strictly limited number of controlled operations at one time has led to the notion that the momentary availability of attentional resources is limited (Kahneman, 1973). This is one usage of the term *mental energy*, and it is the one discussed in the present chapter. A second sense in which the notion of a pool of mental energy might be used is the total reservoir which may be depleted in the course of extended strenuous mental activity, thereby leading to fatigue. It seems plausible that older people have fewer reserves of mental energy in this sense also, but the theme will not be pursued here.

In summary, it is postulated that mental energy is required for the effective functioning of certain mental operations. In general, the *controlled* operations that require allocation of mental energy (or attention or processing resources) are those which are unpracticed or those which require novel combinations of existing operations. It is speculated that the momentary amount of energy available to perform a given task at a given time declines with age. If this is so, it follows that older subjects should be more heavily penalized in tasks requiring novel controlled processing, and there is mounting evidence to this effect (Hasher & Zacks, 1979).

The present chapter focuses on the notion that a reduction in available mental energy is *one* of several major factors underlying declining cognitive efficiency in the elderly. We will deal largely with deficits in episodic and semantic memory, but the implications of the current view for other cognitive abilities will also be pointed out. Specifically, the chapter explores three main themes. The first is an account of age differences in memory and related abilities in terms of encoding and retrieval processes. The basic idea to be examined is that the deeper and more elaborate encoding processes associated with higher levels of retention require more attentional resource (Johnston & Heinz, 1978). If older subjects have a smaller pool of available mental energy (that is smaller reserves of attentional resource), it follows that their encoding, and perhaps retrieval, processes will be impaired whenever the limit of processing resources is exceeded. Even if the limit is not exceeded, it is possible that a smaller pool of resource is associated with impaired processing, although that is a matter for empirical exploration. It is also possible that older people do not differ in the amount of mental energy they have available, but are less willing to expend it. In either event, it would be expected that tasks tapping automatic processes would show a lesser age-related deficit than tasks requiring controlled processing.

The second theme is an examination of the parallel between the effects of aging and the effects of other variables on memory performance. There are interesting similarities in the pattern of memory deficits observed in old age, alcoholic intoxication, and fatigue (Craik, 1977b; Craik & Simon, 1980). Of particular interest is the observation that encoding under divided attention conditions also yields the same pattern of memory deficits as is observed with older and intoxicated people (Craik, 1982), leading to the speculative conclusion that division of attention diverts processing resources from relevant encoding processes in much the same way as encoding processes receive insufficient resources in aging, intoxication, and fatigue. That is, it is suggested that intoxication and fatigue, like old age, are conditions in which attentional resources are depleted and that all these conditions can be mimicked by division of attention in young, alert, sober subjects.

The third theme to be explored briefly is that the memory deficits observed in older subjects are "production deficiencies" in the sense that the subjects are *capable* of carrying out more effective encoding and retrieval operations but do not spontaneously do so (see also Chapter 7). This analysis leads to an interesting question, namely, *why* do older subjects not encode more efficiently if they are capable of doing so? The analysis also leads to the important conclusion that if older subjects still possess these capabilities, it is presumably possible to rectify their inefficient processing through procedures that constrain and guide the relevant mental operations.

## Theoretical Background

In this section we outline the theoretical assumptions that underlie our approach to the study of age changes in memory and thereby set the scene for the subsequent description of some empirical studies.

The first and most general point is that few absolute statements can be made about age differences in memory performance. Rather, overall performance must be understood as a complex set of interactions between the subjects tested, the materials used, and the task or goal set by the experimenter (Jenkins, 1979). Thus, final statements about memory and aging are unlikely to take the simple form of "memory becomes 10% less efficient with each decade" and more likely to consist of conclusions such as "age-related losses in memory are minimized by using highly meaningful materials, an encoding task that induces semantic processing of these materials, and a retrieval test that reinstates the original learning context." That is, conclusions are likely to be relative, not absolute, in character.

The view of remembering adopted in the present chapter is the set of ideas characterized by Craik (1981) as a general processing view of human memory. This composite view stems from the theoretical notions of several researchers, notably Jacoby (Jacoby & Craik, 1979; Jacoby & Dallas, 1981), Kolers (1975, 1979) and Tulving (1974; Tulving & Thomson, 1973). In outline, the idea is that past experience in some organized form largely determines the analysis and interpretation of the incoming stimulus array. The specific analytic operations performed on a particular event are retained in the form of a record (the memory trace) or form an encoded "description" (Norman & Bobrow, 1979) of the event, although not all theorists (e.g., Kolers, 1979) share this view. Typically, only some aspects of the event are analyzed or encoded on any one occasion; the specific subset is determined by the subject's accumulated relevant past experience ("semantic memory" in Tulving's terms) and the subject's temporary goals, expectations, and mental set. For example, highly familiar events or well-practiced operations will require relatively little analysis, and such events are poorly remembered at a later time. Conversely, tasks or materials that lead to rich and extensive analysis (especially "deeper" semantic analysis) are typically well remembered subsequently (Craik & Tulving, 1975). Thus, memorial performance is apparently a function of the extensiveness of the initial analytic operations (Kolers, 1975, 1979). At the time of retrieval, the same processing operations must be reinvoked to give rise to the experience of remembering. This qualitative similarity between encoding and retrieval processes (the encoding specificity principle) may be shaped and guided by the materials themselves, by identical or similar contexts, by retrieval cues, and speculatively by reconstructive processes that involve interactions between general knowledge of the to-be-remembered event and information in the encoded memory record of the event.

In this scheme, memory deficits could arise in a number of ways. Most obviously, if deeper and more extensive encoding processes require greater amounts of attentional resource, a reduction in attentional resources would result in deficient encodings. Similarly, retrieval operations may also demand attentional resources, and their unavailability might result in less extensive and less efficient retrieval. This speculation may require qualification in that some part of the retrieval process may be relatively automatic and thus not require attention (Jacoby & Dallas, 1981; Mandler, 1980). According to these theorists, recognition consists of a familiarity judgment which is rapid and relatively effortless, augmented when necessary by an effortful reconstructive process—conceivably, it is only the latter process that is attention-demanding. Thus, a reduction in attentional resources would yield a decrement in retrieval only to the extent that reconstructive processes must be involved. Finally, memory deficits might arise from a mismatch of encoding and retrieval processes—that is, if the qualitative nature of the mental operations differed at encoding and retrieval, successful remembering would be less likely to occur. It should be stressed that these are the deficits that might occur as a function of the processing framework described in the preceding paragraphs; other memory deficits (amnesias, fugue, repression) might occur for quite different reasons.

In the following sections, various empirical results will be described in an attempt to illustrate the processing deficit viewpoint. First, some studies of memory for events (episodic memory) will be reported, followed by studies of semantic memory. Following a description of the results, the adequacy of the theoretical viewpoint will be evaluated.

## Empirical Studies

### *Aging and Divided Attention*

Before describing some new experiments from our own laboratory, we shall briefly review some of the work that suggests a parallel between the effects of aging and the effects of divided attention. First, it is well established that dividing the subject's attention during presentation of a word list leads to a decrement in subsequent free recall of the words. The decrement is not uniform, however, but is confined to the early (secondary memory) portion of the list (Anderson & Craik, 1974; Baddeley, Scott, Drynan, & Smith, 1969; Murdock, 1965). This same pattern has also been found in older subjects as opposed to young subjects (Craik, 1968; Raymond, 1971) and in intoxicated as opposed to sober subjects (Jones, 1973). It is not the case that *any* disruptive activity gives rise to this pattern, as a task interpolated between presentation and recall leads to a decrement in primary memory but not in secondary memory (Glanzer & Cunitz, 1966). A plausible explanation of the pattern observed under divided attention, aging, and intoxication is that a reduction in attentional resources reduces the subject's ability to carry out deep and elaborate processing—both within and between words—and that this reduction in semantic processing is more detrimental to secondary memory than to primary memory (e.g., Baddeley, 1966).

A further similarity between divided attention and aging is seen in the relation between list length and free recall. It has been known for some time that the number of words recalled from a list increases as the length of the list increases, and that the relation between list length and number of words recalled is approximately linear (Murdock, 1960). That is, the relation can be expressed as

$$R = a + bL$$

where R = the number of words recalled, L = list length, and $a$ and $b$ are constants. Craik (1968) suggested that the intercept constant $a$ largely reflects a relatively stable primary memory component, whereas the slope constant $b$ is an index of secondary memory efficiency. This suggestion was supported by empirical evidence showing that $b$ increased as the lists were made more familiar and amenable to organization; for example, it was found that $b$ increased progressively from lists of unrelated words and lists of animal names to lists of English country names (English subjects were used). Craik also found that $b = 0.15$ for young adult subjects, whereas $b = 0.03$ for a group of subjects whose average age was 65. Mandler and Worden (1973) reported a study in which subjects freely recalled words from lists of 30, 60, or 120 words. The words were presented either under a condition in which subjects paid full attention to the words or under a condition in which subjects performed a concurrent task. The slope constants were 0.37 and 0.05 under the full and divided attention conditions respectively. In a similar study carried out in our laboratory, young subjects listened to word lists of different lengths under full attention conditions, or under the constraint to classify each word as starting with a letter from A–L or from M–Z and as spoken by a male or a female speaker; all subjects knew that they were to recall the words later. The equations relating recall to list length were:

| | |
|---|---|
| Full attention | $R = 4.95 + 0.22L$ |
| Divided attention | $R = 4.30 + 0.10L$ |

Thus, divided attention had relatively little effect on the intercept but was again found to have a substantial effect on the slope. The similarity between the effects of aging and divided attention is attributed to a common decrement in the efficiency with which words are encoded and retrieved.

A third similarity to be mentioned briefly is that both under conditions of divided attention during learning (Mandler & Worden, 1973) and in a group of older subjects (Rankin & Kausler, 1979) the experimental groups made more semantic errors in a subsequent recognition memory test than did the young (full attention) control groups. That is, the experimental groups showed a substantially greater tendency than controls to select synonyms of presented words in the recognition test. This interesting result strongly implies that older people and *divided-attention* subjects do encode something of the meaning of the words learned but that the encoded meaning is less specific and precise. That is, enough of the word's meaning has been encoded to enable the subject to choose that general category at the time of recognition, but not enough to enable him to differentiate between the correct word and a semantically similar distractor item. These findings will be discussed again later in the chapter.

A fourth point relating divided attention to aging and to alcoholic intoxication is that these variables typically interact in their effects on memory performance. For example, old subjects are particularly penalized by tasks requiring divided attention (Inglis & Caird, 1963; Kirchner, 1958). Similarly, intoxicated subjects perform particularly poorly when their attention is divided between two tasks (Levine, Kramer, & Levine, 1975; Moskowitz & de Pry, 1968). Further, older subjects are more vulnerable to the detrimental effects of alcohol on performance (Parsons & Prigatano, 1977). The consistent presence of these interactive effects strongly suggests that some common process is being tapped in all cases. Our suggestion is that a common pool of attentional resource is depleted by aging, divided attention, and alcoholic intoxication.

It is worth pointing out that divided attention is used here simply as a technique for reducing the amount of resource available for a specific task and that, according to the present argument, as the demands of the secondary task increase, performance on the primary task should increasingly resemble that of the older or intoxicated subject. In addition, there may well be deleterious effects on performance arising from the requirement to organize the division of attention between the two tasks, but such specific effects of divided attention will not be addressed in the present chapter.

What factors underlie the poorer memory performance of subjects who are old or intoxicated, or whose attention is divided? The present suggestion is that encoding processes are less efficient under these conditions, and this suggestion is supported by a number of findings in the literature. Encoding processes for words may be broken down into intra-item and inter-item processes (Mandler, 1979); it appears to be inter-item processing that is principally affected. For example, several investigators have shown that the formation of inter-item organization is impaired in older subjects (Hultsch, 1969; Laurence, 1966) and this result has also been found with alcoholically intoxicated subjects (Parker, Alkana, Birnbaum, Hartley, & Noble, 1974; Rosen & Lee, 1976). Intra-item encodings may be less affected by the presumed withdrawal of attentional resources, as indicated by the finding that recognition is less impaired than is recall by the aging process (see Craik, 1977a). Plausibly, then, it is the formation of new connections between items that is impeded by a lack of attentional resource. Other deeper types of processing are also detrimentally affected by aging both in the processing of word lists (Eysenck, 1974, 1977) and with more complex verbal materials. In the latter category, for example, Cohen (1979) and Till and Walsh (1980) have shown that older subjects fail to draw inferences as readily as young people do from sentences and short segments of text. It is attractive to postulate a failure of deeper, more elaborate processing under intoxication and divided attention also, but so far the evidence is scanty. In the case of alcoholic intoxication, indeed, there is some evidence contrary to a processing deficit explanation (Hartley, Birnbaum, & Parker, 1978).

In summary, there is good evidence that aging and divided attention have similar effects on memory. Both sets of effects can be characterized as failures of adequate encoding, more specifically as failures to form new inter-item connections, and failures to engage in deeper processing. It might be expected that retrieval operations would be similarly impaired (e.g., Craik & Jacoby, 1979) but there is no compelling evidence to this effect, except perhaps that aging (Schonfield & Robertson, 1966) appears to impair recognition less than it impairs recall. It is also attractive to believe that alcoholic intoxication has effects on memory that are similar to the effects of aging (Craik, 1977b), but here also the evidence is less than complete. The basic decrement postulated to underlie these processing deficits is a lack of mental energy or attentional resource. The adequacy of this speculation will be reassessed after some new empirical studies are considered.

## *Depth of Processing and Aging*

Eysenck (1974, 1977) has suggested a processing deficit hypothesis to account for age differences in memory performance. According to this view, deeper (that is, semantic, associative, and inferential) processes typically require more effort and attention to achieve, and it is these processes that older subjects fail to carry out—with a resulting impairment in memory performance. Eysenck's notion apparently predicts an interaction between age and type of processing, with older subjects showing the greatest decrement at deeper levels, and he did obtain this result (Eysenck, 1974). Another line of argument put forward by Craik (1977a) appears at first to lead to a different prediction. Craik suggested that the older person's processing was inefficient rather than truly defective and that if processing was guided by means of an orienting task, the older subject's memory decrement might be overcome. This reasoning suggests that whereas old subjects would show a decrement in a free learning situation (because they do not spontaneously carry out deeper processing), *no* age decrement might be found at any level of processing when orienting tasks are provided to guide processing. Implicit in this argument is the idea that sufficient attentional resources are potentially available to older subjects (contrary to earlier suggestions in the present chapter) but that for some reason these resources are not mobilized effectively.

A study by White (described by Craik, 1977a) found an interaction between age and level of processing (greater age decrement at deeper levels) in recall, even though orienting tasks were used. This result thus supports Eysenck's position. However, in a subsequent recognition task within the same experiment

White found no age decrement at any level of processing, although a substantial age decrement remained in the free learning condition; this second result fits Craik's position. A possible resolution of the two views is that older people are inefficient at both encoding and retrieval processing. It is not sufficient to "repair" only encoding (by means, say, of an orienting task) because older subjects still exhibit a decrement if retrieval is unguided, as it is in free recall. This is our account of White's free recall data. When both encoding and retrieval are "repaired"—as in the combination of orienting tasks at encoding with a recognition test at retrieval—the age decrement is minimized, or even eliminated as in White's recognition data. We argue that recognition repairs retrieval processing in older subjects, in the sense that recognition is typically much more effective than free recall in guiding the memory system to reconstruct the same traces (Tulving, 1974) or operations (Kolers, 1973) that were formed when the target items were initially encoded. In free recall, subjects must presumably rely more on self-initiated reconstructive operations, and it may be this part of the retrieval process that older subjects perform less efficiently.

Thus, whereas *typically* older subjects will show greater decrements at deeper levels of processing because such encodings usually demand more effort and attention (Eysenck & Eysenck, 1979; Johnston & Heinz, 1978), there is nothing absolute or inevitable about this position. If deeper processing is made easy or accessible by some means, then the older person will make use of the constraints provided by the task or the material to accomplish those deeper types of processing. If some nominally shallow level of processing is made particularly difficult or effortful to accomplish (e.g., Craik & Tulving, 1975, Exp. 5), then older subjects might well show a greater memory decrement at that level. *Depth* of processing is defined in terms of where the qualitative type of processing lies between sensory surface structure on the one hand and semantic, associative, inferential information on the other. However, access to a specific type of information will depend not only on its depth, but on the task, the materials, and the expertise of the subject (Jenkins, 1979). Deeper levels will *usually* require more effort and attention, but this usual state of affairs must be qualified by consideration of these other factors.

A recent study by Yokubynas (1979) nicely illustrates some of these points. Yokubynas utilized the paradigm devised by Craik and Tulving (1975) in which subjects are asked questions relating to a presented word's typescript, rhyming characteristics, or semantic characteristics, followed by recall and then recognition of the words. Figure 1 shows that in recall deeper processing was associated with larger age decrements both in the case where the initial question led to a positive response (e.g., to do with religion–*priest*) and where it led to a negative response (e.g., a piece of furniture–*leopard*). These recall results thus replicate the findings of Eysenck (1974) and White (cited by Craik, 1977a). In recognition, Yokubynas found very much the same pattern of results in the negative condition, but no interaction (and virtually no age decrement) in the positive

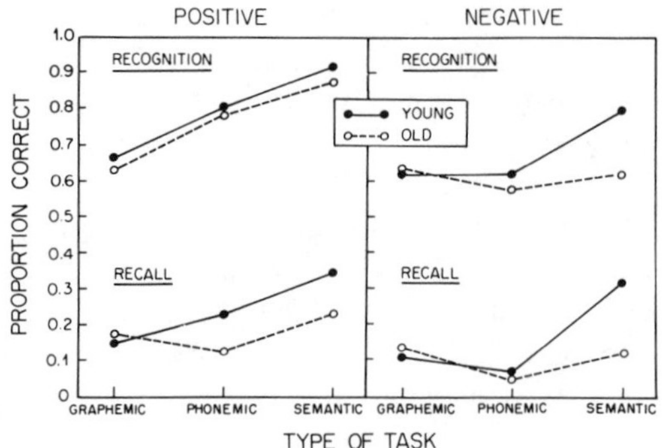


Fig. 1. Recall and recognition as a function of encoding condition and age (Yokubynas, 1979).

condition. Thus, the latter condition replicates the recognition findings in White's experiment. A plausible explanation of these results is that the age decrement is eliminated when a highly compatible encoding condition is combined with a retrieval condition that guides processing effectively.

In our own laboratory we had independently conducted an experiment that replicated Yokubynas's study, but with divided attention as the variable of interest rather than age. That is, subjects answered the orienting task questions about the visually presented words either under conditions of full attention or under conditions in which they had to perform a simultaneous auditory task. Figure 2 shows that the memory deficit normally found under divided attention conditions was eliminated in the conditions that combined positive responses to the orienting task with recognition testing. In other conditions, the divided attention group shows the greatest memory deficit at deeper levels of processing. All in all, the similarity of these results to those of Yokubynas is remarkable and adds further weight to the notion that the effects of aging and divided attention are very similar.

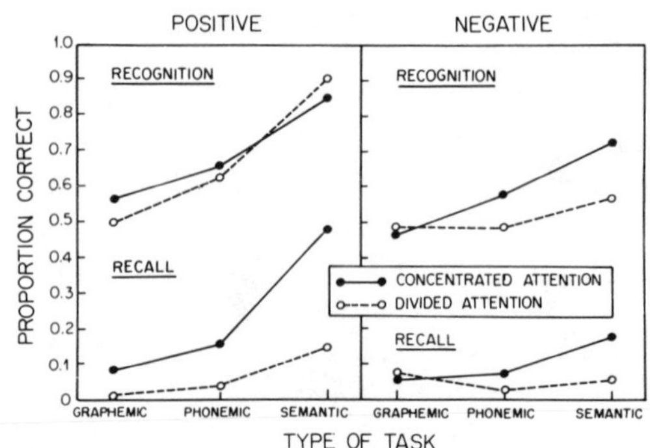


Fig. 2. Recall and recognition as a function of encoding condition and concentrated or divided attention.

The general notion that an age-related processing deficit at encoding and retrieval can be repaired by constraining and guiding the processes involved can also be demonstrated in other ways. It is known that pictures of objects are associated with higher retention levels than the corresponding names of the objects (Paivio, 1971). Paivio's account of this effect is that visual imagery is a particularly effective memory code and that pictures are more likely than words to evoke such imagery. If pictures facilitate these more effective encoding processes, it follows from the arguments made in the preceding paragraphs that older subjects should benefit more than younger subjects from pictorial presentation, especially if retrieval processes are also constrained by the use of recognition testing. By the same argument, age differences should be greatest when the names of objects are presented and retention is tested by free recall. This hypothesis was tested in a study by Rabinowitz, Ackerman, and Craik (unpublished). Lists of 32 objects were presented to young and older subjects, 16 of the objects as words and 16 as line drawings. After each of two such lists, subjects recalled as many as possible of the 32 items. Following the recall task for the second list, recognition tasks for both lists of items were administered; in all cases the recognition stimuli were words, even when the items were presented as drawings. The results are shown in Table 1.

The table shows substantial age decrements in free recall of both words and pictures, a reduced age decrement in word recognition, and essentially no age difference in picture recognition. We argue that pictures give relatively easy access to deep levels of processing, they "drive" the encoding processes to a much greater extent than do word stimuli, and the inefficient encoding processes of older subjects benefit particularly, especially when the pictorial stimuli are combined with a subsequent recognition test.

The same pattern of results was obtained in a further study by Rabinowitz, Ackerman, Craik, and Hinchley (1982) by manipulating encoding *instructions*, as opposed to varying the stimuli. In this second study, younger and older subjects were given lists of unassociated noun pairs to learn. Three different groups were instructed either (1) simply to learn the pairs as best they could, (2) to think of some commonality—some common property or characteristic of the two words in each pair, or (3) to form an interactive image of the two objects

*Table 1. Age Difference in Recall and Recognition of Pictures and Words*

| | Recall | | Recognition | |
|---|---|---|---|---|
| | Words | Pictures | Words | Pictures |
| Young | .33 | .52 | .73 | .84 |
| Old | .17 | .36 | .63 | .83 |

*Table 2. Proportions of Words Recalled after Different Encoding Instructions*

| | Learn | Commonality | Imagery |
|---|---|---|---|
| Young | .56 | .89 | .83 |
| Old | .40 | .75 | .84 |

named in each word pair. The retention test was cued recall—one word from each pair was provided as a cue for the second word. Table 2 shows that subjects of both age groups benefited from the instructions to find a commonality or create an image but that the older group again showed a greater benefit. The age decrement fell from 16% in the case of free learning to zero in the case of interactive imagery. As in the previous study, the age decrement was eliminated by combining an encoding condition that induced effective processing with a retention test that induced effective retrieval processes.

To summarize, we have argued (with other authors, notably Eysenck, 1974, and Perlmutter & Mitchell, Chapter 7) that older subjects exhibit a processing deficit in that they often fail to carry out deeper, inferential processing at both encoding and retrieval. Our suggested reason for this failure is that deeper processing typically requires more attentional resources. However, older people are still capable of carrying out effective encoding and retrieval processes if their processing is constrained and guided by the materials and the task.

## *Age Differences in Semantic Memory*

The experiments described in the preceding section involved memory for episodic events. Are there also age differences in retrieval of information from semantic memory, and do attentional resources play a similar role in this situation? Two recent experiments by Byrd explored these issues.

Byrd's first experiment contrasted generation and decision processes in semantic memory using a technique developed by Freedman and Loftus (1971). In the generation task, subjects were shown a category name followed after 2 seconds by a further presentation of the category name with an initial letter; the subject's task was to generate an exemplar of the category beginning with that letter. Thus, the stimulus *fruit–p* might yield the response *peach* or *plum*. In the decision version of the task, the subject was presented with the category name followed after 2 seconds by the category name and an exemplar; his task was to decide as rapidly as possible whether the exemplar belonged to the category—thus, *fruit–apple* should lead to a positive response and *fruit–chair* to a negative response. The generation and decision trials were either intermixed randomly or were blocked together; thus, only in the latter case did subjects know what type of trial would follow the first *category name only* slide. Loftus (1976) has demonstrated that blocking reduces response times in the *fruit–p* generation case, presumably by setting subjects to generate exemplars as soon as the first category name slide is shown. The present studies sought to ascertain whether blocking would have a similar effect on the decision task and a similar effect for old and young subjects.

Figure 3 shows that generation (*fruit–p*) took substantially longer than decision (*fruit–apple*), that old subjects were slower than young subjects, and that blocking speeded responses in all cases. Of greater interest is the finding that blocking speeded the generation task more than the decision task, but only for young subjects (the three-way interaction was reliable). Thus, in the generation task young subjects were able to take greater advantage of their knowledge of the type of trial coming up; presumably they marshalled their attentional resources to prepare to generate exemplars of the category shown on the first slide. Apparently older subjects did not "set" themselves to the same degree. The blocking manipulation was less effective in the decision task, perhaps because the stimulus drives processing to a greater extent. That is, the generation task requires a lot of self-initiated processing before a response can be made, whereas the decision task stimuli (*fruit–apple; animal–horse*) are more compatible with semantic memory structures and, speculatively, may drive the analysis and response in a somewhat more automatic way. If this account is correct, the present results again show that older subjects are at the greatest relative disadvantage to

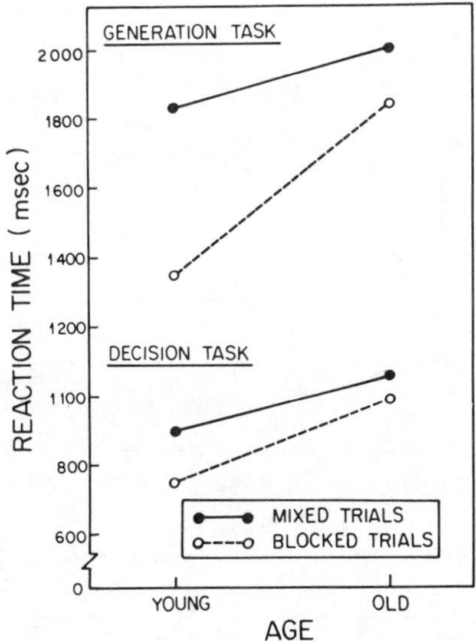


Fig. 3. Generation and decision times as a function of age and whether trials were mixed or blocked.

younger subjects when they must rely on self-initiated, conscious, controlled processes (Shiffrin & Schneider, 1977), and in this sense the present results resemble the findings from episodic memory studies.

If older subjects are relatively unimpaired in tasks utilizing automatic processes (Hasher & Zacks, 1979), it follows that they should show as great a priming effect as young subjects do in the decision task described above. The priming effect in this situation refers to the observation that response times are speeded when the same category is presented in successive trials. Loftus and Loftus (1974) demonstrated such a priming effect with the category–letter generation task; they also showed that the priming was relatively transient in that when questions from the same semantic category were separated by two trials using different categories, the reduction in generation time to the second question was virtually eliminated. The suggestion, then, is that the category priming effect reflects automatic processing and that there should be no age differences in the effect.

In Byrd's second experiment, subjects were shown a series of category–exemplar slides as in the decision task described above. In this study each decision slide appeared alone in the trial; it was not preceded by the relevant category name. Throughout the series of trials, categories were repeated (same category name but a different exemplar—e.g., *fruit–cherry, fruit–apple*) either with no further trials intervening (lag 0) or with one or two different-category trials intervening (lag 1 and lag 2, respectively). As in the previous experiment

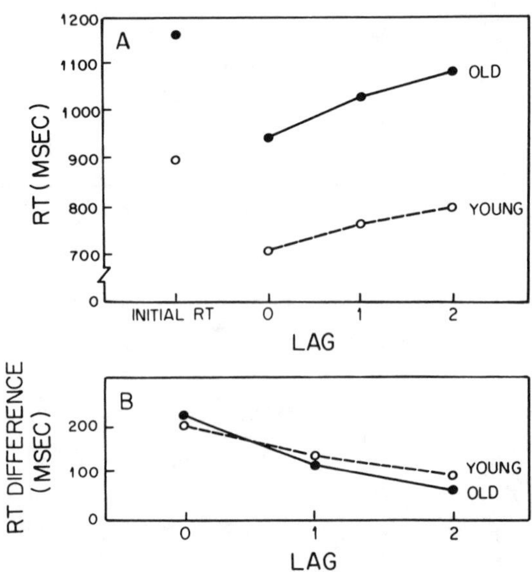


Fig. 4. Reaction times in a category-decision task as a function of age and lag.

the subject's task was to decide rapidly whether the exemplar was a member of the category name accompanying it on the slide.

The upper part of Figure 4 shows the absolute reaction times for old and young subjects. Both groups reacted more rapidly to repeated categories relative to the initial appearance of that category, but this priming effect declined from over 200 msec at lag 0 to 100 msec or less at lag 2. The interesting finding is that whereas older subjects took longer to respond in absolute terms (Figure 4A), there were no age differences in either the size of the priming effect or its decline over intervening trials (see Chapter 5 for a similar result). The implication of this finding is that there appear to be essentially no age differences in automatic processing even, as in this case, when the processing clearly involves semantic structures. Thus, the pattern of age decrements documented in this chapter cannot be described universally in terms of a greater decrement at deeper levels of processing; when deeper (semantic) processing involves automated procedures, age differences are minimal (Hasher & Zacks, 1979; Howard, Lasaga, & McAndrews, 1980). This conclusion adds further weight to our general position that age differences appear to the extent that effortful processing operations, requiring considerable attentional resources, are involved.

## *Summary of Empirical Results*

The general position advocated in the present chapter is that age differences in memory performance can be attributed to inefficiencies in encoding processes and probably in retrieval processes also. We have suggested that the decreased availability of attentional resources in older people reduces the amount of spontaneously initiated deep, elaborate, and inferential processing carried out and that this reduction in turn is associated with lower levels of retention. We do not wish to imply that *no* semantic processing is carried out; rather, it seems that the semantic processing achieved is more general in character (Craik & Simon, 1980; Rabinowitz & Ackerman, Chapter 8). That is, older subjects may encode events in "the same old way" from one occasion to the next, rather than encoding each event distinctively in terms of its specific context. This postulated decreasing specificity of encoding may lie behind the observation that both older people and subjects under divided attention conditions make more false alarm responses to synonyms of target words in a recognition task (Mandler & Worden, 1973; Rankin & Kausler, 1979). Loss of contextual specificity in older people's encodings is also evident in the finding (Raymond, 1971) that older subjects import more intrusions from previous lists into their current list recall in a free recall test. It appears that older subjects do not delimit each item so precisely in terms of the temporal, semantic, and other factors specific to each list. A similar finding has been reported for amnesic patients (Huppert & Piercy, 1976) and for normal subjects under divided attention conditions (Allport, cited by Craik,

1977b). Generally, it appears that various abnormal conditions act to reduce the adequacy and extensiveness of an item's encoding. Some aspects of a perceived event—its basic physical attributes and its general meaning, for example—are encoded relatively easily and automatically, whereas further aspects such as inferential and contextually specific details of meaning appear to be more optional, and they may not be encoded unless guided by orienting tasks that facilitate such further processing.

A related point, which gains some support from the studies reviewed in previous sections, is that automatic aspects of information processing appear to remain essentially intact in older subjects (Hasher & Zacks, 1979; Howard *et al.*, 1980). It is the more effortful conscious processes that are impaired, and in this sense the results from older subjects are like findings with amnesic patients that conscious, episodic aspects of memory show large decrements, whereas less specific procedural aspects of memory (knowing how) show relatively little impairment (Cohen & Squire, 1980; Moscovitch, Chapter 4). Both Mandler (1980) and Jacoby and Dallas (1981) have recently suggested that recognition memory may be based on a relatively automatic judgment of familiarity plus a more effortful retrieval component. Putting these suggestions together with the preceding ideas, we may speculate that older subjects' recognition processes should be impaired only in the latter respect.

Finally, it may be worth stressing that it is not sufficient to characterize age losses in memory under the description "the harder the task, the greater the age decrement." A number of cases do fit that description; these are cases in which encoding or retrieval processes are repaired, and whereas all subjects benefit from the help provided, older subjects typically benefit more (e.g., Hulicka & Grossman, 1967; Schonfield & Robertson, 1966). This pattern of results occurs in our view because older subjects largely retain the ability to encode and retrieve effectively but do not carry out these effective operations unless constrained and guided by tasks or instructions. Younger subjects, on the other hand, carry out such operations spontaneously to a greater extent and thus their performance improves less markedly when guiding tasks or instructions are provided. But not all results show greater age decrements at lower levels of performance. For example, retention levels in the Peterson and Peterson short-term memory paradigm decline equally for old and young subjects as a function of retention interval (see Figure 6 in Craik, 1977a). Second, both Yokubynas's results (Figure 1) and White's data (Craik, 1977a) show an equivalent decline in recognition memory for young and old subjects as a function of shallower depths of processing. As a third example, Rabinowitz and Ackerman's data (Chapter 8, Experiment 2) show cases in which older subjects equal younger subjects' performance levels, both at high levels of retention (high associates, intra-list cues) and at relatively low levels of retention (high associates, extra-list cues), whereas at intermediate levels of retention, a large age decrement is found (low associates, intra list cues). It is not just difficulty level that determines the age decrement;

other *qualitative* aspects of encoding and retrieval processes must also be considered.

## Conclusions: Possible Reasons for Age Decrements in Memory

In view of the emerging consensus that older people are able to carry out effective processing but do not do so spontaneously, it may reasonably be asked *why* older subjects exhibit such a production deficiency. One possible candidate is a failure of metamemory; perhaps older subjects have poorer insight into their own memory processes. At first sight this is an attractive hypothesis since it fits the production deficiency picture—older subjects do not realize that they should use associations or imagery to improve their performance. However, several studies have failed to find age differences in metamemorial knowledge (e.g., Lachman & Lachman, 1980; Perlmutter, 1978). It is certainly true that older people have poor insight into their memory processes, but so do young people, even bright young college students. It is apparently not the knowledge about memory that changes with age so much as the likelihood that an effective strategy will be used.

A second plausible candidate is that older people have had less recent practice at remembering, especially in dealing with the rather academic (and often meaningless) materials presented to them in verbal learning studies. Both Baltes and Willis (Chapter 19) and Rabbitt (Chapter 5) stress the important role of practice in ameliorating apparent age deficits. The lack of practice hypothesis does seem a very reasonable one and is particularly plausible if remembering is regarded as a set of skilled procedures (Bartlett, 1932; Kolers, 1979). However, lack of practice is unlikely to be the complete story in our view. Perlmutter (1978) has found "typical" patterns of age decrement with subjects who were younger and older university faculty members. Even allowing for some age-related drop off in intellectual activity, it seems probable that Perlmutter's older subjects continue to think, solve problems, and learn abstract verbal materials on a day-to-day basis. The converse case is that memory losses in the elderly are by no means restricted to artificial laboratory situations; older people typically complain of poorer memory for everyday incidents and events which they presumably continue to experience and thus "practice" as before.

Thus, whereas lack of practice may well underlie some memory decrements in older people, it is unlikely to be the only cause. In the present chapter we have argued that a decline in attentional resources (or mental energy) is a further major factor. This speculation is at least plausible from what we know of age changes in brain structure and function (e.g., Petit, Woodruff, Chapters 1 and 3) and from what we know of age-related declines in somatic energy levels (Sacher, 1978).

The speculation is given added credibility by a consideration of the strong parallels between the effects of aging, alcoholic intoxication, and divided attention, documented in the present chapter. We postulate that reduced attentional resources lead to an attenuation or shrinkage in the richness, extensiveness, and depth of processing operations at both encoding and retrieval. Automatic processes are left relatively unimpaired (because they require no attentional resources, by definition), whereas deliberate, effortful, and conscious processes are affected to the greatest extent. More specifically, older subjects' encodings will contain less associative and inferential information; their encodings go less beyond the information given. Similarly, we have suggested that an encoded event is less modified by the specific context in which it occurs for the older person and that this difference leads to a less distinctive (and thus less memorable) encoding of the event.

The hopeful aspect of this point of view is that if these postulated age changes are truly *inefficiencies* rather than absolute losses of function, the possibility of developing remedial procedures clearly exists. The work with orienting tasks and instructions that guide and constrain processing both during encoding and retrieval suggests techniques that might be tried and provides strong encouragement for their successful development.

ACKNOWLEDGMENTS

The authors are grateful for extremely useful suggestions on a previous draft of the chapter from Susan Kennedy, Jan Rabinowitz, and Sandra Trehub.

## References

Anderson, C. M. B., & Craik, F. I. M. The effect of a concurrent task on recall from primary memory. *Journal of Verbal Learning and Verbal Behavior*, 1974, *13*, 107–113.

Baddeley, A. D., Scott, D., Drynan, R., & Smith, J. C. Short-term memory and the limited capacity hypothesis. *British Journal of Psychology*, 1969, *60*, 51–55.

Bartlett, F. C. *Remembering: A study in experimental and social psychology*. Cambridge: Cambridge University Press, 1932.

Cohen, C. Language comprehension in old age. *Cognitive Psychology*, 1979, *11*, 412–429.

Cohen, N. J., & Squire, L. R. Preserved learning and retention of pattern-analyzing skill in amnesia: Dissociation of knowing how and knowing that. *Science*, 1980, *210*, 207–210.

Craik, F. I. M. Two components in free recall. *Journal of Verbal Learning and Verbal Behavior*, 1968, *7*, 996–1004.

Craik, F. I. M. Age differences in human memory. In J. E. Birren & K. W. Schaie (Eds.), *Handbook of the psychology of aging*. New York: Van Nostrand Reinhold, 1977. (a)

Craik, F. I. M. Similarities between the effects of aging and alcoholic intoxication on memory performance, construed within a level of processing framework. In I. M. Birnbaum & E. S. Parker (Eds.), *Alcohol and human memory*. Hillsdale, N.J.: Lawrence Erlbaum, 1977. (b)

Craik, F. I. M. Encoding and retrieval effects in human memory: A partial review. In J. B. Long & A. B. Baddeley (Eds.), *Attention and performance*. Hillsdale, N.J.: Lawrence Erlbaum, 1981.

Craik, F. I. M. Selective changes in encoding as a function of reduced processing capacity. In F. Klix, J. Hoffman, & E. van der Meer (Eds.), *Coding and knowledge representation: Processes and structures in human memory*. Amsterdam: Elsevier, North-Holland, 1982.

Craik, F. I. M., & Tulving, E. Depth of processing and the retention of words in episodic memory. *Journal of Experimental Psychology: General*, 1975, *104*, 268–294.

Craik, F. I. M., & Jacoby, L. L. Elaboration and distinctiveness in episodic memory. In L. G. Nilsson (Ed.), *Perspectives on memory research*. Hillsdale, N.J.: Lawrence Erlbaum, 1979.

Craik, F. I. M., & Simon, E. Age differences in memory: The roles of attention and depth of processing. In L. W. Poon *et al.* (Eds.), *New directions in memory and aging*. Hillsdale, N.J.: Lawrence Erlbaum, 1980.

Eysenck, M. W. Age differences in incidental learning. *Developmental Psychology*, 1974, *10*, 936–941.

Eysenck, M. W. *Human memory: Theory, research, and individual differences*. New York: Pergamon, 1977.

Eysenck, M. W., & Eysenck, M. C. Processing depth, elaboration of encoding, memory stores, and expended processing capacity. *Journal of Experimental Psychology: Human Learning and Memory*, 1979, *5*, 472–484.

Finch, C. E., & Hayflick, L. *Handbook of the biology of aging*. New York: Van Nostrand Reinhold, 1977.

Freedman, J. L., & Loftus, E. F. Retrieval of words from long-term memory. *Journal of Verbal Learning and Verbal Behavior*, 1971, *10*, 107–115.

Glanzer, M., & Cunitz, A. Two storage mechanisms in free recall. *Journal of Verbal Learning and Verbal Behavior*, 1966, *5*, 351–360.

Hartley, J. T., Birnbaum, I. M., & Parker, E. S. Alcohol and storage deficits: Kind of processing? *Journal of Verbal Learning and Verbal Behavior*, 1978, *17*, 635–647.

Hasher, L., & Zacks, R. T. Automatic and effortful processes in memory. *Journal of Experimental Psychology: General*, 1979, *108*, 356–388.

Howard, D. V., Lasaga, M. I., & McAndrews, M. P. Semantic activation during memory encoding across the adult life-span. *Journal of Gerontology*, 1980, *35*, 884–890.

Hulicka, I. M., & Grossman, J. L. Age group comparisons for the use of mediators in paired-associate learning. *Journal of Gerontology*, 1967, *22*, 46–51.

Hultsch, D. F. Adult age differences in the organization of free recall. *Developmental Psychology*, 1969, *1*, 673–678.

Huppert, F. A., & Piercy, M. Recognition memory in amnesic patients: Effects of temporal context and familiarity of material. *Cortex*, 1976, *12*, 3–20.

Inglis, J., & Caird, W. K. Age differences in successive responses to simultaneous stimulation. *Canadian Journal of Psychology*, 1963, *17*, 98–105.

Jacoby, L. L., & Craik, F. I. M. Effects of elaboration of processing at encoding and retrieval: Trace distinctiveness and recovery of initial context. In L. S. Cermak & F. I. M. Craik (Eds.), *Levels of processing in human memory*. Hillsdale, N.J.: Lawrence Erlbaum, 1979.

Jacoby, L. L., & Dallas, M. On the relationship between autobiographical memory and perceptual learning. *Journal of Experimental Psychology: General*, 1981, *110*, 306–340.

Jenkins, J. J. Four points to remember: A tetrahedral model of memory experiments. In L. S. Cermak & F. I. M. Craik (Eds.), *Levels of processing in human memory*. Hillsdale, N.J.: Lawrence Erlbaum, 1979.

Johnston, W. A., & Heinz, S. P. Flexibility and capacity demands of attention. *Journal of Experimental Psychology: General*, 1978, *107*, 420–435.

Jones, B. M. Memory impairment on the ascending and descending limbs of the blood alcohol curve. *Journal of Abnormal Psychology*, 1973, *82*, 24–32.

Kahneman, D. *Attention and effort*. Englewood Cliffs, N.J.: Prentice–Hall, 1973.

Kirchner, W. K. Age differences in short-term retention of rapidly changing information. *Journal of Experimental Psychology*, 1958, *55*, 352–358.

Kolers, P. A. Memorial consequences of automatized encoding. *Journal of Experimental Psychology: Human Learning and Memory*, 1975, *1*, 689–701.

Kolers, P. A. A pattern-analyzing basis of recognition. In L. S. Cermark & F. I. M. Craik (Eds.), *Levels of processing in human memory*. Hillsdale, N.J.: Lawrence Erlbaum, 1979.

Lachman, J. L., & Lachman, R. Age and the actualization of world knowledge. In L. W. Poon *et al.* (Eds.), *New Directions in Memory and Aging*. Hillsdale, N.J.: Lawrence Erlbaum, 1980.

Laurence, M. W. Age differences in performance and subjective organization in the free recall of pictorial material. *Canadian Journal of Psychology*, 1966, *20*, 388–399.

Levine, J. M., Kramer, G. G., & Levine, E. N. Effects of alcohol on human performance: An integration of research findings based on an abilities classification. *Journal of Applied Psychology*, 1975, *60*, 285–293.

Loftus, E. F. How to catch a zebra in semantic memory. In R. Shaw & J. Bransford (Eds.), *Perceiving, acting and knowing*. Hillsdale, N.J.: Lawrence Erlbaum, 1976.

Loftus, G. R., & Loftus, E. F. The influence of one memory retrieval on a subsequent memory retrieval. *Memory and Cognition*, 1974, *2*, 467–471.

Mandler, G. Organization and repetition: An extension of organizational principles with special reference to rote learning. In L.-G. Nielsson (Ed.), *Perspectives on memory research*. Hillsdale, N.J.: Lawrence Erlbaum, 1979.

Mandler, G. Recognizing: The judgment of previous occurrence. *Psychological Review*, 1980, *87*, 252–271.

Mandler, G., & Worden, P. E. Semantic processing without permanent storage. *Journal of Experimental Psychology*, 1973, *100*, 277–283.

Moskowitz, H., & de Pry, D. Differential effect of alcohol on auditory vigilance and divided-attention tasks. *Quarterly Journal of Studies on Alcohol*, 1968, *29*, 54–63.

Murdock, B. B., Jr. The immediate retention of unrelated words. *Journal of Experimental Psychology*, 1960, *60*, 222–234.

Murdock, B. B., Jr. Effects of a subsidiary task on short-term memory. *British Journal of Psychology*, 1965, *56*, 413–419.

Norman, D. A., & Bobrow, D. G. On data-limited and resource-limited processes. *Cognitive Psychology*, 1975, *7*, 44–64.

Norman, D. A., & Bobrow, D. G. Descriptions: An intermediate stage in memory retrieval. *Cognitive Psychology*, 1979, *11*, 107–123.

Paivio, A. *Imagery and verbal processes*. New York: Holt, Rinehart, & Winston, 1971.

Parker, E. S., Alkana, R. L., Birnbaum, I. M., Hartley, J. T., & Noble, E. P. Alcohol and the disruption of cognitive processes. *Archives of General Psychiatry*, 1974, *31*, 824–828.

Parsons, O. A., & Prigatano, G. P. Memory functioning in alcoholics. In I. M. Birnbaum & E. S. Parker (Eds.), *Alcohol and human memory*. Hillsdale, N.J.: Lawrence Erlbaum, 1977.

Perlmutter, M. What is memory aging the aging of? *Developmental Psychology*, 1978, *14*, 330–345.

Rabinowitz, J. C., Ackerman, B. P., Craik, F. I. M., & Hinchley, J. L. Aging and metamemory: The roles of relatedness and imagery. Submitted for publication, 1982.

Rankin, J. L., & Kausler, D. M. Adult age differences in false recognitions. *Journal of Gerontology*, 1979, *34*, 58–65.

Raymond, B. Free recall among the aged. *Psychological Reports*, 1971, *29*, 1179–1182.

Rosen, L. J., & Lee, C. L. Acute and chronic effects of alcohol use on organizational processes in memory. *Journal of Abnormal Psychology*, 1976, *85*, 309–317.

Sacher, G. A., & Duffy, P. H. Age changes in rhythms of energy metabolism, activity, and body temperature in *Mus* and *Peromyscus*. In H. V. Samis, Jr., & S. Capobianco (Eds.), *Aging and biological rhythms*. New York: Plenum Press, 1978.

Schaie, K. W. Methodological problems in descriptive developmental research on adulthood and aging. In J. R. Nesselroade & H. W. Reese (Eds.), *Life-span developmental psychology: Methodological issues.* New York: Academic Press, 1973.

Schonfield, D., & Robertson, B. Memory storage and aging. *Canadian Journal of Psychology,* 1966, *20,* 228–236.

Shiffrin, R. M., & Schneider, W. Controlled and automatic human information processing: II. Perceptual learning, automatic attending, and a general theory. *Psychological Review,* 1977, *84,* 127–190.

Till, R. E., & Walsh, D. A. Encoding and retrieval factors in adult memory for implicational sentences. *Journal of Verbal Learning and Verbal Behavior,* 1980, *19,* 1–16.

Tulving, E. Cue-dependent forgetting. *American Scientist,* 1974, *62,* 74–82.

Tulving, E., & Thomson, D. M. Encoding specificity and retrieval processes in episodic memory. *Psychological Review,* 1973, *80,* 352–373.

Yokubynas, R. *Depth of processing and aging.* Unpublished doctoral dissertation, Carleton University, 1979.

CHAPTER 12

# Classification Style Differences in the Elderly

Mary W. Laurence and A. John Arrowood

*Department of Psychology*
*University of Toronto*
*Toronto, Ontario, Canada*

Bruner's (1966) suggestion that categorization skills are basic to a number of other cognitive operations—for example, concept formation, memory, problem solving—has been actively pursued in research with children (see Kagan & Kogan, 1970, for a review). Several recent studies have gone on to compare the classification skills of elderly persons with those of young adults (e.g., Cicirelli, 1976; Denney, 1974; Denney & Denney, 1973; Denney & Lennon, 1972; Kogan, 1974). Almost all have reported a diminished use among the elderly of classification based on conceptual category membership and an increase with age in the number of groupings in which there was no obvious similarity in the objects grouped together. These results have proceeded typically from a paradigm in which subjects are given only one opportunity to sort display material (geometric figures or pictures of familiar objects) into as many groupings as suggest themselves, but with the constraint that no single item can appear in more than one grouping.

Somewhat earlier, Olver (1961; Olver & Hornsby, 1966) developed an equivalence-grouping task for children which permitted study of a wider range of classification behavior. She asked 6- to 11-year-old subjects to select from a display of 42 watercolor drawings of familiar objects a group of pictures that "are alike in some way." When the child had made his selection and offered his reason for the particular grouping, the pictures were returned to their original positions in the display and he was asked to form another group. Thus, the full set of pictures was available each time a grouping was made. This procedure had the advantage of permitting a subject to classify an object in as many different ways as he wished. Olver found that younger children formed many groups which were sentential ("the *bunny* ate the *carrots*") or perceptible ("they are all *yellow*") in nature. Older children, by contrast, tended to group primarily on the basis of concept name or superordinate characteristic ("they are all *food*").

To our knowledge, Olver's method has not been used to assess the classification skills of elderly persons, nor have systematic comparisons been made among groups of elderly subjects drawn from different backgrounds and current life circumstances. Such comparisons are highly desirable to determine the extent to which factors other than age *per se* may affect classification strategies in the elderly. Will diminishing social and intellectual competence, for example, be accompanied by a return to greater use of classification strategies and preferences typical of the younger and less cognitively developed of Olver's subjects? It was to explore whether or not performance styles and competencies on a multitrial classification task would differ among different types of elderly subjects that the study to be reported here was undertaken.

## Method

### *Subjects*

Subjects were drawn from three different sources. Twenty-four University of Toronto undergraduates (7 men and 17 women) participated in partial fulfillment of a course requirement. Their mean age was 20 years. Twenty-four alumni (11 men and 13 women) from the University of Toronto classes of 1918 to 1922 who had responded to a mail appeal for volunteers comprised a noninstitutionalized sample of elderly subjects. Their mean age was 75 years, and all were active and self-sufficient people living in their own homes in the community. Their educational background suggests a level of intelligence at least equivalent to that of the subjects who were currently students. A further 20 elderly subjects, all men, were drawn from the residential facility of the local veteran's hospital. Their mean age was 78 years. None of them had attended university and all required continuing medical supervision, although they were ambulatory within the restricted setting of the hospital. They were demonstrably less fit physically and intellectually than the other elderly subjects. They were selected as subjects by the head nurse on their ward who used the criterion that they would be capable of understanding and following the instructions and would be motivated to participate. Thus, the two groups of elderly subjects, though roughly equivalent in age, represented discriminably different levels of physical, intellectual, and social competence.

We had intended to include a fourth group of elderly subjects in this research but were only partially successful in this aim. Eleven residents (4 men and 7 women) of a home for the aged volunteered their services as subjects. They were all physically mobile, mentally alert, and under no particular medical supervision. They had surrendered their freedom of choice about shelter, menus, and meal schedules to the institutional management but otherwise were able to come and go freely in the community to shop, visit friends, or attend clubs and recreational activities. Thus, they lived, by choice, in a somewhat more protected environment than did the alumni subjects, though less protected than that of the hospital subjects. Their educational background and inferred overall intelligence were also intermediate to that of the other two elderly groups. Three had attended university; the rest had partial or complete high-school education. We ended up with only 11 volunteers after one early participant expressed unfounded fear to the other residents that participation might adversely affect their continued residence in the home. Data from these 11 will be presented for illustrative purposes but will not be included in the main analyses to be reported.

## *Materials*

Two sets of 48 drawings each, done in pen and colored pencil on 7.6 × 12.7 cm (3 × 5 in.) index cards, were prepared. Following Olver (1961), the drawings were of familiar objects (e.g., sofa, cup, lightbulb, lawnmower) and varied in terms of the number of colors in which each was drawn. Some were monochromatic, some were multicolored. This was done in order to provide visual variety and an additional basis on which classification could occur. Half the subjects in each group were tested on one set of drawings, half on the other.

## *Procedure*

Subjects saw all 48 cards at once. Cards were mounted on a large, portable, hinged display board which opened to reveal a 6 × 8 card matrix already in place. Within sets, the arrangement of cards was identical for all subjects. The original placement of the cards, however, had been randomly determined.

Subjects were tested individually. They sat at a table in front of the display board and were asked to remove from the array "as many cards as are alike in some way." If elaboration was requested, they were told to "put together what you think of as going together." When the subject had made his initial selection, the experimenter recorded the cards chosen and asked the subject to indicate the basis for selection. The drawings were then returned to their original places in the array, and the subject was asked to form another group. The task was repeated for as long as the subject was able (or willing) to generate new groupings. This led to a highly variable amount of time necessary to complete the experimental task. Typically, however, 20–25 minutes sufficed. These procedures parallel Olver's (1961) study with children except for the unlimited number of repetitions of the task which we permitted. This was done in order to determine whether differences among subject groups would exist in the number of groupings which they could or would generate and to provide every opportunity for a subject to form as many different kinds of groupings as he might wish.

## *Measures*

Subjects' responses were classified into one of five categories:

1. *Categorical-inferential:* all items are exemplars of the same superordinate concept—e.g., "animals," "means of transportation."
2. *Relational-thematic:* all items pertain to a common overriding theme, though in and of themselves the constituent items are *not* independent exemplars of any single concept—e.g., "connected with eating—lunchbox, table, chairs, barbecue, grocery cart." This category is very similar to what Olver and Hornsby (1966) call a key-ring complexive structure, which consists in taking a theme and linking various items to it by choosing attributes that form relations between each item and the central theme.
3. *Descriptive-analytic:* all items share a common perceptible feature—e.g., "all made of wood," "all metal."
4. *Sentential:* typically two or three items are put together in sentence form to make a declarative statement.
5. *Multiple groupings:* these are used for the small minority of responses (5% overall) in which several subgroupings were included under a single label—e.g., "cleaning—balloons, darts and dartboard, broom, dustpan, mop, candlesticks, lamp."

The first three categories follow the classification schemes of Cicirelli (1976), Kogan (1974), and others. The sentential category is included to tap possible parallels to a response style found frequently among Olver's youngest subjects.

All response protocols were classified independently by each of the coauthors. This procedure yielded reliability coefficients for the various subject groups and classificatory categories which ranged from +.82 to +.96, with an overall reliability of +.90. In the few instances where disagreement about classification category existed, it was resolved by joint discussion.

# Results

The classificatory basis of grouping for each of the three sets of subjects and the mean number and size of grouping are displayed in Table 1. Ignoring age and competence criteria for the moment, one notes that categorical-inferential groupings accounted for 60.5% of all groupings produced. Relational-thematic, sentential, and descriptive-analytic groupings were noticeably less frequent at 15.4%, 10.8%, and 8.3% respectively.

The arc–sine transformation recommended by Kirk (1968) for use with percentage data was performed on the proportion of each subject's groupings that fell into each of the four substantive classificatory categories. Separate analyses of variance carried out on these transformed scores yielded significant differences among subject groups in the use of categorical-inferential ($F$,2,65 = 4.65, $p < .02$), relational-thematic ($F$,2,65 = 3.54, $p < .05$), and sentential ($F$,2,65 = 49.52, $p < .0001$) bases of grouping.

The pattern in Table 1 is clear and consistent. The student and the alumni subjects show remarkably similar bases of grouping. Both adopt a categorical-inferential basis for the majority of their groupings and show much less reliance on relational-thematic or descriptive-analytic modes. Sentential groupings are virtually nonexistent. On the other hand, the hospital subjects rely heavily and equally on categorical-inferential and sentential groupings, which together account for 87.1% of their total output.

Table 1 also records the differences across the three subject groups in the mean number of groupings generated ($F$,2,65 = 5.69, $p < .01$) and in the mean size per grouping ($F$,2,65 = 6.54, $p < .005$). The first of these two analyses

*Table 1. Classification Behavior*

| | Students | Alumni | Hospital | $F(2,65)$ | $p$ | Home for the aged |
|---|---|---|---|---|---|---|
| Percentage categorical-inferential groupings | 67.6 | 63.1 | 43.8 | 4.7 | <.02 | 67.0 |
| Percentage relational-thematic groupings | 17.0 | 17.2 | 9.8 | 3.5 | <.05 | 12.3 |
| Percentage descriptive-analytic groupings | 10.6 | 10.1 | 1.6 | 1.8 | — | 4.1 |
| Percentage sentential groupings | 1.4 | 0.0 | 43.3 | 49.5 | <.0001 | 11.4 |
| Percentage multiple groupings | 3.3 | 9.7 | 1.6 | 4.2 | <.02 | 5.2 |
| Mean number of groupings | 15.0 | 11.2 | 9.7 | 5.7 | <.01 | 8.6 |
| Mean size per grouping | 5.8 | 8.9 | 2.9 | 6.5 | <.005 | 6.2 |
| Number of subjects | 24 | 24 | 20 | | | 11 |

provides the first evidence of any statistically significant difference between the student and the alumni subjects. The alumni generated significantly fewer groupings than did the students ($t = 2.43$, $p < .02$). The alumni also generated significantly more multiple groupings than did the students ($t = 2.64$, $p < .02$). Otherwise, the performance of the two groups is indistinguishable on quantitative grounds. The two elderly groups did not differ in the number of groupings produced, although they did differ in the mean size of grouping ($t = 5.64$, $p < .001$). This significance derives primarily from the very large number of 2- and 3-item sentential groupings by the hospital subjects.

There were no differences between subjects tested on the two sets of pictures, nor (insofar as it was possible to test for them) were there any sex differences on any of the measures reported above.

## Discussion

The most dramatic feature of the data is the similarity in classificatory style of the hospital subjects and Olver's 6-year-olds (1961). She reported that 34% of the young children's groupings were of the categorical-inferential type; our hospital subjects had 44% of their groupings of this sort. Among Olver's 6-year-olds, 61% of the groupings consisted of two items only; the comparable figure for the hospital group was 58%. Finally, 31% of all groupings by her youngest subjects were sentential in nature; this compared with 43% among the hospital subjects. As Olver considered older children, she noted an increase in categorical-inferential groupings, an increase in the mean size of groupings, and a marked decline in sentential style. In the present study, as we move from the hospital to the alumni subjects, we observe a comparable pattern. Although the parallel is not perfect (Olver's 6-year-old subjects made heavy use of the perceptible, that is, descriptive-analytic basis of grouping; the hospital subjects did not), the similarities in classification style between healthy 6-year-olds and hospitalized 78-year-olds far outweigh the differences.

Among the subject groups in the present study, the differences in performance are not, as might be expected, between young and elderly subjects but between the two samples of elderly persons. As suggested earlier, there is virtually no difference between the student and alumni groups in classification style, but there are statistically significant differences between the two elderly groups on three of the four substantive measures. It is not the case that the hospital subjects are incapable of grouping on what is generally considered to be the most mature (categorical-inferential) basis, since nearly half of their groupings are of this kind. The hospital subjects do, however, appear to be much more readily ensnared by what Olver and Hornsby call "the sequential form of the sentence as a powerful determinant of the connections between things'' (1966, p. 83)—that is, ''squirrel, sun, and dog (squirrel and dog like to sit in the sunshine)'' or ''lightbulb, broom, sofa (fixing a burnt-out bulb, pull up sofa to replace, use broom to clean up mess).'' Many of the hospital subjects also show high redundancy and perseveration, as the groupings formed by one of them make explicit: items such as tent, canoe, coffee pot, hot plate, and cup appeared in various combinations under such headings as ''used when living in a tent,'' ''going out to hunt with a tent,'' ''for making tea in a tent,'' and ''used in a tent.'' Although this kind of performance is consistent with many of the stereotypes about the cognitive functioning of elderly people, it should be emphasized that none of the alumni subjects showed such redundancy or perseveration.

Obviously, age *per se* cannot account for cognitive style. It remains to consider what other factors might be pertinent. Our elderly subject samples differed along a number of potentially relevant dimensions, namely, educational level, independence of life style, and physical health. Clearly, in the present study, these factors are confounded—and necessarily so, given the sources of subjects available to us. The alumni were not only better educated than the hospital group but also most physically fit and socially independent. Because we have no data that predate their hospitalization, we have no way of knowing whether the hospital subjects ever functioned at a level comparable to the alumni. Nevertheless, there are at least two reasons for hypothesizing that educational factors may be less relevant than physical and social ones in accounting for the differences in classificatory style observed here. First, other data (Cicirelli, 1976) suggest that differences in educational level do not appear to account for age changes in classification among the elderly. Second, and more directly, nowhere in the present study is there any statistically significant difference between the alumni and the 11 home-for-the-aged subjects, despite the fact that the latter sample is much closer in educational level to the hospital subjects than to the alumni subjects. As for the hospital subjects, although it was their physical condition that rendered them incapable of continuing to lead a ''normal social life,'' the isolation from various social experiences which hospitalization imposes may well have contributed to their lower performance.

We reiterate that educational, physical, and social factors are confounded in this study—as, indeed, at least physical and social factors are in everyday life. We are tempted, however, to make a virtue of necessity and suggest that, as neurological, intellectual, and social competence decline, so does the quality of classificatory behavior. Our data provide a clear-cut demonstration that for classification behavior there is no inevitable decline with age *per se* and that different kinds of old people approach a classification task as differently as do 6-year-olds on the one hand (hospital group) and university students on the other (alumni).

By this comparison with 6-year-olds, we do not wish to imply that the hospital subjects have returned to a ''second childhood.'' The performance of the two age groups certainly has quantitative similarities, but we have no way of knowing whether the qualitative processes that brought them to the same end are comparable. We suspect that they probably are not and, in support of this view, point to at least two clear-cut differences between 6-year-olds and our hospital subjects: first, to the redundancy and perseveration among the elderly group—a phenomenon not observed among Olver's 6-year-olds; and, second, to the almost total absence of descriptive-analytic groupings among the elderly—a mode much favored by the children and one grounded in the perceptible features of the stimulus material rather than in the respondents' own experiences.

## References


Bruner, J. S. On cognitive growth. In J. S. Bruner, R. R. Olver, & P. M. Greenfield (Eds.), *Studies in cognitive growth.* New York: Wiley, 1966.

Cicirelli, V. G. Categorization behavior in aging subjects. *Journal of Gerontology,* 1976, *31,* 676–690.

Denney, D. R., & Denney, N. W. The use of classification for problem solving: A comparison of middle and old age. *Developmental Psychology,* 1973, *9,* 275–278.

Denney, N. W. Classification abilities in the elderly. *Journal of Gerontology,* 1974, *29,* 309–314.

Denney, N. W., & Lennon, M. L. Classification: A comparison of middle and old age. *Developmental Psychology,* 1972, *7,* 210–213.

Kagan, J., & Kogan, N. Individual variation in cognitive processes. In P. H. Mussen, *Carmichael's manual of child psychology* (Vol. 1). New York: Wiley, 1970.

Kirk, R. E. *Experimental design procedures for the behavioral sciences.* Belmont, Calif.: Brooks/Cole, 1968.

Kogan, N. Categorization and conceptualizing styles in younger and older adults. *Human Development,* 1974, *17,* 218–230.

Olver, R. R. *A developmental study of cognitive equivalence.* Unpublished doctoral dissertation, Radcliffe College, 1961.

Olver, R. R., & Hornsby, J. R. On equivalence. In J. S. Bruner, R. R. Olver, & P. M. Greenfield (Eds.), *Studies in cognitive growth.* New York: Wiley, 1966.

CHAPTER 13

# Changes with Age in Problem Solving

David Arenberg

*Gerontology Research Center*
*National Institute on Aging*
*Baltimore, Maryland*

Reasoning is among the most cherished of man's abilities. It is, however, an aspect of cognitive performance which has proved more difficult to study than several others such as intelligence, memory, and learning. As a result, the reasoning literature is more meager and less systematic than the literature in other areas; and, not surprisingly, that picture is reflected in the area of reasoning and aging as well.

Typically, problem solving is used to study reasoning quantitatively. Sometimes performance is measured by the number of problems solved correctly; at other times the problems are designed so that finer aspects of the solutions can be quantified. An extensive review of problem-solving performance and aging can be found in Rabbitt (1977), and subsequent research was reviewed by Giambra and Arenberg (1980). The most recent review of the area is by Denney (1982).

As in other areas of cognitive performance and aging, most problem-solving research is cross-sectional. Many of these studies show age differences with old groups performing less well than young adults. It is recognized among cognitive investigators in aging that in a cross-sectional study age and birth cohorts are confounded and, therefore, age differences may reflect cohort differences and/or age changes. Group differences found in cross-sectional studies are sometimes referred to as "age/cohort" differences.

Longitudinal studies provide direct measures of change within individuals, but such studies are not without their problems. In a longitudinal study, age is confounded with time-of-measurement effects; that is, something may be happening during the course of the study which could account for or contribute to nonmaturational performance changes within individuals over time. Attrition is also a problem in longitudinal studies. Some participants leave the study for various reasons including death and declining health. It is unlikely that those who drop out are representative of the initial study group. As a result, longitudinal samples may be biased; typically, the better performers continue in the study.

Sequential strategies have been designed to avoid or minimize some of these problems (see Schaie, 1977), but they are not panaceas. These strategies require independent samples of several birth cohorts and several age groups at different times of measurement. Sequential analyses can provide group estimates of age changes to confirm longitudinal findings and can also provide estimates of nonmaturational changes over time.

The data segment of this chapter consists of 13 years of an ongoing longitudinal study of concept problem solving carried out in the Baltimore Longitudinal Study of Aging (BLSA). Several types of analyses of number of problems solved correctly are included: (1) cross-sectional age differences; (2) longitudinal changes following a six-year interval; (3) estimates of age change for many birth cohorts; and (4) estimates of nonmaturational change over time for many age groups. In addition, some longitudinal analyses are reported for measures of effectiveness in reaching solutions. This segment is followed by some comments on the current status and future directions of problem solving and aging.

Data collection in the longitudinal study of concept problem solving was initiated in 1967. At that time, two general types of problem-solving tasks had been used in more than one cross-sectional study of aging. Jerome (1962) and his colleague, Young (1966), had shown clear and consistent age differences in performance on complex logical problems developed by John (1957). Cross-sectional results from a longitudinal study using modifications of such problems (see Arenberg, 1974) were quite consistent with the age differences reported by Jerome and by Young. In those problems, the task is to light a goal light by a sequence of button presses involving other lights which are logically related. Arrows indicate which lights are logically related. Subjects are instructed about the possible relations that arrows represent. Each arrow indicates the direction of the relation, but the specific relation must be determined by the subject. In the studies by Jerome and Young, solutions required appropriately sequenced inputs within rather narrow time periods. The major modification introduced in Arenberg's longitudinal study was to make the task subject-paced.

The other general type of task used in studies of aging was concept problem solving. Wetherick's studies (1964, 1966) were of that kind. Unlike the studies with problems of the type used by John, consistent age differences in performance had not been found in the concept studies. It should be pointed out that in some of Wetherick's studies the old and young groups had been matched on nonverbal intelligence, and this almost certainly reduced age differences that may have existed. In 1967, therefore, when this longitudinal study was initiated, even the cross-sectional picture of problem solving and aging was not clear, and no data were available at all to answer the longitudinal question, whether reasoning changed with age. At that time, gerontologists were becoming increasingly more aware that cross-sectional studies are not dependable portrayals of change in an individual (or a group) with age even in the area of intelligence where many such studies had been reported. One purpose of this longitudinal study was to provide descriptive, quantified measures of change in problem-solving performance among an elite group of men.

As will be seen in the results thus far, cross-sectional age differences are quite apparent. The longitudinal results are not nearly so clear cut, but they are probably attenuated by biases due to attrition. The estimates of age change based on sequential analyses are showing substantial aging effects only for the oldest birth cohort. No evidence of nonmaturational changes over time is emerging.

## The Longitudinal Study of Concept Problem Solving

In addition to gross measures involving number of problems solved correctly, the problems were designed to provide measures of how effectively each problem was solved. One way to investigate effectiveness is to allow subjects to select the instances. Then each selection can be evaluated for the amount of information gained. There was also the possibility that the pattern of selections would help us understand how a subject goes about solving problems. Typically, in concept problems, the experimenter selects the sequence of instances; this is referred to as a reception paradigm. In that way, the amount of information available to a subject can be controlled. Obviously this has great appeal; experimenters like to maintain tight control. It ensures that all subjects have the same amount of information at each point in the problem. When subjects are permitted to select instances, the general procedure referred to as the selection paradigm, that kind of control is relinquished. Furthermore, under typical conditions, logically equivalent selections can result in substantially different amounts of information gain. A procedure described by Arenberg (1970) was developed to minimize that problem in a selection paradigm.

In all of the problems in this study, there are four binary dimensions. The four dimensions are labeled A, B, C, and D; and the values for each dimension are 1 and 2. Therefore, the two attributes of dimension A are A1 and A2, the two attributes of B are B1 and B2 and so forth. Each instance consists of one attribute from each dimension, for example, A1, B2, C2, D1. The subject's task is to identify the concept by selecting instances which the experimenter designates as positive or negative. Using this information, the subject attempts to identify the concept with as few selections as he can. That is the solution to the problem.

The problems are presented as poisoned-food problems. Previous experience with less educated subjects had shown that some people have much difficulty understanding even simple concept problems when abstract dimensions are used. By using the language of poisoned foods, these difficulties were substantially reduced. In the language of poisoned foods, the attributes are foods, the selections (or instances) are meals, the concepts (solutions) are poisoned foods, and the designations are "Died" (positive) and "Lived" (negative).

So, in simple (one-attribute) problems, subjects are told that one of the eight foods has been poisoned and their task is to discover that poisoned food. In order to obtain information to solve the problem, they select meals. Each meal consists of one A food, one B food, one C food, and one D food. Each meal is designated "Lived" or "Died" by the experimenter. Whenever the poisoned food is included in a meal, the experimenter says, "Died"; meals which do not include the poisoned food are designated "Lived." Subjects are instructed to solve the problem with as few meals as they can but not to offer a solution until they are certain they have enough information to solve the problem.

Six different types of problems are used in this study, and a subject attempts to solve two of each type, 12 problems in all. Two types are one-attribute problems, that is, the concept is defined by one of the eight attributes (A1, A2, B1, B2, C1, C2, D1, D2). The only difference between these two types of simple, one-attribute problems is that in one the designations are predominantly positive and in the other they are predominantly negative.

The other four types are two-attribute problems; two are conjunctive and two are disjunctive. In the conjunctive problems, subjects are told that there are two attributes which together define the concept. Any instance which includes both of the attributes is a positive instance, an exemplar of the concept. Any instance which does not include both attributes (one or both are missing) is a negative instance, a nonexemplar of the concept. Subjects are told that two foods are poisoned but that a meal is fatal only if both are included. One type of conjunctive problem has low initial information, that is, the first instance is designated negative. Regardless of the selection, the designation is "Lived." This eliminates 6 of the 24 possible solutions. The other type of conjunctive problem has high initial information, that is, the first instance is designated positive ("Died"). This eliminates 18 of the 24 possible solutions.

Similarly, there are two types of disjunctive problems—one with high initial information and one with low initial information. In a disjunctive problem, a concept has two defining attributes, but an instance is designated positive if either attribute (or both) is included. An instance is designated negative only when neither attribute is included. Subjects are told that two foods are poisoned and that either is fatal. In a disjunctive problem with high initial information, the first instance is designated negative ("Lived"); this eliminates 18 of the 24 possible solutions. In a disjunctive problem with low initial information, the first instance is designated positive ("Died"); this eliminates 6 of the 24 possible solutions.

With binary dimensions, conjunctive and disjunctive problems are virtually mirror images of each other. A positive designation in one is equivalent to a negative designation in the other. Logically they are identical (and that helps when we use computers to administer and analyze these problems). As a result, it is possible to compare performance on conjunctive and disjunctive problems of the same type (i.e., high with high initial information and low with low). Conceptually, however, ''bothness'' and ''neitherness'' sometimes seem different and frequently are dealt with differently by problem solvers.

In order to minimize the memory component of the task, subjects are required to write every selection and its designation throughout each problem. They are also encouraged to write notes whenever they believe that would be helpful. Furthermore, the entire procedure is subject-paced. Subjects decide when to make a selection and when to identify a solution. They are given as much time as they need to solve each problem. While they are solving a problem, the concept rule for that problem type is prominently displayed. Any procedural question is answered by the experimenter. The six problems in a block are presented in four different orders, but the two one-attribute problems always precede the four two-attribute problems. For each subject, the six problems in the second block are presented (after a rest of about 10 minutes) in the same order as the first block.

Participants in the Baltimore Longitudinal Study of Aging are predominantly white, educated men[1] living in the Baltimore–Washington area and employed (or retired) as managers, scientists, or professionals (see Stone & Norris, 1966). The study group is sometimes described as ''self-recruited,'' because of the fact that most participants were recruited by men already in the study. The BLSA was initiated in 1958 with a small group recruited by Dr. W. W. Peter. The men spend two and one-half days (every year or two) at the Gerontology Research Center in Baltimore participating in many physiological, biochemical, and behavioral studies.

## *Results*

The data were collected from 1967 through 1979. First are the analyses of the gross measure of number of problems solved correctly. These begin with cross-sectional data, proceed in some detail with the two-point (at least six years apart) longitudinal data, and end with some regression analyses based on first-time data to provide estimates of age changes and estimates of nonmaturational changes over time. (These are analogs of Schaie's cross-sequential and time-sequential analyses but use slopes instead of mean differences because the data

[1] Beginning in 1978, women were included in the Baltimore Longitudinal Study; however, only the data for the men are reported here.

are collected continually.) Then some longitudinal analyses of the effectiveness measures are presented.

*Cross-sectional Data.* Table 1 shows the cross-sectional means of number of problems correct for the seven age groups from the 20s to the 80s; the numbers of subjects in each age group (N) are also given. The table shows that there is a monotonic decrease from youngest to oldest.

*Longitudinal Data.* By the end of 1979, 376 men had returned for a repeat session. Of these, 87% (327) had a correctness measure for all twelve problems the second time. These are the men whose longitudinal correctness data are presented below.

Table 2 shows the mean number of problems correct for the first and second sessions for seven age groups. For this select group of men who continued in the Baltimore program and were able to attempt all 12 problems both times, the means decrease monotonically both times. The mean change measures, however, are not so consistent; nevertheless, the mean changes are positive for the youngest groups and negative only for the men who were in their 60s or 70s when first measured. The relationship between age and magnitude of change can be seen more directly using the correlation of age and individual change ($r_\Delta = -.08$). It is interesting to note that this relationship between age and magnitude of change occurs only in the second block. For the six problems in the first block, the age correlation with change in number of problems correct is only $-.028$; for the same six problems in the second block, the age correlation is $-.094$ ($p < .05$). It is possible that switching back to the types of problems previously encountered in the first block is more interfering for the older men after six years of aging.

Smaller groups of logically identical problems can be examined in the same way to determine whether particular types of problems contribute to these changes in overall performance with age. In the four simple (one-attribute) problems, the decreases with age are small, but they are virtually monotonic at both times. For this select group of subjects, however, magnitude of change is marginally related to age ($r_\Delta = -.07$).

*Table 1. Cross-Sectional Means—Number of Problems Correct*

| | *N* | Mean |
|---|---|---|
| 20s | 71 | 10.4 |
| 30s | 143 | 9.7 |
| 40s | 154 | 9.0 |
| 50s | 142 | 8.2 |
| 60s | 118 | 8.0 |
| 70s | 101 | 6.6 |
| 80s | 22 | 5.4 |

*Table 2. Longitudinal Means—Number of Problems Correct*

| | *N* | Mean 1st | Mean 2nd | Change |
|---|---|---|---|---|
| 20s | 10 | 10.3 | 10.8 | 0.5 |
| 30s | 31 | 10.1 | 10.2 | 0.1 |
| 40s | 96 | 8.9 | 9.2 | 0.4 |
| 50s | 86 | 8.4 | 8.5 | 0.1 |
| 60s | 69 | 8.5 | 8.1 | −0.4 |
| 70s | 31 | 6.9 | 6.7 | −0.2 |
| 80s | 4 | 3.5 | 4.5 | — |
| All | 327 | 8.6 | 8.6 | 0.1 |

The complex problems with high initial information tend to be easier than their low-initial-information counterparts. The typical monotonic decreases are emerging for the four high-initial-information problems. Mean magnitude of change is also clearly age-related. The age correlation is $-.09$ ($p < .05$).

In the four low-initial-information problems, too, the monotonic decreases with age are seen at both times. Magnitude of change, however, is not related to age; the age correlation is zero.

The two-attribute problems with high initial information are major contributors to the relationship between age and change in total number of problems correct. It should be noted that these are not the most difficult problems. For every age group, problems with high initial information are correctly solved more frequently than those with low initial information. The differences are even more evident among the effectiveness measures (to be presented later); problems with high initial information are solved much more effectively than are problems with low initial information.

*Estimates of Age Change.* The fact that first-time data have been collected for 13 years makes it possible to calculate estimates of age changes within birth cohorts. This is conceptually similar to Schaie's cross-sequential analysis with independent samples except that to estimate age changes, within-cohort slopes are used rather than differences between means. Schaie samples each birth cohort at two (or more) points in calendar time. The two samples within a cohort are tested at different mean ages; that is, the second sample is measured seven years later than the first and is seven years older. In the BLSA, intake of new longitudinal participants occurs continually over time. Data are not collected during narrow time periods with long intervals between. Therefore, means at discrete times cannot be compared. Instead, for each birth cohort, first-time measures are plotted against calendar time. Declines with age within cohorts should show up as negative regressions of performance on time. Figure 1 is an example of a plot of number of problems correct for the cohort born from 1887 through 1896. Such slopes can be calculated for seven birth cohorts (there were only seven subjects in the cohort born prior to 1887 and, therefore, that cohort is not discussed) for

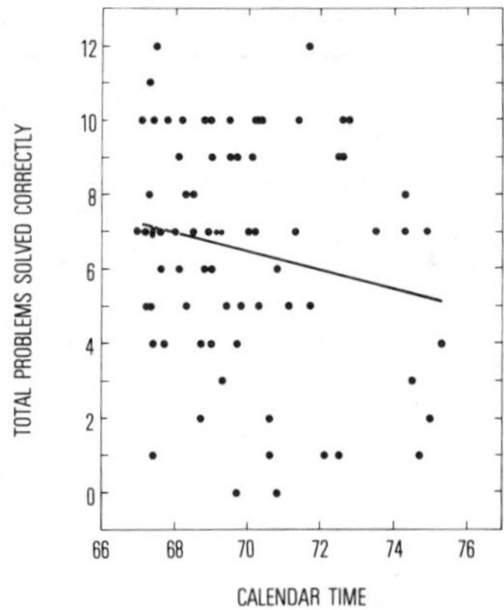


Fig. 1. Number of problems solved correctly in the first testing session for men born between 1887 and 1896. The abscissa is the date of testing.

number of problems correct. The results can be seen in Table 3. These slopes are near zero except for the cohort born from 1887 through 1896. That is the cohort plotted in Figure 1. Estimates of substantial age declines are showing up only for the oldest cohort, the men who were in their 70s at the beginning of the study.

These men can also be categorized into age groups to plot performance on calendar time. This is similar to Schaie's time-sequential analysis. If there is some systematic *nonmaturational* effect occurring during the 13 years of the study, it should show up as nonzero regressions within age groups as well as within birth cohorts. Table 4 shows the slopes for number of problems correct for the seven age groups in the cross-sectional analysis. All of these slopes are small and all but one are positive. The common age-group slope is .04, which is not statistically different from zero.

The slope of −.25 for the cohort born from 1887 through 1896 can be compared with zero and with the common age-group slope. Both comparisons

*Table 3. Birth Cohort Slopes—Number of Problems Correct First Time*

| | *N* | Slope (per yr.) |
|---|---|---|
| 1947–56 | 45 | .12 |
| 1937–46 | 135 | .09 |
| 1927–36 | 87 | −.03 |
| 1917–26 | 156 | −.09 |
| 1907–16 | 138 | .02 |
| 1897–06 | 109 | .00 |
| 1887–96 | 75 | −.25 |
| 1877–86 | 7 | — |

*Table 4. Age Group Slopes—Number of Problems Correct First Time*

| | N | Slope (per yr.) |
|---|---|---|
| 20s | 71 | .08 |
| 30s | 143 | .06 |
| 40s | 154 | .03 |
| 50s | 142 | .05 |
| 60s | 118 | .03 |
| 70s | 101 | .05 |
| 80s | 22 | −.11 |
| Common | | .04 |

are statistically significant. The estimate of age change for the earliest-born cohort indicates a decline of one problem correct every four years. This is substantially larger than the mean longitudinal change of the oldest groups when measured directly (longitudinal repeated measures). Sequential analyses of independent samples avoid many of the attrition problems inherent in repeated measures (longitudinal) analyses. It is likely that the mean changes seen longitudinally are positively biased. In order to be included in the longitudinal analyses, the men not only had to continue in the study for at least six years after the first measures but had to solve all 12 problems both times. There is some evidence that these criteria are positively biasing, particularly for the older groups. In other words, the older participants who are included in the analyses are a highly select group, and their measures of change are likely to be underestimates of the actual changes (if everyone could be measured).

*Effectiveness Measures.* The problems were designed in such a way that each solution could be quantified in terms of information gain. For each selection (after the first) in every problem, the number of possibilities eliminated is determined as well as the number of possibilities that could be eliminated by an optimal selection at that point. These are converted to bits of information; then the ratio of the subject's bits and the optimal bits is calculated. These ratios range from zero (no additional information) to one (maximal information gain). The effectiveness measure for a subject is the mean of these ratios for all of his selections in a single problem. Within each problem, this measure is highly correlated with the number of selections required to solve that problem.

For each subject, effectiveness measures were averaged for problems which are logically identical: simple (one attribute), complex (high initial information), and complex (low initial information). Decade means of these averages for the simple problems are presented in Table 5 for the 391 subjects who had a valid average at both times of measurement (at least six years apart). These means decline monotonically with age when first measured and also when retested. Furthermore, the youngest group is improving and the men in their seventies

*Table 5. Longitudinal Means—Effectiveness Measures, Simple Problems*

| | *N* | Mean 1st | Mean 2nd | Change |
|---|---|---|---|---|
| 20s | 10 | .82 | .87 | .04 |
| 30s | 35 | .79 | .79 | −.01 |
| 40s | 105 | .77 | .76 | −.01 |
| 50s | 105 | .73 | .71 | −.02 |
| 60s | 80 | .71 | .68 | −.03 |
| 70s | 49 | .64 | .58 | −.06 |
| 80s | 7 | .58 | .58 | — |

(when first measured) are showing the largest mean decline. The correlation of magnitude of change with age is $-.14$ ($p < .05$).

Similar results are emerging for the complex problems with high initial information (see Table 6). The age group means decline virtually monotonically at both times of measurement. Again, those in the youngest group are improving and the men in their seventies (initially) are showing the largest mean decline. The correlation between age and magnitude of change is $-.12$ ($p < .05$).

Although the effectiveness measures are substantially lower for the complex problems with low initial information, the pattern of results is somewhat similar to those of the other two types of problems (see Table 7). Age group means decline virtually monotonically at both times of measurement. The youngest group is improving; but, unlike the results of the other problem types, the men in their seventies (initially) are not declining substantially. For these problems the correlation between age and magnitude of change is only $-.05$.

These effectiveness data indicate substantial age differences cross-sectionally; and longitudinally, the youngest group is showing consistent improvement whereas the men in their seventies are declining. All correlations between age and change are negative, indicating that the magnitude of change in effectiveness is related to age with the oldest men tending to decline the most, quite similar to the results for number of problems correct.

One of the ways the effectiveness means are deflated is by overtly redundant

*Table 6. Longitudinal Means—Effectiveness Measures, High Initial Information*

| | *N* | Mean 1st | Mean 2nd | Change |
|---|---|---|---|---|
| 20s | 10 | .88 | .91 | .03 |
| 30s | 32 | .84 | .85 | .00 |
| 40s | 94 | .79 | .79 | −.01 |
| 50s | 93 | .76 | .76 | −.01 |
| 60s | 72 | .71 | .72 | .01 |
| 70s | 37 | .66 | .58 | −.09 |
| 80s | 4 | .75 | .47 | — |

*Table 7. Longitudinal Means—Effectiveness Measures, Low Initial Information*

| | N | Mean 1st | Mean 2nd | Change |
|---|---|---|---|---|
| 20s | 10 | .66 | .72 | .06 |
| 30s | 32 | .66 | .65 | −.01 |
| 40s | 99 | .62 | .64 | .02 |
| 50s | 86 | .61 | .59 | −.02 |
| 60s | 64 | .57 | .58 | .01 |
| 70s | 38 | .52 | .50 | −.02 |
| 80s | 3 | .41 | .54 | — |

selections, that is, repetitions of selections previously made within a problem. These, of course, are totally noninformative. Such repetitions occur mostly in the two-attribute problems with low initial information. They occur most frequently in problems solved incorrectly, less frequently in problems solved correctly by the elderly, and quite infrequently by the young. It should be noted that subjects know such repetitions are noninformative. Later in the same problem when subjects review their previous selections, they often discover the repetitions. When they do, they frequently attempt to cross them out on the paper, sometimes commenting with a four-letter expletive.

It appears that after many selections are made, the older subjects have substantial difficulty reviewing their selections and planning and carrying out their next selection. They seem to be suffering from information overload, and one way to deal with this is not to compare the tentative next selection (written but not yet verbalized to the experimenter) with all of the previous selections. When they make that comparison, they may lose sight of why they made the selection. As a result, they sometimes omit comparing their tentative next selections with their previous selections. Young subjects appear not to have that difficulty.

It seems therefore, that in complex problems, even when access to all current information is available for review (thereby reducing the memory load), the older men nevertheless experience information overload, and that contributes to their lower effectiveness (relative to younger men).

## *Summary of Results*

Consistent cross-sectional age differences are found both in number of problems solved correctly and in measures of effectiveness. Furthermore, the direct measures of change (longitudinal, repeated measures) tend to be age-related; typically, the younger men improve and the older men decline. This is supported by the indirect estimates of change using regression analyses (sequential procedures) within birth cohorts and within age groups. Only the earliest born (oldest) birth cohort (in their 70s at the beginning of the study) are showing evidence of substantial decline with increasing age. These data indicate that in concept problems requiring reasoning, but with all current information available for review to reduce memory load, older men do not perform as well as younger men; and for many of the older men, performance declines in six or seven years. It is tempting to dismiss these longitudinal data because the mean declines are small and the correlations between age and magnitude of change are very small. These longitudinal findings, however, are almost surely conservative assessments of mean changes (due to the positive bias likely for the older, highly attrited groups). The substantial estimate of decline with age seen in the sequential analysis of the earliest born cohort is an indication that declines with age are larger than those found longitudinally for the highly select group of older men. Taken together, these preliminary analyses indicate that concept-problem-solving performance of even well-educated older men is not only poorer than that of young men, but declines with age even over a period of six or seven years.

## Current Status and Future Directions

The literature on problem solving and aging was recently reviewed by Rabbitt (1977). I believe I am not distorting the tone of his chapter to describe the status at that time as disappointing. The domain of psychology labeled *problem solving* has a history of disarray. Not surprisingly, then, the area of problem solving in geropsychology is not well organized. What is surprising is the paucity of research. Rabbitt was struck by the contrast between the vast literature on problem solving in children and the scanty literature in aging.

Last year, my colleague, Leonard Giambra, surveyed the literature since Rabbitt's chapter and found about another dozen studies after 1974. One interesting aspect of the most recent studies is a focus on what is sometimes referred to as "intervention" studies. In these studies, experimental procedures are used to improve problem-solving performance of the elderly.

Some studies have shown that specific training improves performance of the elderly immediately after training. Of more practical significance, perhaps, are the results of a few recent studies which were designed to determine whether training has any lasting effects on problem-solving performance. Some training procedures were found to improve performance some time after training. Most intriguing was the finding by Labouvie-Vief and Gonda (1976) that the control group, which received no training but had practice equivalent to the trained groups, showed sustained effects (about two weeks later) equal in magnitude to that of the trained groups. These investigators interpreted this outcome as evidence that practice allows subjects to develop their own strategies, and that self-developed strategies are as likely to be retained as strategies provided in the training conditions. It is rather reassuring to me that the elderly can develop skills in solving unfamiliar problems without intervention when given opportunity to become experienced with the tasks.

One aspect of cognitive intervention research baffles me. Some investigators seem to assume that if performance of the elderly can be improved by training, then differences or changes with age in such performance are not attributable to maturation. Frankly, I do not understand this reasoning. If we provide a hearing aid to an older person whose hearing has declined with age, and that person can hear better when he uses the device, I doubt that we would say that this is evidence that the hearing impairment was not maturational. If we teach a mnemonic procedure to an older person whose memory has declined with age, and that person can remember better when he uses the mnemonic, why is that evidence that the memory impairment was not maturational?

One direction of research that Rabbitt advocated to account for age differences and changes in problem solving is to dissect complex performance into components. He suggested that contributions of memory, learning, information-processing rate, attention, and other cognitive components must be assessed to improve our understanding of problem solving and what happens to problem-solving performance with advancing age. I concur wholeheartedly.

Giambra has embarked on an ambitious enterprise in this direction. After many years of research in the mainstream of concept learning, Giambra concluded that group means based on one or a few problems per subject are not likely to enhance our knowledge about how an individual solves a complex problem. He decided that it is necessary to study individuals through many problems in order to understand how they go about solving. He has each subject solve more than 100 complex concept problems and attempts to model their performance. During some of the problems, subjects "think aloud" as they solve. The models are generated from the "thinking aloud" protocols and tested with the other problems. A successful model must predict performance throughout each problem.

The components of each person's model include some of the components mentioned by Rabbitt. Memory is very important. Each model includes parameters for how many instances are retained during the solution, which are retained, which aspects of instances are attended to, and how the information is organized. Giambra has succeeded in developing a model for a few subjects including a 96-year-old man. It will be extremely interesting if commonalities of the models can be found among problem solvers of the same age, of the same proficiency, or of the same combination of age and proficiency.

Recently, I had the opportunity to read a manuscript (Charness, 1981) describing an age study of rated tournament chess players in Canada. It was possible to obtain measures of components (such as memory) of the complex performances on chess problems. Even when the ratings of the players were statistically controlled, age was related to some memory measures accounting for performance on the chess problems. Age, however, was not related to performance on the chess problems, suggesting that a compensatory mechanism, such as more efficient search, allowed the older chess players to perform as well as the young. The memory decrement is rather surprising to me because I had a general impression that highly practiced memory skills were not affected by aging. When I played duplicate bridge, I frequently observed skilled players in their seventies who had no difficulty maintaining card counts during a hand and, at the end of a session, reconstructing virtually all the hands they had played. But now there is some evidence that highly practiced memory skills are age-related even among proficient performers.

So where do we stand and where are we going? At the descriptive level, it seems clear that there are age differences in problem-solving performance. Longitudinal data are scanty; and, based on what is available thus far, mean changes with age are small and tend to be found only late in life. It is likely, however, that these means are underestimates of changes with age due to the positive biases typically operating in longitudinal studies; and the effects of these biases are likely to be even larger in these problem-solving studies because only a select subgroup of returning subjects can be included.

These results are similar to many of the cross-sectional and longitudinal findings in studies of intelligence test performance. In Botwinick's recent review of intelligence and aging, he stated, "By and large, longitudinal studies show less decline than do cross-sectional ones; they may also show the decline starting later in life" (1977, p. 590). These results are rather different from the findings for memory-for-designs performance. In general, age differences in cross-sectional comparisons, longitudinal changes, and sequential analyses were quite consistent—small, if any, age effects in early adulthood, modest effects in middle age, and substantial age effects only late in life (Arenberg, 1978, 1982). Not surprisingly, different aspects of cognitive performance are showing somewhat different patterns of decline with age, but the finding common to virtually all aspects of cognitive performance is decline late in life.

There are indications of some progress, mostly not yet published, in analyzing components of complex problem-solving performance. Much more research of this type is needed. I would like to conclude on the optimistic note that, at least for some types of problems, when older people become familiar with them, performance improves without training, and the level of performance is maintained beyond the practice session. If that finding holds up generally, then some of the age differences in performance should be reduced by exposure to the problems.

## Acknowledgments

The author is indebted to Karen Douglas, Darrel Gray, Pat Hawthorne, Marian Hedrick, Barbara Hiscock, Steve Kanis, Joan King, Judy Plotz, and

Marcia Swartz for administering and scoring the data and to Judy Plotz for computer analysis of the data, as well.

# References

Arenberg, D. Equivalence of information in concept identification. *Psychological Bulletin*, 1970, *74*, 355–361.

Arenberg, D. A longitudinal study of problem solving in adults. *Journal of Gerontology*, 1974, *29*, 650–658.

Arenberg, D. Differences and changes with age in the Benton Visual Retention Test. *Journal of Gerontology*, 1978, *33*, 534–540.

Arenberg, D. Estimates of age changes on the Benton Visual Retention Test. *Journal of Gerontology*, 1982, *37*, 87–90.

Botwinick, J. Intellectual abilities. In J. E. Birren & K. W. Schaie (Eds.), *Handbook of the psychology of aging*. New York: Van Nostrand Reinhold, 1977.

Charness, N. Aging and skilled problem solving. *Journal of Experimental Psychology: General*, 1981, *110*, 21–38.

Denney, N. W. Aging and cognitive change. In B. B. Wolman & G. Stricker (Eds.), *Handbook of developmental psychology*. Englewood Cliffs, N.J.: Prentice-Hall, 1982.

Giambra, L. M., & Arenberg, D. Problem solving, concept learning, and aging. In L. W. Poon (Ed.), *Aging in the 1980s: Psychological issues*. Washington, D.C.: American Psychological Association, 1980.

Jerome, E. A. Decay of heuristic processes in the aged. In C. Tibbits & W. Donahue (Eds.), *Social and psychological aspects of aging*. New York: Columbia University Press, 1962.

John, E. R. Contributions to the study of the problem-solving process. *Psychological Monographs*, 1957, *71*, 1–39.

Labouvie-Vief, G., & Gonda, J. N. Cognitive strategy training and intellectual performance in the elderly. *Journal of Gerontology*, 1976, *31*, 327–332.

Rabbitt, P. Changes in problem-solving ability in older age. In J. E. Birren & K. W. Schaie (Eds.), *Handbook of the psychology of aging*. New York: Van Nostrand Reinhold, 1977.

Schaie, K. W. Quasi-experimental research designs in the psychology of aging. In J. E. Birren & K. W. Schaie (Eds.), *Handbook of the psychology of aging*. New York: Van Nostrand Reinhold, 1977.

Stone, J. L., & Norris, A. H. Activities and attitudes of participants in the Baltimore Longitudinal Study. *Journal of Gerontology*, 1966, *21*, 575–580.

Wetherick, N. E. A comparison of the problem-solving ability of young, middle-aged and old subjects. *Gerontologia*, 1964, *9*, 164–178.

Wetherick, N. E. The inferential basis of concept attainment. *British Journal of Psychology*, 1966, *57*, 61–69.

Young, M. L. Problem-solving performance in two age groups. *Journal of Gerontology*, 1966, *21*, 505–509.

CHAPTER 14

# The Theory of Fluid and Crystallized Intelligence in Relation to Concepts of Cognitive Psychology and Aging in Adulthood

John L. Horn

*Department of Psychology*
*University of Denver*
*Denver, Colorado*

## Introduction

The principal purpose of this chapter is to lay out some of the major results and conclusions of a series of studies conducted by this investigator and his coworkers (principally Donaldson, Engstrom, and Mason) over the last few years. To comprehend these results and conclusions it is necessary to have some appreciation of the theory and assumptions on which the research has been based. These ideas are not major themes in the research and theory of mainstream cognitive developmental psychology. It is probably worthwhile, therefore, to sketch at the outset some features of the research that is to be reviewed.

The work of preparing this chapter was supported primarily by a grant from the National Institute on Aging (Number R01 AG 058303), but a grant from the National Science Foundation, Research Initiation and Support Program (Number SER77-06935), also was important in providing computing facilities and salaries, and some of the research, as such, was started under grants that were obtained years ago.

## *Major Concepts*

A major focus of the research has been on processes of attention and memory—processes that have been considered rather fully in other contributions to this volume. As noted, however, the guiding theory is rather different from the theories of other chapters. The theory is very broad, very general, and very much concerned with ideas about a life span of development. It deals with concepts and processes that are often referred to under the heading of intelligence. The research of other chapters, in contrast, is based on relatively more focused and

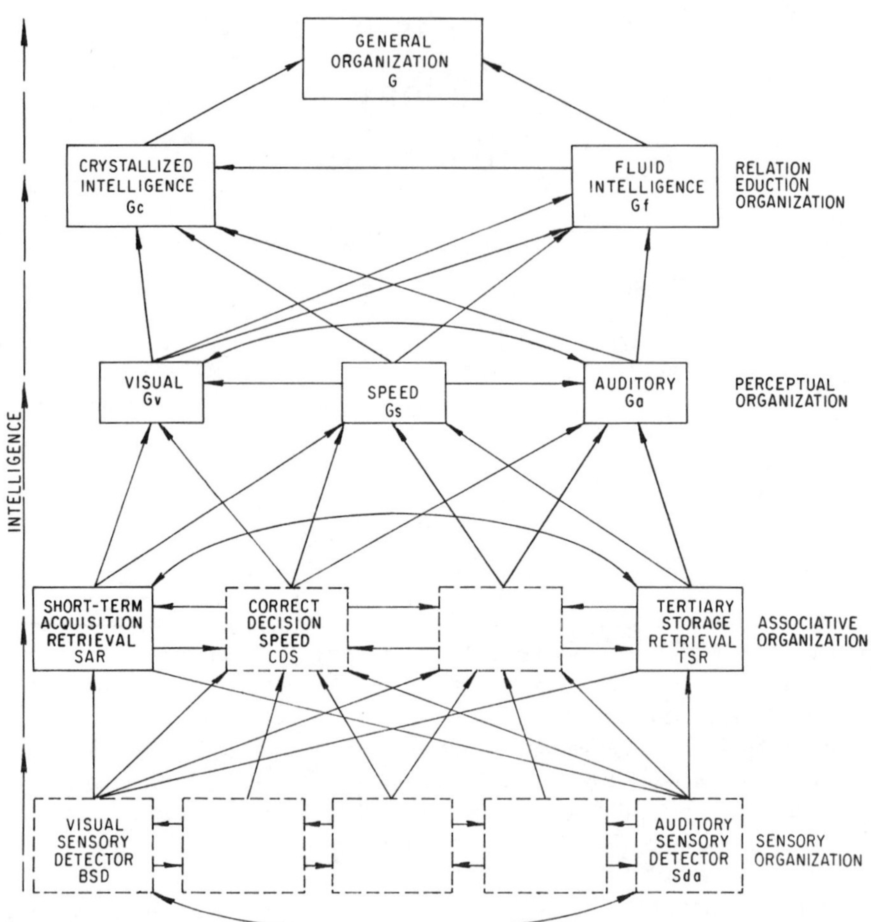


Fig. 1. Schematic representation of intellectual functions. Arrows represent flow of function and development. Sensory detection precedes associational organizations in development and flows into it in function; for example, perceptual organizations prepare information for relation–eduction functions.

fine-grained conceptions of function and development. Within the broad theory of the present chapter, attention and memory represent only a few from among many processes of intellectual functioning. An idealistic objective of the research is to represent operationally all major processes of human intelligence. This ideal is not realized in practice, of course, but as an approach it is important. Empirically, as well as theoretically, memory and attention are considered within a context of approximating a totality of the functioning of intelligence. In the developmental part of the theory, memory and attention are considered in relation to concepts that represent myriads of influences operating over the course of a lifetime. Some consideration is given, also, to physiological-neurological influences, genetics, lifestyle, and even evolutionary change.

Figure 1 is a schematic representation of some of the major concepts of the theory on which the research is based. The rectangles of this figure represent attributes that are defined operationally in ways that are illustrated in Table 1. A manner of talking about the concepts, as in verbal definitions, is indicated in Table 2.

I will not take time to describe the concepts of Figure 1 in any detail. It is important to recognize, however, that most of the concepts (all of those represented as solid-line rectangles in the figure) have been defined empirically and

*Table 1. Examples of Tasks and Scorings Used to Achieve Operational Definitions of Gf/Gc Concepts*

| Concepts and item examples | Descriptions of tasks and scoring |
|---|---|
| SAR: Short-term acquisition–retrieval | Recency and primacy memory, derived from Glanzer and Cunitz (1966) among others. Subject hears words spoken one after another (list lengths from 5 to 18). Recency is recall of last word spoken. Primacy is recall of any of the first three words spoken. Although these two measures are psychometrically independent (i.e., appear to represent independent primary abilities), both help to define SAR, also indicated by paired associates rote memory (Ma primary), span memory (Ms primary), and meaningful serial recall over short periods of time (Mm primary) (See Kelley, 1964; Stankov, Horn, & Roy, 1980).[a] |
| TSR: Long-term storage–retrieval | Clustering in recall, derived from Bousfield and Bousfield (1966), and associations (Horn, 1980). In the clustering task, words of different categories (e.g., vegetables, fish) are presented either in category-blocks or in permuted order. Task is to recall the words some minutes or an hour later. Measure is recall of words of a given category in adjacency clusters. In the associations task, one writes as many words as possible that are similar in meaning to a given word, such as *warm*. |

*Continued*

*Table 1.—Continued*

| Concepts and item examples | | Descriptions of tasks and scoring |
|---|---|---|
| Gs: | Speed | Matching, comparing, marking-a-letter. See Horn (1980). Indicate whether two figures or sets of letters are the same or different. Cross out a given letter in arrays of letters. Average time to provide a correct answer to letter series, matrices, paper folding, vocabulary, analogies, and remote associations tasks. See Horn (1980).[a] |
| Gc: | Crystallized intelligence | Esoteric analogies, remote associations, experiential evaluation. Provide answers to questions such as: Socrates is to Aristotle as Sophocles is to ______? What word associates well with bathtub, prizefighting, and wedding? When is it best not to tell the truth? See Horn (1980). |
| Sda: | Sensory detector: Auditory | Dichotic listening for voices. Derived from Broadbent (1966). Subject hears two voices each pronouncing different words but at the same time.<br>Voice 1 — Voice 2<br>cat pop frog — mom dog toad<br>The task is to reproduce both sets of words if possible. The measure is recall by voice—that is, amount recalled of one voice before recall of other. This behavior, too, is said to indicate the immediate awareness (IMA) variable of some of our earlier research. |
| Gf: | Fluid intelligence | Matrices, topology, letter series. Indicate figure that completes the matrix; find figure where dot can be placed in the same relation to all figures as in example; figure out what letter comes next in series. See Cattell and Horn (1978).<br>In which of the choices on the right can one place the dot so that it is in and out of the circle, square, and triangle in the same way as the dot is in and out for the figure on the left? 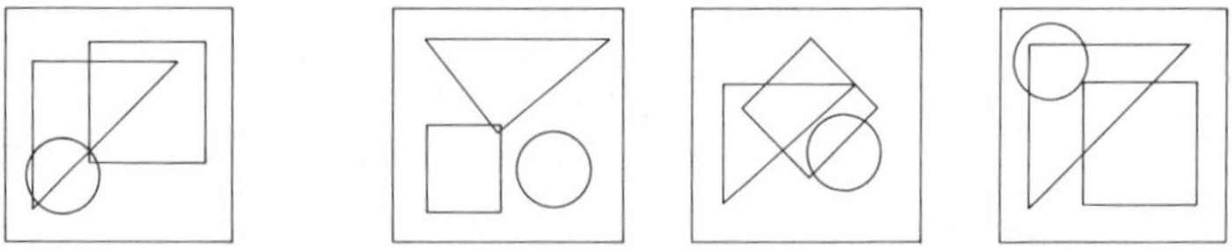<br>Which choice on the right goes in the empty spot in the bottom right corner of the matrix on the left? 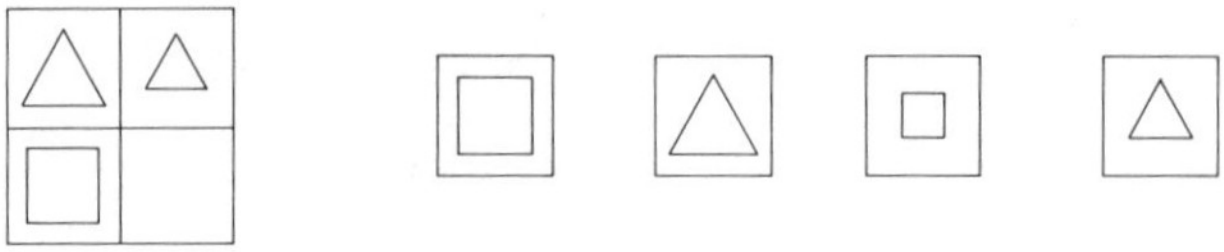 |
| Gv: | Perceptual organization: Visual | Gestalt closure, paper form board, Gottschaldt figures, each based on Thurstone and Thurstone (1941) and representing the Cs, Vz, and Cf primary abilities respectively. Identify |

*Table 1.—Continued*

| Concepts and item examples | Descriptions of tasks and scoring |
|---|---|
| | what is represented by an incomplete figure; show how parts fit into whole; indicate whether figure is embedded in another figure. |
| 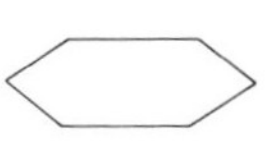 | 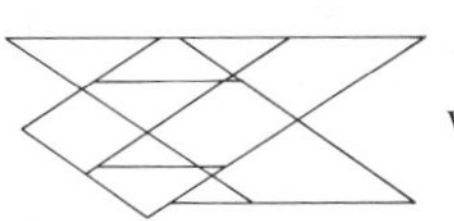 What is this?  |
| | Draw lines in white figure to show how black parts fit in. |
|  | |
| Ga: Perceptual organization: Auditory | Repeated tones, tonal series, cafeteria noise, each based on Stankov and Horn (1980) and representing Tc, ACoR, and SPUD primary abilities respectively. Maintain awareness of order of tones; follow the flow of a series of tones; identify statements embedded in a din of noise. Indicate the tone among the choices that continues the series. 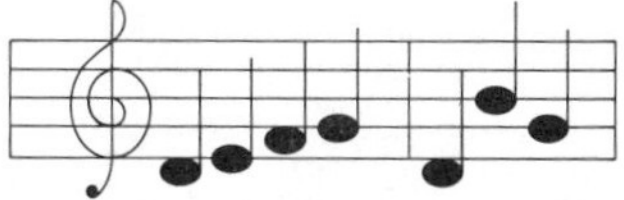 Circle number of tone when tone is heard for the first time.  |
| Sdv: Sensory detector: Visual 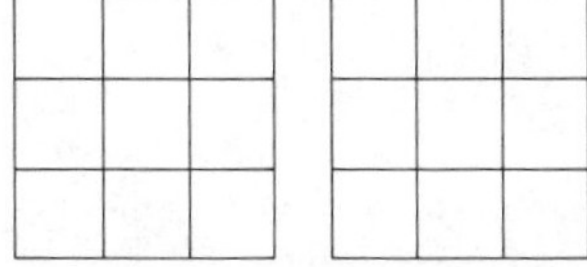 | Matrix vector recall, derived from Sperling (1960). Subject first sees a matrix filled with letters, then sees empty matrix and arrow pointing to a row or column (randomly selected). Task is to fill in letters in designated column or row. Performance indicates that for a second or two a person is aware of more than the 7(±) that has been said to indicate the human's storage capacity for information processing. Such behavior is said to indicate immediate awareness (IMA) or sensory memory (see Kintsch, 1970; Horn, 1978). |

[a]Although measure of CDS in the reviewed studies involved use of some of the same *kinds* of tests as were used to measure Gf and Gc, and some of the different SAR indicators are also based on tests that are in some respects the same, different tests were used to measure each kind of factor in order to maintain operational independence in analyses.

*Table 2. Brief Verbal Descriptions of the Concepts of Gf/Gc Theory*

Sdv and Sda, sensory detectors. These concepts represent the idea that there is sensory reception before there is holding memory and that this reception occurs somewhat separately for different sensory modalities. For an instant or two one is aware of a large amount of impinging stimulation. The span of this awareness is large, but the retention time is short.

SAR, Short-term acquisition–retrieval. This broad factor represents cohesiveness among several memory processes that are themselves distinct. Primary memory and secondary memory are separate processes, for example, but relative to other concepts of Gf/Gc theory the two operate together to indicate a single SAR concept. The concept is no doubt similar to, although operationally broader than, the concept referred to as working memory in many cognitive processing theories (e.g., by Massaro, 1975). It involves holding a relatively small number of items in immediate awareness while doing something with the items, as in dialing a phone number. This holding memory is distinct from the sensory detector functions described above, although clearly the functions are interrelated. The processes of SAR are also distinct not only from the systems of Gf and Gc abilities that are central to most definitions of intelligence, but also, perhaps surprisingly, from a system of fluent retrieval from long-term storage, TSR (see next).

TSR, Long-term storage–retrieval. Both retrieval from the distant past (of months and years ago) and organized (meaningful) memory over short periods of time can be much the same if one makes good sense out of or deeply processes the to-be-remembered material (Craik & Lockhart, 1972). The capacities for deep processing are largely represented in Gf and Gc, but TSR represents an additional set of processes of fluently transforming the processed information into long-term storage (second stage encoding) and accessing this information when needed (retrieval). The classifications formed in this storage are not so much correct as they are possible: to regard *tea kettle* and *mother* as in the same category is not to arrive at a truth so much as it is to see that both can share an attribute, *warmth*. TSR appears to represent ease of forming such conjunctions. It may also represent aspects of perceiving disjunctions, but this has yet to be demonstrated.

Gv, Visual organization. This function is displayed most clearly in tasks in which one must fluently and accurately (not necessarily rapidly) perceive the form of spatial configurations, see how objects change as they move in space, and form correct perspectives of objects in relation to each other.

Ga, Auditory organization. This factor represents facility in perceiving streams-of-sound stimulation, "chunking" such streams appropriately, and keeping different kinds of "chunks" separate in awareness.

Speediness. It has been well documented that speediness in one form or another is a pervasive and important feature of performance on intellectual tasks (see Birren, 1965, 1974 for review summaries). However, it is not clear that speediness represents unitary functioning at any level of analysis (primary, secondary, etc.). Indeed, it seems that speediness under pressure to attend closely to elementary details of otherwise simple tasks (i.e., simple if there are no pressures to work quickly) is distinct from speediness in obtaining correct answers in thinking tasks of the kind that define Gf and Gc. The Gs concept represents the former kind of speediness, as measured by quickness in matching, comparing, and finding various kinds of symbols. Correct-answer speediness in Figure 14-1 represents a finding that quickness in obtaining correct

*Table 2.—Continued*

| |
|---|
| answers to various kinds of reasoning, problem-solving, and comprehension problems is largely independent of the matching, comparing, etc., speediness of Gs. This concept of speed in obtaining correct answers is also largely independent of factors (particularly Gf and Gc) that represent level of difficulty of problems correctly solved. |
| Gc, Crystallized intelligence. This broad function is manifested in a large variety of performances indicating breadth of knowledge and experience, sophistication, comprehension of communication, judgment, quantitative thinking, understanding conventional interpretations, and perhaps most generally, wisdom. |
| Gf, Fluid intelligence. This factor is indicated by many kinds of abilities that are readily accepted as indicating intelligence but are not so clearly indicative of sophistication as are the abilities of Gc. The basic processes of Gf involve identifying complex relations among stimulus patterns and drawing inferences on the basis of comprehending relationships, as measured in thinking tasks wherein performance is not greatly aided by the breadth of knowledge of Gc. |

operationally by replicated factor analytic studies based on goodly samples of variables and subjects. It is also important to recognize that concepts defined in terms of such factoring research are, indeed, concepts—in this case multiple-process concepts.

To say that factors represent concepts is to emphasize that no particular operational definition of a factor is anything more than one way, among many possible ways, of identifying a concept for purposes of empirical study. It is to say, also, that our research is not focused on developing a technology: it is not concerned with establishing a particular test or operational definition for representation of a variable. Instead, the research is aimed at theory development, the establishment of evidence that particular kinds of processes are, or are not, centrally involved in human intellectual functioning and development. A concept such as crystallized intelligence represents a huge universe of somewhat different kinds of ability performances. The operational definition of such a concept in a particular study is merely a sample from this universe, at best a representative sample but in practice almost certainly a biased, arbitrary sample.

To say that factors represent multiple-process concepts is to recognize that we are trying to identify psychological functions that involve interdependent parts, something analogous to the functions of the heart and the parasympathetic nervous system. Just as the functioning of the heart in a living animal involves several distinct processes that nevertheless operate as a unit, so we regard the short-term acquisition and retrieval factor, SAR, as involving a set of processes that function as a unit. The separate processes of SAR include primary memory and secondary memory, for example, both of which can be regarded as independent functions on their own, although at a different level of total function than is represented by SAR. Just as the interdependent processes of heart function are separate from, but related to, the function of the parasympathetic nervous system, so the interdependent processes of SAR function are regarded as separate from, although correlated with, the processes that define the function of fluid intelligence, Gf.

To make these kinds of statements about our approach in research is not to argue that we have great depth of understanding of the processes that are necessary and sufficient to describe any particular function. To the contrary, research is necessary because understanding is lacking. Our strategy in assault on the bastions of poor understanding has been to go to the literature of cognitive psychology in search of paradigms and operational definitions that might tellingly indicate processes that are essential parts of the functions identified in factor analytic research. Before considering this research strategy in detail, a word or two is needed to describe and defend some of our procedures.

## *Some General Features of Procedures*

The general plan of our studies can be said to involve four main steps or assumptions.

1. A concept such as fluid intelligence was defined operationally as a simple unweighted linear combination of scores on several different tests that had been found to be good indicants of the factor.

The idea of using several different tests was justified on grounds that the aim was to represent multiple processes of a concept and cancel out specific factor influences (see Horn & Cattell, 1965, for more detailed development of these ideas). The idea of using unweighted linear combinations was justified on grounds that these are usually more stable under cross-validation than seemingly more elegant weighted combinations (Dawes, 1979; Horn, 1963; Horn, Wanberg, & Adams, 1974; Wackwitz & Horn, 1971).

2. A candidate for a process variable that might help describe a concept was defined by converting a paradigm (e.g., of cognitive psychology) into a set of operations for achieving reliable measure of individual differences. For example, a modification of the Sperling (1960) paradigm was developed to represent a form of immediate awareness that pertains to a large number of elements, but is more evanescent than primary memory. It may be helpful to describe this modification in order to illustrate concretely what is involved in converting a paradigm to a measure.

In our modification of Sperling's paradigm the subject was required to recall letter-elements of several matrices of different orders (see Table 1). In a particular matrix the subject might see the 9 letters of the example shown in Table I. A second or two after exposure to the matrix that is filled with letters, the subject was required to write as many letters as he could recall for a particular row or column that was designated randomly in an empty matrix. Each matrix-pair can be regarded as an item: 15 to 20 such items are needed to achieve reliable measure of individual differences.[1] The measure was thus obtained as the number of letters correctly recalled, summed over 20 matrix pairs. This was interpreted as a measure of breadth of sensory detection, abbreviated BSD. Because many subjects can correctly reproduce most of the elements of a row or column of a matrix, even when the matrix is quite large, and because subjects do not know which row or column of a matrix they will be asked to reproduce, the measure indicates that for a second or two subjects are aware of most of the elements of the matrices. The BSD measure thus indicates awareness of more than merely the 7 items, plus or minus 2, that has been regarded as the human's capacity for information processing (Miller, 1956) or the 4 items, plus or minus 1, that has been regarded as indicating primary memory capacity (Glanzer & Cunitz, 1966).

This modification of the Sperling paradigm thus appears to measure something different from ordinary span memory and primary memory. The modification is not regarded as a measure of an after-image on the retina or some similar elementary perceptual process, however, as in many interpretations of Sperling's results. The measure may represent this, but in fact the time span between presentation and recall is considerably longer than the one-half second, or less, that an after-image might be expected to endure. Also, the BSD measures seem to indicate awareness, not simply passive reaction of the retina. Use of the BSD variable is justified primarly on grounds that it appears to represent a very short-term form of memory or awareness that might be relevant for understanding age differences in general, and age differences in fluid intelligence in particular. Since the time of William James it has been recognized that the human is momentarily aware of a relatively large portion of the blooming, buzzing confusion of stimulation that abounds in the surrounding environment. Such momentary awareness might be an important feature of adulthood changes in intelligence.

Conversion of the Sperling paradigm to a BSD variable and subsequent use of this variable to study age differences in fluid intelligence is an example of procedures that were repeated many times in the research that is discussed in following sections of this chapter. In general, the rationale for this research dictated that if there was an age difference in a function represented by factor measurements such as those of Gf, then possibly some of this difference could be shown to be associated with, and thus be explained as due (in part) to, a process-change that was represented by a variable that was generated by converting a

[1] As a rough rule of thumb, we have found that as many items are needed to obtain satisfactory reliability in measurement of individual differences as subjects are needed in cognitive psychology experiments to demonstrate that an effect is significant at the .01 level. This rule of thumb can be derived from recognition that, as concerns significance, observations are observations, whether of the same subject or of different subjects, and the statistics used to indicate significance convert into the descriptive statistics that (usually) are used to indicate reliability (see Horn, 1971 for discussion of some of these conversions).

paradigm to a measure of individuals. An aging decline of fluid intelligence had been found in previous research. This decline might reflect changes in breadth of awareness of a kind that might be represented in the BSD measures that had been adapted from the Sperling paradigm. Similarly, crystallized intelligence has been found to rise in adulthood, and this might be explained, in part, in terms of cognitive processes that might be represented by measurements adapted from paradigms.

3. To examine the influence of a paradigm-conversion variable on the age differences of a function variable (such as Gf), part-correlation analyses were used. Such analyses can help to indicate whether, and to what extent, one variable (a process variable) can indeed account for age differences in another (function) variable.

In the studies that are to be discussed the developmental continuum was designated as age, specified in half-decade units. For example, self-reported ages of 30, 31, 32, 33, 34 were represented as age 32. This practice might seem odd at first, but it is based on a number of analyses in which several different ways of representing the age variable were tried out. In these analyses it was reasoned that age, as such, is a fallible indicator of a developmental continuum (Wohlwill, 1970), but the best scaling of this indicator is one that yields the largest, consistent correlations (not necessarily linear) with a number of variables that are age-related. The differences in correlations for different ways of scoring age were found to be small in our studies, but results from aggregating over many different age-related variables suggested that the half-decade scoring system yielded the largest correlations and thus in this sense suggested that the half-decade scoring system was best; it seemed to remove some measurement and sampling error associated with reported ages, as such, and yet did not lose discrimination that is lost when subjects are classified into decades or larger categories.[2]

In part-correlation analyses the linear effect of a process variable is removed

[2] In our research we have rejected the rather common practice of comparing groups that are extreme along a developmental continuum, as when college students, say, are compared with residents of a retirement village. I have criticized this practice rather strongly (Horn, 1979) on grounds that because exteme groups can differ significantly on so many variables other than the variable for which interpretation is sought, results are likely to be too ambiguous as to yield really sound interpretations. Obtaining multiple groups along the developmental continuum does not entirely eliminate such amibiguity, of course, but because development is usually orderly (or at least is so regarded in most theories), and the different ways in which extraneous variables can affect group differences need not show this orderliness, the variance of extraneous influences can enter as error in establishing a basis for interpretation of results. Thus, an improved basis for interpretation is established. As noted in the text, we have striven to provide further improvement in the basis for interpretation by sampling comparable subjects in each age period and using control variables of a variety of kinds in part correlation analyses to assess and remove the influence of extraneous variables (see Schonfield, 1972).

from a function variable to yield a part, or residualized, function variable that is then correlated with the age variable, scaled as indicated above. For example, if breadth of sensory detection, as measured in the BSD adaptation of the Sperling paradigm, is responsible for age differences in fluid intelligence, then by estimating all that can be estimated in Gf from BSD (using in this case the linear association) and subtracting this estimate from Gf, one is left with a Gf-residual that has been purged of (fallible) sensory detection influences. Part correlation is used in preference to partial correlation because it is logically sensible to control for breadth of sensory detection, a behavioral variable, in fluid intelligence, another behavioral variable, whereas it seems less sensible to control for a behavioral variable like sensory detection in a status variable like age.

Multiple-part-correlation analyses were also used in our studies. The logic of these analyses is precisely the same as the logic of simple part-correlation analyses. The difference is that whereas only one variable is parted out in the simple analyses, a best-weighted linear combination of two or more process variables is used to estimate the component that is subtracted to yield the residualized function variable in multiple-part-correlation analyses.

The significance of change produced by part-correlation control was evaluated using the analysis of variance fixed-effect model for considering differences between correlations. The .05 level for indicating significance was used throughout our studies. Although the size of difference required for significance varied from study to study, because each was based on a different sample size, generally speaking, a shift in correlation of about .06 or larger was required to indicate significance.

4. For purposes of communicating results, correlations and part correlations were converted to regressions expressed in IQ units. This was done because IQ measures are rather well known and easily comprehended by most psychologists. Usually IQ is thought of as having a mean of 100 and a standard deviation of 15. For this reason it seemed reasonable to communicate correlational and part-correlational results in terms of variables that were scaled to have a standard deviation of 15. Usually the mean was set at 100 for the youngest age group.

The results in Figure 2 illustrate this scaling. Here it can be seen that the measure of fluid intelligence declines about 3.75 IQ units (one-fourth of a standard deviation) per decade of life over a period from 22 to 57 years of age. This particular amount of decline was obtained in an early study and is close to an average over three studies. It was taken as the base, or typical, decline and all other averages were adjusted to this base.

Although perhaps one would not think of breadth of sensory detection as being measured in IQ units, the units of all such psychological variables are arbitrary and thus might as well be expressed in the same convenient units as used for measures of intelligence. When the BSD variable was scaled in this manner, the aging decline was found to be of about the same magnitude as the

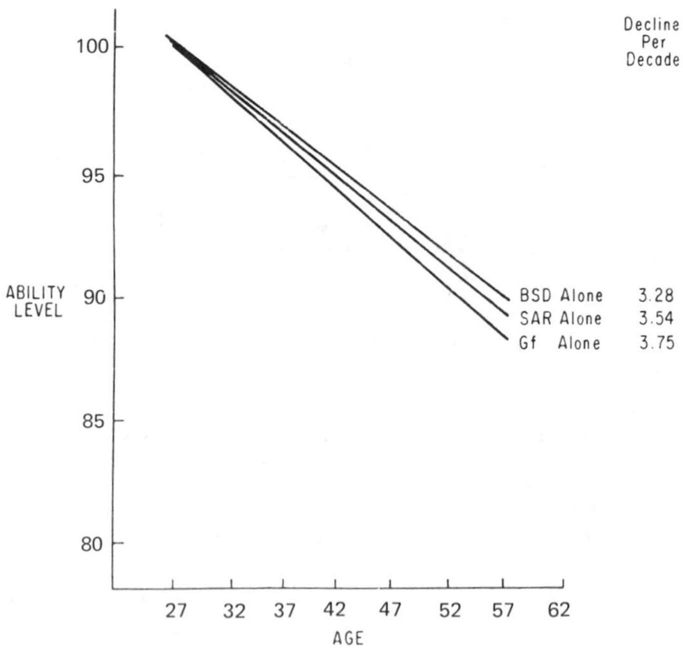


Fig. 2. Aging decline of Gf, SAR, and BSD, each alone.

aging decline for Gf, as can be seen in Figure 2. Here it is shown also that short-term acquisition and retrieval, SAR, declines in adulthood to just about the same extent as Gf and BSD.

In Figure 3 the adulthood aging decline of Gf is shown after the influences of other declining variables has been controlled by part- and multiple-part-correlational analyses. In this figure, and others like it that will be discussed shortly, the residual-Gf variable has been scaled in IQ units in the same manner as Gf itself, and SAR and BSD, were scaled in Figure 2.

## *A Few Comments in Defense of Procedures*

The use of part-correlation analyses seems to bother some people who are accustomed to doing analyses of variance on category variables or who are aware that multiple-regression analyses, path analyses, and structural-equation modeling might be used to accomplish objectives of the kind indicated in our research. To answer such concerns thoroughly requires more space than can be taken here. However, a few answers in overview form can be provided.

In general, analyses should be parsimonious and consistent with plausibility considerations and hypotheses: they should not be merely manipulations to

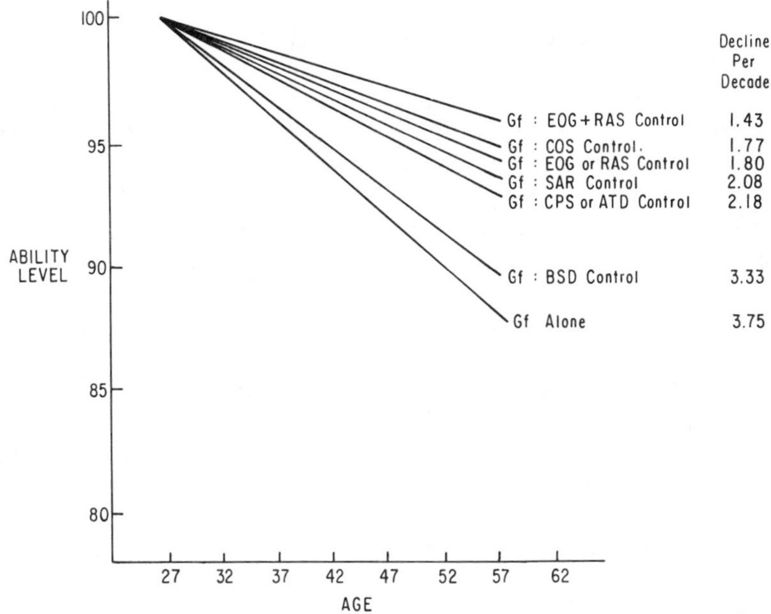


Fig. 3. Aging decline of Gf when BSD, SAR, EOG, and RAS are controlled.

which data can be subjected. For example, plausibility considerations dictate that fluid intelligence probably does not have a cubic relation to age, and even if the relation is quadratic, it is probably only slightly curved—such that it can be parsimoniously represented as monotonic if not linear. Part-correlation analysis is preferrable to analysis of variance (ANOVA) for indicating such a relation because departures from monotonicity, and even departures from linearity, are regarded as part of the error term, a parsimonious representation because the departures are not treated as if they are lawful, replicable features of development; in using ANOVA the opposite is true. Similarly, scoring the age variable in half-decade categories is rationally based on results from analysis and retains discrimination that would be lost by classifying ages into large categories, as is done when ANOVA is used with such data. ANOVA based on extreme-group categories of age is even less defensible. Indeed, although ANOVA is used very widely in behavioral science research, there are good reasons for not using it, as has been documented in several recent articles (e.g., Adam, 1977; Botwinick & Arenberg,1976; Horn, 1979; Horn & Donaldson, 1977; Horn & McArdle, 1980; Humphreys, 1978).

As for an argument that path analysis or multiple-regression analysis or structural-equation modeling should be used in our studies, it should be noted that part-correlation analyses are forms of path analysis, that path analysis is merely a particular form of multiple-regression analysis (namely, a form in which variables are entered into analyses in accordance with hypotheses), that structural-equation modeling is merely a generalization of this hypothesis-directed form of the general linear-model analyses of multiple regression, and thus part-correlation analysis is simply a particular form of these other analyses. Our studies suggest that the major problems of appropriate use of any of these methods stem from possibilities of capitalization on chance and generation of suppressor effects, both of which produce unreplicable and misleading (i.e., improperly interpreted) results. (See, for example, the Monte Carlo and random-variable studies of Horn & McArdle, 1980, particularly and most recently, but also Horn 1965, 1966, 1967; Horn & Engstrom, 1979; Horn & Knapp, 1973, 1974; and Wackwitz & Horn, 1971). Results from these studies suggest that in samples of small-to-moderate size (N less than 250, for example), when theory and knowledge have not been developed to a point at which many complex interrelationships have been established, it is wise to deal with the problems of capitalization on chance and generation of suppressor influences by entering relatively few variables into analyses and entering these primarily on the basis of well-considered hypotheses dictated by plausibility and substantive considerations. Such advice thus leads toward using the simpler linear-model data-analysis procedures, such as those of part-correlation analyses. These are least likely to be misleading because they involve the fewest opportunities to capitalize on chance and generate suppressor effects. They keep one close to the data and provide results that are reasonably easy to communicate; they are simple, direct, and, most important, not likely to mislead.

This defense of part-correlation procedures should not be interpreted as an argument that other procedures should never be used in research of the kind reported in this chapter. There is no absolutely right, one-and-only-one way to analyze data, and there are trade-offs that make one method better for some purposes but not so good for other purposes as another method. The point here is simply that part-correlation methods are appropriate and better for the purposes at hand than are some other methods.

## Subjects and Variables

Results from three specific studies (from among several more) will be described and discussed. Different samples of subjects and variables were used in these studies, but in some major respects these sampling features of the studies are the same. This provides a basis for summarizing the results from all three studies under under one rubric. Results of the specific studies are described in Horn, Donaldson, and Engstrom (1981).

### *Subjects*

In all three of the to-be-summarized studies, the samples of subjects were obtained as paid volunteers from the inmate population of Colorado State Penitentiary (see acknowledgments). The sample sizes were 240, 105, and 147. All the subjects were males.

One must pause to question the use of convict, all-male samples in studies wherein there is an effort to generalize to human development generally. There is no thoroughly satisfying defense of such procedures, but then there is no thoroughly satisfying defense of any other subject-sampling procedures; on balance, the use of male-only, convict samples is about as defensible as the use of any other sample one can obtain with only finite resources. The simple fact is that there is no known way to sample subjects representatively at each level of development in adulthood for research that involves any considerable amount of subject effort. Samples drawn all along an age continuum, from young to old, and samples drawn from similar circumstances of living, although not truly representative of the developmental continuum, are about as representative of this continuum as any sample one can hope to obtain without spending huge amounts of money or being part of a very substantial social effort to provide subjects for developmental studies.

Male convicts of different ages are drawn from rather similar life circumstances, which is to say that at each age in such a sample there is substantial variation in formal education, economic class of father, and other such indicants of life conditions, even as the means and variance on these kinds of variables are comparable from one age to another. For the subtests of the Wechsler Adult Intelligence Scale (WAIS), Corsini and Fassett (1953) found that the covariance among the different abilities and the covariances with age were not notably different for a convict sample as compared with the standardization sample of the WAIS. The suggestion from this kind of work is that although the means for some abilities are lower in convict samples than in the whole population, the interrelationships among variables and thus major lawful relations are much the same for convicts as for any other sample that one might draw.

Also important in our studies is the use of part-correlation techniques to "tease" out and thus control (mathematically) influences of a kind that are represented by such variables as education and socio-economic class.

As for using only males in these studies, it is acknowledged that although males and females no doubt differ in a number of ways that are important for understanding abilities, many of the basic laws of development should have much the same form for both sexes, Moreover, even if basic laws are different for males and females, it is certainly worthwhile to establish lawful relations within either sex considered separately.

Finally, too, although many people who have never been to jail find it difficult to believe, my experience suggests that male convicts in today's world are not so very different from males in general. To put the matter another way, it is not so unlikely as one might think that in the United States a male, at some time in his life, will spend some time in jail; this is perhaps suggested by some recent highly publicized cases in which politicians, labor leaders, and businessmen have gone behind bars.

The use of male-only, convict samples is thus justified on grounds that the basic laws of human intellectual development probably operate for all people in much the same way and that therefore some things about these laws can be learned from careful study of convict samples.

## *Variables*

Table 3 provides a summary of the variables on which the summary to follow is based. This list does not include all variables that have been considered, but the list is representative; it is not merely a culling to show favored results. Table 4 is simply an alphabetical listing of the same variables; it is provided to help the reader to move more easily from summaries of results (in figures to follow) to descriptions of variables and vice versa. Several of the variables will be described in some detail as the rationale for analyses are discussed in the next section.

*Table 3. Variables Used in Three Studies, with Reliabilities ($r_{xx}$)*

| Variables | | $r_{xx}$ | Tests used and combined |
|---|---|---|---|
| Study 1 | | | |
| Gc | Crystallized intelligence | .84 | Vocabulary, analogies, remote associations |
| Gf | Fluid intelligence | .76 | Matrices, letter series, paper folding |
| Ma | Associative memory | .71 | Number–word, word–word paired associates |
| MsB | Memory span backward | .82 | Visual numbers recalled in reverse order |
| MsF | Memory span forward | .81 | Visual letters recalled in order |
| BSD | Sensory detection visual | .73 | Matrix vector recall as in Sperling (1980) |
| Study 2 | | | |
| Gc | Crystallized intelligence | .81 | Vocabulary, esoteric analogies, remote associations |
| Gf | Fluid intelligence | .82 | Matrices, letter series, paper folding |
| SAR | Short-term acquisition–retrieval | .77 | Primacy plus recency plus letters memory span forward |
| SMS | Secondary memory storage | .64 | Primacy, slope as in Murdock (1960) |
| PMS | Primary memory storage | .76 | Recall last word in several lists |

*Table 3.—Continued*

| | Variables | $r_{xx}$ | Tests used and combined |
|---|---|---|---|
| CLR | Clustering in recall | .65 | Adjacency in recall as in the Bousfields (1966) |
| RAS | Recall after sorting | .76 | Words recalled after trials of sorting as in Mandler (1967) |
| ROL | Recall over learning trials | .80 | Words recalled over 10 learning trials as in Tulving (1962) |
| EOG | Encoding organization | .63 | Words in classes of 3, 4, 5, or 6 as in Mandler (1967) |
| SOB | Subjective organization | .31 | Adjacency in successive recalls as in Tulving (1962) |
| SPC | Speed to correct answer | .76 | Average speed to correct answer in several Gf and Gc tasks |
| SPW | Speed to wrong answer | .65 | Average speed to wrong answer in several Gf and Gc tasks |
| CPS | Clerical/perceptual speed | .58 | Matching and comparing as in GATB perceptual speed |
| CAR | Carefulness | .78 | Complement of number wrong in several Gf and Gc tasks |
| PRS | Persistence | .71 | Slowness in abandoning in several Gf and Gc tasks |
| ED | Education | | Years of education reported |
| Study 3 | | | |
| Gc | Crystallized intelligence | .71 | Vocabulary, esoteric analogies, remote associations |
| Gf | Fluid intelligence | .77 | Matrices, letter series, paper folding, visual recognition |
| SAR | Short-term acquisition–retrieval | .84 | Serial recall in several kinds of lists |
| SMS | Secondary memory storage | .70 | Recall of first two words in several lists |
| PMS | Primary memory storage | .64 | Recall of last word in several lists |
| CLR | Clustering in recall | .61 | Adjacency in recall as in the Bousfields (1966) |
| ICM | Incidental memory | .70 | Recall of several events staged throughout testing |
| EOG | Encoding organization | .67 | Word classes of 3, 4, 5, or 6 as in Mandler (1967) |
| CPS | Clerical/perceptual speed | .77 | Cancelling numbers |
| COS | Concentration on slowness | .81 | Little traced in unit time as in Botwinick & Storandt (1974) |
| ATD | Dividing attention | .82 | Marking *a*'s while remembering as in Broadbent and Heron (1962) |
| EIR | Eliminating irrelevancies | .77 | Not monitoring attributes no longer relevant in concept attainment (Rabbitt, 1965) |
| HYP | Forming hypotheses | .92 | Efficiency in asking questions in 20-question game as in Denney and Lennon (1972) |

*Table 4. Variables for Summarized Studies Listed Alphabetically with Internal Consistency Reliabilities for Studies Considered in This Paper*

| Symbol | Variable name | $r_{xx}$ | Study no. |
|---|---|---|---|
| ATD: | Attention dividing | .82 | 3 |
| CAR: | Carefulness | .78 | 2 |
| CLR: | Clustering in recall | .65, .61 | 2, 3 |
| COS: | Concentration on slowness | .81 | 3 |
| CPS: | Clerical perceptual speediness | .58, .77 | 2, 3 |
| EIR: | Eliminating irrelevancies | .77 | |
| EOG: | Encoding organization | .63, .67 | 2, 3 |
| Gc: | Crystallized intelligence | .84, .81, .71 | 1, 2, 3 |
| Gf: | Fluid intelligence | .76, .82, .77 | 1, 2, 3 |
| HYP: | Hypothesis formation | .92 | 3 |
| ICM: | Incidental memory | .70 | 3 |
| Ma: | Associative memory | .71 | 1 |
| MsB: | Memory span backward | .82 | 1 |
| MsF: | Memory span forward | .81 | 1 |
| PMS: | Primary memory storage | .76, .64 | 2, 3 |
| PRS: | Persistence | .71 | 2 |
| RAS: | Recall after sorting | .76 | 2 |
| ROL: | Recall after learning trials | .80 | 2 |
| SAR: | Short-term acquisition–retrieval | .77, .84 | 2, 3 |
| BSD: | Sensory detection visual | .73 | 1 |
| SMS: | Secondary memory storage | .64, .70 | 2, 3 |
| SOB: | Subjective organization | .31 | 2 |
| SPC: | Speed to correct answer | .76 | 2 |
| SPW: | Speed to wrong answer | .65 | 2 |
| TSR: | Long-term storage–retrieval | .78, .72 | 2, 3 |
| USE: | Uses of common objects | .71 | 3 |

# Analyses and Results

The focus of this review will be on adulthood aging decline of fluid intelligence. Control variables that appear low in the hierarchy of Figure 1 will be considered first.

## *Sensory Detection in Relation to Decline of Intellectual Capacities*

As we indicated in previous discussion of Figure 2, breadth of sensory detection, BSD, was found to decline with age to nearly the same extent as fluid intelligence, Gf. This suggests that loss of capacity for becoming aware of surrounding stimuli might be a factor in loss of capacity for solving the kinds of problems that define fluid intelligence. Thus, if breadth of sensory detection is controlled in the relation of age to fluid intelligence, perhaps some (or all) of the decline indicated for the Gf function will be eliminated for the residualized function variable that is defined in part-correlation analysis.

Results are shown in graphic form in Figure 3. Here it can be seen that the results from control of BSD provide little support for the above-stated hypothesis: only a small, statistically not significant change in the age-decline curve for fluid intelligence is effected by control with the BSD variable. This result is not parsimoniously explained as due to lack of reliability in the measure of sensory detection, for the variable has sufficient reliability to establish the hypothesized relationship and the variable is related to age and other variables to an extent that also indicates adequate reliability.

The reason why breadth of sensory detection does not account for decline of fluid intelligence is that the BSD variable is not very strongly related to Gf. This is not a surprising finding, although it might seem to be so to one who is inclined to equate elementary processes of perception with processes that define the *sine qua non* of human intelligence. However, sensory detection is highly developed in many animals other than humans; it is also well developed in humans who are not remarkably intelligent. Such evidence suggests that it is not of the essence of mature human intelligence. Early in this century McKeen Cattell and his coworkers discovered this fact; they found that elementary perceptual processes were not very highly related to variables that could be accepted as indicating intelligence. When put in this framework, a hypothesis stipulating that breadth of sensory detection is related to fluid intelligence can be seen to be not very compelling. Hence, it should not be surprising to find that BSD accounts for very little of the Gf decline, even as it declines itself.

The result indicated for BSD is interesting partly because it points to a larger issue that is often neglected in research on development. This may be referred to as the missing-link issue; there is a missing link in research in which an aging decline for a particular variable is demonstrated and it is inferred that this indicates decline in an important feature of intelligence, but there are no analyses (of the kind outlined above) to show that the variable indeed declines in intelligence. Many things decline with age, but only a very few of these things are related to decline of important features of human intelligence. For example, arm strength declines with adulthood aging, but this is not a feature of Gf decline. Without analyses to demonstrate that a variable does indeed represent an important process of intelligence, results showing that the variable is related to age really tells us very little about the aging of intellectual capacities.

The results summarized in Figure 4 suggest that breadth of sensory detection *is* related to aging decline of memory capacities—working memory, for example. Working memory is often represented operationally by memory span backwards, MsB. As can be seen in the figure, controlling for BSD reduces the aging decline of MsB from about 3.28 to about 2.33 units per decade, a shift that is statistically significant. Such control also reduces the aging decline of forward

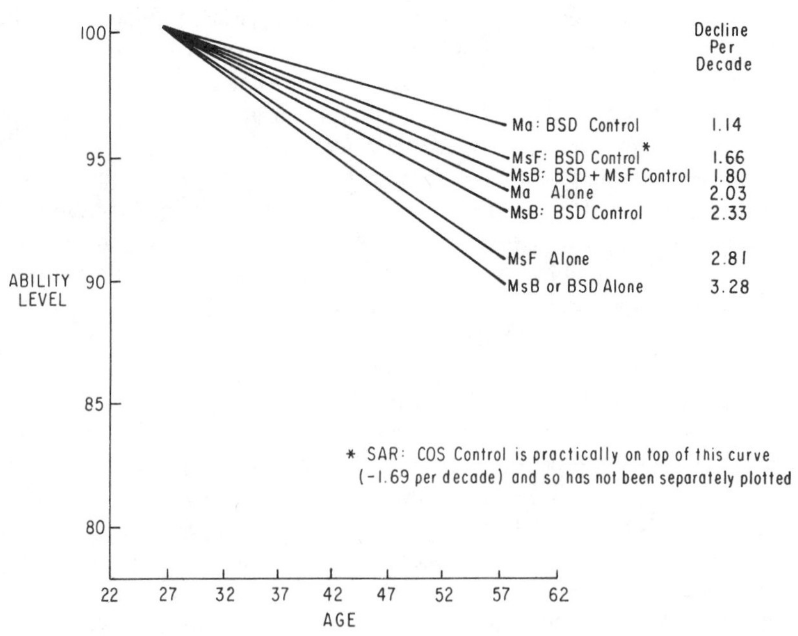


Fig. 4. Aging decline of working memory when measures of sensory detection are controlled.

span, MsF, and nonsense paired associates memory, Ma, each by about 1 unit. When MsF along with BSD is controlled in the aging decline for backward span, the decline is further reduced by about one-half unit to 1.80 units per decade. Such results suggest that a good part of what can be identified as working memory (MsB) is tied up with processes of very short-term apprehension, as measured in BSD and, to a lesser extent, MsF. As we noted previously (in discussion of BSD in relation to Gf), such processes are not themselves very much related to fluid intelligence.

Thus, a failure of a measure of working memory to effect a notable change in the age decline curve for fluid intelligence can be due (in part) to the working memory measure containing sensory detection variance that is not related to Gf decline. This illustrates another kind of missing link in analysis of developmental data and another good reason for using the teasing-out methods of part-correlation analysis.

## *Short-Term Memory, Concentration, Attentiveness, and Speediness Related to Gf Decline*

Returning to a consideration of Figure 3 and processes that might be related to the aging decline of fluid intelligence, we can see that short-term acquisition-retrieval, SAR, is implicated in the decline: controlling for SAR reduces Gf decline from 3.75 to 2.08 units per decade. Thus, short-term memory is a part of the picture of adulthood decline of fluid intelligence abilities. This conclusion is quite consistent with results from analyses and summaries of others (see Reese, 1977, for a cogent summary). Can more be said about the processes associated with Gf memory loss?

Also shown in Figure 3 is a finding that either EOG or RAS, each considered alone, accounts for roughly 2 units of the 3.75 units of aging decline of fluid intelligence. These two variables represent organization in encoding. They are based on a paradigm developed by Mandler (1967). The task of the EOG measure was to sort words in "a way that makes sense to you." The measure itself was simply a count of the number of words sorted into categories of from three to six words. This measure was found to correlate upwards from .7 with RAS, the number of words recalled, as much as 90 minutes later. The correlations between EOG and RAS were nearly as large as their respective reliabilities. Also, as can be seen in Figure 3, controlling for RAS in addition to EOG (or vice versa) did very little to change the Gf decline curve already determined by parting-out EOG (or RAS) alone: either EOG or RAS alone effects almost all of the change in the Gf-decline curve that is effected by the two variables acting together. Thus, both EOG and RAS seem to involve the same organization-in-encoding process, as this is implicated in Gf decline.

If SAR or some other memory variable is added in to multiple-part-correlation control already achieved with EOG or RAS, the Gf decline curve is not further altered by a significant or noteworthy amount. This suggests that organization in encoding accounts for most of the Gf decline that is also described in terms of other short-term memory processes. Thus, it seems that to the extent that SAR represents working memory and working memory is involved in the aging decline of fluid intelligence, the processes involved are some that enable one to achieve good organization of material.

It is interesting in this respect that although EOG is a good predictor of memory, it is obtained under conditions in which the subject is not instructed to memorize. It would be overinterpretation to argue that this alone indicates that spontaneous (in contrast to conscious, effortful) organization in encoding is the "culprit" in aging decline of Gf, but it can be noted that there is other evidence that also suggests this interpretation (see Horn, 1976, for review).

These findings are interesting also because they are found in samples of ostensibly normal adults, and in a midlife developmental period in which intellectual decline is not remarkably large. The aging decrements are similar to memory losses associated with injuries to the hippocampus (and nearby areas of the temporal lobes and limbic system), as seen in Korsakoff's syndrome, for example. These matters will be considered later in this chapter, after some other results have been examined.

The variable labeled COS, concentration on slowness, in Figures 3 and 5

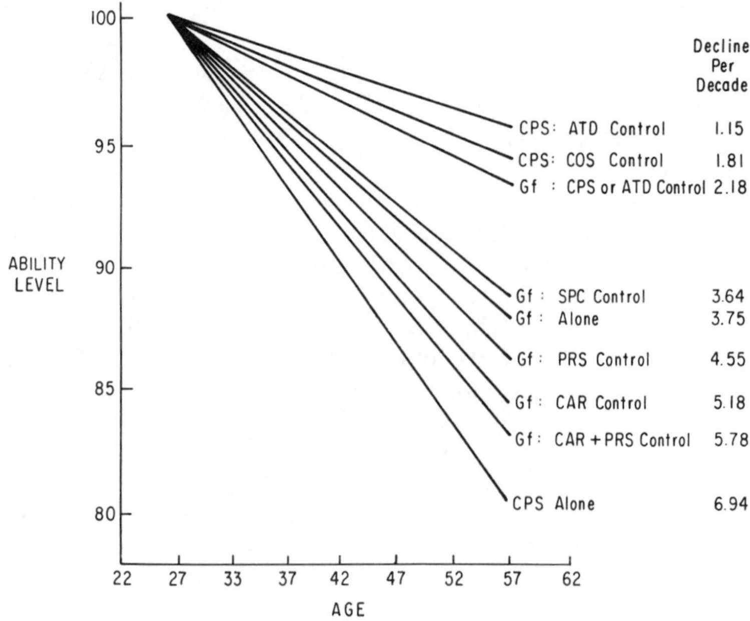


Fig. 5. Aging decline of Gf when speediness and carefulness are controlled.

was entered into the analyses to help indicate how concentration might be implicated in the aging decline of speediness, short-term memory, and fluid intelligence. The measure was derived from some work of Botwinick and Storandt (1974). It was obtained by recording how slowly a person traces simple line drawings under instructions to trace as slowly as possible while always keeping the pencil moving. The task is clearly not one of memory as such, but in the studies of Botwinick and Storandt, as well as in our work, COS had a substantial correlation with short-term memory measures such as span memory, recency, and primacy (obtained from list-learning tasks). It has been known for years that unless one concentrates and attempts to memorize in nonsense-memory tasks, not much memorization is likely to occur. The COS variable, by virtue of its correlation with memory tasks, appears to represent some aspects of this feature of concentration in memory.

It is shown in Figure 4 that COS accounts for a notable amount of the aging decline of short-term memory. Not shown in this figure but indicated by other results are suggestions that the primacy and recency effects, taken together, account for much (although not all) of what is measured in span memory, paired associates memory, serial learning memory tasks, and the combination of these which defines the SAR factor. A substantial part of the aging decline of primary memory and secondary memory is associated with the COS variable. These findings, taken together, suggest that the concentration on attentiveness that is measured in COS is a major determinant of short-term memory aging decline.

The results summarized in Figure 3 suggest that not only is COS a feature of adult memory and memory decline as such, but it is also the feature of the memory decline that is a part of the aging decline of fluid intelligence. This conclusion is suggested first by the results indicating that in simple part-correlation control COS accounts for a noteworthy amount of the aging decline of Gf. (COS is seemingly not at all similar to the reasoning tasks that define Gf.) Secondly, when short-term memory measures are added into this control in multiple-part analyses, the decline of Gf is further reduced by only small amounts; this suggests that most of the Gf decline that is associated with short-term memory is also associated with the features of concentration (or attentiveness) that are measured in the COS variable.

Indeed, it seems that a capacity or inclination for maintaining concentration or close attention to a task is associated with much of the aging decline that is recorded with the variables of our studies. This conclusion is indicated by some of the analyses summarized in Figure 5. The attention-division, ATD, measure of this figure is similar to a paradigm that Broadbent and Heron (1962) used to indicate aging decline in ability to keep two things simultaneously in mind. The task is to cancel letters while also retaining the information of previously presented short essays of the kind used to indicate propositional memory in the work of Kintsch (1974) and his coworkers. Control for this measure of ability to divide attention (which includes memory) reduces fluid intelligence decline to about the same extent as SAR, and, again, additional control with SAR does very little further to change the Gf-decline curve. To add COS to this control effects only a small further change in the decline of fluid intelligence.

Thus, it seems that the attention-division, short-term memory, and concentration variables represent, to a considerable extent, much the same processes of decline in fluid intelligence (this is not to say that these variables do not represent other processes independently, some of which may also decline with age independently of the decline for processes of Gf).

Also shown in Figure 5 are results for speediness processes that appear to be linked with concentration, attention-division, and memory processes that are implicated in the decline of fluid intelligence. The variable representing these speediness processes is labeled CPS. This measure is derived from tasks in which one must judge whether two symbols, such as Aj4T1 and AJ7TJ, are the same or different, or tasks in which one must find a symbol, such as $\zeta$, among sets of other symbols. Measures based on such tasks covary in a manner that indicates a primary factor known as perceptual speed. A finding of several of our early studies is that this factor declines with age in adulthood and accounts for a significant portion of the aging decline of Gf. A finding of the studies here under review is that this variable, too, is associated with the slow-tracing measure of concentration. Also, to a very substantial extent, the aging decline of Gf that is accounted for by CPS is also accounted for by COS. Also, as can be seen in the results of Figure 5, much of the aging decline of CPS, as such, is accounted for by COS (or ATD).

### *Speediness, Carefulness, and Persistence in Relation to Gf Decline*

Thus, aging decline in speed in simple clerical-perceptual tasks is largely due to aging decline in ability or inclination to concentrate on simple tasks and this ability or inclination seems largely to account for the association between aging decline of speediness and aging decline of fluid intelligence. Such findings are not inconsistent with analyses by Birren (1965, 1974) suggesting that adult decline in intellectual capacities is mainly attributable to a slowing of mental processes, but they do suggest a somewhat different interpretation of this hypothesis than is typically advanced. The results suggest that slowing is a consequence, rather than a cause, of decreased intellectual functioning. This interpretation is only suggested; it is not unequivocally indicated by results such as were reviewed in the previous section. There are other results, however, that also support this interpretation.

One relevant finding is that Gf measures obtained under power conditions, in which all subjects attempt all items, show aging decline. This means that older adults (on the average) obtain fewer correct answers than do younger adults to the difficult problems of Gf tasks; thus, a Gf-decline curve does not mean simply that older adults attempted fewer problems near the end of tests than did younger adults.

Also of some relevance in this regard is the finding in Figure 5 illustrating that part-correlation control with SPC brings about very little change in the aging decline curve for Gf. This is a surprising result of some three studies. The SPC variable represents measure of the speediness of obtaining correct answers to relatively difficult problems of the kind that are used to measure Gf or Gc. Such speed-of-solution measures correlate somewhat positively with Gf and Gc, but when care is taken to ensure that quite different problems are used in the speediness measures than are used in the Gf measures, so that operational independence is achieved, the speediness measures effect no significant change on the aging decline that is recorded with power measures of Gf.

Such findings suggest that the ability to solve rather difficult problems of the kind that define Gf declines with age in adulthood but that this decline is not related to slowness in solving such problems even as such slowness in general is somewhat related to ability in solving Gf problems. Thus, it seems that quickness in contrast to slowness in solving Gf problems is a characteristic that persists over age—slow problem-solvers in youth will be slow problem-solvers in later adulthood—and aging of intellectual abilities, as such, is not characterized by development of such slowness in problem-solving. More concretely, the results suggest that when an older person can indeed solve a fluid intelligence problem, he solves it about as quickly (on the average) as a younger person who can solve the problem.

I doubt that these findings are well explained as due to unreliability in the speed-to-correct measures, although this possibility is not entirely ruled out. Our analyses indicate that the specific factor for speed-to-correct scores for different items in the same test and for different tests is very large; therefore one must combine over many items from different tests to build up anything approaching a good measure of a common factor. Thus, one could be capitalizing on chance variation in developing SPC measures, and the further results might simply reflect this fact. Looked at in another way, however, the large specificity for SPC scores indicates that such speediness is not a consistent feature of individual differences in general and thus is not a general feature of individual differences associated with aging.

For these reasons, then, the safest conclusion seems to be that aging decline in fluid intelligence does not reflect aging increase in slowness in solving problems that one can indeed solve.

It seems, also, that the aging decreases in concentration and attention-division that are related to decreases in CPS speediness and to decline of fluid intelligence are not manifestations of increasing carefulness and persistence in working on intellectual tasks, even as such increases do seem to occur (on the average). Results supporting this conclusion are depicted in Figure 5, with the curves showing the effect on Gf decline of controlling for CAR and PRS.

The CAR variable represents carefulness in the sense of striving to make few errors and always give correct answers to relatively difficult problems of the kind that define Gf or Gc. The measure is obtained over a number of tests that were given under speeded conditions. It is the complement of the number of wrong answers given under such conditions—that is, one gets a high score if he is careful to make sure that every answer he provides is indeed a correct answer. It has been known at least since the work of Welford (1958) and his coworkers that older adults tend to be somewhat more careful in this respect (as in others) than younger adults. It sometimes seems to be assumed that such aging increases in carefulness account for aging declines in scores on Gf tests. This assumption is dubious because control for such carefulness not only does not decrease the aging decline for power measures of fluid intelligence, it increases it. Moreover, this increase is significant—from 3.75 to 5.18 IQ units per decade.

The finding of Gf decline with age means that older adults get fewer correct answers than younger adults for sets of Gf problems that all subjects attempt. When similar problems are presented in speeded tests, older adults attempt fewer problems but they produce relatively fewer incorrect answers. They are more careful to make sure that any answer they do give is correct. When this condition of carefulness is taken into account in the control of part-correlation analysis, the aging decline indicated for fluid intelligence is increased. This increase suggests that in unspeeded measures of fluid intelligence the older adult tends to compensate for deficiencies by working somewhat more carefully. Such a result, which has been found in several studies in addition to those considered here, does not support a hypothesis that the aging decline in concentration–attentiveness that has been found to be implicated in fluid intelligence decline is merely a reflection of careful effort to do well on fluid ability tests. It seems, indeed, that older adults are trying harder than younger adults to do well on these tasks (for they are more careful) and that this decreases Gf decline that otherwise would be indicated in the averages.

The persistence variable, PRS, reinforces this conclusion. PRS is a measure of the time spent on problems before finally deciding to abandon a problem. Older adults tend to be somewhat more persistent (in this sense) than younger adults. As in the case of carefulness, this persistence seems to help the older adult to perform somewhat better than otherwise would be the case. The result is that if this advantage is discounted by controlling for individual differences in persistence, the aging decline indicated for fluid intelligence is increased.

### *Spontaneous Alertness, Expectations, and Incidental Memory*

The results summarized in Figure 6 suggest that aging decline of fluid intelligence might be due (in part) to a decline in a kind of spontaneous alertness that may be different from the attentiveness and concentration considered in the previous section. One paradigm-conversion measure that suggests this is ICM, representing a kind of incidental memory measure. The measure was obtained by

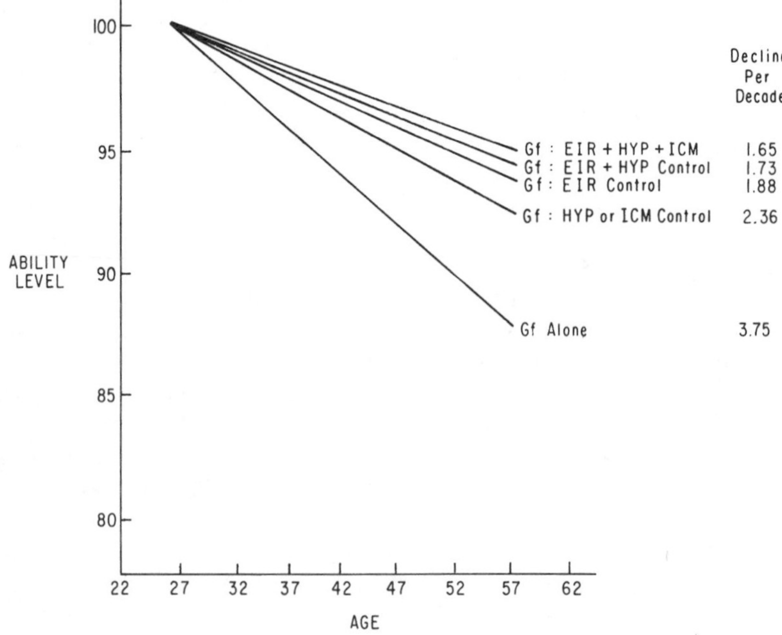


Fig. 6. Aging decline of Gf when EIR, HYP, and ICM are controlled.

staging several rather insignificant events over the course of a testing period that lasted for about an hour and one-half and then having the subject answer questions designed to indicate whether the events were remembered. For example, a line drawing of the dog Snoopy appeared on one of these tests. The subject was required to indicate whether he remembered seeing this dog. Other events had to do with people entering the room and sounds that occurred during the testing. As can be seen in Figure 6, this measure of incidental memory accounted for a statistically significant portion of the aging decline of fluid intelligence.

The variable labeled EIR represents a tendency or ability to eliminate irrelevancies. The broad theory on which the measure is based is similar to that stated by Rabbitt (e.g., 1965), but operationally the variable seems to be rather different from any of Rabbitt's measures. The task was one of concept attainment in which, however, one could designate which attributes were being considered. Also, after a number of trials, it could be determined that particular values of attributes were not relevant. For example, after being told that all possible combinations of green objects are not instances of a concept (a blue, large triangle), one can eliminate green as something to attend to in deciding on the features that determine the concept. If a subject continued to consider green after such exposure, then he would lower his score on the EIR measure. Controlling for this kind of perseveration was found to reduce the aging decline of fluid intelligence, as can be seen in Figure 6.

The HYP measure of Figure 6 was derived from ideas (in cognitive psychology) about the role of hypothesis-formation and anticipation in problem solving. The operations of measurement are based most directly on the work of Denney and Lennon (1972). They had found that in the familiar game of 20 questions older adults ask questions that are not as relevant to solving a problem as the questions asked by younger adults. Our measure based on this game awarded high points if the questions a subject asked tended to divide the possibilities in half and low points if the questions were highly specific (e.g., is it a bread basket?). This measure, too, accounted for some of the aging decline of fluid intelligence.

Taken together, the results obtained with HYP, EIR and ICM seem to indicate that part of the aging decline of Gf reflects a loss in spontaneous alertness about environmental features that could be (but often are not) relevant in problem solving. Relative to younger adults, older adults seem to be somewhat oblivious to things that, while not pointedly relevant to whatever one is doing at a particular moment, turn out to be relevant. This seems to point to a somewhat different quality of alertness than is represented in previously discussed measures of concentration, attention-division, and short-term memory. The alertness in this case involves retention over minutes and hours, as indicated by the incidental memory variable. This storage seems to occur largely in the absence of intention to attend to incidental stimulation or to retain the information of this stimulation.

## *Multiple-Process Involvements in Gf Decline*

The separation of sections in previous discussion was based partly on tradition and common practice (memory is usually considered separately from carefulness, for example) and partly on results suggesting that, indeed, there are separate, independent classes of variables that account for some of the aging decline of fluid intelligence. Our theory is weak, however, in specification of precisely what the processes of decline are and how they operate independently. This weakness results partly because to some extent our variables represent the same processes, and to unknown degrees that are very difficult to estimate. Although measures such as ICM and EOG are operationally independent and seem to be based on notably different kinds of tasks, nevertheless there is a sense in which both might be regarded as measuring the same capacity for incidental memory. We do not know whether that is true; all that our analyses can tell us is the extent to which control by one such variable is redundantly achieved with another such variable. In this respect the analyses are similar to task decomposition analyses such as have been attempted by the two Sternbergs (S. Sternberg, 1966; R. Sternberg, 1978). In common with these last-mentioned efforts at description, our results raise questions in the process of trying to answer questions.

Summarizing over a number of analyses of the kind that were reviewed in previous sections, including analyses with several combinations of variables, we find the following variables to be reasonable initial candidates for representing the major independent processes of all the paradigm-conversion variables we have studied that also pertain to aging decline of fluid intelligence.

- EOG: Organization at the stage of encoding in memory (which accounts for much of the short-term memory involvement in Gf decline)
- COS: Concentration-attentiveness, as in trying to trace very slowly (which also accounts for much short-term memory decline in Gf as well as Gf decline in ability to divide attention and maintain clerical-perceptual speediness)
- EIR: Eliminating irrelevancies in concept attainment (which accounts for much of the incidental memory involvement in Gf decline)
- HYP: Hypothesis formation in the 20-questions game (which, like EIR, accounts for much of the incidental memory involvement in Gf decline)

A problem with controlling for all of several processes at once was mentioned earlier: part-correlation controls involve calculating a multiple regression equation and thus obtaining stable and reliably different regression coefficients for each parted-out variable. Regression coefficients are unstable in cross-validation in small samples, and statistical tests are not always indicative of the "bounce" in the bouncing-beta problem. A rule of thumb that has gained respect among many who have observed the fleeting character of regression coefficients in cross-validation is to require a sample of 100 subjects for each addition of a variable to a regression equation. According to this rule, one would need a sample of 400 to make a case that four distinct processes are involved in Gf decline. In study 3, where measures representing the four processes mentioned above were obtained, the sample size was 147. One must be cautious, therefore, about regarding multiple-part analyses in this sample as indicating separate processes for parted-out variables. If such analyses are suggested primarily by substantive considerations and theory, however, capitalization on chance may be kept to a reasonable minimum and results might be fairly dependable.

Results from entering EOG, COS, EIR, and HYP in multiple-part analysis of the aging decline of fluid intelligence suggest that any three of these variables produce about the same outcome as any other three and that this outcome is not significantly altered by parting out a fourth variable. Moreover, if different combinations of three and four of the other variables that were mentioned in previous sections are entered into multiple-part analyses, the results are again very much the same as when EOG, COS, or EIR is the control variable. In general, starting with Gf decline set at 3.75 units per decade and entering one control variable, Gf decline is reduced by a bit more than one IQ unit per decade; adding a second control variable further reduces the decline by about two-thirds of a unit per decade; entering a third control variable brings the reduction in decline to a bit over 2 units per decade; reductions achieved by further parting-out are minor and appear to be statistically unstable.

Thus, it seems that three basic cognitive processes of relevance for understanding the aging decline of fluid intelligence are represented by the several process-variables indicated in Tables 3 and 4. These processes can be talked about in a number of different ways. For example, they are, in one sense, memory, concentration and alertness; in another sense, they are encoding organization, attentiveness, and expectation formation; and there are still other ways of discussing them. Whichever way they are discussed, however, it appears that there are only three processes represented by our particular operational definitions.

Together these three processes account for only about one-half of the aging decline of fluid intelligence. Thus, processes that have not been represented by the operational definitions of the reviewed studies appear to be involved in the aging losses of fluid intelligence. Perhaps some of these processes have been indicated by other research reported in this volume.

### *The Rise of Crystallized Intelligence*

It is important to recognize that in the same samples of subjects wherein decline of fluid abilities has been found there has been evidence that older subjects perform better than younger subjects on some tasks that are accepted indicants of intelligence. The results (now documented in over a dozen separate studies) have several implications for statements of sound theory about cognitive functioning. They indicate that our statements about experiential and physiological influences in development (particularly in adulthood) should indicate how some abilities improve while others decline. If both the Gf and Gc sets of abilities are regarded as representing the same function, general intelligence, then statements should indicate how the cohesiveness of this function is maintained when parts of it change in somewhat different ways over the course of adult development. Single-influence statements, such as "older adults have had less education than younger adults," do not suffice; they must be augmented with statements indicating how an influence produces both decline and improvement of the abilities of (a singular) intelligence. This is particularly a problem for efforts to specify lawful relationships between neurological functioning and intellectual performances, for it seems evident that there are adulthood decrements in some of the neurological structures and functions that support intellectual behavior, but because there is evidence of improvements in some of this behavior, there must also be corresponding enhancements of neurological functioning. Before discussing issues of this kind, it will be useful to look briefly at some features of adult differences in crystallized abilities.

In our studies much less attention has been given to Gc than to Gf. Only very little can be added to what has been stated about Gc in previous reviews (e.g. Horn, 1975, 1978).

When care is taken to obtain multiple-test measurements with tests that have fairly unifactor relations to Gc, the rise of crystallized intelligence over the "vital years" of adulthood (up to about age 55 to 65 years) is of approximately the same magnitude as the decline of Gf over this period. If part-correlation control with Gf is introduced (in recognition that fallible measurements of Gf and Gc are to some extent confounded), an outside boundary for the average improvement of Gc is estimated to be in excess of 6 IQ points per decade (again, a change that is of roughly the same magnitude as the decline of Gf estimated when the confounding influence of Gc is controlled). Improvements in Gc probably reflect individuals' restructurings of their knowledge systems to make the knowledge increasingly more cohesive, correct, and accessible (as described by, for example, Mandler, 1967; Norman, 1977; Craik & Byrd, Chapter 11). In our research, however, we have had few variables to indicate the precise nature of such restructuring, and we have few ideas about how the restructuring might be manifested in neurological functioning.

Figure 7 provides an indication of some features of the rise of Gc in adulthood. The controls indicated in this figure suggest that part of the improvement in Gc over the adult period of development involves increasing accessibility to information. The TSR (tertiary storage and retrieval) factor, for example, is a measure of facility in recalling facts, connotations—information broadly con-

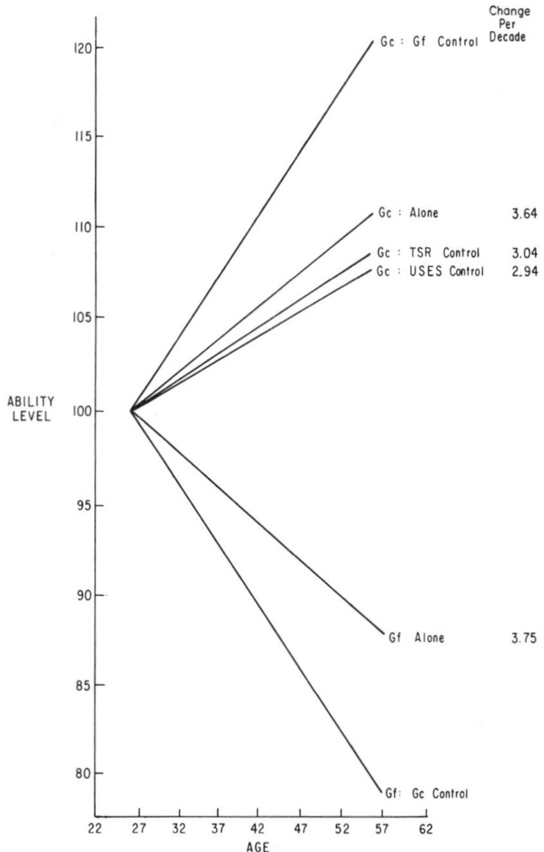


Fig. 7. Age differences in Gc when TSR, USES, and Gf are controlled and age decline in Gf when Gc is controlled.

ceived—from long-term memory storage. This facility may represent, in part, a buildup of information over the life span, resulting in the older person's having more information to access than the younger person (under the assumption that gain is not cancelled by loss). In the first 30 seconds or minute of a task of recalling words that are similar in meaning to the word *warm,* for example, older adults produce almost as many connotations as younger adults, and as the time is extended to 3 minutes (roughly, the asymptote) older adults (on the average) produce more connotations than do younger ones. There appears to be more accessible information for the older adult than for the younger one. The connotations that the older adult accesses in the last two minutes of the above-mentioned task are not necessarily more esoteric or remote (in the sense of infrequency, as in Mednick, 1962) than the connotations accessed by the younger adult.

Aging may also be associated with improvements in getting at information in long-term memory. For example, some of the variables that help describe Gc aging improvements have been interpreted as indicating cleverness or creativity—that is, a flexible structuring of information. For example, in the USES test the task is to specify different ways in which an object (a brick) might be used (as a paper weight, a weapon, etc.). In several studies, this measure has been regarded as an operational representation of creativity. In our work, as indicated in Figure 7, the variable accounts for some of the Gc rise in adulthood. Such findings are not unequivocal, of course, but they suggest that older adults differ from younger adults in having somewhat more flexible access to stored information.

The results just reviewed probably should not be interpreted as taking issue with findings such as Schonfield's (1974; Schonfield & Robertson, 1960) suggesting that older adults have more difficulty than younger adults do in retrieving a particular, sought-after item of information, as in the tip-of-the-tongue phenomenon. The results referred to in Figure 7 indicate that older adults have more knowledge than younger adults (as mainly represented in Gc) and can fluently express this knowledge when prompted to do so; the results do *not* mean that if subjects are given the definition of a word, say, an older person will be able to search through his labels and retrieve the word itself more capably than a younger person (who also knows the word). Indeed, Schonfield's results suggest that the opposite is true. The variables of our studies do not emulate those of Schonfield's work, and our results are not necessarily inconsistent with his. To express connotations from a category is not the same as retrieving a particular item from that category. Our evidence suggests that a facility for expressing connotations of a concept (word or idea) improves with age, at least through the vital years; Schonfield's evidence suggests that a facility for retrieving a particular designated connotation declines, at least in old age. It appears, then, that two distinct processes may be involved in aging changes in accessing information in long-term storage (see Fozard, 1980 for a recent, rather detailed review of additional evidence pertaining to this point).

## *Summing Up*

The evidence of several studies thus indicates that in adulthood important features of intellectual functioning improve, on an average over different subjects, whereas in the same samples of subjects averages for indicants of other important features of intellectual functioning indicate aging decline. A correlation of approximately .5 between Gf and Gc indicates that some of the individuals who improve in Gc also decline in Gf. This correlation, considered with evidence that Gf and Gc have internal consistencies in the neighborhood of .8, indicates that fallible measures of the two constructs have much in common. Some of this overlap can be interpreted as due to inability to achieve pure measures of the two constructs; some of the crystallized abilities of verbal comprehension, for example, intrude in tasks designed to measure Gf. Some of the overlap, however, is probably best interpreted as presenting common determinants (for example, common genetic determinants). The fact that the correlation between Gf and Gc is no larger than it is (relative to the internal consistencies of the fallible measures) and the evidence of age correlations of approximately .25 and −.25 for Gc and Gf respectively indicate that the influences that produce the aging increments are different from those that produce the aging decrements in Gf. No doubt these influences are of a variety of kinds—some experiental, as in learning, and some of a type that an individual can only indirectly experience, as when neurons die. The precise nature of such influences is not indicated by our empirical research and our bibliographical research speaks only indirectly to questions about such influences. Nevertheless it is probably important in a volume such as this one to give some consideration to indirect evidence in order to suggest approaches to further empirical work.

## Brain Function in Relation to Gf and Gc

There is far too much complexity in both neurological functioning and behavioral variations in human abilities to hope for any simple alignments between these two universes of phenomena. A few broad linkups may be indicated, however, by existing evidence and theory. Some such possibilities for Gf will be considered first.

### *Gf Relations to Neurological Gating Functions*

Some of the behavioral defects that have been described as associated with malfunctions in brain areas known as the hippocampus, fornix, thalamus, mamillary bodies, and nearby limbic-diencephalic structures are rather similar to some of the behavioral defects described in the present chapter as associated with aging in adulthood. In particular, descriptions of behavioral defects associated with malfunctions in the above-mentioned neurological areas often suggest that encoding organization, concentration, spontaneous alertness, and similar Gf-decline functions are decreased with brain damage (see Drachman & Arbit, 1966; Hachinski, 1980; Newcombe, 1965; Scoville & Milner, 1957; and Turner, 1969, in regard to the hippocampus; Barbizet, 1963; and Brion, 1969, for evidence pertaining to the mamilliary bodies; Sweet, Talland, & Ervin, 1959, for discussion of fornix functions; and Butters & Crzemak, 1975, and Jahro, 1973, for consideration of several possible limbic-diencephalic functions). In the cases described by Newcombe, Drachman,and Arbit, Scoville and Milner, Turner, and Hachinski, in which there was evidence of hippocampus malfunction of one form or another, the primary intellectual defect appeared to be one of inability to learn in a manner that would allow retention of learned material over minutes, hours, days, or weeks. The skills the patients had acquired prior to the brain malfunction appeared to be largely intact. This suggests that crystallized intelligence was not greatly affected by the damage. Similarly, although a few inabilities to recall information from the distant past (prior to damage) were sometimes described, these did not appear to be central to the patients' inabilities: thus, it seems that tertiary storage and retrieval, TSR, was largely unaffected. Also, in several of the cases, at least, the patient was able to register information and retain it over periods of a few seconds, as in carrying on a conversation; it seems, therefore, that SAR, short-term acquisition and retrieval processes, as such, were not centrally involved in the malfunction. Yet the patients were deeply confused in working out where they were and to whom they were talking. They could not seem to form new, often rather simple, concepts about time and space. It was as if the patient could step through the stages of solution to a problem, seemingly being aware of each stage (suggesting that SAR was intact), without comprehending the total solution in any way that made sense.

Such behavior is very similar to that observed when a subject fails to solve a problem of the matrices and letter series tests that help identify the fluid intelligence factor. As different relations of such a problem are explained, the person seems to be aware of the train of thought—perhaps to comprehend particular relations—but after several steps in the solution are explained, the person seems to draw a total balnk in understanding the overall problem; the answers and the suggestions made to indicate possible answers are arbitrary (that is, as if random) relative to any reasonable inference.

Hachinski (1980) has pointed out that the vascular anatomy of the hippocampus makes this area particularly vulnerable to a variety of injuries that can result from changes in blood pressure. He notes:

> The arteries supplying the hippocampus are arranged in rake-like fashion, branching at right angles to the main trunks and penetrating the hippocampus as end arteries. This feature has led Sharrer (1940) to suggest that whereas a drop in blood pressure is distributed equally in blood vessels branching dichotomously, in the rake-like pattern of the hippocampus, the blood pressure would drop critically before this condition occurs elsewhere in the brain. Hence the hippocampus would be damaged earlier and more severely than the rest of the brain. Furthermore, Coceani and Gloor (1966) point out that the hippocampus lies in the watershed between the carotid and vertebrobasilar arteries territories; any drop in blood pressure renders the hippocampus susceptible to ischemic damage, since the blood flow would cease earliest at the branches furthest away from the blood supply. It is well established that the hippocampus is one of the areas selectively vulnerable to severe falls in blood pressure (Brierly, 1976). It is possible . . . that multiple small areas of brain softenings (infarcts) may occur in patients prone to repeated bouts of profound falls in blood pressure . . . Corsellis (1976) has noted that atherosclerosis and small infarcts are more common in the hippocampus than elsewhere in the brain. (p. 2)

Thus, a *prima facie* case exists for a hypothesis that over the course of a lifetime any of a number of things can happen to bring about decreases—perhaps profound decreases—in blood pressure, decreases which would register first and most noticeably in the hippocampi and be detected in losses in the abilities to concentrate and organize information in fluid intelligence. Such events could be the incipient initiators of other neural events such as McLachlan and Petit have described (Chapters 1 and 2) which lead to the cascade of neuropathology that is seen in clearcut cases of dementia, such as Alzheimer's disease. This is certainly not the whole story of intellectual decline, of course; and although the case is established here for the hippocampus, damage that occurs to areas other than the hippocami may also be important. Furthermore, although encoding organization, concentration, and spontaneous alertness appear to be central to the functioning of fluid intelligence, they are not the whole of this functioning, and several malfunctions in addition to any in the hippocampal areas could be responsible for some of the breakdowns of this form of intelligence.

Some of the behaviors described as typical of Wernicke's aphasia are similar to the behaviors observed when individuals obtain low scores on fluid intelligence tasks. Usually, of course, Wernicke syndromes are regarded as primarily involving language and thus are most readily linked with TSR and/or the knowledge system of Gc. In fact, this may be the major alignment, but it is noteworthy that a dominant feature of Wernicke syndromes is failure to comprehend. Granted that this failure is in comprehension of language, it also appears to involve failure to comprehend in a broader sense—in particular, failure to make sense of information at the level of encoding, rather like the encoding organization failures that have just been referred to as characteristic of aging decline of fluid intelligence. It seems that the retrieval functions of TSR are also affected by damage in Wernicke's area of the brain, but the principal effects in addition to those on TSR may be in the Gf capacities for educing relations and drawing inferences.

### *Possible Neurological Underpinnings of Gc in Relation to Total Function*

Theories about neurological functioning in relation to intellectual functioning must account for the rise in Gc as well as the decline in Gf. However, there are few concrete indications of links between Gc-like performances and neurological functioning.

Dimond (1980) has suggested that white fibers of the brain may carry information of the kind that has been identified as representing Gc (particularly, but possibly also Gf). Dimond recognizes that subcortial, hippocampal, temporal lobe, and related structures are essential to processes of initially recording information and getting it to the cortex, but he suggests that the essential organization of knowledge systems is represented in some unknown way in the white fibers.

Hyden (1973) and Hebb (1949) have suggested that knowledge (of the kind identified by measures of Gc) is stored diffusely throughout the brain in accordance with biochemical structural alterations of neuronal synapses. Thus, Gc might be represented throughout the cortex and in alterations of white fibers. If it is true that limbic system processes are central features of fluid intelligence and given the general activation functions of the limbic system, it seems reasonable to suppose that the activities of the hippocampal and related structures serve the function of activating or charging the activities of white fibers and that together these two kinds of processes enable one initially to make sense of information and get this sensible information deposited in the cerebrum. Once so deposited, the information may be relatively impervious to changes in the hippocampal area.

### *Lateralization Theory in Relation to Gf/Gc Theory*

Gc/Gc theory is sometimes regarded as referring to the same phenomena as are referred to in left-brain/right-brain theory; the two theories might be treated as equivalent in major respects. The present view is, however, that the two theories pertain to rather different phenomena, and thus a hypothesis that they are equivalent will not find support. This is a hypothesis that should be studied carefully in the coming years. Some thoughts about the equivalence of laterality theory and Gf/Gc theory can be roughly summed up as follows.

The encoding-organization, comprehension, and retention effects that were described previously as being associated with damage in the Wernicke and hippocampal areas appear to be most pronounced when the damage is mainly in the left, rather than in the right, hemisphere of the brain. Also, the effects appear to be largely verbal if the damage is mainly in the left hemisphere and largely spatial or auditory if the damage is mainly in the right hemisphere. As is well known, Broca's aphasias occur primarily with damage to the left, not the right, side of the brain. Also, a considerable body of evidence indicates that recognition of, and ability to think with, complex spatial and auditory stimulus-patterns is associated with right brain activity, whereas similar recognition of, and ability to think with, verbal material is associated with activities of the left brain. In short, several lines of inquiry lead to a conclusion that some of the organization that exists among abilities is, at some level, associated with hemispheric organization of the brain.

Beyond this generalization, however, little is known about the relations between the regularities represented by ability factors and the regularities of hemispheric specialization. On first consideration, one might suppose that crystallized intelligence is mainly associated with left brain specialization, while fluid intelligence is mainly supported by right brain activities. However, the abilities of Gc and Gf involve considerably more skills and capacities than have been found to be associated with left brain and right brain specialization. Most lateral specialization has been indicated for relatively simple tasks of recognition and manipulation of stimuli, not for tasks that demand feats of abstraction and eduction of relations and correlates. It is questionable whether there is lateral specialization in performance on these last-mentioned tasks after variance associated with perception of the stimuli has been controlled. Also related is evidence of the kind previously mentioned in discussion of hippocampal function to suggest that damage in both hemispheres affects basic processes of fluid intelligence. Then, too, evidence from several sources suggests that brain damage in either the right or the left hemisphere produces irreversible decrements in fluid abilities but may influence crystallized abilities in only a reversible way. Some of the aphasias associated with damage in Broca's area, for example, are decrements in crystallized intelligence that may be, in part at least, reversible. Thus, it seems that dormant forms of some of these abilities are established in structures outside Broca's area and become activated if the corresponding Broca function is eliminated. At a more general level there is a suggestion that the crystallized abilities are overdetermined, not only in the above-mentioned sense that there are second-team areas that can take over function in the event that the first-team is knocked out, but also in the sense that the neurological supports for the abilities are extensive and in excess of what is minimally required, so that if some of the neurons are destroyed, substantial numbers of remaining neurons can maintain the ability. On the other hand, fluid abilities do not appear to be overdetermined in these ways, and loss of Gf function is therefore roughly proportional to the amount of loss of central nervous system structure. Overdetermined support for crystallized abilities appears to be widespread in the brain, perhaps in both right and left hemisphere, and irreversible decrements in fluid intelligence seem to be associated with damage in widely different parts of the brain. For these reasons, as well as for the other reasons mentioned before, it seems that the behavioral organizations represented by Gf and Gc do not align in any direct way with hemispheric organization of the brain (see Horn & Donaldson, 1980, for a more detailed review).

A major primary ability of crystallized intelligence is verbal comprehension, V. It is reasonable to suppose that V represents an organization of skills that is fairly directly associated with left brain functions of Broca's and Wernicke's areas. It was mentioned previously that some of the retrieval difficulties associated with the left temporal lobe damage of Wernicke's aphasias appear to reflect breakdown in the TSR factor. The behaviors often described as reflecting right-brain activities are similar in several respects to the behaviors that define the broad visualization in Figure 1 and Tables 1 and 2. Also, any of the several primary abilities involved in Gv and Ga could represent right-brain specializations. There are also several other such possible links between what is known about the organization of abilities and right-brain/left-brain functioning. These possible links are not genuine hypotheses, of course, but they represent rudimentary forms of such hypotheses.

## Summary

Review of results from several studies thus leads to a conclusion that losses in capacities for maintaining spontaneous alertness, focused intensive concentration, and awareness of possible organization for otherwise unorganized information are largely responsible for aging decline of those features of short-term memory and performance speediness that are involved in the aging decline of fluid intelligence during the middle years of adulthood, the period between 20 and 60 years of age. These losses are similar to behavioral changes that accompany malfunctions of the temporal lobes, mamillary bodies, thalamus, fornix, the hippocampus, and related limbic-diencephalic structures. Alterations in blood pressure may be a common feature of both the aging and injury behavioral manifestations. The hippocampus, particularly, is exceptionally vulnerable to injuries associated with blood pressure changes. Many factors can produce such injuries—inebriation, blows to the head, hypertension, to name only a few. Over the course of a lifetime there is a good chance that at one time or another one would encounter such factors. Thus, it may be that from time to time throughout normal adult development, some individuals—perhaps many, perhaps all—experience changes in blood pressure that results in multiple small infarcts in the hippocampi and nearby structures, with consequent loss in capacities for maintaining concentration, alertness, and awareness of organizational possibilities. Each such alteration of structure and behavior, considered by itself, could be so small that it would go unnoticed by the individual effected and not be detected by even rather sensitive recorders of change. However, repeated such changes, accumulating over years, could be large enough to be recorded with objective measures of Gf. The evidence reviewed in this chapter suggests that such change might account for roughly one-half of the aging decline of fluid intelligence through the mid-adulthood period. The remaining part of the decline might be due to alterations of other kinds, such as might affect white fibers of the brain or the charge of the neurons in the cerebral cortex. However, once information becomes stored in the complex interlaced firing patterns of cerebral neural structures, it appears to be retained in spite of declines in the gate-opening activation processes of hippocampi-limbic-area structures. Moreover, it seems that some of this complexity promotes more of the same: patterns for neural firing are built from already established patterns; networks are composed from established networks. The capacities thus retained in white fibers are manifested in a crystallized form of intelligence that not only does not decline through the middle years of adulthood, but appears to rise throughout this period. This form of intelligence appears to be linked to a kind of flexibility in thinking that is regarded as a feature of intellectual creativity.

The usual, commonly stated cautions about interpreting cross-sectional data should obtain in thinking about the results summarized in this chapter. These cautions should be accompanied also by awareness that any data set is limited in particular ways and that in several respects cross-sectional data are superior to longitudinal data (Horn & Donaldson, 1980). The sad but inescapable fact is that there is no perfect way to provide evidence on important questions about human development. All studies have flaws. Fortunately, the flaws of one kind of study are not necessarily present in other kinds of studies, and it is possible, therefore, to collate over different kinds of results to build improved conceptions of reality. It is in this sense that the work reviewed in this chapter might be combined with the other research reported in this book to yield an accurate picture of what is presently known about cognitive development in adulthood.

### Acknowledgments

I am grateful to a number of people who helped me with various parts of the research: Mary Halter for doing many tasks of data preparation and writing; Ralph Mason for doing much of the data gathering and data analysis; Bob Engstrom and Gary Donaldson for work ranging from the most mundane aspects of test preparation to the most esoteric and complex aspects of analysis and theory development; Jack McArdle for insightful suggestions regarding data analysis and basic theory; George Levy and his assistants at Colorado State Penitentiary for much of the work that enabled us to gather and retain the data; Bob Short, Pat Ellison, and Vladimir Hachinski for valuable criticisms and comments about neurological functioning; and, most important, the men who served as subjects for conscientious effort in doing tasks that were by no means always fun and easy.

## References

Adam, J. Statistical bias in cross-sequential studies of aging. *Experimental Aging Research,* 1977, *3,* 325–333.

Barbizet, J. Defect of memorizing of hippocampal-manillary origin: A review. *Journal of Neurology, Neurosurgery and Psychiatry,* 1963, *26,* 126–135.

Birren, J. E. Age changes in speed of behavior: Its central nature and physiological correlates. In A.T. Welford & J. E. Birren (Eds.), *Behavior, aging and the nervous system.* Springfield, Ill.: Charles C Thomas, 1965.

Birren, J. E. Psychophysiology and speed of response. *American Psychologist,* 1974, *29,* 808–815.

Botwinick, J., & Arenberg, D. Disparate time-spans in sequential studies of aging. *Experimental Aging Research,* 1976, *2,* 55–66.

Botwinick, J. & Storandt, M. *Memory, related functions and age.* Springfield, Ill.: Charles C Thomas, 1974.

Bousfield, A. K., & Bousfield, W. A. Measurement of clustering and of sequential constancies in repeated free recall. *Psychological Reports,* 1966, *19,* 935–942.

Brierly, J. B. Cerebral hypoxia. In W. Blackwood & J. A. N. Corsellis (Eds.), *Greenfield's neuropathology*. London: Arnold, 1976.

Brion, S. Korsakoff's syndrome. Clinico-anatomical and physiopathological considerations. In G. A. Talland & N. Waugh (Eds.), *The pathology of memory*. New York: Academic Press, 1969.

Broadbent, D. E. The well ordered mind. *American Educational Research Journal*. 1966 *3*, 281–295.

Broadbent, D. E. & Heron, A. Effects of a subsidiary task of performance involving immediate memory in younger and older men. *British Journal of Psychology*, 19662, *53*, 189–198.

Butters, N., & Cermak, L. Some analyses of amnesic syndromes in brain-damaged patients. *The Hippocampus*, 1975, *2*, 377–409.

Cattell, R. B., & Horn, J. L. A cross-social check on the theory of fluid and crystallized intelligence with discovery of new valid subtest designs. *Journal of Educational Measurement*, 1978, *15*, 139–164.

Coceani, F., & Gloor, P. The distribution of the internal carotid circulation in the brain of the Macaque monkey (Macaca mulatta). *Journal of Comparative Neurology*, 1966, *128*, 419.

Corsellis, J. A. N. Aging and the dementias, In W. Blackwood & J. A. N. Corsellis (Eds.), *Greenfield's neuropathology*. London: Arnold, 1976.

Corsini, R. J. & Fassett K. K. Intelligence and aging. *Journal of Genetic Psychology*, 1953, *83*, 249–264.

Craik, F. I. M., & Lockhart, R. S. Levels of processing: A framework for memory research, *Journal of Verbal Learning and Verbal Behavior*, 1972, *11*, 671–684.

Dawes, R. B. The robust beauty of improper linear models in decision making. *American Psychologist*, 1979, *34*, 571–582.

Denney, N. W., & Lennon, M. L. Classification: A comparison of middle and old age. *Developmental Psychology*, 1972, *7*, 210–213.

Dimond, S. J. Memory. In H. Goodglass (Ed.), *Neuropsychology*. Boston: Butterworth, 1980.

Drachman, D. A., & Arbit, J. Memory and the hippocampal complex. II. Is memory a multiple process? *Archives of Neurology*, 1966, *15*, 52–61.

Fozard, J. L. The time for remembering. In L. W. Poon (Ed.), *Aging in the 1980's*. Washington, D.C.: American Psychological Association, 1980.

Glanzer, M., & Cunitz, A. R. Two storage mechanisms in free recall. *Journal of Verbal Learning and Verbal Behavior*, 1966, *5*, 341–360.

Hachinski, V. Relevance of cerebrovascular changes to mental function. *Mechanisms of Aging and Development*, 1980, *10*, 1–11.

Hebb, D. O. *The organization of behavior*. New York: Wiley, 1949.

Horn, J. L. Equations representing combinations of components in scoring psychological variables. *Acta Psychologica*, 1963, *21*, 184–217.

Horn J. L. A rational and test for the number of factors in factor analysis. *Psychometrika*, 1965, *30*, 179–185.

Horn, J. L. On the use of random variables in factor analysis. *British Journal of Mathematical and Statistical Psychology*, 1966, *19*, 127–129.

Horn, J. L. On subjectivity in factor analysis. *Educational and Psychological Measurement*, 1967, *27*, 811–820.

Horn, J. L. Integration of concepts of reliability and standard error of measurement. *Educational and Psychological Measurement*, 1971, *31*, 57–74.

Horn J. L. Psychometric studies of aging and intelligence. In S. Gershon & A. Raskin (Eds.), *Aging: Genesis and treatment of psychologic disorders in the elderly (Vol. 2)*. New York: Raven, 1975.

Horn J. L. Human abilities: a review of research and theory in the early 1970s. *Annual Review of Psychology*, 1976, *27*, 437–485.

Horn, J. L. Human ability systems. In P. B. Baltes (Ed.), *Life-span development and behavior*. New York: Academic Press, 1978.

Horn, J. L. Some correctable defects in research on intelligence. *Intelligence, 1979, 3,* 307–322.

Horn, J. L. Concepts of intellect in relation to learning and adult development. *Intelligence,* 1980, *4,* 285–317.

Horn, J. L.,& Cattell, R. B. Vehicles, ipsatization and the multiple method measurement of motivation. *Canadian Journal of Psychology,* 1965, *19,* 265–279.

Horn, J. L.,& Donaldson, G. Faith is not enough: A response to the Baltes-Schaie claim that intelligence will not wane. *American Psychologist,* 1977, *32,* 369–373.

Horn, J. L., & Donaldson, G. Cognitive development II: Adulthood development of human abilities. In O. G. Brim & J. Kagan (Eds.), *Constancy and change in human development: A volume of review essays.* Boston: Harvard University Press, 1980.

Horn J. L., Donaldson, G., & Engstrom, R. Apprehension, memory and fluid intelligence decline thrugh the "vital years" of adulthood. *Research on Aging,* 1981, *3,* 33–84.

Horn, J. L., & Engstrom, R. O. A comparison of Cattell's screen test and Bartlett's test for the number of factors. *Multivariate Behavioral Research,* 1979, *14,* 283–300.

Horn, J. L., & Knapp, J. R. On the subjective character of the empirical base of Guilford's structure-of-intellect model. *Psychological Bulletin,* 1973, *80,* 33–43.

Horn, J. L., & Knapp, J. R. Thirty wrongs do not make a right: A reply to Guilford. *Psychological Bulletin,* 1974, *81,* 502–504.

Horn, J. L., & McArdle, J. Perspectives on mathematical/statistical model building (MASMOB) in research on aging. In L. W. Poon (Ed.), *Aging in the 1980's.* Washington, D.C.: American Psychological Association, 1980.

Horn, J. L., Wanberg, K. W., & Adams, G. Diagnosis of alcoholism. *Quarterly Journal of Studies on Alcohol.* 1974, *35,* 147–175.

Humphreys, L. G. Doing research the hard way: Substituting analysis of variance for a problem in correlational analysis. *Journal of Educational Psychology,* 1978, *70,* 873–876.

Hyden, H. RNA changes in brain cells during changes in behavior function. In G. B. Ansell & P. B. Bradley (Eds.), *Macromolecules and behavior.* Baltimore: University Park Press, 1973.

Jahro, L., Korsakoff-like amnesic syndrome in penetrating brain injury: A study of Finnish war veterans. *Acta Neurologica Scandinavia* (Supplement), 1973, *54,* 3–156.

Kelley, H. P. Memory ability: A factor analysis. *Psychometric Monographs,* 11. Chicago: University of Chicago Press, 1964.

Kintsch, W. *Learning, memory, and conceptual processes.* New York: Wiley, 1970.

Kintsch, W. *The representation of meaning in memory.* New York: Wiley, 1974.

Mandler, G. Organization and memory. In K. W. Spence & J. T. Spence (Eds.), *The psychology of learning and motivation: Advances in research and theory* (vol. 1). New York: Academic Press, 1967.

Massaro, D. W. *Experimental psychology and information processing.* Chicago: Rand McNally, 1975.

Mednick, S. A. The associative basis of the creative process. *Psychological Review,* 1962, *69,* 220–232.

Miller, G. A. The magical number seven, plus or minus two: Some limits on our capacity for processing information. *Psychological Review,* 1956, *63,* 81–97.

Murdock, B. B. The immediate retention of unrelated words. *Journal of Experimental Psychology,* 1960, *60,* 222–234.

Newcombe, F. Memory for designs task: The performance of ex-servicemen with missile wounds of the brain. *British Journal of Social and Clinical Psychology,* 1965, *4,* 230–231.

Norman, D. A. *Research consideration in the assessment of the (impaired) elderly.* Conference on Cognition and Aging. Battale Research Center, Seattle, Washington, February 1977.

Rabbitt, P. M. A., An age-decrement in the ability to ignore irrelevant information. *Journal of Gerontology,* 1965, *20,* 233–283.

Reese, H. W. Imagery and associative memory. In R. V. Kail & J. W. Hagen (Eds.), *Perspectives on the development of memory and cognition*. Hillsdale, N. J.: Lawrence Erlbaum, 1977.

Schonfield, D. Theoretical nuances and practical old questions: The psychology of aging. *Canadian Psychologist*, 1972, *13*, 252–266.

Schonfield, D. Translations in gerontology—from lab to life: Utilizing information. *American Psychologist*, 1974, *29*, 796–801.

Schonfield, D., & Robertson, E. A. Memory storage and aging. *Canadian Journal of Psychology*, 1960, *20*, 228–236.

Scoville, W., & Milner, B. Loss of recent memory after bilateral hippocampal lesions. *Journal of Neurology, Neurosurgery and Psychiatry*, 1957, *20*, 11.

Sharrer, E. Vascularization and vulnerability of the cornu arrmonis in the opposum. *Journal of Neurology, Neurosurgery and Psychiatry*, 1940, *44*, 483.

Sperling, G. The information available in brief visual presentation. *Psychological Monographs*, 1960, *74*, No. 11.

Stankov, L., & Horn J. L. Human abilities revealed through auditory tests. *Journal of Educational Psychology*, 1980, *72*, 21–44.

Stankov, L., Horn, J. L., & Roy, T. On the relationship between Gf/Gc theory and Jensen's Level I/ Level II Theory. *Journal of Educational Psychology*, 1980, *72*, 796–809.

Sternberg, R. J. Isolating the components of intelligence. *Intelligence*, 1978, *2*, 117–128.

Sternberg, S. High-speed scanning in human memory. *Science*, 1966, *153*, 652–654.

Sweet, W. H., Talland, G. A., & Ervin, F. R. Loss of recent memory following section of fornix. *Transactions of the American Neurological Association*, 1959, *84*, 76–79.

Thurstone, L. L., & Thurstone, T. G. Factorial studies of intelligence *Psychometric Monographs*, 1941, No. 2.

Tulving, E. Subjective organization in free recall of "unrelated" words. *Psychological Review*, 1962, *69*, 344–354.

Turner, E. Hippocampus and memory. *Lancet*, 1969, *2*, 1123–1126.

Wackwitz, J. H., & Horn, J. L. On obtaining the best estimates of factor scores. *Multivariate Behavioral Research*, 1971, *6*, 389–408.

Welford, A. T. *Aging and human skills*. London: Oxford University Press, 1958.

Wohlwill, J. F. Methodology and research strategy in the study of developmental change. L. R. Goulet & P. B. Baltes (Eds.), In *Life-span developmental psychology*. New York: Academic Press, 1970.

CHAPTER 15

# Reallocation of Mental Resources over the Productive Lifespan

## Assumptions and Task Analyses

Roy Lachman, Janet L. Lachman, and Don W. Taylor

*Department of Psychology*
*University of Houston*
*Houston, Texas*

## Overview

Changes in intelligent behavior over the working lifespan are analyzed within an information-processing framework. Methodological issues raised by previous aging research were examined in conjunction with a preliminary task analysis based on computational theory. A survey of the recent literature was first presented revealing that (a) most studies are cross-sectional; (b) few researchers systematically insure age-group comparability; and (c) all older subjects are functional volunteers, possibly unlike subjects who do not volunteer. The assumptions underlying these practices were analyzed. Their consequences are potentially serious enough to undermine most generalizations in the cognitive aging literature. A study using a broad array of cognitive tasks tested the underlying assumptions. Old and young subjects were carefully equated by drawing samples from a homogeneous population of white female schoolteachers. Non-

The work herein described was supported in part by Grant AG-1378 from the National Institute on Aging, and in part by Grant BNS-77-25657 from the National Science Foundation, to the first two authors.

volunteers were induced to participate by payment of a large honorarium, and their performance on a broad array of tasks included some that reflect current trends in information-processing research (metamemory, inference, world knowledge) and others that were chosen because of their popularity in the surveyed literature (WAIS subtests, recall, recognition). They were classified in a four-way ordered set reflecting evolutionary considerations and information-processing theory, into tasks involving information maintenance, location and creation, and system interrogation. The study yielded both methodological and substantive conclusions. Unexpectedly, there was absolutely no effect of voluntarism and no age X voluntarism interactions; thus, the use of older functional volunteers appears methodologically defensible. Results from this carefully equated population proved consistent with the prior literature; the typical lack of comparability of different-aged subject samples has not been misleading at least where conclusions are established by wide replication. Young subjects outperformed older ones on all tasks involving primarily the maintenance of information (e.g., WAIS digit symbol, verbal learning). In tasks involving location of information (e.g., question answering), and those requiring interrogation of the cognitive system (e.g., metamemory), the elderly either equalled or outperformed the young. Results are interpreted as reflecting an adaptive allocation of intellectual resources to maximize the organism's functioning throughout its phylogenetically expected life span.

What is intelligent action and how are we to understand it? That is the core question for a cognitive science, a question that is often considered antecedent to the developmental question: how does a cognitive system change and develop over the life span? But there is another way to look at the relation between cognitive science and the science of cognitive development. The dominant approach in contemporary cognitive science characterizes information-processing systems as consisting of two subsystems: a symbol system and a set of computational mechanisms that operate on the symbol system (Lachman, Lachman, & Butterfield, 1979; Newell & Simon, 1972). Neither component can be characterized independent of its position in developmental time. The symbol system, for example, represents only genetically given content at the beginning of life; but after four score years and ten it represents an individual's knowledge of his universe. The mechanisms that operate on the symbol system are also subject to modification, through experience and the biological aging of the brain. Although it is obvious that cognition changes in an orderly manner throughout adulthood, well prior to the system breakdown associated with senile organic diseases, many "pure" cognitive theories are ageless—ostensibly applicable to adult cognition from puberty to senility or death. For example, Quillian's (1968, 1969) classic theory, the Teachable Language Comprehender, was cast as a computer program that retrived information about the hierarchial relationships of things such as birds, canaries, and animals, and their properties, such as skin and feathers. No one ever asked about TLC, "how old is it?" But it would have been an interesting question; surely the same program cannot model a 17-year-old, a 50-year-old, and a 70-year-old. The student of gerontology does not assume the existence of a prototypical ageless adult. The cognitive gerontologist is interested in the orderly continuity that relates the young adult's cognitive system and the elderly adult's cognitive system. This interest gives rise to a formidable set of methodological and substantive problems. We deal in this chapter with two families of problems, one belonging to each set.

At this point, we should define the limits of our interest and present an overview of the structure of our chapter. We focus on capacities traditionally considered cognitive—that is, the higher mental processes that give rise to intelligent behavior. We leave to others the study of affective or attitudinal consequences of aging. Further, we are concerned with the working life span—age range approximately 20 to 70 years of age. Finally, we are concerned only with age-related cognitive changes that occur in adults who are capable of maintaining their status as productive employed persons; our focus does not extend to deteriorative changes associated with diagnosable pathology or very late life.

Our chapter is divided into two major parts. In Part I we look at the subject selection practices reported over the last 5 years in empirical gerontological journals. We identify and analyze certain assumptions inherent in those practices and report empirical data that call some of these assumptions into serious question. In Part II we describe a large-scale study with both a methodological and a substantive focus. The results resolve one of the serious methodological challenges posed in Part I. The substantive outcomes extend our knowledge of changes in cognitive capacities over the working life span and provide the basis for a principled classification of capacities that is consistent with the thema of contemporary information-processing psychology.

## Assumptions in Empirical Cognitive Gerontology: Subject-Selection Practices

Few psychologists outside the gerontological research community appreciate how difficult it is to adapt traditional experimental methodology to unraveling the determinants of age-related change. This brings us to the first focus of this paper: how can we make valid inferences from gerontological data? A responsible scientist begins the empirical enterprise by making certain assumptions about the observations he is able to make *vis à vis* the observations he would like to make if it were practically possible. Periodic reexamination of the assumptions can help to prevent a kind of experimental drift to observations which deviate more and more from the ideal—perhaps slipping, without fanfare, out of the range that will support the desired inferences. One way to reexamine and highlight key assumptions is to consider the way actual experiments differ from the ideal experiment—the one the scientist would do if it were pragmatically feasible. Each such difference reflects an assumption that actual practice sufficiently approximates the ideal to support the inferences to be drawn. Each investigator assumes that the differences between the experiment he or she is doing and the ideal experiment are so small as to be of no account. The truth may be otherwise, and for this reason we will examine one characterization of the ideal experiment rather closely. Let us journey to a gerontologist's paradise and think up the ideal study, imperfect only insofar as it must be in a world where researchable questions remain. The major apparatus in this study? A time machine, of course, known to have no effect of its own on cognitive functioning. We would recruit perfectly representative elderly subjects of, let us say, age 70. We would test them on a perfectly reliable test and then settle them comfortably in the machine where they would be regressed to their youthful selves, at age 20 perhaps. After testing these 20-year-olds, we would return them to the machine and recreate the 70-year-olds that they were at the start of the experiment. This nearly ideal experiment combines all the advantages of longitudinal and cross-sectional research; it uses the same subjects at different ages and is conducted at a single point in time. Its outcomes are unequivocal: if the 70-year-olds perform better than their 20-year-old selves, age brings improvement in the capacity measured by the task. If the 70-year-olds perform worse, age brings decline. If there is no change, we can even conclude that the capacity is age-independent because the measure was perfectly reliable. The experiments we perform in real life are efforts to approximate, as closely as possible, this nearly ideal state of affairs.

The time machine experiment spares an investigator the deficiencies of traditional longitudinal designs. There is no subject attrition (Riegel, Riegel, & Meyer, 1967); all the young subjects are available for testing when they are old. This observation suggests a nontrivial reason, incidentally, why the ideal study would regress the elderly rather than progress the young. A science of aging must be a science of survivors. Thus, people who have actually gotten old should provide the reference point to which their youthful analogues are compared. Longitudinal designs also suffer from another deficiency not shared by the ideal experiment: the problem of technological obsolescence (Botwinick, 1978). A researcher is often limited throughout a longitudinal study to the conceptual and technological state of the art at its inception. By the time the results are in, the whole enterprise may seem misguided. The cross-sequential, cohort-sequential, and time-sequential designs have attenuated these problems for developmental research in childhood. But in the context of aging research, quasi-experimental arrangements still share most of the difficulties of pure longitudinal design. If one adds these problems to the pragmatic pressures on professional researchers, long-term maintenance of research funding and personal survival, it is not surprising that longitudinal studies are relatively infrequent. The remainder of our discussion concerns the traditional cross-sectional study and the extent to which it approximates the time-machine ideal.

## *The Comparability Problem*

The cross-sectional study can be conceived as an effort to approximate the ideal experiment by finding a sample of young people just like those who would step out of the time machine. This viewpoint exposes the extent to which the validity of a cross-sectional study is contingent on comparable sampling of young and old subjects. If the young people tested are dissimilar in salient respects to the elderly, principled inferences can be drawn only in the case of very robust effects. Where there is no change or when changes are subtle, as is often the case when age brings improvement rather than decline, it is critically important that the age groups be comparable. This observation, of course, is not new; the sophisticated methodological analyses of the last decade (e.g., Baltes & Goulet, 1971; Baltes & Nesselroade, 1970; Schaie, 1970, 1977) might appear to suggest that we are far beyond such low-level advice. Perhaps the time-machine metaphor serves to emphasize the importance of proper subject-selection in making or breaking experimental inference potential, but is this not something we have known for a long time?

If so, it is timely to ask what subject-selection practices are actually in use. To find out, we surveyed four major journals that publish empirical aging research. Our survey included all articles appearing in these journals for the years 1975 to 1979 inclusive that addressed the traditional cognitive issues of information processing, intelligence, learning, and memory. There were 188 such articles.

To see how comparable young and old subjects are in actual practice, we examined the source of subjects in all studies comparing at least one group under 30 years old to one group over 30 in a cross-sectional design. Of the 188 articles, 110 matched this description, and virtually all concerned the effect of age on some cognitive capacity. Some authors carefully cast their conclusions in terms of age "differences," but the introductions and discussions tacitly suggest that such differences are germane to the issue of change. In other words, these studies all assume, to a greater or lesser degree, that the young subjects are similar in critical respects to those who would step out of the time machine in the ideal study.

Table 1 shows how this assumption has been realized over the last 5 years of mainstream cognitive psychogerontology. The far left column lists the 10 most common sources of elderly subjects, plus a catch-all category, *other,* containing several rare sources. Two categories of young subjects, college students and community residents, accounted for 76% of the comparisons surveyed. The other

*Table 1. Sources of Subjects in 113 Studies Published from 1975 through 1979*

| Sources of oldest subjects | | Sources of younger comparison group, number of studies | | | | |
|---|---|---|---|---|---|---|
| Source | Number of studies | "Identical" source | Different source: other | Different source: college students | Unspecified community | Unspecified |
| Community sub-population unspecified | 45 | | 1 | 24 | 20 | |
| Retirement organization | 19 | | 5 | 13 | | 1 |
| Unspecified | 7 | | | 2 | | 5 |
| Staff | 6 | 2 | | 4 | | |
| College alumni | 6 | 3 | | 3 | | |
| Multiple sources | 6 | | 2 | 4 | | |
| Nursing home | 5 | | 1 | 4 | | |
| Hospital patients | 5 | 4 | 1 | | | |
| Newspaper ads | 5 | 2 | 1 | 2 | | |
| College students | 2 | 2 | | | | |
| Other | 7 | 1 | 2 | 4 | | |
| Total | 113 | 14 | 13 | 60 | 20 | 6 |

studies either sampled young and old from an operationally identical source—groups of hospital patients or college alumni, for instance—or from manifestly different sources such as elderly nursing home residents and youthful staff members.

Table 1 illustrates several interesting points. Young subjects come from fewer places than old ones do; the young subjects are college students in over half the studies. The collective gerontological community surveyed appears committed to the idea that whatever kind of 70-year-old steps into the time machine, a college sophomore will probably step out. Assumptions like this one can lead to at least minor mischief. It was once thought that the old are inherently more variable than the young on numerous intellectual measures. However, we have not found this effect when old and young come from the same population (Lachman & Lachman, 1980); and it is quite possible that it is an artifact inherent in sampling homogenous young people and heterogeneous old ones.

Only 12% of the studies have attempted to equate groups by operationally sampling young and old subjects the same way, unless drawing both young and old from "the community" is considered to reflect such comparable operations. However, this designation of subject source is singularly uninformative, giving little or no information about recruitment procedures, population characteristics, or potential sampling biases. Moreover, a number of such studies use ambiguous wording that makes it very clear that *older* subjects come from "the community" but leaves ambiguous whether this was also true of the young. About the most that can be said of subjects from "the community" is that they are not institutionalized, they are not necessarily college students, and the old and young do not necessarily resemble each other with regard to anything but availability.

This may appear a serious indictment of the research community; despite the flight of several methodological jet planes, few real studies have transcended horse-and-buggy problems. Actually, in some circumstances it does not matter. Where effects are robust, they should show up whether the young and old are comparable or not; and where particular methods are widely used, effects can be established by a preponderance of evidence. In other contexts, however, noncomparability may be a serious problem. Age improvements are often more subtle than age declines and may be masked if college sophomores are intellectually more elite than the population from which elderly samples are drawn. Investigators using esoteric measures to test relatively circumscribed theoretical statements may reach misleading conclusions unless they are prepared to replicate their studies using samples from various populations. The researcher seeking an elusive interaction is similarly situated.

There are no magic prescriptions for insuring comparability, since even operational comparability does not insure actual comparability. For example, what is the proper young comparison group for a sample of elderly involutional psychotics? Operational comparability might suggest young psychotics, but the time-machine metaphor suggests that a group of normal young people at risk for involutional psychosis is the appropriate choice. Comparison of young and old college students, for purposes of finding age effects, involves clear operational comparability. But the time-machine metaphor shows the problem: if an elderly college student enters the time machine for regression, what should emerge is a young high school graduate, not a young college student.[1]

Because our own research involves measures which have not been widely studied in a gerontological context, we were most sensitive to the comparability problem. We used an approach which is not novel but which has virtues not reflected in its frequency of use—occupational matching.

The group we chose consisted of schoolteachers. The teaching profession has been extensively studied, and much is known about the education, ability, and demographic origins of American schoolteachers. There are good reasons to believe that teachers are both representative of the general population and comparable at different ages. The most recent studies (Bennett & Erickson, 1971; Betz & Garland, 1974; Havighurst & Neugarten, 1967; Lortie, 1975; National Education Association, 1963, 1972; Schwartzwaller & Lyson, 1978) indicate that schoolteachers originate from a broad range of occupational groupings, with greater representation of middle-class professional and managerial occupations than of working-class manual jobs. The distribution resembles the population at large, and indeed, the National Education Association (NEA) concludes that

[1] This discussion is not meant to imply that such comparisons are never appropriate; there may be specialized questions for which comparisons of different-aged college students are ideal.

"the social backgrounds of teachers come close to representing a cross section of the American public" (NEA, 1963, p. 13). Thus, teachers may be ideal subjects for gerontological research, at least as regards their representativeness of the larger population.

The data on occupational origin and socioeconomic status further support the conclusion that teachers aged 21 to 25 are very likely to be comparable to those aged 61 to 70. Although it is true that in absolute terms more young teachers than old come from middle and upper-middle class family origins, it is also true that this difference reflects long-term population trends such as the diminishing number of farm families in the United States (Betz & Garland, 1974).

The Houston Independent School District, the source of our generational samples, is one of the largest school districts in the United States. Houston teachers have also been extensively studied (Dworkin, 1980) and appear typical of urban teachers in general. We were therefore reasonably certain that young and old teachers were demographically comparable—and thus comparable on demographically determined factors that might correlate with cognitive performance such as socioeconomic mobility. Moreover, teachers of various ages are likely to share common views towards learning and education; such views are clearly likely to influence performance on cognitive tests. Finally, the use of teachers transcends one of the knottiest problems in cognitive gerontology, that of achieving comparability of educational achievement. College graduates of 50 years ago are not comparable to those of last summer. A college education was a rarity in the 1920's and 1930's, and those who acquired one came from an intellectual elite; today, a college education is a far more frequent achievement. To the extent that educational content is matched to expectations of student ability, college students of 50 years ago were probably exposed to a more demanding curriculum than today's students are. The demographic stability of aspiring teachers, in contrast, should have exerted a stabilizing influence on teacher-training curricula. We thus felt confident that age-group comparisons would yield valid inferences regarding age improvement, stability, and decline in an array of cognitive-psychological capacities.

## *The Volunteer Problem*

The foregoing discussion has concerned comparability, which is necessary if age effects are to be reliably inferred from cross-sectional research designs. Even if comparability is achieved, however, there is a further problem—specifying the nature of the population to which the conclusion can be generalized. In order to draw meaningful conclusions from aging studies (or for that matter, from any research), one's subjects must be representative of a known population. If subjects are systematically drawn from a minority of the population to which generalizations are made, there is risk that it is an unrepresentative minority. For example, one would not wish to draw conclusions about university professors from an experiment in which all subjects were professors of, say, architecture. Table 1 confirms the fact that elderly subjects come from a variety of sources, and at first glance there seems to be no problem of representativeness. However, one characteristic is shared by virtually all those elderly people in all those studies—they are volunteers.

Volunteers, of course, are generally considered to be those lovely people willing to donate their time to serve in studies, without inducement other than a researcher's gratitude. But, you may be wondering, are elderly research subjects not commonly paid for their services? Our survey of the literature provides data on this question. Of the 185 studies 49 surveyed reported payment of money to one or more groups, usually including the elderly. The maximum payment offered was $10, and it turns out that a $10 payment attracts only functional volunteers. Gribbin and Schaie (1976) contacted over 2000 subjects by mail, offering $10 to half of them. The $10 incentive increased participation a mere 1½%; and on a broad array of measures, paid and unpaid participants did not differ. It is hard to escape the conclusion that a $10 payment attracts the same people who would serve for nothing, that is, volunteers. Gribbin and Schaie's findings comport well with observations from our own laboratory. When we telephoned teachers and invited them to participate in our research, we found that a $10 incentive produced the same response rate as an earnest request for their assistance. Hence, the gerontological literature is a science of the volunteer elderly, reflecting the assumption that data from old volunteers supports generalizations about old people. The assumption is tenable if either (a) volunteers constitute a substantial proportion of the population, or (b) volunteers are cognitively indistinguishable from nonvolunteers across the target age ranges.

With respect to the first possibility, the empirical findings are not comforting. The attrition problems familiar to survey researchers suggest that volunteers are hard to get; and in Gribbin and Schaie's study, fewer than one in five people were willing to complete questionaires at home and mail them back—for $10 or otherwise. Half of those contacted did not even respond to the solicitation.

The subject-recruitment phase of our own study provides data on the incidence of voluntarism among white, female, metropolitan schoolteachers. We sent, as part of a larger mailing, 888 letters to teachers aged 21 to 25, 41 to 45, and 61 to 70. Of these, 815 were actually delivered. State of the art persuasion techniques were used throughout this mailing (Dillman, 1978). Each letter was personally addressed and hand-signed in blue ink to avoid an impersonal form-letter effect. The return cards were self-addressed and carried colored postage stamps. The letter itself contained an eloquent appeal to the community consciousness and civic spirit of the teachers in facilitating this important research. We said, "We are able to pay you a token fee of $10 in appreciation for participation. This really cannot compensate you adequately for your valuable time, so we are appealing to your public-spirited instincts to participate.'' The underwhelming response is shown in Figure 1; positive responses ran just under 20% overall. When one considers that we asked people to come to our laboratory, while Gribbin and Schaie asked only that they fill out and mail questionnaires, it might seem remarkable that voluntarism rates were so similar in the two contexts. The similarity may reflect the fact that all our subjects were female. The greater willingness of women to volunteer (Rosenthal & Rosnow, 1976), a pattern noted by Gribbin and Schaie, may have offset the somewhat greater demands we made.

Young respondents were more willing to volunteer than middle-aged and older ones; chi-square analysis showed the response patterns of the two older groups to differ from the young but not from each other. Figure 1 may reflect a maximum participation rate when volunteer subjects are recruited from a defined population by the most advanced mail techniques: on the order of 25% of those in their early 20s and 15% of those over 40.

We did not take no for an answer, however; we escalated the aggressiveness of our recruiting by making telephone contact with 114 subjects from each age group who did not return the card. A mature graduate student with a local Texas accent telephoned them and entreated them to be subjects. This ''aggressive subject recruitment'' produced the response rate shown in Figure 2. About twice as many young teachers as middle-aged and older ones agreed to participate in response to the telephone call. Figure 3 pools those who said yes, either to the letter or the telephone call; it shows the participation rate that can be achieved by the two-wave technique. Twice as many young teachers as old ones eventually said yes. Twice as many old as young said no. More young teachers were unreachable, and the response pattern of each age group differs from that of

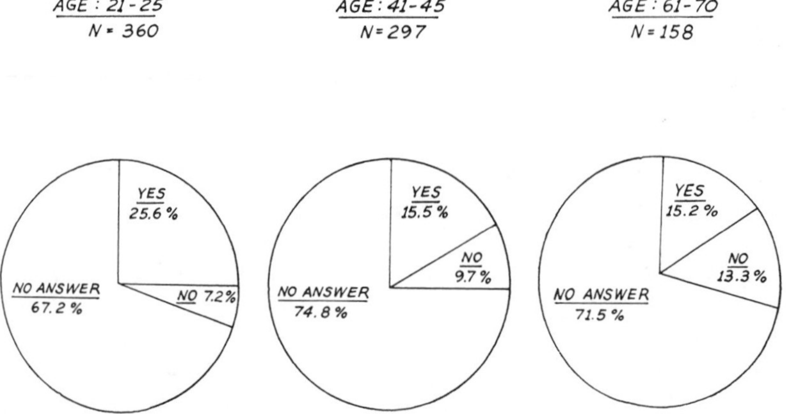


Fig. 1. Response to letters: 8.4% young, 7.8% middle age, and 6.0% of old subjects undelivered. $N$ = delivered letters.

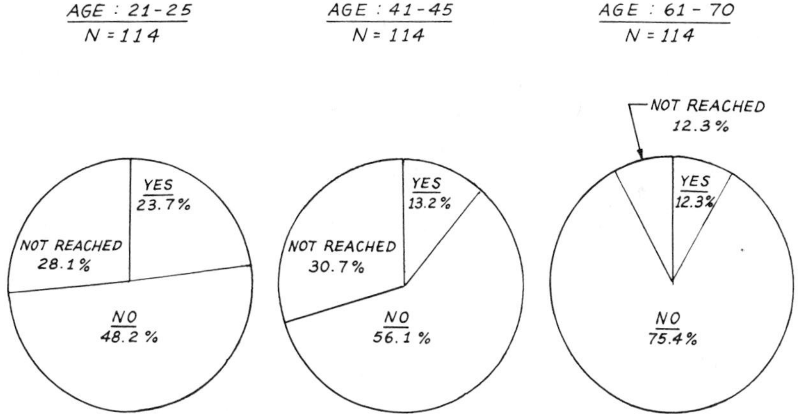


Fig. 2. Response to telephone call recruitment of subjects not answering letter; aggressive recruitment of volunteers.

every other. It certainly appears that volunteers are a minority of the population—a minority of decreasing size as age increases.

The fact that the cognitive psychogerontological literature is based primarily on volunteers, especially elderly ones, is not a problem if volunteers and nonvolunteers are cognitively indistinguishable. Here, however, there is some room for concern.

Voluntarism has been extensively studied in young people, and the evidence suggests that volunteers differ in systematic ways from nonvolunteers—ways that may affect performance on cognitive tasks. The most extensive study of the volunteer subject is that of Rosenthal and Rosnow (1975). On the basis of their

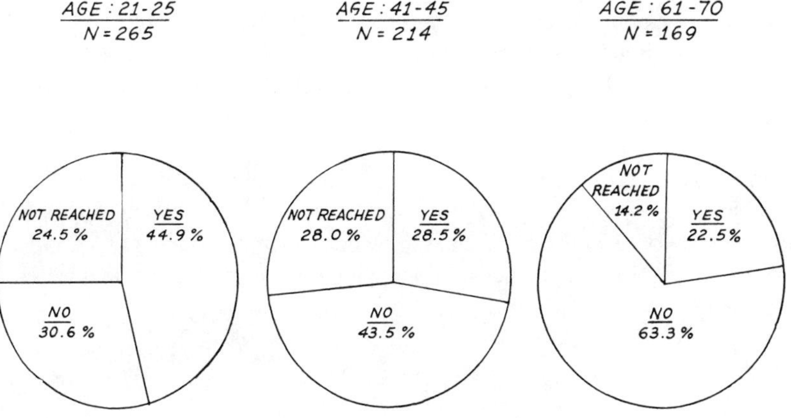


Fig. 3. Responses to recruitment: combined letter and telephone call recruitment of "volunteer" subjects (white female teachers).

own studies and a broad survey of other research, they drew numerous conclusions about the characteristics of subjects who volunteer. They concluded that volunteers tend to be younger than nonvolunteers, especially among females; our own experience supports this conclusion. Rosenthal and Rosnow further concluded, with maximum confidence, that volunteers tend to be better educated and more intelligent than nonvolunteers. These considerations suggest that volunteer experimental subjects may be unrepresentative at any age, but increasingly so at increasing ages.

## A Study of Cognition, Age, and Voluntarism

We were exceedingly sensitive to the potential unrepresentativeness of elderly volunteer subjects following our research on aging and actualization of world knowledge (Lachman & Lachman, 1980). On several measures of world knowledge use, having good ecological validity, we found that our older subjects either equaled or outperformed the young. We wanted to interpret this as evidence that these ecologically valid capacities do not decline; perhaps they even improve with age and experience. But we could not ignore the fact that our older subjects were self-selected volunteers who had answered a call for subjects in a newspaper article about our work, had brought themselves to the university, and were plainly a spunky and spirited lot. If they were also atypically able, an interpretation of their performance as age improvement could be wrong. In order to examine the generality of the Lachman and Lachman (1980) conclusions, a well-defined and homogeneous adult population was identified and sampled. No more than 20% of the young adults agreed to participate; the agreement rate was even smaller among the elderly. It looked as if the only way to handle the volunteer issue issue was to study it directly—vary it and compare volunteers to nonvolunteers. Hence, for the present report, we had to persuade the individuals in our sample who had said no to change their minds, so we could see how they compared, at each age level, to those who had said yes. This variation would permit us to resolve the methodological issue concerning voluntarism, which was one major purpose of the study. But methodological concerns are in service of substantive theoretical issues. Thus, the second and major purpose was to determine which cognitive capacities improve with age, which decline, and which do not change.

### *Subject Selection and Classification*

In order to make our study as close to the time machine ideal as possible, we went to some pains to achieve comparability between our age groups. For the reasons stated above, we drew our samples from the population of Houston schoolteachers actively employed as of November 1, 1979. Furthermore, we included only white female teachers. Men and women enter teaching careers for different reasons, as do whites and blacks (Lortie, 1975). Male teachers comprise a small minority of the teacher population—about 20%—and may be more subject to selection pressures than females. Young and elderly male teachers, therefore, may be less comparable than their female counterparts. Blacks are a larger minority among teachers than men; however, there are reasons to suppose that older black teachers differ from young blacks entering the teaching profession today. For these reasons, we limited our study to white females.

On November 1, 1979, there were 9,079 active teachers in the Houston Independent School District; 9,022 of these make up the useable population as certain data such as sex, age, or ethnicity were unavailable for the other 57. The population contained 7,176 females, of whom 3,447, or 48%, are white. The data on participation willingness were based on 482 teachers aged 21–25, 325 teachers aged 41–45, and 168 teachers aged 61–70.

The data on teacher demography indicated that the oldest and youngest groups are socioeconomically comparable. The middle-aged group, aged 41 to 45, may be comparable as well. However, Betz and Garland (1974) report that the baby boom following World War II somewhat burdened the capacity of the professional and managerial class to supply sufficient teachers when these children reached school age in the 1950s. Consequently, for a time, more teachers were recruited from working-class families. This teacher cohort would now be in their 40s and early 50s, and therefore our middle-aged group could be socially (and hence perhaps cognitively) somewhat more heterogeneous than the oldest and youngest groups. This is but a possibility, requiring further investigation. Along with pragmatic considerations of time and cost, it led us to omit the middle-aged group from the study for the time being.

The design called for 20 volunteers and 20 nonvolunteers in each age group. Subjects were classified as either volunteers or nonvolunteers based on their agreement or refusal to participate in response to the letters or phone calls described earlier. Those who agreed in response to the initial letter were classified as volunteers. Those who had expressly refused, either to the letter or the call, were classified as nonvolunteers. Nonvolunteers were then persuaded to participate by the offer of a handsome honorarium. Once all potential subjects were classified as volunteers or nonvolunteers, actual compensation was equated. A letter was sent to both classification groups indicating that all participants would be paid $80 and suggesting an available date (a Saturday, as all testing was done on weekends). The $80 letter was followed up by more telephone calls to confirm scheduling. Subjects were selected in a random sequence until 20 volunteer and 20 nonvolunteer subjects in each age group were tested. For the old nonvolunteers, we met with 14 refusals before our 20 participants were obtained; for the young nonvolunteers there were 7 (see Figure 4). The 2:1 ratio observed previously appears to hold even with enhanced compensation.

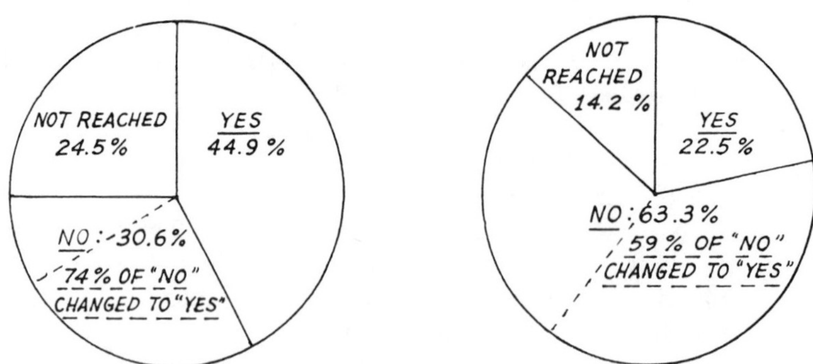


Fig. 4. Responses to recruitment: combined letters and telephone calls and response of "nonvolunteers" to \$80 incentive.

## *Selection and Theoretical Classification of Tasks*

We administered a broad range of measures to these four groups. Some of the tasks were chosen because they have appeared widely in the literature on cognitive gerontology and could therefore provide a check on possible differences between previous conclusions and those in the present design. Other measures were chosen because they reflect our own theoretical interests. An explanation of the theoretical considerations motivating our efforts is worthwhile at this point, before we present detailed descriptions of the tasks we used.

Cognitive capacities related to experience and the use of acquired world knowledge are usually found to resist decline with age. In contrast, those capacities involving acquisition of new skills or content, or adjustment to new situations, deteriorate. Such effects have been described in terms of fluid and crystallized intelligence (Cattell, 1963; Horn & Cattell, 1967), which provides an insightful ordering of capacities. Our objective is to characterize age and cognitive capacity in terms of information processing theory (Lachman, Lachman, & Butterfield, 1979; Newell & Simon, 1972; Simon, 1979). The theory assumes that *homo sapiens* is an information-processing system when engaged in intelligent behavior; that is, that human symbol manipulation is mathematically isomorphic with symbol manipulation in automata. Both are characterized as general-purpose Turing-computable systems capable of recursive functioning. *General purpose* means that the system is capable of producing a wide spectrum of behaviors in dealing with a range of problems whose exact nature need not be specified in advance, a performance which is achieved by the high-speed concatenation of a small set of operations. These systems are recursive in that they are capable of high levels of self-reference.

Systems of this sort contain two major components: a *processor* and a *memory* containing symbol structures. A symbol structure can be represented by a network of nodes and links such as are familiar by now in the cognitive literature. The processor consists of three subcomponents: a set of elementary or primitive symbol-manipulating processes, a transient working or short-term memory to hold the symbol structure being processed, and an interpreter that concatenates the primitives as a function of symbolic instructions in working memory. The primitives can be described in Turing-computable terms; for example, find the next symbol in a sequence, compare two symbols, erase a given symbol.

If the above description of a general-purpose information-processing system correctly characterizes intelligent behavior, then cognitive aging effects must reside in one or another system component. If tasks could be classified in terms of the extent to which various components are involved and the pattern of age effects in each task ascertained then we would be on our way to success in localizing aging effects in particular portions of the information-processing system. At the moment, however, such a classification is stymied by the general-purpose character of the system itself. Experimental tasks involve macrobehavior—that is, task performance necessarily reflects a series of elementary operations which may be extremely long and complex. For this reason, tasks are unlikely to map directly onto hypothetical sequences of a few primitives. The situation is further complicated by the compensatory capability that inheres in generality of purpose; that is, if one route to task completion is blocked, the system is faced with an essentially new task, for which a general-purpose processing device is uniquely designed to devise a solution. Thus, it is possible that the performance of the old and the young on what appears to be the same task may be accomplished by different sequences designed to overcome the deficiencies of each—the relatively impoverished set of symbol structures available to the young, and the potential losses of the old. In spite of these formidable challenges, there may be intermediate ways of classifying tasks so as to highlight predominant task requirements. Such a classification does not finish the job, but it may advance us toward a more refined classification. Incidentally, consistent patterns of age effects within classifications would tend to validate the classification scheme—illustrating how gerontological research may advance the study of age-independent cognitive psychology, as we suggested at the outset.

Table 2 presents our tasks classified in terms of the routines that seem to predominate. A routine as we use the term, is a sequence of primitives defined in terms of an outcome: the *maintenance, location* or *creation* of information, and the *interrogation* of the system itself. Evolutionary and phylogenetic considera-

*Table 2. Experimental Tasks Classified by an Ordered Set of Information Processing Routines*

| Information maintenance routines | Information location routines | Information creation routines | System interrogation routines |
|---|---|---|---|
| WAIS digit–symbol 1 | WAIS information | Inferential answer selection | Meta-inference |
| WAIS digit–symbol 2 | WAIS vocabulary | | Metamemory accuracy |
| WAIS digit–symbol 3 | Question-answering: proficiency speed | | Metamemory efficiency |
| Word recall | Direct-access answer selection | | |
| Word recognition | | | |

tions provided some of the motivation for these groupings. Space precludes development of these considerations here, although we have presented them in preliminary fashion elsewhere (Lachman & Lachman, 1979).

The classifications are not meant to imply that a task involves one or another such routine exclusively. For example, maintenance of information may rely on location of other information, and creation of new information may involve maintenance of old information. Specification of the combinations of routines is a later step in task decomposition. For now, the classifications reflect the single routine that appears to us most directly critical to the completion of a task.

*Information Maintenance.* Five maintenance tasks were included. Three of these were the WAIS Digit–Symbol subtest (Digit–Symbol 1 in Table 2 and 3) and two modifications of it. The first modification (Digit–Symbol 2) involved the same performance as the standard subtest, except that familiar letters of the alphabet were substituted for the unfamiliar symbols. This device can be used to assess the contribution of familiarity to the age decline typically observed in Digit–Symbol performance. The other modification (Digit–Symbol 3) is essentially the procedure used by Storandt (1976) to evaluate the contribution of writing speed to the typical age decline. Subjects merely copied the symbols of the standard Digit–Symbol subtest, rather than coding them from digits. The arrangement of the copying sheets was identical to the standard subtest in these modifications, except that more trials were included to avoid ceiling effects. Other maintenance tasks were a free-recall test of a 24-item word list and a standard word recognition task involving a 40-word list. All these tasks were conceived as maintenance, involving whatever elementary information processes are essential to entering, retaining, and reproducing or recognizing information. The two word-memory tasks did not lend themselves to organizational or other mnemomic strategies, which might introduce an element of information creation. The lists included high- to medium-frequency words so as to be similar to the recall and recognition experiments typically found in the literature.

*Information Location.* Four information-location routines are shown in

Table 2. These differ from maintenance routines in that the source of the correct response is the previously learned repertoire of knowledge that the subject brings to the laboratory, rather than new or arbitrary symbol configurations supplied by the experimenter. Four tasks provided information-location measures: the WAIS Information and Vocabulary subtests and two tests involving question-answering. In one of these tests, subjects answered 72 general knowledge questions, such as "What was the former name of Muhammad Ali?" The questions were first asked in open-ended format, then in multiple-choice format. Question-answering or information location performance can be evaluated in terms of accuracy or speed. Additionally, it can be evaluated in the open-ended context or the multiple-choice context. Certain special questions can be addressed by relating open-ended to multiple-choice performance. These possibilities yield a number of dependent measures of information location capacity, which will be described in detail in conjunction with our presentation of results. The second task providing an information-location measure is labeled "Direct-Access Answer Selection" in Table 2. A multiple-choice test was administered for a set of 25 items that we call *direct-access questions* (Camp, 1979; Camp, Lachman, & Lachman, 1980). Such questions appear to be primarily—and perhaps exclusively—answered by direct location of a concept in memory rather than by constructive or inferential processes. They are of the "you-know-it-or-you-don't" variety; they do not lend themselves to figuring out, and they can give rise to tip-of-the-tongue states. An example is, "What Biblical character lived to the oldest age?" Subjects selected the answer (Methuseleh) from a 4-item multiple-choice set.

*Information Creation.* Inferring the answer to a question entails the creation or construction of information. In the same portion of the study with the 25 previously described direct-access questions, 25 items were intermixed that are predominantly inferential in character (Camp, 1979; Camp, Lachman, & Lachman, 1980). Very few people have directly stored the answers to these questions with the questions themselves; an example is "What horror character would starve to death in northern Sweden in the summertime?" (Answer: Dracula). These items, also presented in multiple-choice format, comprised the only task involving primarily information-creation routines.

*System Interrogation.* Finally, two tasks were included that yielded several measures of system-interrogation capability. System interrogation involves reporting on aspects of the system itself, rather than reporting specific content. The term *metamemory* (Brown, 1975) has been used to describe knowledge about the contents of memory structure. For example, rather than reporting the answer to a question, the subject reports whether the answer is actually present in the memory system. We coined the analogous term *meta-inference* to describe knowledge about the processes used in question answering. Before attempting a multiple-choice test for our direct-access and inferential questions, subjects viewed each question and judged whether inferential or direct-access processes would be required in answering it. In this meta-inference task, the questions were presented along with alternative answers, but the subjects were instructed not to answer the questions at this time. Instead, they were asked to rate, on a 6-point scale, the extent to which the average respondent would have to use inferential processes in arriving at the answer. After all the judgments were made, system interrogation was deemed complete. Then the alternatives were shown and the subject made her selections to provide the data for information location (direct-access) and information creation (inference). Adequacy of meta-inference was evaluated by comparing the subject's assessment to our own classification of the questions, which has been validated in two previous studies (Camp, 1979; Camp, Lachman, & Lachman, 1980).

Conceptually, metamemory is the quality of a person's information about the state of his or her own symbol system. It is measured from subjective judgments of the likelihood that an answer *not* recalled is really available in memory and could be retrieved at other times or by other methods (e.g., recognition). Metamemory was evaluated through use of the feeling-of-knowing procedure devised by Hart (1965, 1966, 1967) and extended in our laboratory (Lachman & Lachman, 1980; Lachman, Lachman, & Thronesbery, 1979) to the measurement of two basic parameters: metamemory *accuracy* and metamemory *efficiency*. Subjects first attempted to answer, in open-ended format, the 72 general information location questions mentioned previously (e.g., What was the former name of Muhammad Ali?). Many of these items ended with a response of "I don't know" or "I can't remember," collectively called "don't know" responses here. Only "don't-know" responses are used in assessing metamemory *accuracy*. Following the answer attempt, a subject indicated on a 3-point scale[2] the likelihood that she would be able to select the correct answer from a multiple-choice set: "very likely," "maybe," and "no." Metamemory accuracy is measured by the percentage of "don't-know" items in each rating category for which a correct selection is actually made when the multiple-choice alternatives are later presented. A subject who chooses the correct alternative in 100% of the "don't-know" items rated "very likely" and achieves only chance performance on those rated "no" would be exhibiting optimal metamemory *accuracy*. Metamemory *efficiency* is the extent to which the subject appropriately allocates time and effort to produce the answer to the open-ended question for those items she thinks she is most likely to answer correctly. The time to say "don't-know" has been related to the subject's prediction of multiple-choice success (Laughery, Thompson, & Band, 1974). An efficient strategy would be to respond "don't-know" rather quickly to items that (subjectively) are probably not there. On the other hand, it would make sense to engage in longer searches,

[2] A pattern of underutilization of the metamemory judgment "no" was found equally prevelant in all groups. Responses falling into this category were combined with those in the "maybe" category for purposes of analysis.

that is, produce longer reaction times, for items that are likely to be retrieved such as items on the "tip of the tongue."

## *General Results*

A study like this generates a truly unbelievable quantity of data, and a detailed presentation would exceed the limits of a chapter. We present those aspects of the results that are most interesting, in the context of the questions we have raised so far. First, what are the effects of voluntarism? Second, is there an interaction between age and voluntarism? Third, what is the pattern of age effects for the four task classifications we have developed? Table 3 presents our major findings. Column 1 lists the tasks previously described for each of the four information processing routines. When several dependent variables are reported for a given task in Table 3, the variables are indented in column 1. Where age differences reach $p < .05$ *or better, the superior age group is listed in column 2. The remaining column list* $F$-ratios and $p$-levels for age, voluntarism, and the age $\times$ voluntarism interaction.

First, the results show that there are absolutely no effects of voluntarism and no age $\times$ voluntarism interactions. Of the 38 comparisons shown in the two major right-hand columns of Table 3, none reaches the .05 level of significance. We are confident that, given samples from as homogeneous and well-educated a population as our teachers, data from volunteer subjects are representative data. There may still be good reasons to pay subjects handsomely, of course, such as attracting a sufficiently large sample or vindicating one's sense of good citizenship; but there are no scientifically mandated reasons to pay at all, and there appears to be no need to buy nonvolunteer subjects at premium prices. It must be emphasized that this conclusion is limited to homogeneous, educated groups of above-average intellectual ability. Quite possibly volunteer effects may still undermine generalizations to heterogeneous, poorly educated, or lower-ability populations; and researchers investigating such variables as educational level and IQ should not discount the possibility of interaction between these variables and voluntarism. Finally, a hard-core group of unapproachable and untested nonvolunteers remains in the target sample (cf. Figure 4). But we succeeded in testing 74% of the sample of young nonvolunteers who were approached and 59% of the elderly nonvolunteers—at least a majority of both age groups.

We now examine the pattern of age effects presented in Table 3. The young teachers performed better on each of the five information maintenance tests. The young transcribed more digit-symbols in the standard WAIS test and on the modified digit-symbol tests using all familiar symbols or uncoded transcription. More words were recalled and recognized by young teachers in these two widely used verbal learning tasks. Clearly, the results replicate major previously established findings on episodic memory in the gerontological literature.

*Table 3. Tasks Classified by Information-Processing Routines: Performance Superiority, F-Ratios, and Significance Levels*

| | | ANOVA sources of variance | | | | | |
|---|---|---|---|---|---|---|---|
| | | Age $df = 1,76$ | | Voluntarism $df = 1,76$ | | Age X voluntarism $df = 1,76$ | |
| Routines | Superior group | $F$ | $p$ | $F$ | $p$ | $F$ | $p$ |
| Information maintenance: | | | | | | | |
| WAIS digit–symbol 1 | young | 48.55 | .001 | 1.44 | ns | <1 | ns |
| WAIS digit–symbol 2 | young | 39.06 | .001 | 1.12 | ns | <1 | ns |
| WAIS digit–symbol 3 | young | 14.82 | .001 | 1.09 | ns | <1 | ns |
| Word recall | young | 20.66 | .001 | <1 | ns | <1 | ns |
| Word recognition | young | 23.38 | .001 | <1 | ns | <1 | ns |
| Information location: | | | | | | | |
| WAIS information | old | 9.44 | .01 | 1.19 | ns | <1 | ns |
| WAIS vocabulary | old | 12.69 | .001 | <1 | ns | <1 | ns |
| Direct-access answer selection | old | 8.93 | .01 | <1 | ns | <1 | ns |
| Question-answering proficiency: | | | | | | | |
| Open-ended | equal | 1.93 | ns | <1 | ns | 1.66 | ns |
| Multiple choice | equal | 1.83 | ns | <1 | ns | <1 | ns |
| Efficiency ratio | trend: old | 2.39 | ns | <1 | ns | 1.02 | ns |
| Question-answering speed: | | | | | | | |
| Open-ended correct (RT) | young | 6.71 | .01 | <1 | ns | 1.39 | ns |
| Open-ended incorrect (RT) | young | 4.32 | .05 | <1 | ns | <1 | ns |
| Information creation | | | | | | | |
| Inferential answer selection | old | 23.73 | .001 | <1 | ns | <1 | ns |
| System interrogation | | | | | | | |
| Meta-inference judgment: | | | | | | | |
| All questions[a] | equal | 1 | ns | <1 | ns | <1 | ns |
| Correctly answered questions[a] | equal | 1.94 | ns | <1 | ns | <1 | ns |
| Metamemory | | | | | | | |
| Accuracy[b] | equal | 1.39 | ns | <1 | ns | <1 | ns |
| Efficiency[b] | equal | 1 | ns | 1.64 | ns | 1.31 | ns |
| Question-answering monitor (open-ended correct divided by attempts to answer) | old | 9.07 | .01 | <1 | ns | <1 | ns |

[a]Each $F$ value for this variable reflects an interaction between source of variance, in the respective column, and type of question (direct access vs. inferential).

[b]Each $F$ value reflects an interaction with a feeling-of-knowing classification.

The older teachers, in all nonlatency information location tasks, equal or outperform the young. WAIS information and vocabulary data yield the typical unadjusted age superiority. Outcomes for the 25 multiple-choice direct-access questions are shown in Table 3 as "Direct-Access Answer Selection", the elderly subjects, as expected, seem to have available symbol systems representing more everyday information. Next, three dependent measures of "Question-Answering Proficiency" are reported: open-ended, multiple choice, and efficiency ratio. The number of correct answers given to open-ended questions is one straightforward measure of location proficiency. Multiple-choice performance is another straightforward measure. Because correct multiple-choice performance suggests that an answer is in store, and failure to produce it initially represents a location failure, an even better measure may be obtained by dividing the correct number of correctly answered open-ended items by the total number of correct answers on both open-ended and multiple-choice tests. This is listed as "efficiency ratio" in Table 3. An efficiency quotient of 1 means that every item actually in store was also located for open-ended answer production. Although this measure does not meet the formal requirements of a ratio—it does not pass through the origin and it may not be linear—its value can nevertheless be quite informative. The trend in the efficiency ratio for the 72 general information questions favors the elderly subjects; however, no demonstrably reliable effects can be inferred for any of the three "Question-Answering Proficiency" variables. When it comes to speed of answering an open-ended question, the young teachers are faster, both when an appropriate answer is produced, "open-ended correct," and when the answer is wrong, "open-ended incorrect."

The task involving 25 inferential multiple-choice questions yielded sharply superior scores for the older teachers. This outcome is presented in Table 3 under "Information Creation." These results suggest that the ability to create new information in the form of novel symbol structures from existing world knowledge improves over the productive lifespan.

System interrogation tasks are subdivided into two apparently independent capacities, meta-inference judgment and metamemory. Two measures of meta-inference judgment are reported. One is the correct-classification rate (as inferential or direct access) for items to which the subject also subsequently selected the correct answer alternative. The other is the correct-classification rate for all items regardless of whether the subject chose the correct alternative. This subdivision was made because Camp, Lachman, and Lachman (1980) found that subjects attempt inferential processing when they do not know an answer, even if the question lends itself primarily or exclusively to direct-access processing. For metamemory, it will be recalled that "accuracy" measures a subject's ability to judge whether currently nonretrievable information is recognizable and therefore part of the subject's long-term store. "Efficiency" measures the appropriateness of time allocations to search for information present or absent in memory. No significant age differences were found for any of these system-interrogation measures, but where there were trends in the data they favored the elderly. The last measure reported in Table 3, "Question-Answering Monitor," is derived from the 72 world information items presented as open-ended questions. It is the ratio of correct answers to attempted answers. Older teachers performed significantly better on this measure. Several factors might account for their superiority. Elderly subjects' greater information stores would elevate the ratio by increasing both the numerator and the denominator. Alternatively, a conservative response bias could elevate the ratio if elderly persons suppress answers unless they are very confident the answers are right. Finally, superior metamemory could result in superior performance on this measure by sharpening discrimination between items actually in store and those not in store, such that attempts to answer would be allocated selectively to items most likely to be answered correctly.

### *Overall Conclusions and Theoretical Analysis*

The absence of any effect attributable to voluntarism was unexpected and even startling, given the general literature on this topic. In contrast, the substantive outcomes on aging present a very reassuring picture of a stable data base for the field of life span learning and cognition. Much greater pains were taken than is typical to insure the comparability of different age groups, resulting in an uncommonly stringent experimental test of aging effects. The results obtained in the word recall and recognition tasks and in the WAIS subtest confirmed those that have been found in many laboratories with many kinds of subject samples. Serious doubts would have been cast on the gerontological data base had these outcomes not been replicated. Broadly replicated results in the literature, thus, establish the reliability of the field's cumulative knowledge and constitute its core.

Regardless of the general outcomes of this study, and despite the fact that increased sample comparability yielded no serious conflicts with prior results, there are many reasons to take pains to insure comparability. Repeated replication is a costly way to build confidence in experimental outcomes, and in many situations a researcher must trust the results of single studies. This will be true in the situations mentioned earlier; when the measure is esoteric or new, when an interpretation depends upon an elusive interaction, when individual differences are apt to be large, or when the experimental effect is expected to be subtle. In these cases, and for all studies located on the frontiers of knowledge, the time-machine metaphor is a useful guide. Occupational matching may provide an excellent solution because if an elderly pharmacist, dentist, or teacher enters the time machine there is a strong expectation that a young pharmacist, dentist, or teacher will emerge. The broad matching of young and old subjects on occupation is likely to equate the two groups on socioeconomic status, personal interest factors, and educational level. Occupational matching is often preferable to matching on single variables, which can actually preclude comparability if the matching variable is systematically related to age. Matching on WAIS raw scores is the best known example of a technique in which similarly performing persons of different ages are guaranteed to represent different populations.

Before discussing the substantive aspects of Table 3, we should mention that the original task classification scheme has been refined to reflect the results of an exploratory factor analysis performed on the data. That analysis and the resulting classification are presented in detail in the appendix to this chapter, to which we refer the interested reader. The factor analysis yielded seven categories rather than four, and we are presently evaluating the implications of the new classification. Because the analysis generally validated three of the original four categories, our discussion is still cast in terms of the original set.

Within each category in the original classification, results are consistent as regards age and processing adequacy. Speed has been accorded special importance in the recent literature on psychological aging, and it appears in the new classification. However, it should be emphasized that in this type of theoretical scheme, the basic organization is around the ultimate products of information processing rather than rates. The fact that young people's information-location capacities are faster but may yield a less adequate product has no single interpretation at present. It may reflect longer searches through the more extensive set of symbol structures available to the old, or the operation of compensatory routines in the older subjects. A more complex, but intuitively satisfying, explanation may be that older subjects apply system interrogation routines before production of an answer, thus adding measurable time.

In addition to providing some answers, the data in Table 3 raise some major questions. Why should the young outperform the old on information maintenance tasks, while the old equal or outperform the young on proficiency measures of the other three task types? Why do information location or creation and system interrogation capacities show no decline (and possibly some improvement) with age? We have been developing an approach based on human evolution, to which we turn for a potential explanation of these results. Our ideas are still in an early stage of development, reflecting a set of orienting attitudes rather than a tight theoretical statement (cf. Lachman & Lachman, 1979). In the case of the present results, the tasks (other than speed measures) that show age decline are those that require a person to adapt internal information-processing routines to externally supplied environmental states and to preserve accurately the information contained in these states. Using evolution-based orienting attitudes as guides, it is clear that the information-maintenance tasks are primarily environment-based, whereas the others are primarily system-based. That is, these tasks require the subject to preserve information from the environment without engaging in any deep symbol interpretation or restructuring. Performance is judged by the extent to which some rather arbitrary state of the environment is preserved; no credit is given for "improving" the stimulus materials to render them more compatible with the real environment outside the laboratory—for instance, by deleting and substituting items to make a memorized word list more like a natural-language sentence. In contrast, the information location and creation tasks and the system interrogation routines require the subject to draw on information that is already preserved. Such information, far from being arbitrary, is consistent with a given individual's entire network of prestored information structures. An age-related shift from facility with arbitrary structures to facility with nonarbitrary ones is adaptive for a system which comes into a relatively stable environment with awesome generality of purpose coupled with limitations on processing capacity. The human information-processing system is equipped to deal with a formidable array of environmental conditions, but it will experience only some of them over its lifetime. It would reflect good system design if young organisms *acquire* new information veridically and readily, while older ones *access* such information with facility. That is, during the phase of life while information structures are being built up, the organism should be most facile at building a veridical representation of those environmental conditions that it actually experiences, relying on its generality of purpose to shape responses to these conditions, and solving the subjectively novel problems generated by that environment. To the extent that ecological conditions are stable, good design should incorporate a gradual shift toward interpreting new environmental inputs as instances of familiar ones—that is, toward reliance on existing structures rather than formation of new ones. The evolutionary hypothesis implies that a well-adapted general-purpose system will spend its resources early in life learning what its world is like; later in life its resources are better spent perfecting its responses to that world and perhaps stereotyping them. This account is consistent with the concepts of fluid and crystallized intelligence (cf. Cattell, 1963; Horn, Chapter 14; Horn & Cattell, 1967). Fluid intelligence may be the ability to form a set of representations of the world and strategies for dealing with it, while crystallized intelligence may be the ability to make appropriate use of the representations and strategies previously formed. For the reader who is familiar with the concepts of *data-limited* and *resource-limited* processing (Norman & Bobrow, 1975), these terms capture essential properties of the dimension along which a shift occurs over the lifespan. The child and youth are more adept at data-limited processing, which yields to a disposition toward resource-limited processing as the adult matures and then ages.

We are working to expand and refine the notion of an evolved, general-purpose information-processing system that is adapted to maximize its functioning at various stages in its adult development. The ultimate objective is to specify, in terms of Turing-computable symbolic operations, the changes in mechanism that accompany observed changes in performance over the life span. At this point in the history of the discipline, no one can say if the objective is attainable. Developments in artificial intelligence, fixed-age cognitive psychology, and related disciplines suggest that the approach has considerable potential.

# APPENDIX[3]

In order to assess the validity of the preliminary task classification scheme described earlier (Table 2), an exploratory factor analysis was performed on the various dependent measures used in the study (Table 3). If the classification is sufficient, only four factors should emerge from the data; these factors should be composed, respectively, of variables from the tasks classified as information maintenance, information location, information creation, and system interrogation. Furthermore, to the extent that the categories involve independent functions, the resulting factors should be uncorrelated. The question we wanted to ask was this: Would the factor analysis suggest a better scheme for classifying information-processing variables than we were able to produce before seeing any data?

All 19 variables listed in Table 3 were used in the analysis. Changes were made to variables in the system interrogation group as follows: meta-inference judgment scores (for "all questions" and for "correctly answered questions") were computed separately for direct access and for inferential questions; metamemory accuracy and efficiency measures were each included as difference scores—that is, proportion-correct-recognition for questions judged to be probably not answerable was subtracted from the proportion correct for questions judged to be answerable, and an equivalent difference score was computed for the search-time efficiency measure. With these changes, there were thus 21 variables total in the analysis.

Incidental to the factor analysis, complete data were collected on 20 white female undergraduate students recruited, for $10 compensation, from introductory psychology courses. The purpose for including the undergraduate students in the study was to compare their performance to that of both younger and older teachers. Briefly, the comparisons revealed no pattern of differences between the students and the younger teachers.

For the factor analysis, data on the 21 variables for all 100 subjects (80 teachers and 20 students) were analyzed in the BMDP (1979) statistical program package, using Kaiser's Second Generation Little Jiffy method with orthoblique rotation. To minimize theoretical "false alarms," we took a rather conservative approach in interpreting the results of the analysis.

A schematic representation of the rotated factor pattern is presented in Table 4. Although a separation of task variables based on three of the four categories appeared in the results of the analysis, seven rather than four factors were found to exist in the data. There was no support for a factor that could be labeled "Information Creation." This result may be due to the fact that there was only one variable, that is, total correct recognition for inferential questions, that was nominally representative of this class of

[3] We thank Dr. Juliet Shaffer of the Department of Statistics, University of California at Berkeley for her advice and consultation.

*Table 4. Revised Task Classification with Factor Loadings*[a]

| Categories and task variables | Factor 1 | 2 | 3 | 4 | 5 | 6 | 7 |
|---|---|---|---|---|---|---|---|
| Information maintenance, grapheme/pseudographeme manipulation | | | X | | | | |
| WAIS digit–symbol 1 | · | · | (+) | · | · | · | · |
| WAIS digit–symbol 2 | · | · | (+) | · | · | · | · |
| WAIS digit–symbol 3 | · | · | (+) | · | · | · | · |
| Information maintenance, short-term lexical retention | | | | | | | X |
| Word recall | – | + | · | · | · | · | (+) |
| Word recognition | · | · | · | · | · | · | (+) |
| Information location, unspeeded access | | | | X | | | |
| WAIS Information | · | · | · | (+) | · | · | · |
| WAIS Vocabulary | · | · | · | (+) | · | · | · |
| Inference task, total correct (recognition) | | | | | | | |
| Direct access questions | + | · | · | + | · | · | · |
| Inferential questions | · | · | · | (+) | · | · | · |
| Information location, speeded access | X | ? | | | | | |
| Metamemory task | | | | | | | |
| Total correct (recall) | (+) | + | · | · | · | · | · |
| Total correct (recall or recognition) | (+) | (–) | · | · | · | · | · |
| Recall efficiency (recall/total) | · | (+) | · | · | · | · | · |

tasks. However, since this variable correlated substantially with a number of other variables, it appears to involve primarily factors already included in the analysis.

Two of the three remaining *a priori* categories appeared as *sets* of factors in the data, with some intercategory overlap in the factor pattern. Two factors (3 and 7) emerged that clearly represented information maintenance skills (cf. Table 4). These factors have been labeled *grapheme/pseudographeme manipulation* and *short-term lexical retention*, respectively. Since factors 3 and 7 correlated reasonably well (.49) only with each other and not with other factors (interfactor correlations less than +/– .20), there is reason to believe that information maintenance skills, although separable into discrete sets, constitute a coherent group distinct from other types of information-processing skills.

Three factors (1, 2, and 4) emerged that were composed predominantly of information location variables. Of the nine variables that loaded with an absolute value greater than 0.50 on at least one of these three factors, seven were nominal information location

*Table 4.—Continued*

| Categories and task variables | Factor 1 | 2 | 3 | 4 | 5 | 6 | 7 |
|---|---|---|---|---|---|---|---|
| Recall response latency | | | | | | | |
| Correct answers | (−) | · | · | · | · | · | · |
| Incorrect answers | (−) | · | · | · | · | · | · |
| System interrogation, inferential process | | | | | X | | |
| Inference task, judgment of question type | | | | | | | |
| Inferential questions | | | | | | | |
| Number correct | · | · | · | · | (+) | · | · |
| Proportion correct (of correctly answered) | · | · | · | · | (+) | · | · |
| System interrogation, locative process | | | | | | X | |
| Inference task, judgment of question type | | | | | | | |
| Direct access questions | | | | | | | |
| Number correct | · | · | · | · | · | (+) | · |
| Proportion correct (of correctly answered) | · | · | · | · | · | (+) | · |
| System interrogation, content | ? | X | | | | | |
| Metamemory task | | | | | | | |
| Feeling-of-knowing accuracy | (−) | (+) | · | · | · | · | · |
| Question-answering recall monitor | · | + | · | · | · | · | · |
| Search-time efficiency | − | · | · | · | · | · | · |

[a]Only rotated factor loadings equal to or greater/less than +/− .35 are shown; loadings below this cutoff appear as "·". Positive loadings equal to or greater than .35 appear as +; if equal to or greater than .50, as (+). Corresponding negative loadings are represented as − and (−) respectively.

variables, one was the single nominal information creation variable (inferential question-answering), and one was a nominal system interrogation variable (feeling-of-knowing accuracy) that did not load on any other factor. On the basis of the available data, it seems most parsimonious to recategorize the single information creation variable as belonging to the information location set. This reclassifying, at least until other data are available, is justified by noting that before any information can be created in the system through inferential or synthesis processing, existing information to be used as the raw material in the creation process must first be located; that is, information creation must be preceded by information location. In our information creation task the information location stage may have accounted for the most variance in performance.

If we drop information creation as a category, information location variables can then be logically subdivided into two sets, distinguished by the conditions under which information is accessed. When subjects answered questions under relatively unspeeded conditions, their performance on information location variables is represented unambiguously by factor 4. However, when time constraints are imposed on question answering, as they were in the metamemory task, performance is represented well by factor 1 and somewhat ambiguously by factor 2. It is not clear what relation factors 1 and 2 have to each other, especially in view of the category overlap found with the metamemory system interrogation variables also loading on these factors. (Because those metamemory variables have strong information location components, they could as readily be classified with information location speeded-access variables.) Factors 1 and 2 are strongly correlated (.89) with each other and with factor 4 (.73 and .58, respectively). As with the information maintenance factors (3 and 7), the information location factors (1, 2, and 4) correlate well only with each other and not with factors from other categories. This suggests that, as for the information maintenance factors, information location skills or routines, as a group, are relatively distinct from other types of skills or routines and at the same time can be subcategorized meaningfully according to conditions (speeded or unspeeded) under which question-answering performance is evaluated.

An interesting factor pattern emerged with respect to nominal system interrogation variables: there may be no such unitary category. Rather, one's knowledge about inferential and locative processing may be independent categories on the same hierarchical level as information maintenance and location. Knowledge about content might also be a higher-level category; on the basis of our data, however, it could just as well be placed as a subprocess in information location. Perhaps the indeterminancy of system interrogation for content can be explained by noting that good performance on all three of the constituent variables required effective system monitoring (of content) *in conjunction with* effective speeded information location skills (i.e., question-answering ability). This argument is especially appealing in view of the factor pattern that emerged for judgments about locative and inferential processes. Good performance on these four constituent variables did *not* require effective question-answering, but only the ability to judge accurately whether a particular question's answer could be found "in store" or had to be inferred. As it turned out, one factor (factor 5) was composed only of the two judgment variables concerned with inferential questions, and the other (factor 6) was composed only of the two judgment variables dealing with direct-access questions. The two process judgment factors (5 and 6) did not correlate well with each other (or with any other factors), supporting the possibility of two independent processes. Thus, when relatively "uncontaminated" system interrogation (of process) variables are considered, they are found to group themselves independently of variables in the other categories, and according to the conclusion ("direct access" or "inferential") of the judgment required of the system.

The classification scheme initially proposed was preliminary, and the factor analytic procedures we carried out were exploratory. Considering that our purpose was to determine whether the classification could be refined on empirical grounds, we are encouraged by the results of the analysis. With some qualifications, there is empirical support for the potential consistency and validity of an ordering scheme for experimental tasks grouped according to the hypothetical information-processing routines they require. The next step may be to examine similar tasks in detail in an attempt to identify and possibly localize in the information-processing system particularly elementary routines that support normal cognitive activity.

# References

Baltes, P. B., & Goulet, L. R. Exploration of developmental variables by manipulation and simulation of age differences in behavior. *Human Development,* 1971, *14,* 149–170.

Baltes, P. B., & Nesselroade, J. R. The developmental analysis of individual differences on multiple measures. In J. R. Nesselroade & H. W. Reese (Eds.), *Life-span developmental psychology: Methodological issues.* New York: Academic Press, 1973.

Bennett, W. S., & Erickson, E. L. Teacher profile. In L. C. Deighton (Ed.), *Encyclopedia of education.* New York: MacMillan, 1971.

Betz, M., & Garland J. Intergenerational mobility rates of urban school teachers. *Sociology of Education,* 1974, *47,* 511–522.

Botwinick, J. *Aging and behavior: A comprehensive integration of research findings.* New York: Springer, 1978.

Brown, A. L. The development of memory: Knowing, knowing about knowing, and knowing how to know. In H. W. Reese (Ed.), *Advances in child development and behavior* (Vol. 10). New York: Academic Press, 1975.

Camp, C. J. *Direct access versus inferential retrieval across the adult lifespan.* Unpublished doctoral dissertation, University of Houston, 1979.

Camp C. J., Lachman, J. L., & Lachman, R. Evidence for direct-access and inferential retrieval in question answering. *Journal of Verbal Learning and Verbal Behavior,* 1980, *19,* 583–596.

Cattell, R. B. Theory of fluid and crystallized intelligence: A critical experiment. *Journal of Educational Psychology,* 1963, *54,* 1–22.

Dillman, D. A. *Mail and telephone surveys: The total design method.* New York: Wiley, 1978.

Dworkin, A. G. The changing demography of public school teachers: Some implications for faculty turnover in urban areas. *Sociology of Education,* 1980, *53,* 65–73.

Gribbin, K., & Schaie, K. W. Monetary incentive, age and cognition. *Experimental Aging Research,* 1976, *2,* 461–468.

Hart, J. T. A methodological note on feeling-of-knowing experiments. *Journal of Educational Psychology,* 1966, *57,* 347–349.

Hart, J. T. Memory and the feeling-of-knowing experience. *Journal of Educational Psychology,* 1965, *56,* 208–216.

Hart, J. T. Memory and the memory-monitoring process. *Journal of Verbal Learning and Verbal Behavior,* 1967, *6,* 685–691.

Havighurst, R. J., & Neugarten, B. L. *Society and education,* (3rd ed.), Boston: Allyn & Bacon, 1967.

Horn, J. L. & Cattell, R. B. Age differences in fluid and crystallized intelligence. *Acta Psychologica,* 1967, *26,* 107–129.

Lachman, J. L. & Lachman R. Theories of memory organization and human evolution. In R. C. Puff (Ed.), *Memory organization and structure.* New York: Academic Press, 1979.

Lachman, J. L. & Lachman, R. Age and the actualization of world knowledge. In L. W. Poon, J. L. Fozard, L. S. Cermak, D. Arenberg, & L. W. Thompson (Eds.), *New directions in memory and aging: Proceedings of the George Talland Memorial Conference.* Hillsdale N.J.: Lawrence Erlbaum, 1980.

Lachman, J. L., Lachman, R., & Thronesberry, C. Metamemory through the adult life span. *Developmental Psychology,* 1979, *15,* 543–551.

Lachman, R., Lachman J. L., & Butterfield, E. C. *Cognitive psychology and information processing: An introduction.* Hillsdale, N.J.: Lawrence Erlbaum, 1979.

Laughery, K. R., Thompson, B., & Band T. *How do we decide to terminate a memory search?* Paper presented at the meeting of the Psychonomic Society, Boston, November 1974.

Lortie, D. C. *Schoolteacher: A sociological study*. Chicago: University of Chicago Press, 1975.

National Educational Association. *The American public school teacher, 1965–1966*. Washington, D.C.: NEA, 1967.

National Education Association. *Status of the American public school teacher, 1970–1971*. Washington, D.C.: NEA, 1972.

Newell, A., & Simon H. A. *Human problem solving*. Englewood Cliffs, N.J.: Prentice–Hall, 1972.

Norman, D. A., & Bobrow, D. G. On data limited and resource limited processes. *Cognitive Psychology*, 1975, *7*, 44–64.

Quillian, M. R. The teachable language comprehender: A simulation program and theory of language. *Communications of the ACM*, 1969, *12*, 459–476.

Quillian, M. R. Semantic memory. In M. Minsky (Ed.), *Semantic information processing*. Cambridge, Mass.: M.I.T. Press, 1968.

Riegel, K. F., Riegel, R. M., & Meyer, G. A study of the drop-out rates in longitudinal research on aging and the prediction of death. *Journal of Personality and Social Psychology*, 1967, *4*, 342–348.

Rosenthal, R., & Rosnow, R. L. *The volunteer subject*. New York: Wiley, 1975.

Schaie, K. W. A reinterpretation of age-related changes in cognitive structure and functioning. In L. R. Goulet & P. B. Baltes (Eds.), *Life-span developmental psychology: Research and theory*. New York: Academic Press, 1970.

Schaie, K. W. Quasi-experimental research designs in the psychology of aging. In J. E. Birren & K. W. Schaie (Eds.), *Handbook of the psychology of aging*. New York: Van Nostrand Reinhold, 1977.

Schwartzwaller, H. K., & Lyson, T. A. Some plan to become teachers: Determinants of career specification among rural youth in Norway, Germany and the United States. *Sociology of Education*, 1978, *51*, 29–43.

Simon, H. A. *Models of thought*. New Haven: Yale University Press, 1979.

Storandt, M. Speed and coding effects in relation to age and ability level. *Developmental Psychology*, 1976, *12*, 177–178.

CHAPTER 16

# Attention Switching in Higher Mental Process

David Schonfield

*Department of Psychology*
*University of Calgary*
*Calgary, Alberta, Canada*

Use of the phrase *higher mental processes* involves the tacit assumption of a high-low dimension. Low points of this dimension presumably indicate that the route from input leads directly to output. Words such as *route* and *lead* in that sentence tend to evoke images of maps and space, but obviously the language is metaphorical so long as *mental* processes are under discussion. There is no neurological insinuation that low mental processes are confined to lower anatomical sections of the brain. Time, not space, serves as the necessary, albeit insufficient, measure or criterion for deciding whether the route is direct, whether a marriage between cue and appropriate performance has or has not been arranged beforehand. To deserve the label of a higher mental process, there must at least be a time lapse between problem and solution, between input cue and output behavior.

When a shotgun wedding between a stimulus and a response is consummated, some prearranged association or previous marriage between the partners can be taken for granted. In the case of reflexes and instinctive behavior, the marriage between stimulus and response has been, one might say, preordained in heaven. However, an immediate match between stimulus and response in the human species is usually due to experience and knowledge, or, as Horn (Chapter 14) might say, an aspect of crystallized intelligence. Because of experience, a red light suddenly noticed by the driver of a car will result in the driver's pressing the brake—an immediate *stop* reaction. For a person seeking a red-light district, a red light would produce a *go* reaction, although perhaps not quite so immediately. Different goals or *Aufgaben* (Ach, 1905) provide a context and set for varying the encoding of external cues. When one is driving, the red light symbol is *translated* at once into an almost universal reaction, and when one hears or sees the words "red light," the translation is also immediate into a common semantic meaning. Higher mental processes are not demanded.

Other translating situations do require higher mental processes. The mental route from symbols or information to meaning and implications with respect to an intended goal may demand many separate conscious translations or stages—and that takes time. Moving from one discrete conscious translation attempt to another seems to warrant the description of attention switch, even though, in some sense and for some people, attention remains consistently focused on the final outcome. Switching attention, whether intentional or unintentional, implies conscious awareness, although perhaps only in retrospect, of different trains of thought. The next step in the argument is, of course, that these internal attention switches tend to cause special age-associated difficulties and strains. I will also suggest that the necessity to switch attention seems to increase with age: thoughts tend to become more discrete. On the other hand, age, insofar as it is correlated with experience, also has its advantages. The exercise or repeated performance of the same types of translation processes speeds up the practiced operations, telescopes them, obviates the necessity of attending to them, and thus reduces the frequency of attention switches. What begins as a laborious series of translation episodes ends in a readied shotgun marriage between cue and responses—mediators are relinquished.

To change the metaphor, what we may be losing on the swings with age, we may be gaining on the roundabouts through experience. This will only occur in areas in which we have had experience and probably only up to a certain age. In real old age—that means as usual, 10 years older than a speaker's or author's chronological age—we usually lose a little more because of age than we have gained by experience. The drop with age among Houston schoolteachers in what Lachman, Lachman, and Taylor (Chapter 15) call *information maintenance* demonstrates a greater loss than gain before the seventies, whereas for information location, information creation, and system integration the experience roundabouts make up for the age swings.

Dare one state the paradox that an individual's progress in solving problems involves replacing higher mental processes by lower mental processes, by replacing fluid intelligence with crystallized intelligence, replacing deep processing with shallow processing? The allusion to levels of processing, nevertheless, masks the perennial conundrum of whether deep processing and spread of elaboration can occur nonconsciously. It is worthy of an aside to recollect that unconscious elaboration is exactly what Freud was trying to uncover. Be that as it may, the concept of translation as used here includes both conscious and nonconscious translations. Nonconscious translations should be considered as automatic processes (Hasher & Zacks, 1979) and would not involve switches of attention, whereas a sequence of conscious translations normally would.

A cursory analysis of an example given by Arenberg (Chapter 13) may clarify the idea of consecutive, conscious translation processes. A participant in his experiment must discover the poisoned food, which in this conjunctive problem requires two interacting dishes. The experimenter has already provided information that a person having eaten, say lamb, peas, ice cream, and coffee had survived. Arenberg describes this as an''A1, B1, C1, D1-negative example,'' with living considered a negative attribute. The participant then has to discover the fate of some other diner and eventually asks, ''Lamb, carrots, ice cream, and coffee?'' The experimenter says, ''Lives.'' Let us guess the participant's internal translation processes. ''It can't be peas or carrots that are poisoned. No, it can be peas or carrots. But it can't be peas or carrots and lamb, and it can't be peas or carrots and coffee. Nor, peas and carrots—what was the other one? I've gone through lamb. Did I do coffee or ice cream? Let's look at my notes. I bet it wasn't the coffee; coffee is never poisoned. Where was I? Not peas and carrots. No; yes, peas and carrots. Lamb or beef—we haven't had them. Or have we? Did he die? etc., etc., etc. What should I ask now? Let's have something to make him die.''

Many of these silent talking-to-oneself statements—perhaps these should be termed TTOs, given the predilection of ''not old'' psychologists for translating into abbreviations—can be considered as separate conscious translations of information acquired earlier and as requiring attention switches. Other statements seem to follow one from the other through a strategy that directs the outcome of one translation into another conclusion without returning to earlier information, without constant switches of attention. Labels were provided to a variety of concept-formation strategies by Bruner, Goodnow, and Austin (1956), and no doubt further light on age differences in switching attention might be shed by asking participants to verbalize their strategies. Yet, it seems intuitively obvious that if there is no logical strategy, which is likely to be the case of inexperienced concept formers, many switches of attention are usually necessary, and that, it is suggested, may be the reason for the negative correlation with age that Arenberg reports for his experiment. However, someone with relevant experience or appropriate crystallized intelligence, and even perhaps someone without experience, but possessed of the necessary fluid intelligence to create an appropriate strategy, will require fewer separate translation processes. These alternative bases for solving problems are worthy of reemphasis, because of the implications for older problem solvers. Horn (1980) subscribes to the view that the same task may be performed by one person with the aid of crystallized intelligence and by another via fluid intelligence and the same individual can use both on the same problem. A case could perhaps be made for suggesting that fluid intelligence is likely to require more frequent switches of attention than crystallized intelligence, all other things being equal. Reducing attention switches would then be a reason for the aged to prefer to rely on experienced methods where possible, rather than tackling new problems in new ways.

As to Arenberg's finding that age is not correlated with the magnitude of change in difficult problems with low initial information, his figures suggest that this may be due to an initially low level of performance. Many of his oldest subjects presumably could not manage even one of the conjunctive problems first time round and did not improve. Indeed, I would be reluctant to ask most Calgary volunteers to undertake those onerous concept-attainment puzzles, because of the danger that volunteers would not return for other experiments and word of mouth about the torture would dry up my potential pool of volunteers. Admittedly, the Lachmans' persuasive power over granting agencies might produce sufficiently large bribes to replenish the subject pool, but that would create a new future problem. Were the munificent handout to participants in future studies ever to cease, it is possible that disappointment over rewards might affect the performance of Calgarians, notwithstanding the findings from Houston's schoolteachers (Chapter 15). In any case, it would not be surprising for Calgarian volunteers to say, after hearing about the poisoned foods, "I do not care which food was poisoned, I would not go to that restaurant for a meal!"

The suggestion that covert switches of attention cause special difficulties with increasing age can be considered as a corollary of the conclusion drawn from many studies that division of attention is an age-related problem. The division-of-attention hypothesis dates back at least to Kay's findings of over 20 years ago (reported in Welford, 1958), where old and young subjects had to press a key corresponding to a light illuminated one back or two back, rather than responding to the light concurrently illuminated. A divided-attention explanation was suggested for the results in a Calgary experiment on dichotic listening (Schonfield, Trueman, & Kline, 1972). And Horn (1980; Chapter 14) now also emphasizes the factorial loading of divided attention tests. Craik and Simon (1980) place divided attention on the same pedestal as depth of processing, the highest possible honor, in their general interpretation of age decrements in learning and memory. It is obvious that a division of attention requires at least one switch of attention, and usually many more. The new thesis proposes that the necessity to switch attention underlies the age-associated difficulty in divided attention tasks. More pertinent in the present context is the proposition that internal switches of attention are characteristic of higher mental processes. Not surprisingly, it is my opinion that age difficulties in attention switches derive from, or are at least linked to, retrieval problems (Schonfield, 1965). While one thought or idea occupies attention, others must be stored in memory and reclaimed when needed. These retrieval episodes will tend to take longer in older than in younger individuals.

A recent Calgary experiment by Fager (1980) for his Master's thesis tackled the issue of age changes in attention using a reaction-time paradigm. Choice reaction times for older and younger participants were obtained when subjects were, and when they were not, preoccupied with another task. Care was taken to ensure that the interrupted assignment demanded equal attention from young and old. The results showed, as anticipated, that switching time, defined as preoccupied reaction time minus normal reaction time, was greater for the old. Although age-related differences were also found between responding to a light on the right compared to one on the left, which requires further investigation, the overall outcome gives reasonably solid support for the switching hypothesis in a perceptual-motor skill. No apology presumably is required for drawing analogies between perceptual-motor tasks and higher mental processes, given Bartlett's (1958) viewpoint that thinking should be treated as a skill.

Now, let us turn to the idea that *frequency* of switching attention increases with age, which is much harder to explain and to justify. Further, it seems almost contradictory to suggest that aging produces both an increase and greater difficulty in switching. However, difficulty refers to extra time or blocking in situations that demand a switch, whereas the increase should be considered as additional superfluous switches relative to the young. The increase occurs because activities tend to become more separated, and the same activity tends to be broken into more components or subunits, as we age. The predominant idea underlying frequency increase with age derives from Bartlett's pithy saying that actions do not care for themselves. Elsewhere, I translated this to the dry generalization that functioning requires more vigilance with age (Schonfield, 1974). In other words, an activity and component stages of an activity tend to require greater proportions of attentional capacity from older than from younger individuals. As a result, less attention capacity is available for preparing a future sequence of activity, and, also, a more distinct subgoal marker emerges. An additional suggestion is that preset—prior preparation for commencing an activity—becomes more significant in the later years of life. Preset was given great emphasis in the beautiful, but often overlooked, monograph that Woodworth (1958) wrote toward the end of his life. Preparing for the next unit while attending to the present one would, of necessity, require a division and switches of attention, with their age-associated difficulties discussed earlier. Discrete subgoals will hinder smooth sequences of subunit performance and may arouse an internal *stop* command when a subunit is completed. The *stop* command might, at least temporarily, be accompanied by forgetting that further activity was required. The forgetting or necessary remembering is not of *what* has to be done, but that anything has to be done. Such remembering to remember in its relation to age was discussed in a recent publication (Schonfield & Stones, 1979). The various threads in the foregoing arguments and their conceptual coordination are quite a mindful, to coin a phrase. Nevertheless, various authorities have made pronouncements that seem to coincide with these ideas about frequency and difficulty in switching, and there are scattered findings in the literature that provide for some aspects of this analytic framework.

An image of Lewin's (1936) topological figures representing regions of life space might be helpful in making these abstract notions more concrete. The proposed increase in frequency of attention switches with age would be represented by a greater number of regions, while the difficulty in switching would be shown by a thickening of boundaries between regions. And, indeed, Kounin (1941), a student of Lewin, stated that the older the individual the more difficulty he will have in the performance of a task that requires him to be influenced by more than one region. He further added that the field tended to be structured into many parts and became less integrated in old age.

A rather precise statement, similar to the views expounded here, appears in the following quotation from Pavlov[1]:

> As he [man] ages, patterns of action no longer function as wholes, such as he needs to think only of a goal or total effect of a given pattern. On the contrary, as he ages, he has to think of and supervise each step or normally subordinate action in order to get through the intended total action.

A few observations from everyday life and from experimental laboratories can be added. Szafran (cited in Welford, 1958) performed an experiment in which participants had to throw some hundred little loops at a bull's-eye. Because the purpose of the study was to investigate age differences in correcting errors, the loops were numbered and the appropriate loop had to be placed by the experimenter in a subject's hand before each throw. Older participants usually, but not usually younger participants, turned to look at their hands as the loops were placed in them. I would want to interpret this as a need to create a preset for the next activity. In Smith's (1974) experiment on cumulative part learning of paired associates, the joining of the already mastered parts took much longer for older people, compared to age differences in learning the separate parts. The explanation, according to the views outlined earlier, is that boundaries of established mental units are less permeable in old people and therefore more difficult to combine with other mental units. There is also Horn's (1980) factor-analytic investigation, in which the marker test for the fluid intelligence drop with age was tracing a figure as slowly as possible. There, the problem seems to be that of switching attention backwards and forwards between the task of tracing and the task of tracing slowly.

In the first aging study I ever ran, summarized in Welford's (1958) book, a participant had to press a button on every trial when ready with an answer. This was necessary in those unsophisticated days, so that time taken was marked on an event recorder activated when the button was depressed. Most of the older, and a few of the younger, participants consistently forgot to press the button before giving their answer, even though they were reminded to do so after each trial. The verbal response to which attention was being paid had no associative

[1] The late W. S. Taylor kindly drew my attention to Pavlov's pronouncement, but, unfortunately, I have so far been unable to trace the specific reference.

link with the button-pressing requirement. Subjects did not remember to remember. Being preoccupied with producing a verbal response, they were not preset for an additional subunit of activity. This is slightly different from the everyday experience of going upstairs and forgetting what one was going to fetch. In those cases, one remembers to remember, but *what* to remember is forgotten. Let me jump now many decades to a recent personal experience by which time *I* have become *they*, the elderly *they*. A new coffee machine in the outside office has a container into which water is poured, subsequently dripping into the coffee jug. The easiest way to be a water-carrier from the faucet is to transport it in the coffee jug. That is what I did, turning on the electric switch for heating the coffee, but forgetting to transfer the water from jug to container. This I discovered some time later when water, rather than coffee, greeted my coffee break. So, I turned off the electricity and poured the water into the container, but then forgot to turn on the electricity, discovering this on my next thirsty search for coffee. There is no question that I could also have done this 30 or 40 years ago, especially when tired. Fatigue, as well as time pressure (Simon, 1979), may mimic aging. In general, however, the tendency not to prepare for a succeeding subunit of a task, while performing an earlier one, seems more prevalent in older than in younger populations.

This motley array of observations can be considered as separate pieces of incomplete jigsaw puzzles. Younger psychologists might be able to join the pieces together more readily than older psychologists. Nevertheless, experience of aging will help in discovering where the pieces fit in. Performing experiments is a good substitute for experience, providing one acts as the experimenter oneself and does not solely rely on research assistants. That will reduce surprises by creating a more general understanding and sensibility concerning aging processes. It will allow one to bet that the results of some experiments are likely to be confirmed, whereas others are unlikely to be supported, without the necessity of an enormous investment in longitudinal studies. My wife used to say that the great advantage of being married to a gerontologist was that as she became older, she became more interesting to her husband. The same is true for gerontologists' examination of their own age changes. Growing older is recommended to every gerontologist.

## References

Ach, N. *Ueber die Willenstaetigkeit und das Denken*. Goettingen: Vandenhoeck und Ruprecht, 1905.

Bartlett, F. C. *Thinking*. London: Allen & Unwin, 1958.

Bruner, J. S., Goodnow, J. J., & Austin, G. A. *A study of thinking*. New York: Wiley, 1956.

Craik, F. I. M., & Simon, E. Age differences in memory: The roles of attention and depth of processing. In L. W. Poon, J. L. Fozard, L. S. Cermak, D. Arenberg & L. W. Thompson

(Eds.), *New directions in memory and aging: Proceedings of the George Talland Memorial Conference*. Hillsdale, N.J.: Lawrence Erlbaum, 1980.

Fager, D. S. *Effect of preoccupation on age differences in reaction to time*. Unpublished Master of Science thesis, University of Calgary, 1980.

Hasher, L., & Zacks, R. T. Automatic and effortful processes in memory. *Journal of Experimental Psychology: General,* 1979, *108,* 356–388.

Horn J. L. Concepts of intellect in relation to learning and adult development. *Intelligence,* 1980, *4,* 285–317.

Kounin, J. S. Experimental studies of rigidity. *Character and Personality,* 1941, *9,* 251–272.

Lewin, K. *Principles of topological psychology*. New York: McGraw-Hill, 1936.

Schonfield, D. Memory changes with age. *Nature,* 1965, *208,* 918.

Schonfield, D. Translations in gerontology—From lab to life: Utilizing information. *American Psychologist,* 1974, *29,* 796–801.

Schonfield, D., & Stones, M. J. Remembering and aging. In J. F. Kihlstrom & F. J. Evans (Eds.), *Functional disorders of memory*. Hillsdale, N.J.: Lawrence Erlbaum, 1979, 103–139.

Schonfield, D., Trueman, V., & Kline, D. Recognition tests of dichotic listening and the age variable. *Journal of Gerontology,* 1972, *27,* 487–493.

Simon, E. Depth and elaboration of processing in relation to age. *Journal of Experimental Psychology: Human learning and memory,* 1979, *5,* 115–124.

Smith, S. L. *Age differences in part and whole learning*. Unpublished doctoral thesis, University of Calgary, 1974.

Welford, A. T. Aging and human skill. London: Oxford University Press, 1958.

Woodworth, R. S. *Dynamics of behavior*. New York: Holt, 1958.

CHAPTER 17

# Studying Cognitive Performance in the Elderly

## A Biopsychosocial Approach

Jerry Avorn

*Division on Aging*
*Harvard Medical School*
*Boston, Massachusetts*

## Introduction

The concept of a biopsychosocial model of human health and illness has been known intuitively to clinicians and researchers since the times of the earliest shamans and was explicated more recently by Engel (1977) in a more formal manner. This approach conceptualizes the person in health and illness as a part of a network of systems, from the molecular to the societal. Proper understanding of health or illness can thus come only with understanding of the role played by each level of organization in the day-to-day (or minute-to-minute or year-to-year) functioning of the organism.

In the medical literature, this model is most often used to admonish physicians not to focus on biological processes within a patient to the exclusion of the psychological and social factors that so often contribute to the development or experience of disease. In the present context, however, my focus will be shifted to examine the biological and social factors associated with cognition in the elderly, and how they interact with the ''purely'' psychological phenomena discussed in other chapters. My conclusions will nonetheless be similar to those

This work was supported in part by a grant from the Robert Wood Johnson Foundation.

who have used this approach in clinical medicine. Just as consideration of an individual's psychosocial situation can add critically important insights to the diagnosis of his or her medical situation, so an assessment of the subject's biological and social condition may be important in understanding and in explaining psychological performance. Further, if these observations are true in general, their relevance becomes even greater in the case of the elderly.

In the pages that follow, I will leave aside the thorny question of how the aging process *itself* (in the absence of other perturbations) inherently affects cognitive functioning; this has been addressed in detail in previous chapters. Rather, I will focus on the impact on cognition of biological and social phenomena that are not inherent in the aging process itself but may be epiphenomena of it. Nonetheless, these aging-related processes may, as we will see, exert profound influences on cognition in the elderly—influences which are often mistaken for changes due to old age.

## The Biological Issues

### *The Nature of Normal Biological Aging*

It is perfectly acceptable to take any number of undergraduates or middle-aged volunteers, ask them if they are in good health, and, if they answer in the affirmative, include them in a study of cognition as ''normals.'' One is on much thinner ice in applying this screening approach to those over 65 (with the risk rising further with each succeeding year of age). Whereas nearly all college sutdents are free of major physiological deficit, one cannot make this assumption with 70-year-olds. The normal aging process is associated with a gradual and usually clinically silent deterioration of function (and consequent loss of reserve capacity) of most organ systems. Contrary to lay and professional assumptions that aging begins in earnest around age 65, this loss of function begins in early middle age and continues progressively until death. As a result, each successive decade beings with it a further subtle diminution in such functions as nerve conduction velocity, cardiac output, vital (pulmonary) capacity, renal glomerular filtration rate, and so on. In general, this slow physiological decline goes on for decades without producing the overt symptoms of disease (Shock, 1960).

The way in which this gradual loss of biological reserves interacts with other factors to produce what we recognize as disease is beyond the scope of this chapter. What is relevant here is the way in which such deterioration can remain clinically inapparent and yet potentially influence behavior. For instance, we know that advanced renal failure is associated with progressive mental failure that can range from lethargy to confusion to coma. We also know that normal aging is associated with a milder progressive loss of renal function (Rowe, Tobin, Andres, Norris, & Shock, 1976). As with most biological phenomena, severity of renal impairment will be distributed along a quasi-normal curve for any given age group. For most elderly people, this loss of function will not cause any symptoms or even subclinical deterioration of mental function. However, for an indeterminate number, the extent of deterioration may be larger, or the ability to compensate may be smaller, and mild renal failure may blunt cognition or performance somewhat, even in the absence of diagnosed kidney disease. The more sensitive our measures, the more likely they are to pick up such subtle changes. Are we then to attribute such performance decrements to aging *per se*? Such a conclusion would be unwarranted if an age-matched comparison group with better renal function did not show such a decrement.

Similar arguments can be made for other variable aspects of biological aging with undetermined (but potentially important) effects on mental functioning. Two conclusions are apparent. First, a great deal more work must be done on the effects on cognition of the ''normal'' deterioration of some homeostatic mechanisms that comes with age. Second, a brief health-status checklist is not an adequate means of controlling for biological contaminants in psychological studies of the elderly.

## *Non-Specific Presentation of Illness in the Elderly*

An axiom of clinical geriatrics is that diseases which have ''classical'' presentations in younger patients can have deceptively atypical presentation in the elderly. Hyperthyroidism and hypothyroidism, rather common disorders, provide good examples. The middle-aged patient with hyperthroidism is likely to have a rapid heartbeat, feel anxious and sweaty, complain of intolerance of heat, and note rapid weight loss. Conversely, the young hypothroid patient will be lethargic, have a slow pulse, note cold intolerance, and be gaining weight despite an effort to diet. Yet, the elderly patient with either disorder may manifest virtually none of these ''typical'' findings and present merely with a syndrome whose name has been borrowed from the pediatric literature—''failure to thrive'' (Rowe & Besdine, 1982).

Similar examples can be cited for other conditions. ''I just don't feel myself'' can be the presenting complaint for congestive heart failure, anemia, diabetes, and a variety of other conditions that are more easily distinguished from one another in the non-aged patient. Of particular relevance here is the observation that mental impairment can be the main presenting complaint for a variety of illnesses, including all of those just noted. For the clinician, this means that a careful search for somatic illness must be undertaken in every elderly patient with intellectual deterioration. For the researcher, this is one more reason for obtaining a clean bill of health on any elderly subject in a study of cognition and age, lest one compare sick elders with healthy young controls and misattribute the causes of any differences found.

## *Drugs and the Elderly*

The use of both prescription and over-the-counter drugs is critically important in any consideration of mental functioning in the elderly. Utilization of drugs of all kinds is much higher in those over 65 (Petersen, Whittington, & Payne, 1979).

The elderly are more likely than the young to use prescription drugs and are more likely to seek nonprescription relief for aches, tension, or insomnia. Equally importantly, the normal decrease in liver and kidney function that comes with age greatly enhances the chance of side effects or overdosage, since the normal means of metabolizing and excreting drugs are functioning at a diminished rate. Both these factors combine to increase the risk of drug interactions, in which the danger of an entire collection of remedies is greater than the sum of the risks from each (Kayne, 1978).

Together, these observations raise considerable concern over the role of drugs in the mental performance of the elderly. Because depression, anxiety, and insomnia are so common among the elderly (perhaps as a result of the stressful and alienated roles they often find themselves in), they are among the largest consumers of tranquilizers (usually benzodiazepines such as Valium and Librium) and antidepressants (generally tricyclics). While it has been well documented that such drugs are often overused in the nursing-home setting, less is known about the effects of these drugs among the noninstitutionalized elderly. Controlled trials suggest that even small doses of such agents can cause mental impairment in aged subjects. Drugs given for other purposes (such as alpha-methyldopa and reserpine, in common use to treat hypertension) can also have profound effects on mental status (Eisdorfer & Fann, 1973).

Here again clinicians and researchers face a situation analagous to that described above—for the former, a careful drug history and a trial off non-life-sustaining medications is a mandatory part of the diagnosis of mental failure in the elderly. For the latter, it makes little sense to assess mental functioning if one cannot be sure one is studying a nondrugged subject.

Two points bear special mention in relation to the situation facing researchers. First, because of the long duration of effect of many drugs on the aged central nervous system, one may need to wait several days before the pharmacologic effects have subsided. Thus, even "an occasional sleeping pill or Valium" may be enough to impair performance in an elderly subject, depending on when the last "occasion" was and on how sensitive the test instruments are.

Second, our own work casts doubt on the adequacy of screening questionnaires to document the exact extent of drug use in the elderly. In a study of 100 consecutive nondemented elderly outpatients, we found that only a third of the patients recalled all of the medications their physicians had been prescribing for them. Interestingly, tranquilizer use was highly correlated with inability to recall medications (Avorn, Griffin, & Costa, 1981).

## *The Epidemiology of Senile Dementia*

A final problem confronting those trying to study cognition in the elderly deals with the prevalence of organically caused *primary* dementia among noninstitutionalized elders. As discussed in previous chapters, there is now consensus that about 60% of cases of "senility" are caused by Alzheimer's disease, a specific neuropathological entity of unknown cause that is associated with fairly clear anatomical changes (senile plaques and neurofibrillary tangles) and, recently, biochemical changes as well (choline acetyl transferase deficiency). About another 20% of cases of senile dementia are associated with equally distinctive vascular changes (multi-infarct dementia) that seem to produce mental impairment by occlusion of blood supply to isolated areas of the brain. The remaining 20% or so of the dementias are thought to be secondary to all other causes combined (Hughes, 1978).

Various epidemiological studies suggest that about 10% of noninstitutionalized people over 65 suffer from some degree of dementia, often mild. This number rises to about 30% when the population 85 and over is considered (Arie, 1974; Kay, 1972). It is crucial to bear in mind that people with these conditions (generally Alzheimer's disease or multi-infarct dementia) are intellectually impaired because of specific disease states, and *not* because of "the mental deterioration of aging." The fact that Alzheimer's-type dementia and multi-infarct dementia occur predominantly *in* the elderly should not cloud this conceptually critical point. (The situation with cerebrovascular accidents is somewhat analogous. By far the greatest number of strokes occur in the elderly. Yet a stroke is a particular disease entity [cerebral thrombosis, embolus, or hemorrhage] that *most* elderly people do not experience. Although predisposing conditions due to aging are important, it would be incorrect to suggest that aging is the cause of strokes.)

One must therefore take special pains to distinguish the mental impairment of such primary senile dementia from whatever other changes occur in the course of *normal* aging. The ultimate best test of whether underlying central-nervous-system disease is present is the postmortem examination of the brain, but this is obviously a cumbersome means of classification. Much work is now going on to verify antemortem means of determining the presence or absence of primary brain disease in elderly patients with mental impairment. Such tools will be critical in studying subjects in cross-sectional and longitudinal studies of cognitive changes with age (Feinberg, Fein, Price, Jernigan, & Floyd, 1980).

## Social Psychological Issues

### *Selection Bias*

A great deal has been written about sample selection as a source of confusion in documenting changes in cognitive function related to aging. Classical in this area are the longitudinal studies of Schaie and Labouvie-Vief (1974) in which they demonstrated that the supposed inferior performance of older subjects in cross-sectional studies could be explained to a very great extent by the fact that those born earlier in the century did less well on tests of intelligence than those born later, *whatever* the subject's age. Viewed longitudinally, Schaie and his co-workers found that much of the deterioration attributed to aging was eliminated (or even reversed) when subjects were followed over several years, although some decrements were found consistently in the late 60s and 70s.

An analogous case of sampling bias concerns the social background of subjects. To begin with, the historical experience of today's elderly is such that they are much less likely to have reached higher education than are the young and middle-aged population, explaining some (but not all) of the findings described above. Rather than taking this into account, many investigators have further skewed their cross-sectional samples by comparing community-dwelling elderly people with that ubiquitous control animal, the undergraduate. An extreme version of this approach is the use of general practitioners' patient lists to locate "normal" elders, who are then compared with university students. The "aging"-related deficits that can emerge from such studies are bound to be as misleading as they are impressive.

The use of volunteers could in theory pose similar problems. Elders who come forward to participate in a study, having read a notice in the newspaper, may well be as atypical as the archetypal undergraduate. One could speculate that such elders might be unrepresentatively bright, or motivated, or bored, or inactive when compared with themselves decades earlier, or with the students decades hence. Happily, recent work by the Lachmans (Chapter 15) seems reasuring on this count, indicating that volunteers in their sample do not seem to differ appreciably from nonvolunteers for the variables studied.

Solutions to these potential methodological problems are conceptually simple but can be quite cumbersome in practice. Use of longitudinal rather than cross-sectional research will solve some the problems mentioned but does not deal with other contaminants (such as mandatory retirement or bereavement) that are not truly "aging" but may affect performance. These are discussed below. However, as Hartley,Harker,and Walsh (1980) point out, there is much in cross-sectional methodology worth retaining. One approach would be to match subjects in terms of formal education, health status, and perhaps even level of day-to-day activity, whatever their age. Until now, much of the literature has failed to address these important variables, and we must be correspondingly insecure about the conclusions thus reached.

## *The Epiphenomena of Aging*

Other factors impeding the study of cognition throughout the life span are the social and psychological changes that are (often arbitrarily) imposed on the elderly in our particular society but are not inherent in the aging process itself. The possible contribution of these factors becomes clear when one imagines the hypothetically perfect experiment to control for the selection errors mentioned above. If one could match 70-year-olds with 30-year-olds for level of education, health status, socioeconomic status, and even a baseline battery of tests administered at age 20, there would still remain variables that might strongly affect the performance of the 70-year-old because he or she is an older person living in the current society, not because 70 years have elapsed since birth.

Mandatory retirement is one such example. Although most studies have failed to find any consistent pattern of decrement in health or mental status attributable to retirement (see Bond, 1976; Streib & Schneider, 1971), nonetheless it seems likely that profound psychosocial changes occur in many individuals as the result of loss of employment (Butler, 1975). Being labeled as one no longer competent to function productively can in theory have a great impact on performance in a wide variety of tasks; this is discussed further below. Of more concrete interest here is the possibility that loss of day-to-day cognitive challenges such as are found in even the most routine work might exert a negative influence on other tests of intellectual performance.

We know, for instance, that many of the tests used to measure cognitive ability are very sensitive to the effects of practice and that performance may improve asymptotically with repeated trials. One could hypothesize that an environment (such as that of work) that demands repeated trials at tasks of pattern recognition, memorization, reaction time, and so forth might well prime a subject for successful performance on laboratory tests of similar skills. Conversely, an environment (such as that experienced by many elderly retirees) devoid of such challenges might put such subjects at a relative disadvantage in the laboratory situation as well as in life. A related formulation of mindful as opposed to mindless activity has been posited by Langer, Blank, and Chanowitz (1978) in connection with the elderly as well as other groups.

Retirement, with the consequent removal of many cognitive challenges (even those of the assembly line), is not an attribute of aging *per se;* it is an epiphenomenon of aging that results from our present social system. For instance, in one recent study of healthy retirees living in Boston, the most common problem cited (by 36% of those interviewed) was concern with "keeping busy" (Sheldon, McKewan, & Byser, 1975). We are in great need of further work on the extent (thus far mostly conjectural) to which these factors affect cognitive performance apart from senescence itself.

A similar case can be made for social isolation of the elderly and bereavement. These, too, are primarily results of social forces—the former because of our trend toward an age-segregated society and the latter because women have tended to marry men older than themselves who then go on (in large part because of tobacco-induced illnesses) to die at a younger age. Beyond the cognitive impoverishment that such situations can create, they are the cause of considerable clinical depression as well. The potential role of depression in lowering performance on cognitive tasks has been addressed previously. What would be the impact on the performance of the elderly of a society that did not impose such (potential) psychological handicaps? We cannot know for certain, although some suggestive evidence comes from the anthropological literature. Additional cross-cultural studies might shed light on this important question.

## *Labeling and Learned Helplessness*

The concept of learned helplessness has been validated repeatedly in a variety of settings, particularly by Seligman (1975) and his colleagues. The simplest paradigm is that of the dog initially exposed to aversive stimuli (e.g., electric shock) that it cannot avoid. When its environment is then altered so that it *can* escape or avoid the shocks (e.g., by jumping across a barrier to another part of its cage), it fails to do so. This behavior is in marked contrast with that of naive animals, who are able to avoid the shock after a few trials. The previously conditioned animal has learned that it is helpless, though this is not now in fact the case (Overmier & Seligman, 1967). A number of investigators have examined this paradigm in the context of more familiar situations. Human subjects put in situations in which they cannot control rewards or aversive experiences tend to learn less well and in general perform more poorly than subjects who can control (or think they can control) their environment—even when the extent of aversive or pleasant input is identical across all groups (Fosco & Geer,1971; Langer, 1979; Thornton & Jacobs,1971).

Since the initial aversive-stimulus work in this area, some important conceptual refinements have been made that extend the applicability of the learned-helplessness paradigm to wider areas, including cognitive functioning in the elderly. The message of loss of control or incompetence need not be transmitted by shocks or loud noises. Rather, the same results can be found when helplessness is inferred by the subject from subtle environmental cues, such as being labeled as "assistant" rather than "boss" (Langer & Benevento,1978).

Of particular relevance to the elderly in this connection is the set of labels and expectations that are often attached to old people in an "ageist" society (Butler, 1975; Rodin & Langer, 1980) that they are inept, "over the hill," ineffectual. To what extent might these expectations affect performance on cognitive tasks? We cannot know for certain, but the data from other fields are intriguing. Of particular interest are the experiments of Rosenthal and Jacobsen (1966) in which school children identified to their teachers as slow learners did in fact perform more poorly even though their assignment to that label was random. There is no reason to assume that this effect would not also be seen among the elderly. Elderly who are put in nursing homes suffer from an even more intense stigmatization (Goffman, 1963). This is all the more debilitating when institutionalization is not the result primarily of physical illness but is rather the result of inadequate availability of sheltered housing, home help, or other community-based supports for the frail elderly (Avorn, 1982).

Nursing homes are generally organized according to a medical model (Kane & Kane, 1978) and thus encourage patients to take on the often passive characteristics of the sick role (Parsons, 1951). Elders are helped to perform various life-sustaining activities of daily living, many of which they could not do for themselves. However, the hospital-like orientation of the nursing home and the drive for quick, efficient "processing" of patients through baths, dressing, meals, and so forth often result in the residents' having activities done for (or to) them that, with more time, they might have done for themselves (Avorn & Langer, 1982). The extent to which this can depress performance on cognitive tasks is a critical question for gerontologists.

To determine how such helping behavior might induce a performance decrement, we conducted a randomized trial in a long-term care facility (Avorn & Langer, 1982). A simple 10 piece jigsaw puzzle was designed to measure psychomotor skills similar to those required in daily life. Seventy-two elderly nursing home residents were randomly assigned to three groups. The "helped" group was actively assisted by an experimenter to complete the puzzles during four sessions; the "encouraged only" group met for an equal number of sessions but were instead urged to do the puzzle themselves. A "no contact" group was tested before and after the training sessions but had no intervention.

Competence (speed, accuracy) of puzzle performance was measured by blind raters for all groups. Consistently, "helped" subjects performed less well on posttest than did "encouraged only" subjects. Further, "helped subjects" also performed less well than the "no contact" group, although all groups were equivalent at pretest. While "helped" subjects showed a performance decrement from pretest to posttest, the other groups improved. Other posttest measures, such as self-confidence and self-esteem, were also markedly lower in "helped" compared to "encouraged" groups.

These findings suggest that helping institutionalized elderly patients at simple pyschomotor tasks can significantly reduce their ability to perform such tasks. The effect involves more than lack of practice, since the decrement was not seen in the "no contact" group. Our findings are complementary with earlier work (Langer & Rodin, 1976; Rodin & Langer, 1977) which indicated that enhancing the sense of control experienced by institutionalized elderly can result in improvements in their mental health and level of functioning (see also Langer & Avorn, 1982).

## *The Problem of Ecological Validity*

The congruence of laboratory-based tests of cognition with the real world inhabited by elderly subjects has two important aspects. First is the question of the potential handicap imposed by tasks for which younger subjects (such as undergraduates) are well practiced (and, indeed, selected) but which older subjects rarely confront in this form: paired-associate learning, digit span, and the like. This objection questions the *validity* of findings drawn from such culturally biased testing. A separate objection does not address validity but instead questions the *relevance* of many laboratory-based findings to the day-to-day mental functioning of people in the world. According to this view, even if it is true that old people are inherently and reliably deficient in memorizing nonsense syllables or copying abstract images presented to them, does this really tell us much of use about their ability to function in normal day-to-day situations? After all, as Baltes and Brim (1979) point out, many intelligence tests used today to study performance differences between old and young people were initially developed for school children or college students, to predict their success in the classroom. We have no *a priori* reason to expect these tests to be fair or relevant to the elderly. The issue of ecological validity has been addressed cogently by Hartley, Harker, and Walsh (1980).

The twin questions of validity and relevance of psychometric tests have recently been in the spotlight in connection with their use in tracking students of various cultural and socioeconomic backgrounds. It is appropriate that the same hard questions of bias and irrelevance in such tests be raised for another minority group, the elderly.

There is still another side to the complex issue of real-world relevance, and that deals with the orientation of the subject. It is clear that motivation and attention are key determinants of performance on virtually all tests of cognitive function. The elderly subject is likely to be different on these two dimensions from his or her younger counterpart. The need to prove oneself or succeed in a university-based testing situation may well diminish (and quite appropriately) with advancing age. Loss of the desire to "go that extra mile" to attend to and succeed at a task (even one that is not irrelevant, but especially one that is) may well be a common concomitant of aging—although whether this is the result of the social factors discussed earlier or a normal adaptive part of the human life span is an open question. Here, again, the prevalence of depression can be expected to add further to this effect. Despite some attempts to control for motivation and attention, a great deal of further work is necessary on this issue. Until then, it will be impossible to know whether elderly subjects do less well on a particular task because they can not do any better or because they do not care to do any better.

## Conclusions

The preceding pages have presented a brief overview of the ways in which biological and social factors may perturb the measurement of cognitive performance in the elderly. These observations remind us of the need for a comprehensive biopsychosocial assessment of all forces impinging on cognition in the elderly, whether in the laboratory or in clinical situations. The concern here ranges beyond appropriateness of methodology, although that is of critical importance. Beyond this is the larger question of how we conceptualize the relation between aging and intellectual function. For it is our view of this that will shape future research and, on a larger scale, will help to determine the way aging is viewed by policymakers, practitioners, and the elderly themselves.

As Giambra and Arenberg (1980) point out, what methodology one uses in this field is determined in large measure by theoretical schemata currently in favor. As a corollary, investigators trying to document the decrepitude of the elderly will come to use tools that bolster their view most effectively, as will those who hold the opposite point of view. But the arrow is double-headed. Findings derived from particular methodologies (such as those based on psychometric-style intelligence testing) in turn help to shape the theoretical underpinnings of the field itself and *could* create a cycle in which, in the worst outcome, we might come to know more and more about things that meant less and less.

Beyond the fields of psychology and gerontology themselves, the study of cognitive function in the elderly has fallout in the wider world as well. The social construction of reality, in which our ideas about the aged shape our observations of them and ultimately our policies for them, has been well summarized by Estes (1980). For example, disengagement theory in social gerontology (Cumming & Henry, 1961) held that it is normal and adaptive for elderly people to withdraw from the world of activities and social relations that characterize youth and midddle age and for such withdrawal to be reciprocated. This view, based on observations of people who in many cases were facing or had experienced forced retirement, in turn provided intellectual authority for many of the programs from which it took its ideological lead. Although this model has now fallen from favor, we must be careful not to replace it with others that confuse the results of medical or social pathology with those of senescence itself.

# References


Arie, J. Dementia in the elderly: Diagnosis and assessment. In *Medicine in Old age*. London: British Medical Association, 1974.

Avorn, J. The social context of geriatric practice. In J. Rowe & R. Besdine (Eds.), *Health and disease in old age*. Boston: Little Brown 1982.

Avorn, J., & Langer E. Induced disability in nursing home patients: A controlled trial. *Journal of the American Geriatrics Society*, 1982, *30*, 397–400.

Avorn, J., Griffin K., & Costa, M. Knowledge of medications in elderly outpatients: Effect of psychoactive drugs. *Clinical Research*, 1981, *29*, 254a.

Baltes, P. B. & Brim, O. G. (Eds.). *Life-span development and behavior*. New York: Academic Press, 1979.

Bond, K. Retirement history study's first four years: Work, health, and living arrangements. *Social Security Bulletin*. Department of Health, Education, & Welfare. Washington, D.C.: 1976.

Butler, R. N. *Why Survive? Being old in America*. New York: Harper & Row, 1975.

Cumming, E., & Henry, W. E.: *Growing old: The process of disengagement*. New York: Basic Books, 1961.

Eisdorfer, C., & Fann, W. E. (Eds.). *Psychopharmacology and aging*. New York: Plenum Press, 1973.

Engel, G. L. The need for a new medical model: A challenge for biomedicine. *Science*, 1977, *196*, 129–136.

Estes, C. *The aging enterprise*. San Francisco: Jossey–Bass, 1980.

Feinberg, I., Fein, G., Price, L. J., Jernigan, T. L., & Floyd, T. Methodological and conceptual issues in the study of the brain-behavior relations in the elderly. In L. W. Poon (Ed.), *Aging in the 1980's: Psychological issues*. Washington, D.C.: American Psychological Association, 1980.

Fosco, E., & Geer, J. Effects of gaining control over aversive stimuli after differing amounts of no control. *Psychological Reports*, 1971, *29*, 1153–1154.

Giambra, L. M., & Arenberg, D. Problem solving, concept learning, and aging. In L. W. Poon (Ed.), *Aging in the 1980's: Psychological issues*. Washington, D.C.: American Psychological Association, 1980.

Goffman, E. *Stigma: Notes on the management of spoiled identity*. Englewood Cliffs, N.J.: Prentice–Hall, 1963.

Hartley, J. T., Harker, J. O., & Walsh, D. A. Contemporary issues and new directions in adult development of learning and memory. In L. W. Poon (Ed.), *Aging in the 1980's: Psychological issues*. Washington, D.C.: American Psychological Association, 1980.

Hughes, C. P. The differential diagnosis of dementia in the senium. In K. Nandy (Ed.), *Senile dementia: A biomedical approach*. New York: Elsevier/North Holland, 1978.

Kane, R. L., & Kane, R. A. Care of the aged: Old problems in need of new solutions. *Science*, 1978, *200*, 913–919.

Kay, D. W. K. Epidemiological aspects of organic brain disease in the aged. In C. M. Gaitz (Ed.) *Aging and the brain*. New York: Plenum Press, 1972.

Kayne, R. C. (Ed.), *Drugs and the elderly*. Los Angeles: University of Southern California Press, 1978.

Langer, E. The illusion of incompetence. In L. Perlmuter & R. Monty (Eds.), *Choice and perceived control*. Hillsdale, N.J.: Lawrence Erlbaum, 1979.

Langer, E., & Avorn, J. Impact of the psychosocial environment of the elderly on behavioral and health outcomes. In R. Chellis & J. Seagle (Eds.), *Congregate housing for older people*. Lexington, Mass.: D.C. Heath, 1982.

Langer, E., & Benevento, A. Self-induced dependence. *Journal of Personality and Social Psychology*, 1978, *36*, 886–893.

Langer, E., & Rodin J. The effects of enhanced personal responsibility for the aged: A field experiment in an institutional setting. *Journal of Personality and Social Psychology*, 1976, *34*, 191–198.

Langer, E., Blank, A., & Chanowtiz, B. The mindlessness of ostensibly thoughtful action: The role of placebic information in interpersonal interaction. *Journal of Personality and Social Psychology*, 1978, *36*, 635–642.

Overmier, J. B., & Seligman, M. Effects of inescapable shock upon subsequent escape and avoidance learning. *Journal of Comparative and Physiological Psychology*, 1967, *63*, 23–33.

Parsons, T. Social structure and dynamic process: The case of modern medical practice. In *The Social System*. New York: The Free Press, 1951.

Petersen, D. M., Whittington, F. J., & Payne, B. P.: *Drugs and the elderly: Social and pharmacological issues*. Springfield, Ill.: Charles C Thomas, 1979.

Rodin J., & Langer, E. Long-term effects of a control-relevant intervention among the institutionalized aged. *Journal of Personality and Social Psychology*, 1977, *35*, 897–902.

Rodin, J., & Langer, E. Aging labels: The decline of control and the fall of self-esteem. *Journal of Social Issues, 1980, 36*, 12–29.

Rosenthal, R., & Jacobson, L. *Pygmalion in the classroom*. New York: Holt, Rinehart & Winston, 1968.

Rowe, J. W. & Besdine, R. *Health and disease in old age*. Boston: Little, Brown, 1982.

Rowe, J. W., Tobin, J. D., Andres, R. A., Norris, A., & Shock, N. W. The effect of age on creatinine clearance in men. *Journal of Gerontology*, 1976, *31*, 155–163.

Schaie, D. W., & Labouvie-Vief, G. Generational versus ontogenetic components of change in adult cognitive behavior: A fourteen-year cross-sequential study. *Developmental psychology*, 1974, *10*, 305–320.

Seligman, M. *Helplessness: On depression, development, and death*. San Francisco: W. H. Freeman, 1975.

Sheldon, A., McKewan, P. S., & Byser, C. P. *Retirement: Patterns and predictions*. National Institute of Mental Health, DHEW publication No. ADM 74–79. Washington, D.C.: U.S. Government Printing Office, 1975.

Shock, N. W. Age changes in physical functions in the total animal. In B. Strehler (Ed.), *The biology of aging*. Washington, D.C.: AIBS, 1960.

Streib, G. F., & Schneider, C. J. *Retirement in American society in fact and process*. Ithaca, N.Y.: Cornell University Press, 1971.

Thornton, J. W., & Jacobs, P. D. Learned helplessness in human subjects. *Journal of Experimental Psychology*, 1971, *87*, 369–372.

CHAPTER 18

# Memory Functioning in Late Adulthood

Irene M. Hulicka

*Faculty of Natural and Social Sciences*
*State University College at Buffalo*
*Buffalo, New York*

## Introduction

This chapter is primarily about people rather than about research findings. I chose a humanistic rather than a rigorous scientific approach to the memory functioning of older people for three reasons. The first is my reaction to two new scholarly books on human memory. Although both authors dealt adequately with representative samples of theoretical and research literature, neither paid the slightest attention to the individuals in whom the processes presumably occur; indeed, the authors conveyed the impression that efficiency of processing material from stimulus input with losses along the way to response output is more dependent on factors such as temporal sequencing and experimenter instructions than on the characteristics of the individuals through and presumably by whom the material is processed. Perhaps because of justified emphasis on scientific rigor, scientists may have inadvertently relegated the person, without whom there could be no memory, to secondary or even tertiary importance.

The second reason for taking a humanistic approach is the contention that scientific gerontologists might ask meaningful new questions and provide better tests for good hypotheses if they spent more time observing and interacting with elderly people in their natural environments. The third reason is that despite familiarity with much of the research and theoretical literature on memory and aging, there is a great deal that I do not know, and that indeed is probably not known by any scientist or academician about the memory functioning of old people and about the problems they encounter when memory deficits develop. For example, how do memory problems affect meeting the demands of life in a nonlaboratory environment? What use do old people make of memory? What constraints on their choice of activities are created by memory deficits? What strategies are used to adapt to memory impairment? For theoretical as well as practical reasons, it may be advantageous to combine information collected painstakingly in the laboratory with new information about memory functioning and about how older people anticipate, assess, adapt to, and are affected by real or attributed memory problems.

## Five Problems of Potential Significance

### *Fear of Memory Impairment*

Questions might be raised about the prevalence and intensity of fear of memory impairment, and when such fear exists, whether and how it affects behavior, general psychological well-being, and perhaps even memory itself. If anxiety can affect performance on laboratory tasks of little personal significance, it seems likely that fear of memory impairment could affect psychological well-being and general efficiency. Although a systematic record has not been kept, during the past year at least 14 of my middle-aged acquaintances have commented on fear of eventual memory impairment, and some mentioned plans for the future, influenced by fear of memory loss.

Many years ago, a middle-aged lady with a very sharp memory told me that she would often wake up during the night in cold terror beset by the dread of being a "lost soul," confused and helpless because of memory problems. Her worst fears were justified. By age 80 she lived in a confused jungle in which she did not know where she lived, nor that her children were her children. Ironically, she was consistently aware of her memory problems and viewed her memory as the tragedy of her life. Immediately prior to an accidental fall, she wrote and mailed a letter which described fairly accurately her gardening activities and the activities of, but not her relationship to, household members. She wrote, "I am keeping pretty well except that my memory is so bad. I would rather be dead than to have lost my memory. Perhaps if I settle down to write I will be able to straighten things out in my mind. It will be my birthday in less than three weeks. I will be 84, but I don't want to live long. It is too terrible with such a bad memory." She died three days later.

A number of questions are worthy of attention. Is intense fear of memory loss, such as this lady experienced, common? What are the characteristics and backgrounds of people who do and do not experience fear? What are the antecedents and consequences of fear of memory loss? How valid is the assumption of at least some professionals that the person with severe memory loss is too out of contact to be aware of the loss and confusion, and hence that memory loss, unlike cancer, for example, is a relatively painless affliction? Is memory loss ordinarily accompanied by flat affect or by intense emotional suffering such as this lady experienced?

Peculiarly, this lady's correspondence typically reflected better contact with reality than her conversation did, although occasionally the first half of a letter would be to one person and the second half to another. Perhaps her better retention of letter-writing than conversational skills was relatively unique, or may be characteristic only of habitual letter writers. She may have performed fairly well in writing letters because she had control over the content of her communications, did not have to contend with competing demands and stimuli, and could work at her own speed. Her comment about straightening things out in her mind suggests that letter writing might have been a self-selected strategy for reducing confusion.

## *The Meaning and/or Accuracy of Self-Assessment of Memory Problems*

The scientific literature is in essential agreement that elderly adults perform less well on tasks involving memory than young adults do. Consistent with the results of laboratory research, a very common complaint of elderly persons is "My memory is not as good as it used to be." Lowenthal and her colleagues (1967) reported that 66% of community-dwelling people over age 75 evaluated their memory ability negatively. However, as others have pointed out (e.g., Poon, Fozard, & Treat, 1978) older people's complaints about memory problems tend to be rather global. Perhaps because of little evidence of interest on the part of listeners, the precise nature of memory problems and conditions under which they occur are usually not specified or, if specified, have received little attention in the scientific literature. Until quite recently, scientific interest in self-assessment of memory functioning has typically been limited to one or two general questions incorporated into a questionnaire on a variety of other topics (e.g., Lowenthal *et al.*, 1967) or a few general questions which are asked in clinical settings.

However, during the past five years there has been increasing awareness of the potential value of attending more closely to the nature of complaints about memory problems and relationships between complaints and performance on laboratory tests of memory. For example, Kahn, Zarit, Hilbert, and Niederehe (1975) asked subjects not only to respond on a five-point scale to the general question, "Do you have trouble with your memory?" but also to describe memory problems relative to changes in recent and remote memory. Their results indicated that although self-assessment was not related to performance scores on objective tests of memory, the number of complaints was associated with score on a measure of depression. Intuitively, it seems logical to predict that people who believe their memory to be deteriorating would feel depressed. However, Kahn and Miller (1978) suggested that memory complaints are symptoms of depression. More information about relationships among complaints, actual memory problems, and depression is needed before firm conclusions are offered about the existence and direction of cause-and-effect relationships. Also needed is information about the nature and seriousness of complaints in relation to efficiency of handling everyday problems and to performance on laboratory and clinical tests of memory.

Poon, Fozard, and Treat (1978) recommended the development of a systematic diagnostic instrument to help an individual articulate his memory complaints. However, they suggested that even given an instrument with specific and concrete examples which tap various dimensions of memory to aid the individual in rank-ordering his memory problems, it is improbable that the individual would be able to evaluate his own memory adequately. The reasons for the pessimism were not given.

Recognizing the need for information about self-assessment of memory problems, Czaja and I have collected some fairly extensive pilot data (see Acknowledgments). The self-assessment of memory questionnaire included: (1) evaluation of present memory for 17 categories of data, for example, appointments, dates, road directions, names of old and new acquaintances, how to do things, responsibilities, and cultural information, by circling excellent, very good, good, fair, or poor, and comparison of present memory for such events to memory 10 years ago by circling better, same, or worse; (2) whether during the past year difficulty had been encountered at least twice in remembering any of 16 items such as events that happened five or more years ago, appointments, where something was put, what someone had said, what one was going to say oneself, something that should be done, and how to do something; (3) overall evaluation of memory efficiency; (4) comparison of overall memory efficiency to one's own memory 5 and 10 years ago, and to that of the perceived average person, the average young adult, and the average like-aged person; (5) signs of memory problems that had been noted, for example, memory for two or more events running together, memory for past events fuzzier and less complete, taking longer to remember, and more effort required to remember. Additional items were included to obtain information about emotional reactions to memory problems, inconveniences resulting from memory problems, relative importance of items remembered and not remembered, strategies used to bolster memory, and circumstances under which difficulty in remembering would be most or least likely. To compare self-assessed memory to formal measures of memory, the logical memory and digit span tests from the Wechsler Memory Scale, and a free recall and a paired associate task of names and occupations were also administered.

*Table 1. Age Distribution in the Pilot Study*

| | Mean age | Range | *N* |
|---|---|---|---|
| Young | 25 | 18–35 | 17 |
| Young-middle | 44 | 36–50 | 20 |
| Middle | 57 | 51–65 | 21 |
| Young-old | 70 | 66–75 | 17 |
| Old-old | 82 | 76–90 | 13 |

The age distribution of the 88 community-dwelling people who participated in the pilot study is summarized in Table 1. Mean ages are not absolutely accurate because subjects were asked to circle a 5 year age range rather than to indicate exact age. Use of the mid-point of a 5-year age span probably resulted in a slight underestimation of correlations between measures.

The results for the formal measures of memory were routine. Age correlated significantly with the free recall ($N = -.35$) and paired associate ($N = -.27$) scores but not with the logical memory ($r = .02$) and digit span ($r = .08$) scores.

Figure 1 summarizes the numerical results of the self-assessment of memory measure and correlations of self-assessed memory score with scores on the formal measures of memory. The self-assessed memory score correlated significantly but not strongly with three of the four formal memory tests: logical memory, digit span, and free recall. The absence of a significant correlation

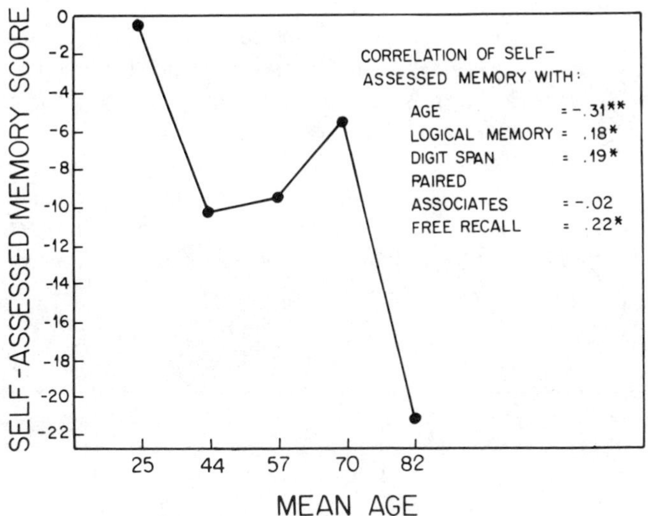


Fig. 1. Self-assessed memory score for five age groups.

between self-assessed memory score and the paired associate task perhaps supports the pessisism of Poon *et al.* (1978) about self-assessment; the paired associate task involved names, and many respondents commented on their inability to remember names.

There was a significant negative correlation between age and self-assessed memory score. Groups with mean ages of 44 and 57 had substantially lower self-assessed mean memory scores than the group with a mean age of 25. Peculiarly, the young-old group with a mean age of 70 had a somewhat higher mean self-assessment score than the groups aged 44 and 57; perhaps people in this age group were counting their blessings. The oldest group with a mean age of 82 presented by far the most negative self-evaluation of memory functioning. Moreover, members of this group tended to provide the most detailed supplementary information about their memory problems. Self-assessed scores ranged in magnitude from +30 to −38, and within each age group there was considerable variability. The distribution of scores by quartiles, presented in Table 2, indicates that in each age group one or more members had high or low self-assessment scores. Forty-one percent of the young and also the young-old subjects had scores in the first quartile in comparison to only 8% of the very old group. Conversely, only 6% of the scores of the young group were in the fourth quartile, in contrast to 62% of the scores of the oldest group. These data suggest that many people note subjective evidence for memory decline rather early in middle age and that by very late adulthood the tendency is much more common.

Of course, legitimate questions could be raised about the reliability and validity of the self-assessed memory scores; for example, subjects were asked to remember if they had had problems remembering categories of items within the past year. It could be argued that the low correlations between the self-assessed memory scores in the formal tests of memory reflect negatively on the validity of the self-assessed scores. However, that argument could also be reversed. Possibly the two types of instruments tap different aspects of memory and neither type provides a very accurate measure of the overall adequacy of memory functioning. Very recently, Zelinski, Gilewski, and Thompson (1980), using a self-assessment instrument which, like the one Czaja and I used, helped the respondent to define situations in which memory problems occur, concluded that older adults are much better at defining problems than was previously believed.

*Table 2. Distribution of Self-Assessed Memory Scores by Age*

| | Y(25) | Y-M(44) | M(57) | Y-O(70) | O-O(82) |
|---|---|---|---|---|---|
| 1st quartile | 41% | 25% | 19% | 41% | 8% |
| Middle quartiles | 53% | 45% | 57% | 35% | 31% |
| 4th quartile | 6% | 30% | 23% | 23% | 62% |

Whether self-assessment can or does provide a reasonable estimate of adequacy of memory functioning, precise information about self-perceived memory strengths and weaknesses, quirks, and deterioration might be of considerable scientific value and at least as useful as the information derived from formal measures for guiding the design of memory improvement intervention programs. Further, just as fear, whether justified or not in terms of real danger, can affect behavior, so also concern about memory functioning, whether justified or not in terms of demonstrated deterioration, might affect behavior in significant ways. Peculiarly, virtually no attention has bcen devoted to objective or external assessment of memory functioning in normal everyday situations. True, relatives often report that "mother's memory is slipping" or "mother is so forgetful." However, generally, these reports are no more precise than the self-report that "my memory is bad." Methods for external observers to record instances of apparent memory problems could be developed, and such records, although they could not provide a comprehensive nor completely valid assessment of another person's memory functioning, could provide clues about the frequency and nature of memory problems and allow for comparisons between observed memory performance and scores on clinical, laboratory, and self-assessed measures of memory functioning.

## *The Progress of Memory Disability*

It is true that rigorous memory studies have provided information about age differences in sensory, primary and secondary memory, encoding, search time, and retrieval. But what does such information mean to the individual in his or her attempts to cope with the exigencies of life? What symptoms of decreased memory efficiency are noted by the individual or by his or her associates? Is there a relatively universal pattern of afflictions for those who are afflicted? Apart from considerabe data concerning availability of information in relation to the developmental stage at time of acquisition (e.g., Botwinick & Storandt, 1974; Lachman & Lachman, 1980) and time since acquisition (e.g., Bahrick, Bahrick, & Wittlinger, 1975), and some data which support Freud's propositions about motivational selectivity in remembering, what is known about the *content* of memories that cease to be available?

The first signs of memory loss that were clearly obvious to herself and to others in the lady who was terrified about the possibility of losing her memory was the nonavailability of relatively inconsequential information such as the birthdates of friends and the names of the spouses of her neighbors' children, while important information necessary for fulfilling her many family and work responsibilities was still available. People of all ages in our pilot study also indicated that they were more likely to have trouble remembering unimportant than important things. I used to attempt to reassure the fearful lady by suggesting that as her energy declined, she was using her available energy wisely by concentrating on important matters. She liked the explanation.

Consistent with *ad hoc* hypotheses about energy conservation and memory selectivity based on importance are comments by Rabbit (1977): "The question of 'energy,' that is, the role of motivating factors in decrement with age, has been almost totally neglected in laboratory experiments but recurs forcefully whenever real life problems are examined." He pointed out that a research strategy which is used too seldom is to ask intelligent older people how they carry out activities and as an example of valuable research described a study in which Birren (1969) asked elderly, successful professionals to comment on their perceptions of changes in methods of coping with demands made of them. Birren's old subjects showed "recognition of the necessity for conserving time and resources of energy ('conservation of the individual') and the ability to distinguish between critical and extraneous tasks" (p. 623).

Although one must be aware of the danger of generalizing from one set of limited observations, it might be of interest to relate observations about the fearful lady's initial selective memory loss to research on attention to irrelevant stimuli and to theoretical propositions such as the effortful and automatic processing distinction. The observed pattern of memory loss is not consistent with research findings that with increased age there is a decrease in ability to ignore irrelevant stimuli (Rabbitt, 1965) and to *discriminate* relevant from irrelevant stimuli (Wright & Elias, 1979). Of course, the comparison might not be appropriate in that mental operations involved in memory and visual search tasks are not identical, and further, quite possibly laboratory tasks are of lower relevance to individuals than personal memory tasks are. Hasher and Zacks (1979) suggested that the pattern of age-associated decrement in performance depends on the degree to which effortful processing is required. Hoyer and Plude (1980) discussed the effortful-automatic processing distinction in terms of degree of practice and pointed out that well-practiced skills require no mental effort or concentration and hence can be performed effortlessly or automatically. In the progress of the lady's memory loss, it is true that well-practiced skills such as skills used for gardening and letter writing were retained reasonably well, long after serious symptoms of memory impairment were obvious to associates. Of greater interest than her ability to perform such activities is the fact that she *remembered* to perform them, that is, she remembered to order seeds, pick the strawberries, transplant the tomatoes, and do the laundry and the mending. The skills used in transplanting might require automatic or effortless mental processing, but it is doubful whether remembering to do the transplanting could be described as automatic. Probably her memory was supported, and hence the effort required was reduced, by the presence of external cues such as seasonal changes, the migration of birds, the size of the plants, the routines of family members, and the delivery of mail. The development of or increase in mental confusion and forgetfulness frequently observed in newly institutionalized elderly patients is probably due, in part, to a reduction in the number of supportive external cues—functioning in a new environment typically requires more energy or effort at any age.

Perhaps in order to expand knowledge about the intricacies and sequencing of memory disabilities in relation to age we should broaden our approaches to the study of memory. Greater effort should be directed toward relating laboratory findings to behavior in naturalistic settings, and similarly observation of behavior in naturalistic settings should be used as a guide to hypotheses to be investigated in the laboratory. Increased attention to systematic observations of the non-laboratory behavior of and introspective reports from young, middle-aged, and older adults, including those who do not manifest or complain about decrements in memory efficiency, could provide preliminary information pertinent to questions such as: What is the nature and form of initially perceived memory decrements, and how do the perceived decrements affect the individual's competence to manage personal affairs? Are there individual differences depending on disease, personality, life events, or realistic demands, or is there a fairly universal pattern for the sequence of memory loss? Are childhood memories ordinarily accessible long after severe impairment for later life memories? If and when the individual engages in life review, are there events of recognized importance for the review process which are not accessible? If so, how does the nonavailability of such memories affect emotional satisfaction with the review process? Incidentally, nonsystematic observations suggest that an individual heavily engaged in life review will exert considerable effort to obtain information that memory indicates exists but cannot provide. Such attempts to retrieve information, including use of external sources, might represent meaningful examples of effortful processing.

## *The Subjective Experience of Memory Impairment and the Strategies Employed*

In response to our questionnaire item about reactions to difficulty in remembering, age groups did not differ in choice of adjectives which were checked, but older people tended to check more adjectives, that is, several relating to fear, humiliation, frustration, worry, embarrassment, anxiety, and uneasiness, in contrast to just one or two by younger people.

An 83-year-old man with few overtly observable signs of memory impairment talked of the utter confusion and terror that he experiences occasionally when, to use his own words, "my memory goes blank." He said, for example, that sometimes after shopping, he does not know where he is, nor even where he should be going. When asked how he ordinarily handles the problem, he said that the first time it happened he wandered aimlessly with great uneasiness, then saw a bus and knew that it was his bus. Once on the bus, he came to himself and his fear subsided. He commented that since then, when he has the lost feeling, he *remembers* to look for a bus stop with the hope that when the right bus comes, he will recognize it. Further, he generalized from this experience, in that whenever he has a serious memory gap he tries to find something familiar, and as he said, "so far it has worked."

A lady with extensive memory impairment attempted at my request to describe the experience of a severe memory lapse. She used the analogy of the terror of being lost in a big dark space, with the occasional elusive glimmer of light from a faint memory that she would attempt to reach but seldom could. She said that she seemed to be unable to escape from the darkness by her own efforts—escape might involve a change in the situation, such as a request from her husband which would cause what put her into darkness to lose significance, or on other occasions, someone would provide the information which had eluded her, an experience which she described as being taken by the arm and led to the light where she could remember well enough to understand. Parenthetically, although her memory impariment was dreadful, she retained a good vocabulary; and on those few occasions that she was able to remember or was given the essential elements of a situation, she reasoned well.

Rabbitt (1977) commented:

> In view of the deterioration of memory and perceptual motor performance with advanced age the right kind of question may well be not "why are old people so bad at cognitive tasks" but rather "how, in spite of growing disabilities, do old people preserve such relatively good performance? (p. 623)

Our elderly questionnaire respondents indicated that they do the expected things such as using lists and notes, asking others to remind them, practicing, and going over in their minds things associated with the items to be remembered. Clearly, the remarkable self-sufficiency that some elderly people maintain despite objectively demonstrable cognitive deterioration cannot be explained fully by utilization of such mundane props as list-making. Rabbitt (1977), using data from a study by Birren (1969), concluded that older people are not simply passive victims of cognitive degeneration of which they are helplessly unaware. On the contrary, he argued, in comparison to younger people, older people tend to conserve and exploit their intellectual resources and to have a more subtle perception of points at which the complexities of decisions exceed their capacities and thereby to avoid unnecessary blunders. Very important is Rabbitt's contention that we shall miss the point if we attend only to decrements in performance with age without also studying adaptations to decrements in performance.

Birren's (1969) elderly subjects recognized the need for advice. As we noted earlier, one elderly person tried to adapt to memory lapses by directing himself to a familiar situation, and another "tried to straighten things out" by writing letters. Quite possibly conservation of time and energy and discrimination between critical and extraneous tasks are among the adaptive strategies used by older people. A careful study of self-selected adaptive strategies, in addition to enhancing our understanding of life-span cognitive changes, might significantly enrich cognitive skills training intervention programs.

### *Potential Effects of Self-Perceived and Attributed Memory Problems on Self-Concept and on Interpretations of Behavior*

Almost certainly, adequacy of memory functioning is an important determinant of the self-concept of older people. In recent social contacts with 17 people over the age of 80, I noted that 13 spontaneously commented on their memory functioning, with 6 complaining about poor memory and 7 expressing gratitude for a good memory.

Further, nonsystematic observations suggest that persons with adequate memories guard themselves zealously against slurs on their memory. For example, at a nursing home I found a 92-year-old host conversing with a grandson and his girlfriend. Because he was reminiscing about the childhood escapades of a granddaughter who visited him occasionally, I was aware that he had misidentified the young woman as his granddaughter, and assumed the young man was her friend. Subsequent information indicated that although the grandson, who had reached adulthood since his last visit, had identified himself, the grandfather, who had a hearing impairment and had been asleep when the company arrived unexpectedly, had not registered the information correctly. The mistake was a reasonable one—the girlfriend and granddaughter were of approximately the same age, size, and coloring and both called him grandpa. When the grandfather realized his mistake, he was terribly embarrassed. He requested that a message be sent to the grandson to explain the error—and six months later checked to confirm that it had been sent and received. In addition to a desire to absolve himself of an apparent discourtesy, he clearly did not want to be viewed as a confused old man.

Also of interest would be the study of defense mechanisms used by persons with severe memory impairments. An elderly lady asked who was the mother of her own daughter. In response to the question "Who do you think her mother is?" she replied tartly, "I asked my question first." Although she was acutely aware of her memory impairment she may have wanted momentary respite from the awareness.

Attention should be directed to potential consequences of the well-known tendency for professionals and family members to attribute behavioral deficits or peculiarities of the elderly to memory or other cognitive impairments. The following example is all too typical. An otherwise excellent meal served by a 78-year-old lady was marred by a salad dressing in which Chlorox had been used instead of vinegar. Concerned relatives attributed the error to poor memory and general intellectual decline and conferred about the need to place her in a home as a potential danger to herself and others. Actually, examination of background events indicated that her error had involved the reasonable use of a well-established habit, and the only relevant impairment was olfactory not cognitive. Various houseguests had assisted with the housework. Someone had erroneously put the chlorox in the cupboard when the vinegar was kept. The two containers were of approximately the same size, shape, and color. She had reached into the cupboard for the vinegar, had not looked at the label and had not tasted the concoction, which she had made well hundreds of time (an example of automatic processing).

Subsequently, some of the people who had shared the Chlorox incident were guests in another home. A young woman asked the hostess for hair spray and was told that there was none. A few minutes later she laughingly reported that she had found in the bathroom cabinet just what whe was looking for, an aerosol can of the right size and shape, and had drenched her hair with Lysol. Though her error was less reasonable than that of the elderly lady, her audience merely twitted her about absentmindedness. No one suggested that she be institutionalized because of cognitive impairment.

As social scientists, we might do well to examine the extent and frequency of inappropriate treatment and mistreatment of elderly people because of the ease of drawing on cognitive decline as an explanation. Do scientists bear any responsibility for the existence of a double standard and for mitigating its effects? Attention to relationships between real, attributed, or self-assessed memory problems and depression should be continued, along with new attention to possible relationships between memory problems and self-concept, happiness, efforts to maintain or relinquish autonomy, adventuresomeness and opportunities for adventuresomeness.

## Content of Memories in Old Age: Case Studies

The remainder of the chapter will be used to present case studies examining the content of topics introduced spontaneously by five elderly people in personal coversations. Although interested in obtaining information about the relative accessibility of early and late memories and preoccupation with life review, I was more interested in what memories are accessible to older people, what memories they draw on in what circumstances, and what use they make of memories in structuring conversation.

Knowledge of the background of the individuals greatly facilitated categorizing the topics which they introduced, particularly by approximate age at time of remembered event. Notes were taken during some of the conversations, and this was apparently perceived as natural because it was known that I was assisting in the preparation of a book on the history of the local community.

However, some of the records were prepared soon after rather than during the conversations and hence are less than perfect because of my fallible memory. Of course, I should have used a tape recorder, but I did not, primarily because of the conversations occurring while I was on vacation and did not have access to one.

## *Case 1*

The topics introduced by this 82-year-old lady (Table A) during several conversations, totalling approximately five hours, support the notion that childhood memories are retained best. She talked a great deal about her childhood and her parents and siblings. Although she could name in order of birth her seven brothers and sisters and most of their spouses, she could name only as many as four of her own nine children, with those named varying from one attempt to another. She requested help to learn the names of her children and their spouses and seemed genuinely pleased when, after considerable practice, she listed them without error. She tended to introduce a topic for which she had an incomplete memory and to ask for the details to be filled in. She invariably expressed appreciation when information was provided. Although she may have been seeking assistance in the life review process, the need for increased clarity or decreased confusion seemed to guide her requests for help.

## *Case 2*

The conversations with the 80-year-old lady (Table B) took place during a period of several hours, the day before she suffered a disabling stroke. Apart from the skimpiness of

**Table A. An 82-Year-Old Lady**

| Content/time of event | Number of topics | Quality and/or content |
|---|---|---|
| To approximately age 16 | 21 | Clear, complex memories |
| Approximately age 16 to 25 | 6 | Clear, complex memories |
| Approximately age 25 to 40 | 3 | Fragmentary memories, with requests for help, e.g., I know I went to Europe but I can't remember who went with me |
| Approximately age 40 to 70 | 3 | Fragmentary memories, with requests for help |
| Approximately age 70 to 82 | 11 | Confused and fragmentary, e.g., correctly remembering a visit with Tom, but believing visit was with brother Tom rather than son Tom |
| Present situation | 12 | Clear, simple, e.g., comments about food, objects in the room, events seen through window |
| Memory | 8 | Clear, complex statements lamenting her loss of memory |

**Table B. An 80-Year-Old Lady**

| Content/time of event | Number of topics | Quality and/or content |
|---|---|---|
| Approximately age 10 | 1 | Clear, complex memories |
| Approximately age 20 to 35 | 6 | Clear, complex memories |
| Approximately age 35 to 80 | 32 | Clear, complex memories most involving mutual acquaintances or mutual experiences |
| Approximately age 65 to 80 | 6 | Clear, complex memories, e.g., death of husband and son, changed living arrangements, a trip |
| Present situation | 7 | Clear, simple, e.g., weather, meal, garden |
| Questions | 14 | Clear questions about my opinion, activities, family, mutual acquaintances, etc. |

childhood memories, the memories which she selected for conversational topics tended to be drawn from the entire life span. There was some evidence of life review and attempt to reach closure; she said for instance, that she had prepared her will two years earlier, mentioning a sentimental bequest to her granddaughter. More interesting was a probable tangential reference to a situation dating back to early adulthood. As a beautiful and lively young woman, she married a quiet, older man who did not accompany her to the community dances, where she was the belle of the ball. As a small child, I had heard fragments of gossip about infatuated men. At age 80, on what was the last fully alive day of her life, she stated, without providing background information, that no matter what people said, she would go to her grave knowing that she had been a good wife and that she had never done anything to be ashamed of. Perhaps she wanted to set the record straight with herself and a confidante.

## *Case 3*

The conversations with the 91-year-old lady (Table C) occurred during an evening spent with her, her daughter and son-in-law, her brother whom she had not seen recently, and two other people. She demonstrated good superficial cover-up for quite severe memory impairment. Her 21 statements about the immediate situation, though appropriate and socially gracious, reflected no knowledge of who her guests were. Although 10 years earlier she had demonstrated excellent memory for childhood events, when her brother

**Table C. A 91-Year-Old Lady**

| Content/time of event | Number of topics | Quality and/or content |
|---|---|---|
| Immediate situation | 21 | Questions or statements about food, clothes, weather, etc. |
| Approximate age 20 to 25 | 7 | Clear complex memories |

sought information from her about their grandparents and events that had occurred when they were children, she was unable to provide even fragmentary information. When the host and a guest played the piano and violin, she commented several times, "They are not doing it right. I should be playing." The piano was yielded to her, and several times she played well a few bars of a mutually selected composition then abruptly switched to her current favorite. Her brother asked that she be given the music for a song popular during their youth. She played it through, then, addressing herself primarily to her brother, articulated clearly, with some encouragement from him, memories of seven incidents when as a young woman she had been the pianist for a dance band. Subsequently, she lapsed into superficial vagueness. Her daughter said that she was more alert during the brief interval after playing the old music than she had been for months. The music, reinforced by the presence of her brother, had apparently served as a stimulus for recall of early adulthood events.

## *Case 4*

The conversations with this lady at age 96 and 100 (Table D) took place in a nursing home and over lunch in a coffee shop. I had not met her previously, but we knew about each other from the mutual friend with whom I visited her. She demonstrated no obvious signs of memory impairment. Her autobiographical reports appeared to be offered more

**Table D. A Lady of Ages 96 and 100**

| Content/time of event | Number of topics | Quality and/or content |
|---|---|---|
| Approximately to age 20 | 8 | Clear, complex memories |
| Approximately age 40 to 70 | 3 | Clear, complex memories |
| Very recent | 5 | Clear statements about activities of past week |
| Statements of historical interest | 4 | Clear, complex memories |
| Questions to me | 8 | Questions reflected memory of what she had heard about me or general interest |
| Questions to her friend | 5 | Questions reflected memory for and interest in her friend's activities |
| Just before her 100th birthday | | |
| Approximately age 45 | 1 | Clear, complex report of a trip and work experience |
| Adulthood | 1 | A somewhat confused anecdote about a nephew which involved some temporal disorientation |
| Previous week | 5 | Clear, simple statements about recent activities |
| Questions to her friend | 4 | Questions reflected memory for and interest in her friend's activities |
| Present situation | 13 | Clear simple statements about flowers that had been given to her, food, etc. |

for my information and entertainment than for life review purposes. The items of historical interest were also offered for my edification, since she knew I was unfamiliar with the geographical area. Her questions to me and to her friend reflected interest and courtesy. She appeared to be more other-oriented than self-centered.

When I visited her a few days before her 100th birthday, this lady was alert and socially gracious. However, she seemed less able than four years earlier to draw on her memory, and in one of the two anecdotes which she told it was apparent that events which she described as recent must have occurred many years previously. She was almost excited about her birthday and the anticipated festivities.

## *Case 5*

This is my most complete report, derived from approximately 150 hours spent over a 3-year period with a man who was 90 when I first began to record the content of the conversational topics introduced by him. Categorizing the content of his conversations was faciliated because his personal history could be subdivided neatly into age and geographical categories as follows:

| | | |
|---|---|---|
| To age 20 | Location I | Europe |
| Age 21–65 | Location II | Farm in western Canada |
| Age 65–89 | Location III | New farm, 500 miles from previous farm |
| Age 90–93 | Location IV | Nursing home in strange city |

About three quarters of the conversations reported were with one or more other persons involved, primarily family members or neighbors from one of the two farm locations. It was possible to categorize fairly well 1,061 topics introduced by him, according to historical periods, general content, and relationship to guest. The record is reasonably complete, except for an underrecording of comments concerning the immediate situation, for example, his current physical condition, meals, the weather, events in the home, and observations through the window. Also, if when several people were present it was not clear who had initiated a topic, it was not recorded.

Table 3 summarizes the distribution of 1,061 topics which he introduced spontaneously by four content categories. Category I, personal memories, constituted 58% of his topics, 25% being memories about himself and 33% being memories about or shared with his guest or guests; Category II, questions reflecting interest in his guest, 30.5%; Category III, comments about the immediate situation, 6.5%; and Category IV, politics, 5%. (Apparently he minimized political topics when I visited him; his knowledge of American as well as Canadian politics exceeded mine.)

The first column of Table 4 summarizes the distribution of the 614 personal memories by historical period. The percentage of personal memories was relatively constant over the development periods of childhood and youth, young adulthood, middle age, and old age. The last column indicates that the percentage of personal memories which were about or shared with his guests rather than about himself alone increased steadily by developmental period, an increase from 23% to 83%. This trend of course makes sense; by age 90 there was almost no one with whom he could share memories of events during

*Table 3. Content of Topics Introduced by a Man Aged 90–93*

| | | N | Percentage |
|---|---|---|---|
| Category I | Personal memories | 614 | 58% |
| | Memories about self | (265) | (25%) |
| | Memories about or shared with guest | (349) | (33%) |
| Category II | Questions reflecting interest in guest | 325 | 30.5% |
| Category III | Immediate situation | 70 | 6.5% |
| Category IV | Politics | 52 | 5% |
| Total | | 1,061 | |

his youth, whereas there were some people with whom he could share memories of events that occurred during his middle and late adulthood.

Table 5 presents the content of his topical choice by category of guests. He had more shared experiences and was generally closer to his sister, offspring, and neighbors from Location II than to neighbors from Location III, most of his grandchildren, and professionals. For the first three categories of guests, proportionately more of his conversational efforts were guest-directed than for the three less familiar categories of guests.

The pattern of this gentleman's choice of conversational topics suggests that his memory for all periods of his life was equally good and that he had no memory fixation on or preference for a single developmental period. Further, his selection of memories for use in conversation appeared to be strongly influenced by his desire to be a courteous host. Possibly also guests served as stimuli for the retrieval and selection of specific memories. One-third of his conversational topics involved memories about his guests or memories of experiences shared with his guests, and almost as many topics were questions about their

*Table 4. Distribution of Memories of a Man Aged 90–93*[a]

| Developmental period | Number of memories | Percentage of personal memories by developmental period | Percentage of memories by developmental period that were self- versus other-oriented: Self-alone | Shared with or about guest |
|---|---|---|---|---|
| Up to age 20 | 138 | 22% | 77% | 23% |
| Approximately 21–40 | 146 | 24% | 55% | 45% |
| Approximately 41–65 | 160 | 26% | 30% | 70% |
| Approximately 66–89 | 123 | 20% | 19% | 81% |
| Approximately 90–93 | 47 | 8% | 17% | 83% |

[a]By developmental period and by memories of self versus shared memories.

*Table 5. Distribution by Category of Guests of Topics Introduced by Man Aged 90–93*

| Category of guest and frequency of association | Total of topics introduced | Self-oriented topics | Other-oriented topics: shared memories and questions | Topics about present situation or politics |
|---|---|---|---|---|
| Sisters: Frequent contacts until age 65, sporadic thereafter | 99 | 14% | 78% | 8% |
| Offspring and spouses: most offspring left home by age 16 but visited at least once a year | 492 | 25% | 65% | 10% |
| Neighbors, Location II: frequent contacts with neighbor families from age 21 to 65, sporadic thereafter | 139 | 20% | 70% | 10% |
| Neighbors, Location III: met after age 65 | 71 | 31% | 56% | 13% |
| Grandchildren: variable | 231 | 31% | 55% | 14% |
| Professionals: associated with nursing home | 29 | 17% | 45% | 38% |

activities, with many of the questions utilizing memories about their interests and families. Further, some of his memories about himself, particularly when his guests were young people, reflected their interest in learning about the "old days."

His choice of conversational topics suggests that perhaps some old people may talk about memories of their childhood and youth, not because memories from other developmental periods are less available, but rather because such memories are judged to be of greater interest to audiences with whom the old person has no shared experiences. A 90-year-old might decide judiciously that his personal experiences of 20 years ago would be of little interest to a relatively new acquaintance, while his personal experiences of 70 years ago, because of relative uniqueness, might be interesting. And many of the very elderly may converse primarily with acquaintances with whom they have few shared experiences.

The reports on topics introduced by five individuals, which at best can be described as a rather casual and partial pilot study, suggest that careful attention to elderly persons' topical choices in conversation might provide information about memory functioning in old age that cannot be easily obtained from laboratory studies alone. For example, laboratory studies on ease of retrieval of information in relation to age at time of acquisition have been fraught with difficulty because of the virtual impossibility of being sure that the respondents had acquired the information. Of the three people in my sample whose memory could be described as good, all introduced memories from the entire life span, and all appeared to be able to draw on memories from any period with equal facility. Only one of the five individuals fitted well the stereotype that elderly people remember childhood events better than events that occur later in life. A variation of the personal conversation approach which might be more efficient and definitive for addressing the question of retrieval in relation to age at acquisition was used by two of my undergraduate students during the past semester. They simply asked their grandmothers to talk about important events in their lives up to the age of 10, from 11 to 20, from 21 to 30, and onward, and recorded the responses on tape. Both grandmothers, in the late 70s, provided completely coherent, very interesting life histories, and neither manifested any evidence of inability to recall significant personal events during any period. Of course, the choice of events to be reported was theirs. Incidentally, the taped life review approach might also yield some interesting information about self-perceived age changes in goals, values and problems.

The observation that a lady whose memory was apparently severly impaired was, under what might have been rather ideal conditions, able to remember a number of events from early adulthood is consistent with the extensive data from laboratory research with respect to the efficacy of retrieval cues (Hultsch, 1975). Quite possibly, lack of cues for recall might account for some of the retrieval difficulties manifested by the elderly in natural settings; this possibility should be investigated and, if supported, evaluated in the design and assessment of memory-training intervention programs. Once an 80-year-old man and his 75-year-old sister gave me permission to read letters they had written to each other when they were young adults. On the basis of the letters, it was possible to prepare 20 questions for each person about items which they had definitely known at one time about trips, friends, celebrations, and family problems. Ten questions were asked of each person individually. The 80-year-old answered four correctly, the 75-year-old three. Subsequently, when they were together for the first time for several years, a conversation was initiated about their early adulthood, and during the conversation, 10 new questions were directed to each of them. Both answered correctly nine of the new questions and all but one of the old questions.

The case study data demonstrate emphatically the importance of memories to very old people. Well over half of the topics introduced by the five elderly people involved memories of past events. By contrast, in reunion conversations among three young men (aged 19 to 21) who had attended high school together and five middle-aged people (aged 50 to 60) who had grown up in the same community, only approximately 10% and 30% of the conversational topics involved long-term memories. Probably memory for past events constitutes an increasingly important component of internally elicited intellectual activity with increased age. It was noticed that the 90- to 93-year-old gentlemen had a tendency to offer self memories more frequently, and sometimes with no obvious external elicitor, if visual problems had prevented him from reading or if he had had fewer guests than usual. Although concentration on remembered events, and particularly self-memories, might reflect intensification of the life review process, it is also possible that memories are used to compensate for a low level of intellectual, social, and perhaps also sensory stimulation and for the fact that there is seldom legitimate reason to attend to plans for anticipated activities. Many elderly people might frequently experience periods of several hours during which memories are their major source of stimulation and entertainment. If, indeed, memory for past events does become increasingly important during very late adulthood, what are the consequences of severe memory impairment to the individual?

In conclusion, it should be emphasized that the thesis of this chapter is not that the experimental laboratory approach should be discarded. Rather it recommends that the scientific study of memory functioning in old age should be enriched, complemented, and supported by careful observational work involving direct interaction with and subjective reports from older adults. Attention should be directed to the nature, meaning, and consequences of memory impairment, to manifestations of memory deficits and strengths, and to adaptive strategies used by older people. Information from naturalistic observation might add valuable new dimensions to the study of hypothetical memory mechanisms and their functions, suggest new hypotheses, and identify new problems worthy of rigorous investigation, and perhaps provide clues for the solution of old problems. Attempts to develop cognitive training programs represent commendable efforts to test and/or apply in real life findings from the laboratory. However, a participant in a cognitive training program might have been all too accurate when she said to the program director, "Lady, your training program deals with your problems rather than mine." Perhaps as scientists we have impeded scientific progress by focusing almost exclusively on problems generated by conflicting theoretical propositions and inconsistent research findings, while devoting little attention to the problems and natural behavior of the categories of people we have sought to understand.

## Acknowledgments

Sincere appreciation is extended to the following people for their assistance in the collection of the self-assessment of memory data: Dr. Susan Whitbourne, Pete Manzi, and David Sperbeck of the University of Rochester; Dr. William Fowler, Kathy Cannon, and Peter Nelson of the Veterans Administration Center, Bath, New York; and Sydney McDougall of Buffalo. Dr. Sara Czaja deserves special acknowledgment as co-investigator.

# References


Bahrick, H. P., Bahrick, P. O., & Wittlinger, R. P. Fifty years of memory for names and faces: A cross-sectional approach. *Journal of Experimental Psychology: General,* 1975, *104,* 54–75.

Birren, J. E. Age and decision strategies. In A. T. Welford & J. E. Birren (Eds.), *Interdisciplinary topics in gerontology* (Vol. 4). Basel: S. Karger, 1969.

Botwinick, J., & Storandt, M. *Memory related functions, and age.* Springfield, Ill.: Charles C Thomas, 1974.

Hasher, L., & Zacks, R. T. Automatic and effortful processes in memory. *Journal of Experimental Psychology: General,* 1979, *108,* 356–388.

Hoyer, W. J., & Plude, D. J. Attentional and perceptual processes in the study of cognitive aging. In L. W. Poon (Ed.), *Aging in the 1980's: Psychological issues.* Washington, D.C.: American Psychological Association, 1980.

Hultsch, D. F. Adult age differences in retrieval: Trace dependent and cue dependent forgetting. *Developmental Psychology,* 1975, *11,* 197–202.

Kahn, R. L., & Miller, N. E., Adaptational factors in memory function in the aged. *Experimental Aging Research,* 1978, *4,* 273–289.

Kahn, R. L., Zarit, S. H., Hilbert, N. M., & Niederehe, M. A. Memory complaint and impairment in the aged: The effect of depression and altered brain function. *Archives of General Psychiatry,* 1975, *32,* 1569–1573.

Lachman J. L., & Lachman, R. Age and the actualization of world knowledge. In L. W. Poon, J. L. Fozard, S. Cermak, D. Arenberg, & L. W. Thompson (Eds.), *New directions in memory and aging: Proceedings of the George A. Talland Memorial Conference.* Hillsdale, N. J.: Lawrence Erlbaum, 1980.

Lowenthal, M. F., Berkman, P. L., Buehler, J. A., Pierce, R. C., Robinson, B. C., & Trier, M. L. *Aging and mental disorder in San Francisco.* San Francisco: Jossey–Bass, 1967.

Poon, L. W. Fozard, J. I., & Treat, N. J.. From clinical and research findings on memory to intervention programs. *Experimental Aging Research,* 1978, *4,* 235–253.

Rabbitt, P. M. An age decrement in the ability to ignore irrelevant information. *Journal of Gerontology,* 1965, *20,* 233–238.

Rabbitt, P. M. Changes in problem solving ability in old age. In J. E. Birren & K. W. Schaie (Eds.), *Handbook of the psychology of aging.* New York: Van Nostrand Reinhold, 1977.

Wright, L. L., & Elias J. W. Age differences in the effects of perceptual noise. *Journal of Gerontology,* 1979, *34,* 704–708.

Zelinski, E. M., Gilewski, M. J., & Thompson, L. W. Do laboratory memory tests relate to everyday remembering and forgetting? In L. W. Poon, J. K. Fozard, L. S. Cermak, D. Arenberg, & L. W. Thompson (Eds.), *New directions in memory and aging. Proceedings of the George A. Talland Memorial Conference.* Hillsdale, N. J.: Lawrence Erlbaum, 1980.

CHAPTER 19

# Plasticity and Enhancement of Intellectual Functioning in Old Age

## Penn State's Adult Development and Enrichment Project (ADEPT)

Paul B. Baltes and Sherry L. Willis

*College of Human Development*
*The Pennsylvania State University*
*University Park, Pennsylvania*

## Objectives of ADEPT

The Penn State Adult Development and Enrichment Project, with the acronym ADEPT, is a basic research program aimed at examining the modifiability of intellectual functioning in later adulthood and old age. Intelligence as referred to in ADEPT research indicates performance on psychometric tests of intelligence rather than process-oriented indices of cognitive functioning. The ADEPT domain of psychometric intelligence is defined primarily by the theory of fluid-crystallized intelligence. Later adulthood and old age covers the age range from approximately 60 to 80 years of age.

The research program consists of a series of interrelated, short-term, longitudinal studies that extend over varying portions of time, from approximately one

ADEPT is supported by a grant from the National Institute on Aging (No. R01 AG00403) to Paul B. Baltes and Sherry L. Willis. Results reported cover data analyses up to 1980.

Paul B. Baltes is now at Max Planck Institute for Human Development and Education, Lentzeallee 94, 1000 Berlin 33, Federal Republic of Germany.

month to close to two years. Throughout, the emphasis is on the study of the range of intraindividual modifiability (plasticity) in psychometric intelligence that can be effected. Training strategies are primarily educational in nature. They include practice and instructional programs that are geared towards the teaching of problem-solving skills relevant for adequate performance on selected intelligence tests. Abilities chosen as targets for intervention center on fluid intelligence. Assessment of training effectiveness considers two dimensions of generalization: training transfer to a broader spectrum of intelligence than is addressed in training, as well as maintenance of training effects over time.[1]

## On Variability and Plasticity in Intellectual Aging

Our general perspectives on the state of the art in life-span and gerontological research on intelligence have been summarized elsewhere (Baltes & Labouvie, 1973; Baltes & Willis, 1979a,b; Willis & Baltes, 1980). For the present purpose, only selected observations are offered. For example, during the recent decade, research on psychometric intelligence in adulthood and old age has moved at an increasing rate from a descriptive cataloguing of the average course of intelligence (Horn, 1970, 1978; Schaie, 1979) to a differential and causal-analytic posture (Baltes & Labouvie, 1973; Baltes & Willis, 1979a; Botwinick, 1977). Descriptive evidence on average trends continues to be important in our search for a better understanding of life-span intelligence. However, in our view, one of the current frontiers is in examining variability in its various meanings. Three such meanings of variability are discussed here: interindividual, interability, and intraindividual. For the latter meaning of variability, we reserve the term *plasticity*.

### *Variability*

A first meaning of variability refers to *differences between individuals* (interindividual differences). Interindividual differences are of multiple sorts. For example, they can denote within-cohort differences, such as static dif-

[1] ADEPT includes one additional set of intervention analyses dealing with transfer of cognitive training to aspects of personality functioning. This research is being conducted for two reasons. A first is ethical and deals with the question of possible negative side effects of sustained cognitive training on personality functioning in the elderly. The second is substantive and deals with the interface between ability and personality. Several aging- and intelligence-related measures have been constructed for that purpose involving such dimensions as locus of control in intellectual and aging contexts (Lachman, Baltes, Nesselroade, & Willis, submitted). Preliminary analyses show that there is no negative side effect on personality as a function of training. The evidence on more specific relationships involving personality and intellectual ability is not yet fully analyzed.

ferences at a given point in time or longitudinal differences between ontogenetic trajectories of distinct individuals. Another type of interindividual differences concerns between-cohort variation. For example, descriptive evidence has suggested that there is much interindividual variability in the level and direction of intellectual functioning between cohorts. Schaie's (1979) groundbreaking work using cohort-sequential designs is a symbol of the evidence.

Descriptive research has also shown much evidence for a second type of variability, *interability variation*. This phenomenon appears under the label of *multidimensionality*. Multidimensionality refers to the need to consider intelligence not as a unified construct, but as a system of abilities with varying courses of ontogeny. Three research programs are particularly convincing on this point. One is research with the Wechsler scale demonstrating differential change functions for distinct categories (verbal versus performance) of the WAIS (Botwinick, 1977). The second and third, and perhaps most persuasive, are the ones associated with Thurstone's primary mental abilities and Cattell and Horn's theory of fluid-crystallized intelligence. In this research, rather distinct age-change functions for different psychometric factors of intelligence have been reported (Cattell, 1971; Horn, 1970, 1978; Schaie, 1970, 1979).

In general, it is our opinion that descriptive research on age-, cohort-, and ability-related variability has shown that there is little power, conceptual or empirical, in organizing the development of adult and gerontological intelligence around a single overarching framework such as universal (across individuals and abilities) decline. On the contrary, we interpret the evidence as suggesting much variability and relatively little age-related invariance. Exceptions are the fluid-crystallized (or similar) distinction and the notion that, for advanced old age (beyond age 70) and for samples of older persons suffering from noted loss of health, more general decline can be observed (Baltes & Willis, 1979a; Schaie, 1979). Except for these qualifications, however, the striking feature of descriptive aging research is one of much variability, both between persons and within persons for distinct abilities.

## *Plasticity*

The third major meaning of variability denotes variability at the *individual* level of analysis, again either at one point in developmental time or over the course of life. In this framework, variability becomes intraindividual modifiability or plasticity. In ADEPT, we are addressing this question of intraindividual variability for a specific age group, that of older persons. Rather than comparing individuals *of different ages or cohorts,* our primary effort is to identify *the range and conditions* of individual modifiability within a given age range.

The term plasticity is used, then, to indicate the range of functioning at the individual level, whether ontogenetic (how variable is the individual course of development?) or concurrent (how variable is performance at a given point in ontogenetic time?). Why do we assign much importance to questions of plasticity? In general, it is our position that theories of psychometric intelligence that do not include or consider statements about plasticity are incomplete (Baltes & Baltes, 1980; Baltes & Willis, 1979a). There are three main reasons. One is related to conceptions of intellectual aging, the second to the nature of psychometric intelligence and its relationship to processual models of cognition, the third to questions of social policy and the optimization of human development.

*Plasticity and Conceptions of Intellectual Aging.* We do not claim that intellectual aging is completely variable and plastic. Such an extreme view would seriously undermine the basics of the field of developmental psychology which requires some acknowledgement of invariance of ontogenetic process (Baltes & Baltes, 1980; Wohlwill, 1973). However, we do postulate that gaining knowledge about conditions and range of plasticity is legitimate and that such knowledge requires an explicit orientation toward such knowledge and a particular methodology.

In general, the theoretical and methodological orientation associated with research on plasticity involves exposing the same individuals to different life conditions including learning programs. The strategy requires a direct or quasi-experimental form of intervention. In the past, such an orientation and such methodology have not been the mainstream of research in psychological gerontology. Using an interventive approach, we learn not only about how intellectual aging looks in a given set of circumstances, but also how it could look if conditions were different (Baltes & Danish, 1980; Baltes & Willis, 1977). Thus, similar to research on testing the limits and learning diagnostics (Brown & French, 1979; Guthke, 1976; Schmidt, 1971), the focus is on examining the range of intellectual aging under conditions not normally existent in either the living ecology of older persons or in the standard assessment situation provided by classical tests of psychometric intelligence. Note here that, for ethical reasons, our research into plasticity is restricted to conditions assumed to be performance-enhancing. From a theoretical point of view, the study of conditions related to performance decrement is equally important.

*Plasticity and Process Research.* The second major reason why we consider research on plasticity important involves the question of the how and why of psychometric intelligence. Research on modifiability and plasticity of psychometric intelligence facilitates another desirable movement in developmental research on intelligence, that of reaching a stronger interface between psychometric intelligence on the one hand and processual research on cognition on the other.

Work on psychometric intelligence has been predominantly a static-correlational enterprise with a primary focus on product rather than process. Cognitive research, contrariwise, has been oriented primarily toward understanding the mechanisms associated with the processing of information. On a conceptual level, the need for a rapproachment between a psychometric-correlational and a cognitive-processual approach toward understanding intelligence has been suggested with dogged perseverance for several decades. Recently, there appears to be a growing commitment to moving beyond rhetoric and isolated work to demonstrate the usefulness of such a rapproachment on the empirical and programmatic level as well (e.g., Resnick, 1976; Sternberg & Detterman, 1979). We believe that research on the modifiability or plasticity of psychometric intelligence is one of the steps in that direction. Such research leads quickly to questions about processes and mechanisms involved in intelligence test performance, thereby requiring explicit attention to models and conceptions of cognition and information processing.

*Plasticity and Social Policy.* The third main reason why research on plasticity is important relates to questions of social policy. Descriptive research with its focus on averages and normative patterns can lead easily to misinterpretations of the potential of older persons and the comparative level of functioning if different age groups are contrasted. For example, descriptive work on average decline in short-term memory or fluid intelligence can be taken as suggesting that older persons are deficient in cognitive effectiveness. At the same time, such an interpretation would not consider the substantial degree of interindividual variability observed nor the fact that whatever decline is observed in aging is relatively small in terms of proportion of variance accounted for (Schaie, 1979, 1982). In fact, Schaie argues that, despite whatever decline is observed in old age, a central impression must be the large number of older persons who either do not experience any decline into the 70s or who in the 70s function at levels above the mean observed for younger age groups.

Research on plasticity augments such a perspective of large interindividual variability in intellectual aging. Research on plasticity leads not only to information about how older persons perform in a given situation but also to what they would be able to do if conditions were different. It examines, even in the presence of decline, whether and how it is possible to use intervention strategies to achieve, for example, age-equivalent levels of functioning. As a consequence, research on plasticity is inherently aimed at providing a knowledge base apt to suggest procedures for optimization (Brandtstädter & Schneewind, 1977) and redistribution of education resources according to a life-span perspective (Baltes & Willis, 1979b; Reinert, 1980; Schaie & Willis, 1978). In this sense, research on plasticity contributes to a foundation of social policy that is inherently preventive, corrective, and equity-oriented rather than discriminatory or defeatist.

## Context and Hypotheses of ADEPT Research

In addition to the general background summarized in the preceding section, there are two more specific domains of research and theory that set the context for the ADEPT research program and index our own belief systems about research priorities in the field of intellectual aging. A first domain is given by ecological and performance considerations of aging behavior. The second is provided by our view and application of Horn and Cattell's theory of fluid-crystallized intelligence.

### *Intellectual Aging: Role of Performance Factors and Ecological Deficits*

*On Performance versus Potential.* Much of our thinking about intellectual aging has been stimulated by the conceptual distinction between performance and potential (capacity) as well as by considerations of the ecology in which elderly persons are living. Related considerations provide the context for the general hypotheses or propositions tested in ADEPT as also evident in Figure 6, shown later in this chapter.

The performance–potential (capacity) distinction appears in a variety of concepts including the differentiation between performance and competence (Bijou, 1971; Botwinick, 1977; Flavell & Wohwill, 1969). While the conceptual distinctions are not always clear, we accept their basic premise. Performance refers to observable behavior, and any given observable behavior is but a sample of the intellectual behavior that a given individual could display. Potential denotes that level (or range) of performance that individuals exhibit if alternative conditions are considered or introduced. The goal is to specify the conditions under which different classes and levels of intellectual behavior occur. Our position may be misinterpreted because the language chosen is similar to that used often in behaviorism. A behavioristic constraint is not intended. The conditions for performance variation can include nonenvironmental and cognitive determinants.

Accepting the significance of a capacity–performance distinction leads to the conclusion that the organization of knowledge about intelligence is facilitated if the data base includes, from the beginning, empirical statements about plasticity. This is so because an observed level of functioning is but one (though concededly important) possible behavior or developmental outcome. In fact, one could take the position that potential or capacity is inherently an unknown, dialectical quantity (see also Figure 6; Riegel, 1976). What is known only is a given outcome resulting from the transaction of capacity with experience; and experiences, of course, can differ markedly, especially if a lifelong view of development is taken.

Recognizing the facts that intellectual behavior is regulated by conditions of performance and that information about variability and plasticity due to performance factors is an important ingredient for a comprehensive theory of intelligence leads to the conclusion that theories of performance (rather than theories about latent abilities and their interrelationships) are a neglected theme in research on psychometric intelligence. It appears to us that psychometric research on intelligence has ignored such an emphasis to such a degree that the resulting body of psychometric theory is out-of-balance. We know relatively little about the questions of how, why, and under which conditions of performance on intelligence tests.

*Intellectual Aging and Performance Factors.* What about the role of performance factors in the study of intellectual aging? First, there is an *ecological* argument. The need for understanding the conditions for intellectual performance is enhanced in all situations in which individuals do not represent normative or "average" situations of living. Examples are members of some socially disadvantaged groups. In the past, related arguments have been made especially for members of minorities or other intellectually disadvantaged populations. In each of these instances, the position is that the performance conditions for such "disadvantaged" individuals are not at a comparable level of optimization as is true for the mainstream or for socially advantaged segments of a population.

We believe that the elderly often live in "disadvantaged" conditions. On a general level, this view is illustrated in the work of Lawton and his colleagues (Lawton & Nahemow, 1973). As to intellectual functioning, although the evidence is far from adequate, one of us argued several years ago (e.g., Labouvie, Hoyer, Baltes, & Baltes, 1974) that it is likely that many older persons live in environments which are not conducive to high levels of intellectual functioning. Another example of an ecological deficit view of psychological aging is Margret Baltes's and her colleagues' research on the social ecology in nursing homes (Baltes & Baltes, 1980; Barton, Baltes, & Orzech, 1980) and its role in the aging-related increase of dependence.

The second rationale for suggesting a lowered performance context for intellectual functioning in old age is *ontogenetic* in the life-span development sense. To what degree is performance on intelligence tests an aspiration or a desirable developmental goal (task) of older persons? It does not appear to us that performance on intelligence tests is a particularly salient goal in the life of many elderly persons. Rather, note that psychometric tests of intelligence are more appropriate for the developmental tasks characteristic of the first part of the life span (Havighurst, 1948). Intelligence tests have been developed with a substantive focus on education and occupational life, both important characteristics of young adulthood. It appears difficult to argue that a similar demand for intelligence-related performance exists in the environmental system of older persons.

As a consequence of both perspectives (ecological, ontogenetic), it is our general position that the level of intellectual performance observed in older persons, if observed without performance-enhancing conditions, is probably an underestimate of what older persons could do if they attended to and practiced the intellectual tasks involved. The growing body of evidence on enhancement of intelligence- and cognition-related performance of older persons (for additional reviews, see Denney, 1979; Labouvie-Vief, 1976; Sterns & Sanders, 1980) appears to be in agreement with such a position.

*Quantitative versus Structural Change in Intellectual Aging.* There is another conceptual reason why a performance orientation is salient in the study of intellectual aging. This rationale deals with the relative importance of developmental-structural determinants at various stages of the human life span.

In the area of cognition, developmental structuralism, such as Piaget's, has been one fruitful approach suggesting fairly invariant sequences and mechanisms of cognitive development in childhood and adolescence. However, theoretical and empirical work stemming from childhood-based structuralism has not yet been extended very fully to the second part of the life span. There are several conceptual efforts to push such an enterprise using, for example, dialectical-contextualistic (e.g., Clayton & Birren, 1980; Labouvie-Vief, 1980; Labouvie-Vief & Chandler, 1978; Riegel, 1976; Schaie, 1977–1978), multivariate-structural (Baltes, Nesselroade, & Cornelius, 1978; Reinert, 1970), but also evolutionary (Brent, 1978) perspectives as the main ingredients for formulating a posture of continued structural development in adulthood.

In future work, such "structuralistic" efforts are important and we underscore their importance. At the same time, particularly where existing data bases are concerned, it appears to us that the current center piece of explanation of adult-developmental change in psychometric intelligence is one of accounting for quantitative rather than structural variability. A performance orientation appears to offer a parsimonious strategy for that task, without prejudging the long-range fruitfulness of a structural-qualitative addition or alternative.

## *Theory of Fluid-Crystallized Intelligence as Framework*

*Definition.* The second specific context for ADEPT is provided by Cattell and Horn's theory of fluid-crystallized intelligence (Cattell, 1971; Horn, 1970, 1978; Horn & Cattell, 1966, 1967). Our intent in this regard is not to use our research program as a vehicle for testing features of that theory. This could be possible, but it is not our primary intent.[2] Rather, we see the theory as a useful, developmental framework for measurement of psychometric intelligence and our work as contributing to knowledge associated with the theory, namely, about the degree and conditions of plasticity associated with tests indexing some of the abilities making up the theory. The work reported here, then, is seen primarily as offering supplemental rather than confirmatory or falsificatory information on Cattell and Horn's theory.

[2] At the same time, we should acknowledge that our decision not to utilize the present work for purposes of testing the Cattell-Horn theory has substantive reasons as well. The theory, in our view, is not sufficiently precise or developed to permit unequivocal predictions when it comes to the role of experience and the direction of causality.

The meanings of fluid and crystallized intelligence are the following. Both represent broad (second-stratum) dimensions of psychometric intelligence. *Fluid intelligence* (Gf) involves problem solving in tasks dealing with complex relations and novel (relatively culture-free) materials. It is "characterized by processes of perceiving relationships, educing correlates, maintaining span of immediate awareness in reasoning, abstracting concept formation, and problem solving" (Horn, 1978, p. 220). *Crystallized intelligence* (Gc), on the other hand, operates in ways and areas in which the intellectual judgments are not novel but involve educational and cultural knowledge. Like fluid, "crystallized intelligence also involves the processes of perceiving relationships, educing correlates, reasoning, etc. . . .but the content of the tasks that best characterize Gc indicates relatively advanced education and acculturation" (Horn, 1978, p. 221–222). Developmentally, fluid intelligence is prior to crystallized intelligence, both from a temporal and causal point of view. It is also seen as reflecting strongly the neurophysiological state of the organism.

*Role in ADEPT Training Research.* Specifically, the fluid-crystallized (Gf/Gc) theory provides a useful rudimentary theory base for cognitive intervention research in aging for two main reasons. A first strength is its life-span perspective on quantitative developmental change. For the present purpose, this feature sets the theory apart from some of its competitors such as Guilford's structure-of-intellect model. According to the theory, the two broad dimensions of intelligence exhibit differential "average" or normative change patterns across the life span. Fluid intelligence is said to develop early in the life span and to follow a normative pattern of gradual decline beginning in early adulthood, whereas crystallized intelligence is postulated to show a longer trajectory of increment and a fair amount of stability for most of adulthood into old age.

Because fluid intelligence is the dimension assumed to exhibit aging-related decline, our choice was to concentrate on the system of fluid abilities. The emphasis on examining the range of short-term modifiability in fluid performance does not negate the possibility that an average pattern of decline in fluid intelligence functioning could occur in certain circumstances. Nor do we interpret the Cattell–Horn theory to suggest necessarily that such decline was irreversible, although with the heavy emphasis on neurological and other biological antecedents of fluid intelligence (Horn, 1970), some researchers might reach this conclusion. There is, however, another feature of fluid intelligence that suggests that it is subject to experiential modifiability. This feature involves its comparative standing on a dimension of "degree of learning." While crystallized intelligence is associated with overlearning, performance on fluid tasks is assessed in contexts or with materials that are relatively novel. Thus, one could expect fluid performance enhancement as amount of learning or experience with fluid task increases.

The second main reason for choosing the Gf–Gc theory as framework concerns its measurement characteristics and their relevance for the assessment of training effectiveness. A major task of cognitive training research is to work within a theory and measurement framework that permits (a) definition of training substance and (b) assessment and evaluation of training effectiveness in a multivariate and systems context (Glaser & Resnick, 1972). The hierarchical and multivariate theory of fluid-crystallized intelligence offers this opportunity. For the most part, the theory makes available a battery of ability-indexed tests and statements about their interrelationships at different levels of aggregation, such as first- and second-stratum factors. Using such a model of measurement permits an orderly approach to the specification and assessment of intervention, both in terms of expected effect patterns as well as in terms of scope (breadth) of training transfer.

## General Design Characteristics

The various short-term longitudinal studies conducted in ADEPT share several design characteristics and objectives. Although these characteristics are not identical for each one of the studies, they are sufficiently general to warrant an introductory summary rather than repetitive presentation.

### *Subjects*

Because the studies were conducted over a period of several years, it was not possible to draw the participants in the various studies from the same parent population and then randomly assign the individuals to the different projects. Each of the studies is based on an independent strategy of sample selection and random subject assignment. However, all participants come from the same general area and for each project from several community sites. Thus, on the average, the study samples represent fairly comparable parent populations.

Specifically, all participants come from rural Central Pennsylvania. They are volunteers, live in community settings, and were recruited through various local organizations such as churches or senior citizens centers. Participants were reimbursed, on the average, approximately $2.00 per hour for their participation, with the funds being paid more often to organizations rather than individuals.

In terms of subject characteristics, aside from being volunteers and affiliated with at least one community organization, the participants on the whole were fairly unselected. In terms of health, the only requisites were physical mobility, to permit attendance at a local testing site, and adequate sensory (vision, hearing) and psychomotor (writing) ability to engage in psychometric testing. The age level of the participants ranged typically from 60 to 80, with an average age of approximately 70. In accordance with demographic characteristics, the samples usually included a larger number of women than men, at a ratio of better than 2:1. In terms of education, most samples are above the mean level for their cohort-census for Central Pennsylvania. Mean number of years of schooling is close to 11 years, which is about 2–3 years above the median educational level of their age/cohort.

In general, then, participants are positively selected in terms of health and education when compared with census data for the region involved. However, because the participants come from many communities and because of reasonably large within-study variability, it is our conclusion that the samples are fairly heterogeneous and representative of a large segment of the total population of older persons living in Central Pennsylvania.

## *Measurement Battery*

The general framework of the measurement space used in ADEPT is summarized in Table 1. First, in line with the Gf–Gc theory, its two major second-stratum dimensions were included: fluid intelligence and crystallized intelligence. In addition, one of the other broad dimensions of psychometric intelligence, speediness, was incorporated. Then a set of relatively pure primary mental abilities representative of the three general dimensions were identified as marker factors with associated tests. The hypothesized relationships between the broad factors and tests of primary mental abilities summarized in Table 1 are based primarily on Cattell (1971) and Horn (1970, 1975, 1978). As a total package, the measurement battery overrepresents the dimension of fluid intelligence. This strategy was chosen because training is focused on that dimension and a refined assessment within the second-stratum factor of fluid intelligence is desirable.

At the present time, the assessment of training transfer presented in this manuscript is based for the most part on a subset of the 17 tests shown in Table 1. These tests are set in italics. Their selection is guided by the wish to achieve a refined assessment of transfer within the fluid domain and a more gross assessment of transfer to crystallized intelligence and the factor of perceptual speed. One of the training studies reported (attention training), in addition, involves tests of memory span and a battery of tests designed to measure attention and other aspects of information processing. This latter training study is still in process and awaits final data collection and analysis, and only very preliminary findings are reported in this chapter. The tests chosen or developed for the attention/memory domain include letter matching, letter digit, continuous paired associates, number–word, Stroop, concentration, and word recognition. These tests are designed to index four categories of attention: perceptual discrimination, selective attention, attention switching, and concentration–vigilance. In format and rationale, the tests are constructed in analogy to work on information processing (e.g., Hunt, Frost, & Lunneborg, 1973; Posner & Mitchell, 1967).

*Table 1. Schematic Design of Measurement Battery: Hypothesized General Intellectual Dimensions, Hypothesized Primary Mental Abilities, and Marker Tests*[a]

| General dimension | Primary ability | Test | Source |
|---|---|---|---|
| Gf | CFR | *Culture Fair Test (Scale 2, Form A)* and *Power Matrices (Scale 3, Form A [1963 ed.] and Form B [1961 ed.])* | Cattell & Cattell, 1957, 1961, 1963 |
| | CFR | *ADEPT Figural Relations Test (Form A)*[b] | Plemons, Willis, & Baltes, 1978 |
| | CFR | *Raven's Advanced Progressive Matrices (Set II)* | Raven, 1962 |
| Gf | I | *ADEPT Induction Test (Form A)*[b,c] | Blieszner, Willis, & Baltes, 1981 |
| | I | *Induction Composite Test*[b] | Ekstrom *et al.*, 1976; Thurstone, 1962 |
| Gf | Ms | Visual Number Span | Ekstrom *et al.*, 1976 |
| | Ms | Auditory Number Span Backwards | After Ekstrom *et al.*, 1976 |
| | Ms | Auditory Number Span Backwards with Delayed Recall | After Ekstrom *et al.*, 1976 |
| Gf/Gc | CMR | Verbal Analogies I | Guilford, 1969a |
| | CMR | Word Matrix | Guilford, 1969b |
| Gc | EMS | Social Translations (Form A) | O'Sullivan & Guilford, 1965 |
| | EMS | Social situations (EPO3A) | Horn, 1967 |
| Gd | V | Verbal Meaning (9–12) | Thurstone, 1962 |
| | V | *Vocabulary* (V-2, V-3, V-4)[b] | Ekstrom *et al.*, 1976 |
| Gs | PS | Finding A's | Ekstrom *et al.*, 1976 |
| | PS | *Number Comparison* | Ekstrom *et al.*, 1976 |
| | PS | *Identical Pictures* | Ekstrom *et al.*, 1976 |

[a]Most training research reported in this manuscript includes all measures set in italics. Research on attention training also included Memory Span (Ms) and newly developed attention measures as reported in text. Based on Baltes *et al.*, 1980.

[b]Tests labeled ADEPT have been developed by the investigators for assessment purposes in cognitive training research.

[c]Induction and Vocabulary are composites of several ''subtests'' (see text). The Induction Composite subtests include Letter Sets (Ekstrom *et al.*, 1976), Number Series, and Letter Series (Thurstone, 1962).

As we have mentioned already, the intervention analyses reported in this chapter are based on test scores at the primary ability level. We have conducted factor-analytic research, however, that yields information on the structure of the 17 tests shown in Table 1 (Baltes, Cornelius, Spiro, Nesselroade, & Willis, 1980). These structural analyses provided information on the nature of the interrelationships of the tests contained in Table 1 as well as on the relationships at the factor level. Such information is important because past research using the Gf–Gc theory has assumed largely that there is factorial invariance across the adult life span into old age. At the same time, there is evidence from other life-span work on the structure of psychometric intelligence (Baltes, Nesselroade, & Cornelius, 1978; Cunningham, 1980; Reinert, 1970) suggesting structural transformation rather than invariance, namely, a change with aging from a highly differentiated structure in adulthood towards one that exhibits features of integration (or dedifferentiation or neointegration).

With ADEPT data based on $N = 109$ elderly subjects (age range 60–89), we obtained evidence to support such an integration position for old age. Specifically, on the level of test correlations, the $17 \times 17$ matrix showed fairly high intercorrelations, with the majority in the range from .4 to .6. Moreover, when comparing different factor models, varying in degree of differentiation versus integration, "integrated" models with fewer factors (including one containing a general factor) provided better fits to the data using COFAMM (Sörbom & Jöreskog, 1976) as a strategy of confirmatory factor analysis. Thus, while the intervention analyses reported in this manuscript are based on test scores (thereby representing psychometric intelligence at the level of primary abilities), it is important to keep in mind these factor analytic outcomes reported in Baltes *et al.* (1980). They suggest a high degree of relatedness (commonality) among the tests and, in addition, some structural transformations that are not in complete agreement with Gf–Gc findings reported for younger adults. Such a high degree of commonality, for example, may suggest that transfer of training from one ability to another is more likely in older than younger adults.

## *Rationale and Substance of Training*

What distinguishes ADEPT training research from earlier training research involving intellectual aging by others and us? As reviewed, for example, by Denney (1979), there has been an increasing number of cognitive intervention studies during the last decade. Many of these earlier studies resulted in positive outcomes. Few, however, were programmatic in the sense that they considered: (a) a theory-based selection of intervention targets, (b) theory-based definition and assessment of scope of intervention transfer, and (c) maintenance of intervention effects beyond immediate posttest. These are the special features of ADEPT training research.

The present chapter provides intermediate results of five independent but related training studies. A first study (Hofland, Willis, & Baltes, 1981) focuses on the role of retesting itself as a condition of training. The remaining studies deal with training of ability-specific cognitive skills. Three first-stratum abilities of the second-order dimension of fluid intelligence are the target of a total of four cognitive training studies: *figural relations* (Willis, Blieszner, & Baltes, 1981; Willis, Blieszner, & Baltes, submitted), *induction* (Blieszner, Willis, & Baltes, 1981), and *attention/memory* (Willis, Cornelius, Blow, & Baltes, 1982). Results from the last training study are highly tentative.

The training studies reported here reflect two levels (strategies) of cognitive intervention.

*Test Practice.* A first level involves minimal intervention procedures in that only *test familiarity* or *test sophistication* is manipulated. This was implemented by conducting a study using retesting with identical tests, under no-feedback conditions, as the independent variable. The goal of this research was to obtain baseline information on plasticity as a function of testing experience alone.

This strategy of intervention has a long history (Greene, 1941; Vernon, 1954). In recent decades, however, some exceptions such as the controversy about the role of coaching in educational selection tests (e.g., Pike, 1978; Wing, 1980) notwithstanding, the question of practice and its role in performance on intelligence tests has received comparatively little interest. This is particularly true for research on aging.

*Factor (Ability)-Specific Problem-Solving Skills.* The second and more direct level of training involved the instruction on *ability-specific problem-solving skills* associated with the three primary factors defining fluid intelligence: figural relations, induction, attention–memory. For each of the three primary abilities indexing fluid intelligence, a training program was developed. Each training program consisted of material and instructions for five one-hour training sessions. The content of the training programs was based on a task analysis of marker tests (rules required for solution and task format) for each of the intelligence factors. In the task analysis, rules and problem-solving strategies required for solution of test items were identified.

For example, in the case of figural relations, the intelligence test used for program development was the Culture Fair Test (Scale 2) consisting of four subtests (figure series, figure classify, matrices, topology). From the task analysis, relational rules (e.g., size, shape, position) utilized in solving items were identified. Training problems were then developed based on the most frequently occurring relational rules. Only the relational rules were used in developing training items; none of the training items was identical to those on the test itself.

A similar strategy of defining training substance was employed in the development of training programs for the two remaining factors of fluid intelligence. In the case of the induction factor, the induction tests from the ETS Kit of Factor-Referenced Tests (Letter Sets) and Thurstone's (1962) PMA battery (letter series, number series) were used as criteria for program development. For the attention/memory factor, training content was taken from the seven tests mentioned above defining four categories of attention/information processing: perceptual discrimination, selective attention, attention switching, and concentration–vigilance.

Training was conducted by one instructor in small groups ranging usually from four to eight persons. The primary instructional strategy utilized in training is best characterized as an adaptation of verbal rule learning which has been effective in both prior problem solving (Wittrock, 1963, 1966) and Piagetian training research (Beilin, 1976). Emphasis was also placed on presenting the material and the rules with much concern for individual styles of problem solving rather than focusing on a single set of correct solution strategies. Training sessions for the different ability-specific programs varied in format. However, in general, the five training sessions focused on the relational rules associated with the various test problems. For example, training on figural relations (involving the four types of problems defining the figural-relations subtests) consisted of individual practice with paper and pencil training materials, oral feedback by the instructor, and group discussions of problems. The fifth and last session consisted of an overall review of the types of problems indexing the fluid factor considered in the training study.

## *Assessment of Training*

Two major criteria are used in assessment of training. The first deals with scope or breadth of training, the second with maintenance of training over time.

*Transfer of Training (Scope).* Scope or breadth of training is examined within a theory-based measurement paradigm provided by the Gf–Gc model of intelligence. With the Gf–Gc model as measurement framework (see Table 1), training is assessed not only with regard to the target ability factor for which a training program was developed, but also with regard to other ability dimensions contained in the Gf–Gc model, including perceptual speed. The tests used in a given training assessment are ordered along a continuum of near-transfer to far-transfer. In line with this ordering, a hierarchical, theory-based pattern of differential training effects (differing in magnitude) is predicted.

The structure of the predicted transfer pattern for each of the studies follows both from the Gf–Gc model (e.g., its factor space) and the degree of similarity of the transfer measures to the content of the training program. It was not expected that the range of training transfer would cover all dimensions of the Gf–Gc model. What is always expected, however, is that training itself would be effective, as assessed at the nearest measure of transfer, most notably with the test developed for that purpose. Near (within-ability) transfer might also involve a training effect on several tests most similar to the target ability trained, usually indexed by tests marking the same ability factors. As to transfer beyond the ability trained, we should also note that, in line with the high degree of integration of psychometric intelligence obtained (Baltes *et al.*, 1980) in elderly persons, some transfer to abilities other than the target ability was expected. In general, however, the breadth of transfer is seen as a question of empirical analysis, except for the prediction that if training extends to additional factors or abilities, it should be ordered hierarchically in magnitude.

*Maintenance of Training.* The second criterion for assessment of training involved its maintenance with time. All evaluation measures, therefore, are given at several posttraining occasions: one week, one month, and six months following training. If training effects were to be interpreted as representing modification of the level of functioning on the "latent" target fluid ability, the extent of temporal maintenance of such effects is critical.

Following training, no further efforts are made to have participants continue practice with problem-solving skills or engage in related activities. In line with general conceptions of memory, therefore, one could argue that maintenance of training would display the typical pattern of a forgetting curve.

The intervention studies contain an additional condition of performance associated with retesting. The repeated testing involved in assessment of the maintenance of training is expected to represent a performance-related enhancement condition. This is especially true for test-naive populations such as the elderly. Retest effects must be distinguished from ability-specific transfer of training effects. In contrast to ability-specific training effects, we predict that, by and large, retest effects are general (extending across all abilities) rather than hierarchically ordered. Description and analysis of retest effects associated with posttraining assessment, however, are not presented in any detail in this chapter (see, however, Blieszner *et al.*, 1981).

*Design and Analysis.* All studies are based on a treatment-control group comparison, with random assignment to the respective condition. In all but one instance, the control groups are no-contact control groups, that is, control subjects participate in assessment sessions only. There is no effort made to provide control subjects with a time- and setting-equivalent amount of experience comparable to the five training sessions delivered to the treatment subjects.

Two studies in progress, however, are aimed at specifying further the role of the nature of contact *per se* as a possible treatment condition and the confounded effect of retesting as a function of multiple posttraining assessments. The first study (Willis *et al.*, 1982), reported here in the context of attention/memory training, compares two levels of control: no-contact with social contact. The second study (not yet analyzed) uses a design that varies systematically the frequency of posttraining assessment.

Data analysis of the various studies involves, for the most part, analysis of variance, covariance, and the systematic application of planned comparisons and *a posteriori* tests. In each instance, an effort is made to achieve first an overall assessment and then a test with maximum statistical power. In addition, the statistical procedures selected are such that the structure of the measurement space is not altered. Thus, whenever assessment instruments are selected to represent particular cognitive abilities, univariate analyses rather than multivariate analyses (requiring computation of composites with unknown test validity) are used.

A final note on data standardization: In order to permit a base of comparison, data from the training studies are transformed to a common metric, separately for each of the assessment instruments involved. The metric used is derived from the performance of the control group at the first posttraining occasion. This procedure is the best estimate for level of performance at baseline. Using the control group's performance at the first posttest as criterion, the metric is set at a mean of 50 with a standard deviation of 10. This procedure facilitates comparative assessment and evaluation of the magnitude of the effects shown in the figures summarizing training outcomes.

## Results of Intervention Studies

In the following, main results from the five studies are presented. More detailed information is contained in the publications listed in conjunction with each of the projects.

### *Retesting or No-Feedback Practice*

A first study (Hofland, Willis, & Baltes, 1981) deals with the examination of the effect of practice with intelligence tests *per se*. Two timed measures (Culture Fair, induction composite) of fluid intelligence were used representing the fluid abilities of figural relations and induction. Thirty older subjects (mean age: 69 years) participated in eight one-hour practice (retest) sessions distributed over approximately one month. At each session, the same tests were administered. No feedback on individual performance was given.

Based on indirect evidence involving younger adults, we expected performance improvement for anywhere from two to five retest sessions. Figure 1 summarizes the outcome for elderly adults showing mean percentage for correct solutions for each of the two fluid measures. Statistically, there is a continuous incremental trend in performance across the eight retest trials. Total improvement in mean scores on both measures is slightly more than one standard deviation. No apparent asymptote is reached after eight trials.

The Hofland *et al.* study itself does not permit examination of two ques-

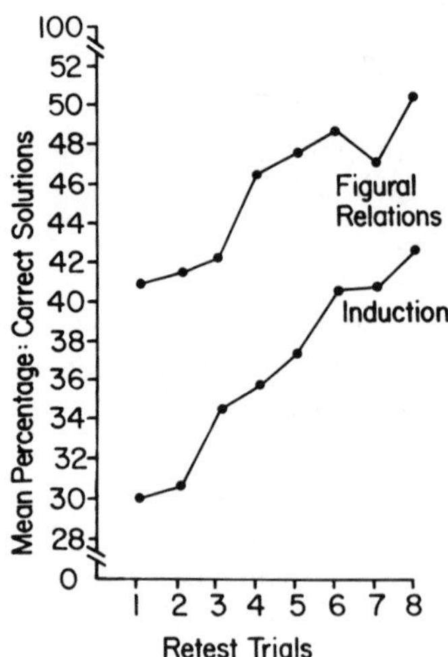


Fig. 1. Mean percentage of correct solutions across retest trials for tests of figural relations and induction. (After Hofland, Willis, & Baltes, 1981.)

tions: (a) whether participants would have reached a similar level of performance if the tests had been given in an extreme power (no time limit) condition at the first retest occasion; and (b) whether retesting itself leads to transfer of training to other ability tests. Relevant studies are currently in progress and initial findings on the role of power versus speeded conditions of assessment are contained in Hofland *et al.* (1981).

However, the data were analyzed for changes in test validity as a function of practice and for evidence on interindividual differences in performance trends. When correlating retest performance with a set of external marker tests (reasoning, memory span, crystallized knowledge, and perceptual speed), there is very little evidence for a testing-related change in the validity of the two retests. Thus, in terms of correlational validity, what is measured at the eighth retest, is similar to what the two tests measured at the beginning of the eight retest trials. Correspondingly, performance increment with retesting does not appear to reflect increasing test specificity associated with the acquisition of test-specific performance skills. Rather, the observed retest increments, in line with one of Greene's (1941) early interpretations, are likely the result of increments in solution strategies (level and/or speed) associated with the two ability factors, figural relations and induction.

As to interindividual differences in performance gains with retesting, intertrial stability coefficients were computed. Throughout, these stability coefficients are very large and approximate the level of estimated reliabilities. We take this information as evidencing that performance improvement as a function of retest practice is similar for all levels of initial functioning. This conclusion is further supported by the finding that trial-related interindividual variability does not show substantial changes, although there is a slight increase in variability toward the last trials of the retest schedule.

## *Training of Figural Relations Ability*

In earlier ADEPT pilot research (Plemons, Willis, & Baltes, 1978), it was already possible to show that performance of elderly persons on figural relations could be enhanced by means of an eight-session training program. That study also showed transfer of training as predicted by the theory, with no transfer to two training-far tests, induction and verbal comprehension.

This pilot evidence has now been enriched by two additional ADEPT studies dealing with figural relations. A first (Willis, Blieszner, & Baltes, 1981) is a replication of the Plemons *et al.* work using an improved training program and an extended battery of tests permitting a more refined assessment of transfer of training. A second study (Willis, Blieszner, & Baltes, submitted) extends the same training program into a two-year longitudinal design involving multistage training. This procedure involved a second application of the training program to the same persons after the three posttests for the first stage of training were completed.

*Replication and Extension.* The results for the new training study (Willis *et al.*, 1981) targeting on figural relations are based on 58 older adults with a mean age of approximately 70 years. Seven tests served as criterion measures at the three posttraining occasions. Figure 2 summarizes the outcome.

Based on statistical analysis, both the predicted training effect on training-near measures and the predicted pattern of differential transfer were judged to be significant. The pattern of training transfer is maintained across all three post-

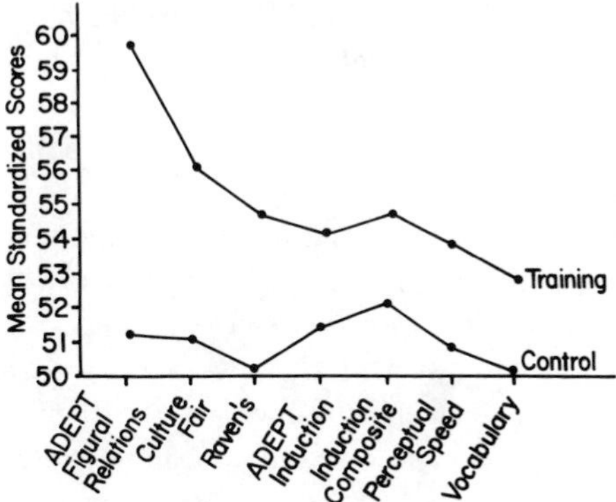


Fig. 2. Standardized mean scores on seven transfer measures for training and control groups averaged across three posttraining occasions. (After Willis, Blieszner, & Baltes, 1981.)

tests, spanning a six-month period. On the nearest transfer measure, the magnitude of training corresponds to approximately one standard deviation if quantified in terms of the baseline performance of the control group at the first posttest.

If the statistical analysis is conducted separately for each of the seven assessment instruments, significant differences (in favor of the figural relations training group) are obtained for the three nearest transfer measures: ADEPT figural relations, Culture Fair, and Raven. However, training is also to some degree effective for the four far-transfer measures. When increasing the statistical power by using a repeated measures analysis of covariance conducted on just the four far-transfer measures, a significant treatment main effect for the four far-transfer tests is obtained as well.

*Two-Stage Training*. Sixty-three percent ($N = 36$) of the subjects completing the Willis *et al.* (1981) replication and extension study agreed to participate in and completed a second stage of figural relations training. This resulted in a two-stage training project extending over a total period of approximately 18 months.

Approximately four months after the six-month posttest for stage 1, participants received five additional hours of training of figural relations involving the same trainer and training program as in stage 1. Subsequent to stage 2 training, subjects were given again three posttests (one week, one month, six months) using the same battery of transfer measures as was true for posttesting of stage 1. Various control analyses for dropout effects were also conducted using stage 2 performance as the dependent variable. There was no strong evidence that stage 2 participants differed in intellectual performance during stage 1 from those subjects who did not continue from stage 1 into stage 2 or did not complete stage 2.

Figure 3 shows the main outcomes related to effect of training and training transfer. Statistical analyses supported the conclusion that averaged over both stages (a) training was effective and (b) training resulted in differential transfer. On the individual level of assessment instruments, significant training effects were found for ADEPT figural relations, Culture Fair, Raven, and perceptual speed. Planned comparisons also indicated that the overall pattern of test performances did not differ for stage 1 and stage 2.

Did stage 2 add anything significant to stage 1 beyond ensuring long-term maintenance of training effectiveness? It appears to us that there is no good evidence that stage 2 training contributed to the level of performance reached by the training subjects following stage 1 training. Stage 2 performance on near-transfer measures is higher than that following stage 1. However, differences between stage 1 and stage 2 are accountable in terms of retesting rather than ability-specific training.

This two-stage training study of figural relations, then, can be seen as a further replication and longitudinal extension of the results obtained with one

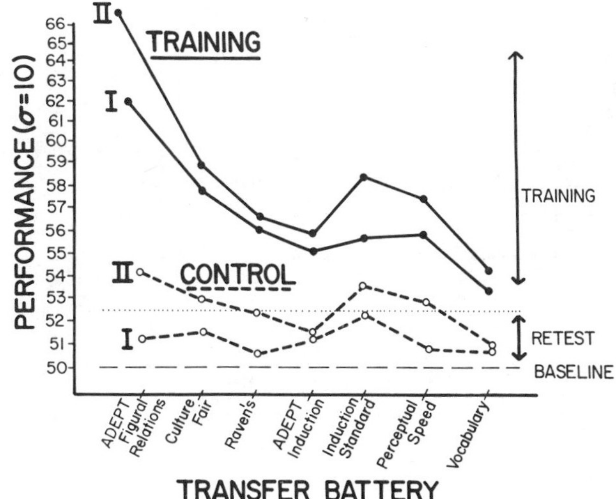


Fig. 3. Standardized mean scores on seven transfer groups following two stages of training (data are averaged for each stage across three posttraining occasions. (After Willis, Blieszner, & Baltes, submitted.)

stage of training. What is particularly noteworthy is not only that training was effective but that the pattern of differential transfer was maintained across two stages of training. On the nearest test of transfer (ADEPT figural relations), the magnitude of training (in addition to retest benefits) is about 1.2 standard deviations as measured by the baseline performance of the control group.

## *Training of Induction*

The next intervention study (Blieszner, Willis, & Baltes, 1981) concentrated on induction, the second of the three markers of fluid intelligence. Within the fluid-crystallized model, induction has been defined as the eduction of relationships in reasoning tasks that do not have semantic content.

Three published tests indexing induction were identified as substantive domain: letter sets, number series, and letter series. These tests served as the content for which task analyses were performed to determine relational rules (strategies) necessary for solving induction-type problems. The most frequently occurring relational rules were then used to develop items for the nearest test of training transfer (ADEPT induction test) and for problems used in the training sessions. Training consisted, as was true for figural relations, of five one-hour training sessions.

A total of 52 older persons (average age: 70) participated. Figure 4 displays the main outcomes. Training was effective, though to a lesser degree than was

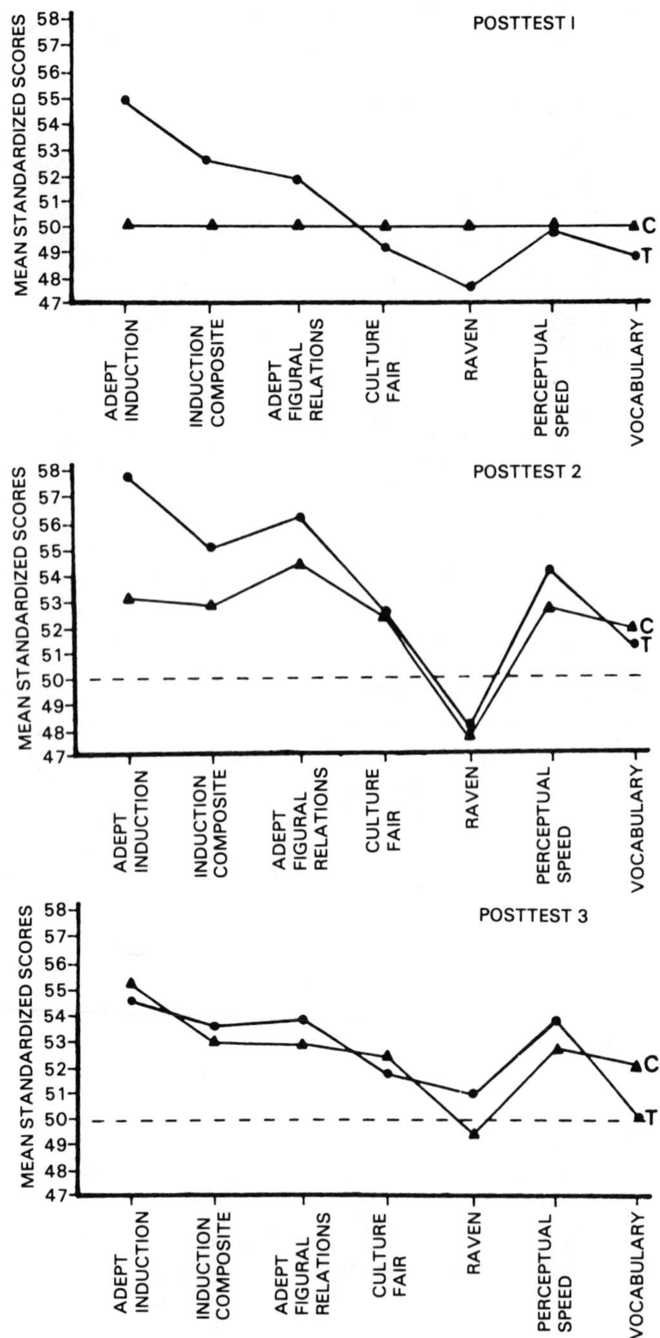


Fig 4. Standardized mean scores on seven transfer measures for training and control groups at three posttraining occasions. (After Blieszner, Willis, & Baltes, 1981.)

true for figural relations. There is statistical evidence for (a) a significant training effect on the nearest test of transfer and (b) a differential pattern of transfer at the first two posttests. At the third posttest, however, the control group (both as a function of retest increments and perhaps because of dissipation of training effect on the part of the training group) has reached the same level of performance as the training group. The fact that the second nearest test of transfer (induction composite), while in the appropriate direction, did not reach statistical significance indicates that induction training was rather specific if compared to the outcome involving training of the ability of figural relations.

Is the plasticity of induction less than that of figural relations? We are not sure yet. Informal assessment of the effectiveness of the induction program during training by the trainer and the second author suggested (already prior to data analysis) that the program may not have been developed optimally. This is an alternative explanation for the fact that induction training was less effective and narrower than training on figural relations. That alternative interpretation is also supported by the fact that induction and figural relations exhibited comparable increments due to retesting alone (Figure 1). Research is in progress to examine this question in a replication study using a modified training program. That study is also designed in such a manner that the effect of training can be identified independent of the effects of retesting. This is accomplished by adding subgroups that are posttested for the first time at occasion 2 and occasion 3, respectively.

## *Training of Attention/Memory*

Development of a training program for the third major ability indexing the second-stratum factor of fluid intelligence focused on several cognitive processes considered to be associated with attention-memory (Willis, Cornelius, Blow, & Baltes, 1982). This research is not yet complete. Thus, only preliminary data, restricted to near transfer (within attention/memory) and the first posttraining assessment, can be reported at this time.

There is some question whether attention/memory should be seen as an intrinsic part of the Gf/Gc realm or as primarily a nonintellectual performance factor more similar to broad speededness than to fluid intelligence. The theoretical and empirical relationship between attention/memory and fluid intelligence is not precise, in part because Horn and his colleagues (1975, 1978; Horn, Donaldson, & Engstrom, 1981) are in the process of refining the meaning and multivariate location of various indices of memory and attention. Our research focus derives from earlier writing, where Cattell and Horn (Horn & Cattell, 1967; Horn, 1970) had identified at the primary ability level a memory component of fluid intelligence. In addition, we consider work on information processing aimed at relating attentional to memory processes. Relevant work on attention and memory processes includes that of Hunt, Frost, and Lunneborg (1973) and, in the aging literature, that of Botwinick and Storandt (1974), Rabbitt (1977), and Craik (1977). Historically, the memory component of fluid intelligence is indexed by measures of secondary memory with backwards memory span serving as a marker test. In our own conception, and very much in line with Horn's current writings, we relate memory functioning of the fluid type to work in the information-processing literature.

Whether this attempt to combine memory as a component of fluid intelligence with memory–attention processes of the information-processing kind will be successful is an open question at present. In addition to the attention/memory training study reported here, we have research in progress (Cornelius, Willis, Nesselroade, & Baltes, submitted) that is aimed at identifying the correlational and factorial relation between the measurement system summarized in Table 1 and the attention/memory tests used in the present intervention study.

Table 2 summarizes the attention/memory measures used. The tests were modified for administration in group settings and for use with older adults. Scoring of the tests involved number of correct answers in a time-limited situation. The given tests deal with four dimensions of attention/memory: *perceptual discrimination* (speed and accuracy in discriminating similarities and differences in perceptual tasks), *selective attention* (ability to focus on a task or stimulus while ignoring irrelevant aspects), *attention switching* or reorientation (ability to shift attention from one task to another and back), and *concentration–vigilance* (sustained attention to or persistence in simple tasks over long periods of time).

The attention/memory training program was delivered in five one-hour sessions with groups of three to eight subjects. The first four sessions each dealt with one of the four dimensions of attention. Practice problems were derived from the marker tests; none of the training problems was identical in content with the test items. For example, in the training session involving selective attention, subjects were shown rows of colored stars and dots and asked to count as fast as possible the items of a given color (ignoring shape), or to count the items of a

*Table 2. Attention/Memory Training Study: Assessment Battery*

| General dimension | Test | Source |
|---|---|---|
| Perceptual discrimination | Letter Matching | Hunt, 1978 (after Posner) |
| Selective attention | Underwood Letter-Digit Task | After Underwood, 1975 |
| | Stroop Color-Word Interference | After Stroop, 1935 |
| Attention switching | Continuous Paired Associates | After Atkinson & Shiffrin, 1968 |
| | Number–Word Test | After Wickens, 1970 |
| Concentration–vigilance | Concentration | After Düker & Lienert, 1959 |
| | Word Recognition | ADEPT, 1979 |

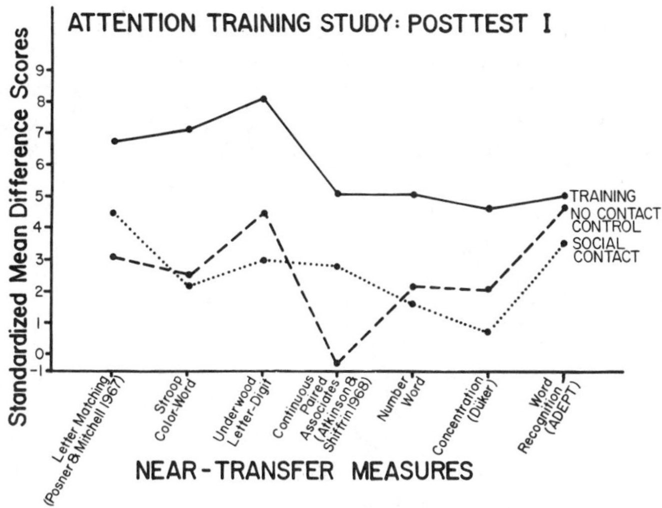


Fig. 5. Standardized mean scores on seven attention/memory measures for training and two control groups at first posttraining occasion. (After Willis, Cornelius, Blow, & Baltes, 1982.)

given shape (ignoring color). Instructional materials included a trainer's manual and individual practice booklets for each of the sessions, and subjects were encouraged to identify performance strategies of their own. The fifth session was devoted to a review of all four attention/memory dimensions.

Figure 5 summarizes available results of the attention/memory training study. Data are based on three randomly assigned groups and a total of $N = 77$ participants with an average age of approximately 70 years. Two no-training control groups were used—one corresponding to past no-contact control groups. The other control group participated in five sessions of social contact with an ADEPT leader. Substance of these social-contact control group sessions involved discussion surrounding questions of life review and friendship.

The results presented in Figure 5 are restricted to assessment of near-transfer *within* the attention/memory domain. Moreover, the data are based on the first posttraining occasion only. Assessment of additional transfer to the measurement battery used in previous training research is not yet complete. Statistical analysis of the data presented indicates a highly significant overall effect of training using a multivariate analysis of variance as strategy of significance testing. Univariate follow-ups specify further that there is significant improvement on three (letter matching, Stroop, continuous paired associates) of the seven tests. Strong suggestive evidence for improvement on two additional tests of the seven (letter–digit and number–word) is present also. Note further in Figure 5 that the direction of the effects is consistent.

The available analyses, then, suggest that there is improvement on attention/memory tests on the one-week posttest following five hours of training. The pattern of outcomes is a rather consistent one. Further analyses are aimed at examining whether this near-transfer is supplemented by far-transfer to other dimensions of the domain of psychometric intelligence, and whether training effectiveness is maintained over longer periods of time.

## Conclusions

The entire research program of ADEPT is not yet completed, nor is it fully analyzed. In particular, we await final analysis of the transfer and delayed posttests regarding the attention-training study and outcomes from the replication and extension of the induction training project. The latter is especially important because these results will permit us to be more precise in interpretation of the differences in breadth of training effectiveness observed when comparing figural relations with induction. In addition, this study will help us in specifying more clearly the role of retest effects and their interaction with training effects when assessing training maintenance over several posttraining occasions.

The following observations, then, are preliminary. Yet, we believe that the outcomes are sufficiently consistent to warrant a few tentative conclusions. In general, we conclude that findings from both the retest and ability-specific training studies suggest considerable plasticity in fluid intellectual performance in old age.

### *Retest Effects*

Manipulation of test familiarity associated with retest effects provides the first data base for evidence on plasticity. Substantial retest effects occurred under minimal practice conditions in which subjects received no experimenter-guided feedback on individual performance.

The strongest evidence for the impact of testing *per se* is contained in the Hofland *et al.* (Figure 1) study. This study, because of its direct focus on retesting as a treatment condition with few tests, involved massed practice. Therefore, it represents the best learning situation concerning retesting effects in ADEPT research. In this study, a continuous performance increment (without apparent asymptote) for the two fluid measures was observed. In our view, this is a remarkable outcome. The finding gains additional significance because the retest measures do not appear to change their factorial validity as retesting progresses.

Note further that retest effects, though of a lesser amount, are also found in the control groups of the training studies. These data are not presented extensively in this chapter but are contained in the original papers. Control groups who participated in from three to six posttraining assessments showed consistent improvements in their performance on practically all tests as a function of retesting. What is also important to recognize is that, as predicted, retest effects in the control groups are fairly general. Contrary to the ability-specific training effects, they occur more equally for all tests. In the past (e.g., Hoyer, Labouvie, & Baltes, 1973; Plemons *et al.*, 1978), we interpreted this generalized retest pattern as indexing primarily the operation of general (ability-nonspecific) performance factors. Following Greene's (1941; see also Wing, 1980) early suggestion, however, the acquisition of ability-specific skills as a function of retest experience is a viable alternative interpretation. One example of such an ability-specific interpretation of retest effects is to view them as an increase in the speed it takes to solve test items rather than as an increase in the level of difficulty of cognitive tasks involved. Because most of the tests used in this study are timed, such an interpretation is plausible and deserves more careful examination.

In the absence of age-comparative data, it is difficult to make statements about age differences or age changes in magnitude and scope of retest effects. In other words, are the retest effects observed in elderly persons larger than those reported or expected for younger age groups? We cannot answer this question. However, we are persuaded that the retest effects seen are substantial and that, if retest effects are taken as one index of plasticity, older persons continue to show a marked ability to benefit from testing experience. It is also noteworthy that this ability to benefit from retesting alone seems to apply to elderly of all levels of functioning who have participated in ADEPT research.

### *Ability-Specific Training and Transfer*

Results of the three ability-specific training studies (figural relations, induction, attention/memory) are also consistently in favor of a position of marked plasticity. In principle, enhancement of fluid performance was demonstrated for all three dimensions of fluid intelligence. The extent of breadth and maintenance of training, however, varied.

At present, the evidence for plasticity is strongest for the ability dimension of figural relations (Figures 2 and 3). Marked, sustained, and broad-based transfer resulting from training of figural relations ability has been found in three studies. In the case of induction ability (Figure 4), our results are less impressive. Improvement due to training, while significant, is restricted to near transfer. Whether this outcome pattern is specific to induction (i.e., whether induction ability is less trainable) or a result of inadequate design (deficiencies in training program as well as lack of retest control) is unanswered. Research in progress is aimed at clarifying these possibilities. Results on the third fluid dimension, attention/memory, are incomplete. However, the available evidence (Figure 5) again indicates a very consistent pattern of performance enhancement on all near-transfer measures. Such an outcome appears to be a necessary condition for finding more broad-based transfer in subsequent analyses.

How significant, empirically and theoretically, are the findings on intervention effectiveness? A first observation on the significance of the observed training effects concerns *breadth* and *order* of transfer. Especially for figural relations, breadth of transfer is large, covering all measures contained in the transfer battery, although at the individual test level some of the transfer effects are nonsignificant. Such breadth of transfer is a remarkable outcome. Although one must be careful not to conclude that the findings point unequivocally to modification of "latent" abilities, the results do support the notion that training of figural relations results in enhancement of performance on a broad battery of ability tests ranging from Gf to Gc and perceptual speed. It is also noteworthy that, by and large, magnitude of transfer was ordered and in line with predictions derived from the theoretical measurement model.

A second observation regarding the significance of the observed training effects deals with their *magnitude*. On near-transfer measures (including the effects of retesting itself), the magnitude is approximately one standard deviation when assessed in terms of baseline conditions. As it turns out, this magnitude is at least as much or more than what Schaie (1979, 1982) reports as the best estimate for longitudinal age decrements in the primary mental abilities from age 60 to 81. Schaie (1982) finds values between one-half and one standard deviation when cumulating successions of seven-year longitudinal decrements to yield 21-year estimations of decline from age 60 to 81. This age range is similar to the cross-sectional age range covered in ADEPT research.

Comparing Schaie's descriptive findings on longitudinal age decline with ADEPT intervention work on the near transfer measures, then, shows that performance improvement in ADEPT is equivalent to 20-year longitudinal age decline observed in the same age range. Note that this level of improvement is reached after a relatively brief intervention: five one-hour training sessions. Thus, it appears likely that, in terms of ability indicators used in ADEPT, intellectual decline during the sixties and seventies (if it occurs) can be slowed down, halted or even reversed if proper education interventions are designed and implemented.

We realize, of course, that this conclusion is restricted in several respects. For example, it is restricted to the age cohorts studied and to fairly healthy elderly community residents able and willing to participate in training research of the type presented. Moreover, the results do not imply that older persons benefit more from cognitive training experience than younger adults. This is possible, but at present, an untested proposition. We must emphasize the role that birth cohorts may play in restricting the generalizability of the present findings. There are historical changes in health, education, and social ecology that modify not only the level of cognitive functioning of elderly cohorts and their intellectual plasticity but also the life history of other age groups living at a particular point in time (Baltes & Schaie, 1976). Age-comparative assessment of plasticity, therefore, will need to consider the use of cohort-sequential designs if the interpretation is aimed at isolating the role of chronological age from the effect of historical change. What is shown, then, in the present data is that elderly persons of a particular birth cohort, if they are exposed and attend to performance-enhancing conditions, do benefit substantially from cognitive training; furthermore, that plasticity at the individual level in the elderly is at least as large as average aging-related decrements observed in longitudinal research based on comparable birth cohorts.

## *Implications: Toward an Integrative View*

We began this chapter by summarizing our observations on the role of plasticity and variability in intellectual assessment. The present findings support the theoretical significance of these perspectives from an empirical point of view. We added observations on the role of ecological and performance deficits in the area of psychometric intelligence, noting that elderly persons are likely to suffer from such deficits. Again, the present findings are in concert with such a position, although they do not represent a direct test. Thus, it is likely that when reduced levels of intellectual functioning on psychometric tests are observed in older persons, these are in part due to ecological and performance deficits. This conclusion is particularly important because it applies to that dimension of psychometric intelligence, fluid abilities, that is postulated to show regular and marked aging decline.

Before we proceed to discuss further theoretical implications, it is desirable to digress somewhat to state what the findings and observations do not imply. It has become a dominant theme to view our research as bearing directly on the question of whether there is intellectual decline with aging (Baltes & Schaie, 1976; Horn & Donaldson, 1976, 1977; Schaie & Baltes, 1977). The present studies are not designed to contribute a direct answer to that question. The research is not age-comparative but deals with in-depth examination of one age group, the 1975–1980 elderly from about 60 to 80 years of age. However, in conjunction with earlier descriptive research on interindividual variability including cohort effects, the findings do speak to the need for developmental theories of psychometric intelligence that incorporate not only features of normative age change (such as is true for the bulk of Horn's writings), but also features dealing with the conditions for and range of variability and plasticity (Baltes & Baltes, 1980; Baltes & Willis, 1979a).

*Performance versus Potential (Latent Reserve).* This digression aside, what are the other implications? In the introduction to this chapter, we also used the distinction between abilities as indicators of performance and abilities as indicators of potential or capacity. Figure 6 summarizes our current view on this matter, preliminary as it is. The figure emphasizes first that observed *performance* is but one assessment of what individuals can do. Although we are not sure, we acknowledge that life-long intellectual performance functions in current cohorts are likely to follow an incremental-plateau-decremental trajectory. The trajectories, however, vary considerably by ability and individual (Baltes & Willis, 1979b).

How can we combine a view of plasticity of gerontological intelligence with the notion that there is aging-related decline in performance? Performance is but one level of achievement. Figure 6, therefore, also emphasizes that there is room for performance enhancement at all ages. This is illustrated in Figure 6 by graphing a second life-span function of intelligence indexing maximum *potential*. In our view, *the level of maximum potential is inherently an unkown or dialectical quantity*. As we learn about conditions for plasticity in performance, the curve for maximum potential is continuously redrawn. However, in line with general notions of biological decline (Strehler, 1977), we acknowledge that the "maximum" level of performance may be lower in old age than in adulthood. Approximation to maximum level would be measured by considering "optimal" conditions of performance such as would be true when graphing world records by age in marathon running (Fries, 1980). When applying such a testing-the-limits

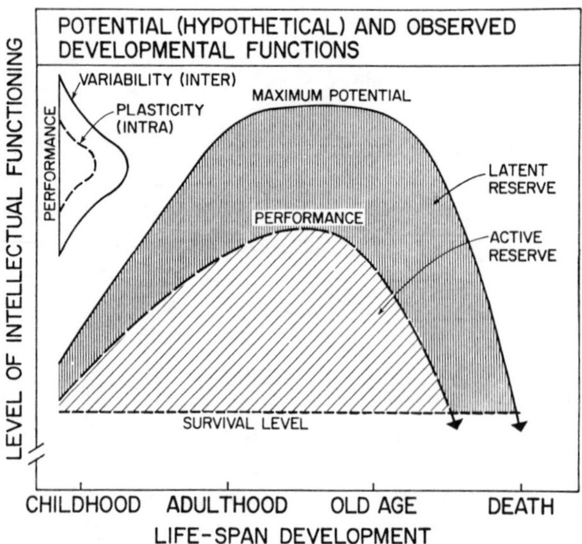


Fig. 6. Life-span development of intellectual performance: Conceptual relationships between potential, performance, and two types of reserve (active and latent).

approach to intellectual aging, we believe (as Fries found for marathon running) that the best older persons would be in the highest percentiles of young adults.

In biology and medicine, the concept of a reserve has been introduced to communicate a similar view. Organisms have reserves that can be called upon if special demands are made (Fries, 1980; Strehler & Mildvan, 1963). In adulthood, for example, the reserves for heart and lung functioning are a multiple of what is necessary during resting stages. In Figure 6, we define as *active reserve* (evidenced in performance) that portion of intellectual potential that has been put into operation. *Latent reserve,* on the other hand, includes that portion of intellectual potential that could be activated if additional energy and time were invested. For most behaviors and certainly for intellectual aging, then, we suggest that there is much latent reserve. Rarely, such as in highly trained athletes or ''mental'' experts, would the level of performance approximate the maximum potential. Most individuals, including the elderly, therefore, if they choose to do so or are exposed to supportive conditions, can improve their performance. Thus, even in the face of aging-related decline of maximum potential, many older persons could maintain high levels of intellectual functioning. What will be necessary for the elderly is to invest more effort in a given class of behavior than would be true for younger adults.

Figure 6 contains an additional piece of information which completes the gist of our current thinking about intellectual aging. It postulates that there are life-stage differences in the proportional relationship between latent and active reserve. In psychometric intelligence and current cohorts, we postulate a smaller difference between maximum potential and performance for the first part of life. We believe this is so because, for childhood and young adulthood, cultural-ecological conditions are aimed at optimization of intellectual performance. Beginning in adulthood and especially in old age, on the other hand, we assert that the ecology is less supportive of high performance on intelligence. This performance deficit in old age is perhaps also enhanced by intraorganismic conditions of late life that assign little priority to high-level functioning in psychometric intelligence.

*Aging as Selective Optimization.* In another context, Baltes and Baltes (1980; see also Brent, 1978) have proposed to use the term *selective optimization* to characterize a process of individuation with aging. They argue that, both for biological and environmental reasons, aging involves an increase in biological vulnerability associated with a decrease in environmental adaptability. However, that process (a) varies widely by individuals and (b) results in individual selective and compensatory effects.

This perspective of selective optimization fits the present data. In light of the need to invest, with aging, more and more effort into maintaining high levels of functioning, older persons may choose a strategy of specialization (Brent, 1978) or selective optimization (Baltes & Baltes, 1980) focusing on those classes of behavior judged to be most adequate to the individual's life situation. Yet, if older individuals are prompted, attend, and practice in other areas, such as psychometric intelligence, their performance can be enhanced markedly. In line with a selective optimzation hypothesis, older individuals *can* maintain or even increase their levels of intellectual functioning.

Thus, we believe that the research reported permits the establishment of another linkage, namely that between intelligence and personality. The findings of plasticity can be coordinated with a position that views aging as a process of selective optimization. When older individuals exhibit lower intellectual performance, this does not necessarily mean that they cannot achieve higher levels in principle. Certain older individuals might have opted out, either because investment is too high or because other domains of behavior are more attractive.

We acknowledge that these concluding observations are tentative and preliminary. Not all of them are supported by empirical evidence, nor is it likely that such a simple view will be a panacea. Yet, until they are falsified, we consider taking the views expressed as a conceptual guide in our future explorations into the conditions for variability and plasticity of psychometric intelligence in old age.

## Summary

Penn State's Adult Development and Enrichment Project (ADEPT) consists of a series of short-term longitudinal studies aimed at examining the extent of and conditions for modifiability (plasticity) of intellectual performance in old age. Study designs include consideration of theory-guided transfer to other abilities (tests) and maintenance of training at several post-training occasions (1 week, 1 month, 6 months). The measurement focus of ADEPT is on Cattell and Horn's model of fluid-crystallized intelligence.

Targets of intervention are three abilities, all indexing fluid intelligence: figural relations, induction, and attention. Conditions for studying modifiability in the sense of enhancement include manipulation of test familiarity (e.g., retest experience) and of ability-specific problem-solving skills by means of educational training. A progress report summarizing a total of five relevant studies is presented.

In general, modifiability of intellectual performance in the target abilities selected for enhancement is substantial. Training also results in a fair amount of transfer to other tests (perhaps abilities) and the skills are maintained over at least one month following training. The overall results suggest (a) the existence of much latent potential (reserve) for intellectual performance in the elderly, (b) the need for articulation of performance theories, and (c) the general notion of emphasizing knowledge about interindividual variability and intraindividual plasticity (including lack thereof) as a critical feature of any theory dealing with intellectual aging. The findings are seen also as convergent with a theory of aging as selective optimization.

ACKNOWLEDGMENTS

Many thanks are due to several colleagues, Paul A. Games and John R. Nesselroade; research assistants Rosemary Blieszner, Frederic Blow, Steven W. Cornelius, Brian F. Hofland, Marjorie E. Lachman, and Avron Spiro, III; and support staff, Rosalie K. Ammerman, Carolyn S. Nesselroade, and Myrtle A. Williams, who collaborated in many phases of the research program. We acknowledge also the helpful comments by Margret M. Baltes, Steven W. Cornelius, and Elizabeth Loftus on an earlier draft of this manuscript.

## References

Atkinson, R. C., & Shiffrin, R. M. Human memory: A proposed system and its control processes. In K. W. Spence & J. T. Spence (Eds.), *The psychology of learning and motivation: Advances in research and theory* (Vol. 2). New York: Academic Press, 1968.

Baltes, P. B., & Labouvie, G. V. Adult development of intellectual performance: Description, explanation, and modification. In C. Eisdorfer & M.P. Lawton (Eds.), *The psychology of adult development and aging*. Washington, D. C.: American Psychological Association, 1973.

Baltes, P. B., & Schaie, K. W. On the plasticity of intelligence in adulthood and old age: Where Horn and Donaldson fail. *American Psychologist,* 1976, *31,* 720–725.

Baltes, P. B., & Willis, S. L. Toward psychological theories of aging and development. In J. E. Birren & K. W. Schaie (Eds.), *Handbook of the psychology of aging*. New York: Van Nostrand Reinhold, 1977.

Baltes, P. B., & Willis, S. L. The critical importance of appropriate methodology in the study of aging: The sample case of psychometric intelligence. In F. Hoffmeister & C. Müller (Eds.), *Brain function in old age*. Heidelberg: Springer, 1979. (a)

Baltes, P. B., & Willis, S. L. Life-span developmental psychology, cognition, and social policy. In M. W. Riley (Ed.), *Aging from birth to death.* Boulder: Westview, 1979. (b)

Baltes, P. B., & Danish, S. J. Intervention in life-span development and aging: Issues and concepts. In R. R. Turner & H. W. Reese (Eds.), *Life-span developmental psychology: Intervention.* New York: Academic Press, 1980.

Baltes, P. B., & Baltes, M. M. Plasticity and variability in psychological aging: Methodological and theoretical issues. In G. Gurski (Ed.), *Determining the effects of aging on the central nervous system.* Berlin: Schering, 1980.

Baltes, P. B., Nesselroade, J. R., & Cornelius, S. W. Multivariate antecedents of structural change in development: A simulation of cumulative environmental patterns. *Multivariate Behavioral Research,* 1978, *13,* 127–152.

Baltes, P. B., Cornelius, S. W., Spiro, A., III, Nesselroade, J. R., & Willis, S. L. Integration vs. differentiation of fluid-crystallized intelligence in old age. *Developmental Psychology,* 1980, *16,* 625–635.

Barton, E. M., Baltes, M. M., & Orzech, M. J. Etiology of dependence in older nursing home residents during morning care: The role of staff behavior. *Journal of Personality and Social Psychology,* 1980, *38,* 423–431.

Beilin, H. Constructing cognitive operations linguistically. In H. W. Reese (Ed.), *Advances in child development and behavior* (Vol. 11). New York: Academic Press, 1976.

Bijou, S. W. Environment and intelligence: A behavioral analysis. In R. Cancro (Ed.), *Contributions to intelligence.* New York: Grune & Stratton, 1971.

Blieszner, R., Willis, S. L., & Baltes, P. B. Training research on induction ability in aging: A short-term longitudinal study. *Journal of Applied Developmental Psychology,* 1981, *2,* 247–265.

Botwinick, J. Aging and intelligence. In J. E. Birren & K. W. Schaie (Eds.), *Handbook of the psychology of aging.* New York: Van Nostrand Reinhold, 1977.

Botwinick, J., & Storandt, M. *Memory, related functions and age.* Springfield: Charles C Thomas, 1974.

Brandstädter, J., & Schneewind, K. A. Optimal human development: Some implications for psychology. *Human Development,* 1977, *20,* 48–64.

Brent, S. B. Individual specialization, collective adaptation and rate of environmental change. *Human Development,* 1978, *21,* 21–33.

Brown, A., & French, L. The zone of potential development: Implications for intelligence testing in the year 2000. *Intelligence,* 1979, *3,* 255–277.

Cattell, R. B. *Abilities: Their structure, growth and action.* Boston: Houghton, 1971.

Cattell, R. B., & Cattell, A. K. S. *Test of "g": Culture Fair (Scale 2, Form A),* Champaign, Ill.: Institute for Personality and Ability Testing, 1957.

Cattell, R. B., & Cattell, A. K. S. *Measuring intelligence with the Culture Fair tests: Manual for Scales 2 and 3.* Champaign, Ill.: Institute for Personality and Ability Testing, 1961.

Cattell, R. B., & Cattell, A. K. S. *Test of "g": Culture Fair (Scale 3, Form A, 1963 Edition; Form B, 1961 Edition, Second).* Champaign, Ill: Institute for Personality and Ability Testing, 1963.

Clayton, V. P., & Birren, J. E. The development of wisdom across the life span: A reexamination of an ancient topic. In P. B. Baltes & O. G. Brim, Jr. (Eds.), *Life-span development and behavior* (Vol. 3). New York: Academic Press, 1980.

Cornelius, S. W., Willis, S. L., Nesselroade, J. R., & Baltes, P. B. *Convergence between attention variables and factors of psychometric intelligence in older adults.* Manuscript submitted, College of Human Development, The Pennsylvania State University, 1982.

Craik, F. I. M. Age differences in human memory. In J. E. Birren & K. W. Schaie (Ed.), *Handbook of the psychology of aging.* New York: Van Nostrand, 1977.

Cunningham W. R. Age comparative factor analysis of ability variables in adulthoood and old age. *Intelligence,* 1980, in press.

Denney, N. W. Problem solving in later adulthood: Intervention research. In P. B. Baltes & O. G. Brim, Jr. (Eds.), *Life-span development and behavior* (Vol. 2). New York: Academic Press, 1979.

Düker, H., & Lienert, G. A. *Konzentrations-Leistungstest.* Göttingen: Hogrefe, 1959.

Ekstrom, R. B., French, J. W., Harman, H., & Derman, D. *Kit of factor-referenced cognitive tests* (1976 Rev.). Princeton, N.J.: Educational Testing Service, 1976.

Flavell, J. H., & Wohlwill, J. F. Formal and functional aspects of cognitive development. In D. Elkind & J. H. Flavell (Eds.), *Studies in cognitive development: Essays in honor of Jean Piaget.* New York: Oxford University Press, 1969.

Fries, J. F. *The plasticity of aging.* Unpublished manuscript, Department of Medicine, Stanford University, Stanford, California, 1980.

Glaser, R., & Resnick, L. Instructional psychology. In P. H. Mussen & M. Rosenweig (Eds.), *Annual review of psychology.* Palo Alto, Calif.: Annual Reviews, 1972.

Greene, E. B. *Measurement of human behavior.* New York: Odyssey, 1941.

Guilford, J. P. *Verbal analogies test, I.* Beverly Hills, Calif.: Sheridan Psychological Services, 1969. (a)

Guilford, J. P. *Word matrix test*. Beverly Hills, Calif.: Sheridan Psychological Services, 1969. (b)

Guthke, V. J. Entwicklungsstand und Probleme der Lernfähigkeitsdiagnostik. *Zeitschrift für Psychologie*, 1976, *184*, 215–239.

Havighurst, R. J. *Developmental tasks and education*. New York: McKay, 1948.

Hofland, B. F., Willis, S. L., & Baltes, P. B. Fluid intelligence performance in the elderly: Retesting and conditions of assessment. *Journal of Educational Psychology*, 1981, *73*, 573–586.

Horn, J. L. *Social situations—EP03A* (Unpublished test). Denver: University of Denver, Department of Psychology, 1967.

Horn, J. L. Organization of data on life-span development of human abilities. In L. R. Goulet & P. B. Baltes (Eds.), *Life-span developmental psychology: Research and theory*. New York: Academic Press, 1970.

Horn, J. L. Psychometric studies of aging and intelligence. In S. Gershon & A. Raskin (Eds.), *Geriatric psychopharmacology: The scene today*. New York: Raven, 1975.

Horn, J. L. Human ability systems. In P. B. Baltes (Ed.), *Life-span development and behavior* (Vol. 1). New York: Academic Press, 1978.

Horn, J. L., & Cattell, R. B. Refinement and test of the theory of fluid and crystallized intelligence. *Journal of Educational Psychology*, 1966, *57*, 253–270.

Horn, J. L., & Cattell, R. B. Age differences in fluid and crystallized intelligence. *Acta Psychologica*, 1967, *26*, 107–129.

Horn, J. L., & Donaldson, G. On the myth of intellectual decline in adulthood. *American Psychologist*, 1976, *31*, 701–719.

Horn, J. L., & Donaldson, G. Faith is not enough: A response to the Baltes–Schaie claim that intelligence does not wane. *American Psychologist*, 1977, *32*, 369–373.

Horn, J. L., Donaldson, G., & Engstrom, R. Apprehension, memory, and fluid intelligence decline in adulthood. *Research on Aging*, 1981, *3*, 33–84.

Hoyer, W. J., Labouvie, G. V., & Baltes, P. B. Modification of response speed deficits and intellectual performance in the elderly. *Human Development*, 1973, *16*, 233–242.

Hunt, E. B. Mechanics of verbal ability. *Psychological Review*, 1978, *85*, 109–130.

Hunt, E. B., Frost, N., & Lunneborg, C. L. Individual differences in cognition: A new approach to intelligence. In G. Bower (Ed.), *Advances in learning and motivation* (Vol. 7). New York: Academic Press, 1973.

Labouvie-Vief, G. Toward optimizing cognitive competence. *Educational Gerontology*, 1976, *1*, 75–92.

Labouvie-Vief, G. Beyond formal operations: Uses and limits of pure logic in life-span development. *Human Development*, 1980, *23*, 141–161.

Labouvie-Vief, G., & Chandler, M. Cognitive development and life-span developmental theories: Idealistic versus contextual perspectives. In P. B. Baltes (Ed.), *Life-span development and behavior* (Vol. 1). New York: Academic Press, 1978.

Labouvie, G. V., Hoyer, W. J., Baltes, P. B., & Baltes, M. M. Operant analysis of intellectual behavior in old age. *Human Development*, 1974, *17*, 259–272.

Lachman, M. E., Baltes, P. B., Nesselroade, J. R., & Willis, S. L. *Cognitive training research with the elderly: Ethical issues and transfer to personality*. Manuscript submitted, College of Human Development, The Pennsylvania State University, 1982.

Lawton, M. P., & Nehemow, L. Ecology and the aging process. In C. Eisdorfer & M. P. Lawton (Eds.), *The psychology of adult development and aging*. Washington, D.C.: American Psychological Association, 1973.

O'Sullivan, M., & Guilford, J. P. *Social translations, Form A*. Beverly Hills, Calif.: Sheridan Psychological Services, 1965.

Pike, L. W. *Short-term instruction, testwiseness and the scholastic aptitude test: A literature review with research recommendations*. Princeton, N.J.: Educational Testing Service, 1978.

Plemons, J. K., Willis, S. L., & Baltes, P. B. Modifiability of fluid intelligence in aging: A short-term longitudinal training approach. *Journal of Gerontology*, 1978, *33*, 224–231.

Posner, M. I., & Mitchell, R. A chronometric analysis of classification. *Psychological Review,* 1967, *74,* 392–409.

Rabbitt, P. Changes in problem solving in old age. In J. Birren & K. W. Schaie (Eds.), *Handbook of the psychology of aging.* New York: Van Nostrand Reinhold, 1977.

Raven, J. C. *Advanced progressive matrices, Set II* (1962 revision). London: Lewis, 1962.

Reinert, G. Comparative factor analytic studies of intelligence throughout the human life span. In L. R. Goulet & P. B. Baltes (Eds.), *Life-span developmental psychology: Research and theory.* New York: Academic Press, 1970.

Reinert, G. Educational psychology in the context of the human life span. In P. B. Baltes & O. G. Brim (Eds.), *Life-span development and behavior* (Vol. 3). New York: Academic Press, 1980.

Resnick, L. B. (Ed.). *The nature of intelligence.* Hillsdale, N.J.: Lawrence Erlbaum, 1976.

Riegel, K. F. The dialectics of human development. *American Psychologist,* 1976, *31,* 689–700.

Schaie, K. W. A reinterpretation of age-related changes in cognitive structure and functioning. In L. R. Goulet & P. B. Baltes (Eds.), *Life-span developmental psychology: Research and theory.* New York: Academic Press, 1970.

Schaie, K. W. Toward a stage theory of adult cognitive development. *Journal of Aging and Human Development,* 1977–78, *8,* 129–138.

Schaie, K. W. The primary mental abilities in adulthood: An exploration in the development of psychometric intelligence. In P. B. Baltes & O. G. Brim, Jr. (Eds.), *Life-span development and behavior* (Vol. 2). New York: Academic Press, 1979.

Schaie, K. W. The Seattle Longitudinal Study: A twenty-one year exploration of psychometric intelligence in adulthood. In K. W. Schaie (Ed.), *Longitudinal studies of adult psychological development.* New York: Guilford, 1982.

Schaie, K. W., & Baltes, P. B. Some faith helps to see the forest: A final comment on the Horn and Donaldson myth of the Baltes–Schaie position on adult intelligence. *American Psychologist,* 1977, *32,* 1118–1120.

Schaie, K. W., & Willis, S. L. Life-span development: Implications for education. *Review of Educational Research,* 1978, *6,* 120–156.

Schmidt, L. R. Testing the limits im Leistungsverhalten: Möglichkeiten und Grenzen. In E. Duhm (Ed.), *Praxis der klinischen Psychologie* (Vol. 2). Göttingen: Hogrefe, 1971.

Sörbom, D., & Jöreskog, K. G. *COFAMM: Confirmatory factor analysis with model modification.* Chicago: National Educational Resources, 1976.

Sternberg, R. J., & Detterman, D. K. (Eds.). *Human intelligence: Perspectives on its theory and measurement.* Norwood, N.J.: Ablex, 1979.

Sterns, H. L., & Sanders, R. E. Training and education of the elderly. In R. R. Turner & H. W. Reese (Eds.), *Life-span developmental psychology: Intervention.* New York: Academic Press, 1980.

Strehler, B. L. *Time, cells, and aging.* New York: Academic Press, 1977.

Strehler, B. L., & Mildvan, A. S. General theory of mortality and aging. *Science,* 1960, *132,* 14–21.

Stroop, J. R. Studies in interference in serial verbal interactions. *Journal of Experimental Psychology,* 1935, *18,* 643–661.

Thurstone, T. G. *Primary mental abilities, grades 9–12, 1962 Revision.* Chicago: Science Research Associate, 1962.

Underwood, G. *Attention and memory* (1st ed.). New York: Pergamon Press, 1975.

Vernon, P. E. Practice and coaching effects in intelligence tests. *Educational Forum,* 1954, *18,* 209–280.

Wickens, D. Encoding categories of words: An empirical approach to meaning. *Psychological Review,* 1970, *77,* 1–15.

Willis, S. L., & Baltes, P. B. Intelligence and cognitive ability. In L. Poon (Ed.), *Aging in the 1980's: Psychological issues.* Washington, D.C.: American Psychological Association, 1980.

Willis, S. L., Blieszner, R., & Baltes, P. B. *Multi-stage training on the fluid ability of figural relations in the aged.* Manuscript submitted, College of Human Development, The Pennsylvania State University, 1980.

Willis, S. L., Blieszner, R., & Baltes, P. B. Training research in aging: Modification of performance on the fluid ability of figural relations. *Journal of Educational Psychology,* 1981, *73,* 41–50.

Willis, S. L., Cornelius, S. W., Blow, F., & Baltes, P. B. Training research in aging: Attentional processes. *Journal of Educational Psychology,* 1982.

Wing, H. Practice effects with traditional mental test items. *Applied Psychological Measurement,* 1980, *4,* 141–155.

Wittrock, M. C. Verbal stimuli in concept formation: Learning by discovery. *Journal of Educational Psychology,* 1963, *54,* 183–190.

Wittrock, M. C. The learning by discovery hypothesis. In L. S. Schulman & E. R. Keisler (Eds.), *Learning by discovering: A critical appraisal.* Chicago: Rand McNally, 1966.

Wohlwill, J. *The study of behavioral development.* New York: Academic Press, 1973.

# Index